MULTICULTURAL LITERATURE AND RESPONSE

MULTICULTURAL LITERATURE AND RESPONSE

Affirming Diverse Voices

Lynn Atkinson Smolen and Ruth A. Oswald,
Editors

 LIBRARIES UNLIMITED

AN IMPRINT OF ABC-CLIO, LLC
Santa Barbara, California • Denver, Colorado • Oxford, England

Library of Congress Cataloging-in-Publication Data

Multicultural Literature and Response : Affirming Diverse Voices / Lynn Atkinson Smolen and Ruth A.
Oswald, Editors.
    p. cm.
  Summary: "This compelling book emphasizes the critical role of quality multicultural literature and
reader response in today's schools and libraries"—Provided by publisher.
  Includes bibliographical references and index.
  ISBN 978–1–59884–474–0 (pbk. : acid-free paper) — ISBN 978–1–59884–475–7 (ebook)
1. American literature—Minority authors—Study and teaching. 2. Children's literature, American—Study
and teaching. 3. Minorities in literature—Study and teaching—United States. 4. Cultural pluralism—
Study and teaching. 5. Ethnic groups in literature—Study and teaching. 6. Ethnicity in literature—Study
and teaching. 7. Children—Books and reading—United States. 8. Young adults—Books and reading—
United States. 9. Multicultural education—United States. 10. Reader-response criticism—United States.
I. Smolen, Lynn Atkinson. II. Oswald, Ruth A.
PS153.M56M85   2011
810.9′8071—dc22   2010043808

ISBN: 978–1–59884–474–0
EISBN: 978–1–59884–475–7

15 14 13 12 11   1 2 3 4 5

This book is also available on the World Wide Web as an eBook.
Visit www.abc-clio.com for details.

Libraries Unlimited
An Imprint of ABC-CLIO, LLC

ABC-CLIO, LLC
130 Cremona Drive, P.O. Box 1911
Santa Barbara, California 93116-1911

This book is printed on acid-free paper ∞

Manufactured in the United States of America

Lynn dedicates this book to her father, Kenneth Biddle Atkinson,
who inspired in her a love of language and literature
and a passion for writing.

Ruth dedicates this book to her daughter, Lori,
an amazing teacher and lover of literature.

Contents

Acknowledgments

We wish to acknowledge the wonderful authors who worked tirelessly to write the excellent chapters in this book. We greatly appreciate their expertise and efforts. We are particularly indebted to the multicultural authors who kindly allowed us to interview them and include excerpts from their interviews in this book. Hearing the voices of multicultural authors brings readers to a better understanding of their work and helps them gain an insider's view of the writing process. These authors include Joseph Bruchac, Doreen Rappaport, Angela Johnson, Pat Mora, Virginia Driving Hawk Sneve, and Laurence Yep.

Finally, we thank our editor, Blanche Woolls, for her valuable feedback and ongoing support. We are also very grateful for the editing of the chapters in the book provided by John Casper, Sarah King, David Smolen, and Barbara Moline. Additionally, we thank Stella Muñoz Rodríguez for her careful editing and proofreading of the Spanish titles, names, songs, and poems. We also appreciate the assistance from the librarians at the Akron Summit County Public Library in gathering the books and other resources for chapters one and two.

Introduction

"Multicultural literature is one of the most powerful components of a multicultural education curriculum, the underlying purpose of which is to help to make the society a more equitable one."

—Bishop, 1993, p. 40

As editors, our goal for *Multicultural Literature and Response: Affirming Diverse Voices* is to encourage educators and teacher librarians to use the rich array of quality multicultural books to support multicultural teaching and learning. We believe that a book on this topic is timely considering the increasing diversity in our schools. According to the National Center for Education Statistics (2010), 45 percent of the U.S. public school population enrolled in kindergarten through twelfth grade comes from diverse racial and ethnic backgrounds.

In this book, the distinguished group of contributing authors, many of whom have an insider perspective of the culture represented in the literature they describe, discuss multicultural literature and provide teachers and teacher librarians with concrete ways to integrate this literature into the curriculum. Our goal is to highlight the importance of multicultural literature as a vital way to make people aware of the need for social justice in our society and throughout the world. Our hope is to bring quality, authentic multicultural literature titles to the forefront and inform teachers and librarians of the wide range of genres and themes that are available in this literature. Authenticity means that ethnic and cultural groups are represented as they are today, not just as they were in the past, and that the distinctive characteristics of each group are represented, avoiding the merging of subcultural groups into one group (Yokota, 1993). We encourage librarians, educators, and parents to include this literature in their collections and response activities on a regular basis with *all* children and young adults.

In this book we introduce readers to quality multicultural literature in all genres throughout the curriculum and throughout the year, not as an add on or separate entity, but as an integral part of literature used to support teaching and learning. For example, when children study poetry, poems by authors of color should be included as an important part of the collection. The same is true when they study fiction and nonfiction. Additionally, when children engage in author or illustrator studies, authors or illustrators of color need to be included in their study. The contributors to this book abide by Louise Rosenblatt's (1994) transactional theory of reader response by including a variety of ways to use these books in classrooms throughout the school day. We advocate using multicultural literature for artistic expression, dramatic expression, written expression, and discussion across the curriculum to support readers' efferent and aesthetic responses.

The editors and authors of this book fervently believe that multicultural literature should be included in the school curriculum and in library programs. They are strongly committed to addressing issues of social justice and believe that educators and librarians risk superficiality if they fail to discuss social issues and inequalities. This means guiding readers to go beyond identifying topic, plot, or main idea, and teaching them to be critical thinkers as they identify issues and themes that might not be stated directly in the text. This is often called inferring or reading between the lines, and it supports thoughtful literacy. It is important for all students to understand how various groups have been marginalized in comparison to the mainstream culture and to try to understand inequalities, discrimination, oppression, and social justice (Cai, 1998).

ORGANIZATION

As the editors of this book, we are honored to introduce our chapters and contributors, an impressive community of authors who have come together to discuss the richness of multicultural literature, and to present multiple paths of response to this literature and ways to affirm diverse voices so that this literature continues to be published and reaches the hands of *all* children.

Chapter 1—"Introduction to Multicultural Literature"—Ruth A. Oswald and Lynn Atkinson Smolen define multicultural literature and discuss why it is essential for our diverse society as well as for the progress of the multicultural education movement in our country. Interviews with two authors are featured as part of the discussion about authors of multicultural literature who write inside versus outside of their culture. Criteria for selection of multicultural literature is included as well as a discussion of culturally responsive teaching with examples of how teachers can include multicultural literature in their curriculum.

Chapter 2—"Integrating Multicultural Literature Into the Curriculum"—Lynn Atkinson Smolen, Ruth A. Oswald, and Sandra Jenkins elaborate on the rationale for integrating multicultural literature into the curriculum. Other topics presented in this chapter include different models for integrating multicultural literature into the curriculum, multicultural twin texts, text sets, and thematic units. These approaches are defined and examples of multicultural books are described. Detailed descriptions of response activities for many of the books are also included.

Chapter 3—"Voices of Multicultural Authors"—Darwin L. Henderson and Teresa Young present the voices of four prominent authors of multicultural children's and young adult literature: Pat Mora, Lawrence Yep, Virginia Hawk Sneve, and Angela Johnson based on personal interviews and information from their books. Through the eyes of these authors, readers gain insight into these authors' views of culture and authenticity and writing that is multicultural.

Chapter 4—"The Power of Illustrations in Multicultural Picture Books: Unfolding Visual Literacy"—Francis S. Broadway and Douglass M. Conkle discuss notable illustrators of multicultural books, various styles and media of picture book illustrators, and share some student work samples in response to multicultural books. They highlight and discuss in detail Eric Velasquez's illustrations in *The Sweet Smell of Roses* (Johnson, 2005).

Chapter 5—"Exploring African American Children's Literature"—Claudette S. McLinn, Yolanda A. Reed, John A. Casper, and Sarah King describe the rich heritage of African American children's literature. They group the books under the following themes and genres: family and friends; identity and self-concept; poetry and rhymes; school and community; imagination; traditional literature; spirituality; historical perspectives; holidays and special days; and biographies and autobiographies. They describe many of the books and provide a variety of literature response activities for children and youth. In addition they include a historical timeline of the literature that stretches from 1746 to the present day.

Chapter 6—"Taking a Critical Look at Native Americans in Children's Literature"—Donna Sabis-Burns discusses how Native Americans have been portrayed in a degrading manner in the past and points out stereotypes to be aware of when selecting books that depict Native Peoples. She discusses the American Indian Youth Literature Award and the criteria used by the award committee to select children's literature that authentically and accurately portrays Native Americans. In her discussion of themes for Native American children's literature, she emphasizes the importance of selecting literature that portrays a variety of tribal nations, books that portray Native Peoples' contemporary life styles, and literature that highlights social justice themes. She includes a valuable table that provides examples of quality Native American books with examples of culturally sensitive (what to do) and culturally inappropriate (what not to do) response activities for the books.

Chapter 7—In "The Journey Continues: Exploring the Literature of Asian and Pacific Island Children," Avis M. Masuda and Michele M. Ebersole begin their chapter by describing the cultural groups represented under the broad category of Asian Americans and the importance of Asian American literature. They discuss this literature for young children under the following themes: traditional literature; celebrations, ethnic food, and traditions; immigration stories; bridging cultures; adoption stories; surviving the internment camp; and immigration stories. They have grouped the Asian American literature for young adolescents under the following themes: identity; model minority stereotype; 1.5 generation; and traditions and culture as part of identity. In addition to describing the themes and the literature, they also include response engagements. In the second half of the chapter, Ebersole and Masuda discuss Pacific Island literature. They begin this section by describing the many cultural groups that make up the Pacific Island peoples and the historical development of the children's literature of this region. They have grouped this literature for children into the following themes: regional literature, myths and legends explaining natural phenomena, and culture and language. They also discuss Pacific Island literature for youth, which mostly consists of novels. Throughout this section they discuss engagement activities for Pacific Island literature.

Chapter 8—"Latino Literature for Children and Adolescents"—F. Isabel Campoy and Alma Flor Ada begin by discussing Latinos in the United States and the distinctiveness amongst the many parallel groups such as Mexicans, Puerto Ricans, Dominicans, and Cubans. They then highlight the commonalities that all Latinos share: a mutual link to their history, a similar view of the world, and a strong connection to the Spanish language. In this chapter, they provide an extensive overview of Latino children's literature. They discuss the historical development of this literature, emphasizing the contributions of José Martí, Pura Belpré, Ernesto Galarza, Piri Thomas, George Ancona, Hilda Perera, Rudolfo Anaya, Nicholasa Mohr, and Alma Flor Ada. They also discuss Latino children's books, categorizing them into the following themes: preserving the oral traditional folklore; transmitting history, cultural achievements and everyday life from Spain and Latin America; sharing personal memoirs; depicting Latino life and culture; celebrating Latino poetic voices; giving free rein to fantasy; and writing for the stage. For each of these themes they provide examples of response activities that emphasize reflection, critical thinking, and a social justice stance.

Chapter 9—"Stories from the Mountains: Appalachian Literature for Children and Adolescents"—Carolyn Brodie provides a brief history of Appalachia, a beautiful region of the United States, and a brief description of the people of this region who are proud of their land, heritage, and community. She discusses the rich literature of this region and groups the books under the themes of love of place, family and intergenerational stories, spirituality and religion, individualism, self-reliance and pride, and neighborliness and hospitality. She also discusses Appalachian books that have won the Caldecott and Newbery Awards and books representing the predominant genres of poetry and folklore. Additionally, she suggests response activities for the literature she describes.

Chapter 10—"Representations not Representation: Exploring Middle East Children's Literature" In this chapter, Ruth McKoy Lowery discusses how Middle Easterners are misunderstood and often maligned as a result of horrific incidents such as the September 11, 2001 terrorist attack on the twin towers in New York City. She describes the demography of Middle Easterners and emphasizes their diversity, pointing out that many Middle Easterners are not Arab. She also gives a brief overview of Middle Easterners in the United States in the twenty-first century. She then discusses books about Middle Easterners using the following categories: immigrant experiences in the United States; American-born experiences; global experiences; immigrant experiences outside the United States; and Middle Eastern native experiences. She emphasizes the importance of including books about Middle Easterners in the classroom as a way of building cross-cultural understanding and includes examples of ways to integrate this literature into the curriculum with response activities in language arts and reading, mathematics, science, social studies, and art.

Chapter 11—"Supporting English Language Learners' Literacy Development with Culturally Relevant Books"—Nancy L. Hadaway and Terrell A. Young discuss how to use multicultural books as part of a culturally relevant pedagogy to support English language learners in the classroom. They include tables with lists of bilingual books, books about English language learners, and text-sets for English language learners. The books are accompanied with valuable information on the cultural background of the book and the suggested proficiency level and grade level for use.

Chapter 12—"Do Tell! Multicultural Folk Stories in the Classroom and Library"—Jacqueline K. Peck shares the importance of stories and storytelling to support an understanding of self and others. She presents principles of good storytelling as well as examples of appropriate multicultural literature to use for this form of expression. She also provides extension activities for storytelling and additional resources on this topic.

Chapter 13—"Linking Audiovisuals to Multicultural Literature"—Meghan Harper provides an update on quality audiovisuals to support the use of multicultural literature. She presents a rationale for using audiovisuals with multicultural literature, discusses in detail how to select quality audiovisuals, and provides a valuable list of multicultural books connected to audiovisuals.

Chapter 14—"Using Multicultural Mentor Texts to Teach Writing"—Barbara Moss collaborates with Christine Kane, a classroom teacher, to present a culturally relevant teaching protocol for using multicultural books as mentor texts to teach writing. They provide guidelines for selecting multicultural texts, a two-phase instructional sequence for teaching with multicultural mentor texts, and ways to use mentor texts for teaching grammar and text structures.

Chapter 15—"Reading Fluency and Multicultural Literature"—Belinda Zimmerman and Timothy Rasinski join Tracy Foreman, a classroom teacher, to present many instructional activities that incorporate multicultural literature to develop reading fluency. They include detailed descriptions of the fluency development lesson, the oral recitation lesson, book bits, audio assisted reading, and reader's theater. A wonderful list of poems, songs, and readers theatre scripts in many languages is also included.

Chapter 16—"Promoting Multicultural Literature and Literacy: Awards, Conferences, Library Initiatives, and Outreach Programs"—Barbara A. Ward reports how multicultural literature is being promoted across the nation through ever-growing literature awards, conferences, library initiatives, and outreach programs that have multicultural literature as their main focus. Lists of the major awards for multicultural literature, conferences featuring multicultural literature as its main attraction, and useful Web sites that feature multicultural literature are included. These resources are excellent starting places for teachers who want to begin to incorporate multicultural literature in their classrooms and librarians who want to include these books in their library programs.

The appendices in this book provide readers with additional information about multicultural literature. These appendices are the following:

- Appendix A: A Selected List of Multicultural Authors and Illustrators
- Appendix B: Multicultural Book Awards
- Appendix C: Publishers and Distributors of Multicultural Literature

REFERENCES

Bishop, R. S. (1993). Multicultural literature for children: Making informed choices. In V. J. Harris (Ed.), *Teaching multicultural literature in grades K–8*, (pp. 35–54). Norwood, MA: Christopher-Gordon.

Cai, M. (1998). Multiple definitions of multicultural literature: Is the debate really just "ivory tower" bickering? *The New Advocate, 11*(4), 311–324.

Johnson, A. (2005). *A sweet smell of roses*, illustrated by E. Velasquez. New York, NY: Simon & Schuster.

National Center for Education Statistics. (2010). The condition of education 2010. Retrieved from http://nces.ed.gov/programs/coe/press/index.asp.

Rosenblatt, L. M. (1994). *The reader, the text, the poem: The transactional theory of the literary work*. Carbondale and Edwardsville, IL: Southern Illinois University Press.

Yokota, J. (1993). Issues in selecting multicultural children's literature. *Language Arts*, 70, 156–167.

I

Introduction to Multicultural Literature

Ruth A. Oswald and Lynn Atkinson Smolen

WHAT IS MULTICULTURAL LITERATURE?

Multicultural literature has been defined in a variety of ways depending on cultural specificity. Thousands of years ago, Confucius proposed the importance of honest language and correct naming. As cited in Freedman (2002), "Calling things by their right names makes it possible for us to speak truthfully about them" (p. 6). Whereas naming is important, this is not to imply that there is one right definition of multicultural literature. However, the way multicultural literature is defined reflects belief (stance) and impacts literature choices as well as how the literature will be used.

According to Harris and Hodges (1995), multicultural literature is "writing that reflects the customs, beliefs, and experiences of people of differing nationalities and races" (p. 158). Many definitions are more inclusive including religious groups, and others are even broader and include individuals with disabilities, gender issues, and sexual orientation. Cai (1998) argued that the controversy over definition simply has to do with how many and which cultures should be covered in multicultural literature and determining the parameters of the prefix "multi."

Because purpose determines the definition of multicultural literature, it is important to note that this text is for teachers, teacher librarians, and educators to use as a resource to promote the multicultural education movement. As explained by Banks and Banks (2001):

multicultural education is an idea, an educational reform movement, and a process whose major goal is to change the structure of educational institutions so that male and female students, exceptional students, and students who are members of diverse racial, ethnic, language, and cultural groups will have an equal chance to achieve academically in school.

(p. 1)

According to Cai (1998), multicultural literature is a critical component of this movement, a tool that can be used to reach its goal: diversity and equity in education (p. 318). This approach goes beyond merely introducing students to many cultures and developing an appreciation for underrepresented groups. The focus is on social equity, justice, removal of prejudice, praxis (reflection and action), and fostering a genuine respect and understanding of the experience and history of oppressed groups (Banks, 2004, p. 15). Nieto (1992) emphasized that multicultural education is for *all* students. Bishop (1997) built upon Nieto's affirmation and added that multicultural literature is also for *all* students and defined multicultural literature as "books that reflect the racial, ethnic, and social diversity that is characteristic of our pluralistic society and of the world" (p. 3). This definition aligns nicely with the purpose of this text.

WHY IS MULTICULTURAL LITERATURE ESSENTIAL FOR OUR MULTICULTURAL SOCIETY?

The United States is a multicultural nation that includes Whites, African Americans, American Indians and Alaska Natives, Asians, Native Hawaiians and other Pacific Islanders, and Latinos (U.S. Census Bureau, 2000). Moreover, the population of the United States includes people from many different religious groups such as Christian, Jewish, and Islam within which each contains diversity. According to the National Center for Education Statistics (2008), minority students make up 43 percent of the public school enrollment, 20 percent of school-age children speak a language other than English at home, and about 5 percent speak English with difficulty. Hispanic students now make up one in five public school students, but these students as well as other minority students are disproportionately clustered in high-poverty schools. Norton (2009) emphasized the increasing need for "cross-cultural understanding" with the demographic shifts that continually occur in the United States (p. 1).

Educators, teacher librarians, and researchers understand the important contribution that quality, multicultural literature can make in classrooms across our nation to enhance learning and understanding for all students. Cullinan (1989) used the metaphors of a mirror and a window to emphasize the potential that children's literature offers. We see our own experiences in literature (the mirror), and then an author "invites us to look through a (window), and we respond, to see the world through another's eyes" (p. 424). Gates and Mark (2006) reported that many have used the Cullinan mirror metaphor to emphasize the need for multicultural literature to assure that all children can see themselves in books and also see those who are outside of their cultural world in literature. All students need to see positive representations of themselves and their cultures in literature.

Through the window of literature, however, we are allowed to enter worlds not physically open to us—to view, to empathize, and to participate emotionally in ways that may ultimately change the way we see ourselves and the society in which we live. Only through repeated immersion into those other cultural experiences will we as a society begin to appreciate the struggles, the pain, and the horror that our sisters and brothers of other backgrounds have suffered. Only then will we begin truly to develop the respect needed to appreciate and honor our unique diversity as a country.

(p. 2)

According to Banks (2004), it is important to move students beyond mere exposure to cultures outside of their own toward an appreciation and understanding of unique cultural experiences, culminating in social action that promotes decision-making on important social issues followed by advocacy and action to help solve these issues.

In order to provide educational equity for all students, it is critical that educators understand the theory of multicultural education and integrate the curriculum and materials to support these goals into practice. Gay (2001) noted the lag that exists between multicultural education theory and practice. When quality, multicultural literature is integrated into the curriculum, it enriches the classroom context for learning in important ways as it validates the culture of individual students and develops an understanding and respect for other cultures that can lead to social action.

CRITERIA FOR SELECTION OF MULTICULTURAL LITERATURE

The first consideration, when selecting multicultural literature, should be the purpose of the literature. Bishop's (1997) five functions of multicultural literature are helpful when determining purpose. Will the literature provide knowledge, offer varying perspectives, promote appreciation for diversity, scaffold critical inquiry, or provide enjoyment? Once purpose is established, it is important for educators to be acquainted with criteria to determine honesty, authenticity, and quality in multicultural literature. Temple, Martinez, and Yokota (2006) emphasized that with the increased number of multicultural books available, it is important to select quality books. They presented the following criteria for teachers and teacher librarians to apply:

- Do the author and illustrator present authentic perspectives? An insider's mind-set and point of view should be maintained to portray a cultural group authentically.
- Is the culture portrayed multidimensionally? Cultural groups should be presented multidimensionally to help readers realize the depth and breadth of experiences within cultures.
- Are cultural details naturally integrated? These details are necessary to make the story come alive but should not impede the flow of the story.
- Are details accurate and is the interpretation current? Details must be accurate and true to the situation in which they are presented. Inaccuracies may indicate careless research and presentation.
- Is language used authentically? The language and dialect spoken by characters should authentically portray the kinds of interactions that are typical of those characters, and terminology that refers to aspects of culture should be acceptable by contemporary standards.
- Is the collection balanced? It is important to present children with a balanced collection of multicultural books (pp. 109–112).

Bishop (1997) noted that "judging authenticity is neither an exact science nor an objective exercise. Teachers and teacher librarians can bring to the reading of a book only their own individual backgrounds and life experiences" (p. 16). As they put forth effort to learn about other people and their cultures and their literature, they are better equipped to make good decisions about individual books. If teachers and teacher librarians lack this background knowledge of the historical, cultural, or literary traditions of a group, they can turn to knowledgeable reviewers. It is also important for these educators to acquaint themselves with respected authors and illustrators of multicultural literature and to follow their work. The remaining chapters in this book will acquaint readers with many of these esteemed authors and artists. Finally, as Bishop (1997) emphasized, it is important to remember:

reading literature, especially fiction, no matter what culture it reflects, ought to be an aesthetic experience. In our search for social significance and our desire for social change, we dare not forget that a well-written piece of literature is a work of art. It may be serious and cause readers to reflect or to become angry or to see something familiar in a new way; it may be informative and diminish ignorance; but it does so through readers' engagement with the literary work. In classrooms where multicultural literature is to have an effect, that experience is primary. Other goals can be achieved when readers are given the time and the opportunity, with a knowledgeable teacher as facilitator, to make thoughtful responses to their reading and to enrich their own readings by interacting with others whose responses may or may not be similar.

(p. 6)

AUTHENTICITY AND THE DEBATE

One of the issues related to authenticity in multicultural books that continues to be debated is the issue of authority regarding authorship of these books. Most multicultural books are written by someone from the culture itself, such as Virginia Hamilton writing about African Americans; but some multicultural books are written by someone outside the culture, such as Eve Bunting who has written about other groups besides her own cultural group. Can authors outside the culture create authentic literature about a culture other than their own? Bishop (1997) explained that this question is complex and is partly a political question that is therefore connected to issues of power, ownership, and definition. "Given the history of race relations in this country, people who see themselves as members of oppressed groups are not always willing to trust people whom they identify as members of the oppressing group to tell their stories, particularly in light of a history of stereotyping, distortions, and patronizing of such groups in literature" (p. 16).

Hancock (2008) agreed that scholars have debated the authenticity of multicultural literature written by authors inside and outside of the culture and reported that most agree that to achieve authenticity, "the author must either be of the culture or take on the perspective of other people living in the culture" (p. 213). Some authors such as Paul Goble who actually lived with the Plains Indians for more than a decade before authoring *Storm Maker's Tipi* have received genuine recognition for an outsider perspective. Bishop (1997) also acknowledged that "the farther a writer's background, knowledge, and experiences are from the culture of the person or people about whom he or she is writing, the greater the necessity for the author to fill in the cultural gaps, the greater the effort needed to do so, and the greater the risk of mistakes" (p. 17).

In an attempt to gather further information about the authenticity debate regarding insider versus outsider authorship of multicultural literature, the authors conducted personal interviews with two authors who are representative of each of these stances, Doreen Rappaport and Joseph Bruchac (D. Rappaport, personal communication, February 19, 2008; J. Bruchac, February 26, 2008). Doreen Rappaport, has written books about cultures that differ from her own, such as *Martin's Big Words: The Life of Martin King, Jr.*; *Freedom River*, the story of John Parker, an African-American businessman who bought his own freedom and then helped many others to obtain their freedom through the Underground Railroad; *The Flight of Red Bird: The Life of Zitkala-Sa*, the story of Gertrude Bonnin who was born to a Sioux mother and White father, left her

Why do you write? What is your purpose?

Rappaport: My purpose is to let kids know. I write what I write for a couple of reasons. One, because I think that there are some incredible stories that kids do not know. There is a lot of churning over of all the same stuff, all the time. In history and in books, there are just so many stories of ordinary people like all of us who do extraordinary things, and I want kids to learn about them. I also want them to understand that there is a process in life. One of the things I write about shows that there is not immediate gratification, and that you have to hold on in life if you want to get somewhere. The Civil Rights Movement and the Slavery Resistance and the Jewish Resistance during the Holocaust, and how women fought back . . . . . . all of these things were about people who stepped out of their role, and they took the chance of what that would mean in life. Some of them put their lives in personal danger; other people risked humiliation, so I want kids to see that there's a process, and I think history shows them that there's process. And I think it will also make them value themselves a lot more and their families.

You often write about people outside of your own culture; how did you develop those interests?

Well, my involvement in the Civil Rights Movement led me to Black History. And that kind of led me to re-looking at the whole history and the way I had been taught . . . because I was taught there were presidents, that's the kind of history I learned. During the Civil Rights Movement, I met these everyday people, these ordinary people, who were risking their lives for freedoms that you and I took for granted, and that made me realize that those stories had to be told. And that led me to think of the Women's Movement, and that led me to think about Hispanics, and that led me to think about people with disabilities . . . so it was a gradual process from the initial involvement in the Civil Rights Movement to a re-thinking of the teaching of the presentation of history.

Have some people questioned you regarding writing outside of your culture?

Never. It's amazing. I have to say it; I thought it would come, but it never came. Maybe it is because my research is meticulous, and people learned who I am. It is the only conclusion I can come to. There was a time in the late 60's, when African Americans were very upset by Whites telling their stories because we usurped so much, but I never had a problem.

What disadvantages do you think you have as an author writing outside of your culture?

I could never be a Black storyteller. I think there is something that comes from your own culture. Do you know Andrea Pinkney's work? Or Joe Bruchac's? They carry with them the whole essence of what it means to be African American or Native American, and I have to try to learn that. I have to try to immerse myself and feel the experience . . . The greatest compliment I have received is from the professor at Rutgers who said to me, "If I didn't know you weren't Chinese, Doreen, I would have thought you were." He said, "You told it." But I studied all the poetry and the images, from the way peach blossoms open and what were the important flowers that came out. I mean, these are details that are crucial to setting the scene. I think I have to work very hard . . . maybe it's why I don't write fiction with those subjects . . . I don't know; I might think it's a little too risky.

Are there any advantages to writing outside one's culture?

You learn a lot. You sure learn a lot. You make a lot of new friends. It broadens your world like crazy. I mean I've learned the most fabulous things. I've been privileged and honored. I went to Zitkala-sa, the reservation. I met her 82 year old niece. I was the only white person she talked to about Zitkala-sa's life . . . I met with South Dakota storytellers. You know, it's just great!

Figure 1.1.
Doreen Rappaport.

Indian culture to attend a boarding school at the age of eight and experienced a loss of her identify as she moved between the Indian and White cultures; and *The Long-Haired Girl: A Chinese Legend*, the retelling of a Chinese legend about a young Chinese girl who saves her village from the threat of drought. An excerpt from an interview with Doreen Rapport (personal communication, February 19, 2008) is included in Figure 1.1.

Joseph Bruchac is a storyteller, and many of his writings are about the land of his heritage in the Adirondack Mountain foothills and his Abenaki ancestry, the part of his ethnic background "by which he has been most nourished" (http://www.josephbruchac .com/bruchac_biography.html, accessed on September 25, 2010). Joseph has authored more than 70 books for adults and children, including *The First Strawberries, Tell Me a Tale, Skeleton Man, Dawn Land, Squanto's Journey, and Sacajawea*. He has received numerous honors including the Lifetime Achievement Award from the Native Writers Circle of the Americas in 1999. An excerpt from an interview with Joseph Bruchac (personal communication, February 26, 2008) is included in Figure 1.2.

Why do you write; what is your purpose?

Writing is something which I always felt impelled to do, since my earliest years of becoming literate, and I believe that the idea of self-expression and letting that voice speak that is within you is a very big part of it. I think it is true of someone who is an artist of any kind, whether you are doing visual art or if you are writing stories.

As an author who writes inside of your culture, how do you feel about the issue about authenticity when authors write outside of their culture?

Well, it's a complicated thing. My culture, quite frankly, is a mixture of European-American, contemporary American Indian, Northeastern Adirondack. I mean, I can't say I'm fully native in any part of my culture, you know what I mean? It's a complicated thing. So to write authentically about Abenaki history, I have to do a great deal of research. I'm not a nineteenth or eighteenth century Abenaki Indian. So I have to do a great deal of research to represent it accurately. Recently I wrote a novel about Geronimo. I surely am not a Chiricahua Indian. You know, and to do that required an equal amount of research, and not just book research...travel, speaking directly with Chiricahua people, and having people review what I've written who are within the culture. In the case of that book, I gave the entire manuscript to a friend of mine who is a direct descendent of one of Geronimo's closest cousins who was with him in the whole period of the Apache captivity. And when he called me back, and said, "Hey, Joe, I finished reading that novel, and I want to say something about it." I kind of went, "Oh, what's he going to say?" He said, "Joe, this sucker's good!"

And you were relieved?

I was relieved, but you know, I would never dream of trying to publish something that was so specifically about other people, other places, other languages, other cultures without going through that kind of vetting process, without spending a long time. My novel about the Navaho Code Talkers; it took me a decade to get to the point where I felt I could begin to write that novel. I was interested in the subject twenty years before I ever wrote the book. So, having said that, let me back up. It does not matter if you are in or outside of a culture. What matters is what you do to get inside that culture as a writer. Which means, you don't have to have a blood quantum but you do have to have the ability to listen and to learn...I would never say that anyone would have to be Abinaki to write about the Abinakis well, but I would say that they would have to work a little harder to get rid of some of the weight of assumption that has already been placed on their shoulders...

(Continued)

> *What advantages do you think you have as an American Indian writer when writing about American Indian cultures?*
> I think I have no advantages at all, because I think I start at the same place everyone else does. I just make use of my mind and my opportunity to listen and to read. I think that's the only thing I have . . . that predilection to listen and to read, because there is nothing genetic about it at all. If I have any advantages, I seem to have been given the gift from the Creator of self-expression, and the way to say things in a way that is memorable. I consider that a gift, and I try to do everything I can to nurture that gift and to honor it.
>
> *What do you wish for, in terms of your legacy as an author of multicultural literature?*
> A few good readers.

Figure 1.2.
Joseph Bruchac.

Both Doreen Rappaport and Joseph Bruchac believe that an author can write about a culture outside their own with authenticity if they do careful research and have personal experiences within the culture they write about. Furthermore, Bruchac underscores the importance of having people who are from the culture and authorities on the time period and particular context check the accuracy and authenticity of the writing. Minfong Ho (2002) also made the point that an author's empathy is extremely important when writing about a particular culture. She states,

All things being equal, if the writer is of the same skin color and speaks the same language as the people she writes about, then of course she's more likely to portray them with more sensitivity than someone who is completely different. Yet I feel that none of those factors—race, sex, class, even language—matters as much as experience and empathy. If someone has lived and worked so closely within another community that she has assimilated their experiences, then I think she can come to feel what they feel. After all, empathy, like that leap of imagination, can bring someone over to 'the other side.' And if the someone is a writer, then building a suspension bridge back is the only natural thing to do to help bring others across.

(p. 97)

CULTURALLY RESPONSIVE TEACHING

It is widely recognized that the cultural gap between children, teachers, and other educators in public schools is great and increasing; and the diversity in our public PK-12 schools continues to increase significantly. The National Center for Education Statistics (2008) reported:

The percentage of racial/ethnic minority students enrolled in the nation's public schools increased from 22 percent in 1972 to 31 percent in 1986 to 43 percent in 2006. This increase in minority enrollment largely reflects the growth in the percentage of students who were Hispanic. In 2006, Hispanic students represented 20 percent of public school enrollment, up from 6 percent in 1972 and 11 percent in 1986.

(p. iv of *The Condition of Education 2008*)

According to Futrell, Gomez and Bedden's (2003) discussion of teaching in the "new America," statistical projections have indicated that the percentage of students of color will increase, reaching 51 percent by 2050. In addition, approximately 25 percent of children live in poverty. In their call for the preparation of culturally responsive teachers, Villegas and Lucas (2002) reported that more than one in seven children between the ages of five and 17 spoke a language other than English at home, and more than one-third of these children had limited proficiency in English.

According to Sleeter and Grant in 2003, over 90 percent of teachers were White; and this percentage was increasing. Sleeter (2001) reported that the research in this area was limited and that predominantly White institutions have generally not responded to this cultural gap between teachers and students in public schools. She recommended that preservice programs either address the issue by recruiting more teacher candidates from culturally diverse communities or by trying to develop the multicultural knowledge base of predominantly White cohorts of teacher candidates.

Varian (2008) investigated the beliefs and practice of six educators who had been identified as using "culturally responsive teaching" in their classrooms. This study clarified what these educators believed to be important in their "culturally aware" classrooms. In addition, the study explored how personal and professional experiences shaped the teachers' beliefs that impacted their practice, with the hope that the insights generated by these educators will provide greater understanding of how a culturally relevant pedagogy can enhance the school experiences of children whose diverse sociocultural backgrounds come together in a multicultural classroom setting. Varian found a strong connection between beliefs and practices. She found that the instructional practices of these teachers were constructivist in approach. Moreover, they were strategies consistent with good instruction for all student populations. These teachers had a strong interest in learning about their students' home culture. They also carefully incorporated those cultures into classroom life in a variety of ways. Finally, the teachers sought to empower the students encouraging them to become responsible for their learning and preparing them not only academically but for the world beyond school.

These teachers' beliefs were greatly influenced by their parents who were all socially active in their communities and who placed a high regard on education. They were also influenced by their own firsthand experiences of immersion in new cultural experiences, either for travel, study, or service. In addition, witnessing or learning about social injustice had deeply affected these teachers' awareness of diversity. The findings from this study support the need for the inclusion of firsthand experiences for teacher candidates in diverse classroom settings with teachers who practice culturally responsible pedagogy. In addition, practicing teachers and teacher librarians need ongoing professional development on the topic of culturally responsive teaching, including effective mentoring programs to allow teachers to observe excellent educators who practice this pedagogy. An emphasis on research to explore how more teachers and teacher librarians can become culturally responsive educators in their classrooms is important for all students.

In spite of many initiatives, there continues to be a significant achievement gap between culturally diverse students and White students. For example, on the National Assessment of Education Progress (NAEP) mathematics and reading assessments, the test scores of African Americans and Hispanics have been consistently and notably lower than those of White students. Research has shown that culturally and linguistically diverse children, who often flounder in school, are inadequately prepared for higher education and seek unskilled employment (Cochran-Smith, Davis, & Fries, 2004). In spite of this disturbing scenario, there is reason for hope. Many schools are looking for ways to successfully educate all of their students, and many researchers are focusing on the identification of instructional strategies that are effective for educating students from diverse backgrounds.

Banks (2004) reported that "for multicultural education to be implemented successfully, institutional changes must be made in the curriculum; the teaching materials; teaching and learning styles; the attitudes, perceptions, and behaviors of teachers and administrators; and the goals, norms and culture of the school" (p. 4). Culturally relevant teaching is part of multicultural education and refers to the way teachers interact with students and the way they teach. Ladson-Billings (1994) explained that culturally responsive teaching is a pedagogy that acknowledges the importance of the inclusion of students' cultural references in all aspects of learning. It is a model of teaching that focuses on academic achievement, cultural competence, and sociopolitical consciousness (Ladson-Billings, 2001). In her study of teachers who were successful educators of African-American children, Ladson-Billings (1994) identified the following tenets of culturally relevant teaching:

- students whose educational, economic, social, political, and cultural futures are most tenuous are helped to become intellectual leaders in the classroom;
- students are apprenticed in a learning community rather than taught in an isolated and unrelated way; students' real-life experiences are legitimized as they become part of the official curriculum;
- teachers and students participate in a broad conception of literacy that incorporates both literature and oratory;
- teachers and students engage in a collective struggle against the status quo; and
- teachers are cognizant of themselves as political beings (pp. 117, 118).

The body of research on how people learn and more specifically, how language and culture may influence learning is growing. Rosenblatt's (1994) transactional view of reading has important implications for culturally responsive instruction. She noted that what readers experience and take away from a reading experience is shaped by their cultural and social experiences as well as the stance or approach to the particular text. The implication of Rosenblatt's theory is that teachers need to allow for multiple interpretations of text because each reader brings prior knowledge based on personal experience to the response to particular texts.

Bell's research (2003) supported instruction for culturally diverse students that is more student-centered with the teacher taking a facilitative role. Sleeter and Grant (2003) reported that culturally relevant instruction relies on effective communication between the teacher and students. They stated, "The important point is that academic learning can be greatly enhanced when teachers learn the cultural style of the child well enough to connect effectively with the child within the child's zone of proximal development" (p. 50).

McLaughlin and McLeod (1996) reported on promising instructional approaches connected to culturally relevant pedagogy. One of the most promising instructional approaches to stimulating learning is cooperative learning that benefits culturally diverse students because it requires them to negotiate roles using linguistic and social strategies. Exemplary schools also sought to build on, rather than replace, their students' native languages using students' primary languages either as a means of developing literacy skills, as a tool for delivering content, or both. A thematic approach to curriculum offers several benefits to students with limited background knowledge. This approach focuses on a topic in depth, over an extended period of time, from multiple perspectives and gives these students an opportunity to acquire the necessary background knowledge (Peregoy & Boyle, 2005).

Moll, Amanti, Neff, and Gonzalez (1992) focused on bridging the differences between home and school cultures and assisted Arizona teachers in making these connections. This approach was based on the belief that cultures possess "funds of knowledge" that teachers can access to make academic material more relevant to students. Teachers visited students' homes in an attempt to understand their cultural backgrounds as well as gather material for their curriculum. This approach was confirmed by Ladson-Billings (1995a) when she declared that culturally competent teachers utilized students' culture as a vehicle for learning. She noted that school was often perceived by African American students as a place where they could not be themselves.

The importance of teachers' passion for teaching children from diverse cultures and also their high expectations for student achievement is well documented in the literature (Gay, 2002; Ladson-Billings, 1995b). Reeves (2004) reported the findings from research conducted on the Norfolk Public School system, a complex urban system. In spite of dismal achievement scores, teachers and administrators in Norfolk believed their students could improve achievement. This school system demonstrated that the relationship between poverty and student achievement could be negligible. They reduced the achievement gap between White and African American students at three grade levels with the African American group continuing to improve.

In her discussion of culturally responsive instruction and new literacies, Au (2001) stated, "cultural responsiveness in literacy instruction can bring students of diverse backgrounds to high levels of literacy by promoting engagement through activities that reflect the values, knowledge, and structures of interaction that students bring from the home" (p. 1). Au believed that if these students were to compete with their mainstream peers, their instruction must take them beyond the basics to higher level thinking with text. She was concerned that there was a pattern of mandated programs in low-income schools. These programs generally focused on lower-level skills and gave students of diverse backgrounds little opportunity to develop higher-level thinking about text. Au supported literature-based instruction that included quality multicultural literature because it built upon the strengths that students brought from their home cultures and fostered higher-level thinking.

Lewison, Leland, and Harste (2008) considered personal and cultural resources as an entry into critical literacy. They believed that educators' goal should be to "make the classroom community feel comfortable to all students, especially newcomers" (p. 25). The curriculum should honor students' experiences and first languages, putting students at the center of the curriculum. Lewison et al. point out that it is important that students' issues move from personal to social because meaning has social and cultural dimensions. "By moving from the personal to the social, students are able to explore how historical practices, power relationships, and cultural systems of meaning all are at play in daily life" (p. 32). Multicultural literature plays an important part in this critical literacy curriculum because these texts invite conversations about justice, equity, and honoring diversity.

HOW CAN TEACHERS INCLUDE MULTICULTURAL LITERATURE IN THEIR CLASSROOM?

The first step toward the integration of multicultural literature into the curriculum is to include a rich collection of this literature within the classroom library. Socioeconomic factors can lead to inequities in students' access to books outside of the classroom, so it is critical that schools offer quality literature representative of many cultures and on a variety of reading levels to all students. This is often a financial challenge for classroom teachers since most school districts do not have a budget that includes support for building and maintaining classroom libraries. However, many teachers persevere to overcome this obstacle with diligent efforts to build their libraries through grant writing, soliciting support from parent-teacher organizations, purchasing used books at garage sales, and discards from library sales.

Teachers and teacher librarians can work together to add appropriate books to the school's library. These books can be rotated to classrooms to support a multicultural experience. Books may also be borrowed from public libraries for temporary use. When all else fails, teachers may save bonus points from student book clubs to obtain free books, and yes, spend money from their personal income to add quality literature to their classroom libraries.

It is important for teachers and teacher librarians to understand the importance of including multicultural literature that is authentic, respectful, and culturally accurate in their classrooms and libraries. Students need access to books in which they can see themselves and not just their physical appearance, but in which they can see their culture and language as well. During Ruth Oswald's years as an elementary classroom teacher, this concept became clear to her as she observed a young, African-American reader claim the book, *Honey, I Love* by Eloise Greenfield as she carried the book around the classroom showing it to classmates, repeating the poems, and then tucking it into her desk. This example supports the Cullinan (1989) mirror metaphor used to emphasize the need for multicultural literature to assure that students can see themselves in books. Ruth began to look in earnest for multicultural picture books with illustrations and language that represented her student population as well as the full spectrum of cultures.

Ruth also came to realize that she needed books in her classroom library that represented cultures that were not familiar to her students, which supports the Cullinan (1989) window metaphor used to emphasize the need for multicultural literature to assure that students have opportunities to experience cultures that are different from their own. After moving into higher education, Ruth was teaching a graduate children's literature course and many of her students were practicing teachers. During the study of multicultural literature, one teacher shared that because there was not much diversity in her classroom, she did not believe she had to worry about including multicultural literature in her classroom library or instruction. It is critical to the education of all of our children for teachers to understand that diversity should be embraced and that we all benefit when we value our own culture as well as differing cultures. This mindset is critical to foster the understanding of social justice and to overcome xenophobia, the fear or hatred of foreign cultures or people. The use of multicultural literature is one of the most powerful ways for teachers to honor students' culture and to encourage cross-cultural understanding.

In Donna Lanyi's fifth/sixth multi-age classroom, the topic of oppression came up in a book discussion while reading *Miles' Song* by Alice McGill, about a 12-year-old slave boy who wants to learn to read. The students were talking about the concept of oppression but did not have a name for it. They mentioned purposefully holding others back, keeping them down, not letting others get better in life. Through their discussion, Donna mentioned that there was a word for this concept–oppression. The children loved learning new words they thought others might not know and ran with it. Interestingly, the word continued to be a theme in many of the books groups read that year such as *Stones in Water* by Donna Jo Napoli and *The Boys of St. Petri* by Bjarne Reuter and Anthea Bell, books about the German occupation in World War II, and *Year of Impossible Goodbyes* by Sook Nyul Choi about the Russian occupation of Korea. As they read and discussed these books, these young readers became very adept at recognizing the concept and using the word oppression/oppressed. Donna and her students never looked up the definition; they came to understand the word more fully through the theme in literature and their discussions. This is a wonderful example of student-centered curriculum as discussed by Lewison et al. (2008). Donna based curriculum on what was important to her students and not on preplanned lessons; she was prepared to face uncertainties as to what happened in the classroom. As explained by Lewison et al., teachers like Donna are conscious of the theories that guide actions in the classroom, and the curriculum does not happen by accident. These teachers believe that "... all students are capable and bring a wide range of experiential, cultural, and linguistic resources to the classroom," and they find "... ways to regularly use these resources and give them a place of prominence in what counts in our classrooms" (p. 28).

Multicultural literature was always an important feature in Linda Collins' work as an English as a second language (ESL) teacher and supervisor in a large urban district. In the classroom, students were always excited to see their own faces, traditions, and points of view expressed in their readings. They made many associations and enthusiastically shared personal connections that related to the literature. Through reading and discussing literature that represented diverse cultures, her ESL students found common ground that connected them to one another as well. Seeing themselves and their experiences represented in books gave each one of them a sense of pride and underscored for them the importance of their own life events and increased their interest in their class work. It also allowed different students to provide a voice of authority and insightful expertise on topics regarding their particular backgrounds.

Later, as a district supervisor working with ESL and bilingual staff, Linda Collins organized workshops for teachers and instructional assistants to reinforce with them the importance of using multicultural literature as well as ways to incorporate it into regular instruction. Seeing the response of diverse staff members to multicultural literature and the events represented in the books validated the earlier reactions Linda had observed from her students. The staff members also embraced the opportunities to share life experiences and connect on a deeper level with the texts and one another. They came to realize the importance of seeking out multicultural literature and incorporating it into their work with students.

Joanna Newton's teaching career began when she served as a Peace Corps volunteer as a teacher of English as a foreign language in a village school in Armenia. By the end of her service, she learned that language is more than just a means of communication; language is the single most important vehicle one can use to affect change. Joanna carries this lesson with her today as she works with a culturally, linguistically, and economically diverse group of second-grade students. The theme in her class that guides their work is, "Words are powerful!" Joanna exposes her students to powerful words in all forms, from read alouds of multicultural children's literature to responses to the poetry of Langston Hughes, to the examination of speeches such as Dr. King's "I Have a Dream" that have changed the course of history. Joanna's students are constantly on the lookout for powerful words as they read, write, or speak to others. When they find these powerful words, they share them with each other and put them on the "Wow Words" word wall. Once a word is on this word wall, students are challenged to use it in their writing or speech. Joanna reports that, at any given time, her students might be "ecstatic" or "perplexed" or "distressed."

As part of the weekly word study in Joanna's second-grade classroom, students are encouraged to understand English vocabulary by examining the Latin and Greek roots from which it came. When her Spanish speakers realize that their language fits into English, they come alive with the excitement that words can bring. Suddenly their personal vocabularies expand from just that of simple sight words. Joanna's students know that words are powerful and that their words matter (personal communication, August 17, 2009).

These are just a few examples of how culturally competent teachers include multicultural literature in the curriculum. Bishop (1997) identified five functions of multicultural literature; it can

1. provide knowledge or information,
2. change how students view the world by offering varying perspectives,
3. promote or develop an appreciation for diversity,
4. give rise to critical inquiry, and provide enjoyment and illuminate human experience (pp. 4, 5).

As children engage in reading multicultural literature, participate in critical discussions about these texts, work cooperatively in small groups, and share information with others through writing and discussion, the chances are increased that their thinking will move beyond the basics toward critical levels of understanding. All children deserve culturally responsive instruction through authentic multicultural literature.

REFERENCES

Au, K. H. (2001, July/August). Culturally responsive instruction as a dimension of new literacies. *Reading Online, 5*(1), http://www.readingonline.org/newliteracies/lit_index.asp?HREF =au/index.html.

Banks, J. A. (2004). Multicultural education: Historical development, dimensions, and practice. In J. A Banks & C. A. M. Banks (Eds.), *Handbook of research on multicultural education* (2nd ed., pp. 3–29). San Francisco, CA: Jossey-Bass.

Banks, J. A., & Banks, C. A. M. (Eds.). (2001). *Multicultural education: Issues and perspectives* (4th ed.). Boston, MA: Allyn & Bacon.

Bell, L. (2003). Strategies that close the literacy gap. *Educational Leadership, 60*(4), 32–34.

Bishop, R. S. (1997). Selecting literature for a multicultural curriculum. In V. J. Harris (Ed.), *Using multiethnic literature in the K–8 classroom* (pp. 1–19). Norwood, MA: Christopher-Gordon Publishers, Inc.

Cai, M. (1998). Multiple definitions of multicultural literature: Is the debate really just "ivory tower" bickering? *The New Advocate, 11*(4), 311–324.

Cochran-Smith, M., Davis, D., & Fries, K. (2004). Multicultural teacher education: Research, practice, and policy. In J. A. Banks (Ed.), *Handbook of research in multicultural education* (2nd ed., pp. 931–936). San Francisco, CA: Jossey-Bass.

Cullinan, B. (1989). *Literature and the child.* New York, NY: Harcourt Brace Jovanovich.

Freedman, R. (2002). *Confucius: The golden rule.* New York, NY: Arthur A. Levine Books.

Futrell, M. H., Gomez, J., & Bedden, D. (2003). Teaching the children of a new America: The challenge of diversity. *Phi Delta Kappan, 84*(5), 381–383.

Gates, P. S. & Mark, D. H. (2006). *Cultural journeys.* Lanham, MD: Scarecrow Press, Inc.

Gay, G. (2001). Curriculum theory and multicultural education. In J. A. Banks & C. A. M. Banks (Eds.), *Handbook of research on multicultural education* (pp. 25–43). San Francisco, CA: Jossey-Bass.

Gay, G. (2002). *Culturally responsive teaching: Theory, research and practice.* New York, NY: Teachers College Press.

Hancock, M. R. (2008). *A celebration of literature and response* (3rd ed.). Upper Saddle, NJ: Pearson Education, Inc.

Harris, T. L., & Hodges, R. E. (Eds.). (1995). *The literacy dictionary.* Newark, DE: International Reading Association.

Ho, M. (2002). Ask the author: Minfong Ho. In C. Temple, M. Martinez, J. Yokota, & A. Naylor (Eds.), *Children's books in children's hands: An introduction to their literature* (2nd ed., p. 97). Boston, MA: Allyn and Bacon.

Ladson-Billings, G. (1994). *The dreamkeepers.* San Francisco, CA: Jossey-Bass.

Ladson-Billings, G (1995a). But that's just good teaching! The case for culturally relevant pedagogy. *Theory into Practice, 34*(3), 159–165.

Ladson-Billings, G. (1995b). Toward a theory of culturally relevant pedagogy. *American Educational Research Journal, 32,* 465–491.

Ladson-Billings, G. (2001). *Crossing over to Canaan.* San Francisco, CA: Jossey-Bass.

Lewison, M., Leland, C., & Harste, J. C. (2008). *Creating critical classrooms.* New York, NY: Lawrence Erlbaum Associates.

McLaughlin, B., & McLeod, B. (1996). *Educating all our students: Improving education for children from culturally and linguistically diverse backgrounds.* Final Report of the National Center for Research on Cultural Diversity and Second Language Learning. Vol. 1, University of California, Santa Cruz.

Moll, L. C., Amanti, C., Neff, D., & Gonzalez, N. (1992). Funds of knowledge for teaching: Using a qualitative approach to connect homes and classrooms. *Theory into Practice, 31*(2), 132–141.

National Center for Education Statistics. (2008). *The condition of education 2008,* http://nces.ed.gov/programs/coe/press/index.asp.

Nieto, S. (1992). *Affirming diversity: The sociopolitical context of multicultural education.* New York, NY: Longman.

Norton, D. E. (2009). *Multicultural children's literature: Through the eyes of many children* (3rd ed.). Boston, MA: Pearson Education, Inc.

Peregoy, S. F., & Boyle, O. F. (2005). *Reading, writing, and learning in ESL: A resource book for K–12 teachers* (4th ed.). Boston, MA: Pearson.

Reeves, D. B. (2004). *Accountability for learning: How teachers and school leaders can take charge.* Alexandria, VA: Association for Supervision and Curriculum Development.

Rosenblatt, L. M. (1994). The transactional theory of reading and writing. In R. B. Ruddell, M. R. Ruddell, & H. Singer (Eds.), *Theoretical models and processes of reading* (4th ed., pp. 1057–1092). Newark, DE: International Reading Association.

Sleeter, C. E. (2001). Preparing teachers for culturally diverse schools: Research and the over-whelming presence of whiteness. *Journal of Teacher Education, 52*(2), 94–106.

Sleeter, C. E., & Grant, C. A. (2003). *Making choices for multicultural education: Five approaches to race, class, and gender* (4th ed.). New York, NY: John Wiley & Sons, Inc.

Temple, C., Martinez, M., & Yokota, J. (2006). *Children's books in children's hands* (3rd ed.). Boston, MA: Pearson Education, Inc.

U.S. Census Bureau (2000). http://www.census.gov/main/www/cen2000.html.

Varian, N. A. (2008). *Beliefs and instructional practices of culturally relevant educators: A qualitative study.* Unpublished doctoral dissertation, The University of Akron, Ohio.

Villegas, A. M., & Lucas, T. (2002). Preparing culturally responsive teachers. Rethinking the curriculum. *Journal of Teacher Education, 53*(1), 20–32.

MULTICULTURAL BOOKS

Bruchac, J. (1995). *Dawn land.* Golden, CO: Fulcrum Publishing.

Bruchac, J. (1997). *Tell me a tale: A book about storytelling.* San Diego, CA: Harcourt Children's Books.

Bruchac, J. (1998). *The first strawberries,* illustrated by A. Vojtech. New York, NY: Puffin.

Bruchac, J. (2003). *Skeleton man.* New York, NY: HarperCollins.

Bruchac, J. (2007). *Squanto's journey,* illustrated by G. Shed. New York, NY: Voyager Books.

Bruchac, J. (2008). *Sacajawea.* New York, NY: Sandpiper.

Choi, S. N. (1993). *Year of impossible goodbyes.* New York, NY: Yearling.

Goble, P. (2001). *Storm maker's tipi.* New York, NY: Antheum.

Greenfield, E. (2002). *Honey, I love,* illustrated by J. S. Gilchrist. New York, NY: Amistad.

McGill, A. (2000). *Miles' song.* Boston, MA: Houghton Mifflin Books for Children.

Napoli, D. J. (1999). *Stones in water.* New York, NY: Puffin.

Rappaport, D. (1995). *The long-haired girl: A Chinese legend.* New York, NY: Dial.

Rappaport, D. (1999). *The flight of Red Bird: The life of Zitkala-Sa.* New York, NY: Puffin.

Rappaport, D. (2000). *Freedom river,* illustrated by B. Collier. New York, NY: Hyperion Books.

Rappaport, D. (2001). *Martin's big words: The life of Martin Luther King, Jr.,* illustrated by B. Collier. New York, NY: Jump at the Sun.

Reuter, B. (1996). *The boys from St. Petri* (A. Bell, Trans.). New York, NY: Puffin.

2

Integrating Multicultural Literature Into the Curriculum

Lynn Atkinson Smolen, Ruth A. Oswald, and Sandra Jenkins

INTRODUCTION

Multicultural literature has been described by experts on literature as both a window and a mirror (Gates & Mark, 2006). It is a window on the world, opening up views for readers to learn about the world, its geography, history and cultures. It is a mirror reflecting the traditions, values, and beliefs of diverse readers. When readers read about characters that look like them and reflect their way of life, their self-identity is affirmed, and they get the message that their way of life is valued (Norton, 2009).

In the increasingly diverse U.S. society, multicultural literature should be an essential part of the fabric of the learning environment (Banks, 2004). However, multicultural literature is often relegated to the back shelf of libraries, book stores, and classrooms. It should not be treated as an after-thought or an add-on in the curriculum. It should not just be brought out on Martin Luther King's Day or Cinco de Mayo. It should be an integral part of the curriculum, representing all Americans. However, teachers and teacher librarians need guidance not only in how to select multicultural literature but also in how to use it in their daily lessons, linking it to key skills, concepts, and standards.

A number of literacy experts have suggested ways for integrating multicultural literature into the curriculum. Norton (1990) suggested that teachers use a five-phase model for studying multicultural literature by exploring the following genres in each phase:

- phase one: traditional literature;
- phase two: traditional tales from one area;
- phase three: autobiographies, biographies, and historical nonfiction;
- phase four: historical fiction; and
- phase five: contemporary fiction, biography, and poetry.

Norton (1990) pointed out that by starting with traditional literature students gain insight into the values of a particular culture. Historical fiction, biography, and informational literature provide readers with essential background information on a particular culture to help them understand themes and important issues in contemporary fiction, biography and poetry.

Rasinski and Padak (1990) suggested that teachers use Banks' levels of multicultural education, starting with level one and building toward levels three and four:

- level one, the contributions approach, focuses on heroes, holidays, and discrete cultural elements;
- level two, the additive approach, focuses on content, concepts, themes, and perspectives which are added to the curriculum without changing its structure;
- level three, the transformation approach, alters the structure of the curriculum to enable students to view concepts, issues, events, and themes from the perspective of diverse ethnic and cultural groups; and
- level four, encourages students to make decisions on important social issues and take action to help solve them (Banks, 2004, p. 15).

The value of using Banks' levels is that students get a more in-depth understanding of the culture they are reading about, avoiding the superficiality of only reading about heroes, celebrations, food and festivals. Furthermore, they develop important background knowledge on different cultures, which helps them interpret characters' actions, settings, and events in multicultural books.

Another way to integrate multicultural literature into the curriculum is by using twin texts, text sets, and thematic units as suggested by Hancock (2008). Depending on the situation, teachers and teacher librarians can start with twin texts (two books that are matched in theme or topic), incorporating these into a broader unit of study; and then once they feel comfortable with this, they can have students read books in a text set (six–eight books that are matched in theme or topic), focusing on a particular theme over a short period of time. As teachers and teacher librarians become even more comfortable with multicultural literature, they can collaborate to develop thematic units that integrate multicultural literature into several different subject areas and tie the thematic unit to content standards. When teachers work closely with teacher librarians, it is possible to expand this approach across grade levels.

No matter how teachers and teacher librarians integrate multicultural literature into the curriculum, it is critical that they use guided discussions (Vacca & Vacca, 2008) with the books. With this approach, teachers guide students to have a greater understanding of the cultures they are reading about so that they do not misinterpret what they read. Allington and Johnston (2002) found that in high-achieving classrooms, students spent significant amounts of time engaged in purposeful talk about their reading and learning.

In this chapter we discuss ways for teachers and teacher librarians to use multicultural literature in twin texts, text sets, and thematic units within the curriculum as suggested by Hancock (2008). We provide examples of each of these and suggest response activities for the books. According to Harvey and Goudvis (2007), comprehension strategy lessons should move from close to home to more global issues or cultures and places further removed from most students' lives. Having students read books that are related in some way provides them with opportunities to make text to text and text to world connections. Harvey and Goudvis stated

Readers naturally make connections between books and their own lives. Once they have heard a wealth of stories and narratives, they begin to connect themes, characters, and issues from one book to another. When children understand how to connect the texts they read to their lives, they begin to make connections to the larger world. This nudges them into thinking about bigger, more expansive issues beyond their universe of home, school, and neighborhood.

(p. 92)

Moreover, these connections can be broadened by Internet projects (Castek, Bevans-Mangelson, & Goldstone, 2006). This approach benefits students because they develop literacy and technology skills at the same time. This chapter recommends Internet sites that can be used with some of the twin texts, text sets, and thematic units. Examples are discussed for different grade-level clusters.

MULTICULTURAL TWIN TEXTS

Table 2.1 shows examples of multicultural twin texts. The books have been matched based on thematic connections between the books. There are examples of twin texts that match poetry with an informational book, a picture book with an informational book, and a historical fiction book with biography.

Table 2.1.
Multicultural Twin Texts

Book 1	Book 2	Recommended Grade	Genre and Culture
My Dadima Wears a Sari, K. Sheth (2007)	*I is for India*, P. Das (1997)	Primary	Picture book and non-fiction; Indian-American
My Colors, My World/Mis colores, mi mundo, M. Gonzalez (2007)	*The Desert in My Mother/El desierto es mi madre*, P. Mora (1994)	Primary	Picture book and poetry, bilingual
Esperanza Rising, P. Ryan (2000)	*Harvest* by G. Ancona (2001)	Intermediate	Fiction and non-fiction (photo essay) Mexican-American
This School is Not White, D. Rappaport (2005)	*Through My Eyes,* R. Bridges (1999)	Intermediate	Picture book and biography African American
The Bus Ride, W. Miller (1998)	*Dear Mrs. Parks: A Dialogue with Today's Youth,* R. Parks (1997)	Intermediate	Picture book and informational book African-American
The Forbidden School-house:The True and Dramatic Story of Prudence Crandall & Her Students, S. Jurmain (2005)	*Miss Crandall's School for Young Ladies and Little Misses of Color,* E. Alexander & M. Nelson (2007)	Intermediate	Nonfiction and Poetry African-American

(*continued*)

Table 2.1. (continued)

Book 1	Book 2	Recommended Grade	Genre and Culture
Code Talker: A Novel About the Navajo Marines of WWII, J. Bruchac (2005)	*Quiet Hero The Ira Hayes Story*, S.D. Nelson (2006)	Middle	Fiction and biography American Indian
Blues Journey, W. Myers (2007)	*Jazz ABZ*, W. Marsalis (2005)	Middle	Poetry and biography African-American
Salsa Stories, L. Delacre (2000)	*Red Hot Salsa: Bilingual Poems on Being Young and Latino in the United States*, L. Carlson (2005)	Middle	Short story and poetry Latino American
Sweetgrass Basket, M. Carvell (2005)	*Rattlesnake Mesa Stories From a Native American Childhood*, E. Weber (2004)	Middle	Fiction and biography American Indian
Fire From the Rock, S. Draper (2007)	*Remember: The Journey to School Integration*, T. Morrison (2004)	Middle	Fiction and nonfiction African American

The following are some examples of these twin texts and response activities to use with them.

I Have a Dream by Dr. Martin Luther King, Jr. (1997), a picture book illustrated by 14 outstanding multicultural artists, is an exquisite book that can be used to familiarize intermediate and middle school students with the eloquent language and powerful message in Dr. King's famous speech delivered in Washington, D.C., in 1963. In the back of the book, the artists reflect upon the message in the portion of the speech they illustrated. After reading the speech once through, students can turn to one of the sections of the speech and write a response regarding what they think and feel about the message. They can then turn to the back of the book and compare their reflection to that of the artist. They could also write about the effectiveness of different artists' interpretations of the portions of the speech they illustrated and what aspect of the speech appears to have inspired the illustration. These artists have used different styles and mediums in their illustrations. Students might paint or draw their interpretation of a portion of the King speech, experimenting with one of the mediums. They could also discuss the different styles used by the artists. Information on illustration style is found in a *Book Links* article by Hancock (September, 2007). Teachers can share this information with students on different styles of illustration.

Pairing this book with *Remember the Bridge: Poems of a People* by Carol Boston Weatherford (2002) powerfully provides students with background knowledge for why Dr. King gave his speech in 1963. On each page spread, Weatherford's poems on the struggles and accomplishments of African Americans are paired with a historical black and white photo. Students can read "I Am the Bridge," which is accompanied by a photo of the crowd at the Washington, D.C. march, and write a response on what they think the bridge symbolizes and how Dr. King's speech might be interpreted as the bridge for his people. They might also discuss what they think the connection is between Dr. King's anguish over explaining discrimination to his young daughter in the poem, "Martin's Letter," to the words in his speech:

I have a dream that one day, down in Alabama, with its vicious racists, with its governor having his lips dripping with the words of interposition and nullification, one day, right there in Alabama, little black boys and little black girls will be able to join hands with little white boys and white girls as sisters and brothers.

(p. 27)

Weatherford gathered the photos for her book from prints and photographs in "libraries, museums, historical societies and state archives" (Weatherford, 2002, p. 52). She not only used photos to illustrate poems she had written but also wrote poems in response to some of the photos she found. Students could search for historical photos on the Internet (for example, see the digital library at http://www.lib.umich.edu, accessed on October 02, 2010) and might then write poems in response to one or more of the photos they have selected.

In the picture book, *When Marian Sang: The True Recital of Marian Anderson*, Pam Muñoz Ryan (2002) portrays key episodes from the life of acclaimed African American contralto, Marian Anderson, who became a powerful symbol to her oppressed people during the early 1900s. After reading this picture book orally to students, ask them to complete a K-W-L (Ogle, 1986) chart, listing questions they would like answered. They could then look for answers to their questions in Russell Freedman's (2004) biography, *The Voice That Challenged a Nation: Marian Anderson and the Struggle for Equal Rights*, which provides readers with an in-depth and insightful account of this great vocalist's life and musical career in the context of African Americans' struggle for civil rights. They could also find information on this vocalist at the Penn Library Web site, http://www.library.upenn.edu/exhibits/rbm/anderson/, accessed on October 02, 2010 in which they can view a video clip of Marian Anderson singing on the steps of the Lincoln Memorial as well as other video clips of her performances and interviews.

Both Freedman (2004) and Ryan (2002) include in their books words from spirituals that Marian Anderson sang highlighting the challenges she faced with social injustice and her moral strength and courage in the face of prejudice and discrimination. Students could listen to some of these spirituals, which are available on recordings and listed in the discography in the back of both books. They might write reflections on how they think spirituals echoed the challenges faced by Anderson during her lifetime.

A key episode in Anderson's life was when she returned to America after being celebrated in the opera houses of Europe only to be denied the right to perform at Constitution Hall in Washington, D.C., because of a whites-only policy. Students could research segregation and the history of Jim Crow at http://www.nps.gov/malu/forteachers/jim_crow_laws.htm, accessed on October 02, 2010, and write about their personal feelings about this social practice.

In response to the description in the books of Marian Anderson's life, students could create a biopoem following Hancock's (2008) suggested format, which provides an interesting way to respond to the personality, values, and experiences of a biographical subject. The following is an example:

Marian

Courageous, dedicated, remarkably gifted contralto singer,
Daughter of John and Anna, sister of Ethel May and Alyse.
Who loved her church, music, and her family.
Who experienced prejudice, segregation, and feelings of humiliation.
Who aspired to be a great opera singer and perform at the Metropolitan Opera House.
Who became a symbol to her people.
Who sang on the steps of the Lincoln Memorial when denied the right to perform at
    Constitution Hall.
Native of South Philadelphia,

Anderson

For a more extensive writing activity, students could craft a biographical sketch on Marian Anderson or another African American involved in the struggle for human rights. The outstanding authors, Patricia and Fredrick McKissack, provide students with guidance on how to write biographies at http://teacher.scholastic.com/writewit/ biograph/index.htm. At this site, they show students how they converted their first draft on Frederick Douglass to a final draft. They also guide students step by step through the writing process and provide a place on the Web site where students can publish their biography electronically.

After listening to or reading *When Marian Sang* and discussing the historical background of the era of Jim Crow, the students could perform a reader's theater production of the book. A reader's theater script is available at http://www.pammunozryan.com/rt/ when_marian_sang_rt.pdf, accessed on October 02, 2010. Students could intersperse their performance by singing the Negro spirituals in the book or playing excerpts from "Marian Anderson Spirituals" available at http://www.amazon.com/Spirituals/dp/ B00000GV4D, accessed on October 02, 2010.

Langston's Train Ride, a beautifully illustrated picture book by Robert Burleigh (2004), tells how Langston Hughes was inspired to write "The Negro Speaks of Rivers," while watching the sun shimmering on the Mississippi River during a train ride to Mexico to visit his father. The poem is included towards the end of the book, and an afterword provides a short biography of the poet. An excellent pair for this book is *Langston Hughes*, a picture book of Hughes' poems edited by Rampersad and Roessel (2006) and illustrated by the acclaimed artist Benny Andrews. In this book there are a variety of poems that Hughes wrote, including "Words like Freedom" in which he expresses his strong feelings about social justice and freedom. Students could research the social injustices African Americans have experienced and then write a poem about their feelings regarding social justice and freedom. A good Web site to find information on the history of African Americans is at http://www.pbs.org/wnet/aaworld/history/ index.html, accessed on October 02, 2010. Rampersad and Roessel's (2006) book includes the poem "The Weary Blues," one of the first poems where Hughes began to experiment with including musical motifs from the blues, jazz and spirituals. Students should read this poem aloud to get a feeling of its beat and rhythm. They could then listen to blues, jazz and spirituals to see if they detect the same rhythm and beat as in this poem. A good Web site for this is http://www.pbs.org/jazz/beat/ discography_artist_armstrong.htm, accessed on October 02, 2010. Here students can listen to examples of jazz over different historical periods. Students could also read this poem chorally, with some students reading the longer lines and others the repetitive parts.

Weedflower by Cynthia Kadohata (2006) is a historical fiction novel for the middle school level about Sumiko, a 12-year-old Japanese American girl who is sent with her family to an internment camp on a Mohave Indian reservation in Arizona after the Japanese bomb Pearl Harbor. In the camp, Sumiko struggles with despair but manages to make some friends, including a Mohave boy. She learns from him that the camp is on land taken from the Mohave reservation and finds that the tribe's plight is similar to that of the incarcerated Japanese Americans. This book can be paired with *The Children of Topaz* by Tunnell and Chilcoat (1996), an informational book about a Japanese-American internment camp with primary sources such as photos, samples of children's writing, and other materials. Students could create a Venn diagram comparing and contrasting the plight of the Japanese Americans during World War II with the Mojave and other Native American tribes, whose land was taken away from them. Using this graphic organizer as a starting place, students could write a report comparing and contrasting the plight of the Japanese Americans with that of the Mojave. In addition, after reading *Weedflower*, students might write a diary entry, assuming the character of Sumiko, and write about how they feel about being taken from their home and living in an internment camp.

MULTICULTURAL TEXT SETS

Text sets are collections of books that have been grouped around a particular theme or themes. The grouping of books encourages students to make intertext connections. An informational book can provide background knowledge for a fiction book on the same topic and vice versa. Following the reading of an informational book, students can read a book of poetry on the same topic and make aesthetic connections to the information learned in the nonfiction book. Often text sets consist of six to eight books that represent a variety of genres and are on varying readability levels. Table 2.2 shows examples of multicultural text sets that teachers can use in primary, intermediate, and middle school classrooms.

Text Sets for the Primary Grades

Children's Relationships with Grandparents and Others

Children benefit from strong bonds with a grandparent, a great uncle, or an unrelated older adult. These intergenerational relationships teach them important lessons about life and help them realize the value of having a strong, loving connection with someone special who has gained wisdom and perspective on life. Additionally, children broaden their world view, acquire an historical perspective, and learn about their family's cultural heritage. They also gain special knowledge or skills such as a craft, a recipe, or family stories from these older people. The books in this text set invite students to read about special relationships children enjoy with older adults and learn why intergenerational connections are important.

Grandpa's Face, a picture book by Eloise Greenfield (1988), is a story about the warm bonds between a young, African American girl and her grandfather. Tamika, who loves the warmth of her Grandpa's face, is one day frightened by the ugly scowl he makes in

Table 2.2.
Multicultural Text Sets

Intergenerational Relationships	Heritage	Great Athletes	Social Justice	Self-identity	Harlem Renaissance
Grandpa's Face, E. Greenfield (1988)	*Keepers*, J. Watts (1997)	*Promises to Keep*, S. Robinson (2004)	*Sweetgrass Basket*, M. Carvell (2005)	*Becoming Naomi Leon*, P. Ryan-Muñoz (2004)	*Jazz*, W. Myers (2006)
Mrs. Katz and Tush, P. Polacco (1992)	*Show Way*, J. Woodson (2005)	*We Are The Ship*, K. Nelson (2007)	*Out of Bounds*, B. Naidoo (2003)	*The Skin I'm In*, S. Flake (2007)	*Jazz ABZ*, W. Marsalis (2005)
Grandfather Counts, A. Cheng (2003)	*Dia's Story Cloth*, D. Cha (1996)	*Beisbol!*, J. Winter (2001)	*The Breadwinner*, D. Ellis (2001)	*A Different Beat*, C. Boyd (1996)	*The Sound That Jazz Makes*, C. Weatherford (2000)
Indian Shoes, C. Leitich (2002)	*The Keeping Quilt*, P. Polacco (1988)	*Louis Sockalexis*, B. Wise (2007)	*Freedom Walkers:* R. Freedman (2006)	*Thief of Hearts*, L. Yep (1995)	*Jazz on a Saturday Night*, L. Dillon & D. Dillon (2007)
Abuela, A. Dorros (1991)	*Circle Unbroken*, M. Raven (2004)	*Champions on the Bench*, C. Weatherford (2006)	*Revolution is Not a Dinner Party*, Y. Compenstine (2007)	*Bud, Not Buddy*, C. Curtis (2005)	*Duke Ellington*, A. Pinkney (1997)
Fox Song, J. Bruchac (1993)	*Dumpling Soup*, J. Rattigan (1993)	*Hoop Kings*, C. Smith (2004)	*Tasting the Sky*, I. Barakat (2007)	*A Step from Heaven*, A. Na (2001)	*Ella Fitzgerald*, A. Pinkney (2002)

The Key Collection, A. Cheng (2003)	Bee-Bim Bop! L. Park (2007)	Sixteen Years in Sixteen Seconds, P. Yoo (2005)	Peaceful Protest: The Life of Nelson Mandela, Y. McDonough (2002)	Jimi & Me, J. Adoff (2007)	Langston's Train Ride, R. Burleigh (2004)
Grandma Lai Goon Remembers, A. Morris (2002)	Sienna's Scrapbook Our African American Heritage Trip, T. Parker (2005)	Wilma Unlimited, K. Krull (1996)	César: ¡Sí, se puede!/Yes, we can!, C. T. Bernier-Grande (2004)	Who Am I Without Him?, S. Flake (2004)	Langston Hughes (Poetry for Young People), A. Rampersad & D. Roessel (Eds.) (2006)
Lots of Grandparents, S. Rotner & S. Kelly (2001)	The Empanadas that Abuela Made, D. Bertrand (2003)	Float Like a Butterfly, N. Shange (2002)			Shimmy Shimmy like My Sister Kate, N. Giovanni (1996)
Momma, Where Are You From?, M. Bradby (2000)	Mim's Christmas Jam, A. Pinkney (2001)	Just Like Josh Gibson, A. Johnson (2004)			The Entrance Place of Wonders, D. Muse (2005)
	Blue Bowl Down, C. Millen (2004)	Joe Louis America's Fighter, D. Adler (2005)			Ellington Was Not a Street, N. Shange (2004)

the mirror while practicing a part for a play. Her fears are quieted when Grandpa takes her on one of their talk-walks in the park and reassures her that he loves her and would never use that mean expression with her. Greenfield's prose is beautiful, especially when describing Grandpa's expressive face. Floyd Cooper's realistic illustrations, with their warm earth tones, emphasize the tenderness of this story.

Patricia Polacco's (1992) picture book, *Mrs. Katz and Tush*, tells a warm, loving story about the friendship between a lonely, elderly Jewish woman and a young African American boy. The relationship begins when Larnel asks Mrs. Katz if she would like to adopt a tailless cat. She enthusiastically agrees to do this if he will help her care for it. During Larnel's visits, Mrs. Katz reminisces about her home in Poland and the life she spent with her late husband, Myron. The two of them celebrate Passover and other special occasions over the years until finally a kaddish is said when Mrs. Katz passes away. The exuberant, colorful illustrations emphasize the joy and love expressed in this story for the primary grades.

Grandfather Counts, a picture book by Andrea Cheng (2003), tells about the warm bonds that develop between a young girl and her Chinese grandfather, who comes from China to visit the family in the U.S. At first, Helen and Gong Gong, her grandfather, are not able to talk to each other because of the language barrier. However, gradually, they learn to communicate with gestures and teach each other some basic words in English and Chinese. This text for the primary grades is accompanied by bright and colorful illustrations.

Cynthia Leitich's (2002), *Indian Shoes*, is a collection of short stories for the intermediate grades about Ray, a young Seminole-Cherokee boy, and his Grandpa Halfmoon. Having lost his parents when he was little, Ray is raised by his grandfather in Chicago and rural Oklahoma. Ray and his Grandpa enjoy each other's company and become involved in various humorous events. In one episode, Ray has to wear his grandfather's pants as the ring bearer at a wedding when they discover that his pants are missing. Each short chapter could be read as a separate read aloud.

Abuela by Arthur Dorros (1991) is a fanciful story about a small Latina child who goes on an adventurous tour of New York City with her grandmother, her *abuela*. They fly in the sky, somersaulting through the clouds, visiting different places. Elisa Kleven's sparkling illustrations add to the delight of this picture book for young readers. The text is sprinkled with Spanish words and phrases which are explained in context. There is also a Spanish/English glossary in the back.

In *Fox Song* by Joseph Bruchac (1993), Jamie, a young Abenaki Indian girl, feels the morning sun on her face but does not want to get up for fear she will lose the image of her beloved grandmother in her mind. Having recently lost Grama Bowan, Jamie remembers the precious times she spent with her, learning about the Abenaki world view: gathering berries, stripping birch bark from trees to make baskets, sipping maple syrup, and watching for animal tracks in the snow. She finally gets out of bed, walks through the woods to a tree where her Grama Bowan used to sit, and sings the fox song she taught her. Suddenly, a red fox appears at Jamie's side to listen to the song, helping her realize she will never be alone, as her Grama Bowan used to say. The oil paintings in this picture book for the primary grades beautifully convey the tenderness of this story.

Andrea Cheng (2003) tells about the warm, reassuring relationship between 10-year-old Jimmy and his Chinese grandmother and explores connections across cultures and generations in *The Key Collection*, a short novel for more advanced readers. Jimmy enjoys Ni Ni's company, her delicious Jiao zi (dumplings), her wonderful stories, and her fascinating objects, such as the key collection, that relate to her homeland in China. He does not want Ni Ni to move to California to live with her daughter. However, after time passes, he learns there are ways to bridge the distance between them and to make new friends.

In the photo essay, *Grandma Lai Goon Remembers: A Chinese-American Family Story* by Ann Morris (2002), we learn about the activities that Grandma Lai Goon enjoys with her grandchildren, including showing them an old family album from China, teaching them how to write Chinese characters, and showing them how to make Chinese dolls. Directions for making the dolls, playing the pebble game, and making the buns are included in this book for the primary grades. Using the same format, Ann Morris has written other books featuring grandmothers from different ethnic groups. Each book also includes activities that children can do with their grandmothers.

Lots of Grandparents (Rotner & Kelly, 2001) introduces photos of grandparents with different abilities and from diverse ethnic backgrounds, engaging with their grandchildren in a variety of activities. The photos in this book for the primary grades are accompanied by a very simple text.

Response Activities

The books in this text set are excellent for inspiring discussion about children's loving relationships with their grandparents and other older adults. They could discuss questions such as: What special activities do they engage in with their grandparents? What crafts, recipes, games, or stories have they learned from their grandparents?

Using Ann Morris' (2002) photo essay, *Grandma Lai Goon Remembers*, or another book in her series as a model, children could write their own book on a grandparent or other special senior citizen with whom they are close. They could interview this person, record the facts about his or her life, and compose these details into a book. They might also collect photos, old recipes, directions for making a craft, and a family story to include. Additionally, they could draw a family tree to show the person's relationship in the family lineage.

Using Marie Bradby's (2000) picture book, *Momma, Where are You From?* as a model, students could write a "where I'm from" poem, taking on the persona of their grandmother, grandfather, or another older adult. This pattern poem uses sensory images to convey the nostalgia and memories from a person's life. Table 2.3 shows a pattern framework (adapted from www.swva.net/fred1st/wif.htm, accessed on October 02, 2010) for the poem that students could use. Bradby's book is reminiscent of George Ella Lyon's poem, "Where I'm From," which can be found on her Web site: http://www.georgeellalyon.com/where.html, accessed on October 02, 2010. This Web site also includes an audio clip of George Ella Lyon reading her poem as well as suggestions for ways teachers can use this poem's format for other activities.

Heritage: Making Connections Across Time

Family stories, heirlooms, customs and traditions are all important symbols of a person's cultural heritage. Books with themes of cultural heritage can help readers make connections across time and recognize the value of learning about their own heritage. Included in this text set are books that explore traditions such as storytelling, celebrations, crafts, and recipes.

Table 2.3.

Pattern Framework for Poetry

I am from _____(everyday item), from _____(item important in life) and _____.

I am from the _____(description of town. adjective, adjective, sensory detail).

I am from the _____(flower or something that has a distinctive smell), the _____(flower or something that has a distinctive smell).

I am from _____(family custom) and _____(family characteristic), from _____(family member's name) and _____(another family member's name) and _____(family name).

I am from the _____(description of family habit or activity) and _____(another family habit or activity). From _____(something you heard as a child) and _____(something else you were told as a child).

I'm from _____(symbol of your religion or beliefs) and from _____(further description of your religion or beliefs).

I'm from _____(place of birth and family heritage or culture), _____(two types of food or dishes that represent your family). From the _____(short family anecdote) and _____(another short family anecdote).

I am from _____(trunk, box or other place where family pictures and other memorabilia are kept) and _____(description of the value of these items).

In *Keepers* by Jeri Watts (1997), Kenyon enjoys his grandmother's stories and wants to be selected as "the keeper" of these stories, however, Grandmother tells him that only girls can be keepers. He proves that he can also be "the keeper" by writing these stories in a book and presenting the book to Grandmother on her birthday. This picture book for the primary grades, accompanied with Felicia Marshall's full page acrylic illustrations, provides a glimpse into African-American family life in a small community.

Story quilts have been used by different cultural groups to pass down history and heritage from one generation to the next. To gain a deeper meaning from story quilts, an individual must be familiar with the art form and particular culture. Jacqueline Woodson (2005) provides a wonderful example of story quilts in *Show Way*, a Newbery Honor book. Passed down from generation to generation in the African-American community, show ways help family members learn about the struggles past generations endured such as slavery, the depression era, and the fight for civil rights. This picture book for primary and intermediate readers is complemented with multimedia arranged in splendid quilt patterns.

Readers learn about the role of story quilts in the Hmong culture in *Dia's Story Cloth* (Cha, 1996), a nonfiction book for the intermediate grades. The illustrations feature hand-embroidered craftsmanship that tells the story of a family's escape from their war-torn homeland in Laos to America. A detailed history of the Hmong people and their journey to freedom is included in the back of the book.

Patricia Polacco's (1988) *The Keeping Quilt* tells the story of a cherished quilt that is passed down from one generation to the next in a Jewish family. The quilt, created from scraps by Anna's Russian immigrant mother, reminds the family of their Russian homeland. It has served functions such as a picnic ground cover, a baby blanket, and a *chuppah* (canopy) at a wedding, as well as a symbol of family values and beliefs. Polacco highlights the quilt in each illustration as the only splash of color in the black and white drawings in this picture book for young readers.

Besides quilts, many other crafts have served to connect generations across time. Margot Theis Raven's (2004) *Circle Unbroken: The Story of a Basket and its People* explains the importance of sweetgrass basket-making to the Gullah. As her grandson listens, Grandma tells the story of how her great grandfather became a basket weaver in Africa and then brought this craft to America as a slave. Each generation since has learned the art of basket weaving. As community members weave, they reflect upon their people's past. This picture book does an excellent job of introducing primary through intermediate readers to the rich heritage of the Gullah people who live off the coast of the Carolinas.

Traditional dress is an important part of heritage. In India, wearing a sari is a celebrated coming-of-age event in a young girl's life. In *Mama's Saris* (Makhijani, 2007), the reader meets seven-year-old Marisa who is eager to wear one of her mother's saris for her birthday. After searching through a collection of saris, mother and daughter find the perfect sari for Marissa's birthday party. Marissa prepares for her upcoming party adorned in the traditional sari and Hindu accessories. The vibrant acrylic colors in the illustrations capture the excitement of this young girl's celebration of feeling grown-up in this picture book for the primary grades.

Family celebrations are another important aspect of heritage. These events always include food and often have singing and dancing. In *Dumpling Soup* by Rattigan (1993), seven-year old Marisa and her multiethnic family make preparations for the New Year celebrations in their home in Hawaii. Marisa helps to prepare the *mandoo* (dumplings) for the traditional holiday soup, but her dumplings are not big and plump like those of the adults and she is nervous about how her family will react. All turns out well when her grandfather shows his approval, and the family asks for seconds. Hsu-Flanders' full-page watercolor illustrations convey the lushness of the tropical Hawaiian landscape and the warmth and love in this family.

Bee-Bim Bop! by Linda Sue Park (2007) introduces young readers to Korean culture through their food. In this book, a young girl helps her mother prepare bee-bim bop, a traditional Korean rice dish with meat and vegetables. Told in rhyme, many of the verses include the steps and ingredients for this delicious dish. Park includes a recipe and a note with information about this traditional dish. Watercolor illustrations by Ho Baek Lee are cartoon-like and provide a whimsical feel to the rhythm of the text.

Diane Gonzales Bertrand's (2003) *The Empanadas that Abuela Made/Las empanadas que hacía la abuela*, a bilingual cumulative story, introduces readers to grandmother's recipe for making empanadas, a traditional Latin American dish. The process of making empanadas from cooking pumpkin, to making and rolling the dough, to baking them in the oven is told using a repetitive, rhythmic text that is very appropriate for beginning readers. The pen and ink glossy illustrations show the family working together to create this delicious dish. A recipe in Spanish and English is included in the back of the book.

Mim's Christmas Jam by Andrea Davis Pinkney (2001) takes place during the Christmas season in 1915 and tells the story of an African-American family who miss their "pap" who is in New York City building the subway system. Mim insists that she and the children make a batch of "belly-hum jam" and send it to pap. Pap's supervisors have just announced that there will be no break for the holiday. However, with one taste of Mim's jam the supervisors acquiesce and allow the workers to have a day off. Brian Pinkney's scratchboard illustrations are a wonderful complement to this delightful picture book for the primary grades.

In *Sienna's Scrapbook: Our African American Heritage Trip* Toni Trent Parker (2005) creates a book that is a combination of diary, scrapbook, and travel guide. As they travel from Hartford, Connecticut to Winston-Salem, North Carolina to attend a family reunion, Sienna gains new knowledge and appreciation of her African American-American heritage from visits to historical sites along along the way. Illustrator Janell Genovese uses a variety of media including doodles, photographs, and historic memorabilia to illustrate Sienna's family vacation in this book for the intermediate through middle school grades.

Response Activities

Kenyon's grandmother in *Keepers* is a keeper, a female member of the family who "holds on to the past until she can pass it on to the next" (Watts, 1997, unpaged). Students can become keepers, like Kenyon, and locate a family photo, interview family members to gather background information, and write a narrative to accompany the picture. They could then present their photo and story to the class. Another option would be to create a me-box, a decorated shoebox containing three items of family or cultural significance.

Using *Show Way* (Woodson, 2005), *The Keeping Quilt* (Polacco, 1988)*, or Dia's Story Cloth* (Cha, 1996) as a model, students can gather photographs, crop them with photo editing software, and create artifacts similar to story quilts. The students can then write a description of the framed artwork.

Based on great grandfather's experience of weaving a grass basket coiled tight enough to hold water as a rite of passage, in *The Circle Unbroken* (Raven, 2004), students can write in reflective journals on the rites of passages or challenges they have experienced. In *Mama's Saris* (Makhijani, 2007), Marisa is given permission to wear a sari despite her young age. Students can reflect in journals about a time when they were allowed to do something new such as walk to school by themselves or go to a friend's sleepover.

After reading about foods from different cultures, students can create shape poems inspired by information on this topic. A shape poem is a poem that describes an object and is written in the shape of the object. More information can be found on shape poems at http://www.readwritethink.org/student_mat/student_material.asp?id=44, accessed on October 02, 2010.

Mim's Christmas Jam (Pinkney, 2001) tells a story related to a favorite family recipe. Students can create a class recipe book in which each person contributes a favorite family recipe. After the book is complete, students can host a food festival and invite families to bring dishes. A contest can be held to choose the favorite dish.

Text Sets for Intermediate Grades

Great Athletes

Great athletes inspire a sense of wonder and awe at their prowess and amazing physical accomplishments. They train with one goal in mind: to be the best. In the past, there have been many American athletes who had to overcome obstacles to succeed, including racism and discrimination. Despite these hurdles, many athletes of color persevered and pursued their dream to be a champion. When they succeeded, they opened doors for others to achieve their goals. This text set includes biographies of athletes who were among the first in their sport to achieve greatness. Many of the biographies included are written and illustrated in picture book format. Also included in this text set are a few fiction books and poetry collections. The recommended grade level for this text set is grades three–six.

Sharon Robinson (2004) chronicles Jackie Robinson's career in *Promises to Keep* and pays tribute to this famous athlete who conquered the color barrier to become the first African-American to play professional baseball. Told from a daughter's point of view, the author provides insight into less known facts about her father such as the effect stardom had on his family. Contemporary photos accompany this book.

Another book on Jackie Robinson, *First in the Field* (Dingle, 1998), describes the discrimination Robinson endured throughout his life. This biography explores Robinson's life and includes black and white photographs, a bibliography, and a chart "Milestones in Black Sports" (pp. 45–47). listing important names and dates. This chart could be used to prompt an inquiry project into African American sports.

Kadir Nelson's (2007) *We Are the Ship: The Story of Negro League Baseball* traces the history of this league and its players through nine plus innings. Each chapter is connected to an inning. Within the pages of each inning, the reader meets teams, players, and owners, providing insight into life on the road in the Negro Leagues. In the ninth inning, the reader is introduced to Jackie Robinson. The end of the Negro League is described in an extra inning in the last chapter. Nelson's extraordinary paintings, inspired by authentic memorabilia, bring baseball and the players to life. The book also includes a foreword by Hank Aaron, an author's note, and a list of African American players who made it to the major leagues. For more information about Hank Aaron, students can read Golenbock's (2001) *Hank Aaron, Brave in Every Way*.

Another great baseball player, Roberto Clemente, is introduced to readers in *Roberto Clemente: Pride of the Pirates* (Winter, 2005), an easy-to-read picture book biography. Told in verse and illustrated with watercolors, this book describes Clemente's life in Puerto Rico and his rise to greatness. For more information about Latino baseball stars, students can read *Beisbol!* (Winter, 2001). In this book, Jonah Winter has created acrylic trading card illustrations as well as baseball card statistics for 14 Latino baseball pioneers and legends. The book provides brief information on each player.

Louis Sockalexis: Native American Baseball Pioneer (Wise, 2007) explores the life of Louis Sockalexis, the first American Indian to play major league baseball. Illustrated with oil paintings by Bill Farnsworth, this book describes when 12-year-old Louis discovers and falls in love with baseball and then relates his experiences in high school and college where he is recruited by the manager of the Cleveland Spiders. Louis' first debut in the major leagues was in 1897, and Wise provides a play-by-play narrative of that day.

Just like Louis Sockalexis, Jim Thorpe was also an American Indian athlete. In Don Brown's (2006) picture book biography, *Bright Path: Young Jim Thorp*, readers learn of Jim's troubled life as a child. Jim's father sent him to Carlisle Indian School, where his athletic ability was discovered and encouraged. He went on to participate in the Olympics and play professional football and baseball.

In *Champions on the Bench*, Carole Boston Weatherford (2006) tells the story of a young boy named Cleveland who wanted to play baseball like his heroes Hank Aaron and Willie Mays. He finally gets his chance in 1955 with the Cannon Street All Stars, an African American Little League team in South Carolina. Cleveland's team is very successful and advances to the state finals, but their opponents, an all white team, refuse to play with them because of their color. The Cannon Street All-Stars go home feeling defeated, but their coach encourages them to not give up and to keep practicing for another opportunity to play in the finals. Weatherford includes an author's note at the end of the book, which provides more information about The Cannon Street All-Stars and tells how the team received acknowledgement and recognition in 2002.

In the basketball arena, there have been many names associated with greatness. Charles R Smith Jr. (2004) has written *Hoop Kings*, a unique poetry book honoring 12 NBA "kings" with poetic lyrics. Each poem is accompanied with a digital image of the king. As each player had his own style, each poem is written in a unique style that represents Smith's view of the basketball king.

For a basic introduction to the vocabulary associated with basketball, readers can turn to *Hoops with Swoopes* (Swoopes, 2001) which features photographs of Sheryl Swoopes, Women's National Basketball Association star, demonstrating various basketball words (dribble, pass, bounce). The glossy photographs by Susan Kuklin and simple, expressive words make this book accessible to younger students.

Aquatic sports legends are less known; however, their contributions and achievements are no less significant. Sammy Lee and Duke Kahanamoku were athletes who chased their dream of achieving Olympic greatness. Both athletes were successful; however, their stories were lost until recently. Sammy Lee was a Korean-American who pursued his dream of becoming an Olympic diver. In *Sixteen Years in Sixteen Seconds* (Yoo, 2005) readers meet young Sammy Lee who was coming of age in the 1930s–1940s. Yoo uses a narrative style enhanced with full-page acrylic illustrations to tell Sammy's story. Sammy's father dreams of his son's future career in the medical field, whereas Sammy dreams of becoming an Olympic diver. The reader learns how Sammy was able to achieve both dreams. *Surfer of the Century* (Crowe, 2007) tells the story of Duke Kahanamoku, an outstanding Hawaiian athlete, in picture book format. This book tells how Duke became a six-time Olympic medal winner. Enhanced with bold, full-page colorful images created with colored pencils, this book is a visual delight.

Boxing enthusiasts are sure to recognize the names Joe Louis and Muhammed Ali. Joe Louis became known as the best heavyweight fighter of all times. David Adler (2005) describes Joe Louis' climb to the top of the heavy-weight boxing world in *Joe Louis: America's Fighter* despite struggles with discrimination most of his life because of his race. During World War II, he became a symbol of America when he fought and defeated German heavy-weight Max Schmeling. Acrylic illustrations by Terry Widener complement Adler's narrative.

Muhammed Ali showcased his skill and demonstrated how he could float like a butterfly and sting like a bee. Two excellent books on Muhammad Ali's life are *Float Like A Butterfly* by Ntozake Shange (2002) and *Twelve Rounds to Glory* by Charles R Smith, Jr. (2007). Although the information in these books is similar, the presentation is very different. Shange's book uses simple text and rap-style verse. In *Float Like a Butterfly*, readers meet the young Cassius Clay as he confronts segregation in the southern United States. As a child, his bike is stolen and as a result, he decides to learn how to box. Written in picture book format, this book is appealing to a younger audience. Full page illustrations by Edel Rodriguez give the illusion that Cassius is larger than life.

Smith's (2007) *Twelve Rounds to Glory*, is a book on Muhammed Ali written for an older audience. Smith's (2007) writes in verse to tell the reader the story of this great athlete. Brian Collier's collage illustrations are bold, adding additional reader appeal. Each chapter is equated to a round and each round opens with a quote from Ali, family, friends, or competitors. Smith states that he believes his book is an excellent tribute to "the greatest boxer of all" (Smith, 2007, unpaged). This book also includes Ali's most current appearances at the 1996 Olympics and the 2005 opening of the Muhammad Ali Center in Louisville, Kentucky.

Female athletes have had to overcome gender bias as well as racial discrimination to achieve greatness. In Sue Stauffacher's (2007) *Nothing but Trouble*, the reader meets Althea Gibson who as a young girl growing up in Harlem was considered nothing but trouble. Althea's athletic skill catches the attention of Buddy Walker who becomes her coach. As a result of her increased skills, Althea is invited to the Cosmopolitan, an upscale tennis club in Harlem, where she continues to improve her tennis skills. Eventually, she goes on to become the first African-American woman to play at Wimbledon.

Kathleen Krull (1996) introduces readers to Wilma Rudolph's great athletic ability in the *Wilma Unlimited: How Wilma Rudolph Became the World's Fastest Woman*. After being stricken with polio at age five, Wilma an African-American, works hard to overcome this crippling disease, learns to walk again, and becomes a talented runner. Eventually, she advances to the Olympics to become the first American woman to win three gold medals in running. This inspiring story is told against the backdrop of David Diaz's dark hues of browns.

Response Activities

The following activities provide students with opportunities to respond to the biographical texts in this text set using podcasting, interviewing, writing, and role playing.

Students can research and create a script of a memorable sports event such as the day Jackie Robinson broke the color barrier in baseball, or the day Sammy Lee won an Olympic medal. They can then create a digital recording of their scripts. Audio podcasts of these live events can be broadcast over the school's PA system or converted to an audio file and inserted into the classroom Web site.

Students can respond to the biographies by role playing sports figures. Working with a partner, one student can play the role of an athlete and the other one can be a reporter doing an interview. They could then work collaboratively to write a newspaper sports story on the athlete to be published in the class newspaper. A sample newspaper story template that guides students through the five W's of newspaper writing is available at http://readwritethink.org/lesson_images/lesson249/format.pdf, accessed on October 02, 2010.

Another example of a dramatic response is for one student to play the role of a sports agent who is responsible for publicity of a sports legend. Working in small groups, students can choose a sports legend and create publicity for him or her through a Power Point presentation, an iPod presentation, a flyer announcing an upcoming meet and greet created on Microsoft Publisher, or a poster announcing a sporting event. The students can then give presentations to their classmates who act as athletic financial supporters.

Working in small groups, students can choose a sports figure from one of the biographies and create a timeline of the athlete's life using the biography selection and rationale template available at http://www.readwritethink.org/lesson_images/lesson26/RWTa34-1.pdf, accessed on October 02, 2010. Each group can then create a collage to accompany the timeline with words and images similar to the bold format used by Charles Smith (2007) in *Twelve Rounds to Glory*. Groups can then write a historical narrative for the timeline.

Text Sets for the Intermediate/Middle Grades

Social Justice

Throughout the world people suffer from social and political injustice. In many countries, the group in power discriminates against, suppresses, and mistreats those who are considered different in race, ethnicity, religion, national origin, tribal group, or political affiliation. In many cases, those who are oppressed are killed or badly injured. However, despite brutal and unfair treatment, there are numerous examples of disenfranchised groups throughout the world that have protested their mistreatment and have gradually gained civil rights and better treatment. Middle school readers will gain much insight from reading books such as the following on how persecuted groups still maintain their dignity and learn how to overcome their difficulties.

Sweetgrass Basket by Marlene Carvell (2005) is a story told by two Mohawk sisters in alternating first-person, free-verse narratives, about their experiences in the Carlisle Indian Boarding School at the turn of the twentieth century. After their mother's death, their well-intentioned father sends the two girls off to the boarding school. At the school, they are treated cruelly, and every attempt is made to take away their Indian identity. Despite this mistreatment, the girls cling secretly to their language and the few precious items they own that represent their heritage, and, in particular, the sweet-grass basket their deceased mother made by hand. Mattie is falsely accused by the school's director, Mrs. Dwyer, of stealing her brooch. She is publicly shamed and attempts to run away from the school. When she returns, Mrs. Dwyer has her locked in a shed where she gets sick from exposure. The book ends with Mattie's tragic death, however, despite the sadness, the author leaves the reader with hope. From this gripping story, the reader learns of the displacement and forced assimilation that many Indians experienced in boarding schools.

Against the background of the historical development of apartheid in South Africa and the resistance against it, Beverley Naidoo's (2003) book, *Out of Bounds: Seven Stories of Conflict and Hope*, features short stories that follow a time line from 1948 to 1995 and feature different perspectives, voices, and themes related to this oppressive period in the history of South Africa. The reader gains insight into what it was like for people of different colors and races to live during this oppressive political period. These stories powerfully reveal the dehumanizing way in which people of different colors and races were classified by the South African government into racial groups and given passes indicating their classification, thus determining where they lived, where they went to school, and what kind of life they were allowed to live. They also illustrate how Blacks gradually gained the inner strength to resist the oppressive regime and eventually bring about social justice. Each of the seven stories is set in a different decade to illustrate the changing political status in South Africa. A timeline of apartheid at the end of the book helps the reader interpret the political background of these stories.

The Breadwinner by Deborah Ellis (2001) tells the story of Parvana, an 11-year old Afghani girl, and her family during the time of the cruel and inhumane regime of the Taliban in war-torn Afghanistan. Once a well-off family, war has had a devastating effect on them, and their dire circumstances force them to live in a one-room apartment in a partially bombed building. Parvana is not allowed to attend school and her mother, once a journalist, is not allowed to work outside the home. When the Taliban come to arrest the father on a pretext that he was educated outside the country, the family is left with no way to support itself because there is no older son, and women are not allowed to work or even leave their homes unless accompanied by an adult relative. The family decides to disguise Parvana as a boy and have her go to the marketplace to earn a living for her family. Realizing that her family depends on her, Parvana shows strong determination, courage, and ingenuity. She goes to the marketplace daily and brings back food so her family can survive. From this book, the reader learns of the terrible oppression that people endure under autocratic regimes in many places around the world. The reader also learns from Parvana how children in times of war and oppression can have strong character and be of great help to their families. This book is the first in a trilogy. The next book is *Parvana's Journey* (Ellis, 2003), which follows Parvana as she searches for her mother and sister in northern Afghanistan.

Russell Freedman's (2006) *Freedom Walkers: The Story of the Montgomery Bus Boycott* is a clearly written photo essay that recounts in detail the events leading up to the Rosa Parks incident as well as the experiences of those unsung heroes who made many personal and political sacrifices to participate in the Montgomery Bus Boycott. On almost every page spread, the reader encounters fascinating black and white photos of those involved in this important historic event, including well-known individuals such as Rosa Parks and Martin Luther King, Jr. and those less known. Freedman also provides chapter notes that are fully documented and an extensive bibliography.

Revolution Is Not a Dinner Party (Compestine, 2007) takes place in the 1970's during the Cultural Revolution in China. Through the eyes of Ling, a young upper-class Chinese girl who lives in Wuhan with her parents who are dedicated doctors, the author provides in sight into the terror and brutality that the Chinese people endured under Mao Ze Dung's rule. The repression gradually escalates as Ling witnesses the mistreatment of her neighbors, friends, and family. At school, she is ostracized and mistreated by bullies who view her as a class enemy. Ling and her mother are devastated when the Red Guard arrests her father and takes him to an undisclosed place. Throughout the tumultuous times, Ling fights to maintain her dignity, sustained by the memories of her brave father and his dream of freedom.

In *Tasting the Sky: A Palestinian Childhood*, Ibtisam Barakat (2007) describes her childhood experiences in Ramallah, Palestine, in the aftermath of the 1967 Six-Day War. This memoir begins with Ibtisam being hauled off a bus by Israeli soldiers to a detention center with no explanation. After hours of waiting in fear, she is finally released; however, this experience has a profound effect on her and prompts her to recall her childhood and reflect on her life as a refugee. The story is framed by two letters, the first, at the beginning, is addressed to no one and the second, at the end, is addressed to everyone. Throughout the book, Barakat shares vignettes from her young life in poetic prose, poignantly drawing a picture of what it was like to live in an occupied land shattered by conflict. The descriptive language powerfully depicts scenes and brings the author's daily world to life with descriptive language such as, "my feelings escape like birds" (p. 5), "he walked like a king with his tomato-red crown" (p. 101), and "words hang on the vines like grape clusters" (p. 11).

Two highly acclaimed biographies about César Chávez, the Mexican-American activist who fought for political and social justice for migrant workers during in the latter part of the twentieth century, contribute to this text set: *César: ¡Sí se puede! Yes, We Can!* (Bernier-Grand, 2004) and *Harvesting Hope: The Story of César Chávez* (Krull, 2003). Bernier-Grand's (2004) book tells the story of Chávez in free verse, accompanied by David Diaz's beautiful folk-art drawings. This book can be paired with the more traditional biography, *Harvesting Hope: The Story of César Chávez*

(Krull, 2003), a Pura Belpré award winner, to provide students with an additional view of Chávez's life.

Response Activities

Students can make personal responses to the books in this text set in a variety of ways. One example is for students to write an obituary on a character in one of the books. Their obituary can reflect the life of the character and describe what they learned about him or her. They can consider questions such as: What did the person stand for? For what will the person be remembered? How was the person viewed by others in the story? What did this person accomplish? How should the person be remembered? What did the person's life mean to others?

Students can also develop a readers' theater script to role-play an episode in one of the books. Working in groups, students can first identify and discuss the events they intend to script and then determine if they want to retell the events as told in the book or write an innovative twist. Acting out the scripts encourages children to take on new personalities and express themselves with a different voice (Young & Ferguson, 1998).

Another response activity involves students in creating a book review movie using iMovie '08 software (Macintosh) or a similar video editing software. In small groups, each focusing on one of the books in one of the themes, students can produce a movie featuring pictures and audio files downloaded from the Internet. They can then add narration to the movie by including information on each book and author and their own critiques of the books. A further step for ambitious projects would be to upload the iMovie into the school Web site, YouTube, or MacWeb Gallery for families and other schools to view. Or, students could upload the iMovie onto iPods to share with others. This activity provides an excellent way for students to share information learned from the books they read and see text-to-text connections.

Another suggested response activity involves drama. Students can write a short play based on one of the books and act it out. For example, students could use information from Freedman's (2006) *Freedom Walkers: The Story of the Montgomery Bus Boycott* and the *Eyes on the Prize* (PBS, 2006) video series and then write a short play on the Montgomery Bus Boycott. They can form small groups, each focusing on a different scene and then dramatically perform the play they create or read it into a digital recorder as a radio drama.

Self-identity Text Set (Middle School)

Finding one's own identity and developing self-esteem are common issues for pre-teens and teens. In their childhood many adolescents are reassured by their parents that they are attractive, smart, and loved, however, when they enter middle school they suddenly discover that they have to make their own way in the world. They have to get along with their peers and develop their own unique identity. This is difficult for all adolescents, but it is particularly difficult for those who are perceived as different in some way by their peers. These individuals often face teasing, bullying, and ostracism by their peers. This situation is exacerbated when adolescents have to deal with issues related to race and ethnicity.

The books in this text set all relate to the theme of developing self-esteem and discovering one's own identity. Some books are about children or adolescents who are bicultural; their parents are from different cultural or ethnic backgrounds and must find their identity somewhere between those two backgrounds. Other books feature youngsters who have to deal with negative attitudes toward their skin color; they are perceived by their peers as too dark-skinned. Other books feature youngsters who struggle with tensions between their home culture and the school culture and the school's devaluing of their heritage.

In Pam Muñoz Ryan's (2004) *Becoming Naomi Leon*, Naomi is a shy, brown-skinned, 11-year-old girl who considers herself nothing special. Having been abandoned by their mother at an early age, she and her younger brother, Owen, have been raised by their great-grandmother in a low-income trailer park. When her dysfunctional mother, Skyla, suddenly reappears in their lives, Naomi faces serious problems because Skyla wants to take her home to live with her and her boyfriend, so she can collect child support. Gram and the two children escape to Mexico to find the children's father to seek his support in the custody battle. This flight turns into a quest not only for Naomi's father but also for her own identity. One day, dressed in a Mexican blouse and *huaraches*, she looks in the mirror and sees a girl who appears to "fit in with all the other brown girls in the barrio" (Ryan, 2004, p. 170). Naomi enters a radish-carving contest at a festival in Oaxaca and this becomes an opportunity for her to discover her roots, find her father, and celebrate the artist within her. At the end of the novel, Naomi has grown into a person who is much more self-assured of who she is.

In the gritty novel, *The Skin I'm In* by Sharon Flake (2007), seventh grader Maleeka is harshly teased by her peers because of her dark skin, her handmade clothes, and her good grades at an urban middle school. Maleeka befriends Charlese, a mean-spirited trouble maker who goads Maleeka into bad behavior as payment for the fashionable clothes that she brings to school for her to wear. Ms. Saunders, the new English teacher, encourages Maleeka to develop her writing skills and her self-identity. She finally develops a stronger self-identity and gains the courage to stand up to Charlese. Towards the end of the novel she declares, "Call me by my name! I am not ugly. I am not stupid. I am Maleeka Madison, and, yeah, I'm black, real black, and if you don't like me, too bad 'cause black is the skin I'm in!" (Flake, 2007, p. 167). Flake's book can be compared to *A Different Beat* by Candy Dawson Boyd (1996), which also deals with issues of skin color.

In Lawrence Yep's (1995) young adult novel, *Thief of Hearts*, Stacy, the daughter of a Chinese-American mother and an Anglo father, has always felt like everyone else in her middle school. One day her parents ask her to befriend Hong Ch'un, a new girl from China, but Stacy is reluctant. On Hong Ch'un's first day at school, some items of sentimental value disappear and are found in her backpack. The other students accuse her of being a thief and Stacy feels obligated to come to her defense. When she does this, the other students treat her like an outsider, accusing her of siding with Hong Ch'un because she is Chinese. Feeling disgraced, Hong Ch'un disappears. Stacy, her mother, and Tai-Paw, her great grandmother, take a trip to Chinatown to see if they can find her. Throughout the ordeal, Stacy struggles with her identity, trying to figure out how she can be both Chinese and American at the same time, and not be like the thief of hearts.

In *Bud, Not Buddy*, (Curtis, 2005) readers meet 10-year-old, African-American Bud who is on a mission to find his father who he believes is a bass player in a jazz band. The only clue he has about his father is a small poster, which deeply upset his mother before her death. Now orphaned and on the run from an abusive foster home, Bud has set out on a journey to find his father and discovers himself along the way.

In *A Step From Heaven* by An Na (2001), readers meet Ju, a young Korean immigrant and her family living in California. Ju struggles with English and the cultural barriers of being an immigrant in America. Her family is plagued by financial woes and her alcoholic father's abusive, behavior. One day, the abuse becomes too much. Ju is faced with needing to make a decision that will change the lives of her mother, brother, and herself. This book was the recipient of The Printz Award for Young Adult Literature.

In Jaime Adoff's (2007) *Jimi & Me*, readers meet 13-year-old Keith who is from a biracial family. Keith and his mother are left penniless after his father, a record producer, is murdered. Keith moves from Brooklyn, New York, to small-town Ohio. He works through his grief by playing Jimi Hendrix songs on his guitar. Written in verse, interspersed with lyrics from Hendrix songs, the reader follows Keith's life as he discovers himself.

Despite the reality that interracial families are significantly increasing in the United States, there are relatively few books with biracial protagonists. In *What Are You? Voices of Mixed Race Young People*, Pearl Fuyo Gaskins (1999) has collected interviews, essays, and poetry from over 40 young adults aged 14–26 who describe the prejudice and frustrations they face as a result of their biracial identity.

Response Activities

In *Becoming Naomi Leon* (Ryan, 2007), Naomi, Owen, Gram, and their friends arrive in Oaxaca in December when two important festivals occur: the festival of La Noche de los Rábanos, a regional festival in which detailed scenes are carved from giant radishes and Las Posadas, a celebration that occurs before Christmas in which believers engage in a reenactment of Joseph and Mary's search for a room in Bethlehem. To view photographs of the festival of the La Noche de los Rábanos, students could go to the author's Web site at http://www.pammunozryan.com/radishes.html, accessed on October 02, 2010. To learn more about Las Posadas, students could read *Las Posadas* by Diane Hoyt-Goldsmith (1999) and then compare the description of the festival to that in the novel.

Naomi is talented at wood carving, a traditional art in Oaxaca. For the La Noche de los Rábanos, she carves a lion out of a large radish, which is later admired by her father. Students could go to http://www.ivory.com/PureFun_IvoryProjects_SoapCarvingTips .htm, accessed on October 02, 2010, to get instructions on soap carving and then try their hand at carving animals out of soap or potatoes. They could then display their creations in the classroom.

Naomi discovers herself and her inner strengths in this novel. Students could write an acrostic poem using the letters of their name, and expressing what is special about them. To model this form of poem, the teacher could show students an example using Naomi's name as shown below:

Never giving up her efforts to solve her problems
Actively searching for her father in Oaxaca
Openly thrilled to find that she belongs in Mexico
Maker of beautiful carvings from wood and radishes
Increasingly self-assured and proud of who she is.

After reading *The Skin I'm In* (Flake, 2007), students could go to Sharon Flake's Web site at http://www.sharongflake.com/media/, accessed on October 02, 2010, which features a video clip of students performing a readers' theater based on excerpts from Maleeka's diary about Akeelma, an African slave on a slave ship. After viewing this clip, students could read these excerpts as a readers' theatre performance. They could also discuss why they think writing in a diary helped Maleeka face some of her problems in the story.

Students can discuss why they think Maleeka complied with everything Charlese told her to do even though Charlese mistreated her. They can then discuss examples similar to this in their own lives or in the life of someone they know.

After reading one of the novels in this text set, students can write character journal entries, taking on the persona of the main character in the book. They could express how the character feels about what he/she goes through in the novel. For example, if they choose to take on the personal identity of Maleeka in *The Skin I'm In*, they could express what she feels about the bullying and harassment that she suffers from her peers in her middle school.

Many of the novels in this text set lend themselves to dramatic performance. For example, students could form groups, each choosing a scene from one of the novels and then create a frozen tableau of the scene. The observers of the performance could then tap one or more of the actors on the shoulder to ask what the actor is thinking and how the he or she feels about what is happening in the scene.

In Yep's (1995) *Thief of Hearts*, Tai-Paw tells Stacy a tale that directly connects to her struggle with her self-identity. Students could think about a family story that has special meaning to them and write about it in their journal. They could consider questions such as: Who told them the story? Why is it an important story to their family or to them? What special meaning does the story have to them in their lives today?

Students could learn more about Chinatown. They might visit Chinatown if they live near one, or they could learn more about Chinatown in San Francisco at: http://www.sanfranciscochinatown.com/, accessed on October 02, 2010. Students could discuss why they think Chinatown was formed in San Francisco and other cities in the United States and why they think these places are still important to Chinese Americans today.

Christopher Paul Curtis' (2005) *Bud, Not Buddy* is set in the 1930s. Students can form jigsaw groups, each group focusing on researching different 1930s events, such as the Great Depression, President Roosevelt's New Deal, and jazz musicians. After the students have completed their research, they can build a classroom timeline of the 1930s and illustrate their timeline with photos downloaded from the Internet. They could also explore music of the time period and discuss how the music expressed the times.

Books about self-identity lend themselves to a variety of response activities. In *Bud, Not Buddy*, Bud writes his own rules for survival. Students can critique Bud's list of rules, comparing them to actual situations in the story in which the rules either helped or hindered his self-discovery. Students can also draft their own survival rules. An Na's (2001) *A Step From Heaven* ends with Ju achieving her dream of going to college. Students can consider what might happen to Ju in college and beyond. They can write a sequel to the book considering how being a survivor of family violence might affect Ju's future. In Jaime Adoff's (2007) *Jimi & Me*, Keith is comforted by the lyrics of Jimi Hendrix's music. As a class, students can explore the music and life of Jimi Hendrix to discover why Keith felt such a strong connection to him. As students read excerpts from Gaskins' (1999) *What Are You? Voices of Mixed Race Young People*, they can write unsent letters to the young adults in the short stories, reflecting, perhaps, on some of the problems they face themselves.

Text Set: The Harlem Renaissance (Middle School)

The Harlem Renaissance was an African American cultural movement that blossomed in Harlem, New York during the 1920's and 1930's. For the first time in American history, the mainstream White culture took notice of African American literature, music, and art. The musical talents of Bessie Smith, Louis Armstrong, Duke Ellington, and others and the eloquent writing of poets and novelists such as Langston Hughes, Countee Cullen, and Zora Neale Hurston were admired and appreciated by a wider audience. Although the Harlem Renaissance came to an end in the 1930s mainly as a result of the Great Depression, the writers, musicians, and artists during this time influenced future African-American talent and inspired interest in African American artistic work with publishers and record companies. Modern-day artists such as Maya Angelou, Toni Morrison, and Alice Walker were able to blossom as a result of the Harlem Renaissance.

This text set includes poetry, biographies of artists, and books that provide insight into the music style of jazz from the Harlem Renaissance. These books are appropriate for students in grades four through eight.

Jazz is a style of American music in which rhythm, melody and improvisation combine to tell a story. *Jazz* by Walter Dean Myers (2006) features poems about the rhythm, instruments, and vocals of jazz. The poems are beautifully illustrated in full-page acrylics by Christopher Myers. A CD with jazz music accompanies this book. Wynton Marsalis' (2005) *Jazz A-B-Z: An A to Z Collection of Jazz Portrait*, with words that echo the rhythm and syncopation of jazz, would be an excellent companion to this book.

The Sound That Jazz Makes, told in rhyming text by Carole Boston Weatherford (2000) and illustrated with beautiful acrylic paintings by Eric Velasquez, provides a history of jazz. The book introduces some of the great legends of jazz such as Louis Armstrong, Duke Ellington, and Ella Fitzgerald. Reference is also made to current rappers who were inspired by the past legends.

Leo and Diane Dillon (2007) go beyond the boundaries of the written word and illustrations by adding an auditory experience to *Jazz on a Saturday Night* with an accompanying CD. The book and CD provide the teacher with an opportunity to place the students in the audience of a jazz performance by having them read along as they listen to the CD. A short biography of each performer is included in the book and CD in addition to information on jazz instruments and the song "Jazz on a Saturday Night." A good companion for this book is *Rap a Tap Tap: Here's Bojangles, Think of That* also by Leo & Diane Dillon (2002).

The blues was another genre of music that emerged during the Harlem Renaissance. In *Blues Journey*, Walter Dean Myers (2003) describes this music, which combines African and European musical forms and evokes a melancholic mood, often associated with the challenges African-Americans have faced in the United States. Throughout the book, Myers uses call and response, a style characteristic of the blues, as he repeats lyrics of importance. A glossary helps readers understand the terms used throughout the book.

There have been several biographies written about the musicians of the Harlem Renaissance. Caldecott Honor and Coretta Scott King Honor Book, *Duke Ellington: The Piano Prince and His Orchestra* by Andrea Davis Pinkney (1997) tells the story of Duke Ellington's life. Brian Pinkney's scratchboard illustrations complement the text.

The reader meets young Edward, Duke's given name, who would rather play baseball than play notes on the piano until one day when he hears ragtime music being played on a piano. After teaching himself how to play the piano, Duke secures some bookings in night clubs and eventually becomes famous for his style of music.

Ella Fitzgerald, a Picture Book Biography written by Andrea Davis Pinkney (2002) and illustrated by Brian Pinkney, introduces readers to the great jazz vocalist, Ella Fitzgerald. Ella's life is narrated from the point of view of Scat Cat Monroe, imitating scat, a style of music for which Ella was well-known. The story is told in four tracks that follow the singer's successful career from Harlem to Carnegie Hall with stops along the way at Yale and at the Savoy. The book includes a bibliography, videography, and selected discography.

An overview of the culture of the Harlem Renaissance is provided by Hill (2004) in *Harlem Stomp! A Cultural History of the Harlem Renaissance*. The first four chapters provide a historical background of the Harlem Renaissance. The text then continues with chapters that introduce readers to the visual and performing arts of the era.

Langston Hughes, an anthology of the poet's works edited by Rampersad and Roessel (2006), has a four-page biographical introduction, a brief introductory statement for each poem, and footnotes to explain some of the dialect. Benny Andrews' bright, colorful illustrations draw readers into this book.

Langston's Train Ride by Robert Burleigh (2004) takes the reader inside the creative thought behind one of Langston Hughes' first poems, "The Negro Speaks of Rivers." At the age of 18, Langston leaves home and travels by train to be with his father in Mexico. As he travels, he is lulled by the clickety-clack of the train and his mind begins to wander and reflect. As he reminisces on his heritage, words come to him. He has the urgent need to capture these words on paper and begins writing them on an envelope. What evolves is his first poem "The Negro Speaks of Rivers." Illustrated with mixed-media collage by Leonard Jenkins, the artwork in this book beautifully complements the metaphorical images evoked by Langston's poem. Other books that serve as tributes to Langston Hughes include *Love to Langston* by Tony Medina (2002) illustrated by R. Gregory Christie and *Visiting Langston* by Willie Perdomo (2002), illustrated by Bryan Collier.

Today, young adult readers can experience the Harlem Renaissance through poetry collections such as *Here in Harlem* by Walter Dean Myers (2004) and *Shimmy Shimmy Shimmy Like My Sister Kate* by Nikki Giovanni (1996). Intermediate readers can feel the rhythm of Harlem in the book *Ellington Was Not a Street* by Ntozake Shange (2004) and in the poetry collection *The Entrance Place of Wonders* edited by Daphne Muse (2005) and illustrated by Charlotte Riley-Webb.

Author Walter Dean Myers grew up in contemporary Harlem. In the book *Here in Harlem*, Myers (2004) writes of his experiences and the people who played an important part in his life. His poems are fictional accounts of people he either knew or had knowledge of Black and white photographs from Walter Dean Myers' personal collection are placed sparingly on the pages. For a fictional account of life during The Harlem Renaissance, Students can read Walter Dean Myers' (2007) novel, *Harlem Summer*, which has been recognized by Notable Books for a Global Society.

Nikki Giovanni (1996) has compiled a collection of African-American poems in *Shimmy Shimmy Shimmy Like My Sister Kate*. She has included her comments about works of poetry dating as far back as the Harlem Renaissance and up to modern day. These poems are an affirmation and celebration of being African-American. Giovanni also includes brief biographical narratives about the poets featured in this anthology.

For intermediate readers, Ntozake Shange (2004) offers her view of the Harlem Renaissance in the book, *Ellington Was Not a Street*. Illustrated in oils by Kadir Nelson, Shange's book is a recollection of the talented men who visited her father's home when she was a child. Some of these famous men had a significant impact on the world. They include W. E. B. DuBois, Paul Robeson, Duke Ellington, and Dizzy Gillespie. Brief narratives about each individual are included in the back of the book.

Daphne Muse has compiled an anthology of Harlem Renaissance poetry for younger readers in the book, *The Entrance Place of Wonders: Poems of the Harlem Renaissance*. It includes works from Langston Hughes, Countee Cullen, and James Weldon ohnson as well as newly discovered talent. Bold abstract paint and pastel illustrations by Charlotte Riley-Webb accompany each poem. Brief biographical synopses are also included the book.

In addition to print resources, teachers can have students explore internet sites on the Harlem Renaissance. These include the Library of Congress' annotated collection of resources on the Harlem Renaissance (http://www.loc.gov/rr/program/bib/harlem/harlem.html, accessed on October 02, 2010), which offers digital collections, lesson plans, learning activities, and exhibits, and the Schomburg Center for Black Culture at The New York Public Library (http://www2.si.umich.edu/chico/Harlem/). In addition, PBS filmmaker, Ken Burns has created a comprehensive documentary on jazz. For information about this film, including links to teacher lesson plan ideas and student-friendly information, teachers can visit http://www.pbs.org/jazz/classroom/, accessed on October 02, 2010.

Response Activities

Ntozake Shange (2004) in her book, *Ellington Was Not a Street*, mentions numerous artists, writers, and musicians who visited her father's house. Students can work in pairs to research Countee Cullen, Paul Robeson, W.E.B. DuBois, Duke Ellington, and others she mentions in her book. Who were these people? What contributions did they make to the Harlem Renaissance? What works are they famous for? Students can record their findings using a graphic organizer such as a character analysis pyramid. A sample template is available at http://www.teach-nology.com/worksheets/graphic/character/, accessed on October 02, 2010.

Leo Dillon and Diane Dillon (2007) as well as Andrea Davis Pinkney (2002) describe jazz as upbeat and rhythmic. In contrast, The blues is described by Walter Dean Myers (2003) as sad and sometimes characterized by a call-and-response format. Both music styles emerged during the Harlem Renaissance and influenced today's music. Students could listen to musical excerpts from well-known blues and jazz compositions and discuss the mood, tempo, and feeling of the music. While listening to the music, students can create free expression art murals depicting the emotions the music inspires in them.

Leo Dillon and Diane Dillon (2007) introduce jazz as a style of improvisation. Students can complete a concept map that defines improvisation. They can then engage in charades in which they pull an action word from a bag and pantomime the action using only body movements. An alternative is for one student to start a story and then others add on to the story, one sentence at a time. The story can be digitally recorded for later transcription.

Much of the poetry written during the Harlem Renaissance was a reflection of societal woes. Students could write their own poems about current or past societal woes. Teachers can encourage students to perform their original poems at a poetry café. Poetry cafes not only give students the opportunity to write poetry but also to perform their own verses. Students can use technology such as iMovie and record images to accompany their words. They can also use hand gestures, dance, or props to communicate their ideas.

MULTICULTURAL THEMATIC UNITS

Thematic units are an excellent way to integrate multicultural literature across the curriculum and help students make meaningful connections between language arts and other content areas. Two examples are included here: a unit on Foods of the Americas for the primary—intermediate grades and a unit on the Civil Rights Movement for the middle school grades.

Unit for the Primary–Intermediate Grades: Foods of the Americas

Pat Mora (2007) celebrates foods from the Americas in *Yum! ¡Mm Mm! ¡Qué rico! America's Spoutings*. This book can be used as the anchor text in a multicultural unit on food for primary through intermediate classrooms. Table 2.4 contains a web of suggested texts.

With the theme of foods of the Americas, children can make cross-curricular connections with language arts, math, science, social studies, fine arts, and technology. Table 2.5 provides a web of possible connections and response activities for books

Table 2.4.
Foods of the Americas Unit, Grades Two–Four

Ancient Civilizations		American Indian Foods
The Golden Flower (Jaffe, 1996)		*Corn is Maize* (Aliki, 1976)
People of Corn: A Mayan Folktale (Gerson, 1995)	**Unit** **Foods of the Americas** **Grades Two–Four**	*Zinnia: How the Corn Was Saved* (Powell, 2003)
A Quetzcoatl Tale of Corn (Parke, 1992)		*The Popcorn Book* (de Paola, 1978)
Legend of Food Mountain (Rohmer, 1982)		*Dragonfly's Tale* (Rodanas, 1991)
		Giving Thanks: A Native American Good Morning Message (Swamp, 1995)
Growing Foods	**Hispanic and Southwestern Foods**	**Food Facts and Recipes**
The ABC's of Fruits and Vegetables and Beyond (Charney & Goldbeck, 2007)	*Delicious Hullabaloo* (Mora, 1998)	*Yum! ¡Mm Mm! ¡Qué rico! America's Sproutings* (Mora, 2007)
From Seed to Plant (Gibbons, 1991)	*Domitila: A Cinderella Tale From the Mexican Tradition* (Coburn, 2000)	*Let's Eat! What Children Eat Around the World* (Hollyer, 2004)
From Seed to Pumpkin (Kottke, 2000)	*The Empanadas that Abuela Made* (Bertrand, 2003)	*Bread, Bread, Bread* (Morris, 1993)
Legend of Food Mountain (Rohmer, 1982)	*Chiles for Benito* (Baca & Accardo, 2003)	*Everybody Brings Noodles* (Dooley, 2002)
Desert Giant: The World of the Saguaro Cactus (Bash, 2002)	*Pumpkin Fiesta* (Yacowitz, 1998)	*The Kids' Multicultural Cookbook* (Cook, 1995)
		Let's Eat/¡A comer! (Mora, 2008)

Table 2.5.

Response Activities for Foods of the Americas Unit, Grades Two–Four

Ancient Civilizations	**Unit** **Foods of the Americas** **Response Activities** **Grades Two–Four**	**American Indian Foods**
Participate in either an Internet scavenger hunt or webquest: http://www2.scholastic.com/ browse/search?query=Aztec %20webquest http://library.thinkquest.org /27981/, accessed on October 03, 2010. Using print materials, have students retrieve information about ancient civilizations. Students can report their findings in a 3-2-1 format. Create masks which depict the various sun gods using self-drying modeling clay or commercially produced blank masks.		Create an anticipation guide to use before introducing *The Popcorn Book*. Explore the myths and history behind popcorn. For more information and recipes about popcorn visit, http:// www.popcorn.org. Bring in samples of sweet corn and maize. Students can explore the differences using their senses. Students can then write a haiku poem. A sample template is available at http:// www.readwritethink.org/files/ resources/lesson_images/ lesson1072/haiku_pattern.pdf, accessed on October 03, 2010. Re-enact one of the legends about corn. Students can write reader's theatre scripts based on one of three legends: *People of Corn*: *A Mayan Folktale*; *Zinnia: How the Corn was Saved*; *A Quetzalcoatl Tale of Corn*

Growing Foods	**Hispanic and Southwes-tern Foods**	**Food Facts and Recipes**
Pumpkin Science. Create a visual which shows the growth process of a pumpkin. Pumpkin Math. Measure the circumference of various classroom pumpkins. *Legend of Food Mountain* illustrates the importance of rain. Use this book to begin investigating the water cycle and its effect on soil erosion and plant growth. *Desert Giant: The World of the Saguaro Cactus* intro-duces readers to edible plant life that grows in the desert. Continue to explore the de-sert ecosystem.	Share the rhyme "Choco-late Rhyme" from *Tortillita Para Mama and Other Nursery Rhymes*. This is a Spanish counting rhyme; students can clap and play along. After reading *The Empa-nadas That Abuela Made*, students can list the steps for making empanadas and then write step-by-step directions for preparing an ethnic treat.	As a class, do a word sort with a list of common foods. As you share Pat Mora's book *Yum! ¡Mm Mm! ¡Qué rico! America's Sproutings*, map the regions of origins of the foods Mora introduces. After sharing Pat Mora's book, students could create a special meal using one of the foods from the book. Explore the food pyramid at http://www.mypyramid.gov/kids/ index.html Investigate the recommended daily servings of fruits and vegetables.

related to this theme. Topics such as growing and harvesting foods, preparing foods, reading myths related to food, and learning about culinary cultural traditions are some of the topics that are suggested here.

To introduce Pat Mora's (2007) *Yum! ¡Mm Mm! ¡Qué rico! America's Spoutings*, a beautifully illustrated book of haiku poetry on fruits, vegetables, and spices of the Americas, teachers can bring cranberries, papayas, chili peppers, and other foods featured in Mora's book into the classroom for students to explore. Students can see, smell, touch, and taste these foods and then record their discoveries on a senses chart at (http://www.eduplace.com/graphicorganizer/pdf/sense_eng.pdf, accessed on October 02, 2010). Teachers can then either read this book aloud to the class or have students jigsaw the different sections of the book and share important information on each food.

To make connections to health, students can study the nutritional value of the foods featured in *Yum! ¡Mm Mm! ¡Qué rico! America's Sprouting* and categorize the foods using the food pyramid at http://www.foodpyramid.com/food-pyramids/healthy-eating-pyramid/.

To make connections to science, students can explore topics such as plant growth, water conservation, and ecosystems in books such as *From Seed to Plant* (Gibbons, 1991), *The Pumpkin Book* (Gibbons, 1999), *The Water Cycle* (Kalman, 2006), and *The Drop Goes Plop: A First Look at the Water Cycle* (Godwin, 2005). They can engage in activities such as planting seeds, estimating the circumference of a pumpkin, measuring the growth of plants and charting the data on a graph, creating graphic organizers on the process of plant growth, and learning about how to conserve water.

For connections to science and art, students can learn about the saguaro cactus of the southwestern United States in *Desert Giant: The World of the Saguaro Cactus* (Bash, 2002). Bash's book describes the life cycle, the ecosystem, and the interdependent relationships of animals and plants of the saguaro cactus. The seeds and fruit of this plant are an important food source for birds and other desert animals. The saguaro cactus is also very important as a food source and cultural symbol to the Tohono O'odham, a Native American tribe that lives in the Sonoran Desert. This tribe harvests the blooms and fruits of the saguaro cactus to make jellies, jams, syrup, and wine. Using information and pictures in Bash's book and in *Cactus Hotel* (Guiberson, 1991), students can form groups to make *papier-mâché* saguaro high rises with nesting places and animals such as jackrabbits, bobcats, Gila monsters, javelin pigs, and woodpeckers that live in the saguaro ecosystem. Each group can focus on a different aspect of this plant; one group can create a spring cactus with flowers in bloom; a second group can create a summer cactus with fruit; a third group can create a dead cactus with animals that make their homes in the decomposing plant; a fourth group can create the stages of a young saguaro from seedlings, to small cacti, to one that depends upon a nurse plant as suggested at http://www.shopgpn.com/guides/rr/62.pdf, accessed on October 02, 2010.

Many of the foods described in Mora's (2007) book originate from Mexico, Central America, and South America. For example, the Aztecs of ancient Mexico first discovered chocolate and introduced it to Spanish explorers. Robert Burleigh's (2002) *Chocolate: Riches from the Rainforest* provides detailed information about how the indigenous peoples in these areas used chocolate for money as well as for other valuable purposes. This book might inspire children to make hot chocolate. Using the traditional Latino "Chocolate Rhyme" in *Tortillitas Para Mama and Other Nursery Rhymes* (Griego, 1981), they can recite this rhyme as they stir hot chocolate in a large pot.

A number of the foods in Mora's book can be tied to the myths of ancient indigenous peoples of the Americas. These indigenous peoples depended on water, soil conditions and the weather to grow crops for their survival. They created myths to explain the phenomena they had to deal with to grow their crops such as drought, floods, and rain. A number of these myths have been adapted into picture books for children and can be read and shared in literature circles in this food unit. *Legend of Food Mountain* (Rohmer, 1982) is an Aztec myth which tells a story about the importance of rain to growing corn. *Golden Flower* (Jaffe, 1996) is a Taino myth that describes how the island of Puerto Rico was created from a pumpkin seed. *People of Corn* (Gerson, 1995) is a Maya myth that underscores the importance of corn to this ancient civilization. *Dragonfly's Tale* (Rodanas, 1991) is a Zuni tale that tells how these people were blessed by the Corn Maiden with an abundant harvest but lost this blessing after a food fight and had to face famine. *Zinnia: How the Corn Was Saved* (Powell, 2003) is a Navajo legend about a young boy sent on a quest to save his tribe's crops by planting zinnias in a vegetable garden. Children can read these myths and discuss what natural phenomena they help explain.

Corn is featured in Mora's book. Young children can compare information about corn in this book to information about this plant in Aliki's (1976) book, *Corn Is Maize: The Gift of the Indians* and to Gail Gibbons' (2008) book, *Corn*. Aliki's book explains how Native peoples of North America grew and prepared corn and Gibbons' book tells the history of corn, explains how corn is grown, and describes the byproducts of corn. Based on information from these books, students can write haiku poems about sweet corn or Indian corn. A sample haiku template is available at http://www.readwritethink .org/files/resources/lesson_images/lesson1072/haiku_pattern.pdf

Cooking is a natural activity for a unit on food. Students can explore a variety of recipes that contain food from the Americas. Two cookbooks that are good resources for this are *The Kids'Multicultural* Cookbook (Cook, 1995) and *The Multicultural Cookbook for Students* (Webb & Roten, 2009). Stories can also be a starting place for cooking. In Bertrand's (2003) *The Empanadas That Abuela Made/Las empanadas que hacía la abuela*, readers meet a family gathering together to make empanadas. Students can use the recipe in this book to make this wonderful traditional Latino dish.

UNIT FOR THE MIDDLE SCHOOL LEVEL: THE CIVIL RIGHTS MOVEMENT

A study of the Civil Rights Movement in the United States is an excellent topic for middle school students to explore. Many quality books have been written by outstanding authors on this movement, using different genres, including fiction, nonfiction, and poetry. The unit proposed here is organized into five different subtopics:

1. Social Injustices
2. Life During the Civil Rights Movement
3. Protests, Boycotts, and Marches
4. School Integration
5. Leaders and Role Models

The unit includes information and response activities related to social studies, language arts, math, and the performing arts. Table 2.6 provides a web of response activities to be used in this unit.

Table 2.6.

Response Activities for Civil Rights Movement Unit, Grades Five–Eight

	Unit **The Civil Rights** **Movement** **Response Activities** **Grades Five–Eight**	

School Integration
Electronic Field Trip
http://www.americanhistory
.si.edu/brown/resources/.
This resource is produced by
The Smithsonian's National
Museum of American History
to accompany its exhibit
"Separate Is Not Equal: Brown v
Board of Education." The resources provided for educators and students on this site
include a bibliography, timeline,
teacher's guide and two electronic field trips. The electronic
field trips include a tour of the
exhibit by the curators and a
question and answer segment.

Social Injustices
Reader's Theatre. Choose a
poem from one of the following anthologies: *Remember the*
Bridge, Birmingham 1963, or *A*
Wreath for Emmett Till. Students work in small groups and
divide the poem into speaking
parts. They rehearse and perform their poetry
selection for the entire class.
Frozen Tableau. Begin by
projecting a photograph or
illustration onto a large screen.
Engage in conversation with the
students. Describe what you see;
can you identify people; what
emotion is being expressed.
Next, student volunteers pose
themselves as if they were the
photograph. A reporter visits
each person and asks questions.

Leaders and Role Models
Radio Drama. After researching a specific historical event
and the leaders of the event,
students create a radio drama.
Emphasis should be placed on
character development.
Students should consider the
emotions of each character and
try to convey this to the
audience in an historical
context. These radio dramas
could be recorded and played
back at a later time.

Life During the Civil
Rights Era
Oral History. Locate primary sources such as
interviews and journals
documenting the events
throughout the Civil
Rights Movement (*Oh*
Freedom! Kids Talk About
the Civil Rights Movement
With the People Who
Made It Happen). Discuss
point of view. Share how
primary sources are useful
resources. Choose an event
from U.S. History that
occurred during the Civil
Rights Movement (i.e.,
Bus Boycott, School Inte-
gration, Peace March). Locate people in your
community that remember
these events. Students can
design interview questions
that spark discussion and
provide an oral history of
the event. The students
should have enough facts
about the event and frame
their questions around the
thoughts and feelings of the
person being interviewed.

Protests, Boycotts and
Marches
Internet Visit the National
Parks Web site and create a
travel brochure for one of the
49 places in the United States
which have been declared of
historical significance to the
Civil Rights Movement. http://
www.nps.gov/history/nr/travel/
civilrights/, accessed on
October 03, 2010.
"We Shall Overcome Historic
Places of The Civil Rights
Movement." Each of these 49
places is shown on a US map
and a brief synopsis of the
historical significance is provided.

To provide opportunities for student inquiry on life during the Civil Rights Era, teachers can arrange a classroom library of fiction, nonfiction, and poetry. Recommended titles are included in Table 2.7.

To begin this unit, students can brainstorm what they know about topics such as social justice, school integration, the Montgomery Bus Boycott, sit-ins, Rosa Parks, and Martin Luther King, Jr. The teacher can then read aloud selected poems from Rappaport's (2006) *Nobody Gonna Turn Me 'Round* and Weatherford's (2002) *Remember the Bridge*. Students can journal their responses to the poems, focusing on the emotions the poems provoke and then share their reactions with the class.

Table 2.7.
Civil Rights Movement Unit, Grades Five–Eight

School Integration	Unit	Social Injustices
Remember: The Journey to School Integration (Morrison)	**The Civil Rights Movement Grades 5–8**	*Riding to Washington* (Swain)
Freedom School, Yes! (Little-sugar)		*Mississippi Trial, 1955* (Crowe)
Through My Eyes (Bridges)		*Brimingham, 1963* (Weatherford)
The Power of One: Daisy Bates and The Little Rock Nine (Fradin)		*Remember the Bridge* (Weatherford)
This School Is Not White! (Rappaport)		*A Wreath for Emmett Till* (Nelson)
Fire From The Rock (Draper)		*Getting Away With Murder: The True Story of the Emmett Till Case* (Crowe)
Leaders and Role Models	**Life during The Civil Rights Era**	**Protests, Boycotts and Marches**
My Brother Martin: A Sister Remembers Growing Up With the Rev. Martin Luther King, Jr. (Farris)	*Oh, Freedom! Kids Talk About the Civil Rights Movement With the People Who Made It Happen* (King & Osborne)	*Freedom Walkers: The Story of the Montgomery Bus Boycott* (Freedman)
Let It Shine! Stories of Black Women Freedom Fighters (Pinkney)	*Nobody Gonna Turn Me 'Round: Songs and Stories of the Civil Rights Movement* (Rappaport)	*Freedom on the Menu: The Greensboro Sit-Ins* (Weatherford)
Fight On! Mary Church Terrell's Battle for Integration (Fradin)	*Witness to Freedom: Young People Who Fought for Civil Rights* (Rochelle)	*Mississippi Challenge* (Walter)
Delivering Justice: W. W. Law and the Fight for Civil Rights (Haskins)	*A Sweet Smell of Roses* (Johnson)	*A Dream of Freedom: The Civil Rights Movement From 1954 to 1968* (McWhorter)
John Lewis in the Lead: A Story of the Civil Rights Movement (Haskins)	*Abby Takes a Stand* (McKissack)	*Freedom's Children* (Levine)
I Am Rosa Parks (Parks & Haskins)	*White Socks Only* (Coleman)	*Now Is Your Time: The African-American Struggle for Freedom* (Myers) 1991
I Have a Dream (King)	*The Other Side* (Woodson)	*Dear Mrs. Parks: A Dialogue With Today's Youth* (Parks)
	The Watsons Go to Birmingham - 1963 (Curtis)	

To build students' background on the racism and prejudice that existed in the South in the first half of the twentieth century, teachers can read aloud *White Socks Only* (Coleman, 1996) and *The Other Side* (Woodson, 2001). In *White Socks Only*, an African-American girl is threatened with a whipping from a white man after she mistakenly takes a drink from a "whites only" water fountain. In *The Other Side*, a white girl and an African-American girl who live on opposite sides of a fence, develop a friendship despite being told to avoid each other.

To explore what life was like during the civil rights protests of the 1950s and 1960s, students can read books that give first person accounts. *Oh Freedom! Kids Talk About the Civil Rights Movement With People Who Made it Happen* (King & Osborne, 1997) contains oral history essays based on students' interviews with relatives who experienced these times. Other first person accounts include *Witness to Freedom: Young People Who Fought for Civil Rights* (Rochelle, 1993) and *Freedom's Children: Young Civil Rights Activists Tell Their Stories* (Levine, 1993). Students can examine different points of view and the use of primary sources for research when discussing these books. They can also choose an event during the Civil Rights Movement such as the Montgomery Bus Boycott, the integration of Central High School in Little Rock, Arkansas, or the Peace March on Washington, D.C., to research. Students can then interview individuals in their community who lived during the event and write a report on their findings or present the information in a Power Point slide presentation. To help them with the oral interview process, students can access http://www.roots web.ancestry.com/~usgwkidz/query2.htm, accessed on October 02, 2010, which describes how to conduct an oral history interview and includes suggested interview questions and http://www.readwritethink.org/lesson_images/lesson928/chart .pdf, accessed on October 02, 2010, which has a graphic organizer for gathering oral histories.

To learn about the injustices that led to the protests of the 1950s and 1960s, students can read poetry books, such as *A Wreath for Emmett Till* (Nelson, 2005), a wreath of sonnets about Emmett Till, a 14-year-old African-American boy who was murdered for allegedly whistling at a white woman in Mississippi in 1955, and *Birmingham, 1963* (Weatherford, 2007) a free verse poem about the Birmingham, Alabama church bombing in which four African-American girls were killed. In response, students can form groups and choose a poem from one of these books to create a reader's theater performance for the class.

A number of books provide students with insight into the protests, marches, and boycotts of the 1950s and 1960s. Russell Freedman (2006) has compiled powerful first person accounts and photographs of the Montgomery Bus Boycott in the photo essay, *Freedom Walkers: The Story of the Montgomery Bus Boycott*. Other books that provide information about this event include *Rosa* (Giovanni, 2005) and *Freedom Riders: John Lewis and Jim Zwerg on the Front Lines of the Civil Rights Movement* (Bausum, 2006). *Freedom on the Menu: The Greensboro Sit-ins* (Weatherford, 2005) tells the story of the Jim Crow laws which prohibited African-Americans from sitting at soda counters and led to the Greensboro sit-ins. In response to these books, students can write a diary entry in which they pretend to have been involved in one of these events. In the entry, they can describe their feelings and reactions to what they witness.

School integration was a very important issue during the Civil Rights Movement. Readers can learn about this issue from Ruby Bridge's first-person account in *Through*

My Eyes: The Autobiography of Ruby Bridges (Bridges, 1999) in which she describes her fear and excitement as a six-year old girl going to a new school that was integrated by law for the first time in 1960. They can also learn about this issue in the photo-essay, *Remember: The Journey to School Integration* (Morrison, 2004). Morrison's book conveys the emotions surrounding the School Integration Movement through use of historical photographs and her own reflective writing on each of the photos. Students can compare what they learned from these books about school integration to Sharon Draper's (2007) novel, *Fire From the Rock*, a fictionalized retelling of the life of Sylvia, an African-American honors student who was chosen as one of the first students to integrate Central High School in Little Rock, Arkansas. Told against the backdrop of life in racially tense Little Rock in 1957, this book leads to excellent discussions and text-to-self connections. These three books provide information on school integration through three different genres and lend themselves to critical thinking. Students can critique these books in small groups in terms of which book they find most compelling, or they can compare and contrast the information from the different perspectives of the books and display their thinking in a graphic organizer.

To learn about civil rights leaders and role models, students can read one or more of the many biographies that are available. They can read *Martin's Big Words* (Rappaport, 2001) which has short quotes from a number of Martin Luther King's speeches and is beautifully illustrated with collages by Brian Collier. Students also can read, *My Brother Martin: A Sister Remembers Growing Up With the Rev. Martin Luther King, Jr.* (Farris, 2003), a memoir written by his sister which provides a snapshot of life in the South during Dr. King's youth. They can also read Nikki Giovanni's (1996) poem, "The Funeral of Martin Luther King, Jr." and compare it to Martin Luther King's "I Have A Dream" speech, which is full of historical references and figurative speech. King's speech is available in an audio/video version at http://www.americanrhetoric.com/speeches/mlkihaveadream.htm, accessed on October 02, 2010 and in hard copy at http://teachingamericanhistory.org/library/index.asp?documentprint=40, accessed on October 02, 2010. Comparing these two literary works offers students the opportunity to examine the inter-text connections between these two works and the chance to learn about the historical context in which Giovanni wrote her poem. In response to reading biographies on leaders in the Civil Rights Movement, students can work in pairs to role play an interview with one of the important figures of the Civil Rights Movement. One student can play the interviewer and the other can play one of the leaders of the Civil Rights Movement on a talk show. They can record their interviews on a digital recorder and transfer them to a podcast on the school Web site.

To further explore the Civil Rights Movement, students can go on the Smithsonian National Museum's electronic field trip, which is based on the exhibit, "Separate Is Not Equal: Brown v. Board of Education," commemorating the fiftieth anniversary of Brown v. Board of Education. The resources on this site include a bibliography, timeline, teacher's guide, and two electronic field trips. To find out more information, students can visit the Smithsonian National Museum's Web site, http://www.americanhistory.si.edu/brown/resources/ A possible culminating activity for this unit is for students to revisit the poetry collections and photo essays recommended above. Based on the insight they now have into the Civil Rights Movement, students can participate in frozen tableau, a form of drama. They can locate a photograph from the 1950s or 1960s and pose as if they were in the photograph. They can then reenact the photographic moment for the entire class. This can then lead to a class discussion of the importance of the event portrayed in the photograph.

FINAL THOUGHTS

Integrating multicultural literature throughout the curriculum adds cultural richness and depth to enhance understanding and critical thinking for all learners. This integration offers content, concepts, and perspectives that can enable students to view issues and events from the perspective of diverse ethnic and cultural groups and support the levels of multicultural education proposed by Banks (2004). Discussion in the classroom and library is the essential ingredient to support deep respect and understanding of diverse cultures. As explained by Samway and Whang (1996), students must have a safe, supportive classroom environment before they will openly share their questions, ideas, and opinions in regard to issues. Teachers can make the difference if they establish a trusting community with ground rules for attentive listening and no put-downs. "Through openended discussions, we can all deepen our understanding of often controversial issues, while experiencing what it means to live in and develop a democratic world" (p. 121).

REFERENCES

Allington, R. L., & Johnston, P. H. (2002). *Reading to learn: Lessons from exemplary fourthgrade classrooms*. New York, NY: Guilford.

Banks, J. A. (2004). Multicultural education: Historical development, dimensions, and practice. In Banks, J. A., & Banks, C.A.M. (Eds.), *Handbook of research on multicultural education* (2nd ed., pp. 3–29). San Francisco, CA: Jossey-Bass.

Castek, J., Bevans-Mangelson, J., & Goldstone, B. (2006). Reading adventures online: Five ways to introduce the new literacies of the Internet through children's literature. *The Reading Teacher, 59* (7), 714–726.

Gates, P. S., & Mark, D. H. (2006). *Cultural journeys*. Lanham, MD: Scarecrow Press, Inc.

Hancock, M. R. (September, 2007). Art styles in picture books: A window into visual literacy. *Book Links*.

Hancock, M. R. (2008). *A celebration of literature and response: Children, books, and teachers in K-8 classrooms*, 3rd ed. Upper Saddle River, NJ: Pearson.

Harvey, S., & Goudvis, A. (2007). *Strategies that work*, 2nd ed. Portland, ME: Stenhouse Publishers.

Norton, D. E. (1990). Teaching multicultural literature in the reading curriculum. *The Reading Teacher, 44*, 28–40.

Norton, D. E. (2009). *Multicultural children's literature: Through the eyes of many children*, 3rd ed. Boston, MA: Pearson Education.

Ogle, D. (1986). K-W-L: A teaching model that develops active reading of expository text. *The Reading Teacher, 39*, 563–570.

Rasinski, T. V., & Padak, N. D. (1990). Multicultural learning through children's literature. *Language Arts, 67*, 576–580.

Samway, K. D., & Whang, G. (1996). *Literature study circles in a multicultural classroom*. Portland, ME: Stenhouse Publishers.

Vacca, R., & Vacca, J. A. (2008). *Content area reading*, 8th ed. Boston, MA: Allyn & Bacon.

Young, T. A., & Ferguson, P. M. (1998). From Anansi to Zomo: Trickster tales in the classroom. In M. F. Opitz (Ed.), *Literacy instruction for culturally and linguistically diverse students: A collection of articles and commentaries* (pp. 258–274). Newark, DE: International Reading Association.

CHILDREN'S AND YOUNG ADULT LITERATURE

Adler, D. (2005). *Joe Louis America's fighter*, illustrated by T. Widener. Orlando, FL: Gulliver Books.

Adoff, J. (2007). *Jimi & me*. New York, NY: Hyperion Books for Children.

Alexander, E. & Nelson, M. (2007). *Miss Crandall's school for young ladies and little misses of color: Poems*, illustrated by F. Cooper. Honesdale, PA: Wordsong.

Aliki. (1976). *Corn is maize: The gift of the Indians*. New York, NY: Crowell.

Ancona, G. (2001). *Harvest*. Tarrytown, NY: Marshall Cavendish.

Baca, A., & Accardo, A. (2003). *Chiles for Benito*, illustrated by J. Colin, translated by A. Accardo. Houston, TX: Piñata Books.

Barakat, I. (2007). *Tasting the sky: A Palestinian childhood*. New York, NY: Farrar, Straus & Giroux

Bash, B. (2002). *Desert giant: The world of the saguaro cactus*. San Francisco, CA: Sierra Club Books for Children.

Bausum, A. (2006). *Freedom riders: John Lewis and Jim Zwerg on the front lines of the Civil Rights Movement*. Washington, D.C.: National Geographic.

Bernier-Grand, C. T. (2004). *César: ¡Sí, se puede!/Yes, we can!*, illustrated by D. Diaz. New York, NY: Marshall Cavendish.

Bertrand, D. (2003). *The empanadas that Abuela made/Las empanadas que hacía la abuela*. Ill, illustrated by A. P. DeLange. Houston, TX: Piñata Books.

Boyd, C. D. (1996). *A different beat*. New York, NY: Puffin Books.

Bradby, M. (2000). *Momma, where are you from?* illustrated by C. K. Soentpiet. New York, NY: Orchard Books.

Bridges, R. (1999). *Through my eyes: The autobiography of Ruby Bridges*. New York, NY: Scholastic.

Brown, D. (2006). *Bright path: Young Jim Thorpe*. New Milford, CT: Roaring Brook Press.

Bruchac, J. (1993). *Fox song*, illustrated by P. Morin. New York, NY: Philomel Books.

Bruchac, J. (2006). *Code talker: A novel about the Navajo Marines of WWII*. New York, NY: Dial Books.

Burleigh, R. (2002) *Chocolate: Riches from the rainforest*. New York, NY: Henry N. Abrams.

Burleigh, R (2004). *Langston's train ride*, illustrated by L. Jenkins. New York, NY: Orchard.

Carlson, L. (2005). *Red hot salsa: Bilingual poems on being young and Latino in the United States*. New York, NY: Henry Holt.

Carvell, M. (2005). *Sweetgrass basket*. New York, NY: Dutton Children's Books.

Cha, D. (1996). *Dia's story cloth*, illustrated by C. Cha & N. T. Cha. New York, NY: Lee & Low Books.

Charney, S. & Goldbeck, D. (2007). *The ABC's of fruits and vegetables and beyond*, illustrated by M. Larson. Woodstock, NY: Ceres Press.

Cheng, A. (2003). *Grandfather counts*, illustrated by A. Zhang. New York, NY: Lee & Low Books.

Cheng, A. (2003). *The key collection*, illustrated by Y. Choi. New York, NY: H. Holt.

Coburn, J. (2000). *Domitila: A Cinderella tale from the Mexican tradition*, illustrated by C. McLennan. Walnut Creek, CA: Shen's Books.

Coleman, E. (1996). *White socks only*, illustrated by T. Geter. Morton Grove, IL: A. Whitman.

Compestine, Y. C. (2007). *Revolution is not a dinner party: A novel*. New York, NY: H. Holt.

Cook, D. (1995). *The kids' multicultural cookbook*. Charlotte, VT: Williamson Books.

Crowe, C. (2002). *Mississippi trial*. New York, NY: Dial.

Crowe, C. (2003). *Getting away with murder: The true story of the Emmett Till case.* New York, NY: Phyllis Fogleman Books.

Crowe, E. (2007). *Surfer of the century: The life of Duke Kahanamoku*, illustrated by R. Waldrep. New York, NY: Lee & Low.

Curtis C. P. (1995). *The Watsons go to Birmingham-1963.* New York, NY: Laurel Leaf Books

Curtis, C. P. (2005). *Bud, not Buddy.* New York, NY: Yearling.

Das, P. (1997). *I is for India.* Parsippany, NJ: Silver Press.

de Paola, T. (1978). *The popcorn book.* New York, NY: Holiday House.

Delacre, L. (2000). *Salsa stories.* New York, NY: Scholastic.

Dillon, L., & Dillon, D. (2002). *Rap a tap tap: Here's Bojangles, think of that.* New York, NY: Blue Sky Press.

Dillon, L., & Dillon, D. (2007). *Jazz on a Saturday night.* New York, NY: Blue Sky Press.

Dingle, D. T. (1998). *First in the field: Baseball hero Jackie Robinson.* New York, NY: Hyperion Books for Children.

Dooley, N. (2002). *Everybody brings noodles*, illustrated by P. Thornton. Minneapolis, MN: Carolrhoda Books.

Dorros, A. (1991). *Abuela*, illustrated by E. Kleven. New York, NY: Dutton Children's Books.

Draper, S. M. (2007). *Fire from the rock.* New York, NY: Scholastic.

Ellis, D. (2001). *The breadwinner.* Toronto, ON: Douglas & McIntyre.

Ellis, D. (2003). *Parvana's journey.* Berkeley, CA: Groundwood Books.

Farris, C. K. (2003). *My brother Martin: A sister remembers growing up with the Rev. Martin Luther King, Jr.*, illustrated by C. Soentpiet. New York, NY: Simon & Schuster Books for Young Readers.

Flake, S. (2004). *Who am I without him? Short stories about girls and the boys in their lives.* New York, NY: Jump at the Sun/Hyperion Books for Children.

Flake, S. (2007). *The skin I'm in.* New York, NY: Jump at the Sun.

Fradin, D. B., & Fradin, J. B. (2003). *Fight on! Mary Church Terrell's battle for integration.* New York, NY: Clarion Books.

Fradin, J. B., & Fradin, D. B. (2004). *The power of one: Daisy Bates and the Little Rock nine.* New York, NY: Clarion Books.

Freedman, R. (2004). *The voice that challenged a nation: Marian Anderson and the struggle for equal rights.* New York, NY: Houghton Mifflin.

Freedman, R. (2006). *Freedom walkers: The story of the Montgomery Bus Boycott.* New York, NY: Holiday House.

Gaskins, P. F. (Ed.). (1999). *What are you? Voices of mixed race young people.* New York, NY: Henry Holt & Company.

Gerson, M. (1995). *People of corn: A Mayan story*, illustrated by C. Golembe. Boston, MA: Little, Brown.

Gibbons, G. (1991). *From seed to plant.* New York, NY: Holiday House.

Gibbons, G. (1999). *The pumpkin book.* New York, NY: Holiday House.

Gibbons, G. (2008). *Corn.* New York, NY: Holiday House.

Giovanni, N. (Ed.) (1996). *Shimmy shimmy shimmy like my sister Kate: Looking at the Harlem Renaissance through poems.* New York, NY: Henry Holt.

Giovanni, N. (1996). *The selected poems of Nikki Giovanni: 1968–1996.* New York, NY: William Morrow.

Giovanni, N. (2005). *Rosa*, illustrated by B. Collier. New York, NY: Henry Holt & Company.

Godwin, S. (2005). *The drop goes plop: A first look at the water cycle.* Minneapolis: MN: Picture Windows Books.

Golenbock, P. (2001). *Hank Aaron brave in every way*. San Diego, CA: Harcourt.

Gonzales Bertrand, D. (2003). *The empanadas that Abuela made/Las empanadas que hacía la abuela*, illustrated by A. Pardo DeLange. Houston, TX: Piñata Books.

Gonzalez, M. (2007). *My colors, my world/Mis colores, mi mundo*. San Francisco, CA: Children's Book Press.

Greenfield, E. (1988). *Grandpa's face*, illustrated by F. Cooper. New York, NY: Philomel Books.

Griego, M. C., Bucks, B. L., Gilbert, S. S., & Kimball, L. H. (1981). *Tortillitas para Mamá and other nursery rhymes: Spanish and English*, illustrated by B. Cooney. New York, NY: Holt, Rinehart and Winston.

Guiberson, B. Z. (1991). *Cactus hotel*, illustrated by M. Lloyd. New York, NY: Henry Holt.

Haskins, J. (2005). *Delivering justice: W. W. Law and the fight for civil rights*, illustrated by Benny Andrews. Cambridge, MA: Candlewick Press.

Haskins, J. (2006). *John Lewis in the lead: A story of the Civil Rights Movement*, illustrated by Benny Andrews. New York, NY: Lee & Low.

Hill, L. C. (2004). *Harlem stomp! A cultural history of the Harlem Renaissance*. New York, NY: Little Brown.

Hollyer, B. (2004). *Let's eat! What children eat around the world*. New York, NY: Henry Holt.

Hoyt-Goldsmith, D. (1999). *Las posadas: An Hispanic Christmas celebration*, photos by L. Migdale. New York, NY: Holiday House.

Jaffe, N. (1996). *The golden flower: A Taino myth from Puerto Rico*, illustrated by E. O Sanchez. New York, NY: Simon & Schuster Children's Publishing.

Johnson, A. (2004). *Just like Josh Gibson*, illustrated by B. Peck. New York, NY: Simon & Schuster.

Johnson, A. (2007). *A sweet smell of roses*, illustrated by E. Velasquez. New York, NY: Aladdin Paperbacks.

Jurmain, S. (2005). *The forbidden schoolhouse: The true and dramatic story of Prudence Crandall and her students*. Boston, MA: Houghton Mifflin Books for Children.

Kadohata, C. (2006). *Weedflower*. New York, NY: Atheneum Books for Young Readers.

Kalman, B., & Sjonger, R. (2006). *The water cycle*. New York, NY: Crabtree Publishing.

King, C., & Osborne, L. B. (1997). *Oh, freedom! Kids talk about the Civil Rights Movement with the people who made it happen*. New York, NY: Knopf.

King, M. L., Jr. (1997). *I have a dream*. New York, NY: Scholastic.

Kottke, J. (2000). *From seed to pumpkin*. New York, NY: Children's Press.

Krull, K. (1996). *Wilma unlimited: How Wilma Rudolph became the world's fastest woman*, illustrated by D. Diaz. San Diego, CA: Harcourt Brace.

Krull, K. (2003). *Harvesting hope: The story of* César Chávez, illustrated by Y. Morales. San Diego, CA: Harcourt.

Leitich, C. (2002). *Indian shoes*, illustrated by J. Madsen. New York, NY: Harper Collins.

Levine, E. (1993). *Freedom's children: Young civil rights activists tell their own stories*. New York, NY: Putnam.

Littlesugar, A. (2001). *Freedom school, yes!*, illustrated by F. Cooper. New York, NY: Philomel Books.

Makhijani, P. (2007). *Mama's saris*, illustrated by E. Gomez. New York, NY: Little Brown.

Marsalis, W. (2005). *Jazz A-B-Z: An A to Z collection of jazz portraits*, illustrated by P. Rogers. Cambridge, MA: Candlewick.

McDonough, Y. (2002). *Peaceful protest: The life of Nelson Mandela*, illustrated by M. Zeldis. New York, NY: Walker & Company.

McKissack, P. (2005). *Abby takes a stand*, illustrated by Gordon James. New York, NY: Viking.

McWhorter, D. (2004). *A dream of freedom: The Civil Rights Movement from 1954 to 1968*. New York, NY: Scholastic.

Medina, T. (2002) *Love to Langston*, illustrated by R. Gregory Christie. New York, NY: Lee & Low Books.

Millen, C. (2004). *Blue bowl down*, illustrated by H. Meade. Cambridge, MA: Candlewick.

Miller, W. (1998). *The bus ride*, illustrated by J. Ward. New York, NY: Lee & Low.

Mora, P (2008). *Let's eat/¡A comer!* New York, NY: Harper Collins.

Mora, P. (2007). *Yum! ¡Mm Mm! ¡Qué rico! America's sproutings*, illustrated by R. López. New York, NY: Lee & Low Books.

Mora, P. (1998). *Delicious hullabaloo*, illustrated by F. X. Mora. Houston, TX: Piñata Books.

Mora, P. (1994). *The desert is my mother/El desierto es mi madre*, illustrated by D. Lechon. Houston, TX: Piñata Books.

Morris, A. (2002) *Grandma Lai Goon remembers: A Chinese-American family story*, illustrated by P. Linenthal. Brookfield, CT: Millbrook.

Morris, A. (1993). *Bread, bread, bread*, illustrated by K. Heyman. New York, NY: Harper Collins.

Morrison, T. (2004). *Remember: The journey to school integration*. Boston, MA: Houghton Mifflin Company.

Muse, D. (2005). *The entrance place of wonders: Poems of the Harlem Renaissance*, illustrated by C. Riley-Webb. New York, NY: Harry N. Abrams.

Myers, W. D. (1991). *Now is your time: The African-American struggle for freedom*. New York, NY: HarperCollins.

Myers, W. D. (2003). *Blues journey*, illustrated by C. Myers. New York, NY: Holiday House.

Myers, W. D. (2004). *Here in Harlem*. New York, NY: Holiday House.

Myers, W. D. (2006). *Jazz*, illustrated by C. Myers. New York, NY: Holiday House.

Myers, W. D. (2007). *Harlem summer*. New York, NY: Scholastic.

Na, A. (2001). *A step from heaven*. Asheville, NC: Front Street.

Naidoo, B. (2003). *Out of bounds: Seven stories of conflict and hope*. New York, NY: Harper Collins.

Nelson, K. (2007). *We are the ship: The story of Negro baseball*. New York, NY: Jump at The Sun.

Nelson, M. (2005). *A wreath for Emmet Till*, illustrated by P. Lardy. Boston, MA: Houghton Mifflin.

Nelson, S. (2006). *Quiet hero: The Ira Hayes story*. New York, NY: Lee and Low.

Park, L. S. (2007). *Bee-bim bop!* illustrated by H. B. Lee. New York, NY: Clarion.

Parke, M. (1992). *A Quetzalcoatl tale of corn*. Carthage, IL: Good Apple Inc.

Parker, T. T. (2005). *Sienna's scrapbook: Our African American heritage trip*, illustrated by J. Genovese. San Francisco, CA: Chronicle Books.

Parks, R., & Haskins, J. (2000). *I am Rosa Parks*, illustrated by Wil Clay. New York, NY: Puffins Books.

Parks, R., & Reed, G. J. (1997). *Dear Mrs. Parks: A dialogue with today's youth*. New York, NY: Lee and Low.

Perdomo, W. (2002) *Visiting Langston*, illustrated by B. Collier. New York, NY: Lee & Low.

Pinkney, A. D. (1997). *Duke Ellington: The piano prince and his orchestra*, illustrated by B. Pinkney. New York, NY: Hyperion.

Pinkney, A. D. (2000). *Let it shine! Stories of Black women freedom fighters*, illustrated by S. Alcorn. San DiegoCA: Harcourt.

Pinkney, A. D. (2001). *Mim's Christmas jam*, illustrated by V. Pinkney. San Diego, CA: Harcourt Children's Books.

Pinkney, A. D. (2002). *Ella Fitzgerald: The tale of a vocal virtuosa*, illustrated by B. Pinkney. New York, NY: Jump at the Sun.

Polacco, P. (1988). *The keeping quilt*. New York, NY: Simon Schuster Books for Young Readers.

Polacco, P. (1992). *Mrs. Katz and Tush*. New York, NY: Bantam.

Powell, P. H. (2003). *Zinnia: How the corn was saved, A Quetzalcoatl tale of corn*, illustrated by K. Benally. Flagstaff, AZ: Salina Bookshelf.

Rampersad, A., & Roessel, D. (Eds.) (2006). *Langston Hughes*, illustrated by B. Andrews. New York, NY: Sterling Publishers.

Rappaport, D. (2001). *Martin's big words*, illustrated by B. Collier. New York, NY: Hyperion.

Rappaport, D. (2005). *This school is not White*, illustrated by C. James. New York, NY: Hyperion Books.

Rappaport, D. (2006). *Nobody gonna turn me 'round: Songs and stories of the Civil Rights Movement*, illustrated by S. Evans. Cambridge, MA: Candlewick.

Rattigan, J. K. (1993). *Dumpling soup*, illustrated by L. Hsu-Flanders. Boston, MA: Little, Brown & Company.

Raven, M. T. (2004). *Circle unbroken: The story of a basket and its people*, illustrated by E. B. Lewis. New York, NY: Farrar, Straus and Giroux.

Robinson, S. (2004). *Promises to keep: How Jackie Robinson changed America*. New York, NY: Scholastic.

Rochelle, B. (1993). *Witnesses to freedom: Young people who fought for civil rights*. New York, NY: Lodestar Books.

Rodanas, K. (1991). *Dragonfly's tale*. New York, NY: Clarion.

Rohmer, H. (1982). *Legend of Food Mountain*, illustrated by G. Carrillo. San Francisco, CA: Children's Book Press.

Rotner, S. & Kelly, S. (2001). *Lots of grandparents*. Brookfield, CT: Millbrook Press.

Ryan, P. M. (2000). *Esperanza rising*. New York, NY: Scholastic.

Ryan, P. M. (2002). *When Marian sang: The true recital of Marian Anderson*, illustrated by B. Selznick. New York, NY: Scholastic Press.

Ryan, P. M. (2004). *Becoming Naomi León*. New York, NY: Scholastic Press.

Shange, N. (2002). *Float like a butterfly*, illustrated by E Rodriguez. New York, NY: Jump at the Sun.

Shange, N. (2004). *Ellington was not a street*, illustrated by K. Nelson. New York, NY: Simon & Schuster.

Sheth, K. (2007). *My dadima wears a sari*, illustrated by Y. Jaeggi. Atlanta, GA: Peachtree.

Smith, Jr. C. (2004). *Hoop kings*. Cambridge, MA: Candlewick.

Smith, Jr. C. (2007). *Twelve rounds to glory*, illustrated by B. Collier. Cambridge, MA: Candlewick.

Stauffacher, S. (2007) *Nothing but trouble: The story of Althea Gibson*, illustrated by G. Couch. New York, NY: Alfred A. Knopf.

Swain, G. (2008). *Riding to Washington*, illustrated by David Geister. Chelsea, MI: Sleeping Bear Press.

Swamp, J. (1995). *Giving thanks: A Native American good morning message*, illustrated by E. Printup, Jr. New York, NY: Lee & Low.

Swoopes, S. (2001). *Hoops with Swoopes*, illustrated by S. Kuklin. New York, NY: Jump at the Sun.

Tunnell, M. O., & Chilcoat, G. W. (1996). *The children of Topaz: The story of a Japanese-American interment camp based on a classroom diary*. New York, NY: Holiday House.

Walter, M. P. (1996). *Mississippi challenge*. New York, NY: Aladdin Paperbacks.

Watts, J. (1997). *Keepers*, illustrated by F. Marshall. New York, NY: Lee & Low.

Weatherford, C. B. (2000). *The sound that jazz makes*, illustrated by E. Velasquez. New York, NY: Walker Books for Young Readers.

Weatherford, C. B. (2002). *Remember the bridge: Poems of a people*. New York, NY: Philomel.

Weatherford, C. B. (2005). *Freedom on the menu: The Greensboro sit-ins*, illustrated by J. Lagarrique. New York, NY: Dial Books.

Weatherford, C. B. (2007). *Birmingham, 1963*. Honesdale, PA: Wordsong.

Weatherford, C. B. (2006). *Champions on the bench*, illustrated by L. Jenkins. New York, NY: Dial Books.

Webb, L. S., & Roten, L. G. (2009). *The multicultural cookbook for students: Updated and revised*. Westport, CT: Greenwood.

Weber, E. (2004). *Rattlesnake mesa: Stories from a Native American childhood*, photographs by Richela Renkun. New York, NY: Lee & Low.

Winter, J. (2001). *Beisbol! Latino baseball pioneers and legends*. New York, NY: Lee & Low.

Winter, J. (2005). *Roberto Clemente: Pride of the Pirates*, illustrated by R. Colon. New York, NY: Antheneum.

Wise, B. (2007). *Louis Sockalexis: Native American baseball pioneer*, illustrated by B. Farnsworth. New York, NY: Lee & Low.

Woodson, J. (2001). *The other side*, illustrated by E. B. Lewis. New York, NY: Putnam's.

Woodson, J. (2005). *Show way*, illustrated by H. Talbott. New York, NY: G. P. Putnam's Sons.

Yacowitz, C. (1998). *Pumpkin fiesta*, illustrated by J. Cepeda. New York, NY: HarperCollins.

Yep, L. (1995). *Thief of hearts*. New York, NY: HarperCollins.

Yoo, P. (2005). *Sixteen years in sixteen seconds: The Sammy Lee story*, illustrated by D. Lee. New York, NY: Lee & Low Books.

3

Voices of Multicultural Authors

Darwin L. Henderson and Teresa Young

Multicultural literature refers to literature by and about people who are members of groups considered to be outside the sociopolitical mainstream of the United States. Most frequently, the term, multicultural literature, refers to books about people of color in this country–African American, Asian American, Native American, Hispanic (Bishop, 1997). Whereas this definition is one that is most generally accepted, books about other underrepresented groups such as religious minorities, regional cultures, and individuals with disabilities are frequently included in the definition of multicultural literature. It also includes "any persons whose lifestyle, enforced or otherwise, distinguishes them as identifiable members of a group other than the mainstream" (Taxel, 2003, p. 143).

One of the most effective ways to support diversity of all kinds is through children's literature. In recent years, children's literature has been infused throughout the entire curriculum to support the various content areas. Prior to its use in social studies, science, history, and math, children's literature was employed most effectively in the reading and language arts portions of the curriculum. Teachers designed units of study by selecting various types of books written for children. When this approach was implemented, it enabled the teacher and student to move beyond the limitations of a single textbook. The use of multiple sources of information made learning more interesting, offered a broader point of view, and most importantly, provided for the diverse interests, life experiences, and capabilities of students in inclusive classrooms.

Donna Norton (2003) suggests that multicultural literature has value and significance for the following reasons:

- Through multicultural literature, children who are members of racial or ethnic groups realize that they have a cultural heritage of which they can be proud and that their culture has made important contributions to the United States and to the world.

- Pride in their heritage helps children improve their self-concepts and develop cultural identity. Reading about individuals who have successfully solved their own problems and made notable achievement helps raise the aspirations of children who belong to underrepresented groups.
- Learning about other cultures allows children to understand that people who belong to racial or ethnic groups other than theirs are real people with feelings, emotions, and needs similar to their own–individual human beings, not stereotypes.
- Children discover that whereas not all people may share their personal beliefs and values, individuals can and must learn to live in harmony.
- Children of the majority culture learn to respect the values and contributions of minority groups in the United States and the values and contributions of people in other parts of the world.
- Children broaden their understanding of history, geography, and natural history when they read about cultural groups living in various regions of their country and the world.
- The wide range of multicultural themes also helps children develop an understanding of social change (Norton, 2003, p. 457).

Perhaps multicultural literature's most important value is the opportunity it affords children to access the diverse literary traditions of other cultures. The sharing of sensitive, culturally accurate, and positive literature of high literary quality offers children an opportunity to connect with the unique qualities of humanity throughout the world.

Another avenue to explore multicultural literature is through the author and the stories they create for children and young adults. Getting to know the author through author studies frames and solidifies the authenticity of the story. Students experience the culture, understand the nuisances of the lived cultural experience, and hear the voice of the author in the stories read.

In this chapter, we share responses from four prominent authors of children's and young adult literature. Angela Johnson, a celebrated writer and MacArthur Fellowship recipient, explores children's search for truth (personal communication, September 9, 2008). In her books she writes about friendship, a sense of community, culture and identity, and the essence of childhood. Pat Mora, poet and author of nonfiction and children's picture storybooks, through her writing expands the boundaries and borders of literary style (personal communication, October 9, 2009). Through style, sound, memory, and experience, she writes in two languages, English interwoven with Spanish words and phrases. Critics have praised her for capturing the nuances of Latino culture and the use of warm, engaging, and evocative language. Best known for her children's books about Rosebud Sioux life and culture, Virginia Driving Hawk Sneve often combines history and legend to create authentic Native American stories (personal communication, October 23, 2009). A former English teacher and school counselor, this award-winning writer "strives to be honest and accurate about the Native American experience portrayed in her work." In her writing, she dispels stereotypes and shows her reading audience that Native Americans have a proud past, a viable present, and a hopeful future. Laurence Yep, a prolific, award-winning author, explores themes of alienated characters that often see themselves as outside their own culture (personal communication, September 19, 2009). Yep states, "I try to write about issues that interest young readers, especially questions of identity." In the following conversations, these outstanding authors share their insights and ideas about writing, culture, and authenticity and what makes a book multicultural.

WRITING

Authors define the writing process variously. Some respond to external stimuli, whereas others are drawn to a particular subject without consciously knowing why that subject interests them. Still others appear to be provoked and feel writing is a meaningful response to their global environment, surroundings, and experiences. Thus, the writing reflects an emotional insight. As readers, we engage with these various writing styles. Rosenblatt (as cited in Klug, Tuner and Feuerborn, 2009) describes the writing experience from the readers' perspective:

Authors use language to produce ideas within the readers concerning the subjects being pursued. Depending on the type of texts, readers may engage in efferent stances, wanting to mine writings for information they provide, or aesthetic stances, which bring to mind sensations, images, feelings, and ideas that are the residue of past psychological events involving those words and their referents . . . [experiencing and savoring] qualities of the structured ideas, situations, scenes, personalities, and emotions that are called forth and participate in the tensions, conflicts, and resolutions as they unfold.

(p. 93)

Rosenblatt asserts that the act of reading requires interactions between the readers, authors, and texts (as cited in Klug, Turner, and Feuerborn, 2009, p. 93). It is these lived through experiences that the writer explores and brings to life for the reader. The reader interacts with the author, creating a reading encounter. Virginia Driving Hawk Sneve (personal communication, October 23, 2009) describes how her everyday experiences inspire her writing:

I am inspired to write by many aspects: how the sun rises over the mountain, something my child said or felt; words some one has spoken or from a story I heard; my own and other's experiences; places I visit. I am open to inspiration from all I hear, see, sense, want, and dislike.

These inspirations help children and young adults see themselves in the story, bridging the connection between the author and the text. Cullinan (1989) used the metaphors of a mirror and a window to emphasize the potential that children's literature offers. "We see our own experiences in literature (the mirror), and then an author 'invites' us to look through a (window), and we respond, to see the world through another's eyes" (p. 424).

In Laurence Yep's books, he tells stories about Chinatown and other times about dragon realms, allowing the reader to look into the mirror of his daydreams. "Writing allows me to daydream all day." For Yep, "writing is that wonderful discomfort when I feel connected to the world in so many special ways–when a two-dimensional canvas of facts and words becomes a three-dimensional world of color and is populated with living, breathing people and creatures" (personal communication, September 19, 2009). He is a storyteller and that is what he does in his books, tells stories that resonant with readers creating a magical connection of emotions and experiences.

The authors we interviewed all described the need to write for their audience and share their honest and accurate perspectives. Angela Johnson (personal communication, September 9, 2008) writes that she is thrilled with the poetry of the language, and she mines for those events that spark a need to write.

I will be talking to someone about a completely innocuous event or subject when out of the blue some phrase or word simply spoken astounds me. Sometimes it's a play on words. Many times it's a sentiment reduced to its purest and clearest form. Other times it's something spoken so profoundly I'm moved to tears and moved to write about it.

And, she hopes this feeling never changes because this is the bedrock for her creativity. These authors are able to explore the everyday nuisances and then seamlessly help readers connect to those experiences.

Pat Mora (personal communication, October 9, 2009) also searches in her writing for ways to connect her experiences and express her creativity. She believes she doesn't choose her subjects, but her subjects choose her. "We don't fully understand, I think, as writers, why we are drawn to certain topics. I enjoy the talking about writing, but I love the mystery of writing, too. As a writer, I come to the page hoping that something inter-esting will emerge. I write because I love the process and because I love language." She shared that she is most interested in what words can do, in the pleasure they can bring, in the way they can break our hearts, and in the magic. The bedrock of creativity is evident because these authors capture their creative moments inducing thoughts and feelings for so many children and young adults.

CULTURE AND AUTHENTICITY

The nature of writing for children and young adults tends to be around themes. However, in multicultural literature, those themes recall culture or elicit a response characterized by a given culture. Pat Mora (personal communication, October 9, 2009) states, "All books are cultural texts and we are each cultural beings." When asked, what do you think your books contribute to cultural understanding? Mora eloquently described the essence of cultural context for her readers:

Culturally, I hope that the reader experiences the movement between languages. Even though a reader may be monolingual, as a result of reading my books, he or she will have a sense of how two languages can live together, and how words can move back and forth between languages. That movement need not be abrupt or a painful experience; it can flow, which is what happens, I think, in bilingual environments.

Expanding on Mora's reflection on the need for cultural understanding, the National Council of Social Studies (NCSS) asserts that cultural studies prepare students to ask and possibly answer important questions. For example, what are the common charac-teristics of different cultures? How do belief systems influence culture? Does the cul-ture accommodate different ideas and beliefs? How do we learn cultural values and beliefs through the language? Typically in schools, these themes appear as units dealing with geography, history, and anthropologyas well as multicultural topics across the cur-riculum (www.socialstudies.org, accessed on September 30, 2010). Further, the NCSS defines culture as

. . . a way to help us to understand ourselves as both individuals and members of various groups. Human cultures exhibit both similarities and differences. In a democratic and multicultural soci-ety, students need to understand multiple perspectives that derive from different cultural vantage points. This understanding will allow them to relate to people in our nation and throughout the world (www.socialstudies.org).

"Too often those in the mainstream make the mistake of thinking that cultural diversity refers only to people who are different from them, but everyone belongs to a culture, and in fact, to several cultural communities" (Galda, Cullinan, & Sipe, 2010, p. 23). Pat Mora (personal communication, October 9, 2009) continues this assertion when she described her audience's experience after reading her books,

At the most basic level, the awareness that the Latino experience is something that the reader, whether Latino or not, can identify with and understand. I believe that literature helps us cross borders. Through a story or a poem, the reader connects and realizes our basic humanity. It is our humanity, it is how we both respect our differences and feel a responsibility to understand our difference that is important. [. . .] That's what literature does for us, that's why we love it. That's why we want our students to love it. It makes us less lonely. It softens us. It reminds us what it means to be human.

Whereas some authors write about culture as a concept focusing on themes, others provide depth in their depictions of cultural experiences that are embedded within characterization, plot, and setting. "Culturally rich books allow readers to look through a window at characters similar to or different from themselves, to recognize their own culture or learn about another" (Galda, Cullinan, & Sipe, 2010, p. 24).

The uniqueness and accurate depiction of individuals within the human family is celebrated in multicultural literature and its illustrations. For some writers and illustrators, cultural details enhance the readers understanding of the story. For example, Jerry Pinkney (as cited in Henderson & May, 2005) attributes his earliest awareness of the uniqueness of people to the neighborhood where he lived as a child. He states that "writers often keep written files or notes; my file was a visual file. . . . Interesting enough, I didn't know at the time that that curiosity would be somehow stored away, and it would find a way to express itself" (p. 274). Pinkney accurately represents cultural details through extensive research, the mood of the story, and the sensory impressions from his childhood. Laurence Yep (personal communication, September 19, 2009) also describes cultural details in his writing as a sensory experience.

Characters and their world are built out of the small details of everyday living. The sounds that tell you what time of day it is. For example, in Chinatown, it would be the clack of mah jong tiles coming down from some open tenement window in the afternoon. Or the sound of a Chinese fiddle in the evening. When I was a boy, a music store would broadcast the Chinese radio station in the late afternoon. What do you smell and when? Even if I were blindfolded, the smell of roast ducks would tell me that I was on upper Grant Avenue in Chinatown where the delicatessens are. From these little sensory details, it's possible to suggest a complex of ideas and history that are connected to them.

Whereas authors weave their personal experiences into their stories, they also conduct extensive research to develop characters that are three dimensional and plots and settings, which are believable. In Angela Johnson's *A Sweet Smell of Roses*, she affirms the importance of characters in their authentic circumstances. When asked about the issues related to authenticity in children's books, she states, "The issue I find

as to authenticity is a writer's ability not to pander or condescend to their audience"
(personal communication, September 9, 2008). Yep (personal communication,
September 19, 2009) reaffirmed the idea about authenticity and believes that

Too often children's writers will read a few books and feel they are now able to write accurately
about a culture. Children's writers might even interview children of that ethnic group, but
unfortunately [. . .] the writers filter the interviews through their own cultural biases. For example,
in the past there have been instances in which all Chinese traditions were mere superstitions and
the solution to the problem was to abandon four thousand years of custom and imitate Caucasian
children.

Clearly, the themes of culture and authenticity permeate the writing by authors of
multicultural literature. Cultural details appear to be skillfully included in their writing.
They describe not just their experiences but they also include accurate portrayals of life
and cultural details in their stories. Virginia Driving Hawk Sneve (personal communication, October 23, 2009) reflects, "the biggest satisfaction from my writing has been
the acceptance of my work by Native people—adults who appreciate the accuracy of
the stories—teachers in reservation schools who welcome my books, and Native children who identify with the characters, plot, and location of my stories."

WRITING THAT IS MULTICULTURAL

"A book is multicultural when its characters reflect varied values, beliefs in the way
they speak, act, eat and interact with others," (Virginia Driving Hawk Sneve, personal
communication, October 23, 2009). The necessity for sharing culturally rich literature
and implementing teaching strategies, which develop an understanding of and positive
attitude towards various cultural groups is evident. As the aforementioned quote indicates, writing that is multicultural helps readers not only widen but deepen their understanding of people underrepresented because of culture, religion, or color. Additionally,
many readers are searching for their own story in literature and multicultural authors
can provide that story. Laurence Yep (personal communication, September 19, 2009)
and Angela Johnson (personal communication, September 9, 2008) described the process of introspection and renewal as what characterizes a good multicultural book.
Johnson shared her feelings about authenticity in her writing that is multicultural,
"I grew up in a small village with few African Americans. I was always searching for
the truth of culture and identity. There is no play book. Everyone has a competing story
or idea of what the truth of cultural identity is or how it may be defined in the context of
a book." Her beliefs about authenticity in multicultural literature make her writing
accessible to so many readers:

As an adult I've been surrounded with people of different cultures, religions, family dynamics,
sexual orientations, and world views. I have to believe the need to write what I experience is so
inborn in my psyche it comes out in my writing. I try to accept and never judge as an adult would
judge and quantify as I am telling a child or teen's story. I don't think there is a difference in the
telling of a story that is multicultural. You must be true to the nature of the characters. Any language that emerges is the language of the story, time, and situation the characters find themselves
in. I write what I know. If I don't know it—I stretch and try to imagine it.

Laurence Yep (personal communication, September 19, 2009) reflected on that belief, "Multicultural literature restores our sense of wonder. Multicultural literature mirrors our very thought processes and satisfies that primal curiosity that makes us human, and on a pragmatic level, is a necessity." The NCSS indicates that "the primary purpose of social studies is to help young people develop the ability to make informed and reasoned decisions for the public good as citizens of a culturally diverse, democratic society in an interdependent world" (www.socialstudies.org). This purpose solidifies the strong need for quality multicultural literature as well as an understanding of what defines multicultural literature as described earlier in this chapter. In the following quote, Pat Mora (personal communication, October 9, 2009) exemplifies this purpose and through her literature perpetuates this goal. "To be productive citizens, students need information, and at another level, they also need multicultural literary experiences. Unless we are attentive, our students are not going to have an accurate picture of the America they will inherit."

Bishop (1997) [. . .] indicated that multicultural literature is for all students and defined multicultural literature as "books that reflect the racial, ethnic and social diversity that is characteristic of our pluralistic society and of the world" (p. 3). Angela Johnson's definition of multicultural literature adds to that explanation,

I'm constantly looking for THAT book. You know the book with just as many males as females; just as many African Americans, Asians, Hispanics and Natives as Caucasians; just as many gays as straights, just as many Jocks as Goths. My idea of multicultural literature is that we get it right and it is a natural conclusion that all writers will include the human condition—involving all kinds of humans. I hope most of my books have a comfort level that draws everyone in and says *all* are welcome.

(personal communication, September 9, 2008)

Through the various interviews described in this chapter, we hope the voices of these multicultural authors help to define but also extend the many definitions of multicultural literature. We also hope that these authors' voices are evident not only in their interviews but in the beautifully written and crafted stories they weave for children and young adults. As Angela Johnson (personal communication, September 9, 2008) stated, "all are welcome," and we contend that the purpose of multicultural literature is to strive to attain that goal.

REFERENCES

Bishop, R. S. (1997). Selecting literature for a multicultural curriculum. In V. J. Harris (Ed.), *Using multiethnic literature in the K–8 classroom* (pp. 1–19). Norwood, MA: Christopher-Gordon Publishers, Inc.

Cullinan, B. (1989). *Literature and the child*. New York, NY: Harcourt Brace Jovanovich.

Curriculum Standards for Social Studies: I. Introduction. (2009). http://www.socialstudies.org

Galda, L., Cullinan, B., & Sipe, L. (2010). *Literature and the child*, 7th ed. Belmont, CA: Wadsworth.

Henderson, D. L. & May, J. (2005). *Exploring culturally diverse literature for children and adolescents*. Boston, MA: Pearson.

Klug, B., Turner, K., & Feuerborn, P. (2009). Affecting literacy and world understandings through creating opportunities to meet real authors. *The Reading Teacher, 63*(1), 92–94.

Norton, D. (2003). *Through the eyes of a child*, 6th ed. Upper Saddle River, NJ: Merrill Prentice Hall.

Taxel, J. (2003). Multicultural literature and the politics of reaction. In D. L. Fox, & K. G. Short (Eds.), *Stories matter: The complexity of cultural authenticity in children's literature* (pp. 143–164). Urbana, IL: NCTE.

MULTICULTURAL BOOKS

Johnson, A. (2007). *A sweet smell of roses, illustrated by E. Velasquez*. New York, NY: Simon & Schuster.

4

The Power of Illustrations in Multicultural Picture Books: Unfolding Visual Literacy

Francis S. Broadway and Douglass M. Conkle

INTRODUCTION

Because illustrations are "images that explain or clarify words and each other" (Nodelman, 1990, p. viii), this chapter is about the meaning, what is explained, and what is clarified in books in which "the function of illustration is the creation and development of characters and the portrayal of the scenes necessary in mood or action to bring [a] story to completion" (Klemin, 1966, p. 16). These picture books are "intended for young children which communicate information or tell stories through a series of many pictures combined with relatively slight texts or no text at all" (Nodelman, 1990, p. vi). Last, these picture books reflect the "human interest, ideology, and the experiences of the [culturally and ethically diverse] people who created it" (Banks, 2004, p. 3). In other words, multicultural picture books recognize "multiple, contested, even seemingly contradictory subject positions" (Letts, 2002, p. 122) albeit, for this chapter, normalized to positions of culture, race and ethnicity. Therefore, to apply and to embody visual literacy and to examine the meaning of illustrations in multicultural picture books, the authors are structuring this chapter into three parts: a critical analysis of illustrations in picture books; an exposition on illustration media used in picture books, specifically how a single illustrator, Eric Velasquez, uses different media within the opus; and examples of kindergarteners and teacher candidates exploring illustration media.

CRITICAL ANALYSIS OF ILLUSTRATIONS

Text and narrative are integral aspects of reading. Thus, this section explicates illustrations as text and illustrations as story. As text, the entirety of a communication, be it visual, linguistic, etc., as a conversation and its situational context (Harris & Hodges, 1995, p. 255), and as narrative that is telling of story (Conkle & Broadway, 2008), illustrations are symbols which elicit meaning.

Illustrations as Text: *Dear Juno*

Both thematically and through narrative in *Dear Juno*, Pak (1999) attempts to challenge, to disrupt, and to complicate the primacy and privilege of writing; however, first Pak establishes that reading has primacy in communication. In other words, in terms of communication, reading, according to Goodman (1968), "an interaction between the reader and written language, through which the reader attempts to reconstruct a message from the writer" (as cited in Harris & Hodges, 1995, p. 207), is a major factor that must be available if communication is to be complete, mastered, and understood. During the story, Pak (1999) creates Juno, a character who cannot read written letter symbols. "Juno looked at the letters and words he couldn't understand" (p. 12), but from the beginning of the story and as a storytelling device such as Juno reading the plane, Pak utilizes pictorial symbols as something that can be read, "And he wondered if any of the planes came from a little town near Seoul where his grandmother lives, and where she ate persimmons every evening before bed" (p. 5).Furthermore, as "Juno looked at the letter that came that day" (p. 6), another symbol, "the special stamp" (p. 6), is read by Juno to communicate, "that the letter was from his grandmother" (p. 6). Naturally, Juno contemplates reading the letter from his grandmother. This letter from his grandmother not only reinforces that reading is the "end," but becomes the catalyst for the plot of the narrative. Reading becomes an element in the storytelling.

Juno declares "Maybe I can read the inside, too" (p. 10) in order to not disturb his parents,

Through the window Juno could see his parents. He saw bubbles growing in the sink. He saw dirty dishes waiting to be washed. He knew he would have to wait for the cleaning to be done before his parents could read the letter to him.

(p. 8)

and since he had

looked at the letter that came that day. It was long and white and smudged. He saw the red and blue marks on the edges and knew the letter came from far away. His name and address were neatly printed on the front, so he knew the letter was for him,

(p. 6)

Thus, Juno is actively engaged in making meaning of actions and symbols: objects. In other words, Juno is reading. Thus, Pak establishes *Dear Juno* as a fable concerning reading; however, instead of reading being the sense-making of the printed word, reading, for this didactic story, is sense-making and representations of objects, actions, and ideas. Pak clearly elucidates that young children engage in reading as meaning making. Rosenblatt (1995) explains

... meaning [that] emerges as the reader carries on a give-and-take with the signs of the page. As the text unrolls before the reader's eyes, the meaning made of the early [texts] influence what comes to the mind and is selected for succeeding signs ...

(pp. 26–27)

Consequently, before reading as it is taught becomes hegemonically defined

... as a complex system of deriving meaning from print that requires all of the following:

a. the skills and knowledge to understand how phonemes, or speech sounds, are connected to print;
b. the ability to decode unfamiliar words;
c. the ability to read fluently;
d. sufficient background information and vocabulary to foster reading comprehension;
e. the development of appropriate active strategies to construct meaning from print; and
f. the development and maintenance of a motivation to read

(U.S. Department of Education: Office of Elementary and Secondary Education, 2002, p. 27).

After Pak has articulated her goals of (1) explicating reading as the primal form of communication and (2) challenging reading as sense-making of the printed word, she demonstrates Juno's reading is not one-to-one pronunciations of words, nor phonetical, but experiential: "'Grandmother has a new cat," Juno said as he handed the letter to his mother. "And she's growing red and yellow flowers in her garden"' (Pak, 1999, p. 14). Juno is communicating to his parents the content of the letter. However, knowing that Juno cannot read writing:

> "How do you know she has a new cat?" Juno's father asked.
> "She wouldn't send me a picture of a strange cat," said Juno.
> "I guess not," said Juno's father.
> "How do you know the flower is from her garden?" asked Juno's mother.
> "She wouldn't send me a flower from someone else's garden," Juno answered.
> "No, she wouldn't," said Juno's mother. (p. 14)
> "Juno's mother read him the letter."

(p. 14)

The reason for reading the letter may be confirmational, but more likely to remind the reader that reading is the sense making of written symbols, thereby cautioning us that Juno is indeed not reading. As the story continues and develops, Pak incorporates illustrations as writing numerous times. Juno writes a letter, "So Juno decided to write one [a letter] (Pak, 1999, p. 19) . . . I'm going to write a letter he told her [his mother]" (p. 21). Juno writes a letter when "after school, Juno ran to his backyard. He picked a leaf from the swing tree—the biggest leaf he could find. 'Yes it will [be a very nice letter],' Juno said, and then he began to draw" (p. 21). In return, Juno's grandmother writes him. "[O]ne day a big envelope came. It was from Juno's grandmother" (p. 28). As has been true throughout the narrative, Juno's grandmother's writing included objects, a box of colored pencils, and a small toy plane (p. 28) as well as illustration, "Next, he pulled out a picture of his grandmother" (p. 28). However, through the exchange of drawings and the telling about Juno's Grandmother's cat, Pak cautions the reader no matter if "it takes a good artist to say so much with a drawing" (p. 25), drawings are misleading and may miscommunicate."Juno looked at the letters and words he couldn't understand. He pulled out the photograph. It was a picture of his grandmother holding a cat" (Pak, 1999, p. 12). This is the first mention of Juno's grandmother's cat. For Juno, a non–"reader," his sense-making of the photograph indicates

> "Grandma has a new cat," Juno said as he handed the letter to his mother.
> "And she's growing red and yellow flowers in her garden."
> "How do you know she has a new cat?" Juno's father asked.
> "She wouldn't send me a picture of a strange cat," said Juno.

> (p. 14)

In order to confirm that Juno's sense-making is correct concerning the cat, Juno's mother reads the written letter, " . . . I have a new cat to keep me company. I named *him* Juno after you" (p. 17, italic added). Whereas Juno cannot sex his grandmother's cat from the picture, through the letter, Juno' grandmother sexes her cat male; however, when Juno reads his grandmother's reply to his letter, he

> pulled out a picture of his grandmother. He noticed she was sitting with a cat and two kittens. He thought for a moment and laughed. Now his grandmother would have to find a new name for her cat—in Korea, Juno was a boy's name, not a girl's."

> (p. 28)

Although the written letter states explicitly the sex of the cat as male, Juno could not determine from the first photograph the sex of his grandmother's cat as if one can easily and visually determine the sex of a cat. Therefore, he deferred to the authority of the written text. However, because the second envelope from his grandmother did not contain a written letter, the second photograph reclaims the authority of illustration as text by stating the true sex of his grandmother's cat. Pak, by no means, is belittling illustrations but rather challenges the equity of written language and pictorial language (illustrations).

Illustrations as Story: *Owen*

As a 1994 Caldecott Honor book, *Owen* (Henkes, 1993), like all quality literature, has multiple stories of which one story is the front book jacket illustration of one mouse behind the fence, Mrs. Tweezers, looking through binoculars to the left and another mouse in front of the fence, Owen, dreamingly with eyes closed and gingerly stepping towards the right, is looking down toward the right as "art work in picture books is most often concerned with storytelling" (Fang, 1996).

In other words, there are Owen's story and Mrs. Tweezers' story. Each story is different. However, in terms of written words and illustrations, there are numerous stories that may be the same if one looks at the illustrations in isolation. For example, Owen, a playful, lighthearted, witty, dancing, clever, jocular mice, gendered "he," has "a fuzzy yellow blanket [and] he loved it with all his heart" (Henkes, 1993, p. 3). "'Fuzzy goes where I go,' said Owen" (p. 4). "'Fuzzy likes what I like,' said Owen" (p. 5); however, his neighbor, Mrs. Tweezers, a mouse, is gendered feminine with a pink ribbon tied around her head, dressed in a pink jacket with yellow cuffs, a skirt with broad yellow stripes that contains narrow pink stripes and a white and pink plaid apron and peers over and around a fence that separates her and her yard from Owen's yard. "'Isn't he getting a little old to be carrying that thing [yellow blanket] around?' asked Mrs. Tweezers" (p. 6); "'Can't be a baby forever,' said Mrs. Tweezers" (p. 13); "'Can't bring a blanket to school,' said Mrs. Tweezers" (p. 18). Hence, one plot within the narrative of *Owen* is that of Owen's maturity—giving up the blanket, his blanket, Fuzzy,

"I *have* to bring Fuzzy to school," said Owen.
"No," said Owen's mother.
"No," said Owen's father.
Owen buried his face in Fuzzy.
He started to cry and would not stop.

(p. 19)

Another plot is Mrs. Tweezers' socialization of Owen.

Two narratives concerning Owen's parents also illustrate the multiple stories within *Owen*. One story is the relationship between Owen and his parents, and the second story is the relationship between Owen's parent and Mrs. Tweezers. Although in both written words and illustrations where Owen's father and Owen's mother are present, they most often talk as one character, one voice such as "Owen's parents hadn't" (Henkes, 1993, p. 6) and "that night Owen's parents told Owen to put Fuzzy under his pillow" (p. 7).

"No kidding," said Owen's mother.
"No wonder," said Owen's father.

(p. 9)

"Fuzzy's dirty," said Owen's mother.
"Fuzzy's torn and ratty," said Owen's father.

(p. 10)

Owen's parents' relationship with Mrs. Tweezers is that, "Mrs. Tweezers [fills] them in" (p. 13) concerning developmental appropriateness: "'Isn't he getting a little old to be carrying that thing [yellow blanket] around?' asked Mrs. Tweezers" (p. 6); age-appropriate behavior: "'Can't be a baby forever," said Mrs. Tweezers (p. 13); and sociocultural norms: "'Can't bring a blanket to school,' said Mrs. Tweezers" (p. 18). In all three situations, "Owen's parents hadn't" (pp. 6, 13, & 18) heard about culturally normative remedies for solutions to Owen's "ills" and "Mrs. Tweezers filled them in" (pp. 6, 13, & 18).

The relationship between Owen and his parents ensues as his parents negotiate their responsibility or role of being hegemonic socializing agents with that of being caring parents. For example, in terms of the Blanket Fairy, "that night Owen's parents told Owen to put Fuzzy under his pillow" (p. 7); Owen's parents then tell him "the Blanket Fairy would leave an absolutely wonderful, positively perfect, especially terrific big-boy gift in its place" (p. 7). However, in one instance Owen's father does not want to "admit weakness, to admit frailty and fragility ... to be seen as a wimp, a sissy, not a real man" (Kimmel, 2005, p. 33). So, "when Owen wasn't looking, his father dipped

Owen's favorite corner of Fuzzy into a jar of vinegar" (Henkes, 1993, p. 14) in order to appease Mrs. Tweezers who asked " 'Haven't you heard of the vinegar trick?' " (p. 13). On the other hand, Owen's mother acts alone in order to appease Owen's crying that would not stop.

> "Don't worry," said Owen's mother.
> "It'll be all right," said Owen's father.
> And then suddenly Owen's mother said, "I have an idea!"
> It was an absolutely wonderful, positively perfect, especially terrific idea.
>
> (p. 20)

In heteronormative fashion, Owen's mother

> Snip, snip, snip.
> Sew, sew, sew.
> "Dry your eyes."
> "Wipe your nose."
> Hooray, hooray, hooray!
> Now Owen carries one of his not-so-fuzzy handkerchiefs with him wherever he goes . . .
>
> (p. 22)

The transformation of Fuzzy from "a fuzzy yellow blanket" (p. 3) to "not-so-fuzzy [yellow] handkerchiefs" (p. 23) by " 'the good mother': open-heart, nurturing, and gentle" (Weems, 1999, p. 28) ends with Mrs. Tweezers looking to the right waving a purple handkerchief over the fence to an Owen looking to the left waving a "not-so-fuzzy [yellow] handkerchief" and the words:"And Mrs. Tweezers doesn't say a thing" (Henkes, 1993, p. 24). In other words, Snyder (2009) summarizes *Owen* as

Give up his blanket! Owen won't even consider the possibility. Nosy neighbor Mrs. Tweezers thinks it's time. Owen relinquishes his Fuzzy and offers suggestions, but his mother comes to the rescue. Parents and children will enjoy the battle of wits between Owen and Mrs. Tweezers.

Roser, Martinez, Fuhrken, and McDonnold (2007) put forth that "readers of picture books frequently draw character depth from the illustrations." Albeit the conversation concerns story rather than character, if the illustrations are isolated from the written text, then another story is posited in addition to the socializing hegemonic enculturation story of the struggle between Mrs. Tweezers and Owen and his parents to produce a story that ends happily ever after with both sides winners and "emphasize[s] the hope for a better future" (Lynch-Brown & Tomlinson, 2008, p. 4) albeit Owen must obey, comply, and be complacent to the rules that are demanded of him hegemonically through the character, Mrs. Tweezers.

An interpretation of the illustrations as sole communicator of the narrative might seek to have Owen's parents facilitate the carefreeness of Owen, but the ultimate meaning of the narrative is that their responsibility as parents is to inculcate Owen into the world where "Mrs. Tweezers doesn't say a thing" (Henkes, 1993, p. 24), especially the world of school, " 'Can't bring a blanket to school,' said Mrs. Tweezers" (p. 18). In other words, Owen's parents must open the "carefully tucked limbs of [the] tiny mouse . . . Owen . . .—with [his] closed and protected bod[y]—convey reticence, anxiety, and timidity about . . . the loss of comforting blankets" (Roser, et al., 2007, p. 553) until those limbs wave smilingly, cheerfully, and respectfully at Mrs. Tweezers. Thus, unlike *Snowy Night* which has a main character that is of color but is not multicultural because "if the illustrator had chosen to give that child a different racial/ethnic identity, the text could have remained unchanged" (Sims, 1982, p. 34), the authors posit that *Owen* is multicultural not because the illustrator chose to color Mrs. Tweezers white and Owen and his parent gray, but because the illustrations indicate two cultures: the white culture of Mrs. Tweezers and Owen's and his parents' culture of color.

From a postcolonial point of view, there exist two cultures in the Henkes' illustrations for *Owen*. These two cultures are divided by a solid, not picket or rail, fence as if "good fences make good neighbors" (Frost, 1914). On one side of the fence is Mrs. Tweezers, a white mouse, and on the other side, in perspective closer to the reader, are Owen and his parents, the mice of color. As a symbol of the dominate (white) culture, Mrs. Tweezers, in the first illustration, peers around the fence, but in remaining illustrations, she looks over the fence. From her elevated, often standing on overturned flowerpots, position of looking over her garden's fortifications, Mrs. Tweezers sends forth proclamations that elicit acknowledgement of ignorance from the mice of color, Owen's parents. Although Owen's and Owen's parent's culture is in reaction to the dominant culture of Mrs. Tweezers, the culture of the mice of color is industrious, caring, nonjudgmental, and tolerant as well as obedient, complacent, and compliant—"loving yet befuddled" (Snyder, 2009). Therefore, there are two cultures in conflict if only as an element of the plot, which in political colonialist terms, the mice of color must become obedient, compliant and complacent. Owen's parents are obedient when they must learn to say "no"; they are compliant when they transform the blanket into handkerchiefs; and they demonstrate complacency when they reluctantly engage in the Blanket Fairy play.

The white mouse must dominate. Mrs. Tweezers dominates to the last words of the story "and Mrs. Tweezers doesn't say a thing" (Henkes, 1993, p. 24). Furthermore, Owen in his dancing, scheming, and rebelling and as "a child [who] outwits both his parents and the neighbor—a rare victory from a child's point of view" (Snyder, 2009) is seemingly unaware that he is becoming like the master and is the colonialist's child who, in the last illustration, is content to have Fuzzy be not a blanket but handkerchiefs as Owen acknowledges the correctness of Mrs. Tweezers' point of view with a wave of one of his yellow handkerchiefs. This final illustration is the only time Owen looks at Mrs. Tweezers, although earlier in the story Owen acknowledges Mrs. Tweezers existence, "Owen stuffed Fuzzy inside his pajama pants and went to sleep" (p. 8). In isolation, the illustrations, as quality literature, tell the "story of a small [rambunctious little] mouse who is determined not to give up his blanket before he starts school" (Short & Pierce, 1994, p. 64) and whose mother produces a solution that satisfies everyone and the story of white cultural dominance and obedience and compliance of a culture of color.

ERIC VELASQUEZ AND VISUAL LITERACY

If during reading, "the reader infuses intellectual and emotional meanings into the pattern of verbal symbols, and those symbols channel his [*sic*] thoughts and feelings" (Rosenblatt, 1995, p. 24), then the authors as readers present or (re)present their reading of the illustrations and verbal symbols, of Eric Velasquez. Furthermore, if reading is efferent, a "stance [that] pays more attention to the cognitive, the referential, the factual, the analytic, the logical, the quantitative aspects of meaning" (Rosenblatt, 1994/2005, p. 12) and aesthetic, a "stance [that] pays more attention to the sensuous, the affective, the emotive, the qualitative" (p. 12), then the authors posit the efferent and aesthetic meaning they found through their transactions with the illustrations of Eric Velasquez. If

there is not necessarily only one 'correct' interpretation of the significance of a given work. Not even an author's statement of his aims can be considered definitive. The text exist as a separate entity, a set of marks on a page, that may or may not fulfill his [sic] intentions and can possess for us more values than he [sic] foresaw,

(Rosenblatt, 1995, p. 108)

then the authors report their understanding, "the full impact of the sensuous, emotional, as well as intellectual force" (p. 106) of Eric Velasquez's illustrations. Hence, by examining Eric Velasquez's illustrations through the various media he employed to create his illustrations, this section explicates the authors' reading of the illustrations with the framework that "the knower, the knowing, and the known are seen as aspects of 'one process' " (Rosenblatt, 1994/2005, p. 3).

Eric Velasquez's picture books' opus with numerous authors includes illustrations that are primarily oil paintings; however, there are acrylic paintings, pastel, charcoal, and graphite (pencil) illustrations (See Table 4.1). These illustrations explain and clarify genres such as modern fantasy, historical and realistic fiction, and biography with settings such as Jamaica; Fredericksburg, VA; and Miami, FL, and there are no patterns among genre, medium, setting, and characters. Oil painting illustrations are used for biographies and historical and realistic fiction as well as white people of the United States and African Americans. For African-American heroes, there are oil paintings and pastel illustrations. Charcoal and pastels illustrations adorn different historical fictions. Thus, Eric Velasquez's diversity of illustration media through diverse genre, characters, and settings of picture books enable texts or stories to be a portrait or thick description, "a description that goes beyond the mere or bare reporting . . . but describes and probes the intentions, motives, meanings, contexts, situations, and circumstances" (Glesne, 2006, p. 27).

Eric Velasquez and African-American Heroes

Before beginning a deep and rich transactional analysis of Eric Velasquez's illustrations through the examination of Angela Johnson's *A Sweet Smell of Roses* (2005), the authors explicate picture books concerning African-American heroes as a means of demonstrating the application of visual literacy and in order to show the complexity of Eric Velasquez's illustrational opus. Although Eric Velasquez illustrated a biography of a white United States citizen, Houdini (Krull, 2005), an extensive number of picture books are about African-American heroes. Chronologically, the illustrations of these books begin as oil paintings. These oil painting are chromatically muted and often staged if not to overdramatize the hero element of individuals who the texts portray as an exceptional everyman (Anonymous, 1995) but nevertheless typical and normal and to emphasize the figurative or realistic rather than narrative nature of the stories and illustrations. In other words, the illustrations often represent the characters in a setting or within a context in order to tell a story independent of the text. Oil paintings that depict events in different cultural times and settings serve as the illustrations for the biographies of Muhammad Ali (Haskins, 2002), Chevalier de Saint-George (Brewster, 2006), David "Panama" Francis (Francis & Reiser, 2002), and Matthew Hanson (Weatherford, 2008); however, with *Jesse Owens: Fastest Man Alive* (Weatherford,

2007), "He [Eric Velasquez] believes the change from oil painting was inspired by the challenging vital subject: 'Something about Jesse Owens cried out for an immediate medium such as pastels' " (backjacket flap).

The biographies of Matthew Hanson (Weatherford, 2008), Jesse Owens (Weatherford, 2007), and Wendell Scott (Weatherford, 2009) are illustrated in pastels. The Jesse Owens illustrations challenged the stoically heroic portrait compositional style of illustrations compared to other Eric Velasquez illustrations. Pastels made the calculated figurative style of oil painting disappear. Whereas in oil painting where the media allows if not demands working and reworking as well as building up, pastels require immediacy that if overworked pastel lapses into murkiness. In other words, the speed in which the artist needs to work in pastels equals the speed of Jesse Owens. Creatively, *Jesse Owens: Fastest Man Alive* begins with "ON YOUR MARK/READY. SET" (Weatherford, 2007, pp. 2, 3). Hence, in *Jesse Owens: Fastest Man Alive*, the

Table 4.1.

Selected Bibliography of Picture Books Illustrated by Eric Velasquez

Medium	Title	Pub. Year	Author
Oil Paintings	*Other Mozart: The Life of the Famous Chevalier de Saint-George*	2006	Brewster, H
	Grandma's Records	2004	Velasquez, E.
	Escape!: A Story of the Underground Railroad	1999	Gayle, S. S,
	Sound That Jazz Makes	2001	Weatherford, C. B.
	David Gets His Drum	2002	Francis, D.
	Champion: The Story of Muhammad Ali	2002	Haskins, J.
	Liberty Street	2003	Ransom,
	Season for Mangoes	2005	Hanson, R.
	Houdini: World's Greatest Mystery Man and Escape King	2005	Krull, K.
	Rain Stomper	2008	Boswell, A.
Charcoal	*A Sweet Smell of Roses*	2005	Johnson, A.
Pastels	*I, Matthew Henson: Polar Explorer*	2008	Weatherford, C. B.
	Jesse Owens: Fastest Man Alive	2007	Weatherford, C. B.
	Racing Against the Odds: The Story of Wendell Scott, Stock Car Racing's African-American Champion	2009	Weatherford, C. B.
Black and White Illustrations	*Tanya and the Tobo Man: A Story for Children Entering Therapy*	1991	Koplow, L.
Paintings in Acrylic with Pencil Cross-Hatching	*The Piano Man*	2000	Chocolate, D.

illustrations are powerful narratives such as the physicality of Jesse Owens sprinting, long jumping, sprinting, and competing in the 400-meter relay, the faces of prisoners in Nazi concentration camps (p. 9) opposite the back of the helmets of Nazi soldiers (p. 10), or the friendship with "tall blond blue-eyed Luz Long" (p. 22). However, the biographies of Matthew Hanson and Wendell Scott return to the representational figurative portrait composition of Eric Velasquez. The portrait representation accents these African Americans as heroes—one who

ventures forth from the world of common day into a region of supernatural wonder: fabulous forces are there encountered and a decisive victory is won: the hero comes back from this mysterious adventure with the power to bestow boons on his fellow man.

(Campbell, 1949/1968, p. 30, italic in the original)

but "a hero ain't nothin' but a sandwich" (Childress, 1973/2003).

A Sweet Smell of Roses

The Eric Velasquez illustrations with Angela Johnson's (2005) *A Sweet Smell of Roses* are charcoal. Out of the different media used by Eric Velasquez, charcoal is a unique medium and the uniqueness of the medium solicits, if not begs, for a transactional analysis. Furthermore, the charcoal is not all charcoal colors. Eric Velasquez has included a color red in the form of flowering roses, the flag of the United States, and a ribbon on a teddy bear. The "from the artist" statement (p. 3) grounds the illustrations in inspiration—art history. "The two men who inspired my work in this book, Harvey Dinnerstein and Burton Silverman, are no strangers to the fine-art community" (p. 3). Lastly, the transactional analysis of *A Sweet Smell of Roses* explicates visual literacy through the usage of the elements and principle of design as a separate axis or integrated into the medium and art history discussion.

Charcoal and Dinnerstein and Silverman

Harvey Dinnerstein stated, "I usually start with a quick sketch in graphite or charcoal to establish my response to the subject" (Frey & Norris, 2008, p. 142). As a student of Harvey Dinnerstein at the Art Students League, Eric Velasquez's use of charcoal in *A Sweet Smell of Roses* establishes his response to the Civil Rights movement, especially marching, and permits a response by the reader to the Civil Rights movement. The response is a steadfast, dedicated call to action for the liberation of the oppressed and the disinherited (Thurman, 1949/1996). Movement as an element of design permeates Eric Velasquez's illustrations in a narrative sense seemingly inspired by Dinnerstein's quest to move the figurative portrait into the narrative. "I [Harvey Dinnerstein] did numerous sketches of people walking, culminating with the drawing *Walking Together, Montgomery,* searching for a graphic image that would express the spirit of the remarkable events we had witnessed" (Frey & Norris, 2009, p. 70). For example, Eric Velasquez's illustration for

When it's time to go,
we skip back hand in hand.
Minnie and me.
Singing freedom songs along
the streets

(Johnson, 2005, p. 24)

incorporates "Minnie and me" leaving the scene of the march,—the narrative and the figurative, becoming the narrative—a uniform with striped-trousers, hand gripping a nightstick, and a male standing, solo-legged, on crutches just like Dinnerstein's *Walking Together, Montgomery* (Frey & Norris, 2008, pp. 29, 71) figuratively includes, in the far right, a male standing, solo-legged, on crutches narratively marching.

"Our drawings [of the Montgomery Bus Boycott], however, celebrated the ordinary men and women of the black community and recorded their passion, pain, and ultimately their triumphant spirit" (Silverman & Dinnerstein, 2006, n. p.). Angela Johnson (2005) concurs, "For each of the names that we know, there are tens of thousands that we do not know. And some of those overlooked names belong to children" (p. 3). Thus, in *A Sweet Smell of Roses*, Eric Velasquez's drawings are of ordinary men and women, of a Civil Rights march.

> As my sister, Minnie, and I slip
> past Mama's door and out of the house
> down Charlotte Street
> Past the early-morning milkman, over the cobbled bridge, and through the curb
>   market. . .
> to where everybody waits to march
>
> (pp. 4–8)

> the ordinary people become more than the black community. The community becomes
> there is a sweet smell of roses as
> we all gather in the center of town. All together.
>
> (p. 20)

Therefore, through charcoal drawings, Harvey Dinnerstein and Burton Silverman immersed Eric Velasquez into their lived experience of the Montgomery Bus Boycott. Likewise, Eric Velasquez immerses the reader of *A Sweet Smell of Roses* into a Civil Rights march.

Charcoal and Color

Although within the illustrations there is the shocking contrast of color, charcoal / red, and value, light/dark—albeit it charcoal/red or charcoal color/paper color, Eric Velasquez's illustrations for *A Sweet Smell of Roses* (Johnson, 2005) is reminiscent of Allen Say's illustrations for *Magic and the Night River* (Bunting, 1978). The choice of Eric Velasquez to use charcoal color in a time when high-definition color is the norm might first be a means to recall the past, the Civil Rights movement, but Eric Velasquez has used color for narratives that are not present-day. Again, in addition to honoring Dinnerstein and Silverman, Eric Velasquez used charcoal colors and red to emphasize the three narratives in Angela Johnson's written text. Eric Velasquez gives the reader three visual narratives: the (red) roses, the (red)-striped flag of the United States, and the (red) ribbon of the teddy bear.

The red roses that appear on the first page of the text and the last page of the text bound the narrative of home. ". . . and there is a sweet smell of roses all through our house" (Johnson, 2005, p. 32). The home narrative is home as place, "a context [for] the development of a sense of self and sense of being in the world" (Whitlock, 2007, p. 2).

In other word, *A Sweet Smell of Roses* as a story begins in the home and returns to the home. In terms of the illustrations between the two rose illustrations, Minnie and me begin their quest

> after a night of soft rain
> there is a sweet smell of roses.
>
> (p. 4)

Ribbon "is a symbol that represents awareness, yet requires no knowledge of a cause" (Moore, 2008, p. 2); hence the red ribbon on the teddy bear is an awareness narrative. Placing the red ribbon on the teddy bear, a symbol of childhood, indicates Minnie and me as children are becoming aware. The awareness narrative begins with the children running "to where everybody waits to march" (Johnson, 2005, p. 8);

> Then we start to march
> Minnie and me
>
> (p, 12)

there is a sweet smell of roses (p. 14, 18, 20, & 32) and "... feeling a part of it all. Walking our way towards freedom" (p. 16). Awareness is achieved

> when it's time to go,
> we skip back hand in hand.
> Minnie and me.
> Singing freedom songs along
> the streets
>
> (p. 24)

and the last illustration with the red ribbon is the narrator and Minnie being hugged:

> She smiles after a while,
> hugging us,
> then takes our hands. And as we tell her about the march,
> the curtains float apart.
>
> (p. 30)

Hence, the awareness narrative is coming to know what Civil Rights means, but more importantly how Civil Right marches are the narratives that carry the stories of the Civil Rights.

The red stripes of the United States' flag are the narrative of the United States. Specifically, the Civil Rights march of *A Sweet Smell of Roses* is an event in the United States. If flags are symbols for "a nation, a legal unity, land, profits, and political power" (Zinn, 1980, p. 59), then Eric Velazquez suggests that the flag should have an alternative meaning by always placing the flag in the hands of the marchers. Therefore, the United States' narrative becomes the ability for the masses to influence change. The red-striped flag appears on the dust cover and the cover sheet for *A Sweet Smell of Roses* and throughout the book is always carried in a crowd of people. The red-striped flag also appears with "There is a sweet smell of roses as more people start marching with us pouring out of the side streets, clapping and singing" (p. 18). Although the illustration does not connect the home narrative and the United States narrative, the interplay of text and illustration connotes that home is the United States.

Interestingly, there are numerous illustrations where the two narrative symbols appear simultaneously, but only one narrative symbol is red. For an example, the illustration on page five, opposite

there is a sweet smell of roses ...
past Mama's door and out of the house
down Charlotte Street,

(p. 4)

contains a vase of roses, but the roses are not red. The ribbon on the teddy bear is red. In this conflict of narratives, the narrative of awareness trumps the home narrative as if awareness happens in the world outside home. The symbols of awareness and the flag of the United States clash when

Then we start to march,
Minnie and me.
We look ahead and walk faster like him. ["Dr. King" (p. 12)]
Clapping in time with our feet.
Looking ahead,
just like him.

(Johnson, 2005, p. 13)

In this illustration, there are three flags, but again the ribbon is red. The awareness of the importance and fear associated with becoming aware has primacy. This is further emphasized on the next page where there is a partial flag, but still the ribbon on the teddy bear is red and the text

You are not right.
Equality can't be yours.

(p. 14, bold in the original)

The juxtaposition of the flag and the teddy bear are a question for the principles of design with coloration of the flag potentially dominating the illustrations and corrupting and compromising the design. However, in the next illustration, the flag is red-striped, and the ribbon on the teddy bear is charcoal.

Freedom!
Freedom!

(p. 19, bold in the original)

gives primacy to the colored red symbol of the United States rather than the awareness narrative.

Also, there are three illustrations in which red does not appear. These illustrations have narratives of their own. One single-page is an illustration of Dr. King:

He talks about peace,
love,
nonviolence,
and change for everybody

(p. 23)

This is Dr. King's narrative. Another single-page red-less illustration is

> . . . to our house on Charlotte Street.
> . . . Then there is Mama, worried face, waiting there for us.

(p. 28)

This is the Mama narrative, the narrative of fear, a fear of which she does not want Minnie and me to become aware, a fear of the United States, and a fear of the destruction of her home. Lastly, there is a double page illustration:

> There is a sweet smell of roses as
> we all gather in the center of town.
> All together.
> All here.
> Listening to Dr. King as the sun gets higher in the sky . . .

(p. 20)

Within this illustration, "Minnie and me" balance two police with one police with his arms crossed and his pistol in clear sight.

Unity, as a principle of design is strong as Minnie and me standing behind POLICE LINES to the extreme right with the bear in plain sight yet there is a stranglehold around the bears neck, which covers up or hides the red ribbon. The policeman stands to the far left, larger than the people behind police lines and in front of the sign FREE-DOM NOW. In terms of perspective, the people behind POLICE LINE gradually become smaller until they disappear behind the policemen. In light of the historical oppressive and oft violent actions of local police, especially during the historic marches of Dr. King in such places as Selma and Montgomery, this illustration explicates that there is no need to be aware of the power of the police; the actions and narratives of the Civil Rights movement could not happen in the United States; and no one would want to call the police setting home, *A Sweet Smell of Roses*, home.

ACTIVITIES

Herein, the authors present two ideas about making public the private transactions formed with reading multicultural picture books. The first activity presents a traditional approach to communicating the meaning making that occurs during reading. Kindergarteners are asked to present first visually their meaning making and then in dialogue with the teacher. The second activity, with early childhood and middle level teacher candidates, focuses on exploring different visual media used to communicate "the creation and development of characters and the portrayal of the scenes" (Klemin, 1966, p. 16).

Visual Literacy and Kindergarteners: An Eric Velasquez Activity

During an innercity afterschool program in which at risk students are offered an extra two hours of school, 12 kindergarteners participated in a transactional analysis of a written and illustrated text activity. The kindergartners were to read Weatherford's *Jesse Owens: Fastest Man Alive* (2007). Through visual (artistic) media and oral (dialogue), the kindergartners presented their reading.

As the kindergarten students gathered on the rug and sat fidgeting with this and poking at that, I, the second author, told them that we were going to be reading books illustrated by Eric Velasquez. On two different days, I held up the book, *Jesse Owens: Fastest Man Alive* (Weatherford, 2007) and a box of chalk pastels because after reading *Jesse Owens: Fastest Man Alive*, I wanted the kindergartens to express their transactions with *Jesse Owens: Fastest Man Alive* with the same art medium that Eric Velasquez used; however, I knew that at least some of the kindergarteners needed scaffolding.

I began to mine their "fund of past experiences" (Rosenblatt, 1995, p. 101) by taking a book walk. During the book walk the kindergarteners formed and shared predictions about the book. As a group, we discussed the predictions in light of the illustrations. Based on the prediction statements and questions about the illustrations, I, as the teacher, gave explanations about Jim Crow and segregation, explanations about Germany and the Olympics, and explanations about Nazism and concentration camps. After these explanations, I solicited additional predictions. Seemingly forgetting about sports and becoming concerned of the morality and ethical treatment for people (Leafgren, 2009); the kindergarteners predicted that Jesse Owens is going to get Hitler and to free those people, the people in concentration camps. I read *Jesse Owens: Fastest Man Alive*.

"On your mark . . . (p. 3) Ready. Set . . . (p. 4) Go! (p. 5)," the first six words of the book right away caught most of the students' attention. As the storyline began to focus on the track competition, the kindergarteners, seizing the here and now, turned their predictions away from morals and ethics to sports. Jesse runs. Jesse jumps. Jesse runs and Jesse runs again. During each event, the kindergartens cheered Jesse on and were excited when he was victorious.

At the conclusion of the story, the kindergarteners transitioned from the reading rug to work tables. I demonstrated how to use the chalk pastels including how to spread the chalk with cotton swabs, and how messy the materials can be. I emphasized to the kindergarteners that the chalk pastels can be messy, there is a need to be careful with dirty fingers, and hands should be washed directly after the visual presentation is finished. Then, each kindergartener chose one sheet from a stack of 12 × 18-inch construction paper of assorted colors and selected a pack of square chalk pastels with 12 assorted colors.

Some of the students drew Jesse on the track (See Figure 4.1.) Some kindergarteners drew stands full of people. Some drew a newspaper clipping, and some drew Jesse with his medals. After the visual pastel representations were finished, I asked the children, one at a time, to "tell me what your picture is about" as a mean of soliciting their meaning-making of *Jesse Owens: Fastest Man Alive*. In other words, I was not privileging the verbal representation but rather asking for a thick description of their transaction with text with the hope of becoming aware of some redundancy (Lincoln & Guba, 1985).

Lisa Garla

Lisa Garla, a self-selected pseudonym for an individual who I will gender—a boy, engaged in the reading of *Jesse Owens: Fastest Man Alive* (Weatherford, 2007) activity twice. Racism was the theme of the first reading of the story, and the second reading of the story is a biography of Jesse Owens. Both these readings transact the psychosocial power of the starter pistol—"*Bang!*" (p.15) and "fires" (p. 25).

"Jesse and the white boy" is Lisa's moniker for race relations. In his transactional expression of the text, Lisa Garla first tried violence as a means to understand racism:

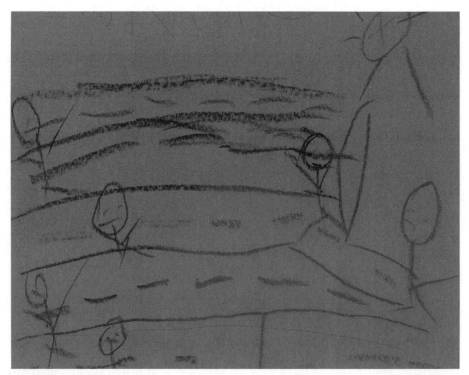

Figure 4.1.
Jesse on the Track

"I hit him and he hit me back," but through a pause, Lisa Garla seemingly realized that violence only begot violence. In a second attempt to communicate his transactions with the text and to combat "racism" in the story, Lisa Garla used the high jump competition. During the history of the long jump (Weatherford, 2007, pp. 21–24) in the sections: "A Leap of Friendship" (pp. 21–22) and "Medal #2: The Long Jump Finals" (pp. 23–24) where Jesse Owens jumps against the "[t]all, blond, blue-eyed Luz Long" (p. 21), Lisa Garla became occupied with

> Finally, Long versus Owens–
> German and American

(p. 23)

> –Jesse Owens' and Luz Long's jump although
> In the end, you soar to a second gold medal, but Long is no sore loser.
> He slaps your back, sealing the bond between you.
> You two talk into the night; new friendship richer than gold.

(p. 24)

Lisa Garla stated:

Then that gun shooted and that gun shooted and then . . . he jumped, he jumped up in the air and he went, he did that (Jesse jumped), and the white boy didn't even do nothing. He was running but, everybody was like (chanting) "YOU SUCK! YOU SUCK! YOU SUCK!" to him.
    (Author's question to Lisa Garla) To whom, the white boy or Jesse Owens?

Figure 4.2.
Jesse Jumping the Highest.

Lisa Garla continued:

The white boy. And then they was like 'YOU SUCK!' and then this one shooted and then the babies was crying about him. . .and then somebody was like no, no, no . . . and then I'm Jesse Owens and I said, no idea, no whitey, you not the boss of me, ahhh. And then I got mad and then he was like, 'NO, I don't like you.' And then I hit him and he hit me back . . . and then I jumped up in the air high. He [whitey] jumped this high (Lisa Garla uses two fingers to show me about an inch of space).

Lisa Garla's transactional experience with the text was profound. Empathically, he even made himself interchangeable with Jesse Owens by stating "and then I [Lisa Garla] jumped high in the air. He [Luz Long] jumped this high" seemingly to fight, to describe, and to probe what he understood to be racism. In other words, Lisa Garla was struggling and attempting to express his complex understanding of the reality of racism.

The starter pistol begins Lisa Garla's second transaction with *Jesse Owens: Fastest Man Alive* (Weatherford, 2007); however, through narrative, which "has two aspects: story, the events or functions in normal chronological sequence, and plot, the artful, subversive rearrangement and thus defamiliarization of the parts of the sequence" (Guerin, Labor, Morgan, Reesman, & Willingham, 2005, p. 334), he tells the story of Jesse Owens. His visual narrative, storytelling (See Figure 4.2), flows across the page from right to left. The first image is of Jesse Owens "jumping the highest." Next, the second image is of Jesse Owens running on the track and with his gold medals—"That's when he was running the track like this (rreeer . . .) and those are his medals" The third image is "when the gun [the brown area] shot off and they had that one race." The fourth image, the line between image two and image three and above and below the images, is of the people sitting. Lisa Garla's second transaction focused on Eric Valesquez's illustrations for "Medal #1: The 100-Meter Dash" and "Medal #3: The 200-Meter Finals" and Weatherford's words:

> and await the starting pistol.
> Your every muscle listens. *Bang!*
> You spring forward, (p. 15–16)
> The pistol fires; you bolt from the starting line

(p. 25)

Pizza Barbara

Another kindergartener, who I will gender—a girl, gave her pseudonym as Pizza Barbara. Pizza Barbara's picture (See Figure 4.3) focused on factual written and visual information contained within both the written and visual text of *Jesse Owens: Fastest Man Alive* (Weatherford, 2007).

> I like the medals.
> I like his hair.
> I like the racing tack.
> I like that jumpin' thing, that one he did a win.
> I like his face (Pizza Barbara).

Therefore, Pizza Barbara made the following comments concerning her illustration:

I drawed his face, I drawed his shirt because he's a people. I draw his next. I draw his eyes. I draw his necklace. I draw his nose. I draw his mouth (Pizza Barbara).

Pizza Barbara's portrait of Jesse Owens, which is suggestive of the snapshot photograph in which the subject of interest is standing erect in the center of the visual field with the subject uncomfortably holding the pose as if this moment is not a fraction of a second, but rather eternality, is reminiscent of Eric Velasquez's figurative portrait illustrations.

Visual Literacy and Teacher Candidates: An Activity

In a university course, Teaching Multiple Texts through Genre, designed to explore ways in which teachers can broaden children's understanding and appreciation of a variety of different text types, print and nonprint, class time is allotted for the exploration of different artistic media, specifically linoleum cuts, watercolor, pastel, scratchboard, and torn paper collage. Although some teacher candidates in this course have taken a course, Integrated Expressive Arts for Early Childhood or are Visual Art Education teacher candidates in which they have explored some of these media as well as

Figure 4.3.
Jesse's Face

studied elements and principles of design, this activity is an excellent time to introduce teacher candidates to different illustrators of color as well as other illustrators.

The explicit exploration of illustration media and illustrations is introduced as a class project, the production of a poster composed of the artwork of the teacher candidates (See Figure 4.4). Based on an idea developed and used by kindergarten teachers Joanne Dreire and Betsy McCormick of the Catlin-Gable School in Portland, OR, the poster consists of artwork created by each of the teacher candidates in the class. This is an example of a project that teacher candidates might use in their future as teachers to produce some collaborative artistic representation of a unit of study in the classroom. The members of the class receive a personal copy of the poster either free or at an additional charge, usually less than five dollars because a portion of course fees is used to support the project. The actual design for the poster is given to an art major who takes the individual artwork and designs the poster. The art student is compensated for time and expertise in design and production as well as the cost of the production.

Figure 4.4.
Alphabetic Art

For the poster in Figure 4.4, each teacher candidate was asked to select out of a hat a letter of the alphabet. This selected letter became the subject of the teacher candidate's artwork and each exploration of a different medium. During the introduction of the project, the elements of design: line, space, shape, direction, size, texture, color, perspective, and value, and the principles of design: balance, gradation, repetition, contrast, harmony, dominance, and unity are presented and discussed through the examination of Loren Long's illustrations for *I Dream of Trains* (Johnson, 2003). A group of three or four students were given a copy of *I Dream of Trains* with which they identified the elements and principles of design. After small group exploration, a whole class discussion occurred in which the focus was on how the teacher candidates can use the elements and principles of design in producing a letter. After the discussion on elements and principles of design, the teacher candidates are told the specific art media: linoleum cuts, watercolor, pastel, scratchboard, and torn paper collage.

One art medium was introduced during one class period throughout the semester. At the time that a particular medium became the topic, the instructor shared numerous picture books in which the illustrator used the specific medium with the teacher candidates. (Refer to Table 4.2, for a list of picture books by illustrators of color that were used as examples during the introduction of a medium.) Although the illustrators were not limited to illustrators of color, for example, woodcuts—Mary Azarian (Azarian, 1981; Martin, 1999) and David Frampton (Bunting, 2001; Frampton, 2007), scratchboard—Beth Krommes (Root, 1999, Swanson, 2008) and Michael McCurdy (Lincoln, 1863/1995; Kay, 1999), watercolor—Peter Catalanotto (Johnson, 1997, Catalanotto, 1999) and Barry Moser (Pochocki, 1993, Rylant, 1998), pastel—Chris Van Allsburg (1983, 1985) and Thomas Allen (Hendershot, 1992 and Turner,

Table 4.2.
Selected Illustration Media and Illustrators of Color

Medium	Illustrator / Example of Work
Collage/Torn Paper/ Cut Paper	Bryan, A. (2003). *Beautiful Blackbird*, Bryan, A. illus. New York, NY: Atheneum Books for Young Readers.
	Bryan, A. *Let It Shine* (2007), Bryan, A. illus. New York, NY: Athenaeum Books for Young Readers. Cotton, C. (2008). *Rain Play*, Steptoe, J. illus. New York, NY: Henry Holt and Co.

Table 4.2. (continued)

Medium	Illustrator / Example of Work
	Dillon, L. & Dillon, D. (2007). *Jazz on a Saturday Night*, Dillon, L. & Dillon, D. illus. New York, NY: Blue Sky Press/Scholastic.
	Dillon, L. & Dillon, D. (2002). *Rap a Tap Tap: Here's Bojangles—Think of That!* Dillon, L. & Dillon, D. illus. New York, NY: Blue Sky Press/Scholastic.
	Krull, K. (2007). *Pocahontas: Princess of the New World*, Diaz, D. illus. New York, NY: Walker & Company.
	Lachenmeyer, N. (2008). *The Origami Master*, Sogabe, A. illus. Morton Grove, IL: Albert Whitman & Company.
	Myers, W. D. (1997). *Harlem*, Myers, C. illus. New York, NY: Scholastic Press.
	Myers, W. D. (2009). *Amiri and Odette: A Love Story*, Steptoe, J. illus. New York, NY: Scholastic Press.
	Perdomo, W. (2002). *Visiting Langston*, Collier, B. illus. New York, NY: Henry Holt and Company.
	Reibstein, M. (2008). *Wabi Sabi*, Young, Ed. Illus. New York, NY: Little, Brown.
Linocut/Woodcut	Bryan, A. (1982). *I'm Going to Sing*, Bryant, A. illus. New York, NY. Bryan, A. (1974). *Walk Together Children*, Bryant, A. illus. New York, NY.
	Delacre, L. (2000). *Salsa Stories*, Delacre, L. illus. New York, NY: Scholastic.
	San Souci, R. D. (2000). *Cut From the Same Cloth: American Women of Myth, Legend, and Tall Tale*, Pinkney, B. illus. New York, NY: Penguin Group.
	Serwadda, W. M. (1987). *Songs and Stories From Uganda*, Dillon, L. & Dillon, D. illus. New York, NY: World Music Press
	Soto, G. (1992). *Neighborhood Odes*, Diaz, D., illus. New York, NY: Harcourt Children's Books.
Pastels	Coerr, E. (1993). *Sadako and the Thousand Paper Cranes*, Young, Ed. Illus. New York, NY: Putnam.
	Krishnaswami, U. (2003). *Monsoon*, Akib, J. Illus. New York, NY: Farrar, Straus and Giroux.
	Little, L. J. (2000). *Children of Long Ago: Poems*, Gilchrist, J. S., illus. Lee & Low Books, Inc.
	Miller. W. (1995). *Frederick Douglass: The Last Day of Slavery*, illustrated by C. Lucas. New York, NY: Lee & Low Books, Inc.
	Rahaman, V. (2008). *Divali Rose*, Akib, J. Illus. Boyds Mills Press.
Scratchboard	Pinkney, A. D. (1994). *Dear Benjamin Banneker*, Pinkney, B. illus. San Diego, CA: Gulliver Books.
	Pinkney, A. D. (1998). *Duke Ellington*, Pinkney, B. illus. New York, NY: Hyperion Books for children.
	Pinkney, A. D. (2006). *Peggony-Po: A Whale of a Tale*, Pinkney, B. illus. New York, NY: Jump at the Sun.

(continued)

Table 4.2. (continued)

Medium	Illustrator / Example of Work
Watercolor	Andersen, H. C. (1999). *The Ugly Duckling*, Pinkney, J., illus. New York, NY: Morrow Junior Books.
	Birtha, B. (2005). *Grandmama's Pride*, Bootman, C. illus. New York, NY: Albert Whitman
	Bradby, M. (1995). *More Than Anything Else*, Soentpiet, C. illus. New York, NY: Scholastic.
	Greenfield, E. (2006). *Friendly Four*, Gilchrist, J. S., illus. New York, NY: Puffin.
	Greenfield, E. (1996). *Night on Neighborhood Street,* Gilchrist, J. S., illus. New York, NY: HarperCollins Publishers.
	Pinkney, J. (2009). *The Lion and the Mouse*, Pinkney, J., illus. New York, NY: Little, Brown Books for Young Readers.
	Say, A. (1989). *The Lost Lake*, Say, A. illus. New York, NY: Houghton Mifflin Harcourt.
	Say, A. (2002). *Home of the Brave*, Say, A. illus. New York, NY: Houghton Mifflin Harcourt.
	Slate, J. (2009). *I Want to Be Free*, Lewis, E. B. illus. New York, NY: Putnam Juvenile.
	Smalls, I. (1996). *Louise's Gift*, Bootman, C. illus. New York, NY: Little, Brown & Company.
	Woodson, J. (2001). *The Other Side*, Lewis, E. B. illus. New York, NY: Putnam Juvenile.
	Yin (2006). *Brothers*, Soentpiet, C. illus. New York, NY: Philomel.

1994) and paper collage—Molly Bank (1996); Ann Grifalconi (Myers, 2002) and Steve Jenkins (2001), books authored by people of color, Johnson (1997) and Myers (2002), were gathered, conspicuously, in order to introduce teacher candidates to authors of color. After the instructor gave some words about the illustrator, each of the picture books was passed around with the instruction to examine the illustrations to determine the distinguishing characteristics of the medium.

Whereas teacher candidates examined the illustrations, the instructor gave an overview of the technical aspects of the medium. For example, that wood (linoleum) cuts are negative images (see the letter "B" in Figure 4.4), and thus teacher candidates need to take into account the positive images (See the letter "T" in Figure 4.4) as well as what will be white and what will be ink" (See the letter "T" in Figure 4.4). Also, the instructor posed questions to the class concerning techniques. For example, how does a watercolorist use watercolors to produce the wash effect utilized often by Jerry Pinkney (2009) or Soentpiet's strong brilliant color (Yin, 2006)? In addition to technique concerns, the criteria of the demonstration of elements and principles of design were discussed in light of the medium. For example, Bryan Collier's (Perdomo, 2002) and Ed Young's (Reibstein, 2008) use of texture in collage versus the texture in Ashley

Bryant's (2003) and the Dillions' (2007) collages. With the examples still in the hands of teacher candidates, the materials were distributed; and teacher candidates were asked to explore the medium before they designed and created their images.

Teacher candidates were given class time to explore the medium. Although a design process (Dunn & Larson, 1989) or a workshop process (Ray & Cleaveland, 2004) is not emphasized, required, or enforced, teacher candidates are asked to think about their design and final project. Throughout the semester or session, the teacher candidates explored each of the media with the same letter. Near the end of the semester, the teacher candidate selected one piece to become their part of the class poster.

CONCLUSION

Broadly speaking, the term "visual literacy" refers to the skills used to construct and understand visual texts (McDougall, 2004, p. 10). According to Braden and Walker (1980, p. 1), "to be visually literate is to be able to gain meaning from what we see and to be able to communicate meaning to others through the images we create" (as cited in McDougall, 2004, p. 26). In other words, "the concept of [visual] literacy has expanded from en/decoding of [visual] text to de/construction of symbolic and iconic forms within visual culture" (Ferneding, 2007, p. 1335); however, if "art becomes one of the subject matters students study in order to understand cultural values and the social sources of power" (Eisner, 1984, p. 260), then visual literacy "focus[es] on developing social and cultural awareness not only aim[s] to enable students to understand how these images are visually constructed, but also how they serve the interests of groups who control those images" (p. 260). Thus, as authors, we wanted to unfold a critical visual literacy that is the "making of meaning through the interaction of different communicative modes [that] requires interaction between two or more discrete sign systems" (Duncum, 2004, pp. 253, 254) through reading multicultural texts, exploring the media employed by Eric Velasquez, and engaging kindergarteners and teacher candidates in visual literacy as reading.

Within this chapter, visual literacy becomes a necessary tool for reading. In other words, with picture books, the written word suffers if there is not equitable concentration on (and teaching about) the illustrations. Specifically, the illustrations are a narrative unto themselves. Illustrations, as narrative, need to be made explicit to all readers. The exposure and reading of the illustrations' narratives becomes extremely important when the contextual lens is multiculturalism, especially in light of the discussion within this chapter. In other words, *Owen* (Henkes, 1993) and Lisa Garla's transactions, through their contextual lens, are multicultural texts.

Owen (Henkes, 1993), a seemingly benign playful and witty text, becomes, through the illustrations, a clash of two cultures: white and of color; *Owen* is a multicultural text albeit to explicate the dominance of hegemonic capitalism. Through his transactions, Lisa Garla's reading of *Jesse Owens: Fastest Man Alive* (Weatherford, 2007) unearths racism through the clash of German/American or Luz Long/Jesse Owens as well as his anchoring of racism symbolically in violence, pistol, and trying to discover and to live the Pandoraian hopefulness (Weigle & Broadway, 2009) of becoming the hero, Jesse Owens, when he, Lisa Garla, is "livin in a time when a hero ain't nothin but a sandwich" (Childress, 1973/2003, p. 74).

In this chapter, we, the authors, are always wrestling and struggling with an understanding concerning the reading of illustrations. If understanding is defined as the

relations among academic knowledge, the state of society, the processes of self-formation, and the character of the historical moment in which we live, in which others have lived, and in which our descendents will someday live. It is understanding that informs the ethical obligation to care for ourselves, and our fellow human beings, that enables us to think and act with intelligence, sensitivity, and courage in both the public sphere—as citizens aspiring to establish a democratic society—and in the private sphere, as individuals committed to other individuals.

(Pinar, 2004, p, 187)

then, our current belief is visual literacy is necessary for the reading of illustrations. We are finding, especially with illustrations in picture books, that each engagement with a picture book necessitates a multicultural transaction no matter how hegemonically obtuse the narrative of the picture book may be. Hence, multicultural picture books are those books that acculturate readers "with worlds they themselves never knew and with which they are unprepared to cope" (Sims, 1985, p. 2), albeit that picture books and the worlds of picture books are, again, mostly culturally hegemonic, but facilitate transactions which may lead to the praxis (Friere, 1970/2000) that is necessary to salvage Earth as a sustainable world of both difference and identity.

REFERENCES

Anonymous (1995 version). *Everyman and other miracle and morality plays* (Dover Thrift Edition). Mineola, NY: Dover Publications.

Banks, J. A. (2004). Multicultural education: Historical development, dimensions, and practice. In Banks, J. A. & Banks, C. A. M. (Eds.). *Handbook of research on multicultural education*, 2nd ed., pp. 3–29. San Francisco, CA: Jossey-Bass.

Braden, R. A., & Walker, A. D. (1980, November). *Reigning catachreses and dogmas related to visual literacy*. Paper presented at the Annual Conference of the International Visual Literacy Association, College Park, MD.

Campbell, J. (1949/1968). *The hero with a thousand faces*. Princeton, NJ: Princeton University Press.

Conkle, D. M., & Broadway, F. S. (2008, April). *Daddy teacher: Male early childhood teacher*. Paper session presented at the American Educational Research Association, New York, NY.

Duncum, P. (2004). Visual culture isn't just visual: Multiliteracy, multimodality and meaning. *Studies in Art Education: A Journal of Issues and Research, 45*(3), 252–264.

Dunn, S., & Larson, R. (1989). *Design technology: Children's engineering*. New York, NY: Routledge.

Eisner, E. W. (1984). Alternative approaches to curriculum development in art education. *Studies in Art Education: A Journal of Issues and Research, 25*(4), 259–264.

Fang, Z. (1996). Illustrations, text, and the child reader: What are pictures in children's storybooks for? *Reading Horizons, 37*(2), 130–142.

Ferneding, K. (2007). Understanding the message of the medium: Media technologies as an aesthetic. In L. Bresier (Ed.), *International handbook of research in arts education* (pp. 1331–1354). Dordrecht, NL: Springer.

Freire, P. (1970/2000). *Pedagogy of the oppressed* (30th Anniversary ed.). New York, NY: Continuum.

Frey, R., & Norris, W. (2008). *Underground together: The art and life of Harvey Dinnerstein*. New York, NY: Chronicle Books.

Frost, R. (1914). Mending wall. In R. Frost, *North of Boston* (pp.11–13). New York, NY: Henry Holt and Company.

Glesne, C. (2006). *Becoming qualitative researchers: An introduction* (3rd ed.). Boston, MA: Pearson Education, Incorporated

Goodman, K. S. (1968). *The psycholinguistic nature of the reading process.* Detroit, MI: Wayne State University Press.

Guerin, W. L., Labor, E., Morgan, L., Reesman, J. C., & Willingham, J. R. (2005). *A handbook of critical approaches to literature* (5th ed.). New York, NY: Oxford University Press.

Harris, T. L., & Hodges, R. E. (1995). *The literacy dictionary: The vocabulary of reading and writing.* Newark, DE: International Reading Association.

Kimmel, M. S. (2005). Masculinity as homophobia: Fear, shame, and silence in the construction of gender identity. In Kimmel, M. S. *The gender of desire: Essays on male sexuality.* Albany, NY: The State University of New York, NY Press.

Klemin, D. (1966). *The art of art for children's books: A contemporary survey.* New York, NY: C. N. Potter.

Leafgren, S. (2009). *Reuben's fall: A rhizomatic analysis of disobedience in kindergarten.* Walnut Creek, CA: Left Coast Press, Inc.

Letts, III, W. J. (2002). Revisioning multiculturalism in teacher education: Isn't it queer. In Kissen, R. M. (Ed.), *Getting ready for Benjamin: Preparing teachers for sexual diversity in the classroom.* Landam, MD: Rowman & Littlefield Publishers, Inc.

Lincoln, Y. S., & Guba, E. G. (1985). *Naturalistic inquiry.* Newbury Park, CA: Sage Publications.

Lynch-Brown, C., & Tomlinson, C. M. (2008). *Essentials of children's literature* (6th ed.). Boston, MA: Allyn and Bacon.

McDougall, J. K. (2004). *Changing mindsets: A study of Queensland primary teachers and the visual literacy initiative* (Ph.D. thesis, Central Queensland University, Australia), http://hdl.cqu.edu.au/10018/18092.

Moore, S. (2008). *Ribbon culture: Charity, compassion and public awareness.* New York, NY: Palgrave Macmillan.

Nodelman, P. (1990). *Words about pictures: The narrative art of children's picture books.* Athens, GA: University of Georgia Press.

Pinar, W. F. (2004). *What is curriculum theory?* Mahwah, NJ: Lawrence Erlbaum Associates.

Ray, K. W. & Cleaveland, L. (2004). *About the authors: Writing workshop with our youngest writers.* Portsmouth, NH: Heinemann.

Rosenblatt, L. M. (1994/2005). The transactional theory of reading and writing. In *Making meaning with texts: Selected essays.* (pp. 1–37). Portsmouth, NH: Heinemann.

Rosenblatt, L. M. (1995). *Literature as exploration* (5th ed.). New York, NY: The Modern Language Association of America.

Roser, N., Martinez, M., Fuhrken, C., & McDonnold, K. (2007, March). Characters as guides to meaning. *The Reading Teacher, 60*(6), 548–559. doi: 10.1598/RT.60.6.5

Short, K., & Pierce, K. (1994, September). Finding ourselves as people and as learners. *The Reading Teacher, 48*(1), 64. Retrieved from Professional Development Collection database.

Silverman, B., & Dinnerstein, H. (2006). Protest in Montgomery: An account by the artists of their journey in 1956 to draw the people of Montgomery and their protest against segregation. In Montgomery Museum of Fine Arts (2006). *Protest in Montgomery: The Montgomery Bus Boycott—An exhibition of drawings executed in March of 1956 by Harvey Dinnerstein and Burt Silverman,* n.p. Montgomery, AL.

Sims, R. (1982). *Shadow and substance: Afro-American experience in contemporary children's fiction.* Urbana, IL: National Council of Teachers of English.

Snyder, S. (2009, October 22). Owen: *Book summary/Is it any good?* [Review of the book *Owen*, by K. Henkes]. Retrieved from common sense media: http://www.commonsensemedia.org/book-reviews/Owen.html/details#whats-the-story.

Thurman, H. (1949/1996). *Jesus and the disinherited*. Boston, MA: Beacon Press.

U. S. Department of Education: Office of Elementary and Secondary Education. (2002, October). *Reading Excellence Act: Non-regulatory guidance for state and local grantees*. Washington, DC: U.S. Department of Education.

Weems, L. (1999). Pestalozzi, perversity, and the pedagogy of love. In W. J. Letts, IV & J. T. Sears (Eds.). *Queering elementary education: Advancing the dialogue about sexualities and schooling* (pp. 27–36). Lanham, MD: Rowman & Littlefield Publishers, Inc.

Weigle, L., & Broadway, F. S. (2009, October). *Pedagogical practices of hope at Akron North High School*. Paper session presented at the Curriculum and Pedagogy Group, Decatur, GA.

Whitlock, R. U. (2007). *This corner of Canaan: Curriculum studies of place & the reconstruction of the South*. New York, NY: Peter Lang Publishing.

Zinn, H. (1980). *A people's history of the United States: 1492-present*. New York, NY: Harper Perennial.

CHILDREN'S AND YOUNG ADULT LITERATURE

Andersen, H. C. (1999). *The ugly duckling*, illustrated by J. Pinkney. New York, NY: Morrow Junior Books.

Azarian, M. (1981). *A farmer's alphabet*. Boston, MA: David R. Godine.

Bank, M. (1996). *Chattanooga sludge: Cleaning toxic sludge from Chattanooga Creek*. New York, NY: Houghton Mifflin Harcourt.

Birtha, B. (2005). *Grandmama's pride*, illustrated by C. Bootman. New York, NY: Albert Whitman.

Boswell, A. (2008). *Rain stomper*, illustrated by E. Velasquez. Tarrytown, NY: Marshall Cavendish Children's Books.

Bradby, M. (1995). *More than anything else*, illustrated by C. Soentpiet. New York, NY: Scholastic.

Brewster, H. (2006). *Other Mozart: The life of the famous Chevalier de Saint-George*, illustrated by E. Velasquez. New York, NY: Harry N Abrams, Inc.

Bryan A. (1974). *Walk together children*. New York, NY: Antheneum.

Bryan, A. (1982). *I'm going to sing*. New York, NY: Antheneum.

Byran, A. (2003). *Beautiful blackbird*. New York, NY: Atheneum Books for Young Readers.

Bryan, A. (2007) *Let it shine: Three favorite spirituals*. New York, NY: Atheneum Books for Young Readers.

Bunting, E. (1978). *Magic and the night river*, illustrated by A. Say. New York, NY: Harper Collins Children's Books.

Bunting, E. (2001). *Ride the tiger*, illustrated by D. Frampton. New York, NY: Clarion Books.

Catalanotto, P. (1999). *Dad and me*. New York, NY: DK Publishing.

Childress, A. (1973/2003). *A hero ain't nothin' but a sandwich*. New York, NY: Speak.

Chocolate, D. (2000). *The piano man*, illustrated by E. Velasquez. New York, NY: Walker Books for Young Readers.

Coerr, E. (1993). *Sadako and the thousand paper cranes*, illustrated by E. Young. New York, NY: Putnam.

Cotton, C. (2008). *Rain play*, illustrated by J. Steptoe. New York, NY: Henry Holt and Co.

Delacre, L. (2000). *Salsa stories*. New York, NY: Scholastic

Dillon, L., & Dillon, D. (2002). *Rap a tap tap: Here's Bojangles—think of that!* New York, NY: Blue Sky Press/Scholastic.

Dillon, L., & Dillon, D. (2007). *Jazz on a Saturday night*. New York, NY: Blue Sky Press/ Scholastic.

Frampton, D. (2007). *Mr. Ferlinghetti's poem*. Grand Rapids, MI: Eerdman's Books for Young Readers.

Francis, P., & Reiser, B. (2002). *David gets his drum*, illustrated by E. Velasquez. Tarrytown, NY: Marshall Cavendish Corporation.

Gayle, S. S. (1999). *Escape!: A story of the Underground Railroad*, illustrated by E. Velasquez. Norwalk, CT: Soundprints.

Greenfield, E. (1996). *Night on neighborhood street*, illustrated by J. S. Gilchrist. New York, NY: HarperCollins Publishers.

Greenfield, E. (2006). *Friendly four*, illustrated by J. S. Gilchrist. New York, NY: Puffin.

Hanson, R. (2005). *Season for mangoes*, illustrated by E. Velasquez. New York, NY: Clarion Books.

Haskins, J. (2002). *Champion: The story of Muhammad Ali*, illustrated by E. Velasquez. New York, NY: Walker Books for Young Readers.

Hendershot, J. (1992). *In coal country*, illustrated by T. Allen. New York, NY: Dragonfly Books.

Henkes, K. (1993). *Owen*. New York, NY: Greenwillow Books.

Jenkins, S. (2001). *Animals in flight*. New York, NY: Houghton Mifflin Books for Children.

Johnson, A. (1997). *The rolling store*, illustrated by P. Catalanotto. New York, NY: Orchard Books.

Johnson, A. (2003). *I dream of trains*, illustrated by L. Long. New York, NY: Simon & Schuster Children's Publishing.

Johnson, A. (2005). *A sweet smell of roses*, illustrated by E. Velasquez. New York, NY: Simon & Schuster Books for Young Readers.

Kay, V. (1999). *Iron horses*, illustrated by M. McCurdy. New York, NY: Putnam Juvenile.

Koplow, L. (1991). *Tanya and the tobo man: A story for children entering therapy* (A. Contos, Trans.), illustrated by E. Velasquez. Washington, DC: Magination Press.

Krishnaswami, U. (2003). *Monsoon*, illustrated by J. Akib. New York, NY: Farrar, Straus and Giroux.

Krull, K. (2005). *Houdini: World's greatest mystery man and escape king*, illustrated by E. Velasquez. New York, NY: Walker Books for Young Readers.

Krull, K. (2007). *Pocahontas: Princess of the new world*, illustrated by D. Diaz. New York, NY: Walker & Company.

Lachenmeyer, N. (2008). *The origami master*, illustrated by A. Sogabe. Morton Grove, IL: Albert Whitman & Company.

Lincoln, A. (1863/1995). *The Gettysburg Address*, illustrated by M. McCurdy. New York, NY: Houghton Mifflin Books for Children.

Little, L. J. (2000). *Children of long ago: Poems*, illustrated by J. S. Gilchrist. New York, NY: Lee & Low Books, Inc.

Martin, J. B. (1999). *Snowflake Bentley*, illustrated by M. Azarian. New York, NY: Houghton Mifflin Books for Children.

Miller. W. (1995). *Frederick Douglass: The last day of slavery*, illustrated by C. Lucas. New York, NY: Lee & Low Books, Inc.

Myers, W. D. (1997). *Harlem*, illustrated by C. Myers. New York, NY: Scholastic Press.

Myers, W. D. (2002). *Patrol: An American soldier in Vietnam*, illustrated by A. Grifalconi. New York, NY: Harper Collins.

Myers, W. D. (2009). *Amiri and Odette: A love story*, illustrated by J. Steptoe. New York, NY: Scholastic Press.

Pak, S. (1999). *Dear Juno*, illustrated by S. K. Hartung. New York, NY: Puffin Books.

Perdomo, W. (2002). *Visiting Langston*, illustrated by B. Collier. New York, NY: Henry Holt and Company.

Pinkney, A. D. (1994). *Dear Benjamin Banneker*, illustrated by B. Pinkney. San Diego, CA: Gulliver Books.

Pinkney, A. D. (1998). *Duke Ellington*, illustrated by B. Pinkney. New York, NY: Hyperion Books for Children.

Pinkney, A. D. (2006). *Peggony-Po: A whale of a tale*, illustrated by B. Pinkney. New York, NY: Jump at the Sun.

Pinkney, J. (2009). *The lion and the mouse*. New York, NY: Little, Brown Books for Young Readers.

Pochocki, E. (1993). *The mushroom man*, illustrated by B. Moser. New York, NY: Simon & Schuster.

Ransom, C. F. (2003). *Liberty Street*, illustrated by E. Velasquez. New York, NY: Walker Books for Young Readers.

Rahaman, V. (2008). *Divali Rose*, illustrated by J. Akib. Honesdale, PA: Boyds Mills Press.

Reibstein, M. (2008). *Wabi Sabi*, illustrated by E. Young. New York, NY: Little, Brown.

Root, P. (1999). *Grandmother winter*, illustrated by B. Krommes. New York, NY: Houghton Mifflin.

Rylant, C. (1998). *Appalachia: The voices of sleeping birds*, illustrated by B. Moser. New York, NY: Sandpiper.

San Souci, R. D. (2000). *Cut from the same cloth: American women of myth, legend, snd tall tale*, illustrated by B. Pinkney. New York, NY: Penguin Group.

Say, A. (1989). *The lost lake*. New York, NY: Houghton Mifflin Harcourt.

Say, A. (2002). *Home of the brave*. New York, NY: Houghton Mifflin Harcourt.

Serwadda, W. M. (1987). *Songs and stories from Uganda*, illustrated by L. Dillon & D. Dillon. New York, NY: World Music Press.

Slate, J. (2009). *I want to be free*, illustrated by E. B. Lewis. New York, NY: Putnam Juvenile.

Smalls, I. (1996). *Louise's gift*, illustrated by C. Bootman. New York, NY: Little, Brown & Company.

Soto, G. (1992). *Neighborhood odes*, illustrated by D. Diaz. New York, NY: Harcourt Children's Books.

Swanson, S. M. (2008). *The house in the night*, illustrated by B. Krommes. New York, NY: Houghton Mifflin Books for Children.

Turner, A. W. (1994). *Sewing quilts*, illustrated by T. Allen. New York, NY: Simon & Schuster.

Van Allsburg, C. (1985). *The Polar Express*. New York, NY: Houghton Mifflin Books for Children.

Van Allsburg, C. (1983). *The wreck of the Zephyr*. New York, NY: Houghton Mifflin Books for Children.

Velasquez, E. (2004). *Grandma's records*. New York, NY: Walker Books for Young Readers.

Weatherford, C. B. (2001). *Sound that jazz makes*, illustrated by E. Velasquez. New York, NY: Walker Books for Young Readers.

Weatherford, C. B. (2007). *Jesse Owens: Fastest man alive*, illustrated by E. Velasquez. New York, NY: Walker Books for Young Readers.

Weatherford, C. B. (2008). *I, Matthew Henson: Polar explorer*, illustrated by E. Velasquez. New York, NY: Walker Books for Young Readers.

Weatherford, C. B. (2009). *Racing against the odds: The story of Wendell Scott, stock car racing's African-American champion*, illustrated by E. Velasquez. Tarrytown, NY: Marshall Cavendish Corporation.

Woodson, J. (2001). *The other side*, illustrated by E. B. Lewis. New York, NY: Putnam Juvenile.

Yin (2006). *Brothers*, illustrated by C. Soentpiet. New York, NY: Philomel.

5

Exploring African American Children's Literature

Claudette Shackelford McLinn, Yolanda A. Reed, John A. Casper, and Sarah King

Since the advent of written language, history has been recorded with the ink and paper of the educated few. Ever since this development, the human experience of our past has echoed through the sanctuaries of our churches, the shelves of our libraries, and the halls of our schools. Literature is the tool that we use to understand who we are, where we come from, and where we are going. It is only through this tool that our children can learn about the events of the past and relate them to the world that they experience first-hand. Over the course of history, the various nations, peoples, and cultures of our world have each contributed to our collective experience in the forms of novels, poems, plays, and works of nonfiction. Each culture's unique perspective and voice is presented in these writings and it is through these works that we can begin to understand and relate to one another in a peaceful and pluralistic global society.

The body of children's literature that chronicles the African-American experience is broad and deep, and it dates back to the earliest days of our nation's history. In this chapter, we will uncover the extensive history and breadth of children's literature written by African-American authors. We will survey the prevalent themes found in this literature by compiling a listing to assist in book selection and curricular-related lessons. Our focus is mostly on African-American authors who may be well known to some readers and less known to others. We believe that it is imperative that children the world over are able to hear the voice of the African-American community in the writings presented here. This is why we have chosen to focus primarily on books written by Black authors. We would be remiss, however, if we did not pay homage to the important works of non-African Americans, which include Arnold Adoff, Verna Aardema, Rachel Isadora, Ezra Jack Keats, Virginia Kroll, Nancy Larrick, Franc Lessac, William Miller, Chris Raschka, Pete Seeger, Robert San Souci, Jan Wahl, Doreen Rappaport, and many others who have enriched African-American children's literature.

The remarkable history of literature representing African Americans is quite extensive in its development and dates back to the early days of our nation. The earliest known work to be recorded by an African American was a poem written by Lucy Terry. Her poem, "Bars Fight," was created when she was 16 years old. The poem records an Indian ambush of two white families on August 25, 1746, in a section of Deerfield, Massachusetts known as the Bars, a colonial word for meadows (Andrews, Foster, & Harris, 2001, p. 719). Phillis Wheatley was the first African American and the second woman to publish a book in the 13 colonies on any subject (Andrews, Foster, & Harris, 2001, p. 770). Wheatley published her first poem, "On Messers, Hussy and Coffin," (Massachusetts Historical Society, 2010) that tells the remarkable survival of these gentlemen in a hurricane off Cape Cod. The poem appeared on December 21, 1776, in the New Port Mercury.

The earliest examples of African-American children's literature took the form of periodicals and were published as early as 1887 when Mrs. Amelia E. Johnson published an eight-page monthly magazine for children entitled, *The Joy*. In 1889, she wrote, *Clarence and Corinne, or God's Way*, and in 1894, *The Hazeley Family*, both books for young readers but with European protagonists (Andrews, Foster, & Harris, 2001, p. 135). W.E.B. DuBois, Augustus Granville Dill, and Jessie Redman Faust served as publishers and editors of the *Brownies' Book*, an early African-American children's periodical, that began publication in 1919 (Andrews, Foster, & Harris, 2001, p. 135). This periodical was published every month for 24 months from January 1920 through December 1921 (Johnson-Feelings, 1996, p. 12).

Despite a small handful of children's books published by black authors during the eighteenth century, it was not until the nineteenth century that the development of the African-American children's book took place. Langston Hughes and Arna Bontemps, who were both prolific authors, wrote books expressly for Black children (Appiah & Gates, 1999, p. 420). In 1932, Hughes and Bontemps coauthored the novel, *Popo and Fifina*; and Hughes published, *The Dream Keeper*, a collection of poetry. Bontemps wrote several more children's stories and published the poetry anthology, *Golden Slippers* (Appiah & Gates, 1999, p. 420). By the 1940s, African-American children's literature continued with notable writers like Jessie Jackson, who wrote the novel *Call Me Charley* in 1945 and Lorenz Graham, author of the *South Town-North Town* series, which were written from 1958 to 1976 (Appiah & Gates, 1999, p. 420). In 1956, Gwendolyn Brooks (2007) published her poetry collection, *Bronzeville Boys and Girls*, which celebrated her Chicago neighborhood and featured poems of joy and imagination through the eyes of Black children. This poetry collection is still in print with a reillustrated edition featuring colorful paintings by artist Faith Ringgold. It must be noted that although a number of African-American authors wrote children's books, the number of books published were very small in volume compared to books published by and about White children (Cooperative Children's Book Center, 2010).

Beginning in the 1960s, when the Civil Rights and Black Power movements reached unprecedented levels of public awareness, a new group of children's authors appeared whose works declared black is beautiful (Appiah & Gates, 1999). Virginia Hamilton, Walter Dean Myers, John Steptoe, Mildred Taylor, and Julius Lester were among the many African-American authors who began writing children's books and young adult novels featuring African-American characters set against a variety of contemporary backgrounds. Mildred Taylor's (1976) *Roll of Thunder, Hear My Cry*, set in a 1930's rural Mississippi community, was the first book in a trilogy portraying the oppression suffered by African Americans under the Jim Crow laws in the South. This gripping book won the Newbery Award in 1977. Julius Lester's (1968) *To Be a Slave*, a collection of reminiscences of slaves and exslaves, powerfully described the wrenching experiences of Black Americans during the period spanning the African slave trade through the Civil War and into the early twentieth century. Lester's book, which selected slave narratives from various sources and arranged them chronologically, was awarded the Newbery Honor Award in 1969, and Lester became the second African American to win this award. Earlier, in 1949, Arna Bontemps (1948) was the first African American to win the Newbery Honor Award for his book, *Story of the Negro*. In 1975, Virginia Hamilton's (1974) *M.C. Higgins the Great*, a story of 15-year-old M.C. whose strength and determination helps to find a way for his family to escape the spoil heap that may one day destroy their beloved home, won the Newbery Award. Hamilton became the first African American to win the Newbery Award for this book. Virginia Hamilton, who wrote books representing many genres, including, Black folk tales, science fiction, realistic fiction, and historical fiction, garnered every major national and international honor for which her work was eligible (Adoff & Cook, 2010). She is, undoubtedly, one of America's greatest authors.

The body of African-American children's literature by African-American authors has been noteworthy both in quality and quantity. Rudine Sims (1982) stated the following:

These books come closest to constituting a body of Afro-American literature for children. They are books that reflect, with varying degrees of success, the social and cultural traditions associated with growing up Black in the United States. In contrast to the social conscience books, they are not primarily addressed to non-Blacks, nor are they focused on desegregating neighborhoods or schools. They differ from the melting pot books in that they recognize, sometimes even celebrate, the distinctiveness of the experience of growing up simultaneously Black in America. Their primary intent is to speak to Afro-American children about themselves and their lives, though as has been pointed out, they are by no means closed to other children. These books must be considered an important component of American children's literature in general.

(p. 49)

Appendix A provides a timeline of African-American children's literature. From this list, teachers, librarians, and students can gain an understanding of the historical development of African-American children's literature.

We have argued that these children's books provide an important way to better understand the African-American experience. African-American literature for children and youth has been collected in libraries, schools, and individual homes, yet many students may not have a clear understanding of the scope and importance of this literature. Over the course of recent history, African-American children's books, as well as a number of publications intended for adults, have been categorized into the African-American history section in many libraries and bookstores. We argue that African-American literature, including children's literature, should be classified into a number of genres or themes. As Virginia Hamilton stated, "There is nothing at all wrong with categories and groupings as long as they serve as informative guides. But what has happened is that categories of books have become institutionalized as a kind of multiple segregation, and woe to the books that can't fit a category" (Adoff & Cook, 2010, p. 39). During African-American History Month, attention is paid to the writings of all African-American authors of all genres and themes in one month's time. As an example of this phenomenon, Hamilton stated (Adoff & Cook 2010):

A long time ago, I first noticed that in the month of February, I am in much greater demand than at any other time of the year; February is of course, the month when Americans justly pay tribute to the historical accomplishments of American blacks. For Black History Week, school children in all white, all black, and racially mixed schools diligently read my books. I dutifully make appearances in classrooms to explain how I write, why, and with what singleness of purpose. Once, upon asking students by what means they came to read my books, they informed me that in February they had to read books by black authors, that the rest of the year they could read anything they wanted.

(pp. 39–40)

African-American authors of children's books, in particular, fit into many genres and themes and should not be confined to be read one month out of the year. To demonstrate the many themes and issues that are important when selecting African-American children's literature, we have grouped a selection of these books into themes to help teachers and librarians integrate them into the curriculum and for parents to select books based on their child's interest throughout the year. The themes and genres found in the following section include the following: family and friends, identity and self -concept, poetry and rhymes, school and community, imagination, traditional literature, spirituality, historical perspectives, holidays and special days, and biographies and autobiographies.

FAMILY AND FRIENDS

Families are as unique as individuals. They look different, act different, and have different customs and traditions. Some are big, and some are small. Some are traditional, and some are far from it. Whereas this information comes as no surprise to an adult, to a child it may be shocking to find that their classmate has two mommies or a sister with a different daddy. Many of these differences come from the culture or ethnic group to which a particular family belongs. Manning and Baruth (2009) stated:

Many African American children grow up in homes that are very different from the homes of children and adolescents from other cultures. Minority extended families function on the principles of interdependence and extensive reliance on networks of people, including blood relatives and close friends called *kinsmen*. A young African American child might be taken into the household of elderly grandparents. In such arrangements, children have a sense they belong to an extended family clan, not merely to their parents. Uncles, aunts, cousins, and grandparents have considerable power within the family unit and may take responsibility for the care and rearing of children and for teaching appropriate skills and values.

(p. 65)

By exposing our students to the wide range of literature that illustrates the differences and similarities our families share, we can help to build bridges between cultures, thus eliminating misunderstanding and promoting cultural awareness. The books in Table 5.1 emphasize the importance of the African-American family in the African-American community as well as the U.S. society as a whole.

Table 5.1.

Family and Friends

Grade Level	Children's Book	Author	Year
Pre-K to Kindergarten	*Amifika*	Clifton	1977
	Baby Says	Steptoe	1982
	One of Three	Johnson	1991
	On the Day I was Born	Chocolate	1995
	Please, Baby, Please	Lee	2002
	Snug in Mama's Arms	Medearis	2004
	Welcome Precious	Grimes	2006
	Homemade Love	Hooks	2002
	My Aunt Came Back	Cummings	1998
	Honey Baby Sugar Child	Duncan	2005
	My Nana and Me	Smalls	2005
	Lord Aunt Hattie	Thomas	1973
	Busy Baby	McMillan	1995
	Eliza's Baby	Thomas	1976
	My Best Friend	Hinds	1996
	Let George Do It	Foreman	2005
	Did I Tell You That I Love You Today?	Jordan & Jordan	2004
	Girls Together	Williams	1999
	Grandma and Me	Weatherford	1996
	Me and the Family Tree	Weatherford	1996
	Two Mrs. Gibsons	Igus	1996
Grades 1–3	*The Hundred Penny Box*	Mathis	1975
	The Patchwork Quilt	Flournoy	1985
	When I was Little	Igus	1992
	Things I Like About Grandma	Haskins	1992
	Just the Two of Us	Smith	2001
	Visiting Day	Woodson	2002
	Daddy Goes to Work	Asim	2006
	Abby	Gaines	1984
	Carousel	Cummings	1994
	Two and Too Much	Walter	1990
	Aunt Flossie's Hat	Howard	1991
	Just Us Women	Gaines	1982
	Me and Neesie	Greenfield	1975
	Working Cotton	Williams	1992
	In My Mama's Kitchen	Nolan	1999

(*continued*)

Table 5.1. (continued)

Grade Level	Children's Book	Author	Year
	Neeny Coming, Neeny Going	English	1996
	Daughter's Day Blues	Pegram	2000
	The Baby on the Way	English	2005
	Peeny Butter Fudge	Morrison	2009
	First Pink Light	Greenfield	1991
	Ma Dear's Apron	McKissack	1997
	Bigmama's	Crews	1991
	The Twins Strike Back	Flournoy	1980
	Who Will I Be, Lord?	Nelson	2009
Grades 4–6	*Justin and the Best Biscuits*	Walter	1978
	Cousins	Hamilton	1990
	Sister	Greenfield	1987
	Your Dad Was Just Like You	Johnson	1993
	Because You're Lucy	Small	1997
	Creativity	Steptoe	1997
	Talk About a Family	Greenfield	1993
	Food in Grandma's Day	Weber	1999
	Home Life in Grandma's Day	Weber	1999
	Roll of Thunder, Hear My Cry	Taylor	1991
	A Blessing in Disguise	Tate	1995
	Francie	English	2007
	Strawberry Moon	English	2001
	Little Sister Is Not My Name	Draper	2009
	Bud, Not Buddy	Curtis	1999

Who Will I Be, Lord? is a wonderful picture book by Vaunda Micheaux Nelson (2009) about the diverse professional roles within the African-American family and the community. The narrator, who is never named but is depicted by illustrator, Sean Qualls, as a young African-American girl, reflects on the different members of her family, describing their various careers and roles within the community. After a description of each family member's career, the narrator follows her portrayal with a question to God: "What will I be Lord?" (Nelson, 2009, n. p.). Nelson writes this book in simple conversational prose that connotes the voice of a young girl, and it is quite touching in its simplicity. In just a few words, Nelson is able to sincerely capture the essence of the diversity of the African-American family, and Qualls' honest and simple watercolor collages effectively depict the loving relationships that the narrator enjoys.

A word wheel is a great activity for young students to use to help them organize and summarize information. Because of the segmented nature of its narrative, *Who Will I Be, Lord?* is a perfect example of the kind of book that works well with this activity. After reading this book aloud, the teacher or teacher librarian can model the activity

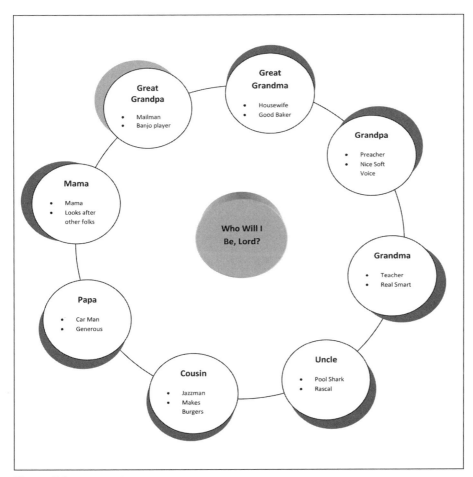

Figure 5.1.
Word Wheel

by drawing a series of concentric circles joined together by the title of the book or, perhaps, the words "Family" or "Careers." In the circles, the teacher or teacher librarian can write the names of the narrator's relatives, their careers, and some of their character attributes. Figure 5.1 provides an example of a word wheel for *Who Will I Be, Lord?*

Students should be encouraged to help contribute to the discussion as the word wheel is constructed. Once the wheel is completed, teachers can take this activity one step further by having students create word wheels about their fellow classmates' families. By pairing up students and having them interview each other about their families, students will be able to learn about the differences and similarities that they share with their classmates. Students could be provided with a series of questions to help scaffold the construction of the word wheel; or to encourage originality and creativity, the students could ask their own questions and create the word wheels in whatever manner they choose.

For older students studying the Great Depression, Christopher Paul Curtis (1999) presents a wonderful tale about the role of family, friends, and community in his celebrated novel, *Bud, Not Buddy*, a book that won both the Newbery and Coretta Scott King Awards in 2000. Set in Flint, Michigan, in 1936, this novel tells the tale of the orphan, Bud, who after multiple experiences with abusive foster parents decides to run away to find his real family. The only clue that he has to go on is a jazz flyer given to him by his mother before she died. Bud believes that the performer on this flyer is his father, and he sets off on an adventure to find him. Along the way, Bud encounters other orphans as well as jobless and homeless people who are all friendly and helpful in his quest. Curtis underscores the importance of community during times of economic hardship and social turmoil while teaching important lessons about society, history, culture, and family.

An effective way to teach the concepts and themes of this children's novel is to teach this book in conjunction with a history unit on the Great Depression. Curtis' novel will help students connect with the abstract ideas of the past by enabling them to identify with characters who lived through the hardships that they read about in their history textbooks.

A great approach to use when reading a novel as a class is character mapping. Character mapping is an especially effective strategy for helping the students recognize attributes of the various characters as well as the different kinds of relationships that those characters share with one another. This activity can also be adapted so students can observe how the characters in the novel evolve over time, giving them a sense of the overall story structure and character development. The teacher or teacher librarian should first model the activity and then guide students in a prereading activity to skim through the chapter to search for character traits. Next, students should draw large boxes on a sheet of paper for each character that they are mapping. In the boxes, the students should write the names of characters and their attributes. Once the chapter or passage has been read, students should finish up their character attributes and then draw arrows from character to character writing words above the arrows that identify the relationship that those characters share. Figure 5.2 provides an example of a character map for *Bud, Not Buddy.*

Bud and Jerry Character Map for Chapter 1

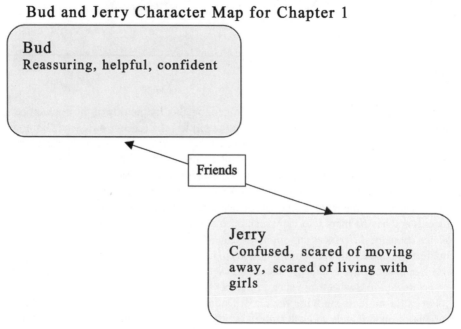

Figure 5.2.
Character Map

This activity can be done for every chapter and students can compare and contrast, for example, Bud from chapter 1 with Bud from chapter 19. This is a very effective way for students to visualize the way that characters change over the course of a novel.

Welcome, Precious by Nikki Grimes (2006) is a beautifully written book about a mother and father welcoming their new baby into the world. Grimes uses rich, poetic descriptions of sights, sounds, and feelings to convey the warmth and love in the baby's new world. An example of this rich language is "the silk of grass, the satin of rose petals" (Grimes, 2006, n. p.). The text is accompanied by Bryan Collier's large, bright illustrations that blend watercolor art and collage. Following a reading of this book, the teacher could point out the descriptive language in the book and ask children what images the language conveys in their minds. This could lead to a writing activity in which students write about a special time with their family and attempt to use descriptive language. Younger children could engage in an interactive writing activity in which each student writes a sentence with descriptions while the other students add their input.

IDENTITY AND SELF-CONCEPT

Literature provides a means for children to make sense of their world. "It tells students who and what their society and culture values, what kind of behaviors are acceptable and appropriate, and what it means to be a decent human being" (Bishop, 1990, p. 561). Brooks and McNair (2009) noted that literature can help students establish beliefs and identities. Hefflin and Barksdale-Ladd (2001) reported that not so long ago, African-American children's literature was scarce. Too many students were unable to find themselves in the literature they read in classrooms. Unintentionally, African-American children could determine that they were not valued in society. Over the past 40 years, there has been an increase in the number of books written by and for African Americans. This is incredibly important for African-American children because when they have the opportunity to read books to which they connect, they not only grow as people but are influenced to develop a love of reading. The books in Table 5.2 affirm African-American children's identity and help to build their self-concept.

Table 5.2.

Identity and Self-Concept

Grade Level	Children's Book	Author	Year
Pre-K–Kindergarten	*Colors Around Me*	Church	1971
	Pretty Brown Face	Pinkney	1997
	No Mirrors in My Nana's House	Barnwell	1998
	Brown Sugar Babies	Smith	2000
	Shades of Black	Pinkney	2000
	Girls Hold Up the World	Pinkett-Smith	2005
	Sweet, Sweet Baby	Steptoe	2005
	Skin Again	Hooks	2005
	Happy to Be Nappy	Hooks	1999
	Billy the Great	Guy	1991

(continued)

Table 5.2. (continued)

Grade Level	Children's Book	Author	Year
Grades 1–3	*An Enchanted Hair Tale*	DeVeaux	1987
	When I Look in the Mirror	Greywolf	1993
	Melanin 'n' Me	Crespo	1995
	Cornrows	Yarbrough	1997
	I Love My Hair!	Tarpley	1998
	Daisy the Doll	Medearis	2000
	Nappy Hair	Herron	1997
	I Want To Be	Moss	1993
	I Like Me!	Coker	1995
	Louise's Gift	Smalls	1996
	Hair Dance	Johnson	2007
Grades 4–6	*The Black Snowman*	Mendez	1989
	Being Me	Parker	2002
	The Shimmershine Queens	Yarbough	1996
	It's All Good Hair	Collison	2002
	Grandpa, Is Everything Black Bad?	Holman	1998
	Handsome Me	Thomas	2002
	Kids Talk Hair	Ferrell	1999
	Beautiful Me	Thomas	2002
	Let's Talk Race	Lester	2005
	Looking Like Me	Myers	2009

Sandra L. Pinkney's (2000) *Shades of Black*, is a book of photographs of African-American children. The text describes the different colors of the children's skin tones by comparing them to something familiar to the students. For example, one child's skin tone is described as being like the "creamy white frost in vanilla ice cream" (Pinkney, 2000, n.p.). Students could create a classroom book with a picture of each student and a color description following the model of Pinkney's book. The teacher can collect all of the pictures and compile the book to be put on display for everyone to enjoy.

Hair Dance! by Dinah Johnson (2007) is a book full of beautiful photographs taken by Kelly Johnson of African-American children. The accompanying text describes the variety of hair styles of the children. Teachers can follow up the reading of the book by leading a discussion on the similarities and differences of the way the students and the characters in the book wear their hair. Next, students could draw self-portraits and write accompanying sentences using details to describe their hair.

Ashley Bryan's (2003) celebrated retelling of a Zambian parable in *Beautiful Blackbird* is a story about how pluralism and multiculturalism benefit society and how our neighbors help us to shape our own identity. Bryan won the 2004 Coretta Scott King Award for his colorful and poetic adaptation of this traditional African tale. The story begins long ago when "the birds of Africa were all colors of the rainbow . . . clean, clear colors from head to tail. Oh so pretty, pretty, pretty" (Bryan, 2003, n. p.). All of the birds are envious of the beautiful blackbird's blackness. Although the blackbird assures his colorful friends that "color on the outside is not what's on the inside" (Bryan, 2003, n. p.), they still wish to share in his gift, so he uses his feathers to paint black markings on each one.

> Our colors sport a brand new look,
> A touch of black was all it took.
> Beautiful Black, uh-huh, uh-huh
> Black is beautiful, UH-HUH!"

(Bryan, 2003, n. p.)

Bryan's colorful cutout collages that accompany this musical tale are the perfect inspiration for an artistic activity that that can inspire a discussion on the importance of multiculturalism and the benefits of being different. Teachers can distribute colorful cutouts of birds that resemble the illustrations in the story, and once the students have chosen them, they could decorate their birds with black construction paper. While the students are completing this activity, the teacher might engage them in a dialogue about identity and the importance of valuing each person's uniqueness.

POETRY AND RHYMES

> Read indiscriminately. Just gobble it up. And don't let anybody suggest to you that this particular poet or fiction writer doesn't have anything to say to you by virtue of his or her race or gender or class or national identity.
>
> —*Rita Dove* (as cited in Alexander, 2005)

The United States has a long history of African-American poets who have contributed to the development of African-American poetry and song. From Phillis Wheatley, a first generation slave who was the first African-American woman to be published, to Rita Dove, the first African-American poet laureate of the United States. Black poets have played an integral part in the evolution of the art of poetry in the United States. Repetition, rhyme, cadence, alliteration, assonance, and intonation; these are all fundamental characteristics of the voice of the African-American people. One need not look far to hear poetry pouring from the mouths of preachers, politicians, activists, artists, and athletes of the Black community. Indeed, the art of language is one of the defining characteristics of the African-American culture. It adds to our national character and is something that we all can be proud of, regardless of our racial heritage or the color of our skin. Our children can learn so much from the writings of poets like Langston Hughes, Lucille Clifton, and Maya Angelou, and there is still much being written today for the ever changing, diversified student population to enjoy.

Without question, one of the most influential and significant African-American authors of the twentieth century is Langston Hughes. This prolific writer of plays, novels, short stories, essays, and poetry, with his literary versatility and his graceful command of the English language, earned his place among the great writers in American history. Recently, there have been a number of children's picture books using Hughes' poetry as the text. Two wonderful examples of such re-imaginings are *My People* (Hughes, 2009), with its minimalist black and white photographs by Charles R. Smith, Jr., recipient of the 2010 Coretta Scott King Award, and *The Negro Speaks of Rivers* (Hughes, 2009) with its strikingly beautiful watercolors by E. B. Lewis, also a recipient of the 2010 Coretta Scott King Honor Award. These critically acclaimed picture books combine the classic poetry of a genuine literary legend with the beautiful visual inter-pretations of these illustrators, allowing the reader to become totally immersed in the artistry of the words and pictures. The two poems in these books are relatively short and thus, the text is sparse. This allows for a wide range of readership, as it can be read by very young students, but still appreciated by older ones. These books will appeal to all audiences, inspiring the minds of our children and moving the hearts of the adults who care for them.

After reading *My People* (Hughes, 2009a) and *The Negro Speaks of Rivers* (Hughes, 2009b) and analyzing the artists' interpretations of these poems, students can read other Langston Hughes poems and decide how to interpret these literary works with their own artwork, using Smith's photographs and Lewis' illustrations as models for different ways to interpret poetry. Providing students with varied mediums such as photography, tempera, watercolor, art pencils, collage, and computer software will give them different ways to interpret Hughes' poetry and will encourage originality in their artwork.

Traditional literature and visual arts are not the only ways to expose young minds to poetry. For almost 30 years now, hip-hop and rap have changed the popular music landscape, bringing African-American art to a genuinely diverse mainstream audi-ence. One of the great things about hip hop is that it is a wonderful medium with which to teach poetry. Obviously, many of the popular rap songs are not appropriate for any classroom, let alone an elementary one, but Nikki Giovanni (2008) has put together a wonderful collection of poetry that incorporates important elements of the genre in *Hip Hop Speaks to Children: A Celebration of Poetry With a Beat*. This collection features poetry from classic poets like Langston Hughes and Gwendolyn Brooks as well as modern rap and hip-hop artists like Common, Kanye West, and Lauren Hill. Accompanying this colorfully illustrated New York Times best seller is an audio CD that features readings and performances by many of the artists highlighted in the book.

Giovanni's book naturally lends itself to a performance activity, allowing students with musical aspirations to show off some of their skills. After playing examples of the performances on CD, teachers and teacher librarians could divide up their students into groups, assigning each group a poem and designating roles for a performance for the class. Students could perform the poem a cappella, or with background beats and rhythms. A Google search for free beats and loops will turn up any number of Web sites featuring background accompaniments for aspiring artists. Teachers should download beats ahead of time in order to avoid any unpredictable content that may be listed on the sites. Once the students are in groups, they could divide up the poem however they like, each taking a stanza or trading off on lines. One student could act as a D. J. if he/she has stage fright, controlling the beats and loops on the computer. Still yet, another student might choreograph dance moves for the rappers to perform.

Families: Poems Celebrating the African American Experience is a collection of poems assembled by Dorothy and Michael Strickland (1994) that emphasize the impor-tance of family in the African-American community. After reading this collection of poems, the teacher could do a lesson on poetry writing based on one or more styles pre-sented in the book. With help, students could then write or dictate their own poems and share them with the class and their families. Table 5.3 lists other books with African-American poetry and rhymes.

SCHOOL AND COMMUNITY

Children's literature depicting successful African-American students has the ability to inspire children to succeed themselves. It can pass along the message that education is important. In a broader context, it is also important for African-American children to see themselves as legitimate members of their communities. Through this type of children's literature, students can discover not only how their culture connects to the

Table 5.3.
Poetry and Rhymes

Grade Level	Children's Book	Author	Year
Pre-K–Kindergarten	*Picture Me in a Poem*	Adams	1980
	Families	Strickland	1994
	Daddy Calls Me	Johnson	1997
	Singing Black	Evans	1998
	The Angel's Lullaby	Thomas	2000
	My People	Hughes/Lewis	2009
	The Negro Speaks of Rivers	Hughes	2009
Grades 1–3	*Poems by Kali*	Grosvenor	1978
	Honey, I Love	Greenfield	1978
	Apples on a Stick	Michele/White	1993
	Pass It On	Hudson	1993
	Meet Danita Brown	Grimes	1994
	ABC's of African American Poetry	Bryan	1997
	The Blacker the Berry	Thomas	2008
	Keep Climbing Girls	Richards	2006
	Freedom Light Sunlight	Lewis	2000
	DeShawn Days	Medina	2001
	Bronzeville Boys and Girls	Brooks	2009
Grades 4–6	*Red Dog, Blue Fly*	Mathis	1995
	Make a Joyful Sound	Slier	1996
	In My Daddy's Arms I Am Tall	Steptoe	1997
	Words With Wings	Rochelle	2001
	Remember the Bridge	Weatherford	2002
	Hip Hop Speaks to Children	Giovanni	2008
	Poetry for Young People	Wilson	2007
	A Wreath for Emmett Till	Nelson	2005
	There Is a Flower at the Tip of My Nose	Walker	2006

classroom, but also to their families and communities (McMillon & McMillon, 2004). This genre/theme includes books about school, community jobs and activities, and interactions among people in communities.

In a primary classroom setting where most children are driven to school, the book, *School Bus*, by Donald Crews (1984) could be used to introduce students to the function of a school bus. The teacher or teacher librarian could follow up this book with a transportation unit that covered other forms of important transportation in their community like public buses, trains, subways, taxis, cars, and bikes. If possible, the teacher or teacher librarian could even arrange a short trip on a school bus.

Virgie Goes to School With Us Boys by Elizabeth Fitzgerald Howard (1999) is about a young African-American girl who wants to go to school with her brothers. Howard's grandfather, Virgie's brother, told her this story which inspired her to write the book. The story takes place after the Civil War when many schools were founded to educate the newly freed slaves. One follow-up activity would be to do a lesson on the barriers that slaves faced even after being freed after the war. Students could also do research on the author.

Table 5.4 provides a list of other books that focus on school and community.

Table 5.4.
School and Community

Grade Level	Children's Book	Author	Year
Pre-K–Kindergarten	*The Best Time of Day*	Flournoy	1978
	School Bus	Crews	1984
	Bright Eyes, Brown Skin	Hudson/Ford	1990
	Jamal's Busy Day	Hudson	1991
	I Remember "121"	Haskins	1991
	When Will Sarah Come?	Howard	1999
	I Need a Lunch Box	Gaines	1988
	From Where I Stand	Hudson	2008
	Mighty Menfolk	Weatherford	1996
	Bippity Bop Barbershop	Tarpley	2002
Grades 1–3	*Shortcut*	Crews	1992
	White Socks Only	Coleman	1996
	Whitewash	Shange	1997
	Something Beautiful	Wyeth	1998
	Virgie Goes to School With Boys	Howard	2005
	Uptown	Collier	2000
	Don't Say Ain't	Small	2003
	Kenya's Word	Trice	2006
	Think Again	Fresh	2002
	The Other Side	Woodson	2001
	I Have a Dream, Too!	Elster	2002
	I'll Do the Right Thing	Elster	2003

Table 5.4. (continued)

Grade Level	Children's Book	Author	Year
	Miss Viola and Uncle Ed Lee	Duncan	1999
	Keena Ford and the Field Trip Mix-Up	Thomson	2009
	Keena and the 2nd Grade Mix-Up	Thomson	2009
	Donavan's Word Jar	DeGross	1994
Grades 4–6	*Going Back Home*	Igus	1996
	A Street Called Home	Robinson	1997
	A Bus of Our Own	Evans	2001
	Off to School	Battle/Lavert	1995
	Destiny's Gift	Tarpley	2004
	The Hard Time Jar	Smothers	2003
	Speak to Me	English	2004
	The Watson's Go to Birmingham	Curtis	1995
	The Gold Cadillac	Taylor	1987
	Broken Bike Boy and the Queen of 33rd Street	Flake	2007

IMAGINATION

If my mind can conceive it, my heart can believe it, I know I can achieve it.

—Rev. Jesse Jackson. (as cited in Myers & Jeeves, 1987)

Over the course of American history, the Black imagination has inspired everything from art, literature, and music to change and social justice. What was a dream to Dr. Martin Luther King, Jr. for U.S. society to be more just in the 1960s is, in many ways, a reality today. Imagination is the catalyst of progress, and nowhere is this gift more vivid than in the mind of a child. According to Lynch-Brown and Tomlinson (2008), imagination and inspiration are two of the benefits children receive from good literature as it helps them to look at their world in new ways and consider ways of living that differ from their own. "Through the vicarious experience of entering a world different from the present one, children develop their imaginations" (Lynch-Brown & Tomlinson, 2008, p. 5). The canon of African-American literature is filled with fantastic stories written to captivate the imagination and inspire the children in our classrooms. From fairy tales to folktales to science fiction, the collection of imaginative African-American children's literature covers every genre, guaranteeing to appeal to every child in the classroom; there's something to inspire everybody. Table 5.5 lists African-American literature that inspires the imagination.

Newbery Honor Award winner, Julius Lester (2005) takes us across the Atlantic in *The Old African*, a beautifully imaginative tale about escapism, illustrated in stunning watercolors by the distinguished Jerry Pinkney. Once an African mystic and now a slave on a plantation, Jaja, the old African, uses his supernatural powers to help ease the pain of his fellow slaves. After an especially brutal beating by the slave master, Jaja decides to use his mystical powers to lead the slaves on the plantation to freedom by walking them back to Africa, across the ocean's bottom. Whereas this is a picture book, the prose is

Table 5.5.

Imagination

Grade Level	Children's Book	Author	Year
Pre-K–Kindergarten	*The Magic Moonberry Jump Rope*	Hru	1996
	Sleeping Cutie	Pinkney	2004
	The Glass Bottle Tree	Coleman	1995
	Albidaro and the Mischievous Dream	Lester	2000
	The Moon Ring	DuBurke	2002
Grades 1–3	*C.L.O.U.D.S.*	Cummings	1986
	Land of the Four Winds	Ellis	1993
	Kofi and His Magic	Angelou	1996
	Madelia	Gilchrist	1997
	You Are Here	Crews	1998
	Cosmo and the Robot	Pinkney	2000
	Stompin' at the Savoy	Campbell	2006
	Jimmy Lee Did It	Cummings	1985
	What's in Aunt Mary's Room	Howard	1996
	Stormy Nights	Hardwell	2007
	Joshua's Masai Mask	Hru	1993
	The Day They Stole the Letter	Mahiri	1989
Grades 4–6	*The Black Snowman*	Mendez	1989
	Adventures of Sparrow Boy	Pinkney	1997
	The Old African	Lester	2005
	Finding the Greenstone	Walker	1991
	Who's Jim Hines	Elster	2008
	The Secret of Gumbo Grove	Tate	1987
	Invisible Princess	Ringgold	1999

challenging, and Lester holds no bars when it comes to his vivid descriptions of the horrors of slavery; teachers and teacher librarians need to make careful judgment regarding whether or not the students are mature enough for this book. The idea of escapism is also a complex one and may be difficult for even fourth or fifth graders to grasp. Still, the idea that imagination can take you away from danger is an important one, and it is essential for young students to remember that dreams can affect change.

By the time students have reached fourth or fifth grade, they will have learned quite a bit about slavery and its place in the history of our nation. Some sort of anticipatory activity would be appropriate to prepare the students for the difficult themes that *The Old African* explores. An anticipation guide or a K-W-L chart (Ogle, 1986) would lay the groundwork for a discussion on the important ideas discussed in the narrative. Following the reading, the teacher could ask the students to imagine what it would be like to be taken from their home, tortured, and forced to do things against their will. Teachers and teacher librarians could facilitate discussion with questions like

- What would you do if someone took you away from your home and family?
- If someone else was being hurt, what would you do to help them?
- When you are unhappy, do you ever daydream of being somewhere else?
- Do you ever pretend that superheroes will come and save the day?
- What would happen if your daydreams came true?
- How could you be a hero in your world?

By relating the narrative in *The Old African* to students' real lives, the story takes on a new meaning, and the important ideas presented here are driven home. These questions, which would also be good prompts for journal writing, are meant to stimulate a discussion about the importance of imagination to the betterment of society, a heavy topic for a child to discuss. However, children have the capacity to believe in themselves as agents of change and this idea needs to be emphasized as often as possible.

Similar themes of escapism and imagination can be found in Virginia Hamilton's (1985) *The People Could Fly: American Black Folktales* which was the Coretta Scott King Award winner in 1986. This book is a beautifully written collection of 24 African-American folktales featuring classic African-American characters like Bruh Bear and Bruh Rabbit. These stories exemplify the strength of the African-American spirit and its ability to endure the inhumanity of slavery. They also express African American's imagination. As Virginia Hamilton states in the introduction to the book, "As slaves, they were forced to live without citizenship, without rights, as property—like horses and cows—belonging to someone else. But no amount of hard labor and suffering could suppress their powers of imagination" (p. x). With its similar themes and stories, this book would be perfect to teach in concert with *The Old African*. This book is appropriate for a wide range of ages and could be taught from third grade to fifth or sixth grade.

Diamond and Moore (1995) suggest an engaging strategy called Radio City to be used with short stories or folktales. This cooperative learning activity mixes the Question-Answer Relationships (QAR) strategy, "which sensitizes readers to different thinking patterns and demands required by various levels of questions" (p. 113), with the basic principles of the jigsaw reading strategy. The teacher or teacher librarian preps the students by reviewing three types of QAR questions to ask about the folktale: right there questions, whose answers are directly stated in the text; think and search questions, which require students to look for information that is implied in the text; and on-my-own questions, which ask for information not in the text and require that readers come up with answers on their own.

After reviewing the QAR strategy, the students can be divided into groups and each group can be given a folktale from *The People Could Fly: American Black Folktales* (Hamilton, 1985). The teacher or teacher librarian, having already divided up each folktale into parts, then assigns each student in the group a part of the text to both read and compose QAR questions related to the main ideas of the text. For example, in the story, "He Lion, Bruh Bear, and Bruh Rabbit," students might develop the following QAR questions:

Right There: What did Man do when he saw He Lion?
Think and Search: Why did things quiet down in the forest after He Lion met Man?
On Your Own: If you were to describe Man in today's world, how would you describe him?

Once students have read over their story and composed their own questions, it is time for the radio part of the activity. Using props like microphones and headphones, each student takes a turn reading his or her passage to the other members of a group, perhaps imitating a D. J. or radio personality. The other students listen and then answer the reader's questions as if they were callers in on a radio talk show. According to Diamond and More (1995), the Radio City activity "creates a literate environment in which students' voices, as well as the author's are heard" (p. 118).

Albidaro and the Mischievous Dream by Julius Lester and Jerry Pinkney (2000) is a fanciful story about children dreaming that they can do anything they desire. After reading this book and discussing this story, the teacher or teacher librarian could lead the students in writing an imaginative class story. Each student could illustrate a section of the story. The class could follow up this activity by reading other imaginative stories.

TRADITIONAL LITERATURE

"Folktales ... offer an excellent opportunity to discuss accurately the history of Africans in America" (Kline, 1992, p. 13). Whereas folktales were first recorded in the late 1880s, Virginia Hamilton began the more recent African-American folktale trend with the publication of *The People Could Fly: American Black Folktales* (1985). Other collections, including popular animal stories, were followed by books about Brer Rabbit from the Uncle Remus stories written by Julius Lester. Jerry Pinkney and Julius Lester both wrote books with stories that originated in other parts of the world, but were reworked to include African-American characters and culture. Other artists wrote books with stories from their own childhoods. "The folktale revival ... continue[s] the emphasis on history and heritage" (Bishop, 1990, p. 560). This genre/theme includes books about not only traditional African stories but also folk tales, fables, myths, and legends from around the world. Table 5.6 lists African-American traditional literature.

Nina Crews' (2004) *The Neighborhood Mother Goose* takes the traditional Mother Goose stories and places them in a modern day Brooklyn neighborhood. After studying the illustrations, students could choose their favorite Mother Goose story and create their own unique illustration through drawing, painting, or photography. The teacher or teacher librarian could compile all of the stories into a book to be placed in the classroom or even the school library. Students could also take turns bringing the book home to share with their families.

Julius Lester's (1994) *John Henry*, which won a 1995 Newbery Honor Award, is an African-American tall tale about a great American hero who was capable of great feats, including the ability to cut through a mountain with a steam drill. This tale is enhanced by Jerry Pinkney's beautiful watercolors. After reading this tale, the teacher or teacher librarian could lead a discussion of the characteristics of tall tales. Students could then read other American tall tales, like Paul Bunyan, Pecos Bill, and Babe the Blue Ox and compare the heroes in these tales with John Henry. Once they are familiar with this type of story, students could then write their own tall tales.

SPIRITUALITY

Although it is still taboo and even sometimes professionally dangerous to bring up the subject of religion in our public schools, part of the multicultural movement is to push toward a more religiously pluralistic classroom and a more understanding and sensitive student population with regard to peoples' beliefs and cultural practices. Yet, there is nothing that makes parents squirm more than the idea of someone else's

Table 5.6.

Traditional Literature

Grade Level	Children's Book	Author	Year
Pre-K to Kindergarten	*The Baby Leopard*	Goss	1989
	Neighborhood Mother Goose	Crews	2004
	The Night Has Ears	Bryan	1999
	What a Truly Cool World	Lester	1999
	Leola and the Honey Bears	Rosales	1995
	The Lion and the Mouse	Pinkney	2009
	Many Colors of Mother Goose	Hudson	1997
Grades 1–3	*Mother Crocodile*	Diop/Guy	1981
	Afrotina and the Three Bears	Crump	1991
	Aesop's Tales	Koram	1992
	John Henry	Lester	1994
	Dragon Takes a Wife	Myers	1995
	Big Jabe	Nolen	2000
	Origin of Life on Earth	Anderson	1991
	Thunder Rose	Nolen	2003
	Way Up and Over Everything	McGill	2008
	The Princess and the Frog	Tarpley	2009
	The Six Fools	Hurston/Thomas	2005
	America's Promise	Powell	2003
Grades 4–6	*Mufaro's Beautiful Daughters*	Steptoe	1987
	Million Fish More or Less	McKissack	1992
	The Hunter Who Was King	Ford	1995
	Her Stories	Hamilton	1995
	The Girl Who Spun Gold	Hamilton	2000
	Aesop's Fables	Hudson	1997
	Lies and Other Tall Tales	Hurston/Thomas	2005
	Sure as Sunrise	McGill	2004

religious beliefs being taught in the classroom. Robert Nash and Penny Bishop have written quite extensively on the topic of incorporating religion and spirituality into the curriculum, and they argue that "pluralistic dialogue about religions and spiritualities in the classroom, as in the world-at-large, requires direct, give-and-take participation with all types of religious otherness. It insists that we allow the 'other' to get under our skins, to engage with us, to disturb us, and even, if the circumstances warrant, to *change* us" (Nash & Bishop, 2006, 31).Indeed, one of the most pernicious types of prejudice is religious prejudice. If left unchecked, religious prejudice can motivate people to do unthinkable things, and as Nash and Bishop state, "in an age marked by acts of terrorism throughout the world, largely based in extremist religious fundamentalisms of all kinds, a globally aware, religiously literate citizen needs to understand the meanings and content of the world's major and minor monotheistic and polytheistic religions" (Nash & Bishop, 2006, p. 32).

Although the majority of students in almost any American classroom will consider themselves to be Christian, there are differences amongst the various Christian denominations' beliefs and practices as well as the significance of those denominations to the communities that they represent. The Black church, for example, has been the one institution that has sustained African Americans throughout their long struggles to overcome slavery, Jim Crow, and other oppressive treatment. Many of the leaders in the Black community have been preachers or have been strongly connected to the Black church, for example, Martin Luther King, Jesse Jackson, Ralph Abernathy, Joseph Lowery, and Al Sharpton. The significant place that the Black church has in the community is different than the place that the church has in the white community. These differences can confuse young people and must be explored in honest and open dialogue at some point in their education. By carefully incorporating multicultural religious and spiritual literature into our curriculum and teaching all religions from an objective and unbiased perspective, we can teach our children to understand and celebrate our differences, preparing them for citizenship in a pluralistic society. Table 5.7 lists books that provide insight into spirituality in the African-American community.

Ashley Bryan (2007) applies his signature cut-paper collages to three traditional spiritual Christian hymns in his 2008 Coretta Scott King Award winning book *Let it Shine: Three Favorite Spirituals*. This picture book adaptation of "This Little Light of Mine," "Oh, When the Saints Go Marching In, " and "He's Got the Whole World in His Hands" would be perfect to be used in a music classroom and could easily be incorporated into a history lesson about the development of African-American music during the early years of our nation. Each page presents a colorful interpretation of several lines of each spiritual. Bryan includes the full songs with music notation at the end of the book along with a short note about the history of the pieces that he chose to use. This vibrant, musically inspired book will appeal to the artist and the musician alike and would serve as a great medium to begin a dialogue about the important place that music and religion have in the African-American community.

One of the great things about the songs that Bryan chose to use in his book *Let it Shine* is that although they are traditional Negro spirituals sung in African-American churches across the country, they are also popular hymns that are sung in all churches as well. Many Christian students will recognize these songs from their own churches and Sunday schools, and this could be a great opportunity for teachers to help students to recognize the similarities that we share as a multicultural community. As noted before, teachers could give a history lesson about slavery and the music created by early American Blacks. These songs were originally written and sung by slaves on plantations. Making the connection between the distant past and the songs with which we are familiar in the present should help students to better understand our history and the important place that African-American art has in our culture.

Julius Lester is a well known author of African-American children's books. His famous children's book, *To Be a Slave* (1968) established him as an important contributor to the African-American cannon. Lester is no stranger to the diverse world of religion. Having been born to a Methodist preacher and converting to Judaism later in life, Lester is a perfect author to use to explore the varying complexities of our different religions. Older students will enjoy Lester's (1999) humorous and creative reimagining of Genesis in his collection of short stories titled: *When the Beginning Began: Stories About God,*

Table 5.7.

Spirituality

Grade Level	Children's Book	Author	Year
Pre-K to Kindergarten	*Who Am I?*	Dulaney	1999
	Little Lumpy's Book of Blessings	Lewis	1998
	Sunday	Saint James	1996
	He Got the Whole World in His Hands	Nelson	2005
	God Smiles When	Hudson	2002
	This Little Light of Mine	Lewis	2005
Grades 1–3	*Rock of Ages*	Bolden	2001
	Madelia	Gilchrist	1997
	Come Sunday	Grimes	1996
	When Daddy Prays	Grimes	2002
	Sunday Week	Johnson	1999
	What a Truly Cool World	Lester	199
	Why Heaven Is Far Away	Lester	2002
	Prayers and Meditations for Little Angels	Nettles	1996
	God Inside of Me	Reese	1999
	Angels Watchin'	Rollins	2003
	Nobody Knows	Rollins	2003
	Heart For Jesus	Bynum	2005
	How Do Alligators Praise the Lord	Franklin	2005
	Three Kings and a Star	Crump	2005
	Bible Stories	Crump	2002
	The Other Little Angel	Crump	1994
	Stand For The Children	Edelman	1998
	Beloved One	Bray	2002
	Madelia	Gilchrist	1997
Grades 4–6	*Color Me Light Of the World*	Carter	1989
	To Everything There Is a Season	Dillon	1998
	African Heritage Short Stories	Jackson	2000
	Music from Our Lord's Holy Heaven	Pinkney	2005
	Lullabies to Dreamland	Williams	1993
	When the Beginning Began	Lester	1999
	I'm Your Child, God, Prayers	Edelman	2002
	Children of Color Storybook Bible	Fuller	1997
	The Creation	Johnson/Ransome	1994
	Let My People Go	McKissack	1998

The Creatures, and Us. In this creative and amusing collection, Lester blends his African-American Christian background with the Jewish tradition of midrashim, exploring the familiar biblical stories with humor and curiosity. Some more conservative Christians may find his irreverent reimagining offensive, but according to the Lester's introduction, "[r]egarding God with a loving irreverence is characteristic of African-American storytelling and is a tone that I have applied in stories about God throughout my career" (Lester, 1999, p. viii). Reading familiar stories presented in this way will help students to understand that different people regard God in different ways, and should help students make connections that will lead to a more pluralistic classroom.

The stories in *When the Beginning Began: Stories About God, The Creatures, And Us* (Lester, 1999) are written using the Jewish tradition of midrash, which according to Lester is a way of interpreting biblical text and commenting on the stories presented therein. According to Lester, "biblical stories eschew details. They say only what is needed to tell the story. Throughout Jewish history, rabbis and laypeople have created midrashim (plural) to answer such questions, and they continue to do so today" (p. vii). The idea of midrash would be a wonderful activity for a creative writing project and would also serve as a great opportunity for students to share the diversity of their various faiths. Students could be asked to bring in their favorite religious stories, perhaps presenting them to the class or small groups. Once each student has chosen a text, they could then be asked to compose questions about the unanswered questions that the text presents. Although this may be difficult for some students, it will be a good exercise in critical thinking. The questions that students compose can then be used as prompts for a piece of creative writing in which students reimagine their story, emulating Lester's style from the book.

Kadir Nelson's (2005) *He's Got the Whole World in His Hands* is a gorgeous depiction of one of the best known songs in the country. The book's illustrations show the connection among the people in the world. Students can create their own pictures showing the connection of the people around the world and put them on display around the room. The teacher or teacher librarian could also teach the students the words to the song and play a recording while the children sing along. There is a recording of Marian Anderson, a famous African-American opera singer, singing this song which would tie in well to this activity.

HISTORICAL PERSPECTIVES

Children's literature depicting the history of African Americans is powerful. Students can "relive the past vicariously" through characters and events brought to life in the text (Norton, Norton, & McClure, 2003, p. 412). "While reading multicultural books, they experience the joys of celebrations as well as the pain of conflict; they learn to comprehend the various perspectives of people who are players in these events" (Diamond & Moore, 1995, p. 225). When African-American students are given the opportunity to study their own history, they come to better understand past conflicts and achievements. These students also develop a feeling of pride in their heritage, which is incredibly important for any child. Other students learn to appreciate the struggles and accomplishments that African Americans have experienced. They also have the opportunity to see how diverse people have worked together to overcome obstacles. This theme includes books about important events and people in history. Table 5.8 lists books related to this theme.

The book *Our People* by Angela Shelf Medearis (1994) presents the history of the people of Africa throughout the years. A follow-up activity could provide the opportunity for

Table 5.8.

Historical Perspectives

Grade Level	Children's Book	Author	Year
Pre-K to Kindergarten	*Our People*	Medearis	1994
	Kumi and Chanti	Johnson	1992
	Little Zend's ABCs	Hall	1993
	Amazing Adventures of ABIOLA	Dean	1994
	Girls of Our People	George	1995
Grades 1–3	*March On!*	Farris	2008
	Now Let Me Fly	Johnson	1993
	I Have Heard of a Land	Thomas	1995
	Grandpa, Is Everything Black Bad?	Holman	1998
	Show Way	Woodson	2005
	A Sweet Smell of Roses	Johnson	2005
	Patchwork Path	Stroud	2007
	Dinner at Aunt Connie's House	Ringgold	1993
	If a Bus Could Talk	Ringgold	1999
	Martha Ann's Quilt for Queen Victoria	Hicks	2007
	I'll Fly My Own Plane	Elster	2002
	An Apple for Harriet Tubman	Turner	2006
	A Children's Story of Los Angeles	Lewis	2002
	Goin' Someplace Special	McKissack	2001
	Remember	Morrison	2004
Grades 4–6	*Dancing with the Indians*	Medearis	1991
	The Friendship	Taylor	1987
	Through My Eyes	Bridges	1999
	Sweet Words So Brave	Brodie/Butler	1996
	From Slave Ship to Freedom Road	Lester	1998
	We Troubled the Waters	Shange	2009
	Walking to the Bus-Rider Blues	Robinet	2002
	The Tallest Tree	Belton	2008
	Boycott Blues	Pinkney	2008
	Child Out of Place	Wall	2004
	Sienna's Scrapbook	Parker	2005

the students to learn more about the inventors mentioned in the story. The teacher or teacher librarian could read stories about Garrett Morgan and Lewis Howard Latimer. Students could then draw or create their own inventions and share them with the class.

A Sweet Smell of Roses by Angela Johnson (2005) presents the Civil Rights Movement through the eyes of children. A follow-up activity to this book could be for the students to complete a sketch-to-stretch based on their feelings and thoughts on the main points of the story. Sketch-to-stretch is an activity developed by Harste, Short, and Burke (1988) that invites students to first visualize how a text makes them feel and then draw or sketch the image in their mind. The students could share their sketches with the whole class and discuss them. The teacher or teacher librarian could conclude the activity by discussing how not only adults, but also children and youth, were involved in the Civil Rights Movement. Students could then discuss whether or not they would participate in a freedom march and reflect on how that would make them feel.

For older students studying American history, Ntozake Shange (2009) has written an inspiring collection of 18 poems in *We Troubled the Waters: Poems* that tell the story of the Civil Rights movement, beginning with the Booker T. Washington School in 1941 and ending at the march on Washington in 1963. Shange's free verse poems accurately reflect life in the South during this period and coupled with the powerful and disturbing oil paintings by Rod Brown, this picture book packs an emotional punch that will shake up children and adults alike.

Choral reading is a great practice to use to teach poetry in the classroom. In preparation for a choral reading, it is often helpful for the teacher to model reading the poem for the class. This is especially important for poetry that follows irregular patterns and phrasing. Students will have a better understanding of how to recite and understand the free verse poems from *We Troubled the Waters: Poems* (Shange, 2009) if the teacher or teacher librarian reads the poems first, asking questions like: What parts of this poem did I read loudly and softly? Why do you think I did this? Where did I pause? Why? and so on. An effective mode of choral reading is to divide the class in half and assign each group different parts of the poem to read aloud. After each team practices their parts several times, the groups should read together passing their parts back and forth as they recite the poem as a whole. Diamond and Moore (1995) observed that choral reading instills students with feelings of pride and success, and they also point out that reluctant readers are less apprehensive about participating when everyone reads at the same time.

HOLIDAYS AND SPECIAL DAYS

Without a doubt, one of the most important dates in the history of the United States is June 19, 1865. On this day Union soldiers arrived in Galveston, Texas, and announced the end of the Civil War and delivered a general order freeing the state's 250,000 slaves. Although the Emancipation Proclamation had been announced over two years earlier, many states still continued the practice of slavery, disregarding the proclamation and ultimately sending our nation into civil war. Texas was the last of these states to fall in line, and on June 19, 1865, the last American slaves were freed from the bonds of slavery. Commemorating this important event in American history is the annual holiday, Juneteenth. Also known as Freedom Day or Emancipation Day, Juneteenth is a state holiday in 32 states and is celebrated through public readings of the Emancipation Proclamation, parades, street fairs, cookouts, family reunions, and other celebrations of American heritage. Although this holiday, which has been celebrated for over 100 years, is meant to be a celebration for all, it is still thought of by many today as an African-American holiday and is only officially observed in 32 of the 50 states. Also, because of the lack of publicity and governmental support, many communities may be completely unaware of this celebration.

Juneteenth is just one example of an important celebration that goes unnoticed by many because of ignorance and misunderstanding. Part of living in a pluralistic society is understanding and participating in holidays and celebrations that may not traditionally be observed by our own family or community. That is why it is imperative that we expose the important celebrations of our diverse populations to our children by integrating them into the curriculum of our schools. Table 5.9 lists books that describe African-American holidays and special days.

Doreen Rappaport's (2002) highly celebrated pictorial biography of Martin Luther King Jr., with its breathtaking watercolor collage illustrations by Brian Collier, is the

Table 5.9.
Holidays and Special Days

Grade Level	Children's Book	Author	Year
Pre-K to Kindergarten	*Hugs and Hearts*	Parker	2002
	Painted Eggs and Chocolate Bunnies	Parker	2002
	Sweets and Treats	Parker	2002
	Parker	Medina	2008
	Christmas Makes Me Think	Nelson	2001
	Juneteenth (On My Own Holidays)	Greenfield	1996
	Waiting for Christmas	Chocolate	1992
	My First Book of Kwanzaa	Saint James	1994
	Kwanzaa Teddy	Ball	2001
	Birthday	Steptoe	1972
	Lulu's Birthday	Howard	2001
	Flower Girl Butterflies	Howard	2004
	The Wedding	Johnson	1999
	Glo Goes Shopping	Hudson	1999
	Amazing Peace	Angelou	2008
	Snowflake Kisses & Gingerbread Smiles	Parker	2002
Grades 1–3	*The Legend of Valentine*	Bond	2001
	Super Fine Valentine	Cosby	1998
	Easter Parade	Greenfield	1998
	Juneteenth (Holiday Histories)	Jordan	2003
	Juneteenth Jamboree	Weatherford	1995
	Jenny Reen and the Jack Muh Lantern	Small	1996
	Christmas Soul	Samuels/Wood	2001
	Celie and the Harvest Fiddle	Flournoy	1995
	A Strawbeater's Thanksgiving	Smalls	1998
	Under the Christmas Tree	Grimes	2002
	Mim's Christmas Jam	Pinkney	2001
	Hold Christmas in Your Heart	Hudson	1995
	K is for Kwanzaa	Ford	1997
	Together for Kwanzaa	Ford	2000

(*continued*)

Table 5.9. (continued)

Grade Level	Children's Book	Author	Year
	A Very Special Kwanzaa	Chocolate	1996
	Santa's Kwanzaa	Thomas	2004
	Just Right Stew	English	1998
	Uh-Oh! It's Mama's Birthday	Thomas	1997
Grades 4–6	*Happy Easter, Everyone*	Morton	2003
	Juneteenth: Freedom Day	Branch	1998
	The Birthday Storm	Draper	2009
	Juneteenth: Celebration of Freedom	Taylor	2002
	The Bells of Christmas	Hamilton	1997
	Freedom's Gifts: Juneteenth Story	Wesley	1997
	Poppa's Itchy Christmas	Medearis	1998
	The Black Snowman	Mendez	1989
	Addy's Surprise: A Christmas Story	Porter	1993
	Complete Kwanzaa Celebration Book	Robertson	1993
	It's Kwanzaa Time	Goss	1995
	The Story of Kwanzaa	Washington	1995
	The Children's Book of Kwanzaa	Johnson	1997
	Jumping the Broom	Wright	1994

kind of book that should occupy shelf space in every single elementary classroom in the country. The recipient of both the Caldecott Honor and Coretta Scott King Awards, *Martin's Big Words*, employs excerpts from Dr. King's own speeches to tell the story of the life of one of our countries greatest civil rights leaders. Rappaport's simple biographical prose, intermingled with King's own words, is accompanied by Collier's symbolic stained glass window; his inspired illustrations are a montage of watercolors and paper-cut collages. Although this kind of book is perfect to be used in lessons on and around Martin Luther King Day, teachers should be teaching this kind of literature throughout the year. Students should think of holidays like Martin Luther King Day as celebrations of civil progress not just the day that they read books about important civil rights heroes. *Martin's Big Words* (Rappaport, 2002), with its focus on the oratory of Dr. King, presents an excellent opportunity for young students to begin learning about the art of public speaking. This picture book would fit perfectly into a unit on civil rights or minority oppression, helping to build a dialogue in the classroom about the social ills that plague our nation. After reading books like these and listening to and watching some of Dr. King's important speeches, the teacher or teacher librarian can provide students with guided questions about how they feel about racism, bigotry, and social injustice. These potent topics should make it easy for students to form the kinds of strong opinions and ideas that lead to good speeches. Once the questions have been answered, the teacher can help students to work their answers into fixed-format speech that can be delivered in front of the class, or perhaps at a school-wide Martin Luther King Day celebration.

Roles:

Passage Master: Selects passages from the book that the group is to read aloud. This student must prioritize the most important passages from each chapter.

Discussion Director: Develops a list of questions that the group will discuss about this book. Questions should be open ended, helping students to think about the big picture as opposed to the little details.

Word Master: Chooses new or unfamiliar words from the text, defines them and uses them in a sentence. Helps the group to build vocabulary fluency.

Illustrator: Draws a picture related to the reading.

Connector: Finds connections between the book and the world outside.

Summarizer: Prepares a synopsis of today's reading.

Travel Tracker: Carefully tracks where the action is happening in today's reading. Uses visual aids like maps to show what is happening in the story geographically by describing where certain key events took place.

Story Mapper: Maps today's reading using a graphic organizer. Students can use any organizer such as: character maps, story elements maps, or Venn diagrams.

Figure 5.3.
Literature Circle Roles

Older students who are studying the history of post Civil War reconstruction will love Ann Rinaldi's (2007) historical novel, *Come Juneteenth*. This exciting tale of friendship, revolving around the actual official end of slavery, is a wonderful way to expose students to this important historical event. Fourteen year-old Luli Holcomb, the daughter of a Texas plantation owner is best friends with Sis Goose, a young mulatto girl who, despite her technical status as a slave, has been raised as a part of the family. Luli finds herself caught in a very difficult place when she learns that two years earlier, President Lincoln emancipated the slaves, and although the nation is still involved in a civil war, the slaves at the plantation are technically free. Luli must choose between family and friendship. This book is quite unapologetic in its descriptions of the harsh realities of the time period, and teachers should be aware that the book does contain some violence, language, and sexual content.

Creating and maintaining an open and ongoing dialogue about the kinds of themes presented in *Come Juneteenth* (Rinaldi, 2007) is the goal of teaching multicultural literacy. Literature circles is a great strategy to employ to help encourage students to have this kind of dialogue, and it is especially effective when teaching a novel, or longer work of fiction. With this strategy, students take on different roles (see Figure 5.3), such as discussion leader, vocabulary enricher, summarizer, and investigator and meet in small groups to discuss the novel one chapter at a time. Students periodically switch roles and, thereby, learn to approach the story from varied angles and perspectives, helping them to understand the multifaceted nature of long works of fiction.

Amazing Peace: A Christmas Poem by Maya Angelou (2008) depicts people of different races and beliefs gathering together to celebrate peace during the holidays. Before reading the book, the teacher should assess the students' background knowledge and understanding of the word "peace." While reading the story, the teacher or teacher librarian could help the students identify peace in the text and in the illustrations. After reading, the teacher could lead a potentially powerful discussion about the diverse beliefs and backgrounds of people and the notion that rather than separating us, bring us together. Students would also have the opportunity to learn about the different holidays that take place during December through other books. The class could conclude the activity by hosting a peace party.

BIOGRAPHIES AND AUTOBIOGRAPHIES

In the mid-twentieth century, African-American children's books were either novels or biographies (Kline, 1992). Biographies about African Americans illustrate obstacles that lie in the way of becoming successful but also show that it is possible to overcome these obstacles. They particularly offer positive role models that demonstrate how to

Table 5.10.
Biographies and Autobiographies

Grade Level	Children's Book	Author	Year
Pre-K to Kindergarten	*Visiting Langston*	Perdomo	2002
	Before John Was a Jazz Giant	Weatherford	2008
	Harriet in the Promised Land	Lawrence	1968
	A Lesson For Martin Luther King	Patrick	2003
	The Empak Heratige Kids	Johnson	1992
Grades 1–3	*Tommy, Traveler/ World of Black History*	Feelings	1991
	Coming Home	Cooper	1994
	Dear Benjamin	Pinkney	1994
	Moses	Weatherford	2006
	More than Anything Else	Bradby	1995
	Malcolm X	Myers	2000
	My Brother Martin	Farris	2003
	Rosa	Giovanni	2005
	Explore Black History	Turner	1998
	Testing the Ice	Robinson	2009
	Coretta A. Scott	Shange	2009
	Ida B. Wells	Myers	2008
	Bridget "Biddy" Mason	Williams/Ford	2005
	Molly Bannaky	McGill	1999
	Young Martin's Promise	Myers	1993
Grades 4–6	*When Harriet Met Sojourner*	Clinton	2007
	I, Mathew Henson	Weatherford	2008
	Langston Hughes	Walker	2002
	Five Great Explorers	Hudson	1995
	Toussant L'Ouverture	Myers	1996
	Talkin' About Bessie	Grimes	2002
	George Washington Carver	Bolden	2008
	I and I–Bob Marley	Medina	2009
	Freedom Light Sunlight	Lewis	2000
	Yes We Can	Thomas	2008
	From Slave to Civil War Hero	Cooper	1994
	Bad News for Outlaws	Nelson	2009

deal with prejudice and oppression. Biographies aid children in understanding how individuals have shaped history and made contributions to our world (Sunanon Webster & Saine, 2007). They are a powerful literary tool in helping to inform and inspire young African-American readers. Authors have written numerous biographies about famous and not so famous African Americans in recent years. Biographies written about more well-known individuals include: Martin Luther King, Jr., Malcolm X, Sojourner Truth, and Rosa Parks. However, authors have also written books about Matthew Henson, Molly Bannaky, and Bridget Biddy Mason. Table 5.10 lists biographies and autobiographies of African Americans.

Lawrence's (1968) *Harriet in the Promised Land* is a biography written as a poem. This book's beautiful illustrations show the mood of the people based on their faces and body language. The teacher or teacher librarian could give background information on Jacob Lawrence and his illustrations as a pre-reading activity. While reading, the teacher could stop on each page and have the students identify the feelings of the characters in the illustrations. The teacher could ask the students to explain why the slaves in the pictures feel the way they do and provide background information about the lives of slaves throughout reading the book.

More Than Anything Else by Marie Bradby (1995) is a picture book biography of Booker T. Washington which has beautifully illustrated paintings by Chris Soentpiet. This book emphasizes Washington's passionate desire to learn how to read, despite the limited opportunities for schooling in his early years. After reading this book, students could generate questions about Booker T. Washington, such as: Why did he have to work in the salt mines? Why didn't he have the opportunity to attend school? Why was he so motivated to learn how to read? The teacher could then provide nonfiction books and Internet sources for the students to research the answers to their questions. To complete the activity, students could write unsent letters to Booker T. Washington describing what interested them about his life and his accomplishments and asking questions about his life not found in their research.

CONCLUSION

The books described in this chapter are just a sampling of the wonderful literature that has been written describing the African-American experience in a positive and authentic manner. These books enrich the lives of children, teachers, librarians, and parents. We encourage all librarians, teachers, parents, and students to explore their school libraries, public libraries, and neighborhood bookstores to search for books written by African-American authors that depict and illustrate the rich and varied experiences of the African-American culture.

APPENDIX A
TIMELINE OF AFRICAN AMERICAN CHILDREN'S LITERATURE

Year   Publication/Historical Event

1746   "Bars Fight" by Lucy Terry. The first poem written by a 16-year-old slave in Deerfield, Mass. Not published until 1895.

1767   "On Messrs. Hussey and Coffin." First poem published by 14 year old Phillis Wheatley in Newport Mercury newspaper. Chronicles their remarkable survival in a hurricane off Cape Cod.

1768   "On Being Brought from Africa to America." Poem written by 15-year-old Phillis Wheatley.

1773   *Poems on Various Subjects: Religious and Moral* by Phillis Wheatley. The first book published by an African American.

1887   *The Joy*, an eight page monthly magazine with poems, short stories and articles edited by Mrs. Amelia E. Johnson. First African American to write Sunday School fiction. First secular publication produced by an African American writer for children.

1888   *The Ivy*, second magazine for children edited by Mrs. Amelia E. Johnson.

1889   *Clarence and Corinne or God's Way* by Amelia E. Johnson. First African American woman to publish a novel for children.

      An Alphabet for Negro Children, Leila A Pendleton

1890   *Morning Glories*, Josephine Henderson Heard. A book of poems.

1893   *Aunt Lindy*, Victoria Earle Matthews

1894   *The Hazeley Family*, Amelia E. Johnson

1895   *Little Brown Baby*, Paul Lawrence Dunbar. A collection of dialect poetry

1905   *Floyd's Flowers or Duty and Beauty for Colored Children*, Silas X. Floyd

1913   *A Child's Story of Dunbar*, Julia L. Henderson

1916   *The Colored Girl Beautiful*, Madame E. Azalia Hackley. An etiquette book.

1920   *Brownie's Book*, a magazine edited by W. E. B. DuBois, Augustus G. Dill and Jessie Faust

      The Upward Path, Myron T. Pritchard and Mary Ovington. A reader for colored children.

      First Steps and Nursery Rhymes, Monroe A. Major

1921   *Unsung Heroes*, Elizabeth Ross Haynes

      The Negro Speaks of Rivers, Langston Hughes. His first nationally published poem.

1922   *The Negro in Our History*, Carter G. Woodson for high school and college students.

1928   *Negro Makers of History*, Carter G. Woodson, for elementary students.

      African Myths Together with Proverbs, Carter G. Woodson

      For Freedom, Arthur Fauset

1932   *Dream Keeper*, Langston Hughes. One of the first classics of original African American poems selected for children.

      Popo and Fifina: Children of Haiti, Langston Hughes and Arna Bontemps

1934   *You Can't Pet a Possum*, Arna Bontemps

1935   *Picture Poetry Book*, Gertrude Parthenia McBrown

1936   *We Sing America*, Marion Cuthbert

1937   *Sad Faced Boy*, Arna Bontemps. First Harlem story for children.

1938   *The Family*, Evangeline Harris Merriweather

      A Children's Story of the Negro, Jane Dabney Shackelford

      Negro Art, Music, and Rhymes for Young Folks, Helen A. Whiting

1939   *African Heroes and Heroines*, Carter G. Woodson

      Negro Folk Tales for Pupils in the Primary Grade, Helen A. Whiting

1940   *Little Brown Baby, Poems for Young People*, Paul Lawrence Dunbar/Bertha Rodgers

      Gladiola Garden, Effie Lee Newsome

      Stories for Little Tots, Evangeline Harris Merriweather

      Janie Bell, Ellen Tarry. One of first African American to produce picture books.

      The Lost Zoo, Countee Cullen. Book of poetry.

1941   *Golden Slippers*, Arna Bontemps. First complete anthology of poetry for children featuring African American poets.

      Word Pictures of the Great, Geneva Turner, Jessie Roy

      We Build Together, Charlemae Rollins

1942   *Hezekiah Horton*, Ellen Tarry. One of the first picture storybooks to be both written and illustrated by African Americans.

      The Fast Sooner Hound, Arna Bontemps

      My Lives and How Fast I Lost Them, Countee Cullen

1944 *Happy Days*, Jane Dabney Shackelford
Play Songs of the Deep, Altona Trent Johns
Dr. George Washington Carver: Scientist, Shirley Graham
1945 *Call Me Charley*, Jesse Jackson
Child Play Magazine, Negro Story Press
Negro Makers in History, Carter G. Woodson
We Have Tomorrow, Arna Bontemps
1946 *My Dog Rinty*, Ellen Tarry/ Mary Hall. A landmark picture book in African American children's fiction.
Tales of Momolu, Lorenz Graham. His first book for children.
1947 *Jasper, the Drummin' Boy*, Margaret Taylor Burroughs
Anchor Man, Jesse Jackson
1948 *The Story of the Negro*, Arna Bontemps. The first African American author to win a Newbery Honor Book award (1949).
1949 *The Drugstore Cat*, Ann Petry
The Story of Phillis Wheatley, Shirley Graham
1952 *The First Book of Negroes*, Langston Hughes.
The Runaway Elephant, Ellen Tarry
1953 *Jean Baptiste Pointe De Sable: Founder of Chicago*, Shirley Graham
1954 *The Story of George Washington Carver*, Arna Bontemps
The First Book of Rhythms, Langston Hughes
Harriet Tubman: Conductor on the Underground Railroad, Ann Petry
1955 *Lonesome Boy*, Arna Bontemps
Booker T. Washington: Educator of Hand, Head and Heart, Shirley Graham
The First Book of Jazz, Langston Hughes
1956 *Bronzeville Boys and Girls*, Gwendolyn Brooks
Did you Feed My Cow? Margaret Taylor Burroughs
The Child's Story of the Negro, Jane Shackelford
The Story of the Negro, Arna Bontemps
The First Book of the West Indies, Langston Hughes
1957 *South Town*, Lorenz Graham
Room for Randy, Jesse Jackson
1958 *Charley Starts From Scratch*, Jesse Jackson
George Washington Carver, Henry Thomas
1959 *Frederick Douglass: Slave, Fighter, Freeman*, Arna Bontemps
1960 *The First Book of Africa*, Langston Hughes
1964 *Tituba of Salem Village*, Ann Petry
Whip Me, Whop Me Pudding and Other Stories, Margaret Taylor Burroughs
Christmas Gif', Charlemae Rollins
The Adventures of Spiders, Joyce Arkhurst
1966 *I, Momolu*, Lorenz Graham
1967 *We Read: A to Z*, Donald Crews
Zeely, Virginia Hamilton
Young Jim, Early Years of James Weldon Johnson, Ellen Tarry
1968 *Harriet and the Promise Land*, Jacob Lawrence. Most well known picture book about slavery.
To Be A Slave, Julius Lester. The second African American author to win a Newbery Honor Book award.
What Shall I Tell My Children Who Are Black?, Margaret Taylor Burroughs
The Soul Brothers and Sister Lou, Kristin Hunter
The House of Dies Drear, Virginia Hamilton
Tessie, Jesse Jackson

1969   *Lillie of Watts*, Mildred Pitts Walter
        Who Look at Me?, June Jordan
        Stevie, John Steptoe. A breakthrough contemporary African American picture book.
        Time-Ago: Tales of Jahdu, Virginia Hamilton
        Where Does the Day Go?, Walter Dean Myers
        A Quiet Place, Rose Blue
        Black Misery, Langston Hughes
        A is for Africa, Jean Carey Bond
        Brown Is A Beautiful Color, Jean Carey Bond
        Black American Leaders, Margaret B. Young
1970   *The Black ABC's*, Lucille Clifton
        Black Troubadour, Langston Hughes/Charlemae Rollins. The 1971 Coretta Scott King, Author Award Winner.
        Some of the Days of Everette Anderson, Lucille Clifton. First of Everette Anderson books.
        Zamani Goes to Market, Muriel and Tom Feelings
        Poems by Kali, Kali Grosvenor
        Uptown, John Steptoe
        Tessie Keeps Her Cool, Jesse Jackson
        I Wish I Had an Afro, John Shearer
        Young Hand in Mine, Sam Cornish
        Mr. Kelso's Lion, Arna Bontemps
        The Picture of Life of Thurgood Marshall, Margaret B. Young
        The Voice of Children, June Jordan
        Coretta Scott King Book Award established
1971   *Moja Means One*, Muriel and Tom Feelings. First African American illustrator to win Caldcott Honor Award.
        It's a New Day, Sonia Sanchez
        Spin a Soft Black Song, Nikki Giovanni
        Ego Tripping and Other Poems for Young People, Nikki Giovanni
        Sidewalk Story, Sharon Bell Mathis
        Colors Around Me, Vivian Church
        Everette Anderson's Christmas Coming, Lucille Clifton
        More Adventures of Spider, Joyce Arkhurst
1972   *The Dragon Takes a Wife*, Walter Dean Myers
        Bubbles, Eloise Greenfield. First book
        Birthday, John Steptoe
        Walk On!, Mel Williams
        Glowchild and Other Poems, Ruby Dee
        The Knee-High Man and Other Tales, Julius Lester
        Little Zeng's ABC's, Chris Hall
1973   Ebony Jr. Magazine created by Johnson Publishing Co., the only African American magazine to follow The Brownies Book.
        Na-Ni, Alexis DeVeaux
        Abby, Jeanette Caines
        Ray Charles, Sharon Bell Mathis
        Good, Says Jerome, Lucille Clifton
        The Adventures of Fathead, Smallhead and Squarehead, Sonia Sanchez
        All Us Come Cross the Water, Lucille Clifton
        The Boy Who Didn't Believe in Spring, Lucille Clifton
        Don't You Remember?, Lucille Clifton
        Everette Anderson's Friend, Lucille Clifton

Lordy Aunt Hattie, Ianthe Thomas
J. D., Mari Evans
Don't Ride the Bus on Monday: Rosa Parks, Louise Meriwether
1974 *The Tiger Who Wore White Gloves*, Gwendolyn Brooks
She Comes Bringing Me That Little Girl, Eloise Greenfield
M. C. Higgins the Great, Virginia Hamilton. First African American author to win the Newbery Medal Award.
My Special Best Words, John Steptoe
Fly Jimmy Fly, Walter Dean Myers
Walk Together Children: Black American Spirituals, Ashley Bryan
Jambo Means Hello, Muriel and Tom Feelings
The Times They Used to Be, Lucille Clifton
Sister, Eloise Greenfield
I Look at Me, Mari Evans
The Legend of Africania, Dorothy Robinson. The 1975 Coretta Scott King, Author Award Winner.
Walk Home Tired Billy Jenkins, Inathe Thomas
New Life: New Room, June Jordan
Langston Hughes: American Poet, Alice Walker
1975 *Song of the Boat*, Lorenz Graham
Me and Neesie, Eloise Greenfield
My Brother Fine With Me, Lucille Clifton
My Daddy Is a Cool Dude and Other Poems, Karama Fufuka
Song of the Trees, Mildred Taylor
The Hundred Penny Box, Sharon Bell Mathis
1976 *Little Man, Little Man: A Story of Childhood*, James Baldwin
Yesterday I Climbed a Mountain, Margery W. Brown
The Adventures of Aku, Ashley Bryan
The First Pink Light, Eloise Greenfield
Eliza's Daddy, Ianthe Thomas
My Daddy's People, Sam Cornish
The Story of Stevie Wonder, James Haskins
Jay and the Marigold, Harriette G. Robinet
Roll of Thunder, Hear My Cry. Mildred Taylor
My Streets a Morning Cool Street, Ianthe Thomas
Ashanti to Zulu, Margaret Musgrove
1977 *Amifika*, Lucille Clifton
African Dream, Eloise Greenfield. The 1978 Coretta Scott King, Author Award Winner.
Daddy, Jeanette Caines
Everett Anderson's 1-2-3, Eloise Greenfield
The Dancing Granny, Ashley Bryan
Good News, Eloise Greenfield
Coretta Scott King, Lillie Patterson
1978 *Honey I Love*, Eloise Greenfield
I Greet the Dawn: Poems by Paul Lawrence Dunbar, Ashley Bryan
The Best Time of Day, Valerie Flournoy
The Twins Strike Back, Valerie Flournoy
Singing Black, Mari Evans
Talk About a Family, Eloise Greenfield
Something on My Mind, Nikki Grimes
I Can Do It By Myself, Lessie Jones Little/Eloise Greenfield
Freight Train, Donald Crews

Everett Anderson's Nine Months Long, Lucille Clifton
Rain, Donald Crews
Escape to Freedom: A Play About Young Frederick F. Douglass, Ossie Davis. The 1980
Coretta Scott King, Author Award Winner.
Jennifer's New Chair, Charles Bible
Benjamin Banneker: Genus of Early America, Lillie Patterson
1979   *Cornrows*, Camille Yarbrough
The Lucky Stone, Lucille Clifton
Hi, Mrs. Mallory, Ianthe Thomas
Jim Flying High, Mari Evans

REFERENCES

Adoff, A., & Cook, K. (Eds.). (2010). *Virginia Hamilton: Speeches, essays, and conversations.* New York, NY: The Blue Sky Press.

Alexander, E. (2005) "An interview with Rita Dove." *The Writers Chronicle, 38*(2), 4–12.

Andrews, W., Foster, F. S., & Harris, T. (Eds.). (2001). *The Oxford companion to African American literature.* New York, NY: Oxford University Press.

Appiah, K. A., & Gates, H. L. (Eds.) (1999). *Africana: The encyclopedia of the African and African American experience.* New York, NY: Basic Civitas Books.

Bishop, R. S. (1990). Walk tall in the world: African American literature for today's children. *Journal of Negro Education, 59*(4), 556–565.

Brooks, W., & McNair, J. C. (2009). "But this story of mine is not unique": A review of research on African American children's literature. *Review of Educational Research, 79*(1), 125–162.

Cooperative Children's Book Center. (2010). Children's Books by and About People of Color Published in the United States. Statistics Gathered by the Cooperative Children's Book Center, School of Education, University of Wisconsin-Madison. Retrieved from Cooperative Children's Book Center, School of Education, University of Wisconsin-Madison http://www.education.wisc.edu/ccbc/books/pcstats.htm.

Diamond, B. J., & Moore, M. A. (1995). *Multicultural literacy: Mirroring the reality of the classroom.* White Plains, NY: Longman Publishers.

Harste, J. C., Short, K. G., & Burke, C. (1988). *Creating classrooms for authors: The reading-writing connection.* Portsmouth, NH: Heinemann.

Hefflin, B. R., & Barksdale-Ladd, M. A. (2001). African American children's literature that helps students find themselves: Selection guidelines for grades K–3. *The Reading Teacher, 54*(8), 810–819.

Johnson-Feelings, D., (Ed.). (1996). *The best of the Brownies' Book.* New York, NY: Oxford University Press.

Kline, L. (1992). *African-American children's literature.* ED#355520 Retrieved from ERIC, www. eric.ed.gov.

Lynch-Brown, C., & Tomlinson, C. M. (2008). *Essentials of children's literature*, 6th ed. Boston, MA: Pearson Education.

Manning, M. L., & Baruth, L. G. (2009). *Multicultural education of children and adolescents*, 5th ed. Boston, MA: Pearson Education.

Massachusetts Historical Society (2010, May 15). African Americans and the end of slavery in Massachusetts. Retrieved from http://www.masshist.org/endofslavery/?queryID=57.

McMillon, G., & McMillon, R. (2004). The empowering literacy practices of an African American church. In F. B. Boyd and C. H. Brock (Eds.), *Multicultural and multilingual literacy and language contexts and practices* (pp. 280–303). New York, NY: Guilford Press.

Myers, D. G., & Jeeves, M. A. (1987). *Psychology through the eyes of faith*. San Francisco, CA: Harper & Row.

Nash, R., & Bishop, P. (2006). Teaching adolescents about religious pluralism in a post-9/11 world. *Religion and Education, 33*(1) pp. 26–47.

Norton, D. E., Norton, S. E., & McClure, A. (2003). *Through the eyes of a child: An introduction to children's literature*, 6th ed. Upper Saddle River, NJ: Merrill/Prentice Hall.

Ogle, D. M. (1986). K-W-L: A teaching model that develops active reading of expository text. *The Reading Teacher, 39*(6), 564–570.

Sims, R. (1982). *Shadow & substance: Afro-American experience in contemporary children's fiction*. Urbana, IL: National Council of Teachers of English.

Sunanon Webster, P. P., & Saine, P. (2007). Reading strategies to enhance comprehension of informational books and biographies of African American heroes of the American Revolution. *Ohio Social Studies Review*, 43(1).

LITERATURE FOR CHILDREN AND YOUNG ADULTS

Angelou, M. (2008). *Amazing peace: A Christmas poem*. New York, NY: Random House.

Bontemps, A. (1948). *Story of the Negro*, illustrated by R. Lufkin. New York, NY: Knopf.

Bradby, M. (1995). *More than anything else*, illustrated by C. K. Soentpiet. New York, NY: Orchard Books.

Brooks, G. (2007). *Bronzeville boys and girls*, illustrated by F. Ringgold. New York, NY: Amistad/HarperCollins. (Original work published, 1956.)

Bryan, A. (2003). *Beautiful blackbird*. New York, NY: Atheneum Books for Young Readers.

Bryan, A. (2007). *Let it shine: Three favorite spirituals*. New York, NY: Atheneum Books for Young Readers.

Crews, D. (1984). *School bus*. New York, NY: Greenwillow Books.

Crews, N. (2004). *The neighborhood Mother Goose*. New York, NY: Greenwillow Books.

Curtis, C. P. (1999). *Bud, not Buddy*. New York, NY: Delacorte Press.

Fitzgerald Howard, E. (1999). *Virgie goes to school with us boys*, illustrated by E. B. Lewis. New York, NY: Simon & Schuster Books for Young Readers.

Giovanni, N. (2008). *Hip hop speaks to children: A celebration of poetry with a beat*, illustrated by A. Vergel de Dios, D. Ward, K. Balouch, J. Tuqeau, & M. Noiset. Naperville, IL: Sourcebooks Jabberwocky.

Grimes, N. (2006). *Welcome, precious*, illustrated by B. Collier. New York, NY: Orchard Books.

Hamilton, V. (1974). *M.C. Higgins, the great*. New York, NY: Simon & Schuster.

Hamilton, V. (1985). *The people could fly: American Black folktales*, illustrated by L. & D. Dillon. New York, NY: Knopf.

Hughes, L. (2009a). *My people*, photographs by Charles R. Smith Jr. New York: Atheneum Books for Young Readers.

Hughes, L. (2009b). *The Negro speaks of rivers*, illustrated by E. B. Lewis. New York: Hyperion Books for Children.

Johnson, A. (2005). *A sweet smell of roses*, illustrated by E. Velasquez. New York, NY: Simon & Schuster Books for Young Readers.

Johnson, D. (2007). *Hair dance!* photographs by K. Johnson. New York, NY: Henry Holt.

Lawrence, J. (1968). *Harriet in the promised land*. New York, NY: Windmill Books.

Lester, J. (1968). *To be a slave*, paintings by Tom Feelings. New York, NY: Puffin Books.

Lester, J. (1994). *John Henry*, illustrated by J. Pinkney. New York, NY: Dial Books.

Lester, J. (1999). *When the beginning began: Stories about God, the creatures and us*, illustrated by Emily Lisker. San Diego, CA: Silver Whistle.

Lester, J. & Pinkney, J. (2000). *Albidaro and the mischievous dream*. New York, NY: P. Fogelman Books.

Lester, J. (2005). *The old African*, illustrated by Jerry Pinkney. New York, NY: Dial Books.

Nelson, K. (2005). *He's got the whole world in his hands*. New York, NY: Dial Books.

Nelson, V. M. (2009) *Who will I be, Lord?* illustrated by Sean Qualls. New York, NY: Random House.

Pinkney, S. L. (2000). *Shades of black: A celebration of our children*, photographs by M. Pinkney. New York, NY: Scholastic.

Rappaport, D. (2002). *Martin's big words*, illustrated by Bryan Collier. New York, NY: Jump at the Sun Books.

Rinaldi, A. (2007). *Come Juneteenth*. Orlando, FL: Harcourt Children's Books.

Shange, N. (2009). *We troubled the waters: poems*, illustrated by Rod Brown. New York, NY: Amistad/Collins.

Shelf Medearis, A. (1994). *Our people*, illustrated by M. Bryant. New York, NY: Atheneum.

Strickland, D. & Strickland, M. (1994). *Families: Poems celebrating the African American experience*, illustrated by J. Ward Honesdale, PA: Wordsong/Boyds Mills Press.

Taylor, M. (1976). *Roll of thunder, hear my cry*. New York, NY: Bantam Books.

6

Taking a Critical Look at Native Americans in Children's Literature

Donna Sabis-Burns

During a lesson on Columbus Day a student eagerly exclaims, "Miss Sabis, those Brown people were stolen from their homes by bad people, just like we were!" While reading Jane Yolen's children's book, *Encounter* (1992) to a former class of mine, one student instantly makes a personal connection to the images and story of a Taino child, stolen from his home with the intent to be sold into slavery. This statement was made by a six-year-old, African-American boy from a lower socioeconomic background in a first-grade elementary class. The young child linked the horrific past of African slavery in America to the often untold story of native peoples sold into Spanish slavery by Columbus and his men. This was not an exercise of intentional critical thought. It was an emotion released directly from the heart.

On the contrary, a few years later while giving a class presentation to my fellow doctoral students on critical thought, I provided each student with a copy of Yolen's *Encounter*, along with several other types of books about Columbus, for their critical review. The assignment was to read each story and then compare and contrast the books and identify how these books portrayed an event in history with varying perspectives. After reading Yolen's book, one student hesitantly asked, "Can you explain this situation about the six native people who were captured and forced to Spain as slaves? I have never heard this before. This can't be true." After I convinced her that it was true, we both sat there in disbelief; she could not believe her parents or teachers never shared this event with her years before in elementary school. Her disbelief made me consider how many more people out there shared the same lack of information. However, it is important to remember that whereas Spaniards committed atrocities against indigenous peoples, they were not the only Europeans to do so, nor were they worse than others.

Literature featuring native peoples has many splendid and important stories. Within these stories is the influence to divulge knowledge, and as Sir Frances Bacon once claimed, "Knowledge is power." Stories of history and contemporary issues among native peoples, both written and oral, retell who we were as a human race, where we have been, and where we are today. Yet have we, as Americans overall, been told truthful accounts of our past and present and the influential figures and events that make such significant means as the stories told to us as a child in children's literature?

Sealy (1984) contended that any educational experience should be one of celebration and sensitivity to cultural diversity, to foster an educated awareness to cultural customs and values, promote communication with people from other countries, and create experiences involving other cultures. Through literature, readers explore lands and cultural mores that they would otherwise not experience (Lowery & Sabis-Burns, 2007). Multicultural literature can provide this authentic learning opportunity through real-life experiences and cross-cultural connections, especially with a plethora of indigenous populations across the United States.

In the 2000 census, 1.5 percent of the total population (4.1 million people) in the United States was identified as Native Americans and Alaska natives. Approximately 1 percent of the overall U.S. student population is Native American (645, 601). Nearly 90 percent of these students attend public schools (Stancavage & NCES, 2006) or schools operated by the federal Bureau of Indian Education (BIE), tribal or community controlled schools under BIE management but operated by local tribal school boards, state-supervised public schools, private schools, and parochial schools.

All native peoples share a distinctive relationship to the federal government. From their first encounters, Tribal nations and federal authorities operated on a government-to-government basis. The tribal-federal relationship was recorded in the U.S. constitution and in treaties, executive orders, legislation, court decisions, and bureaucratic arrangements that establish a binding trust agreement on the part of the federal government "to represent the best interests of the tribes and their members." The keystone of the tribal-federal relationship is *tribal sovereignty*: the "right of a people to self-government, self- determination, and self-education." Tribal sovereignty is complex. Federal law recognizes that tribal sovereignty is inherent; it is not something that another government gives to tribes. Remember, tribal governments, organized political bodies, predate the state and federal government.

Although governments have adapted and evolved, their origins are deeply rooted in history and the tradition and culture that still play an important role today (TEDNA, 2006). Nevertheless, all native peoples share a distinct status as Indigenous peoples that entail the right to self-determination. This information becomes important as we engage in the discussion of children's literature and the complexity of Native American history and contemporary issues often reflected, many times inaccurately, in materials found in school classrooms and libraries. In addition to knowing the unique relationships between native peoples and the federal government, there is also the issue of understanding the preferred terminology.

Appropriate terminology is a critical factor when discussing themes surrounding indigenous populations in the Americas. When discussing issues related to native peoples, the common terms that have emerged include *Native American*, *American Indian*, *indigenous* or *aboriginal* people. The terms *Native American* and *American Indian* are often interchanged and are broadly used in professional literature. However, their use is not consistent among native people as many do not consider either term appropriate. On the other hand, there are some native people who call themselves *Indian* and do not prefer one way over the other. One universal point where agreement seems consistent among native peoples is the use of the traditional name of their people. Whenever possible, it is most appropriate to identify a person from their tribal group or tribal name. Personally, I prefer the use of my tribal group or name such as *Iroquois* or *Tuscarora/Mohawk*, respectively, rather than the term *American Indian*. The reason being is that many people do not realize that people born indigenous to the Americas are part of more than 560 federally recognized tribes, 619 reservations and Alaska native villages, over 250 native languages and varying customs; native peoples live in every corner of the country and its accompanying territories (McCarty, 2000). To be grouped into a simple term of *American Indian* does not identify or capture the unique cultural aspect of that person and the tribal affiliation to which they identify. However, in this chapter, when there are instances where more than one tribal group or nation is being discussed, the term *native peoples* is used interchangeably with *Native American* for clarification purposes.

Through children's literature we are exposed to many enlightening and powerful messages that disperse a plethora of culturally motivated inquiries and historically compelling stories that tell the history of where we have been, where we are, and where we wish to be. Separated by our uniqueness, our differing viewpoints of history, controversial presence, and even at times the division of geographical borders, we can nonetheless come together and refer to literature to serve as both the change agent and connecting bridge linking humankind and humanity.

According to Fox and Short (2004), every child reserves the right to see themselves positively and accurately portrayed in stories and to find truth based on their own experiences instead of negative stereotypes and misrepresentation. Yet literature involving multicultural characters or events written from a European American perspective tends to perpetuate the European American dominance within society (Lim & Ling, 1992). Accurate portrayals of history, contemporary issues, and authentic cultural values are thought to be the cornerstones of experiencing a good story. As children gain the knowledge to critically approach books that involve these events, it is believed that children become able to challenge the status quo and seek more meaningful experiences as they learn their culture or culture that is different than their own. Within the Native American experience is a broad range of unique (though connected) lifestyles. However, according to Roberts, Dean and Holland (2005), the majority of Americans know little about this diversity.

As educators rise to the challenge of teaching accurate content to their students about the diverse cultures spanning the Native American experience, the reliance on text and literature becomes essential. Empirical evidence shows that more multicultural representation is found in conventional textbooks and teaching materials today than in the past; however, the accuracy and depiction of native people is highly questionable (Loewen, 2005). To supplement the classroom textbook, educators can seek a variety of commercial trade books that have been shown to inspire critical thinking about the human condition, to heighten social sensitivity, and to provide additional insight into cultural nuances (Sanchez, 1999; Slapin & Seale, 2000). Even with the increase in published literature regarding indigenous people, Harvey (1999) warned that whereas trade books may contain more well-written narratives, the need for accuracy in historical and contemporary perspectives and the challenging of stereotypes still greatly exists. Brophy (1999) accentuated the power of trade books that are historically and culturally accurate and urged educators to decipher accurate sources from those books that bear distortion, tokenism, omission, inaccuracy, inappropriate representation, lack of humanness, and negative stereotyping of indigenous people and their culture.

Part of the problem in today's classroom is that the educational community has yet to deal with issues related to how Native American cultures and people are represented, or omitted, from the curriculum in our schools (Jones & Moomaw, 2006). While visiting my son's Harvest Day Celebration (in lieu of Halloween), the majority of the fourth grade had handmade, brown paper bag dresses and vests with random geographic designs, complete with headbands and makeshift feathers. The children paraded around the school without a thought of consequence. I shared my concerns with the principal of the school by explaining the possible degradation and mocking to important cultural and spiritual traditions that this activity conjures, to which I received no response.

Educators may not understand the importance of native traditional dress and the honor and meaning behind the symbols that are displayed; feathers are earned or gifted, and hold a very sacred meaning, which may vary from tribal nation to tribal nation. Traditional regalia is worn for certain celebrations or other specific events and is very personal, not as something to wear in disguise. By selecting an item of apparel or a particular art tradition, non native children are encouraged to view native peoples as exotic and different rather than helping children understand the unique, yet similar, characteristics. These topics do not seem to be part of the educator's repertoire of multicultural understanding in many cases. That is why the dependence on and availability of quality, accurate, and contemporary books is critical in classrooms and libraries.

AVAILABILITY

Publishers continue to publish many stories for children and young adults about native peoples in various genres. If you were to visit the school and local public library, you would most likely find a substantial number of books representing an indigenous perspective or historical event or some referenced native-based myth or legend. Whereas a portion of these more recently published books reflect an attempt to include more accurate, appealing and useful books about Native Americans, there still exists an abundance of books that are inaccurate, offensive, and useless (Lindsay, 2003). This widely known issue has not changed much over the past several years.

The Cooperative Children's Book Center in Madison, Wisconsin, has discovered noticeably fewer books about native peoples that contain the amount of high-quality criteria that would qualify them to be included in their recommended lists. Additionally, an online survey of the Horn Book Guide offers a similar conclusion that the number of reviewed books about Native Americans received lower quality rankings than the years prior. Lindsay points out that although reviewers may be better qualified to review books of this nature and hold higher standards to their reviews, the issue remains that there just are not enough solid, quality books about Native Americans. The importance of this statement accentuates the fact that if a small number of good books about native peoples and culture are being published, the number of good books making it into the hands of classroom teachers and librarians also diminish, leaving the students with a stagnant perspective and a status-quo approach to the literature available to them.

STEREOTYPES IN NATIVE AMERICAN LITERATURE

Native American culture is rich and deeply embedded in ancient traditions among its people. Their values, ideas, government, traditions, foods, clothing, music, art, and recreation have been well documented over the past couple of centuries (Diamond &

Moore, 1995). However, stereotypical images of young children in headdresses, passive girls in long, black braids, and the portrayal of native people as savage beasts are reported in many children's books today (McMahon, Saunders, & Bardwell, 1996). By definition, a stereotype is a "fixed image, idea, trait or convention, lacking in originality or individuality, most often negative" (Dowd, 1992, p. 220), which takes away the human qualities of individuals and promotes an unclear understanding of social realities (Verrall & McDowell, 1990).

Books with such presentations are deemed inaccurate and disrespectful and are said to deny the rich diversity among specific native tribes (Lindsay, 2003; Reese, 1999; Stewart, 2002). As Norton (1990) specified, literature is identified as a key component to increasing cultural awareness. It must be carefully selected to accurately reflect customs and values of other native cultures while heightening students' understanding of their beliefs and lifestyles. Furthermore, "using literature that gives inaccurate information can be more harmful than the failure to represent other cultures at all" (Hilliard, 1995, p. 729). As a result, the need to recognize the stereotypes that are often identified in books featuring Native American themes becomes essential.

The earliest stereotypes of Native Americans came from missionaries and explorers who portrayed native people as uncivilized, superstitious, simplistic, perfect for conversion to Christianity, and dependent on the European influences. When the landing of Christopher Columbus took place and the European rivalries over land began in North America, Native Americans became known as "blood thirsty savages" greatly feared by their enemies (Reese, 1998). For the most part, children are influenced by these stereotypes of Native Americans, which lead them to believe that either Native Americans cease to exist after 1890 or that Native Americans are all exotic people who wear feathers and smoke peace pipes (Caldwell-Wood & Mitten, 1991; Reese, 1998). Additionally, Native Americans are stereotyped in many other ways, even in today's culture. During the month of November with reference to Pilgrims and Thanksgiving, teachers often have children make and wear multi-feathered headdresses, a sacred custom traditionally worn only by high-ranking members of the tribal community. There is also the stereotyped caricature of the Native American depicted as a sports mascot. In addition, children still play "cowboys and Indians," often grunting the Hollywood created "Ugh," which has been described by Mihesuah (2002) as "a nonsensical, verbal symbol of the quintessence of Indians" (p. 11). Furthermore, Dorris (1998) lamented, "It's hard to take seriously, to empathize with, a group of people portrayed as speaking ungrammatical language, as dressing in Halloween costumes, as acting 'wild,' as being undependable in their promises of gifts" (p. 19). Because children's books play an important role in shaping children's perception of various cultures, books are more than just entertainment; they are vehicles that transfer cultural knowledge, awareness, and thought and bear the responsibility of upholding the truth of our nation's past.

Howard (1991) posited that an authentic book contains a story that is set within the distinctiveness of characters and settings and reflects the universality of experience throughout the pages. The broad and the specific combine to create a story in which "readers from the culture will know that it is true, will identify, and will be affirmed, and readers from another culture will feel that it is true, will identify, and learn something of value" (p. 92). If the story is not accurate or wrongly portrays a history or culture, Howard (1991) argued that children cannot only walk away with inaccurate information, but this erroneous information can follow them throughout their schooling.

SELECTION CRITERIA

A child leans forward onto her knees, attention keenly fixed on the person sharing the story, eyes filled with wonder and imagination: this is an image of the ultimate childhood experience. Whether a child is sitting in a longhouse listening to elders, around a campsite at dusk, or on a rug in a school classroom, the message of the experience is the same: children love a good story. However, what marks a good story varies from child to child and experience to experience, so we rely on other sources to assist in collecting good books.

Although there are many resources available nowadays to provide assistance in selecting a quality book featuring native peoples, there are a few outstanding thoughts to keep in mind. Book lists are advantageous as a quick reference or as a way to build a classroom library. The lists provide information such as the publisher's information, usually an appropriate age level, a brief description of the story, among other insightful pieces of information. But the most important question that can be asked of that booklist is, "How do they determine what constitutes a 'good' book?"

Susan Jeffers's *Brother Eagle Sister Sky* (1991) is notorious among the native community as an inappropriate book for children for its gross misinterpretations and heavy Eurocentric perspectives of a eulogy offered by Chief Seeathl. Jane Yolen's *Encounter* (1992) often hits the best seller lists as well. Although the story offers a unique perspective of the invasion from the eyes of a Taino child, the language and message that is often left behind is that the Taino were to blame for their perils, that the Taino vanished (not true) and became nothing short of simply the victim."Then there is the issue of Thanksgiving. Whereas the true circumstances of the origin of this holiday were different from what is portrayed in American history books (a celebration of battles won by the English against the indigenous people), there are versions of history that exist throughout that do not highlight the realities as told in books for children. *The Thanksgiving Story*, written by Alice Dalgliesh, is a book published in 1954 and Caldecott Honor, complete with the silver medal on the cover and readily available for checkout from a variety of libraries throughout the county. This story is riddled with outdated, stereotyped images and references to unfriendly Indians such as ". . . some of the men went to see if it was safe. There would be Indians. The settlers had heard all kinds of stories about Indians. So the men carried their guns" (unpaginated). All three of these books have made their way to recommended book lists of some sort.

To reduce the chance of obtaining a less desirable book, it is recommended to use the wide variety of selection criteria questionnaires written and published by respectable authors that are widely available, lists published in peer reviewed journals (preferably by a native reviewer), and refer to the recommended resources later in this chapter for ways to identify good books that are written by Native American authors. Often when evaluating books, there are sets of criteria listed as guidelines in determining accuracy and other important aspects to consider.

According to Barclay (1996), judging the accuracy of cultural content becomes a complicated task, even when using given guidelines. He terms it the "checklist mentality" in which one denounces a book automatically for any stereotype violation. The result becomes failing to acknowledge if the book is perpetuating a myth or some other harmful cultural idea of Native Americans. Barclay (1996) also claims that some stereotypes cannot be avoided. Sanchez (1999) provides the following examples; too many Navajos live in poverty is a fact as well as an archetype. In addition, Sanchez asserts that one's perception of a stereotype can be another's cultural virtue such as contemporary Native Americans living without many modern, materialistic luxuries of today's society. Some believe this as a negative stereotype whereas others may simply see it as a rejection of the dominant cultural tradition of materialism. Therefore, using a guideline is dependent on how it is perceived by the user.

Since indigenous lifestyles may not be well known across the country, it is prudent for educators to refer to existing resources that can assist in evaluating books about Native peoples. One of the most comprehensive resources for evaluating children's literature featuring native peoples is *Through Indian Eyes: The Native Experience in Books for Children* by Beverly Slapin and Doris Seale (1998). Taken directly from their list of selection criteria, when selecting books or materials that include Native Americans one should begin by asking the following questions:

Is the story truthful?
Is the book respectful?
Is there anything in this book that would embarrass or hurt a Native child?
Is there anything in this book that would employ stereotypic thinking in a non-Native child?

Look at picture books:
In ABC books, is "E" for Eskimo?
In ABC books, is "I" for Indian?
In counting books, are Indians counted?
Are children shown playing Indian"?
Are animals dressed as Indians?
Do Indians have ridiculous names, like Indian Two Feet, or Little Chief?

Look at Stereotypes:
Are native peoples portrayed as savages, or primitive craftspeople, or simple people, now extinct?
Are native peoples shown as human beings, members of highly defined and societies?
Are native societies oversimplified and generalized? Are native people all one, one style?
Are native societies presented as separate from each other, with each culture, language, religion, and dress, unique?
Is the artwork a mishmash of generic Indian designs?
Is attention paid to accurate, appropriate design and color; are clothes, dress, houses drawn with careful attention to detail?

Look for Loaded Words:
Are there insulting overtone to the language in the book? Are racist adjectives to refer to native peoples?
Is the language respectful?

Look for Tokenism:
Are native people depicted as stereotypically alike, or do they look just like white people with brown faces?
Are native people depicted as genuine individuals?

Look for Distortion of History:

Is there manipulation of words like victory, conquest, or "massacre to justify Euro-American conquest of the native homelands? Are native nations presented as being responsible for their own "disappearance?" Is the U.S. government only "trying to help"?

Is history put in the proper perspective: the native struggle for self-determination and sovereignty against the Euro-American drive for conquest?

Does the story encourage children to believe that native peoples accepted defeats?

Does the story show the ways in which native peoples actively resisted the invaders?

Are native hero(ines) only the people who, in some way or another, are believed to have aided Europeans in the conquest of their own people?

Are native hero(ines) those who are admired because of what they have done for their own people?

Look at the Lifestyles:

Are native cultures presented in a condescending manner? Are there paternalistic distinctions between them and us?

Is the focus on respect for native peoples and understanding of the sophistication complexity of their societies?

Are native peoples discussed in the past tense only, supporting the vanished Indian myth? Is the past unconnected to the present?

Is the continuity of cultures represented, with values, religions, morals, an outgrowth of the past, and connected to the present?

Is a society portrayed in a distorted or limited way? Are religions described as superstitions with backward or primitive connotations?

Are Indian religions and traditions described accurately, in the context of their civilizations?

Is there an ethnocentric Western focus on material objects, such as baskets, pottery, and rugs?

Does the writer show any understanding of the relationship between material and nonmaterial aspects of life?

Are native peoples shown as relentlessly ecological?

Are native societies described as coexisting with nature in a delicate balance?

Look at the Dialogue:

Do the People speak in either a sort of early jawbreaker or in the oratorical style of the noble savage?

Do the people use language with the consummate and articulate skill of those who come from an oral tradition?

Look for Standards of Success:

In modern times, are native peoples portrayed as childlike and helpless? Does a authority figure— pastor, social worker, teacher—know better than native people themselves what is "good for them?" Are Indian children better off' away from their families?

Are native adults seen as mature individuals who work hard and make sacrifices, in order to take care of their families, and for the well-being of the people?

Do native people and their communities contrast unfavorably with the "norm" of white middle-class suburbia?

Are native people and their communities seen as their own cultural norm?

Does it take "white" standards for native people to get ahead?

Are native values of cooperation, generosity, sharing, honesty, and courage seen as integral to growth and development?

Look at the Role of Women:

Are women completely subservient to men? Do they do all the work, while the look around, waiting for the next hunt?

Are women portrayed as the integral and respected part of native societies that they really are?

Look at the Role of Elders:

Are elders treated as a dispensable burden upon their People to be abandoned in of trouble or famine; querulous, petulant, demanding, nagging, irritating, and boring?

Are elders treated as loved and valued custodians of a People's history, culture, and lifeways? Are they cherished in the words of the writer as they were and in the reality of the lives of the People?

Look for the Effects on a Child's Self-Image:

Is there anything in the story that would embarrass or hurt a native child?

Are there one or more positive role models with whom a native child can identify?

Look at the Author's or Illustrator's Background:

Is the background of the author and illustrator devoid of the qualities that enable them to write about native peoples in an accurate, respectful manner? Is there an ethnocentric bias which leads to distortions or omissions?

Is there anything in the author's and illustrator's background that qualifies them to write about native peoples? Do their perspectives strengthen the work?

A few more questions that are important to ask that are not included in Slapin and Seale's book address information about the author and what Native American reviewers have said about the book:

➤ What was the author's purpose in writing it and what perspectives does the author bring to it? Are his/her ethnic affiliations identified?

➤ Is there appropriate identification of a specific tribe or tribes? Does the author avoid a generalized portrayal of American Indian peoples as being all alike?

➤ What do Native American reviewers or readers say about this book? (www.oyate.org)

Authors and Illustrators:

Sherman Alexie (Spokane/Coeur d'Alene)—author
Shonto Begay (Navajo)—author and illustrator
Jeanne Rorex Bridges (Cherokee)—illustrator
Joseph Bruchac (Abenaki)—author
Joseph Medicine Crow (Crow)—author
Yvonne Wakim Dennis—author
Anthony Chee Emerson (Navajo)—illustrator
Louise Erdrich (French and Anishinaabe)—author
Joy Harjo (Mvskoke/Creek)—author
Thomas King (Cherokee)—author
George Littlechild (Plains Cree)—author & illustrator
Devon A. Mihesuah (Choctaw)—author
Simon Ortiz (http://www.uta.edu/english/tim/poetry/so/ortizbib1.htmAcoma Pueblo)—author
Marcie R. Rendon (Anishinaabe)—author
LaVera Rose (Lakota)—author
Gayle Ross (Cherokee)—author

Hendle Rumbaut (Chickasaw)—author
Cynthia Leitich Smith (Muscogee Creek)—author
Virginia Driving Hawk Sneve (Lakota Sioux)—author
Drew Hayden Taylor (Ojibway)—author
Tim Tingle (Choctaw)—author
Richard Van Camp (Dogrib—Tlicho)—author

EXEMPLARY LITERATURE

American Indian Youth Literature Award

Beginning in 2006, the American Indian Youth Literature Award (AIYLA) was created as a way to identify and honor exemplary writing and illustrations by and about native peoples. Every two years books are selected to receive the award. These books, fiction or nonfiction, represent Native American people in their dedication and fullness of their humanity in either past or present contexts.

Up to three awards may be given every two years—*Best Picture Book*, *Best Middle School Book*, and *Best Young Adult Book*. In the case of picture books, awards will be given to both author and illustrator if they are not the same person. Awards will consist of a beaded medallion and cash prize for each winner and will be announced at the American Library Associated Midwinter Conference. Table 6.1 identifies all previous winners.

General Criteria for the Award

The following provides the criteria for selecting each award winner:

The book allows children and young adults to look, read, recognize, and respond to the text and
   illustrations in a positive manner.Text and illustrations are infused with (or reflect) values and
   worldview of Native American cultures such as significance of community, extended
   family structures, harmony between material and nonmaterial aspects of life, and respect for
   all aspects of Mother Earth. Native American religion and spirituality, if included, is shown
   in a natural, not contrived, way.
Gender is balanced and accurately portrayed.
Text and illustrations depicting race, ethnicity, gender, age, sexual orientation, or class will be
   free of stereotypes.
Authentic and balanced characters will exhibit the wide range of positive and negative human
   emotions, behaviors, reactions, and lifestyles.
*Native American characters will demonstrate the ability to achieve success on their own terms
   and in the context of native cultures or communities.
*Native American characters are portrayed as successful problem solvers rather than dependent
   on non-Indian teachers, social workers, and other authority figures.
References and consultants with expertise in Native American cultures are cited.
Text and illustrations should accurately reflect the traditions, symbols, clothing, housing, and life
   styles of the nation(s) presented in the book, appropriate for the time period of the story.
Women should be accurately portrayed as essential, integral, and powerful members of their communities, and not as subservient drudges or marginalized beasts of burden, as often occurs in
   historical works.
The roles of traditional elders are authentically presented.

Table 6.1.

Recent Winners

Year	Best Picture Book	Best Middle School Book	Best Young Adult Book
2006	*Beaver Steals Fire: A Salish Coyote Story* (2005), by the Confederated Salish and Kootenai Tribes (Illustrator)	*The Birchbark House* (1999), by Louise Erdrich	*Hidden Roots* (2004), by Joseph Bruchac
2008	*Crossing Bok Chitto* (2006) by Tim Tingle	*Counting Coup: Becoming a Crow Chief on the Reservation and Beyond* (2006) by Joseph Medicine Crow, Herman Viola	*The Absolutely True Diary of a Part-Time Indian* (2007) by Sherman Alexie, Ellen Forney (Illustrator)
2010	*A Coyote Solstice Tale* (2009) by Thomas King, Gary Clement (Illustrator)	*Meet Christopher: An Osage Indian Boy from Oklahoma* (2008) by Genevieve Simermeyer, photographs by Katherine Fogden	*Between the Deep Blue Sea and Me: A Novel* (2008) by Lurline Wailana McGregor

Heroes are recognized by native standards.

Books should show the continuity of cultures, with indigenous values, religions, and morals as an outgrowth of the past and connected to the present.

Historical texts portray Native American people as human beings and members of highly defined and complex societies.

THEMES

It is understood that a single teacher or librarian does not have the time to scrutinize over every book and apply every guiding question to be able to share it with children. However, there are a few general thoughts that are critical and must be considered. First, choose books that contain topics from a variety of tribal nations and go beyond the well-known tribal nations. More and more books are being published that include smaller tribal entities from across the country such as the AIYLA winner, *Beaver Steals Fire: A Salish Coyote Story* (2005), by the Confederated Salish and Kootenai Tribes located in Montana. This riveting story teaches the difficulty of bringing fire from the sky world and its importance to people and animals. It reflects Salish culture and historical storytelling topics. Another example is Nicola Campbell's *Shi-Shi-etko* (2005); a well-written, autobiographical novel about a First Nations girl's experience when she is sent away from her family ranch and forced to attend the federal mandated boarding school in 1959. These books bring to life one of many tribal nations that may not be as familiar to many but play a large part in both historical and contemporary events today.

Second, choose books with contemporary native themes. Last fall I accompanied my son on a field trip to the area pumpkin patch. On site was a tipi with a Cherokee woman (an awkward combination) who had been hired to tell native stories to the children. As I entered the tipi, I overheard a few children discussing how the Indians *used* to get their water, and how the Indians *used* to live. Unfortunately, this is a common topic of conversation. Many children grow up believing that native peoples no longer exist. Actually children's books are out there that continue to perpetuate the myth by flat out stating this inaccuracy. Nevertheless, native peoples who drive BMWs, who are doctors, lawyers, and teachers do, in fact, exist today, and they do not look like or speak like Tonto. Muscogee Creek author Cynthia Leitich-Smith (2001) said it best, "I make lousy fry bread. I'm usually feather-free. I don't start conversations with phrases like 'as my grandfather once said' and then burst into poignant lectures about the religious traditions related to my native identity, let alone anybody else's" (para. 1). For that reason, Leitich-Smith's *Jingle Dancer* (2000) and Sherman Alexie's *The Absolutely True Diary of a Part-time Indian* (2007) offer the reader contemporary Native American characters who wear baseball caps, are both women and successful lawyers and business people, who get picked on in school, and who have fights with their best friends. The message stands that native peoples do exist; like others, there are many shapes, sizes and shades of skin tones; they may even have red hair and freckles and speak with a southern accent, but they are very much alive and play a vital role in their community.

Lastly, one other contemporary theme in children's literature featuring Native Americans is choosing books that highlight social justice issues. Social justice is a condition in which people in a society are treated fairly and equally. Social justice found within children's books advocates social action and challenges the status quo. If literature has the potential to inspire children into social action, not only can the reader initiate change, but also the opportunity exists to transform the world around us and make it a better place (McCall & Ford, 1998). Literature has the power to be a motivating agent of change. Many good books offer pro-justice protagonists in Native American literature for children and young adults. For example, Marlene Carvell's *Who Will Tell My Brother?* (2002) shares the plight of a high school boy who attempts to tackle the issue of school mascots at his school. Tim Tingle's *Crossing Bok Chitto: A Choctaw Tale of Friendship & Freedom* (2006) written as a tribute to the native peoples of every nation who aided runaway people of bondage, highlights the coming together of African Americans and Native Americans (Chocktaw) through the bravery of two young children fighting to free a family from slavery.

RECOMMENDED BOOKS

The following list provides quality literature featuring native peoples for children and young adults published within the last 10 years. This list is not exhaustive, but offers award-winning books and others that should be part of every classroom library.

Contemporary Realistic Fiction

Alexie, Sherman. (2007). *The Absolutely True Diary of a Part-Time Indian.* New York, NY: Little, Brown.

Bruchac, Joseph. (2004). *Hidden Roots.* New York, NY: Scholastic.

Carlson, Lori Marie (Ed.) (2005). *Moccasin Thunder: American Indian Stories for Today.* New York, NY: HarperCollins.

Carvell, Marlene. (2002). *Who Will Tell My Brother?* New York, NY: Hyperion Books for Children.

Leitich-Smith, Cynthia. (2001). *Rain Is Not My Indian Name.* New York, NY: HarperCollins.

Leitich-Smith, Cynthia. (2002). *Indian Shoes.* New York, NY: HarperCollins.

Fiction

Bruchac, Joseph. (2001). *Skeleton Man*. New York, NY: HarperCollins.

Picture books

Allen, Paula Gunn & Smith, Patricia Clark. (1996). *As Long As the Rivers Flow: The Stories of Nine Native Americans*. New York, NY: Scholastic.

Campbell, Nicola L. (2005). *Shi-Shi-etko*. Toronto, ON, Canada: Groundwood Books.

Harjo, Joy. (2000). *The Good Luck Cat*. San Diego, CA: Harcourt Brace.

Leitich-Smith, Cynthia. (2000). *Jingle Dancer*. New York, NY: Morrow Junior Books.

Maher, Ramona. (2003). *Alice Yazzie's Year*. Berkeley, CA: Tricycle Press.

Rumford, James. (2004). *Sequoyah: The Cherokee Man Who Gave His People Writing*. Boston, MA: Houghton Mifflin Co.

Savageau, Cheryl. (2006). *Muskrat Will Be Swimming*. Gardiner, Me.: Tilbury House.

Tingle, Tim. (2006). *Crossing Bok Chitto: A Choctaw Tale of Friendship & Freedom*. El Paso, TX: Cinco Puntos Press.

Waboose, Jan Bourdeau. (2000). *Sky Sisters*. Toronto, CAN: Kids Can Press.

Wise, Bill. (2007). *Louis Sockalexis: A Native American Baseball Pioneer*. New York, NY: Lee & Low Books.

Historical Fiction

Carvell, Marlene. (2005). *Sweetgrass Basket*. New York, NY: Dutton Children's Books.

Erdrich, Louise. (2005). *Game of Silence*. New York, NY: HarperCollins.

Spalding, Andrea & Alfred Scow. (2006). *Secret of the Dance*. Victoria, BC: Orca Book Publishers.

Nonfiction

Grace, Catherine O'Neill and Bruchac, Marge. (2001). *1621: A New Look at Thanksgiving*. Washington, D.C.: National Geographic Society.

Medicine Crow, Joseph and Viola, Herman J. (2006). *Counting Coup: Becoming a Crow Chief on the Reservation and Beyond*. Washington, D.C.: National Geographic.

National Museum of the American Indian. (2007). *Do All Indians Live in Tipis?* New York: Collins, in association with the National Museum of the American, Smithsonian Institution, Washington, D.C.

Preschool

Confederated Salish and Kootenai Tribes. (2005). *Beaver Steals Fire: A Salish Coyote Story*. Lincoln, NE: University of Nebraska Press.

Himango, Deanna. (2002). *Boozhoo, Come Play With Us*. Cloquet, MN: Fond du Lac Head Start Program.

Van Camp, Richard. (2007). *Welcome Song for Baby: A Lullaby for Newborns*. Victoria, BC: Orca Book Publishers.

Poetry

Harjo, Joy. (2009). *For a Girl Becoming*. Tucson, AZ: The University of Arizona Press.

National Museum of the American Indian. (2008). *When the Rain Sings: Poems by Young Native Americans*. Washington, D.C.: National Museum of the American Indian. National Museum of the American Indian, Smithsonian Institution.

DO THIS, NOT THAT!

To assist all educators as well as classroom teachers and school librarians in sharing more accurate information regarding native peoples, there are a few topics of discussion that should be mentioned. Taking from an exemplary example of appropriate curriculum that teaches about the inclusion of native peoples in the classroom is the book, *Lessons From Turtle Island: Native Curriculum in Early Childhood Classrooms* by Guy W. Jones and Sally Moomaw (2002). Although the focus is early childhood learning, the basics provided in this publication has far-reaching intentions that reach across the ages of children and young adults. Common pitfalls that well-meaning educators seem to get pulled into, in addition to stereotyping that was mentioned earlier in this chapter, center around cultural insensitivity, inaccurate curriculum and omission of native culture from the curriculum. To avoid these pitfalls, Table 6.2 provides a list of excellent books and activities that can positively impact readers while providing appropriate representation of native culture.

RESOURCES

Fortunately, there are several resources that can help educators gain more experience to adequately evaluate materials and media used in the classroom. Curriculum, books, media, and Web sites all provide opportunities that teach about native peoples and are a dime a dozen. The following list is hand-picked resources that stand out as excellent sources of information.

INTERNET

Techniques for evaluating American Indian Web Sites.
http://www.u.arizona.edu/~ecubbins/webcrit.html. (Last accessed January 23, 2010)
A Web site that provides evaluation criteria for Web pages that represent native peoples.

American Indians in Children's Literature: Critical perspectives of indigenous peoples in children's books, the school curriculum, popular culture, and society-at-large.
http://americanindiansinchildrensliterature.blogspot.com/. (Last accessed January 23, 2010)
The content of the Web site is designed to help people develop a critical stance when evaluating American Indians in children's books.

Oyate.
www.oyate.org. (Last accessed February 9, 2010)
Oyate is a non-profit native organization working to see that the lives and histories of indigenous people are portrayed honestly. This is one of the best resources for adopting quality books (and also knowing which ones to avoid) by native authors and illustrators.

American Indian Library Association Web Site.
http://www.nativeculturelinks.com/aila.html. (Last accessed February 11, 2010)
http://www.ailanet.org/. (Last accessed February 11, 2010)

Table 6.2.
American Indian Books and Activities

Theme	Book Title	Do This . . .	. . . Not That!
Homes and Food	*The Story of the Milky Way* (1995) by Joseph Bruchac (Abenaki) & Gayle Ross (Cheroke). This is a traditional Cherokee story that brings to light the importance of corn to the people. Its history is widespread and crosses many native cultures.	Research the ways corn is celebrated in various native cultures and traditions. Survey food items with native logos. Discuss the implications of caricatures of native peoples and how it perpetuates stereotyping.	Do not use stereotypical caricatures of native people, like those found on Land o' Lakes butter boxes which have a picture of an Indian princess (there were no Indian princesses) or like the Calumet baking power container that has a warrior in full headdress.
Families and Traditions	*Jingle Dancer* (2000) by Cynthia Leitich Smith (Muscogee Creek). A story of a contemporary young girl who turns to her family and community to help her collect jingles for her jingle dress (something shared by generations of women in her family).	Many cultures have their own special dance traditions. Survey other children's books to compare dances and traditions shared across cultures today.	The traditional Native American dance regalia should not be equated with a dance costume in any way. This regalia may represent something sacred, a personal identity or affiliation with a particular tribal Nation. This also applies to costumes worn for Halloween or other non- native celebrations.
Families and Self-Awareness	*Less Than Half, More Than Whole* (1994) by Kathleen (Irish, English and Mohawk) and Michael Lacapa (Apache, Hopi and Tewa). This contemporary story of three boys who notice the different physical characteristics among themselves. A boy's grandfather assists them through sharing photographs of extensive family members to demonstrate how different and special each one is.	Share other books that explore the emotions of children and help them understand similarities and differences among families. A book, *Foster Baby* (1996), written by Rhian Brysjolson which describes a Native American baby in a loving native foster home. Children can also write about their own families and share.	Do not ask children to make up stories about a fictitious Native American family. When this is done it encourages inaccuracies and stereotypes, which in turn perpetuates misconceptions. There was an instance when a native parent entered a classroom where the children were given the assignment to "describe your Indian and what *it* wears . . ." an obvious bad case of objectification.

(continued)

Table 6.2. (continued)

Theme	Book Title	Do This...	...Not That!
Death	*Northern Lights: The Soccer Trails* (1993) by Michael Arvaarluk Kusugak (Inuit). A young Inuit girl loses her mother to sickness and goes through a tough, very sad time. One night she watches her village play a soccer game under the stars and northern lights. Her grandmother shares with her that the lights are the souls of loves ones who have died and are playing soccer in the sky.	Students can discuss the different ways death is celebrated among various cultures. Some cultural groups enter into a fasting time, mourning time, funerals, wakes, and so forth.	Do not ask children to invent Native American myths. Oftentimes stories from Christian, Jewish, and Muslim religions are categorized as "religion" whereas spiritual beliefs from native peoples are referred to as myths. Like stories from the Bible or the Koran, these native stories of traditional beliefs have deep spiritual meanings. We would never ask a child to make up their own Bible story.
Community	*Earth Daughter* (1995) by George Ancona (Acoma Pueblo). This story introduces a young girl, Alicia, who takes the reader through her Pueblo community focusing on the culture, traditions, contemporary family life, and community events. Through this tour the reader gets a sense of lifestyles, artwork, cultural symbols, and everyday life in this community.	Children can compare Alicia's modern home with their own home, or compare and contrast Alicia's modern home with the ancient Pueblo home in a nearby community maintained by Alicia's family. This provides an opportunity for readers to get a sense of how contemporary and traditional life is shared among many indigenous peoples.	Do not let children adopt symbols from another culture into their own artwork. Symbols are specific to native cultures and many are viewed as sacred. As there are no global Native American symbols, portraying Indian symbols as universal misinforms children. It perpetuates the myth that there is one Native American culture rather than hundreds.
Art	*A Rainbow at Night: The World in Words and Pictures by Navajo Children* (1996) by Bruce Hucko.	This story offers the perfect setting to discuss he artwork of authentic Native American artists. Teachers may focus on a particular illustration	Teachers should not have children copy Native American art. While it is important to share and view art from other cultures, there is often symbolism and spirituality

	As an art educator who spent ten years working on the Navajo Reservation he compiled a variety of paintings, drawings, and reflections of several Navajo (Dine) children, ages five to eleven. Each child is asked to reflect on their own culture and community and to represent their thoughts in art.	in this story by having the children talk about the art medium and incorporating Hucko's suggestions that are conveniently located throughout the pages.	underlying the artwork that many people do not know (Navajo weavings). By obtaining authentic artwork children can better appreciate the work while letting them explore their own artistic style and exploration.
Environment	*Did You Hear Wind Sing Your Name? An Oneida Song of Spring* (1995) by Sandra De Coteau (Oneida). This book is an excellent example of sharing the celebration of the circle of life, renewal, and rebirth through song. In this Haudenosaunee (Iroquois) story, the author describes the book as a song of thanks by also describing familiar objects to children while subtly conveying the Oneida worldview.	Compare this story to *Giving Thanks: A Native American Good Morning Message* (2003) by Chief Jake Swamp (Akwesasne Mohawk). Mohawk parents have taught their children to start each day by giving thanks to Mother Earth. Also known as the Thanksgiving Address, this good morning message is based on the belief that the natural world is a precious and rare gift. Students can research how other cultures celebrate life and what rituals are practiced.	While holding the title of "environmentalist" can be perceived as a positive trait, it still falls under the stereotyping pitfall when applied to a specific group of people. There are many native peoples who remain connected to their environment while others do not practice such traditions. Not all native peoples participate in the same rituals and teachers should not lead students to believe there is one size fits all when it comes to the deep cultural underpinnings such as the environment.

Evaluating American Indian materials and resources for the classroom textbooks, literature, DVDs, Videos, and Web Sites.
http://opi.mt.gov/pdf/IndianEd/EvalAmIndianMaterials.pdf. (Last accessed February 13, 2010)
The Montana Office of Public Instruction offers this resource for evaluating a variety of media featuring Native Americans in a comprehensive and culturally sensitive manner.

Children's and young adult author Cynthia Leitich Smith.
http://www.cynthialeitichsmith.com/index.html. (Last accessed February 15, 2010)

TEXTBOOKS

Jones, Guy W., & Moomaw, Sally. (2002). *Lessons from Turtle Island: Native Curriculum in Early Childhood Classrooms*. Redleaf Press.

Seale, Doris, & Slapin, Beverly. (2006). *A Broken Flute: The Native Experience in Books for Children*. AltaMira Press.

Slapin, Beverly, & Seale, Doris. (1998). *Through Indian Eyes: The Native Experience in Books for Children*. University of California, American Indian Studies Center.

ARTICLES

"I" is For Inclusion: The Portrayal of Native Americans in Books for Young People.
Program of the ALA/OLOS Subcommittee for Library Services to American Indian People. American Indian Library Association. American Indian Children's Literature: Identifying and Celebrating the Good. Washington, D.C., June 23, 2007. Compiled by Naomi Caldwell, Gabriella Kaye, Lisa A. Mitten. Updated October 2007. (pdf file)
http://www.ailanet.org/publications/I%20IS%20FOR%20INCLUSION-rev%2010-07.pdf
Goals for Writing and Reviewing Books with Native American Themes by Debbie Reese.
School Library Journal (pdf file) http://www.schoollibraryjournal.com/article/CA153126.html.
Sharing literature that incorporates a critical multicultural perspective requires the integration of addressing the issues of justice and social change and the connections to the developing self-identity within the way we learn to see ourselves in relation to the world (Kincheloe & Steinberg, 1997). Children learn what is given to them and take that knowledge and transform it into power for self-change, self-actualization, and an ability to read the world.

Children learn from the old stories and new books that authentically include Native Americans in present day as well as in the past (Trafzer, 1992). With this exposure and perspective, both native and non native children can set their minds thinking in new and diverse ways. Hopefully, they will build a foundation that refuses social inequality and the suffering that accompanies it within the schooling process. In addition, students from the mainstream culture will be enlightened as well and will learn how to border cross to other parallel cultures. As Kincheloe and Steinberg (1997) stated, understanding difference empowers the oppressed. Children's literature that tells the story of the encounter of Columbus and the Taino people is simply a tool to help reach this goal of empowering the oppressed. The present study provides an opportunity to critically analyze trade books and the contextual connections they bring, both historically and in contemporary times, hopefully leading to a heightened awareness and knowledge base that includes the native voice.

REFERENCES

Barclay, J. (1996). Native Americans in books from the past. *The Horn Book Magazine, 72*(5), 559–566.

Brophy, J. (1999). Elementary students learn about Native Americans: The development of knowledge and empathy. *Social Education, 63*(1), 39–45.

Caldwell-Wood, N., & Mitten, L. A. (1991). *"I" is not for Indian: The portrayal of North Americans in books for young people.* Compiled for the American Indian Library Association, Atlanta, GA.

Diamond, B. J., & Moore, M. A. (1995). *Multicultural literacy: Mirroring the reality of the classroom.* White Plains, MY: Longman.

Dorris, M. A. (1998). "I" is not for Indian. In B. Slapin & D. Seale (Eds.), *Through Indian eyes: The Native experience in books for children* (pp. 19–20). Berkeley, CA: Oyate.

Dowd, F. S. (1992). "We're not in Kansas anymore": Evaluating children's books portraying Native American and Asian cultures. *Childhood Education, 68*(4), 219–224.

Fox, D. L., & Short, K. (Eds.). (2004). *Stories matter: The complexity of cultural authenticity in children's literature.* Urbana, IL: National Council of Teachers of English.

Harvey, K. (1999). Resources for teaching about Native Americans. *Social Education, 63*(1), 51–53.

Hilliard, L. L. (1995). Defining the "multi" in "multicultural" through children's literature. *The Reading Teacher, 48*(8), 728–729.

Howard, E. F. (1991). Authentic multicultural literature for children: An author's perspective. In M. V. Lindgren (Ed.), *The multicolored mirror: Cultural substance in literature for children and young adults* (pp. 91–99). Fort Atkinson, WI: Highsmith Press.

Jones, G. W., & Moomaw, S. (2002). *Lessons from Turtle Island: Native curriculum in early childhood classrooms.* Toronto, CAN: Redleaf Press.

Kincheloe, J. L. & Steinberg, S.R. (1997). *Changing multiculturalism.* Philadelphia, PA: Open University Press.

Leitich Smith, C. (2001). Native now: Contemporary Indian stories. *Book Links, 10*(3). Retrieved from http://www.ala.org.

Lim, S. G., & Ling, A.L. (1992). *Reading the literatures of Asian Americans.* Philadelphia, PA: Temple University Press.

Lindsay, N. (2003). 'I' still isn't for Indian: A look at recent publishing about Native Americans. *School Library Journal, 49*(11), 42–43.

Loewen, J. W. (1995). *Lies my teacher told me: Everything your American history textbook got wrong.* New York, NY: Simon & Schuster.

Lowery, R. M., Sabis-Burns, D. L. (2007). From borders to bridges: Making cross-cultural connections through multicultural literature. *Multicultural Education, 14* (4), 50–54.

McCall, A. L. & Ford, M. P. (1998). Why not do something? Literature as a catalyst for social action. *Childhood Education, 74*(3), 130–135.

McCarty, T. L. (2008). *The impact of high-stakes accountability policies on Native American learners: Evidence from research.* Arizona State University, USA.

McMahon, R., Saunders, D., & Bardwell, T. (1996). Increasing young children's cultural awareness with American Indian literature. *Childhood Education, 73*, 105–108.

Mihesuah, D. A. (2002). *American Indians: Stereotypes and realities.* Atlanta, GA: Clarity.

Norton, D. E. (1990). Teaching multicultural literature in the reading curriculum. *The Reading Teacher, 44*(1), 28–40.

Reese, D. (1998). "Mom, look! It's George, and he's a TV Indian!" *The Horn Book Magazine, 74*(5), 636–644.

Reese, D. (1999). Authenticity and sensitivity: Goals for writing and reviewing books with Native American themes. *School Library Journal, 45*(11), 36–37.

Roberts, L. C., Dean, E., & Holland, M. (2005). Contemporary American Indian cultures in children's picture books. *Beyond the Journal-Young Children on the Web. NAEYC, 9.* 16.

Sanchez, A. R. (1999). "Dangerous Indians": Evaluating the depiction of Native Americans in selected trade books. *Urban Education, 36*(3), 400–425.

Sealy, B. (1984). Measuring the multicultural quotient of a school. *TESL Canada Journal/Review, 1*(2), 21–28.

Slapin, B., & Seale, D. (1998). *Through Indian eyes: The Native experience in books for children.* Los Angeles: American Indian Studies Center.

Slapin, B., Seale, D., & Gonzales, R. (2000). *How to tell the difference: A guide to evaluating children's books for anti-Indian bias.* Berkeley, CA: Oyate.

Stancavage, F. B. & National Center for Education Statistics. (2006). National Indian Education Study. Part 2, the educational experiences of fourth- and eighth-grade American Indian and Alaska Native students. *National Center for Education Statistics, Institute of Educational Sciences*, U.S. Dept. of Education, [Washington, D.C.].

Stewart, M. P. (2002). Judging authors by the color of their skin? Quality Native American children's literature. *School Library Journal, 49*(11), 42–43.

Trafzer, C. E. (1992). "The word is sacred to a child": American Indians and children's literature. *American Indian Quarterly, 16*(3), 381396.

Tribal Education Departments National Assembly [TEDNA]. (2006). A manual for chief state school officers and state education agencies on American Indian and Alaska Native tribal sovereignty, federal education programs for tribal students, and tribal education departments. Boulder, CO: Author.

Verrall, C., & McDowell, P. (1990). Resource reading list 1990: Annotated bibliography of resources by and about native people. Toronto, ON, Canada: Canadian Alliance in Solidarity with the native peoples, p. 157.

MULTICULTURAL BOOKS

Alexie, S. (2007). *The absolutely true diary of a part-time Indian*, illustrated by Ellen Forney. New York, NY: Little, Brown.

Allen, P. G. & Smith, P. C. (1996). *As long as the rivers flow: The stories of nine Native Americans.* New York, NY: Scholastic.

Ancona, G. (1995). *Earth daughter: Alicia of Acoma Pueblo.* New York, NY: Simon & Schuster Books for Young Readers.

Bruchac, J. (2001). *Skeleton man.* New York, NY: HarperCollins.

Bruchac, J. (2004). *Hidden roots.* New York, NY: Scholastic.

Bruchac, J. & Ross, G. (1995). *The story of the Milky Way*, illustrated by Virginia A. Stroud. New York, NY: Dial Books for Young Readers.

Campbell, N. (2005). *Shi-shi-etko*, illustrated by Kim LaFave. Toronto, ON, Canada: Groundwood Books.

Carlson, L. M. (Ed.). (2005). *Moccasin thunder: American Indian stories for today.* New York, NY: HarperCollins.

Carvell, M. (2002). *Who will tell my brother?* New York, NY: Hyperion Books for Children.

Carvell, M. (2005). *Sweetgrass basket.* New York, NY: Dutton Children's Books.

Confederated Salish and Kootenai Tribes. (2005). *Beaver steals fire: A Salish coyote story,* illustrated by Sam Sandoval. Lincoln, NB: University of Nebraska Press.

Crow, J. M. with Viola, H. (2006). *Counting coup: Becoming a crow chief on the reservation and beyond.* Washington, D.C.: National Geographic.

Dalgliesh, A. (1954). *The Thanksgiving story,* illustrated by Helen Sewell. New York, NY, NY: Aladdin.

Erdrich, L. (1999). *The birchbark house.* New York, NY: Hyperion Books for Children.

Erdrich, L. (2005). *Game of silence.* New York, NY: HarperCollins.

Grace, C. O. & Bruchac, M. (2001). *1621: A new look at Thanksgiving,* Photographs by Sisse Brimberg and Cotton Coulson. Washington, D.C.: National Geographic Society.

Harjo, J. (2000). *The good luck cat,* illustrated by Paul Lee. San Diego, CA: Harcourt Brace.

Harjo, J. (2009). *For a girl becoming,* illustrated by Mercedes McDonald. Tucson, AZ: The University of Arizona Press.

Himango, D. (2002). *Boozhoo, come play with us.* Cloquet, MN: Fond du Lac Head Start Program.

Hucko, B. (1996). *A rainbow at night: The world in words and pictures by Navajo children.* San Francisco, CA: Chronicle Books.

Jeffers, S. (1991). *Brother eagle, sister sky.* New York, NY: Dial Books/Penguin.

King, T. (2009). *A coyote solstice tale,* illustrated by Gary Clement. Toronto, ON, Canada: Groundwood Books.

Kusugak, M. A. (1993). *Northern lights: The soccer trails,* illustrated by Vladyana Krykorka. Toronto, ON, Canada: Annick Press.

Lacapa, K. & Lacapa, M. (1994). *Less than half, more than whole,* illustrated by Michael Lacapa. Flagstaff, AZ: Northland.

Leitich-Smith, C. (2000). *Jingle dancer,* illustrated by Cornelius Van Wright and Ying-Hwa Hu. New York, NY: Morrow Junior Books.

Leitich-Smith, C. (2001). *Rain is not my Indian name.* New York, NY: HarperCollins.

Leitich-Smith, C. (2002). *Indian shoes,* illustrated by Jim Madsen. New York, NY: HarperCollins.

Maher, R. (2003). *Alice Yazzie's year,* illustrated by Shonto Begay. Berkeley, CA: Tricycle Press.

McGregor, L. W. (2008). *Between the deep blue sea and me: A novel.* Honolulu, HI: Kamehameha Publishing.

National Museum of the American Indian. (2007). *Do all Indians live in tipis?* New York, NY: Collins, in association with the National Museum of the American Indian, Smithsonian Institution, Washington, D.C.

National Museum of the American Indian. (2008). *When the rain sings: Poems by young Native Americans* (Rev. ed.). Washington, D.C.: National Museum of the American Indian. National Museum of the American Indian, Smithsonian Institution.

Orie, S. D. (1995). *Did you hear wind sing your name? An Oneida song of spring,* illustrated by Christopher Canyon. New York, NY: Walker.

Rumford, J. (2004). *Sequoyah: The Cherokee man who gave his people writing.* Boston, MA: Houghton Mifflin Co.

Savageau, C. (2006). *Muskrat will be swimming,* illustrated by Robert Hynes. Gardiner, ME: Tilbury House.

Simermeyer, G. (2008). *Meet Christopher: An Osage Indian boy from Oklahoma*, with photographs by Katherine Fogden. Tulsa, OK: National Museum of the American Indian, Smithsonian Institution, in association with Council Oak Books.

Spalding, A. & Scow, A. (2006). *Secret of the dance*, illustrated by Darlene Gait.Victoria, BC: Orca Book Publishers.

Tingle, T. (2006). *Crossing Bok Chitto: A Choctaw tale of friendship & freedom*, illustrated by Jeanne Rorex Bridges. El Paso, TX: Cinco Puntos Press.

Van Camp, Richard. (2007).*Welcome song for baby: A lullaby for newborns*. Victoria, BC: Orca Book Publishers.

Waboose, J. B. (2000). *SkySisters*, illustrated by Brian Deines. Toronto, ON, Canada: Kids Can Press.

Wise, B. (2007). *Louis Sockalexis: A Native American baseball pioneer*, illustrated by Bill Farnsworth. New York, NY: Lee & Low Books.

Yolen, J. (1992). *Encounter*, illustrated by David Shannon. New York, NY: Harcourt Trade.

7

The Journey Continues: Exploring the Literature of Asian and Pacific Island Cultures

Avis M. Masuda and Michele M. Ebersole

The cultural diversity within our classrooms is rapidly increasing. More than four out of ten students in the U.S. P–12 classrooms are members of cultural minorities (Eggen & Kauchak, 2010). Our children bring with them a set of values and beliefs or their funds of knowledge (Moll, 1992) from their homes and neighborhood cultures that may complement or clash with the school culture, which may legitimate the social, economic, political, and cultural hegemonic values of the dominant society. Nonetheless, all children are deserving of a multicultural education, regardless of ethnicity, race, or language. According to Nieto (1999), developing a multicultural perspective allows us to question, "What does it mean to be an American?" thus inviting critical discussion of equity and social justice.

In 1993, after 150 years in America, Aoki questioned where Asian Pacific Americans stand with respect to children's literature. She challenged educators to "turn a new page in a new book" (pg. 133) in Asian Pacific American children's literature. Almost 20 years later, have we turned a new page and started a new chapter? Well, we can state that the representation of Asian Americans in literature has grown substantially and there are books, which deal with contemporary issues and concerns (Yokota & Bates, 2005; Yokota, 2009), so yes, we believe we have turned the page and started new critical conversations, but as Maile's story below tells us, there is still much work to be done.

MAILE'S STORY

Maile, a prospective teacher of Asian and Pacific Island ethnicity, enthusiastically shared,

I'm going to do my unit on different cultures and I'm planning to use literature to help me teach about the different cultures. I've already bought several books, *The Five Chinese Brothers*

(Bishop & Wiese, 1938) and *The Story of Ping* (Flack & Wiese, 1933), to help me teach about Chinese culture. I remember reading these books when I was young and I can't wait to use them with my students!

With recent experiences such as this one, we must stop to consider how far have we come in looking at Asian-American children's literature? As teacher and teacher librarian educators, how do we respond when our prospective colleagues still choose to use *The Five Chinese Brothers*? The book has been criticized for the use of ethnic stereotyping by its portrayal of Chinese people looking alike with bright yellow skin and slanted slits for eyes. In examining use of Asian-American children's literature, we ask ourselves, "What does it mean to be an Asian American?"

CULTURAL GROUPS

"Asian" refers to a wide range of people who come from very different geographic locations and have varied cultural experiences from the Far East, Southeast Asia, or the Indian subcontinent (for example, Cambodia, China, India, Japan, Korea, Malaysia, Pakistan, the Philippine Islands, or Vietnam).[1] Chinese, Japanese, and Koreans have been in the United States over several generations, whereas other groups such as the Vietnamese and Cambodians are comparatively recent immigrants (Reeves & Bennett, 2003). The 1965 Immigration Act, the first to drop racial criteria, resulted in an increase in Asian immigration and a panethnic[2] population, which includes more cultures and more varied cultures than ever.

A wide variation is posed by intragroup diversity and within-group diversity based upon country of origin, place of birth, generations in U.S., age, income levels, educational achievement, and so forth (Yokota & Bates, 2005). Further complexity arises with children who have been adopted into non-Asian families. Despite the vast geographic, demographic, and cultural differences, Asian Americans share a deeply rooted heritage of honoring family, tradition, and the telling of stories as a way to perpetuate these values. However, this also means no one single book can represent what it means to be Asian American (Yokota, 2009). Students need access to literature that presents a multidimensional look at culture through "a variety of genres, a variety of perspectives, and a variety of voices" (Yokota, 2009).

WHY THIS LITERATURE IS IMPORTANT

Literature is viewed as an enculturating agent (Rosenblatt, 1995). It has been offered as a vehicle through which adults promote understandings, values, attitudes, mores, and philosophies of life (Norton, 1991; Sims Bishop, 1994). Through literature students can engage in thoughtful discussions (Rosenblatt, 1995), which have the potential to elicit multiple perspectives and multiple voices in pursuit of understanding (Sims Bishop, 1997). Moreover, multicultural perspectives affirm diversity and help us to see reality from a variety of perspectives (Nieto, 1999). Literature is a critical part of people's heritage, and multicultural literature is a tool that can be used to attain equity and social justice, the goal of multicultural education (Cai & Bishop, 1994).

Literature thus plays a powerful role in shaping the perceptions of children, and Asian-American literature allows young readers to see themselves mirrored in books as well as provides windows into new perspectives for readers unfamiliar with Asian-American cultures (Cullinan, 1989). Providing Asian-American students with opportunities to understand the significance of their cultural heritage sheds light on how their storied lives have historically impacted who they are in the present and paves understanding of these strong cultural values in their future lives. For non-Asian readers, high-quality literature can portray authentic depictions of Asian Americans, foster empathy, break down stereotypes and build universality across humanity. Fortunately, there is an increasing amount of high quality literature on Asian-American cultural groups available to us today.

HISTORICAL DEVELOPMENT OF ASIAN-AMERICAN LITERATURE

Until recently, children of color have been virtually invisible in books or projected as stereotypes; however, in the last 40 years, there have been greater numbers of children's literature with children of color portrayed in a positive way. In 1997, Yamate wrote, "...in any given year, while four to five thousand new children's books are published, fewer than ten are by or about Asian Pacific Americans" (p. 97). The Cooperative Children's Book Center (CCBC; 2008) in the School of Education at the University of Wisconsin-Madison documents the number of books published in the United States for children written by and about people of color. Ten years after Yamate's observations, 68 of the 3,000 books documented by the CCBC were about Asian Pacific Americans, and of those books, 56 were by Asian Pacific Americans. This indicates some growth in the number of books by and about Asian and Pacific Islanders; however, there are still disproportionately low numbers of books published by and about Asian and Pacific Islanders. The population of Asian and Pacific Islanders was approximately 4.5 percent of the total population in 2000; yet on average, about 73 out of 3000 books or 2 percent of the books that were documented by the CCBC between 2002 and 2007 were about Asian Pacific Americans. Based on the number provided by the CCBC, there seems to be a growing number of books written by Asian Pacific Americans between 2003 and 2007. In addition, there seems to be an increasing number of children's books that address issues significant to today's Asian and Pacific Island children.

STEREOTYPES IN ASIAN-AMERICAN CHILDREN'S LITERATURE

According to Yokota and Bates (2005), in the 1960s, well-known authors such as first-generation Japanese immigrants, Taro Yashima and Kazue Mizumura, offered realistic representations of settings portrayed in their books, but limitations of the printing presses portrayed Japanese as yellow-skinned people. Many books written by non-Asians perpetuated stereotypes of exotica, Fu Manchu mustaches, short, straight cereal bowl haircuts, buck teeth, myopic vision, ancient clothing, yellow-skinned and slant-eyed.

Pang, Colvin, Tran, and Barba (1992) pointed out key stereotypes in children's literature that depict lives of Asian Americans:

1) Cultural assimilation means fitting into mainstream community. We can instead offer books with a culturally pluralistic theme that posits cultural diversity as an integral asset to the makeup of our nation.

2) Asian Americans are overgeneralized in terms of politeness, servitude, having expertise in martial arts, or stilted speech patterns. It is important to find books that positively and authentically portray Asian-American characters as empowered, real people.

3) Asian Americans are not American citizens or native-born. Story settings that take place in Chinatown, Little Tokyo, and Little Saigon often contradict the notion that Asian Americans are members of the U.S. community.

4) Asian Americans all look alike and dress in traditional clothing. Illustrations should convey that Asian Americans have unique and diverse physical characteristics and are proud, expressive people.

5) Characters are portrayed as foreigners and outsiders. Books with a strong plot and characterization offer credible, accurate depictions that mirror cultural and literary integrity, and reflect a range of human emotions.

6) Asian Americans are passive when confronted by racial ascription. Asian Americans are proactive people in the face of ethnic prejudice. Books used in the classroom should employ historical accuracy, presenting a balanced view of the history of hardship and courage faced by Asian Americans over time.

Aoki (1993) noted authors should transcend stereotypes and avoid the model minority and super-minority syndrome. The stereotype perpetuates the notion that Asian-American youth are passive, studious overachievers and "all Asian students excel in school, have few adjustment problems, and need little help" and is the standard by which other minorities are measured (Nieto, 1999, p. 180).

The model minority myth can be detrimental to the Asian-American community because it can exclude some ethnic communities from distribution of assistance programs, public and private, and understate or demean the achievements of particular Asian Pacific American individuals. Communities that are especially affected are Southeast Asians such as Cambodian Americans, Hmong, Laotian Americans, and ethnic groups from Burma whose communities have much lower education levels and higher poverty rates.

SELECTION CRITERIA

Teachers and teacher librarians should consider four critical factors when using Asian-American literature. First, books used in classrooms should provide readers with "sensitive, positive, and accurate portrayals" (p. 217) of the Asian-American community that negates stereotypes such as those described earlier (Pang, Colvin, Tran, & Barba, 1992). To help dispel stereotypes, recommendations from the Asian American Children's Book Project Committee (cited in Aoki, 1993) include reviewing books for instances in which

1) *Loaded words and images reinforce offensive stereotypes.* Avoid words that suggest that many or most of all Asian Pacific Americans are
   • smiling, calm, serene, quiet, shy, reserved, peaceful;
   • short, stocky, small, buck-toothed, myopic, delicate, stunted;
   • excessively obedient, passive, stolid, docile, unquestioning, overly accommodating;
   • menial (the waiter-houseboy-cook syndrome), servile (as shown through repeated bows) subservient, submissive;
   • artistic, mystical, inscrutable, philosophical, sagacious;
   • quick, dexterous, expert in martial arts;
   • exotic foreigners (even in second, third or later generations), faceless hordes or a Yellow Peril; or
   • sinister, sly, evil cunning, crafty, cruel or a people who place little value on human life.

2) *Illustrations represent Asian Americans with features such as:*

- facial structures, especially eyes to ensure that they are not slanted and without pupils (slits);
- skin color variations from white to black and include shades of brown or tan (not bright yellow); or
- dress appropriate to settings and not confused scenes of pagoda roofs or ancient emperors' courts (can portray the past or how Asian countries look today, not mix with little regard to fact).

Second, students also need to engage with high quality literature that provides a balance of representation of Asian-American cultures (Yokota & Bates, 2005). The first literary trend in the 1970's primarily focused on authors from Japan and China. Notable Chinese American author Lawrence Yep has written science fiction, fantasy, historical fiction, realistic fiction, a biography, an autobiography, and retold fairy tales. His series, *The Golden Mountain Chronicles*, are an impressive series that follow the Young family from China to America and provides historical perspectives on the immigrant experience. As history unfolds, Yep chronicles the family using American-born Chinese protagonists, but the immigration theme remains significant.

Notable author and illustrator, Allen Say, was born and raised in Japan but immigrated to the U.S. when he was 16. His books often reflect themes that show his love of both Japan and the U.S. He has written realistic fiction, retold folktales, and some of his picture books such as *Grandfather's Journey* (1993) and *Tea with Milk* (1980) are autobiographical.

An increasing variety of quality books are now written by Korean, Thai, Cambodian, Hmong, and South Asian (Indian) authors. For example, a recurring theme from Southeast Asian authors centers on immigrant stories. During the 1970–1980 decade, the influx of peoples from these countries reflects a number of immigrant waves. According to Tran (1998),

- 1975: First wave. Comprised of refugees and included employees and military personnel from South Vietnamese governments, those employed by Americans in Vietnam, members of Vietnamese middle class (doctors, engineers, educators, business people);
- 1975–78: Second wave. Group included immediate family members of first-wave as well as Laotian, Cambodian, Hmong (associated with U.S. military) peoples who escaped reeducation camps;
- 1978–80: Third wave. Exodus of boat people from Vietnam, Laos, Cambodia who lived in limbo in refugee camps under harsh camp conditions, mainly farmers, and fisherman from rural areas with little education and no association with military;
- 1980–90: Fourth wave. Group comprised of prisoners released from reeducation camps as well as Amerasian children who were fathered by U.S. soldiers.

Third, even though the issues are complex, literature should provide culturally authentic representations (Short & Fox, 2003; Yokota & Bates, 2005). In considering the complexity of cultural authenticity, Short and Fox (2003) suggest an analysis of the extent to which a book reflects the beliefs and values of a specific cultural group and accurately depicts details about their everyday life and language. Readers from the culture represented in the book need to be able to identify with and feel affirmed by what they are reading. Table 7.1 presents literary qualities and guiding questions for teachers to review books for cultural authenticity.

Table 7.1.
Criteria for Exploring Cultural Authenticity

Literary Qualities
- How well does the author tell the story?
- Is it quality literature?

Believability
- Is this story believable?
- Could it happen?
- In what ways does it feel real?

Power Relationships
- Which characters are in roles of power within the book?
- Who doesn't have power?
- What kind of actions are taken and by whom?
- How is the story resolved?

Response by insiders
- How have people from the culture responded to this book?

Origin of Book
- What is the origin of the book?
- Who was the original publisher and in what country?
- Who is the author?
- Illustrator?
- Translator?
- What are their backgrounds?

Accuracy of details and authenticity of values
- What are the inaccuracies within the details of the book?
- What values are at the heart of the book?
- How do these values connect to the actual lives of people within the culture?
- Does this book reflect a specific cultural experience or could it happen anywhere?

Audience
- Who do you think the author wrote the book for?

Connections for readers
- What are the possible connections to your own life?

Authorship
- How does the author's experiences connect to the setting and characters in this book?
- What are the experiences and/or research on which the book is based?
- Why do you think the author chose this story to tell?

Perspectives
- Whose perspectives and experiences are portrayed?
- Who tells the story?
- What is the range of insider perspectives?

Relationship to other books
- How does this book connect with other books about this cultural experience?
- Do the available books about this culture reflect different perspectives and experiences within that culture?

Source: Adapted from Stories Matter: The Complexity of Cultural Authenticity in Children's Literature, "Why the Debates Really Matter" (Short & Fox, 2003).

Culturally authentic books speak to nuances of their unique heritage, which insiders identify with and recognize. Many Ly, author of *Roots and Wings* (2008), weaves a heartrending story about a Cambodian American youth who comes to grips with self-identity mediated by her ethnic roots, learning that "cultural influence can, sometimes, strangely hibernate in deep layers of our consciousness" (Mo & Shen, 2007, p. 180). Minfong Ho (*The Clay Marble, 1991*) and Kashmira Sheth (*The Keeping Corner, 2009*) open our eyes to the lives of young adolescents that reside within the authors' country of origin. Kashmira Sheth's novel, *Boys Without Names* (2010) is a haunting tale of child labor in Mumbai, India. These books provide rich literary experiences for young adolescents and enlighten them about the cultural backgrounds and experiences of youth living in the home countries of Asian-American immigrants.

Finally, in relation to the last point, books should also explore realistic depictions of the here and now (Yokota & Bates, 2005). For example, Lisa Yee compellingly refutes the stereotype of the model Asian-American minority and the traditional view of women's status in her trilogy, *Millicent Min, Girl Genius* (2004), *Stanford Wong Flunks Big-Time* (2007), and *Totally Emily Ebers* (2008). The same story is told from the perspective of the three different main characters: Millicent, Stanford, and Emily. The first two books feature Asian-American protagonists, Millicent Min and Stanford Wong. These books serve as windows to explore complexities of Asian-American culture and youth identities. Whereas not only groundbreaking in the young adult canon of multicultural literature, Yee's books transcend the model minority myth (Endo, 2009) and use a strong, female Asian protagonist. In these books, readers engage with two very different characters who encounter struggles in some ways unique to Asian Americans and in other ways universal to all American preteens.

One valuable resource available to help select Asian-American children's literature that provides sensitive and accurate portrayals, a balance in representation, cultural authenticity, and contemporary realistic depictions is the Asian/Pacific American Librarians Association (APALA). Founded in 1980, the APALA is committed to working toward a common goal: to create an organization that would address the needs of Asian/Pacific American librarians and those who serve Asian/Pacific American communities. Since 2001, the APALA has awarded authors of adult fiction and nonfiction literature, picture books, and youth literature that reflect Asian/Pacific American heritage to "honor and recognize individual work about Asian/Pacific Americans and their heritage, based on literary and artistic merit" (see http://www.apalaweb.org/, accessed on October 01, 2010).

EXEMPLARY LITERATURE

The APALA Award is presented annually to promote Asian/Pacific American culture and heritage, based on literary and artistic merit. The books were chosen from titles by or about Asian Pacific Americans in the categories of adult fiction, honorable mention for adult fiction, adult nonfiction, honorable mention for adult nonfiction, picture book, honorable mention for picture book, youth literature, and honorable mention for text in youth literature.

In Table 7.2, we have listed the books for children and young adolescents that won the APALA award.

Table 7.2.
APALA Winners

2004–05	2006	2007	2008	2009	2010
			Picture Book Winners		
Wong, Janet S. and Margaret Chodos-Irvine (Illustrator). *Apple Pie 4th of July.* New York, NY: Harcourt, 2002. **Honorable Mention for Illustration in Children's Literature** Myer, Tim and Robert Roth (Illustrator). *Tanuki's Gift.* New York, NY: Marshall Cavendish Corp, 2003. Yin. and Soentpiet, Chris (Illustrator). *Coolies.* New York, NY: Philomel Books, 2001. Na, An. *A Step From Heaven.* Asheville, NC: Front Street, c2001.	Park, Linda Sue and Julie Downing (Illustrator). *The Firekeeper's Son.* New York, NY: Clarion Books, 2004. **Honorable Mention for Illustration in Children Literature** Yoo, Paula, and Dom Lee (Illustrator). *Sixteen Years in Sixteen Seconds: the Sammy Lee Story.* New York, NY: Lee & Low Books, 2005. Lipp, Frederick and Jason Gaillard (Illustrator). *Bread Song.* New York, NY: Mondo Publishing, 2004. Kadohata, Cynthia. *Kira Kira.* New York, NY: Atheneum Books for Young Readers, 2004.	**Illustration in Children Literature Winner** O'Brien, Anne Sibley. *The Legend of Hong Kil Dong: The Robin Hood of Korea.* Watertown, MA: Charlesbridge, 2006. **Honorable Mention for Illustration in Children Literature** Yin. *Brothers.* Illustrated by Chris Soentpiet. New York, NY: Philomel. 2006. Headley, Justina Chen. *Nothing But the Truth.* New York, NY. Little, Brown, and Co., 2006.	**Illustration in Children Literature Winner** Crowe, Ellie. *Surfer of the Century.* Illustrated by Richard Waldrep. New York, NY: Lee and Low, 2007 **Honorable Mention** Barasch, Lynne. *Hiromi's Hands.* New York, NY: Lee and Low, 2007. Easton, Kelly. *Hiroshima Dreams.* New York, NY: Dutton, 2007 **Honorable Mention** Sheth, Kashmira. *Keeping Corner.* New York, NY: Hyperion, 2007	Reibstein, Mark. *Wabi Sabi.* Illustrated by Ed Young. New York, NY: Little Brown, 2008. **Honorable Mention for Picture Book** Sheth, Kashmira. *Monsoon Afternoon.* Illustrated by Yoshiko Jaeggi. New York, NY: Peachtree, 2008. Ly, Many. *Roots and Wings.* New York, NY: Delacorte, 2008. **Honorable Mention for Text in Youth Literature** Hirahara, Naomi, *1001 Cranes.* New York, NY: Delacorte, 2008.	Gilmore, Dorina K. Lazo. *Cora Cooks Pancit.* Illustrated by Kristi Valiant. Walnut Creek, CA: Shen's Books, 2009. **Honorable Mention for Picture Book** Iyengar Malathi Michelle. *Tan to Tamarind.* Illustrated by Jamel Akib. San Francisco, CA: Children's Book Press, 2009. Woo, Sung. *Everything Asian.* New York, NY: Thomas Dunne Books, 2009.

Honorable Mention for Text in Young Adult Literature

Desai Hidier, Tanuja. *Born Confused.* New York, NY: Scholastic. 2002.

Mochizuki, Ken. *Beacon Hill Boys.* New York, NY: Scholastic. 2002.

Park, Linda Sue *A Single Shard.* New York, NY: Clarion Books, 2001.

Honorable Mention for Text in Children and Young Adult Literature

Cheng, Andrea. *Shanghai Messenger.* New York, NY: Lee & Low Books, c2005.

Park, Linda Sue. *Project Mulberry: a novel.* New York, NY: Clarion Books, c2005.

Honorable Mention for Text in Children and Young Adult Literature

Lin, Grace. *Year of the Dog.* New York, NY: Little, Brown and Co., 2006.

Yoo, Paula. *Good Enough.* New York, NY: Harper Collins, 2008.

Honorable Mention for Text in Youth Literature

Russell, Ching Yeung. *Tofu Quilt.* New York, NY: Lee & Low, 2009.

161

PREVALENT THEMES

Several themes are prevalent in Asian-American children's literature. Stories from the country of origin include folklore, celebrations, and traditions. Refugee and immigrant stories illuminate how Asian Americans have had to adjust to a new culture. There are also stories of shared histories such as the internment camps for Japanese Americans during World War II and books that have bridged cultural experiences. Relatively new to Asian-American children's literature are stories of adoption. Books for older readers highlight issues relevant to contemporary Asian-American young adolescents and focus on the intersection of their heritage, identity, and acculturation to life in Western contexts (Davis, 2004). Several authors of contemporary young adult literature reflect realistic portraits of Asian-American youth as characters experience the model minority myth (Aoki, 1993; Nieto, 1999), intergenerational conflicts, wrestling with the physicality of looking different, and the negotiation/constraint of cultural traditions. We begin with themes prevalent in picture books and then move into themes for older readers.

With each themed section, we offer pairings of books and use questions and strategies from Johnson and Freedman (2005) and McLaughlin and DeVoogd (2004) that may be posed as classroom response engagements with children that challenge them to think about texts as representational and to discuss how people may be positioned according to race, class, and gender. These questioning engagements are underpinned by the critical literacy tenet that reading from a critical literacy perspective disrupts the commonplace by examining an idea from multiple perspectives (McLaughlin & DeVoogd, 2004). This encourages children to examine culture from multiple perspectives and voices.

Whereas we offer suggestions for classroom response engagements, we also want to emphasize that critical literacy practices are not intended as stand-alone activities. Critical literacy is not formulaic in method but a practical stance towards how texts work in the social world (Luke, 2000). We support and acknowledge the notion that critical literacy is a way of engaging with texts as part of what fluent, competent readers do (Luke & Freebody, 1997). Helping readers assume a critical stance towards texts, both print and digital, helps them to question the voices behind the texts, analyzing who is represented or not represented and challenge assumptions behind the positioning of people.

ASIAN-AMERICAN LITERATURE FOR YOUNG CHILDREN

Traditional Literature

Sims Bishop (1994) reported that folktales account for about 20 percent of the total number of books from Asian-American cultures. These traditional tales have a place of origin and setting outside the United States and are often the first books available for children of color. Folktales and written forms of traditional oral tales such as legends and myths have played an important role in establishing a basis for Asian-American children's literature. Growing up as third and fourth generation Japanese Americans in Hawaii, the most accessible books with characters that looked like us were in the folktales that we returned to over and over again. One in particular was a treasured folktale of Japan, *Momotaro: Peach Boy* (Tabrah & Whatley, 1972), a classic story of a boy born in a peach who, along with animals he meets during his journey, battles and overcomes the evil *oni* (ogres) that have plundered his village for many years. This beautifully illustrated book by George Suyeoka is now in its sixth printing. Along with *Japanese Children's Favorite Stories* (1958), edited by Florence Sakade, these short stories and fables have been favorite picture books for many young children. Thus, folklore has played a critical role in the development of Asian-American children's literature and has established a basis for children of Asian ancestry to see images of people who look like them in the literature.

Other well-known picture books such as *Lon Po Po: A Red-Riding Hood Story from China* (Young, 1989) and *The Empty Pot* (Demi, 1990) are wonderfully written and illustrated traditional tales that reinforce universal values and are often used by teachers to introduce cultural content to children. More recently, authors and illustrators have attempted to take new perspectives on traditional tales to help children break common stereotypes of Asian characters. Author Kathy Tucker and illustrator Grace Lin (2003) retell the ancient Chinese folktale, *The Seven Chinese Sisters* with "shining black hair and sparkling eyes" (unpaged) which portrays each sister with her own unique features and personality, unlike the stereotyped characters in books like the *Five Chinese Brothers* (Bishop & Wiese, 1938). Author Margaret Mahy and illustrators Jean and Mou-sien Tseng's version of *The Seven Chinese Brothers* (1990) also portrays characters with unique physical features using different colored tones of brown and depicts Asian characters with nonslanted eyes. Table 7.3 lists Asian-American traditional literature.

Response Engagement

Juxtapose *Seven Chinese Sisters, Five Chinese Brothers*, and *Seven Chinese Brothers*.

- How are the pictures of the characters in the *Five Chinese Brothers* and *Seven Chinese Brothers* different?
- How are stereotypes of girls addressed in the *Seven Chinese Sisters*?
- Do you think these books represent the time period of the story accurately?

Celebrations, Ethnic Food, and Traditions

Books about celebrations and cultural traditions from Asian cultures are also readily available. Children's picture books typically describe the New Year celebrations and ethnic foods prepared by different cultural groups. In *Lion Dancer: Ernie Wan's Chinese New Year* (Waters & Slovenz-Low, 1991), six-year-old Eddie Wan prepares to perform his first lion dance in the Chinese New Year celebration in New York. *Dumpling Soup* (Rattigan, 1993) is based on the author's own experience preparing *mandoo*, a

Table 7.3.
Asian-American Traditional Literature

Title	Genre
Momotaro: Peach Boy by Tabrah & Whatley (1972)	Picture book (Folktale)
Japanese Children's Favorite Stories edited by Sakade (1958)	Folktale collection
Lon Po Po: A Red-Riding Hood Story From China by Young, (1989)	Picture book (Folktale)
The Empty Pot by Demi, (1990)	Picture book (Folktale)
The Seven Chinese Sisters by Tucker (2003)	Picture book (Folktale)
The Seven Chinese Brothers by Mahy (1990)	Picture book (Folktale)

Table 7.4.

Celebrations, Ethnic Food, and Traditions

Title	Genre
Lion Dancer: Ernie Wan's Chinese New Year by Waters and Slovenz-Low (1991)	Picture book (nonfiction)
Dumpling Soup by Rattigan (1993)	Picture book (fiction)
Cora Cooks Pancit by Gilmore (2009)	Picture book (fiction)
Bee Bim Bop by Park (2005)	Picture book (fiction)
A Carp for Kimiko by Kroll (1996)	Picture book (fiction)
Ruby's Wish by Bridges (2002)	Picture book (fiction)

Korean dumpling. In this book, seven-year old Marisa helps prepare mandoo for her multiethnic family of Korean, Japanese, Chinese, and Hawaiian origins to commemorate the New Year. In *Cora Cooks Pancit* (Gilmore, 2009), young Cora cooks pancit, a Filipino chicken and vegetable noodle dish, with her mother. While cooking, Cora's mother shares her grandfather's immigration story from the Philippines and shows how culture is shared through family stories and food. Notable author Linda Sue Park expresses a young girl's anticipation and delight while making her favorite Korean dish in *Bee Bim Bop* (2005). These kinds of books often teach children outside the culture about cultural traditions associated with celebrations and reinforce a sense of pride and identity for children who savor these foods and cherish these traditions. Picture books also illustrate a different perspective on traditions such as *A Carp for Kimiko* (Kroll, 1996). Kimiko wants her own carp kite and questions the tradition of flying colorful carps solely for boys outside their homes on Children's Day. Her parents remind her of the unique Japanese traditions reserved for girls, but it still does not quell her desire to have her own kite. In the end, Kimiko learns the importance of preserving tradition and is satisfied when her parents buy her a goldfish. Traditional roles are broken in *Ruby's Wish* (Yim Bridges, 2002), the author's grandmother's story about how a little Chinese girl abandons traditional gender roles when her father allows her to study with the boys and pays for her to attend the university. Table 7.4 lists Asian-American literature related to the themes of celebrations, ethnic food, and traditions.

Response Engagement

Comparison Chart:

- Construct a matrix with students to examine how culture is represented in these books through text and pictures.
- Discussion:
    Why did Kimiko want a carp kite on Children's Day?
    Do you think her parents should have given her a carp kite? Why?
    Do you think it is okay to do things differently from the way we usually do them?

Immigration Stories

Refugee stories are often an important part of the personal histories of Asians who have immigrated to America. These stories tell of Asians who have left their home countries in search of a new home. *My Freedom Trip: A Child's Escape from North Korea* by Frances and Ginger Park (1998) is a picture book based on the Parks' mother's experience. The authors share a powerful story of courage and faith as a young girl escapes from North Korea to South Korea prior to the Korean War.

Moving to America from different Asian countries often creates cultural conflict and raises identity issues for young children. Several picture books help children who may struggle with their identity and the challenges of adjusting to a new culture. In *The Name Jar* (Choi, 2001), a young girl is anxious to find a new name in her new country; but as she reflects on who she is, she realizes that she really wants to keep her Korean name. The deep sense of identity that this character expresses is also reflected in the picture book, *My Name Is Yoon* (Recorvits, 2003) in which Yoon holds on to her Korean values while learning to adapt to a new culture. *Angel Child, Dragon Child* (Surat, 1983) is another powerful story about a young Vietnamese girl who struggles to adjust to her new American school where she is laughed at and bullied. Most of all, she misses her mother who was left behind in Vietnam. These picture books compellingly portray immigrant children's experiences in a new culture. Table 7.5 lists Asian-American literature for young children related to the theme of immigration stories.

Response Engagement

Pair and juxtapose *The Name Jar* and *My Name Is Yoon* and have students discuss:

- How is Yoon's name important to her?
- Is Unhei's name important to her? Why or why not?
- How is your name important to you?

Bridging Cultures

Asian-American authors have also written about cross-cultural experiences and how they have bridged both cultural worlds. *Grandfather's Journey* (Say, 1993) exemplifies the beginnings of the bridging cultures theme. Based on his grandfather's memories, notable author Allen Say shares his grandfather's journey from his homeland in Japan to America. The story depicts his grandfather's and his own love for both Japan and America through simple text and compelling illustrations. In another picture book Say places a new lens on bridging cultures. *Erika-San* (Say, 2009) is about an American girl who falls in love with a picture and image of Japan as a very young child. As she grows into adulthood so does her fascination with Japan and Japanese culture. Upon

Table 7.5.
Immigration Stories for Young Children

Title	Genre
My Freedom Trip: A Child's Escape From North Korea by Park & Park (1998)	Picture book (historical fiction)
The Name Jar by Choi (2001)	Picture book (fiction)
My Name Is Yoon by Recorvits (2003)	Picture book (fiction)
Angel Child, Dragon Child by Surat (1983)	Picture book (fiction)

Table 7.6.
Bridging Cultures

Title	Genre
Grandfather's Journey by Say (1993)	Picture book (fiction)
Erika-San by Say (2009)	Picture book (fiction)

graduation from college, she leaves America to teach in Japan where she falls in love with a Japanese man and makes her new home in the countryside. These books show how one can live in very different cultures and still have a strong sense of personal and cultural identity. Table 7.6 lists Asian-American books related to the theme of bridging cultures.

Response Engagement

Setting Switch:

• Read *Grandfather's Journey* first to talk about how the place might change the story.
• Then read *Erika-San* for comparison.
• Discuss:
• Have you ever lived in a different place? How did you feel about moving to a different place?
• How did the Grandfather feel about living in America? How did he feel about living in Japan?
• How did Erika-San feel about living in America? How did she feel about living in Japan?
• Why do you think Erika-San and Grandfather felt differently about America?

Adoption Stories

Over the past several decades, adopting children from Asian countries has become increasingly common due to different economic, cultural, and demographic factors such as an oversupply of Asian adoptees, large numbers of U.S. couples who are unable to bear their own children, and small numbers of children available for adoption in the U.S. (Le, 2009). To address some of the interracial adoptee topics and issues, a number of authors have written picture books based on their personal experiences. Written in simple language for young children, the picture book *I Don't Have Your Eyes* (Kitze, 2003) recognizes physical differences but celebrates the commonalities that all people share because "We don't look the same on the outside, but in our hearts, we are the same" (unpaged). *I Love You Like Crazy Cakes* (Lewis, 2000) is based on the author's own experience as she travels to adopt a baby girl from China and expresses her deep love and joy that the child has brought into her life. Okimoto and Aoki (2002) share the excitement and anticipation of four different families as they travel overseas to adopt four little Chinese girls in *The White Swan Express*. This humorous, yet joyful story depicts the differences each family brings but also shows the love and bond that ties these families together with this shared experience. These stories are an important addition to children's literature, sharing common stories for the increasing number of Asian children adopted by U.S. couples. Another good resource for adoption stories can be found at http://sarahpark.com/, accessed on October 01, 2010. Table 7.7 lists Asian-American children's books related to the theme of adoption stories.

Table 7.7.
Adoption Stories

Title	Genre
I Don't Have Your Eyes by Kitze (2003)	Picture book (poetry)
I Love You Like Crazy Cakes by Lewis (2000)	Picture book (fiction)
The White Swan Express by Okimoto & Aoki (2002)	Picture book (fiction)

Response Engagement

Ethnic Switch Discussion:

- How did the parents feel about their adopted children?
- Did it matter that the children were of a different ethnicity from their parents?

Table 7.8 lists other recommended Asian-American books for young children.

ASIAN-AMERICAN LITERATURE FOR YOUNG ADOLESCENTS

Surviving the Internment Camp

Asian-American authors have also related their common histories and struggles through children's literature. In 1942 the U.S. government sent 120,000 innocent Japanese Americans to live in internment camps because the United States was at war with Japan in World War II. Authors of Japanese-American ancestry have written about

Table 7.8.
Other Recommended Asian-American Books for Young Children

Title	Grade Range
Dia's Story Cloth by Cha (1998)	Grades 3–5
The Lotus Seed by Garland (1993)	Grades 1–4
Hush! A Thai Lullaby by Ho (1996)	Grades K–1
Year of the Rat by Lin (2008)	Grades 2–4
The Ugly Vegetables by Lin (1999)	Grades K–2
Love as Strong as Ginger by Look (1999)	Grades K–3
Alvin Ho: Allergic to Girls, School, and Other Scary Things by Look (2009)	Grades 2–3
Thanksgiving at Obaachans by Mitsui Brown (1994)	Grades K–3
Filipino Children's Favorite Stories by Romulo, L. (2000)	Grades 1–4
The Whispering Cloth: A Refugee Story by Shea (1995)	Grades 4, 5
Monsoon Afternoon by Sheth (2008)	Grades K–2
Char Siu Bao Boy by Yamate (2004)	Grades K–2
Sixteen Years in Sixteen Seconds—The Sammy Lee Story by Yoo (2005)	Grades 3–5

their experiences or experiences of family members in these relocation camps. Yoshiko Uchida, a well-known and respected author, documents her Japanese-American internment camp experience in young adolescent novel, *Journey to Topaz* (1971). This story deals with ethnicity, citizenship, and cross-cultural relationships. More recently, Cynthia Kadohata (2006) used some of her father's experiences in the internment camp to write *Weedflower*, a novel about a young girl's friendship with a Mohave boy while she struggled to survive in an internment camp on an Indian reservation in Arizona. An excellent companion book to *Weedflower* is *The Children of Topaz: The Story of a Japanese-American Internment Camp Based on a Classroom Diary* by Michael Tunnel and George Chilcoat (1996). This book is based on a classroom diary kept by third grade children who lived in the internment camp in Topaz, Utah. The rich black-and-white photographs portray how children endured the unfair treatment under difficult conditions (Smolen & McDonald, 2008). *Under the Blood Red Sun* by Salisbury (1994), set in Hawaii, highlights the perspective of Japanese Americans after the bombing of Pearl Harbor. In this story, Tomi, a second-generation Japanese American, grapples with the racial tensions on the islands and the temporary internment of both his father and his grandfather.

In addition to the books discussed above, there are also picture books that depict how Japanese-Americans survived life within the internment camps. In *A Place Where Sunflowers Grow*, Amy Lee-Tai (2006) powerfully depicts the hardships and injustices suffered by Japanese Americans in the internment camps. Teachers can pair this book with *Baseball Saved Us* (Mochizuki, 1993) to have students explore how Japanese Americans found creative ways to maintain their sense of hope despite the despair of their circumstances.

In *Heroes* (1995) by Ken Mochizuki Donny, a Japanese American hates playing the part of the enemy every time he plays war games with his friends "because I looked like them" (unpaged). He wants to prove that he is an American and that his father and uncle fought as Americans in the WWII and the Korean War. These powerful stories are important for both children of Asian ancestry and others to learn about the discrimination and unfair treatment endured by Asians in America. Table 7.9 lists Asian-American books for young adolescents related to the theme of surviving the internment camp.

Table 7.9.
Surviving the Internment Camp

Title	Genre
Journey to Topaz by Uchida (1971)	Fiction
Weedflower by Kadohata (2006)	Fiction
The Children of Topaz: The Story of a Japanese-American Internment Camp Based on a Classroom Diary by Tunnel & Chilcoat (1996)	Nonfiction
Under the Blood Red Sun by Salisbury (1994)	Fiction
A Place Where Sunflowers Grow by Lee-Tai (2006)	Picture book (fiction)
Baseball Saved Us by Mochizuki (1993)	Picture book (fiction)
Heroes by Mochizuki (1995)	Picture book (fiction)

Response Engagement

Drama and Role-Switch:
Drama

- The teacher identifies specific incidents in the stories that evoke powerful emotions. For example, in *Heroes*, while playing war Donny is chased by his friends for being the enemy. Have students capture what Donny might be feeling at that particular point in the story.
- The teacher assigns one student to be a sculptor and a partner is assigned to be the block of clay. The sculptor shapes the clay to capture the emotion of the character in the story.
- Role Switch
- Students are assigned roles that are portrayed in each of the stories.
- Discuss the problem from the perspective of their assigned role. For example, in *Heroes*, students immerse themselves in 'being there' as the main character Donny, bystanders, teachers, principals, and others discuss what they perceive to be the problem in this story.
- Discuss what potential actions can you take from your role or position in the story? Are they able to take any actions to help?
- Other questions that might be posed to extend the discussion:
  ○ How would you feel if you were living in the desert like Sumiko in the book, *Weedflower*? (or other character/other physical environment)?
  ○ What would you do in this situation to make Sumiko (or another character) feel better about her (his) life?
- Bring the whole group together for discussion and reflection on discrimination and unfair treatment.

Immigration Stories

One of the most notable Asian-American authors is Laurence Yep, a Chinese American who lived in an African-American neighborhood but grew up in Chinatown, attending a Catholic school. Yep refers to himself as a cultural outsider, a theme that resonates in many of his books. Growing up, he concurs there were no books about Chinese Americans. An imaginative and prolific writer, Yep's books are often about Chinese immigrants, adapting, dragons, science fiction, fantasy, and mystery. From his earlier works, *Dragonwings* (1977), the story of a young boy and his family trying to make a living in twentieth century San Francisco and *Dragon's Gate* (1995), the story of Chinese immigrants working on the transcontinental railroad, Yep continues to write novels which appeal to young adolescents. His latest book, *City of Fire* (2009), is the first in the City Trilogy fantasy series. Yep's books and words help readers attain that special way of seeing into a life we often take for granted. Table 7.10 lists Asian-American books for young adolescents related to the theme of immigration stories.

Table 7.10.
Immigration Stories for Young Adolescents

Title	Genre
Dragonwings (1977)	Historical fiction
Dragon's Gate (1995)	Fiction
City of Fire (2009)	Fiction

Response Engagement

Problem Posing Discussion:

- Do you sometimes view people as odd because they have different beliefs than you do? Can you think of some examples?
- Who has power in *Dragon's Gate?* Which people have little or no power? Is this fair?
- Why do you think people continue to leave their homelands to live in countries like America?

Identity

Many Asian-American authors belong to a hybrid culture, belonging to their Asian community and at the same time being part of the U.S. mainstream. Drawing from their own experiences, they write stories portraying the challenges young adolescents of color face with identity issues. They often relate stories in which insiders in a particular setting position others as outsiders through their social interactions.

Model Minority Stereotype

In the novels, *Millicent Min, Girl Genius*, and *Stanford Wong Flunks Big-Time*, Lisa Yee skillfully uses the model minority stereotype as somewhat of a social liability. Eleven-year old Stanford Wong, the antithesis of the model minority, prefers basketball to school. Millicent Min is academically advanced beyond her 11 years and attends college. There are a few Chinese cultural stereotypes embedded within the novels such as eating dim sum, practicing *feng shui*, and learning *kung fu*. Nuances of traditional values are present in the story. Family plays an important role in both Millicent and Stanford's lives. Their second-generation grandmothers both utilize the oral tradition of storytelling to share insights about their past. Both Millicent and Stanford try to separate themselves from their Chinese-ness, yet both appreciate their Chinese American grandmothers who help them cope with preteen anxieties.

Yee juxtaposes the Min and Wong families portraying them as diverse Asian-American families whose lives are complicated by their social stances. These books both contradict and perpetuate stereotypes, thus providing readers with the requisite background to explore complex issues surrounding Asian-American representation in young adult literature. The power of her books is further enhanced by the use of universal themes added to the complex layers of Millicent and Stanford's hybrid identities as native-born Asian Americans. Readers can engage with two very different Asian-American characters who encounter struggles unique to Asian Americans yet universal to all American preteens. Yee explains that she wanted to "turn perceptions upside-down" by casting Stanford as the antistereotype (see An Interview with Lisa Yee: http://www.cynthialeitichsmith.com/lit_resources/diversity/asian_am/asian_am.html, accessed on October 01, 2010).

Response Engagement

Text Set Project:

- Have three small groups of students read one of Yep's trilogy books in a literature discussion circle: *Millicent Min, Girl Genius; Stanford Wong Flunks Big-Time; Totally Emily Ebers.*

- Engage students in short discussion about the concept of *stereotype*.
- Construct a character web of each book's main character (Millicent, Stanford, Emily) with their individual character traits and stereotypes in the story.
- Next, ask students to draw lines that show connections to other characters and explain why there is a connection.
- Students then analyze characters' perspectives toward each other or the events.
- Create additional text sets around common stereotypes (ethnic, gender, social class, etc.) for students to read. These terms will have to be explained to the students when introducing the text sets.
- Discussion questions:
- *Using ideas about the relationships between Millicent, Stanford, and Emily, what does the author want us to think about social class, gender, age, and ethnicity?*
- *How do these books contradict stereotypes (e.g., social class, gender, age and ethnicity)?*

1.5 Generation

As immigrants, Asian-American young adolescents may encounter conflicts because American values do not always align with traditions of their ancestry (Mo & Shen, 2007). Today's young adolescents are part of a culture of hybridity where they can be apart from as well as part of mainstream culture. These youth are "facing new stereotypes in a new historical context" (Mo & Shen, 2007, p. 178). Some are referred to as the 1.5 generation, or those who immigrated with their parents to the U.S.

An Na's work *A Step From Heaven* (2002), draws upon the impact of being a member of the 1.5-generation of Asian-American youth. These youth encountered challenges of learning to speak English in school and adjusting to the American culture. They experienced effects of racism by being categorized as "Chinese" or "Japanese" and often having to deal with racial alienation and ethnic mockery (Mo & Shen, 2007). In an interview with the author, An Na, she states, "*A Step From Heaven* grew from a need to express some of the longings and frustrations that I felt as an immigrant growing up in America."[See An Na on Writing: http://www.nationalbook.org/anabio .html, accessed on October 01, 2010].

As the story follows Young Ju from her childhood into young adulthood, we witness the angst and hardship of her family's adjustment to the American way of life. She struggles to remain true to her Korean heritage and family traditions and at the same time fit in as an American girl in her school. These struggles are intensified by the domestic conflict created by a depressed, alcoholic, and abusive father.

In *Everything Asian* (Woo, 2009), the difficult transitions faced by 1.5-generation youth are recounted in this book of stories-within-a novel. Joon-a (aka David) Kim and his Korean family work as store proprietors who must traverse the challenges of learning to speak and understand their English-speaking patrons and fellow storeowners within the Peddlers Town mall.

Response Engagements

Mind Portraits:

- Have students draw sketches of the parents and main characters (Young Ju or Joon-a) and write thoughts from the characters' perspective about acculturating to Western culture.

- Students can also include symbols or artifacts that represent important things to Young Ju such as her 9th grade GPA award or a family photo; for Joon-a, a sign of the Peddlers' Town Mall).
- Discussion questions: *A Step From Heaven*
  - What does An Na want readers to understand about Young Ju's immigrant experience?
  - How is Young Ju's viewpoint about living in America different from her parents or brother?
  - What would Young Ju's mom (or dad) say if s/he told the story?
- Discussion questions: *Everything Asian*
  - How might the story be different if Joon-a's dad told the story?
  - What might life be like for you if your family had to move to Korea and run a store where most people didn't speak English?

Looking Different

The comparison of physically looking different used with stereotyping poses problems when living within a predominately White world. *The Fold* (Na, 2008) showcases an Asian-American girl wanting to look more American by undergoing a common eyelid surgery to create the double eye look that Caucasian girls possess. Known as "Asian eyelid surgery," the painful procedure entails stitching a permanent crease into the eyelid so that eyes appear rounder and holds up to the Caucasian standard of beauty. The eyelid issue is also significant in *Good Enough* (Yoo, 2008) as Patti defiantly opposes the operation and acknowledges Asian girls do this because of "pressure from society" (p. 231) or sometimes pressure from elders to assimilate into Western culture.

In *Year of the Dog*, (Lin, 2007), Grace wants to try out for the part of Dorothy in her school play, "The Wizard of Oz." Her White friend Becky explains the impossibility of her being Dorothy because "Dorothy's not Chinese" (p. 70). Grace is devastated; "Like a melting icicle, my dream of being Dorothy fell shattered on the ground. I felt like a dirty puddle after the rain" (p. 70).

Year of the Dog is Lin's memoir of growing up as a Chinese American whose parents wanted her to fit in with other American youth. In an interview, she speaks of being angry or ashamed at being Chinese (see http://cynthialeitichsmith.blogspot.com/2006/01/author-illustrator-feature-grace-lin.html, accessed on October 01, 2010). *Year of the Dog* helps the reader understand Grace's hurt at being called an "Americanized Twinkie" and understand the richness of her Taiwanese heritage. Lin skillfully weaves a tapestry of her identity for the reader through the telling of her mom's stories of growing up in Taiwan, immigrating to America, her family's customs, and finally, accepting not having to belong to one group more than the other.

Nothing But the Truth (and a Few White Lies) (Headley, 2006) examines Patty Ho's search for self-identity as she wrestles with being half Taiwanese and half White in a white community. She is not comfortable in her own skin, being too tall for an Asian and too Asian for White boys. Her ultrastrict Taiwanese mom launches into lengthy lecture tirades in an effort to protect Patty from societal evils and shape her daughter's achievements in front of her Taiwanese friends. When a Taiwanese fortune-teller foresees a white boy in Patty's future, her mom ships Patty off to Stanford Math Camp to help her get into a prestigious university. Even amongst the Asian math campers, Patty struggles with being bi-racial, but eventually learns that her *hapa* (half-Asian, half-White) identity is the best of both worlds or that the "feeling of being home results only from a mutual acceptance between individual and cultural environment" (Mo & Shen, 2007, p. 180).

Response Engagement

Body/clothing switch:

- Are people with particular body types, hairstyles, cars, clothes, or attitudes admired in these books? What body type, hairstyle, car, clothes, or attitudes are not be admired?
- Other possible questions:
  - What does it mean to be an insider or an outsider? Can you think of an example in your school?
  - How would you describe yourself to someone else?
  - Do you behave differently at home than at school? Describe how your behavior might change depending on where you are. How would you like to represent yourself?
  - If you could change your physical image, what would it be and why?
    - Students could create sketches or collages of particular body types, hairstyles, cars, or clothes they admire.
    - Students could write biopoems that describe their ideal or desirable physical image.

Traditions and Culture as Part of Identity

Unlike Grace in *Year of the Dog* (2007), some Asian-American youth may stay away from coethnics who might represent the negative stereotype of forever foreigner in an effort to assert an American identity (Mo & Shen, 2007, p. 174). A good example is Gene Yang's award-winning *American Born Chinese* (2006), which deftly presents three separate comic strip stories that intertwine the fable of the monkey king who wants to be a god; the woes of Jin Wang, the sole Chinese American in school who is constantly picked on and falls in love with an American girl, and Chin-Kee, the negative Chinese stereotype who visits his cousin Danny each year. Danny is so embarrassed by this Chinese cousin that he changes schools every year in an effort to disassociate himself from this racial relationship.

These characters constantly negotiate racial ascription from the larger society and, oftentimes, the traditional influence/constraint from their immigrant family or ethnic community. These tensions produce intergenerational conflicts with parents or other elders. In *Good Enough* (Yoo, 2008, p.13), Patti Yoon's parental pressure to get into HYP ("HARVARDYALEPRINCETON . . ."), get perfect SAT scores, and aspire to role model status of well-known Korean achievers such as Sarah Chang, concert violinist, or Michelle Wie, professional golfer. Patti understands she should not disobey her parents and continues to take practice SAT tests, to study SAT vocabulary words, to draft SAT essays, and to respectfully attend Korean Church on Sundays. However, Patti experiences typical teen angst in wanting to make her own choices from dating to choosing a college. Yoo's work is a light-hearted and entertaining read that emphasizes the superminority syndrome, but nonetheless gets at real life issues faced by Asian-American youth.

Response Engagement

Problem Posing with Pictures: The use of simple language or pictures paired with the following questions can help students understand how words portray particular representations and that connotations behind words carry emotional implications (Johnson &

Table 7.11.
Identity Stories for Young Adolescents

Title	Subtheme
Millicent Min, Girl Genius by Yee (2004)	Model minority stereotype
Stanford Wong Flunks Big-Time by Yee (2007)	Model minority stereotype
A Step From Heaven by Na (2002)	1.5 generation
Everything Asian by Woo (2009)	1.5 generation
The Fold by Na (2008)	Looking different
Good Enough by Yoo (2008)	Looking different & Traditions & culture as part of identity
Year of the Dog by Lin (2007)	Looking different
Nothing But the Truth (and a Few White Lies) by Headley (2006)	Looking different
American Born Chinese by Yang (2006)	Traditions & culture as part of identity

Freedman, 2005). Gene Yang's *American Born Chinese* is an excellent graphic novel to use for this activity to highlight racial stereotypes. Table 7.11 lists Asian-American books for young adolescents related to the theme of identity stories for young adolescents.

- In what ways are words (or pictures) positive or negative?
- What do you think these words to do to those who are labeled as such or called particular names?
- How is Jin-Wang, a second-generation, American-born Chinese boy portrayed?
- How is his cousin, Chin-kee, portrayed in this graphic novel?
- How does the author use graphic images to shape our understanding about these characters?
- What does the author want us to believe?

Students could construct a collage of images they download from Google Images that depict contemporary Chinese Americans and write labels around the pictures.

- How do these images of real people compare to Jin-Wang and Chin-kee?
- How do these collages refute stereotypes?

Table 7.12 lists other recommended Asian-American novels for young adolescents.

OVERVIEW OF PACIFIC ISLAND LITERATURE

Cultural Groups

The Pacific Islanders inhabit a vast region within Oceania that encompasses about one-third of the earth. Oceania has extreme ecological and cultural diversity. The term Pacific Islander is expansive, including individuals from approximately 25,000 islands and representing many diverse populations.[3] Pacific Islander refers to those having origins in any of the indigenous peoples of Hawaii, Guam, Samoa, or any other Pacific Islands within Polynesia, Micronesia, and Melanesia (Grieco, 2001).[4] The Pacific

Table 7.12.

Other Recommended Asian-American Novels for Young Adolescents

Title	Grade Range
Children of Asian America by the Asian American Coalition (2002)	Grades 5–8
Fresh off the Boat by Dela Cruz (2005)	Grades 7–10
1001 Cranes by Hirahara (2008)	Grades 5–8
Rice Without Rain by Ho (1990)	Grades 6+
Wait for Me by Na (2007)	Grades 8+
Mismatch by Namioka (2006)	Grades 7–10
The Not-So-Star-Spangled Life of Sunita Sen by Perkins (2005)	Grades 6–9
Tangled Threads: A Hmong Girl's Story by Shea, (2003)	Grades 6–8

Islands are geographically, ethnically, culturally and linguistically diverse. Each island entity is distinct and varies considerably. There are modernized areas as well as areas that are very remote and are highly traditional. Thousands of different islands exist; there are numerous languages and dialects spoken making language policies within U.S. affiliated political entities complex (Low, Penland, and Heine, 2005).

The linguistic diversity of the Pacific Islands is illustrated by the fact that in most public schools in Hawaii, American Samoa, Commonwealth of the Northern Marianas, and Guam, English is the dominant language; however, national languages are spoken in areas such as the Freely Associated States of the Republic of Palau, the Federated States of Micronesia, and the Republic of the Marshall Islands. Many Pacific Island children are multi-lingual (Spencer, Inouye, & McField, 2007). Compounding the language issues, Klein (2007) noted that in comparison to Asian American or Pacific Islanders that have emigrated to the U.S., some Pacific Islander Americans, Hawaiians, and Chamorros have experienced the scarring effects from colonization of their lands and peoples, resulting in the denigration of their languages and fundamental cultural tenets.

Why this Literature Is Important

Oral storytelling in indigenous groups has played a critical role for passing on history, genealogy, language, rituals and knowledge of the culture (Brislin, 2003). An inherent part of the Pacific Island child's being, storytelling preserves cultural beliefs and traditional practices. Learning about their history and heritage through traditional stories helps Pacific Island children gain understanding of the importance of their people's cultural values. These stories can also help readers unfamiliar with Pacific Island cultures develop cultural understanding, refute stereotypes and increase empathy.

Historical Development of Pacific Island Literature

Challenges arise given the lack of availability, limited accessibility, and narrow scope of Pacific Island children's literature. Such literature, if available, is primarily available within the specific regional location and encompasses more books that might be considered in the realm of traditional literature. Some of these stories have made their way via oral storytelling, such as legends and myths.

Given the language complexities and the remote nature of the islands, it is often difficult to access printed materials that are tailored to the culture of each island community. Many books written by and about Pacific Island communities are written and published locally and are not readily available to wider audiences. Some attempts have been made to increase accessibility and availability of Pacific Island children's literature by using the Internet to share the culture and stories of the people of Guam, Micronesia, and the Pacific through oral storytelling and by encouraging teachers to write and print original works (Dalton, 2000). Additionally, the Pacific Resources for Education and Learning (PREL), an independent organization which serves the educational community in the U.S.-affiliated Pacific Region, has addressed the lack of children's literature by and about Pacific Islanders by offering a guide for teachers to develop their own original works to create more printed materials for children in the Pacific.

With increased technology, there has been greater access to books published in the Pacific; however, there is still a great need to expand the number of stories of Pacific Island cultures to wider audiences. As a result of the limited availability of Pacific Island children's literature, Pacific Island children rarely, if ever, see images of themselves in books.

Stereotypes in Pacific Island Children's Literature

Preconceived notions of Pacific Island residents include exotic depictions of paradise such as children who live in grass shacks, dress in grass skirts, and run away from volcanic eruptions. When reviewing books or other resources, teachers should be wary of stereotypical representations of Pacific Islanders as being lazy, too fun-loving, happy-go-lucky, or unintelligent. They are often seen in roles such as hula dancers, football players, or even bullies and gang members (Klein, 2007; Ooka-Pang, & Cheng, 1998).

The popular media often portrays Pacific Islanders as living in a tropical paradise, wearing leis, drinking tropical drinks under palm trees, and swimming and surfing on beautiful sandy beaches. Images of volcanic eruptions and natives appeasing angry gods by diving into hot lava represent Pacific Islanders as uncivilized or, at best, pleasant, but ignorant people in subsistence social structures (Brislin, 2003). Brislin makes note of the Disney film, *Lilo & Stitch*, as somewhat of a more culturally authentic attempt to portray the Hawaiian cultural value of *ohana* (family) and the natural use of *pidgin*, the Hawaiian Creole English.

Selection Criteria

When reviewing the available literature for Pacific Island children we considered the four criteria discussed in the Asian American section: 1) sensitive, positive, and accurate portrayals of Pacific Island children; 2) a balance of high quality literature that is representative of Pacific Islanders; 3) culturally authentic representations of Pacific Island communities; and 4) contemporary realistic depictions of here and now. As noted earlier, the number of available books about Pacific Islanders is limited in number and scope. Because Pacific Island literature is still evolving and much of the literature is available regionally, it is challenging to meet all four of the selection criteria in providing examples representative of all Pacific Island communities. Rather, these criteria may be used in relation to a particular Pacific Islander population. In this section we provide examples of books available to us in the Pacific region of Hawaii. However, it is important for readers to note that these criteria can be used with any island community.

First, sensitive, positive, accurate portrayals (Pang, Colvin, Tran, & Barba, 1992) of Pacific Island children should be presented. Sensitivity to stereotyping helps to refute the commonplace notion of brown-skinned natives living in an idyllic paradise. We must cautiously consider a more critical eye when perusing children's books often found at airports, grocery stores or tourist destinations that may reinforce a superficial perspective of the region. A book may be a traditional folktale or fairytale variant crafted to incorporate specific characteristics of a place. The main characters are often anthropomorphic animals and creatures of fantasy, rather than people who look like Pacific Island children or their families. Oftentimes there is a moral or a value that is shared as part of the story. Whereas these stories are very popular and add to the base of literature, they may misrepresent or oversimplify Pacific Island culture. Merely providing children with access to books that appear to market cultural diversity may increase students' awareness of cultural differences and diversity, but runs the risk of reinforcing negative stereotypes (Fang, Fu, & Lamme, 1999).

Second, teachers should provide a balance of high quality literature (Yokota & Bates, 2005) that is representative of Pacific Island cultures. Meeting this criterion is particularly challenging due to the lack of available children's literature and limited accessibility. In some Pacific Island communities, such as Hawaii, there are an increasing number of books representative of the culture that are marketable, however; they may not uphold to the high standards of literary criticism. Conversely, there are also well-written stories but written by outsiders, which brings into question authentic representation of the Pacific Island culture. One example of this issue can be raised with the story *Healing Water* written by Joyce Moyer Hostetter (2008). This historical fiction novel depicts the pain and suffering endured by the native Hawaiians with leprosy (now known as Hansen's disease) who were exiled to Molokai's Kalaupapa peninsula in the mid-1800s. Although this adolescent novel is well written and the author has evidenced extensive research about the topic, Hostetter lives outside the culture. Some Hawaiian readers may question the cultural and historical authenticity of the story with respect to the lifestyle of the main character. The Hawaiian language chapter headings may be translated accurately into English, but do not reflect implicit cultural meanings. Oftentimes, these cultural nuances are difficult to capture in a literal translation. In addition, other native Hawaiian readers have noted the tendency of non-resident writers to highlight the moral depravity of Molokai—the stealing, the sexual predators, the lawlessness, and inept managers in Kalawao—more so than books written by residents. For example, the insights and viewpoint provided in *No Footprints in the Sand*, an adult memoir of Kalaupapa by "insider" Henry Nalailelua with Sally-Jo Bowman (2006) can be contrasted with the experience of the character in *Healing Water*. Although told from the perspective of an adult in a time period almost 70 years later, Nalaielua presents a very different story and highlights the full and joyous life he experienced living on Molokai. In this case, Naleilelua's memoir may meet the criterion for cultural authenticity but is an adult book and does not meet the criteria for high quality children's literature as Hostetter's book does. These critical issues are complex and students in Pacific Island communities need opportunities to discuss high quality literature and question authentic representations of their culture. The loss of opportunity to examine different perspectives only continues to silence other voices and perpetuate possible assumptions from outsiders' perspectives.

Third, even though the issues are complex, literature should provide culturally authentic representations (Short & Fox, 2003). Pacific Island communities are comprised of both indigenous peoples as well as large communities of nonindigenous peoples who have lived in the islands over several generations and consider themselves insiders. When examining the complexity of cultural authenticity, one needs to consider whose perspectives and experiences are portrayed. For Pacific Island children, there is an unsettling history of what Brislin (2003, p. 103) calls "an image of a proud people wronged, struggling for a return of their land." Theirs is a history of voices that were silenced and marginalized. Children need opportunities to learn how to view texts as representational. Who is telling the story? What is the range of insider perspectives from the indigenous peoples' viewpoint? These questions open up exploration of power relationships and help students to construct multiple interpretations.

The Pacific Worlds Web site serves as an excellent resource for realistic and culturally sensitive depictions of cultures in the Pacific: http://www.pacificworlds.com/index.cfm, accessed on October 01, 2010, this Web site highlights geographic features of Pacific Island communities, provides teachers with lessons that represent multiple perspectives about these island communities. For example, a discussion question such as, "How did colonization impact the Pacific Island people and their way of life?" compares and contrasts western ways and indigenous ways of thinking, thereby creating an opportunity for students to learn about different viewpoints. Especially noteworthy are the photographs and footprints section, which tell stories from real people who live within the island community. Informational text features issues related to arrival, native place, the sea, the land, stories, visitors, memories, and current and future directions of the people. Language terminology of the culture is provided in addition to other resources such as readings, images, and Web sites.

Finally, Pacific Island children should also explore contemporary depictions of the here and now (Yokota & Bates, 2005). Some Pacific Island communities are populated by different ethnic groups of people who consider themselves insiders, thus, contemporary images of life today includes a diverse population of both indigenous and nonindigenous peoples. For example, in Hawaii today there are many different ethnic groups that immigrated to Hawaii and brought with them their unique cultural heritages and languages. As a result of this cultural blending, a hybridized culture emerged. The term local culture now refers to the wide range of ethnic groups with different status, beliefs, activities, and experiences, yet who share attitudes, experiences, and values among the people of Hawaii (Okamura, 1980). A local literature has evolved over the past 40 years, representing this hybridized culture and a contemporary perspective of life in Hawaii today. *Dance for the Land* (McClaren, 1999) may be considered a book that raises sensitive topics and issues representative of contemporary life. The present day setting, focus on current issues facing children in Hawaii, and authentic feel of the author's language and culture in Hawaii raise critical issues for students to discuss. The main character, 13-year-old Kate, is *hapa haole* (part white and part native Hawaiian) and moves from California to Hawaii with her dark-skinned father and brother. Kate's own light complexion and resistance to her native Hawaiian heritage complicate her struggle to fit into a culture foreign to her. She takes on the role of an outsider to the culture even though she could be considered an insider because of her native Hawaiian ethnicity. Her brother gets involved in the indigenous rights movement, whereas she is called racial names and physically harassed by a boy at school. As Kate faces the adjustments of a new school and new life, she learns about and comes to appreciate her Hawaiian heritage through the hula (dance) and becomes the nucleus of peace in her quarrelsome family. Contemporary stories such as this one can, "expose injustices" (Hade, 1997, p. 256) and help students confront the realities of racial tensions that exist in hopes of leading them toward change for more just relationships.

Exemplary Books

Another resource that teachers can look to for recommendations for literature representative of Hawaii's island culture is the Hawai'i Book Publishers Association Ka Palapala Po'okela book awards (www.hawaiibooks.org, accessed on October 01, 2010). This annual award is presented by the Hawaii Book Publishers Association to recognize the efforts of Hawaii's publishing community. The phrase, ka palapala pookela, can be translated from Hawaiian to mean excellent or exemplary manuscript. In addition, the Samuel M. Kamakau Award is presented to a book with the highest level of achievement in choice of subject, use of language and quality of presentation. Table 7.13 provides information on the Ka Palapala Po'okela winners from 2005 to 2008.

Table 7.13.
Ka Palapala Po'okela Winners

2005	2006	2007	2008
	Children's Hawaiian Culture: *Akua Hawai'i: Hawaiian Gods and Their Stories*, Kimo Armitage, illustrated by Solomon Enos, Bishop Museum Press; Honorable Mention, *Pele and Poli'ahu: A Tale of Fire and Ice*, Malia Collins, illustrated by Kathleen Peterson, BeachHouse Publishing	**Children's Hawaiian Culture**: *Lono and the Magical Land Beneath the Sea* by Caren Loebel-Fried (Bishop Museum Press) Honorable mention: *The Sleeping Giant: A Tale from Kaua'i* by Edna Cabcabin Moran (BeachHouse Publishing)	**Children's Hawaiian Culture:** *Lumpy Poi and Twisting Eels* by David Kawika Eyre, illustrated by Imaikalani Kalahele (Kamehameha Publishing). Honorable mention: *Girls' Day/ Boys' Day* by Minako Ishii (Bess Press).
Children's Illustrative or Photographic Books: *Mr. Miyataki's Marvelous Machine,* Tandy Newsome, illustrated by Don Robinson, (Island Heritage).	**Children's Illustrative or Photographic Books:** *The Hungry Pua'a and the Sweet Sweet Potato,* Leonard J. Villanueva, (BeachHouse Publishing); Honorable Mention, *Pua Polu, the Pretty Blue Hawaiian Flower,* Nona Beamer, illustrated by Caren Keala Loebel-Fried, (Bishop Museum Press).		**Children's Illustrative or Photographic Books**: *From Aloha to Zippy's: A Keiki Alphabet Book* (Bess Press). Honorable mention: *Kraken-ka, The Komodo Dragon* by Jodi Parry Belknap and Tamara Montgomery, illustrated by Joseph D. Dodd (Calabash Books).

(continued)

Table 7.13. (continued)

2005	2006	2007	2008
Samuel M. Kamakau trophy for the Hawaii Book of the Year: *The Fish and Their Gifts/Na Makana a Na I'a* by Joshua Kaiponohea Stender (Kamehameha Schools Press).	**Children's Books— Fiction or Nonfiction:** *My Dog Has Flies: Poetry for Hawai'i's Kids,* Sue Cowing, illustrated by Jon J. Murakami, (BeachHouse Publishing); Honorable Mention, *The Hawaiian Bat: 'Ope' ape'a,* Marion Coste, illustrated by Pearl Maxner, (University of Hawai'i Press).	**Children's Literature:** *Lono and the Magical Land Beneath the Sea* by Caren Loebel-Fried (Bishop Museum Press). Honorable mention: *What Am I? A Hawaii Animal Guessing Game* by Daniel Harrington, illustrated by Susan Brandt (Mutual Publishing).	**Children's Literature:** *The Watercolor Cat* by Shelly Mecum, art by Peggy Chun (Mutual Publishing). Honorable mention: *Lumpy Poi and Twisting Eels* by David Kawika Eyre, illustrated by Imaikalani Kalahele (Kamehameha Publishing).

PACIFIC ISLAND LITERATURE FOR YOUNG CHILDREN

Prevalent Themes

Themes that emerge in Pacific Island literature for young children and adolescents center on: regional literature; myths, and legends that explain natural phenomena, culture and language, and geography and history of the region.

Regional Literature

Regional children's books are typically set in a particular place and often include cultural or ecological characteristics that are unique to that specific location. It is especially important for Pacific Island children to read stories that feature characteristics of their region. For example, Pacific Island children can connect with the literature when they read books that illustrate the flora and fauna they are familiar with instead of always reading books that feature flora and fauna of the U.S. mainland. In Pacific Island communities, many books are written and published locally and may not be readily available to wider audiences. All the themes fall within the regional literature category: myths and legends, which explain natural phenomena; culture and language; and geography and history of the place. These books play an important role; they are meaningful to Pacific Island children, and they educate and inform a wider audience about the authentic and unique aspects of these communities.

Myths and Legends: Explaining Natural Phenomena

Much of the literature available for Pacific Island children is the retelling of traditional tales or written accounts of stories passed down through oral tradition. Some of the stories explain natural phenomena as in *Pele: The Fire Goddess* (Varez & Kanahele, 1991). This beautifully illustrated story retells the ancient legend of Pele, goddess of fire who resides in Kilauea's volcano on the Big Island of Hawaii. Hawaii residents often speak of her

Table 7.14.
Regional Literature

Table	Subthemes
Pele: the Fire Goddess by Varez & Kanahele (1991)	Myths and Legends: Explaining Natural Phenomena
How Maui Slowed the Sun by Tune (1988)	Myths and Legends: Explaining Natural Phenomena
Hawaiian Myths of Earth, Sea, and Sky by Thompson (1988)	Myths and Legends: Explaining Natural Phenomena
Naupaka by Beamer (2008)	Myths and Legends: Explaining Natural Phenomena
The Island-below-the-Star by Rumford (1998)	Myths and Legends
Pacific Island Legends: Tales From Micronesia, Melanesia, and Polynesia by Flood, Strong, & Flood (1999)	Myths and Legends: Explaining Natural Phenomena

fiery temper and the many different physical forms she can take such as a dog, an old woman or a beautiful young woman. It is believed that when Pele is enraged, she shows her anger with a volcanic eruption or lava flow. A video showing Kilauea's volcano and the Halemaumau crater where it is believed Pele lives can be seen at http://www .youtube.com/watch?v=Hec9yK-QQ4o, accessed on October 01, 2010. Another popular Hawaiian character is the trickster, Maui. Depicted as a young boy, this mischievous and magical hero is capable of many amazing feats such as taming the sun in *How Maui Slowed the Sun* (Tune, 1988). Stories in *Hawaiian Myths of Earth, Sea, and Sky* (Thompson, 1988) tells how Native Hawaiian storytellers of the past explained the world around them and other legends like *Naupaka* (Beamer, 2008) explain why the naupaka flower blossoms of the mountains and the sea bloom in perfect halves. In *The Island-below-the-Star* (1998) well-known author, James Rumford, tells an imaginary story of how five brothers sailed from the Marquesas Islands 1500 years ago and found the Hawaiian Islands using traditional navigation methods. *Pacific Island Legends: Tales From Micronesia, Melanesia, and Polynesia* (Flood, Strong, and Flood; 1999) gives older students a sense of Pacific Island culture through poems, legends, history, and folklore. Table 7.14 lists Pacific Island literature related to the theme of regional literature.

Response Engagement

Building prior knowledge:

- What knowledge is important to understand and respect your culture (e.g., reverence and respect for the land)?
- Who is telling the story?
- What are characteristics of this genre? How does oral storytelling support this genre?
- What do we know about the time and place that helped to explain the people's world?
- What does this myth explain about volcanic eruptions in the Pacific Islands?
- What do we learn about the Pacific Islands from these legends?

Culture and Language

Culturally specific books are often localized to describe aspects specific to place. For example, *From Aloha to Zippy's* (Bess, 2007) is an alphabet book that incorporates cultural symbols and icons characteristic to people and places in Hawaii. In this picture book for toddlers, A is for Aloha Airlines Airplane, and Z is for Zippy's, a popular restaurant that serves foods from the many different ethnic cultures in Hawaii. For Pacific Islanders, the Pacific Resources for Education and Learning (PREL) has made available *Island Alphabet Books*, which feature the specific culture's language and children's artwork. Each book includes the complete alphabet for the language, examples for each letter, and a word list with English translations. Books are available in Carolinian, Chamorro, Chuukese, English, Hawaiian, Kosraean, Marshallese, Palauan, Pohnpeian, Samoan, Satawalese, Ulithian, Woleaian, and Yapese. Other word books are also available from the University of Hawaii Press for Asian and Pacific Islanders in Vietnamese, Korean, Hawaiian, Japanese, Samoan, Chamorro, and Filipino.

Poems and songs are another category of place-based literature. Picture books written in rhyme or song, such as *Hula Lullaby* (Kono, 2005) and *Songs of Papa's Island—Micronesia* (Kerley, 1995), provide lyrical stories specific to place. These books can be used as a means of helping children identify and connect with their home culture in the classroom. Table 7.15 lists Pacific Island books related to the theme of culture and language.

Response Engagements

Cultural collage: Students compare pictures from different cultures within the Pacific Islands and engage in classroom discussion:

- What can you learn about this culture from the pictures in this book?
- What language does this group of people speak? Are there any words that you learned in this language from this book?
- Why is language important to the people in this culture?

Geography and History of the Place

Pacific Island nonfiction books describe the unique characteristics specific to the geography of the place. Stephanie Feeney's books for preschool-aged children, *A is for Aloha* (1980), an alphabet book; *Hawaii Is a Rainbow* (1985), a color book; *Sand to Sea: Marine Life in Hawaii* (1989); and *Seasons in Hawaii* (2005) are excellent examples of children's picture books that incorporate the cultural, historical, and

Table 7.15.
Culture and Language

Title	Genre
From Aloha to Zippy's by Bess (2007)	Picture Book (Alphabet book)
Hula Lullaby by Kono (2005)	Picture Book (Poetry)
Songs of Papa's Island—Micronesia by Kerley (1995)	Picture Book (Fiction)

geographic aspects of Hawaii in child-friendly terms. In addition, some books provide descriptions both in English and the language of the place. *A Coral Reef Alphabet Book for American Samoa* (Madrigal, 2001) provides photographs of coral reef life in American Samoa along with descriptions in English and some are translated into Samoan. Oftentimes, children who live on an island in the Pacific, may be subjected to reading books about bears, deer, or eagles, which are not familiar or do not reflect their own experiences. Some nonfiction books that give facts and information specific to the animals in Hawaii, for example, *Kolea: The Story of the Pacific Golden Plover* (Coste, 1998), *Sea Turtles of Hawaii* (Ching, 2001), and *The Hawaiian Bat: `Ope`ape`a* (Coste, 2005), are now available.

Children's picture books that share historical and biographic information are also important to learning about a place. For example, David Kawika Eyre has written a 12-story series documenting the life of Hawaii's King Kamehameha (2009). Biographical picture books such as *Duke's Olympic Feet* (Crowe, 2002) chronicles five key events in Hawaii's Olympic swim champion and internationally recognized surfer, Duke Kahanamoku, between 1911 and 1914. Reading biographies about successful people who look and speak like the people in their culture inspires children. Table 7.16 lists Pacific Island books related to the theme of geography and history of the place.

Response Engagements

In my own backyard: Students research geography and history of a unique aspect of their community

- How does the geography influence the people, plants, and animals who live in this place?
- Were there events in the community's history that influenced the people, plants, and animals that live in this place?
- What would happen if invasive species are brought into island communities (e.g., coqui frogs)?

Table 7.16.
Geography and History of the Place

Title	Genre
A Is for Aloha by Feeney (1980)	Picture book (Alphabet book)
Hawaii Is a Rainbow by Feeney (1985)	Picture book (Concept book—colors)
Sand to Sea: Marine Life in Hawaii by Feeney (1989)	Picture book (Nonfiction)
Seasons in Hawaii by Feeney (2005)	Picture book (Nonfiction)
A Coral Reef Alphabet Book for American Samoa by Madrigal (2001)	Picture book (Alphabet book)
Kolea: The Story of the Pacific Golden Plover by Coste (1998)	Picture book (Nonfiction)
Sea Turtles of Hawaii by Ching (2001)	Picture book (Nonfiction)
The Hawaiian Bat: `Ope`ape`a by Coste (2005)	Picture book (Nonfiction)
Duke's Olympic Feet by Crowe (2002)	Picture book (Fiction)

Pacific Island Literature for Young Adolescents

Literature for Pacific Island young adolescents encompasses primarily novels that are regional literature specific to Hawaii, incorporating culture, language, history, and geography. As noted in the Asian-American literature section, notable author Graham Salisbury continues to engage young adolescent readers with stories and characters of Hawaiian cultural backgrounds. Salisbury weaves history and Hawaiian legend into a modern day tale in his novel, *Night of the Howling Dogs* (2007), and makes clear for readers the importance of place. His story is based upon camping adventures at the site of the 1975 natural disaster at Halape on the southern coast of the Big Island of Hawaii. In *Blue Skin of the Sea* (1992), Salisbury masterfully creates eleven stories about a young boy's life growing up in Kona, Hawaii. Each story is unique and can stand alone; however, the stories are also brilliantly woven together to create a whole. Written about life in the early 1950's, this book describes the main character's life on the Big Island of Hawaii as he comes to grips with being a member of Hawaiian fishing family and his fear of the ocean. Salisbury captures his readers' attention by illuminating issues universal to the human experience, yet powerfully portrays experiences unique to Hawaii's island culture. We share the following questions generated by a class of fifth graders, who read this novel as part of a text set on culture. These questions serve as a good model to inspire lively discussions about racism and inequitable treatment of those from different cultural backgrounds:

Response Engagements

Literature circles: Students read Salisbury's *Blue Skin of the Sea*.

Ask students to generate topics and issues about racism raised in the books. Have students generate questions about these issues. For example,

- Why do people mistreat others when they don't like it when they are themselves mistreated?
- Why do people tease others about their race?
- How can we combat racism when we face it? How do we protect ourselves from racism?
- Why do people judge others by the way they look instead of the way they feel, think, and act?
- Why do people have prejudice against others?
- How can we protect and continue our cultures and traditions?
- Does mistreatment occur mostly to certain cultures?
- How come culture is important?
- Why do people make fun of other people's culture? How do people decide which culture is better or worse?

Then, create text sets to explore these issues. Teachers can select texts related to specific topics, which can help students explore issues to deepen thinking and generate new questions. For example, to address racial teasing a text set including picture books such as *Angel Child, Dragon Child* (Surat, 1983), *Heroes* (Mochizuki, 1995), *Whoever You Are* (Fox, 1997), and *All the Colors of the Earth* (Hamanaka, 1994). Table 7.17 lists other recommended Pacific Island literature for children and young adolescents.

Closing Thoughts

In this chapter we have discussed Asian-American and Pacific Island literature and provided ways teachers might begin to open a dialogue with their students about this

Table 7.17.

Other Recommended Pacific Island Literature for Children and Young Adolescents

Title	Grade Range
Surfer of the Century: The Life of Duke Kahanamoku by Crowe (2007).	Grades K–3
Pulelehua and Mamaki by Crowl (2009)	Grades 2–5
I Had a Dollar in Hawaii by Endicott (1999)	Grades K–3
Surf's Up for Kimo by Germain (2000)	Grades K–2
A Is for Aloha by Goldsberry (2005).	Grades K–1
Koa's Seed by Han (2004)	Grades 3–4
Winter Is for Whales: A Book of Hawaiian Seasons by Hirsch (2007)	Grades K–4
Lullaby Moon by Masters (2002)	Grades K–2
The Royal Waker Upper by Masters (2003)	Grades K–4
To Find a Way by Nunez (1992)	Grades 2–5
Too Many Mangos: A Story About Sharing by Paikai (2009)	Grades K–3
The Last Princess: The Story of Princess Kaiulani by Stanley (2001)	Grades 2–5
Princess Pauahi by Williams (2005)	Grades K–5

important body of work. Literature helps us to understand our own world as well as those of others with which we are not familiar, and although our students come from a wide variety of backgrounds and have many varied perspectives, they are filled with questions about the world around them and can learn much from the broad swath of multicultural literature that is available today.

Changing how we frame the window changes how we view the world (Stevens & Piazza, 2010). By engaging their students in an open and honest dialogue about the differences and similarities that our cultures share, and by incorporating multicultural literature into that discussion, teachers have many opportunities to help their students to be part of a more inclusive and pluralistic society. Literature itself is a cultural tool through which we can see ourselves from different perspectives; the very act of reading has a strong impact on our identity. Sometimes literature can position readers according to race, class, gender, and perspective (Davies & Harre, 1990). By enabling our students to see life through a different set of eyes, we are helping them to see the world in more vivid detail, giving them the vision needed to take part in the globalized society that they will one day be in charge of.

We believe it is important to continue to raise the level of awareness, dispel stereotypes, and work to build empathy as the foundation to work towards a more equitable society of compassion and respect for all humanity. In the classroom and library, we can begin by asking students to think about what assumptions we make about our world and ourselves. We can teach students to look closely at the language used to support these assumptions and beliefs. We can pose questions that help students ponder whether these assumptions hold true for all people across cultures. Using literature whose protagonists struggle with situations that students may face in their own lives challenges them to think about how the world works for or against certain people. Ultimately, a questioning stance helps students develop an awareness of stereotyping and an understanding of injustice. Indeed, this is the first step toward addressing social justice in order to create a more democratic and equitable society.

We believe classrooms and libraries need to be enhanced with high quality literature which presents balanced perspectives, demonstrates sensitivity to stereotyping, and builds appreciation and understanding of diverse cultures. Knowing students and their real issues is an important factor for teachers to consider in selecting books that will move the students to engaged and meaningful discussions. Juxtaposing alternative texts that dispel stereotypes and open doors to cultural understanding moves students to new and powerful insights. Teachers and teacher librarians also need to be asking themselves questions about whether they are providing enough support for students to cope with sensitive issues that magnify and make explicit negative attitudes which may still exist toward race, ethnicity, and culture.

When we visit the local bookstore, traditional favorites, such as *The Five Chinese Brothers* (Bishop & Wiese, 1938), are still prominently displayed and jump out at us. However, as we search deeper and carefully comb through the shelves, we find books that challenge us to uncover Asian-American and Pacific Islander stereotypes. These books reveal the complex layers that shape the lives of contemporary Asian-Americans and Pacific Islanders. Fortunately, we now have access to literature that provides alternatives that help bridge some of the gaps and silences that have existed in the past for Asian-Americans and Pacific Islanders. Students need to be provided with spaces that invite new frames from which to view the world. Doing so will create and build pluralistic communities shaped by the cultural tapestry of the richly diverse voices discussed in this chapter.

REFERENCES

Aoki, E. M. (1993). Turning the page: Asian Pacific American children's literature. In V. J. Harris (Ed.), *Teaching multicultural literature in grades K–8* (pp. 109–135). Norwood, MA: Christopher Gordon.

Brislin, T. (2003). Exotics, erotics, and coconuts: Stereotypes of Pacific Islanders. In P. M. Lester & S. D. Ross (Eds.), *Images that injure: Pictorial stereotypes in the media* (2nd ed., pp.103–112). Westport, CT: Praegar Publishers.

Cai, M., & Sims Bishop, R. S. (1994). Multicultural literature for children: Towards a clarification of the concept. In A. H. Dyson and C. Genishi (Eds.), *The need for story: Cultural diversity in classroom and community* (pp. 57–71). Urbana, IL: National Council of Teachers of English.

Cooperative Children's Book Center. (2008). *Children's books by and about people of color published in the United States*. Retrieved from School of Education, University of Wisconsin-Madison: http://www.education.wisc.edu/ccbc/books/pcstats.htm.

Cullinan, B. (1989). *Literature and the child*. New York, NY: Harcourt Brace Jovanovich.

Dalton, B. (2000). To see one another more clearly: A Pacific children's literature project. *Reading Online*. Retrieved from: http://www.readingonline.org/electronic/elec_index.asp?HREF=rt/5-00_column/index.html.

Davies, B., & Harre, R. (1990). Positioning: The discursive production of selves. *Journal for the Theory of Social Behaviour, 20*, 43–63.

Davis, R. G. (September, 2004). Reinscribing (Asian) American history in Laurence Yep's *Dragonwings*. *The Lion and the Unicorn, 28*(3), 390–407.

Eggen, P. D., & Kauchak, D. P. (2010). *Educational psychology: Windows into classrooms* (8th ed.). Upper Saddle River, NJ: Pearson.

Endo, R. (2009). Complicating culture and difference: Situating Asian American youth identities in Lisa Yee's *Millicent Min, Girl Genius* and *Stanford Wong Flunks Big-Time*. *Children's Literature in Education*, 40, 235–249. doi: 10.1007/s1053-009-9085-0.

Fang, Z., Fu, D., & Lamme, L. (1999). Rethinking the role of multicultural literature in literacy instruction: Problems, paradox, and possibilities. *The New Advocate, 12*(3), 259–276.

Grieco, E. (2001, Dec.). The Native Hawaiian and other Pacific Islander population: *Census 2000 brief*. U.S. Census Bureau. Retrieved from: http://www.census.gov/prod/2001pubs/c2kbr01-14.pdf.

Hade, D. (1997). Reading multiculturally. In V. Harris (Ed.), *Using multiethinic literature in the K–8 classroom* (pp. 253–256). Norwood, MA: Christopher-Gordon Publishers.

Johnson, H., & Freedman, L. (2005). *Developing critical awareness at the middle level*. Newark, DE: International Reading Association.

Klein, S. (2007). *Handbook for achieving gender equity for children*. Mahwah, NJ: Lawrence Erlbaum Associates.

Le, C. N. (2009). Adopted Asian Americans. Asian-Nation: The landscape of Asian America. *Asian Nation*. Retrieved from: http://www.asian-nation.org/adopted.shtml.

Low, M., Penland, D., & Heine, H. (2005, August). The language question in Pacific education: The case of the Republic of the Marshall Islands. Pacific Resources for Education and Learning Research Brief. *Pacific Resources for Education and Learning*. Retrieved from: http://www.paddle.usp.ac.fj/collect/paddle/index/assoc/prel016.dir/doc.pdf.

Luke, A. (2000). Critical literacy in Australia: A matter of context and standpoint. *Journal of Adolescent & Adult Literacy, 43*(5): 448–461.

Luke, A., & Freebody, P. (1997). The social practices of reading. In S. Muspratt, A. Luke, & P. Freebody (Eds.), *Constructing critical literacies: Teaching and learning textual practice*. (pp. 185–226). Cresskill, NJ: Hampton Press, Inc.

McLaughlin, M., & DeVoogd, G. L. (2004). *Critical literacy: Enhancing students' comprehension of text*. New York, NY: Scholastic.

Mo, W., & Shen, W. (2007). Home: A feeling rooted in the heart. *Children's Literature in Education, 38*, 173–185. doi: 10.1007/s10583-006-9023-3.

Moll, L. C. (1992). Funds of knowledge for teaching: Using a qualitative approach to connect homes and classrooms. *Theory into Practice, 31*(2), 132–41.

Nieto, S. (1999). *Affirming diversity: The sociopolitical context of multicultural education* (3rd ed.). Boston, MA: Allyn & Bacon.

Norton, D. (1991). *Through the eyes of a child* (3rd ed.). New York, NY: Macmillian.

Okamura, J. (1980). *Aloha kanaka me ke aloha aina*: Local culture and society in Hawaii. *Amerasia, 7*(2), 119–137.

Ooka-Pang, V., & Cheng, L. (1998). *Struggling to be heard: The unmet needs of Asian Pacific American children*. Albany, NY: SUNY Press.

Pang, V., Colvin, C., Tran, M., & Barba, R. (1992). Beyond chopsticks and dragons: Selecting Asian-American literature for children. *The Reading Teacher, 46*(3), 216–224.

Reeves, T., & Bennett, C. (2003, May). The Asian and Pacific Islander population in the United States: March, 2002. Current population reports. *U.S. Census Bureau*, March 2003, 520–540. Retrieved from: http://www.census.gov/prod/2003pubs/p20-540.pdf.

Rosenblatt, L. (1995). *Literature as exploration* (5th ed.). New York, NY: The Modern Language Association of America.

Short, K., & Fox, D. (2003). The complexity of cultural authenticity in children's literature: Why the debates really matter. In D. Fox and K. Short (Eds.), *Stories matter: The complexity of cultural authenticity in children's literature* (pp. 3–24). Urbana, IL: National Council of Teachers of English.

Sims Bishop, R. (1994). A reply to Shannon the canon. *Journal of Children's Literature, 20*(1), 6–8.

Sims Bishop, R. (1997). Selecting literature for a multicultural curriculum. In V. Harris (Ed.), *Using multiethnic literature in the K–8 classroom* (pp. 1–19). Norwood, MA: Christopher-Gordon.

Smolen, L., & McDonald, S. (2008). Adolescent literature and reader response: 'It's about global awareness and social justice!' *The International Journal of Learning 15*(10), 207–212.

Spencer, M. L., Inoue, Y., & McField, G. P. (2007). Achieving gender equity for Asian and Pacific Islander Americans. In S. S. Klein (Ed.), *Handbook for achieving gender equity for children* (pp. 501–524). Mahwah, NJ: Lawrence Erlbaum Associates.

Stevens, L. P., & Piazza, P. (2010). Dear President Obama and Secretary Duncan: You are looking through the wrong window. *Journal of Adolescent & Adult Literacy, 53*(6), 512–515.

Tran, M. T. (1998). Behind the smiles: The true heart of Southeast Asian American children. In V. O. Pang and L. L. Cheng (Eds.), *Struggling to be heard: The unmet needs of Asian Pacific American children* (pp. 45–57). Albany, NY: State University of New York Press.

U.S. Census Bureau. (2008). American factfinder. The face of our population. Retrieved from U.S. Census Bureau: http://factfinder.census.gov/jsp/saff/SAFFInfo.jsp?_pageId=tp9_race_ethnicity.

Yamate, S. (1997). Asian Pacific American children's literature: Expanding perceptions about who Americans are. In V. Harris (Ed.), *Using multiethnic literature in the K–8 classroom* (pp. 95–128). Norwood, MA: Christopher-Gordon.

Yokota, J. (2009). Asian Americans in literature for children and young adults. *Teacher Librarian, 37*(3).

Yokota, J., & Bates, A. (2005). Asian American literature: Voices and images of authenticity. In D. Henderson and J. May (Eds.), *Exploring culturally diverse literature for children and adolescents: Learning to listen in new ways* (pp. 323–325). Boston, MA: Allyn & Bacon.

WEB SITES WITH RESOURCES FOR ASIAN-AMERICAN AND PACIFIC ISLANDER CHILDREN'S LITERATURE

An Na's Web site http://www.nationalbook.org/anabio.html, accessed on October 01, 2010.

Asian Pacific American Librarians Association Web site http://www.apalaweb.org/, accessed on October 01, 2010.

Cynthia Leitich Smith's Web site http://www.cynthialeitichsmith.com/lit_resources/diversity/asian_am/asian_am.html, accessed on October 01, 2010.

International Children's Digital Library Web site http://en.childrenslibrary.org/, accessed on October 01, 2010.

Pacific Rim Voices Project, Paper Tigers Web site http://www.papertigers.org/, accessed on October 01, 2010.

Philippine Board on Books for Young People celebrates the National Children's Book Day in the Philippines. http://www.pbby.org.ph/index.html, accessed on October 01, 2010.

The Reading Rockets Web site invites us to hear firsthand, the wisdom from notable authors, such as Laurence Yep that has stood the test of time (http://www.readingrockets.org/books/interviews/yep, accessed on October 01, 2010) through video interviews.

Sarah Park's Web site http://sarahpark.com/, accessed on October 01, 2010.

South East Asia booklist http://www.poojamakhijani.com/sakidlit.html, accessed on October 01, 2010.

University of California, Center for Multicultural and Multilingual Research Web site http://www-bcf.usc.edu/~cmmr/Asian.html, accessed on October 01, 2010.

Worlds of Words Web site (http://www.wowlit.org, accessed on October 01, 2010) highlights multicultural and international books, including book reviews and stories of teachers using literature discussion in K–12 classrooms.

MULTICULTURAL BOOKS

Beamer, N. (2008). *Naupaka*, illustrated by C. K. Loebel-Fried. Honolulu, HI: Bishop Museum Press.

Bess, B. (2007). *From aloha to Zippy's*. Honolulu, HI: Bess Press.

Bishop, C. H. (1938). *The five Chinese brothers*, illustrated by K. Wiese. New York,NY: Putnam.

Cha, D. (1998). *Dia's story cloth*, illustrated by Chu and N.T. Cha. New York, NY: Lee & Low Books, Inc.

Ching, P. (2001). *Sea turtles of Hawaii*. Honolulu, HI: University of Hawaii Press.

Choi, Y. (2001). *The name jar*. New York, NY: Dell Dragonfly Books.

Coste, M. (1998). *Kolea: The story of the Pacific golden plover*, illustrated by F.E. Salmon, Jr. Honolulu, HI: University of Hawaii Press.

Coste, M. (2005). *The Hawaiian bat: 'Ope 'ape 'a*, illustrated by P. Maxner. Honolulu, HI: University of Hawaii Press.

Crowe, E. (2002). *Duke's Olympic feet*, illustrated by M. N. Brown. Waipahu, HI: Island Heritage.

Crowe, E. (2007). *Surfer of the century: The life of Duke Kahanamoku*, illustrated by R. Waldrep. New York, NY: Lee & Low Books.

Crowl, J. (2009). *Pulelehua and Mamaki*, illustrated by H. Orme. Honolulu, HI: Bishop Museum Press.

Dela Cruz, M. (2005). *Fresh off the boat*. New York, NY: HarperTeen.

Demi, (1990). *The empty pot*. New York, NY: Henry Holt and Company.

Endicott, J. (1999). *I had a dollar in Hawaii*, illustrated by H. Loffel. Honolulu, HI: Palila Books.

Eyre, D. (2009). *Kamehameha set, part I: The rise of a king*, illustrated by I. Kalahele. Honolulu, HI: Kamehameha Publishing.

Feeney, S. (1980). *A is for aloha*, photos by H. Hamid. Honolulu, HI: University of Hawaii Press.

Feeney, S. (1985). *Hawaii is a rainbow*, photos by J. Reese. Honolulu, HI: University of Hawaii Press.

Feeney, S. (2005). *Seasons in Hawaii*. Honolulu, HI: University of Hawaii Press.

Feeney, S., & Robinson, A. (1989). *From sand to sea: Marine life in Hawaii*, photos by E. Robinson. Honolulu, HI: University of Hawaii Press.

Flack, M., & Wiese, K. (1933). *The story of Ping*. New York, NY: Viking Press.

Flood, B., Strong, B.E., & Flood, W. (1999). *Pacific Island legends: Tales from Micronesia, Melanesia, Polynesia and Australia*, illustrated by C.J. Adams. Honolulu, HI: Bess Press.

Fredericks, A. (2007). *The tsunami quilt*, illustrated by T. Yee. Chelsea, MI: Sleeping Bear Press.

Fox, M. (1997). *Whoever you are*, illustrated by L. Staub. San Diego, CA: Harcourt Brace.

Garland, S. (1993). *The lotus seed*, illustrated by T. Kiuchi. San Diego, CA: Harcourt Brace.

Germain, K. (2000). *Surf's up for Kimo*, illustrated by K. Montes. Haleiwa, HI: Island Paradise Publishing.

Gilmore, D. (2009). *Cora cooks pancit*, illustrated by K. Valiant. Walnut Creek, CA: Shen's Books.

Goldsberry, U. (2005). *A is for aloha*, illustrated by T. Yee. Chelsea, MI: Sleeping Bear Press.

Hamanaka, S. (1994). *All the colors of the Earth*. New York, NY: HarperCollins.

Han, C. (2004). *Koa's seed*, illustrated by K. Peterson. Ewa Beach, HI: Beach House Publishers.

Headley, J. C. (2006). *Nothing but the truth (and a few white lies)*. New York, NY: Little, Brown & Co.

Hidler, T. D. (2003). *Born confused*. New York, NY: Scholastic.

Hirahara, N. (2008). *1001 cranes*. New York, NY: Delacorte.

Hirsch, R. (2007). *Winter is for whales: A book of Hawaiian seasons*, illustrated by Y. Green. Waipahu, HI: Island Heritage Press.

Ho, M. (1990). *Rice without rain*. New York, NY: HarperCollins.

Ho, M. (1991). *The clay marble*. Evanston, IL: McDougal Littell.

Ho, M. (1996). *Hush! A Thai lullaby*, illustrated by H. Mead. New York, NY: Orchard Books.

Hostetter, J. (2008). *Healing water: A Hawaiian story*. Honesdale, PA: Calkins Creek Books.

Kadohata, C. (2006). *Weedflower*. New York, NY: Atheneum.

Kerley, B. (1995). *Songs of Papa's Island*, illustrated by K. Tillotson. New York, NY: Houghton Mifflin.

Kitze, C. (2003). *I don't have your eyes*, illustrated by R. Williams. Warren, NJ: EMK Press.

Kono, E. E. (2005). *Hula lullaby*. New York, NY: Little, Brown, and Company.

Kroll, V. (1996). *A carp for Kimiko*, illustrated by K. Roundtree. Watertown, MA: Charlesbridge Publishing.

Lee-Tai, A. (2006). *A place where sunflowers grow*, illustrated by F. Hoshino, Japanese translation by M.A. Lee. San Francisco, CA: Children's Book Press.

Lewis, R. (2000). *I love you like crazy cakes*, illustrated by J. Dyer. New York, NY: Little, Brown, & Company.

Lin, G. (1999). *The ugly vegetables*. Watertown, MA: Charlesbridge Publishing.

Lin, G. (2007). *Year of the dog*. New York, NY: Little Brown & Company.

Lin, G. (2008). *Year of the rat*. New York, NY: Little Brown & Company.

Look, L. (1999). *Love as strong as ginger*, illustrated by S. Johnson. New York, NY: Atheneum.

Look, L. (2009). *Alvin Ho: Allergic to girls, school, and other scary things*, illustrated by L. Pham. New York, NY: Random House.

Ly, M. (2008). *Roots and wings*. New York, NY: Delacorte Press.

Madrigal, L. (2001). *A coral reef alphabet book for American Samoa*. Honolulu, HI: Pacific Resources for Education and Learning.

Mahy, M. (1990). *The seven Chinese brothers*, illustrated by J. Tseng & M. Tseng. New York, NY: Scholastic.

Masters, E. (2002). *Lullaby moon*, illustrated by T. Yee. Waipahu, HI: Island Heritage Press.

Masters, E. (2003). *The royal waker upper*, illustrated by A. Leung. Waipahu, HI: Island Heritage Press.

McClaren, C. (1999). *Dance for the land*. New York, NY: Atheneum Books.

Mitsui Brown, J. (1994). *Thanksgiving at Obaachans*. Chicago, IL: Polychrome Books.

Mochizuki, K. (1993). *Baseball saved us*. New York, NY: Scholastic.

Mochizuki, K. (1995). *Heroes*, illustrated by Dom Lee. New York, NY: Lee & Low Books.

Na, A. (2002). *A step from heaven*. New York, NY: Penguin Group.

Na, A. (2007). *Wait for me*. New York, NY: Speak (Penguin Group).

Na, A. (2008). *The fold*. New York, NY: G. P. Putnam's Sons.

Nalailelua, H. with Bowman, S. (2006). *No footprints in the sand: A memoir of Kalaupapa*. Honolulu, HI: Watermark Publishing.

Namioka, L. (2006). *Mismatch*. New York, NY: Delacorte (Random House).

Nunes, S. (1992). *To find the way*, illustrated by C. Gray. Honolulu, HI: University of Hawaii Press.

Okimoto, J. D. & Aoki, E. (2002). *The White Swan Express: A story about adoption*, illustrated by M. So. New York, NY: Clarion Books.

Paikai, T. (2009). *Too many mangos: A story about sharing*. Waipahu, HI: Island Heritage.

Park, F., & Park, G. (1998). *My freedom trip: A child's escape from North Korea*, illustrated by D. R. Jenkins. Honesdale, PA: Boyds Mills Press.

Park, L. (2005). *Bee-bim bop*, illustrated by H. Lee. New York, NY: Clarion Books.

Perkins, M. (2005). *The not-so-star-spangled life of Sunita Sen (Originally published as: The Sunita experiment)*. New York, NY: Little, Brown and Company.

Phillips, L. (2004). *Island alphabet books—Carolinian*. Honolulu, HI: Bess Press.

Phillips, L. (2004). *Island alphabet books—Chamorro*. Honolulu, HI: Bess Press.

Phillips, L. (2004). *Island alphabet books—Chuukese*. Honolulu, HI: Bess Press.

Phillips, L. (2004). *Island alphabet books—Hawaiian*. Honolulu, HI: Bess Press.

Phillips, L. (2004). *Island alphabet books—Kosraean*. Honolulu, HI: Bess Press.

Phillips, L. (2004). *Island alphabet books—Marshallese*. Honolulu, HI: Bess Press.

Phillips, L. (2004). *Island alphabet books—Palauan*. Honolulu, HI: Bess Press.

Phillips, L. (2004). *Island alphabet books—Pohnpeian*. Honolulu, HI: Bess Press.

Phillips, L. (2004). *Island alphabet books—Samoan*. Honolulu, HI: Bess Press.

Phillips, L. (2005). *Island alphabet books—Satawalese*. Honolulu, HI: Bess Press.

Phillips, L. (2009). *Island alphabet books—Ulithian*. Honolulu, HI: Bess Press.

Phillips, L. (2009). *Island alphabet books—Woleaian*. Honolulu, HI: Bess Press.

Rattigan, J. M. (1993). *Dumpling soup*, illustrated by L. Hsu-Flanders. Boston, MA: Little, Brown, and Company.

Recorvits, H. (2003). *My name is Yoon*, illustrated by G. Swiatkowska. New York, NY: Farrar, Straus and Giroux.

Romulo, L. (2000). *Filipino children's favorite stories*, illustrated by J. De Leon. North Clarendon, VT: Periplus Editions (HK) Ltd.

Rumford, J. (1998). *The Island-Below-the-Star*. Boston, MA: Houghton Mifflin Company.

Sakade, F. (1958). *Japanese children's favorite stories*, illustrated by Y. Kurosaki. Osaka: Tuttle Publishing.

Say, A. (1980) *Tea with milk*. New York, NY: Houghton Mifflin.

Say, A. (1993). *Grandfather's journey*. New York, NY: Houghton Mifflin.

Say, A. (2009). *Erika-San*. New York, NY: Houghton Mifflin.

Salisbury, G. (1992). *Blue skin of the sea*. New York, NY: Laurel Leaf.

Salisbury, G. (1994). *Under the blood-red sun*. New York, NY: Random House.

Salisbury, G. (2007). *Night of the howling dogs*. New York, NY: Wendy Lamb Books (Random House).

Shea, P. (2003). *Tangled threads: A Hmong girl's story*. New York, NY: Clarion Books/Houghton Mifflin.

Sheth, K. (2007). *The keeping corner*. New York, NY: Hyperion.

Sheth, K. (2008). *Monsoon afternoon*, illustrated by Y. Jaeggi. Atlanta: GA: Peachtree Publishers.

Sheth, K. (2010). *Boys without names*. New York, NY: Balzer + Bray.

Stender, K. (2004). *The fish and their gifts/Na makana a na la*, illustrated by A. Bate, L. Eads, L. Frizzell, P. Herron-Whitehead, K. Lindsey, M. Kakalia, N. Keopuhiwa, K. Puhi, & P. Svendsen. Honolulu, HI: Kamehameha Schools Press.

Stanley, F. (2001). *The last princess: The story of princess Kaiulani*, illustrated by D. Stanley. New York, NY: HarperCollins.

Surat, M. M. (1983). *Angel child, dragon child*, illustrated by V.D. Mai. New York, NY: Carnival Press.

Tabrah, R., & Whatley, K. (1972). *Momotaro, Peach Boy*, illustrated by G. Sueyoka. Waipahu: Island Heritage Publishing.

Thompson, V. L. (1988). *Hawaiian myths of earth, sea, and sky*, illustrated by M. Kahalewai. Honolulu, HI: University of Hawaii Press.

Tucker, K. (2003). *The seven Chinese sisters*, illustrated by G. Lin. Morton Grove, IL: Albert Whitman and Company.

Tune, S. (1988). *How Maui slowed the sun*, illustrated by R. Burningham. Honolulu, HI: University of Hawaii Press.

Tunnel, M., & Chilcoat, G. (1996). *The children of Topaz: The story of a Japanese-American internment camp based on a classroom diary*. New York, NY: Holiday House.

Uchida, Y. (1971). *Journey to Topaz*, illustrated by D. Carrick. Berkley, CA: Heyday Press.

Varez, D., & Kanahele, P. (1991). *Pele: the fire goddess*. Honolulu, HI: Bishop Museum Press.

Waters, K., & Low, M. (1991). *Lion dancer: Eddie Wan's Chinese New Year*, photographs by M. Cooper. New York, NY: Scholastic.

Williams, J. (2005). *Princess Pauahi*, illustrated by R. Racoma. Honolulu, HI: Bishop Museum Press.

Woo, S. J. (2009). *Everything Asian*. New York, NY: St. Martin's Press.

Yamate, S. (2004). *Char Siu Bao boy*, illustrated by C. Yao. Chicago: Polychrome Books.

Asian American Coalition. (2002). *Children of Asian America*. Chicago: Polychrome Books.

Yang, G. (2006). *American born Chinese*. New York, NY: First Second.

Yee, L. (2004). *Millicent Min, girl genius*. New York, NY: Scholastic.

Yee, L. (2007). *Stanford Wong flunks big-time*. New York, NY: Scholastic.

Yee, L. (2008). *Totally Emily Ebers*. New York, NY: Scholastic.

Yep, L. (1977). *Dragonwings*. New York, NY: HarperCollins.

Yep, L. (1995). *Dragon's Gate*. New York, NY: HarperCollins.

Yep, L. (2009). *City of fire*. New York, NY: Starscape.

Yim Bridges, S. (2002). *Ruby's wish*, illustrated by S. Blackall. San Francisco, CA: Chronicle Books.

Yoo, P. (2008). *Good enough*. New York, NY: HarperCollins.

Yoo, P. (2005). *Sixteen years in sixteen seconds-the Sammy Lee story*. New York, NY: Lee.

Young, E. (1989). *Lon Po Po: A Red Riding Hood story from China*. New York, NY: Scholastic.

NOTES

1. According to 2003 Census Bureau estimates, the number of people who reported being Asian is growing at a much faster rate than other races and the population of Asians grew from 11.9 (4.2% of the population) in 2000 to 13.5 million. In 2004 the population projections indicate that the Asian population is expected to grow 213 percent by 2050, to 33.4 million, or 8 percent of the total population (U.S. Census, 2008).

2. A panethnic Asian American identity first developed in Hawaii before World War II as an organized effort by the plantation laborers to protect themselves from being exploited by plantation owners. Panethnic identities developed further as a second Asian generation in Hawaii and native Hawaiians formed voting blocs to unseat racist politicians. This political maneuver manifested a panethnic identity continued to develop in the 1960s on the U.S. mainland. Thus, a collective identity as Asian-Americans was

formed. The hyphenated term has since been changed. See [http://science.jrank.org/pages/9754/Multiple-Identity-in-Asian-Americans-Panethnic-Identity.html, accessed on January 02, 2010].

3. Prior to the 2000 U.S. Census, Asian or Pacific Islander was established under the same racial category; however for the 2000 Census, a separate racial category, Native Hawaiian or Other Pacific Islander was created (U.S. Census Bureau, 2008).

4. Approximately 900,000 or 0.3 percent of the population reported Native Hawaiian or Other Pacific Islander in the United States in 2000. In 2003, Census Bureau estimates indicate that Native Hawaiians and other Pacific Islanders is another quickly growing population and increased 5.8 percent in three years.

8

Latino Literature for Children and Adolescents

F. Isabel Campoy and Alma Flor Ada

This chapter aims to present an overview of what outstanding Latino authors, writing in English or Spanish, have contributed to the field of literature for children and adolescents in the United States, and to identify the most significant themes addressed by their literature. The space limitation to one chapter restricts us from naming all Latino authors and illustrators or all their titles. Instead, we have included representative examples of the themes we identify.

BRIEF OVERVIEW OF THE LATINO CULTURE

Latinos, that is, native speakers of Spanish or their descendants living in the United States, are a product of the intermarriage of Native Americans and people of African descent with Spaniards. Each of these groups represent a great diversity: the Spaniards come from the interweaving of multiple people who have inhabited the Iberian Peninsula through the centuries, Native American cultures are multiple and distinct, and the people of African descent in Spanish-speaking America had also very diverse origins. Additional richness was contributed by people from various lands who immigrated to Latin America at different times and under diverse circumstances. All of this contributed to the birth of a *mestizo* people of unique characteristics; and every Latin American is *mestizo* either by blood, by culture, or both. The Mexican thinker José Vasconcelos coined the term "Raza cósmica," the cosmic race, to refer to the people resulting from such a confluence of origins.

Reflecting the richness of their heritage, Latinos can look and think very differently from one another, even within the same family. Their appearance and demeanor can be as diverse as their class, education, language repertoire, or degree of assimilation into the majority culture.

What unites Spanish-speakers today is the Spanish language and a worldview embedded within the language. This worldview, which can be shared with their descendants, values closely-knit relationships among family and friends, placing human needs above such abstract realities as professional success. In this worldview the concept of honor has great significance; people would like their word to carry as much weight as a signed document. Happiness and joy of life, particularly as expressed through music, song, and dance, are essential to this approach to life in which conversation is valued, elders are respected and cared-for, and generation gaps are not fostered. People of all ages celebrate together at every possible occasion.

The food and music of the celebrations vary from region to region, sometimes within the same country, and these differences should not be taken lightly; one is first Mexican, Puerto Rican, Dominican, or Cuban, and then Latino or Latina. Yet, in spite of significant distinctions, all Latinos share a common sense of history, a common worldview, and a clear link to the Spanish language.

SELECTION CRITERIA

Most of the books included in this analysis have been recognized by the Pura Belpré, Tomás Rivera, and Americas awards committees. Some have received recognition from other award committees such as Newbery, Aesop (American Folklore Association), Once Upon a Story (Museum of Tolerance), Parent's Choice, Christopher Medal, Junior Library Guild or by *Colorín Colorado*, *Críticas*, *Kirkus Review*, *The Horn Book*, *School Library Journal*, *Publishers Weekly*, and other professional journals in print or digital format. Some of the books were written in English, and may or may not have been translated into Spanish. Some appear in bilingual editions. A few have been published only in Spanish.

A clear distinction is made between books for children and children's literature. Many beautiful and informative books belong in children's libraries and children's hands, but they do not represent exactly the artistry necessary to be considered literature. Whereas they could be recommended in a different context, they fall outside the parameters for inclusion here.

The brevity inherent in a chapter make this presentation far from exhaustive and does not allow the exploration of the magnificent literature for children and adolescents published in Spanish in 20 countries. These books should all be present in libraries and schools in the United States and made accessible to Latino children. They deserve to be studied by bilingual teachers and translated and published in the United States.

The chapter also does not include books about Latinos by authors who are not Latinos themselves. Whereas the merit of a book is not determined by the heritage of the author or illustrator but rather by their intention, knowledge, sensitivity, responsibility, and artistry, the experience of a people can seldom be told authentically from the outside. A long contact with the people of the culture and its environment has allowed a few non-Latino writers (Arthur Dorros, Jane Medina, and Tony Johnston are some of them) to create excellent books about Latinos, yet their work falls outside the established scope: literature of merit created by outstanding Latino writers.

OVERVIEW OF THE LITERATURE

Historical Development

The first Spanish speakers to come to the Americas brought with them a rich oral treasury of nursery rhymes, songs, ballads, tongue-twisters, riddles, folktales, and legends that is alive to this day. This oral tradition stems from many sources: old tales from the Arab tradition, ancient Hebrew stories like *The Horse of Seven Colors*, *romances* (the Medieval ballads that gave origin to the Mexican *corrido*) and centuries-old harvest songs like *De colores*. Wherever people of Spanish-speaking descent live, the *Dama Blanca* or *Dama del alba* of the old Spanish legends continues to cry at night looking for her lost children as *La Llorona*, just as Juan Bobo, also known as Pedro Urdemales or Pedro Remales, continues to entertain them with his trickster's deeds. In African tales, the animal characters may have changed but the stories continue to retain their power.

The First Voice: José Martí

It is remarkable that Martís work which transformed forever how writing for children would be viewed in the Spanish-speaking world was created in New York. In 1889, José Martí published *La Edad de Oro* (The Golden Age) a literary magazine for children, which he wrote in its entirety and addressed to all the Spanish-speaking children of the Americas. Through a new style of writing that was light and suggestive, the magazine reflected a new appreciation of the child reader. Only four issues of the magazine were published, but they have been collected into a book that has been constantly reprinted throughout the Spanish-speaking world. This book marks the beginning of a written Latino children's literature.

Sensitive to children's vast interests and wanting to make them true citizens of the world, Martí wrote for them in a variety of genres: original stories and retelling of traditional tales, poetry, biographical sketches, nonfiction information, and essays. Each entry was of outstanding literary quality. In laying the foundation for a way of speaking to children that was light, fresh, engaging, and captivating without the moralizing heaviness of the times; Martí's diverse examples opened up vast possibilities. Whereas *La Edad de Oro* (1889) continues to be published in its entirety as a book, some of its entries have also been published independently. For example, in the United States the long story in verse, *Los zapaticos de rosa* (The Pink Slippers) has been published by Lectorum as a book illustrated by Lulú Delacre (Martí, 1997). It also appears in *El son del sol* (The Sun's Song, 1998) published by Del Sol Books and has been recorded in an original musical arrangement by Suni Paz.

Whereas Martí was a modernist writer, intent on delighting with the beauty of the language and its imagery, he addressed many social issues that are still prevalent today. The young protagonists, the children that he considered to be "the hope of the world," rise up to help create the world he envisioned, "the happy time when all human beings treat each other as friends." He denounces class differences in *Los zapaticos de rosa* (1997), which tells of a generous child ready to give what she treasures to ease someone else's pain. The original story *La muñeca negra* (The Black Doll) addresses the issue of discrimination.

Martí emphasizes that all children of the Americas, regardless of their own particular ethnicity, must recognize "our indigenous mother" and our debt to the indigenous people. This is not a romantic claim, but one born of a deep social consciousness. He uses a variety of literary tools, in prose and verse, to share with children the respect due to all people. His literature denounces any sort of discrimination and oppression and expresses his hope that young people will embrace the concept of equality among all human beings and espouse justice as the means for living in a world at peace.

In addition, he believed that truth and knowledge are the roads to freedom. He wanted children to know about human achievements in all fields: in the works of the great European poets, musicians, and artists as well as in the great achievements of the indigenous populations of the Americas, in particular, those of Mexico, the country he loved so dearly.

In one magnificent essay, Martí invites young readers to accompany him through the World Exhibition in Paris in 1889, using this opportunity to talk about the French Revolution and its ideals. The description of each Latin American pavilion in the Fair becomes a piece of history told as an enchanting tale. Describing the murals in the Mexican pavilion, he asserts, "That's how one should love the motherland, fiercely and tenderly." But even though Martí loved his motherland so fiercely, and the bigger mother, la Patria Grande, as he considered all Latin America to be, he hoped for respect and unity among all people of the Earth.

Martí devoted another of the essays of *La Edad de Oro* entirely to Vietnam, its land, and its people, explaining the teachings of Buddhism with the same respect he explained the beliefs of the ancient Greeks and the Aztecs. "They are like fine silversmiths in all they do," he writes, "be it wood or ivory, armory or weavings, painting or embroidery," [the translation is the authors'] as he dwells on the historical destiny of this land, so many times colonized and conquered, affirming that the peace-loving people who had been repeatedly invaded would eventually have to rebel against foreign colonizers, bringing about much sorrow. It attests once more to his vision that more than half a century later Vietnam would be so significant in the history of the United States.

Cartas a María Mantilla is a compilation of Martí's (1982) letters to the child he very much loved. Fearing his imminent death, as he prepares in Santo Domingo to go to fight for Cuba's independence, he gives María what may be his last advice. He takes a feminist stance, insisting on the importance of education for women, telling the young girl that education will not only provide her with personal enrichment and a means to earn her living but will give her the possibility of knowing true love. Only if she is free to work and be independent will she have the freedom to share her life out of love and not, like most women of her time, out of dependence.

In these letters, Martí elaborates on the art of translation, one of the skills he suggests María can develop. He proposes that translation be transparent and explains how to write for young people in a manner that brings clarity and honesty to the words. His advice has become an inspiration for many Latin-American writers.

Emerging Recognition of Latino Children's Literature

As a *mestizo* people, Latinos have inherited an extraordinarily rich oral tradition. In Florida, along the Mississippi, in New Mexico, Arizona, Colorado, Texas, and California, the old songs, legends, and stories have lived on in the hearts of the people, sometimes taking on new settings and characters and new myths, legends, and stories are developing.

A few significant Latino writers appeared earlier; yet, despite the seminal work of Martí and the richness of the old and new traditions, a literature for and about children and young adults of Hispanic descent, written by Latino authors and drawing on this wealth of material, was virtually nonexistent for most of the twentieth century. In the few instances where non-Latino writers touched upon Latino themes, Latino people were at best romanticized as exotic creatures. Most often, however, they were treated in a stereotypical and pejorative manner.

The transition from a rich oral literature to a written literature for children and adolescents was a slow process for Latinos. Although a significant number of Spanish-speakers have lived for generations on the same land, the division of that land into countries has changed through treaties and wars. When the territory north of the Río Grande was annexed to the United States, the Mexican population living there became citizens of New Mexico, Arizona, Colorado, Texas, or California. As the mainstream language changed from Spanish to English, their cultural identity became a personal challenge for each family and individual. The Puerto Ricans shared a similar experience when their island became a trophy of war after the Spanish-American War in 1898. They also have needed to define their language and identity against the backdrop of stereotypical views propagated by the media to justify the war and territorial takeover. Once such views become part of the general perception, it becomes very difficult to eradicate them.

For most of the twentieth century, authors wanting to portray an authentic view of Latinos, in either Spanish or English, directed their writing to adult readers and usually resorted to small independent presses. Latino literature for children and adolescents came of age only in the 1990s. A few voices paved the way, most significantly Pura Belpré (1909–1992), Ernesto Galarza (1905–1984), Piri Thomas (1928), George Ancona (1929), Hilda Perera (1930), Rudolfo Anaya (1937), Nicholasa Mohr (1938), and Alma Flor Ada (1938).

Pura Belpré [1909–1982]

Born in Cidra, Puerto Rico, in 1909, only 10 years after the publication of *La Edad de Oro*, Pura Belpré, who attended the New York Public Library School program and Columbia University, became the first Puerto Rican librarian in the New York public system. After many years of storytelling in the library, she initiated her publications with retelling traditional tales. In 1932, she published *Pérez and Martina*, a shortened English version of a tale well known throughout the Spanish-speaking world. In 1946, *The Tiger and the Rabbit and Other Tales*, appeared, a collection of stories which shows the rich African heritage of Puerto Rico. This was followed in 1962 by *Juan Bobo and the Queen's Necklace*, a story of the beloved trickster, who was apparently silly and inwardly cunning, and in 1969, by *Oté: A Puerto Rican Folktale*.

After publishing folktales for close to 30 years, in 1961 Pura Belpré published *Santiago*, her first realistic fiction story. The transition to this genre is of great significance. It exemplifies the need among Latino writers to record and celebrate their roots before beginning to look at and re-create their present-day reality.

Santiago is a young boy living in New York who constantly daydreams about his life in Puerto Rico and the pet hen he left behind. It depicts the homesickness and sense of loss of the immigrant and was probably inspired by Pura Belpré's own childhood experiences.

Belpré's last book in English, *The Rainbow Colored Horse*, another folktale, was published in 1978, the same year she received the award of the *Asociación de Literatura Infantil y Juvenil en español y portugués*, during the association's first conference in San Francisco.

Pura Belpré's lifelong involvement in children's literature is a true example of the responsibilities faced by our pioneer authors. She kept the old tales alive by telling them in Spanish in the Bronx Public Library, sometimes with the aid of puppets, for three generations. She used to glow when telling how the grandmothers who walked into her library with their grandchildren had heard the same stories from her. She expanded the life and reach of the tales by publishing them in English so that they could be read by all children. Finally, she was able to re-create for us some of the difficult experiences of living in two worlds and the feelings of the immigrant child. She brought them to light, not only so that children who are undergoing similar experiences could find themselves in a book, but also to extend to other children an awareness of these brown children with sparking eyes and funny accents whose inner richness they may otherwise perhaps never suspect. To share her own childhood, she wrote *Firefly Summer* (1996), published by Piñata Books.

Pura Belpré received numerous well-deserved awards during her lifetime. The American Library Association (ALA) honored her pioneering work by giving her name to the ALA Award for Latino authors of books for children and young adults. *The Storytelling Candle* by Lucía González (2008), illustrated by Lulú Delacre, is a biography of Pura Belpré for children.

Ernesto Galarza [1905–1984]

Determined to provide Latino children in California with quality literature that addressed them directly, Ernesto Galarza, who had come from México when very young, took on the task single-handed. Just as Martí wrote all the pages of *La Edad de Oro* (1889) by himself, Galarza wrote, translated, and published his books, usually illustrating them with photographs he himself had taken. The very humble format of these wonderful little books published under his own imprint, Almadén, as a collection he called Mini-libros, does not obscure the quality of Galarza's poems, many of which have been incorporated into anthologies and reading programs in Spanish and English. The books from the Mini-libros collection have been out of print for many years, although they certainly deserve to be reprinted.

Two of Galarza's most important contributions were, first, singing to the everyday experience of the children of farmworkers and showing them the poetry in the world around them; and second, making the bilingual/bicultural reality a focus of some of his books, by giving a Mexican flavor to some of the traditional English rhymes, initiating a trend that other authors will later follow.

Like Pura Belpré, Galarza was honored by the *Asociación de Literatura Infantil y Juvenil en español y portugués*, during the association's second congress in México City, where Gabilondo Soler [also known as Crí-Crí] was also honored.

Piri Thomas [1928–]

Born Juan Pedro Tomás in Harlem of a Puerto Rican mother and a Cuban father, Piri Thomas's struggle for identity began very early in a vicious street environment of poverty, drugs, and violence. He experienced seven years of incarceration, which fed his determination to put his talent to the service of youth to turn them away from a life of crime. He shared his life experiences in three autobiographical novels *Down These Mean Streets* (1967), *Savior, Savior, Hold My Hand* (1972), and *Seven Long Times* (1974). These experiences also inspired the book *Stories from the Barrio* (1978).

George Ancona [1929–]

Born in New York of Mexican parents, George followed on his father's footsteps looking at the world through the lenses of a camera. His robust photography is nurtured by a creativity that allows him to depict angles and details that could otherwise escape our attention. An extraordinarily caring person, George is known to develop lasting friendships with the protagonists of his books, who he is able to depict in all their humanness. Ancona has published over one hundred books, over two-thirds of which he has also written. He has provided children with the richest and most diverse visual image of the Latino people and their everyday life experiences. The books *Pablo Remembers: The Fiesta of the Day of the Dead* (Ancona, 1993), published also in Spanish as *Pablo recuerda: La fiesta del Día de los Muertos*, and *Barrio: José's Neighborhood* (Ancona, 1998) published also in Spanish as *El barrio de José*, were some of the first books to present with great dignity the life in the barrio. The series of six bilingual books *We Are Latinos/Somos Latinos* (2004) explore the lives of Latino families of various origins, in different parts of the country, focusing in different aspects of their lives. Ancona's view of the cultural manifestations in our cities can take different outlooks. *Fiesta USA (1995)* chronicles celebrations, *In City Gardens* (1996) [In Spanish: *En los jardines de la ciudad*] records the efforts of communities to create communal gardens inside the city, whereas *Murals: Walls that Sing* (2003) is a recognition to the significance of murals within our barrios.

Ancona has also created books to share with children the reality of the lands of their ancestors. He has explored, with his characteristic insight, aspects of Mexican people and culture in *El piñatero/The Piñata Maker* (1994), *Mayeros: A Yucatán Maya Family* (1997), *Charro: The Mexican Cowboy* (1994) among other. The five books of the *Viva México* series (2001) depict different aspects of Mexican life: The folkart, the foods, the people, the past. In *Harvest* (2001), he explores the reality of the farm workers' lives and their poorly recognized contribution to the U.S. society.

Ancona does not limit his topics to Latinos in the United States or in Mexico. He has explored multiple topics including those of disability and artistic expressions. As additional contributions to Latino topics, he has created books about other Latin American cultures as in *Cuban Kids* (2000) and *Capoeira: Dance! Game! Martial Art!* In collaboration with Joan Anderson he published *Spanish Pioneers in the Southwest* in 1989, published also in Spanish as *Los pioneros españoles en el suroeste*. This very important book challenges the unfortunate misconception that the Spanish speakers populating the Southwest were armored men on horseback who came to conquer. In truth, the Spanish settlers mainly were families who cultivated the land and raised livestock. Their farms gave origin to the rich cattle industry and the sheep herds of the Southwest. From them, we inherited the tradition of cultivating grapes, olives, and numerous fruits, as well as two elements essential to the culture of what would become the United States, the horse, and the guitar. Ancona's photographs show the lives of the pioneering Spanish families with precise details.

Hilda Perera [1930–]

This Cuban author had a well-established career before moving to the United States, particularly for the book *Cuentos de Apolo*. She continued publishing in Spain, where in 1975 she received the Premio Lazarillo, the Spanish equivalent to the Newbury Award, for her book *Cuentos para chicos y grandes*.

Rudolfo Anaya [1937–]

Anaya, who writes for all ages, is a giant among Latino writers. His book *Bless Me, Última* (1972) has remained a best seller since its publication in 1972. It is a blessing for young readers that he has decided to extend his work to them by sharing his passion for the Southwestern culture with books of traditional stories and legends like *Maya's Children: The Story of La Llorona* (1997), *My Land Sings: Stories from the Río Grande* (2003) and *The Santero's Miracle: A Bilingual Story* (2004), with picture books like *Roadrunner's Dance* (2000) and *The First Tortilla* (2005) and with stories told in verse, like *Juan and the Jackalope: A Children's Book in Verse* (2009).

Older children will get a combination of history and the power of story with *Serafina's Stories* (2004). Like a New Mexican Scherezade, Serafina, a Pueblo Indian girl, strikes a bargain with the colonial governor in 1680. She will tell him one story each night, and if he likes her story, he will pardon one of the Pueblo Indians who had conspired to incite a revolution. The stories Serafina tells are a combination of European stories that had taken a New Mexican flavor as well as original Indian stories as a demonstration of the mestizo reality essential to New Mexico.

Anaya's (2000) *Elegy on the Death of César Chávez* is an exquisite and inspiring book. Because César Chávez is an American hero, this book belongs in the hands of all youth.

Nicholasa Mohr [1938–]

The issue of identity, common in adolescence, becomes very significant for bicultural people. Latino youths growing up in the U.S. search for their identity both with regard to their parents and grandparents who may speak Spanish and maintain many traditions from back home and the general population. They may feel caught like a hinge, neither fully on one side nor the other.

Nicholasa Mohr was perhaps the first Latino author to address this issue in a children's book. Felita's quest for identity continues to be as authentic today as when the book *Felita* (1979) received the Américas Book Award in 1981.

Alma Flor Ada [1938–]

Alma Flor Ada's writing had been published in Perú and in Spain for 21 years when *The Gold Coin*, which received the Christopher Award, was published in the United States in 1991. Since then, she has published continuously in multiple genres, memoirs (*Under the Royal Palms*), poetry (*Gathering the Sun, Coral y espuma*), and diverse styles, like her fractured fairy tales in letter format (*Dear Peter Rabbit*) or in newspaper format (*Extra! Extra!*) in both English and Spanish. Issues of identity, family, language and cultural preservation, resilience and persistence take many different expressions in her narrative work. Her poetry can be whimsical and humorous or of a delicate lyricism.

Children's Literature in Spanish in the United States: The 1970s and 1980s

The development of bilingual education in the United States during the decade of the 1970s raised awareness of the need for books in Spanish for Spanish-speaking students. As a consequence, some publishing houses from Spain began first importing, and later publishing, literature in Spanish, as in the case of Santillana and its imprint Alfaguara. Small publishing houses developed to produce materials primarily for this population. Some were born initially as nonprofit organizations supported by federal and private foundations, for example, Piñata Books of Arte Público Press in Houston and Children's Book Press in San Francisco. Others were strictly commercial, like Hampton-Brown. Specialized distributors also imported children's literature from Latin America and Spain, in particular Mariuccia Iaconi of Iaconi Books, Linda Goodman, and Teresa Mlawer, owner of Lectorum, which also developed its own publishing house.

In the early 1970s, a group of enthusiastic idealists became aware of the scarcity of information in the field of children's literature in Spanish and the limited communication between authors, illustrators, publishers, and critics in Spanish-speaking countries and those working with Spanish-speaking children in the United States. To bridge this gap, they created the *Asociación Internacional de Literatura Infantil en español y portugués* in San Francisco. The founding members included librarian Mary Frances Johnson, teacher Tim Beard, dedicated book distributor Mariuccia Iaconi (a pioneer in the identification and dissemination of books written in Spanish). With support from Susan Benson at the Organization of American States, BABEL a Title VII resource center in Berkeley, and the University of San Francisco, in 1978, they organized the First Congress of Literature in Spanish and Portuguese in San Francisco. The presenters included children's literature specialists and historians from various countries: Carmen Bravo Villasante from Spain, Efraín Subero from Venezuela, Flor Piñeyro de Rivera from Puerto Rico, Marta Dujovne from Argentina, as well as Carmen Diana Dearden representing Ekaré-Banco del Libro from Venezuela and Gabriel Larrea representing the Secretaría de Educación Pública de México. That year, the award of the Association was given to Pura Belpré who was present to receive it and was introduced by Anne Pellowski.

This landmark event encouraged follow-up sessions. The Secretaría de Educación Pública de México and the Organization of American States cosponsored a second congress in Mexico City with a special symposium in Cocoyoc and a third one in Tucson, Arizona.

In the Second Congress, the association awards were presented by Alma Flor Ada to Ernesto Galarza and Gabilondo Soler (also known as Cri-Crí). During the Third Congress, the award was granted *in absentia* to the Puerto Rican poet Ester Feliciano Mendoza and presented by Flor Piñeyro de Rivera.

Participating countries were Argentina, Bolivia, Colombia, Cuba, Mexico, Panama, Peru, Puerto Rico, Spain, and Venezuela. As a result of those meetings, the International Board of Books for Young People (IBBY) was initiated, strengthened, or expanded in those countries. Right after the Second Congress, CIDCLI, a publishing company devoted to children's literature, was born in Mexico and took as its logo the one that had been developed for that Congress. And as a follow-up to the Mexican Congress, a Children's Literature Book Fair was inaugurated in Mexico City, and continues to function annually. Now, more than 30 years later, the reflections, activities, partnerships, and support that originated during these first congresses are still evolving.

In 1981, Sylvia Cabazos Peña, professor at the University of Houston and an active member in the Asociación, edited *Kikirikí*, which was soon followed by *Cuenta-ca-tún*. Arte Público Press published both of these bilingual anthologies of Latino writers. Although the selections included are of diverse merit, they represent a significant pioneering effort as the first anthologies to gather the writings of Latino authors of children's literature and thus to give recognition to their work.

New courses in Children's Literature in Spanish in the University of Texas at El Paso, the University of Arizona in Tucson, the University of Houston and Saint Thomas University in Houston, Texas, and the University of San Francisco in San Francisco, California, among others, began to bring academic recognition to this field. Whereas these were some of the first courses devoted exclusively to the study and analysis of children's literature in Spanish and Latino children's literature as distinguished from methodological courses on the use of literature in the classroom, other courses have later developed across the nation. Presentations on Latino children's literature are now frequent at regional and national conferences.

For several years, there was a Center for the Study of Children's Books in Spanish at the California State University, Domínguez Hills. It has now been transformed into the Isabel Schon International Center for Spanish Books for Youth in the San Diego Public Library. In 1998, the journal *Cuentaquetecuento*, published in Costa Rica with distribution throughout Latin America, dedicated volume III, no. 3, to Latino Children's Literature, in an effort to bring awareness to Latin Americans of what Latino authors are producing in the United States

The Development of Latino Children's Literature in English in the 1990s and Beyond

The minimal presence of Latino writers in the field of children's literature in the United States began to turn around slowly at the end of the 1980s. Keeping in mind that the number of books for children and young adults published by Latino authors is still very small in proportion to the total number of books published, it is noteworthy that most of them have been published since 1990.

In addition to the previously mentioned developments, several other factors seem to have come into play. Latin American literature (with figures such as Gabriel García Márquez, Mario Vargas Llosa, and Carlos Fuentes) as well as Latino literature (Isabel Allende, Sandra Cisneros, Julia Álvarez, and Oscar Hijuelos) gained great credibility and readership. Some well-established Latino writers (like Rudolfo Anaya and Gary Soto) began to write for younger audiences and Latino writers who were publishing and winning awards in Latin America and Spain (like Hilda Perera and Alma Flor Ada) began to be published and translated into English in the United States. A dedicated group of librarians formed the REFORMA group in the ALA to advocate for, among other goals, authentic literature by Latino authors. As an incentive, they lobbied for several years to establish the Pura Belpré Award, which was finally inaugurated in 1996 to be given biannually.

As the number of quality books produced by African-American authors and illustrators increased and became more visible, Latino authors and illustrators were stimulated and inspired to benefit from this example. At meetings of the United States Section International Board of Books for Young Children (USBBY), American Library Association (ALA), International Reading Association (IRA), National Council of Teachers of English (NCTE) and other similar forums, specialists in the field began strongly encouraging publishers to search for and support Latino writers. Whereas there is much need for improvement, there is now a growing body of literature that can be shared with students.

PREVAILING THEMES

The scope of this section is to present the topics found in Latino literature since 1990. Individual portraits of major Latino authors and descriptions of their most relevant books can be found in the very informative book *Latina and Latino Voices in Literature for Children and Teenagers*, by Frances Ann Day (2003). Internet searches will also contribute up-to-date factual information about the creators in this evolving field. Their names will appear as their works are mentioned as examples of the identified themes.

When analyzed collectively, this body of literature shows seven major themes:

* preserving the oral traditional folklore;
* transmitting history, cultural achievements and everyday life from Spain and Latin America;
* sharing personal memoirs;
* depicting Latino life and culture; ·
* celebrating Latino poetic voices;
* giving free rein to fantasy; and
* writing for the stage.

Preserving the Oral Traditional Folklore

Exiled from childhood, adults may feel profound nostalgia for their early years and want to share the traditions that enriched their own childhood with their children and the children of their children. For Latino authors, the popular oral literature takes on special significance by providing a literature families can share to strengthen their sense of identity and gain confidence through being part of an unending culture. Having themselves experienced the pain of uprootedness, some may want to offer new immigrant children the comfort of the known and familiar. Having loved these traditions, they might all wish to share and preserve them by telling them to all children.

Among those who have collected oral traditional folklore are F. Isabel Campoy and Alma Flor Ada (*¡Pío Peep!*, 2003; *Mamá Goose*, 2004; *¡Merry Navidad!*, 2007; *¡Muu, Moo!*, 2010; *Ten Little Puppies/Diez perritos*), 2011; Lulú Delacre, (*Arroz con leche: Popular Songs and Rhymes from Latin America*, 1989; *Las Navidades: Popular Christmas Songs from Latin America*, 1990; *Arrorró mi niño: Latino Lullabies*, 2006); José Luis Orozco (*De Colores and Other Latin American Folk-songs for Children*, 1994; *Diez deditos/Ten Little Fingers and Other Play Rhymes and Action Songs from Latin America*, 1997); and Suni Paz (*From the Sky of My Childhood/Del cielo de mi niñez*), 1979.

Among those who have retold the old tales are Alma Flor Ada (*Mediopollito/Half-chicken*, 1995; *The Lizard and the Sun/La lagartija y el sol*, 1995; *The rooster who went to his uncle's wedding*, 1993; *Three Golden Oranges*, 1999); Julia Álvarez (*A Gift of Gracias: The Legend of Altagracia*, 2005); Rudolfo Anaya (*My Land Sings: Stories from the Río Grande*, 1999); Carmen Bernier-Grant (*Juan Bobo: Four Folktales from Puerto Rico*, 1994); María Cristina Brusca (*When Jaguars Ate the Moon and Other Stories about Animals and Plants of the Americas*, 1995); F. Isabel Campoy

(*Rosa Raposa*, 2002; *Tales Our Abuelitas Told/Cuentos que contaban nuestras abuelas*, 2006); Carmen Agra Deedy (*Martina the Beautiful Cockroach*, 2007); the Salvadorian J. Argueta retells one of the legends of his country (*Zipitio/El zipitio*, 2007); George Crespo (*How Hwariwa the Cayman Learned to Share: A Yanomami Myth*, 1995); Lulú Delacre (*Golden Tales: Myths, Legends and Folktales from Latin America/De oro y esmeraldas: Mitos, Leyendas y Cuentos Populares de Latino América*, 1996; *Salsa Stories*, 2000); Lucía González (*The Bossy Gallito/El Gallo de Bodas. A Traditional Cuban Folktale*, 1994; *Señor Cat's Romance and Other Stories from Latin America*, 1997); Olga Loya (*Momentos mágicos. Tales from Latin* America, 1997); Nicholasa Mohr (*The Song of El Coquí and Other Tales of Puerto Rico*, 1995); Marisa Montes (*Juan Bobo Goes to Work*, 2000); Pat Mora (*Doña Flor. A Tall Tale*, 2005); and Daniel Moretón (*La Cucaracha Martina: A Caribbean Folktale*, 1997).

Occasionally, the authors may tell new stories that incorporate elements of the traditional literature, as do Julia Álvarez (*The Secret Footprints*, 2000 and *The Best Gift of All: The Legend of la vieja Belen/El mayor regalo del mundo: La historia de la vieja Belén*, 2008); Gloria Anzaldúa (*Prietita and the Ghost Woman/Prietita y la llorona*, 1995), Yuyi Morales (*Just a Minute. A Trickster's Tale and Counting Book*, 2003); and Rosalma Zubizarreta (*The Woman Who Outshone the Sun/La mujer que brillaba más que el sol*, 1991).

The significance of traditional folklore is also manifested in two other ways. First, experiences with the folklore as a child appear in authors' autobiographical memories. Second, the familiarity and enjoyment of the traditional tales has led some authors to write original stories in folktale style, as is the case with Nicholasa Mohr's *Old Letivia and the Mountain of Sorrows* (1996) and Alma Flor Ada's *The Gold Coin* (1991) [in Spanish *La moneda de oro*] and *Jordi's Star* (1996).

Reflection and Practice Related to Preserving the Oral Traditional Folklore

- Ask the students to provide (a) a definition of what is meant by oral traditional folklore, (b) to think on any example they might know of this genre, and (c) to provide a list of people they know who might be knowledgeable of some traditional folklore.
- Invite the students to ask their families for (a) a nursery rhyme, (b) a proverb, (c) a popular song, and (d) an old tale that their families know or learned in their childhood.
- Create a book titled Folklore Our Families Preserved for Us, with the examples collected at home. Suggest different kind of anthologies: riddles, songs, rhymes, or folktales.
- Ask students to read a traditional story from any of the books mentioned in this section in the chapter. Provide an opportunity to share the stories they read and what they learned from the text. Have them compare and contrast the tale with others they have read.

Transmitting History, Cultural Achievements, and Everyday Life from Spain and Latin America

The limits between Latin America and the world of Latinos are not always easy to trace, particularly because there have been historical changes in the physical boundaries. Two-thirds of what was originally Mexico are now the west and southwest of the United States. Puerto Rico was a Spanish colony, but instead of becoming an independent nation as Cuba and the Dominican Republic did, it is part of the U.S. Commonwealth, which also includes Guam and the Mariana Islands. The individual lives of the Latinos may also have developed between two worlds: born and raised in their countries of origin or many of the authors included in this chapter now live and publish in the United States. It is not surprising that these authors would like to enrich the lives of Latino children and their knowledge of the history and cultural achievements of Latin Americans and Spaniards as well as provide a better understanding of their everyday life.

The works in this category appear in different genres:

Historical Narratives

Whereas there is still a scarcity of narratives of this kind, some are very significant. *Before We Were Free* by Julia Álvarez (2002) explores the difficult topic of the dictatorships that have plagued Latin American history. This topic had also been the theme of the excellent books by Jyll Becerra de Jenkins, *The Honorable Prison* (1988) and *So Loud a Silence* (1996).

The Surrender Tree: Poems of Cuba's Struggle for Freedom by Margarita Engle (2008), centers on the issues concerning the struggle for independence. With exquisitely crafted verses Engle addressed in *The Poet Slave of Cuba: A Biography of Juan Francisco Manzano* (2006) the issue of slavery, a very important aspect of Latin American history very seldom included in children's books. Fernando Pico's (1997) *The Red Comb* also addresses this issue.

Colonial life in Colombia is the background for *The Walls of Cartagena* by J. Durango (2008). A more recent historical time, the period following World War II is addressed by Margarita Engle (2009) in *Tropical Secrets: Holocaust Refugees in Cuba*.

In *Journey of Dreams*, M. Pellegrino (2009) describes a harrowing journey in the 1980s of a Guatemalan family trying to escape the army's scorched earth campaign as well as the resilience and love for each other that help them survive and escape to the north.

Realistic Narratives

Narratives in this genre may appear in picture-book format like Lulú Delacre's *Vejigante Mascarader* (1993), depicting a child's desire to participate in a traditional Puerto Rican festivity; Luis Garay's *Pedrito's Day* (1997), a moving presentation of a young child's efforts to survive poverty, and Omar S. Castañeda's *Abuela's Weave* (1993). Or they may appear in books for older readers like Omar S. Castañeda's *Imagining Isabel* (1994).

Biographies

Prominent Latin American and Spanish figures have inspired numerous biographies. Among them are Carmen T. Bernier-Grand (2007), *Frida. ¡Viva la vida! Long Live Life!;* Monica Brown, *My Name is Celia/Me llamo Celia* (2005) and *My Name is Gabito: The Life of Gabriel Garcia Márquez/Me llamo Gabito: la vida de Gabriel Garcia Márquez* (2007) and *Side by Side/Lado a lado* (2010) the biographies of Dolores Huertas and César Chávez in a parallel presentation; Alma Flor Ada and F. Isabel Campoy, *Paths/Caminos* (2000; biographies of José Martí, Frida Kahlo, and César Chávez); *Smiles/Sonrisas* (2000; biographies of Pablo Picasso, Gabriela Mistral, Benito Juárez); *Steps/Pasos* (2000; biographies of Rita Moreno, Fernando Botero, and Evelyn

Cisneros); *Voices/Voces* (2000; biographies of Luis Valdez, Judith F. Baca, and Carlos J. Finlay); the already mentioned Margarita Engle (2006), *The Poet Slave of Cuba: A Biography of Juan Francisco Manzano*; and Pat Mora (2002), *A Library for Juana*, centered on the childhood of Sor Juana Inés de la Cruz and her passion for reading.

The collection *Cuando los grandes eran pequeños* [which means when the great ones were small] by Georgina Lázaros (2006–2009) include poetic biographies devoted to Federico García Lorca, Julia de Burgos, Sor Juana Inés de la Cruz, José Martí, Pablo Neruda, and Jorge Luis Borges. The exquisite book *The Dreamer*, written by Pam Muñoz Ryan (2010) and illustrated by Peter Sis has been inspired by the life of Pablo Neruda.

Nonfiction

Notable are the books of photo-journalist George Ancona, among many others *Carnaval* (1999), *Cuban Kids* (2000), *Fiesta Fireworks* (1998), *Mayeros: A Yucatan Maya Family* (1997) and of Maricel E. Presilla, *Feliz Nochebuena, Feliz Navidad* (1996).

Art

Two magnificent books depicting the richness of Latin American handcrafts are Maricel E. Presilla, *Mola: Cuna Life Stories and Art* (1996) and Maricel E. Presilla and Gloria Soto, *Life Around the Lake: Embroideries by the Women of Lake Patzcuaro* (1996). Multiple expressions of Latin American, Spanish, and Latino art appear in Alma Flor Ada and F. Isabel Campoy, *Blue and Green* (2000) [in Spanish *Azul y verde*] and other books of the Gateways to the Sun/Puertas al Sol collection.

Reflection and Practice Related to Transmitting History, Cultural Achievements and Everyday Life from Spain and Latin America

- Invite the class to divide into five groups. Assign to each group one of the five topics of this section: (a) historical narratives, (b) realistic narratives, (c) biographies, (d) nonfiction, and (e) art.
- Each group can select one of the books mentioned in their group-topic in this chapter and prepare a presentation about the contents of their book to the rest of the class.
- Propose to students to identify an important person in their lives and write a short biography of that person, illustrated with photographs.

Sharing Personal Memoirs

It seems only natural that authors of literature for children and youths would write their autobiographies or vignettes of their life when they were children in a style directed to their readers. Children and young people have a natural curiosity to know about an author's life as a child and how it may have been similar to or different from their own.

Each author's motivation to write is as personal and unique as it would be for any individual. One can write down childhood memories to preserve experiences from oblivion, to honor the people who helped shape earlier memories, to heal wounds, and to soothe the pain of hurtful experiences. The proportionately abundant autobiographical writing among Latinos and Latinas suggests three profound motivations to add to the natural desire of writing about what we know best, our own lives:

First, having been ignored or silenced, having grown up invisible to the eyes of the media and mainstream writing, there is a desire to have one's life recognized.

Second, having felt discrimination and disdain from others toward aspects of life that were dear to us and particularly representative of our family and community, there is a determination to validate their significance by making them part of a literary or artistic pursuit.

Third, for those who have grown up immersed in the literary traditions of the Spanish-speaking world there are numerous examples to serve as powerful inspiration. The Spaniards Juan Ramón Jiménez (*Platero y yo*, 1914) and Alonso Zamora Vicente (*Primeras hojas*, 1995); the Argentinean Norah Lange (*Cuadernos de infancia*, 1957); the Venezuelan Teresa de la Parra (*Memorias de la Mamá Blanca*, 1929/1966); and the Cuban Reneé Méndez Capote (*Memorias de una cubanita que nació con el siglo*, 1964) all contributed to creating a tradition of literary autobiographical writing about one's early years.

Autobiographical picture books authored by Latinos include María Cristina Brusca (*On the Pampas*, 1991); Amelia Lau Carling (*Mamá y Papá Have a Store*, 1998, and *Alfombras de aserrín/Sawdust Carpets*, 2006); Lucha Corpi (*Where Fireflies Dance/Allí donde bailan las luciérnagas*, 1997); Juan Felipe Herrera (*Calling the Doves/Canto de las palomas*, 1995); Francisco Jiménez (*La mariposa*, 2001 and *The Christmas Gift/El regalo de Navidad*, 2000); Carmen Lomas Garza, (*Family Pictures/Cuadros de familia*, 1990 and *In My Family/En mi familia*, 1996); and Amada Irma Pérez (*My Very Own Room/Mi propio cuartito*, 2000 and *My Diary from Here to There/Mi diario de aquí hasta allá*, 2002).

Significant autobiographical narratives have been written by Arcadia López (*Barrio Teacher*, 1992); Nicholasa Mohr (*In My Own Words: Growing Up Inside the Sanctuary of My Imagination*, 1994); Judith Ortiz Cofer (*Silent Dancing: A Partial Remembrance of a Puerto Rican Childhood*, 1990); and Víctor Villaseñor (*Walking Stars: Stories of Magic and Power*, 1994). Pura Belpré (*Firefly Summer*, 1996); María Cristina Brusca (*My Mama's Little Ranch on the Pampas*, 1991); Alma Flor Ada *Under the Royal Palms*, 1998 [in Spanish: *Bajo las palmas reales*], and *Where the Flame Trees Bloom*, 1994 [in Spanish: *Allá donde florecen los framboyanes*]; Ernesto Galarza, (*Barrio Boy*, 1971); Francisco Jiménez (*Breaking Through*, 2002; *Reaching Out*, 2009; and *The Circuit: Stories from the Life of a Migrant Child*, 1997).

After the tragic death of Alicia, her teenage daughter, Lulú Delacre interviewed her friends. She used their words to create *Alicia Afterimage* (2008), a unique book about loss and grieving.

In these authentic texts about their own lives, the authors have contributed a most significant chapter to literature for children and adolescents in the United States. They should be considered essential for any collection that aspires to represent in its entirety the society of the United States.

Reflection and Practice Related to Sharing Personal Memoirs

- Students can choose any book from the library written as a personal memoir by authors of any cultural background. In their presentation to the class students should mention (a) who the author is, (b) what the more salient topics in this memoir are, (c) why they choose it, and (d) what have they learned from reading this book.
- Invite students to write a vignette about a moment in their lives.

Depicting Latino Life and Culture

Many good stories are created from bits of reality and large doses of imagination. Writing about people one knows, streets one has walked, and meals one has eaten can contribute to the power of a story. Authors may also desire to explain life as they see it and perhaps even to make it have the evolution they would *like* to see.

Contemporary realistic narrative is an important aspect of literature for children and adolescents. Whereas each genre has something valuable to offer children, it is in realistic fiction, especially in contemporary narrative, that they can see themselves, their friends, and their individual quests represented.

Whereas the need for authentic Latino books in all genres is great, the need in this genre is particularly noticeable. Among the realistic picture books available some show aspects of Latino life and family relationships like *The Farolitos of Christmas* (1995) and *Farolitos for abuelo* (1997) by Rudolfo Anaya, whereas Luis Felipe Herrera depicts various aspects of Latino children's lives. In *Grandma and Me at the Flea/ Mero mero rematero* (2002) a young child understands the efforts made by his grandmother and other sellers at the flea market, *Desplumado/Featherless* (2004) is one of the few books by Latinos addressing the issue of physical limitations, whereas *Super Cilantro Girl/La superniña del cilantro* (2003) offers, through the fantasy of a girl with super powers, a message of hope. In René Colato's *Play Lotería/El juego de la lotería* (2005), a boy and his grandmother playing a traditional game discover one more dimension of love. Grandparents are very significant in Latino culture. They may live in the child's home and perhaps even be the child's primary caretaker, in most instances they are respected and cherished and a frequent theme in Latino children's literature. A grandmother/grandchild relationship appears in Contrera's (2009) *Braids/Trencitas*; in Vega's *Grandmother, Have the Angels Come?* (2009) a child asks her grandmother to explain the changes brought about by aging; whereas in Soto's *My Little Car* (2006), Teresa asks her grandfather to restore her car. Benjamín Alire Sáenz also addresses the topic of grandparents. In *A Gift from Papá Diego/Un regalo de papá Diego* (1998), a boy dreams he can fly to fulfill his dream of visiting his grandfather in Mexico and in *A Perfect Season for Dreaming/Un tiempo perfecto para soñar* (2008), a grandfather shares with his granddaughter his nine most precious dreams. A hen flying in front of a child's window makes her remember her grandfather who stayed in El Salvador in *La gallinita en la ciudad/The Little Hen in the City* (2006) by Jorge Argueta.

Very young children will recognize themselves and their world in Ina Cumpiano's (2009, 2010) Quinito's books and those who frequently inherit their siblings clothes will appreciate Soto's *If the Shoe Fits* (2002) and those who would like to look like their fathers *The Bushy Moustache* (1998).

The experience of immigration is an essential part of the Latino culture. Whereas many Latinos have lived in the United States for many generations, for a larger number, immigration is a close experience because they are immigrants or children of immigrants or because their friends, neighbors, or coworkers have moved to the United States from Spanish-speaking countries.

The immigrant experience is complex and painful. Even if the immigrant has chosen a new land trusting that life will become better, there is always pain in loosing what has been left behind. In general, people willing to leave their country to move to a different society are resilient, hard working, and courageous because all that is required to make

it in a new land. Children suffer the experience in multiple ways that have not been suf-
ficiently studied or addressed. A book teachers working with immigrant children may
find of great value is Igoa's (1995) *The Inner Life of the Immigrant Child*.

Several Latino authors have addressed the multiple aspects of immigration as experienced by children. In *Friends from the Other Side/Amigos del otro lado* (1993),
Gloria Anzaldúa explores the conflicts that can exist between those that have documentation and those who do not. The nostalgia for the land left behind by children who have
immigrated from El Salvador has been addressed poetically by Jorge Argueta in *A
Movie in My Pillow/Una película en mi almohada.* (2001) and *Xochitl and the Flow-
ers/Xochitl la niña de las flores* (2003). He explores the dream of returning home, held
in the heart of many immigrant children, which gets fulfilled for his protagonist during
a visit to his homeland in *Alfredito Flies Home* (2010), whereas *Money Luna/Luna
lunita lunera* (2005) presents the fears of a young child on a first day at school. René
Colato Laínez has drawn on his experiences as a young immigrant from El Salvador
to create a series of picture books that show the difficulties faced by immigrant children. The important issue of the respect for the child's name is brought up in a delightful way in *I Am René, the Boy/Yo soy René, el niño* (2005) and in *René Has Two Last
Names/René tiene dos apellidos* (2009). The pain of the separation from their parents
experienced by many immigrant children is the topic of Colato's *Waiting for Papá/
Esperando a papá* (2004) and *From North to South* (2010). In *My Shoes and I* (2010)
a father and his son will have to cross the frontier before they reunite with the mother.

The life of farm workers has inspired many authors. Those who come from farm-
working families have provided very poignant descriptions, like in *La mariposa*
(2001) by Francisco Jiménez. The cross-cultural experience of children who may have
grandparents who live in the United States and in Latin America is reflected in *Liliana's
Grandmothers* (1998) by Leyla Torres, whereas grandparents of different language and
culture appear in *I Love Saturdays y domingos* (2002) [in Spanish: *Me encantan los Saturdays y domingos*] by Alma Flor Ada.

Celebrations that bring together families and contribute to maintain alive cultural
traditions are a very important part of Latino life. It is not surprising that they would
appear amply in children's books by Latino authors. Pat Mora has shared the New
Mexico tradition of *Abuelos* (2008). Christmas has inspired her books *The Gift of the
Poinsettia* (1995) and *A Piñata in a Pear Tree: A Latino Twelve Day of Christmas*
(2009). The feast of the *Reyes Magos*, January 6 is the background for her book *The
Bakery Lady* (2001). A family birthday is the topic for *A Birthday Basket for Tía*
(1997). *Delicious Hullabaloo/Pachanga deliciosa* (1998) is an animal fantasy celebra-
tion. A general celebration of life appears in her book *Join Hands!* (2008) and in
Gracias/Thanks (2009).

Campoy and Ada (2006) *Stories to Celebrate/Cuentos para celebrar* (2006) of 12
bilingual books, combining fiction and nonfiction, includes Latino celebrations, like
Cinco de Mayo, Day of the Dead, Three Kings Day, as well as multicultural celebrations as Martin Luther King's Day and others. Ancona has also addressed this topic
with a multitude of books as previously mentioned when describing his work.

A growing body of substantive, realistic chapter books and young adult novels merit
special attention. Gary Soto has been very prolific in this area, as attested by his many
titles that include *Baseball in April and Other Stories* (1990), *Taking Sides* (1991),
Pacific Crossing (1992), *Local News* (1993), *The Pool Party* (1993), *Crazy Weekend*
(1995), *Summer on Wheels* (1995), *Buried Onions* (1997), *The Skirt* (1997), *Petty*

Crimes (1998), *Accidental Love* (2006), *Help Wanted* (2007), *Facts of Life* (2008). These also include, among others, *My Name Is María Isabel* (1993) [in Spanish *Me llamo María Isabel*] and *Dancing Home* (2011) by Alma Flor Ada; *He Forgot to Say Goodbye* (2008) by Benjamín Alire Sáenz; *How Tía Lola Came to (Visit) Stay* (2001), *Finding Miracles* (2004), and *Return to Sender* (2004) by Julia Álvarez; *In the Shade of the Níspero Tree* (1999) by Carmen T. Bernier-Grand; *Dark Dude* (2008) by Oscar Hijuelos reflects the conflicts created by the diverse physical appearances of Latinos; *The Smell of Old Lady Perfume* (2008) by Claudia Guadalupe Martínez; *A Crazy Mixed Up Spanglish Day* (2006) by Marisa Montes; *Felita* (1979) and *Going Home* (1986) by Nicholasa Mohr; *Becoming Naomi Leon* (2004) and *Esperanza Rising* (2000) by Pam Muñoz Ryan; *Cuba 15* (2003) by Nancy Osa; and Matt de la Peña's *We Were Here* (2009) is a novel of self-discovery. The young adult novel, *Marcelo in the Real World* (2009) by Francisco X. Stork, is one of the few books by Latino authors exploring the theme of autism.

Latinos face some very specific concerns and issues. One of them is the right to retain and develop the Spanish language. From the moment of beginning school and sometimes even before, Latino children are faced with societal prejudice against their home language: They see themselves ridiculed, discriminated against, ignored, or teased for speaking a language other than English. Everyone agrees that all children should learn English and learn it well. Conflicts arise when the societal attitude lacks appreciation for bilingualism and does not have the vision to see how enriching it can be to know two languages well.

In addition, parents will usually place a lot of emphasis on having their children learn English as quickly as possible for a number of reasons. If they themselves are having difficulties finding work because they know little English, they want to prevent their children from suffering in the same way. If they have experienced discrimination, they tend to believe that it is related only to language and that the moment their children speak English they will be fully accepted as bona fide Americans. If the parents are trying to learn English, they want their children help them learn, or may need the children to translate for them.

Thus, the children are both getting a push at home to speak English and a message from society that their language is inferior, and most likely no one close to them fully realizes what will happen once they stop using Spanish. The parents do not foresee that their children will indeed become incapable of speaking Spanish beyond very simplest commands or statements of need; this will be true particularly for younger children who communicate with the parents through an older sibling. One day, when it is already too late, the parents will be faced with the painful reality that they can no longer converse with their children around meaningful themes, transmit values, clarify situations, share family history, or reveal to them their deepest feelings and thoughts.

The concern for identity also takes on major importance. How should children relate to parents or grandparents whose language and traditions may be very different from the ones they are acquiring in this country? How much of the old should they retain? At the same time, who are they in relationship to the dominant society, and what aspects of themselves are they willing to give up to become a part of it? Finally, how much would they be accepted if they tried? Other significant issues affecting Latino realities in various settings are the hardships of the farm-working life, the presence of violence and drugs in the barrios, and the rivalries between members of the established community and newer immigrants.

One of the most constantly recurring themes in the literature we are considering is the expression of love for family and, in particular, for grandparents and other elders. Whereas the intergenerational theme is common in books for young readers, it seems to take on a special poignancy among Latina and Latino authors.

Several elements of the Latino reality may contribute to this. First, grandparents represent continuity in families that have left a motherland to move to the United States and in migrant families that move frequently in search of seasonal work. Second, grandparents offer consistency in their very important role as caretakers when parents have to work long hours or even leave the children in their care for prolonged periods. Third, as cultural transmitters, grandparents, and all elders, not only enrich children's lives with their stories, songs, and sayings, but contribute to giving them a sense of pride in who they are.

Reflection and Practice Related to Depicting Latino Life and Culture

- Invite students to read a picture book that depicts some aspect of Latino culture. Ask them to present each book to the class reporting about (a) the characters, (b) the setting, (c) the cultural elements imbedded in the text, (d) what the illustrations bring to the content of the book, (e) anything that is different from their culture and experience; and (f) anything that is the same.
- Ask students to expand their knowledge of the culture they read about by at least reading a second book.
- Ask student to discuss one of the chosen books by following the "Creative Reading Methodology" (Ada, 2000)
  A. **Descriptive phase**. Describe what the book is about answering what, who, when, where, and why questions.
  B. **Personal interpretive phase**. Students reflect on their own experiences and previous knowledge as they relate to the story. Questions may be of the nature of: have you even been a similar situation? How did you feel? If you were involved in a similar event, what would you do? How does the information in the book confirm or contradict your own experiences? How would a situation like this happen in your own home or culture?
  C. **Critical/multicultural/antibias phase**. Students examine the book in view of the tenets of justice and equality. Is it just/fair what happened to the characters in the book? Are they all treated fairly? How are things similar/different in your social group? What would be the consequences in real life of the actions depicted in the book? Who would suffer and who would benefit by attitudes like the ones portrayed? How? Why?
  D. **Creative/transformative phase**. Students are encouraged to see themselves as protagonists of their own lives and reflect on creative and transformative actions that will lead them to be stronger and to promote equality and justice.

Once students understand this process, they can apply it to anything they read.

Celebrating Latino Poetic Voices

Spanish-speaking poets have created beautiful poetry of universal value. There is an ample tradition of popular poetry in every country of the Spanish-speaking world, in which anonymous poets have captured emotions, feelings, dreams, and their view of life and reality in verses that have lived through the centuries because of their quality and appeal.

Poets writing in Spanish also include Nobel Prize winners Juan Ramón Jiménez, Gabriela Mistral, Pablo Neruda, and Octavio Paz as well as numerous international figures such as Miguel Hernández, Antonio Machado, and César Vallejo. Whereas children can enjoy the poetry of almost any poet, many of the most famous poets writing in Spanish have created some poems especially for children. Among these are Rubén Darío, Federico García Lorca, Nicolás Guillén, Juana de Ibarborou, Antonio Machado, Amado Nervo, and Alfonsina Storni.

Among Latino authors there are also some extraordinary poets writing for children. Francisco Xavier Alarcón, a recognized poet who published poetry for adults, has dedicated to children: *Angels Ride Bikes and Other Fall Poems/Los ángeles andan en bicicleta y otros poemas de otoño* (1999), *From the Bellybutton of the Moon and Other Summer Poems/Del ombligo de la luna y otros poemas de verano* (1998), *Laughing Tomatoes and Other Spring Poems/Jitomates risueños y otros poemas de primavera* (1997), *Iguanas in the Snow and Other Winter Poems/Iguanas en la nieve y otros poemas de invierno* (2001), and *Animal Poems of the Iguazu/Animalario del Iguazú* (2008). Rudolfo Anaya created the *Elegy on the Death of César Chávez* (2000), which can be enjoyed by readers of all ages. The Salvadorean poet Jorge Argueta has explored very different topics poetically. The poems of *Trees Hanging from the Sky* (2007) show the imaginary world of dreams and unusual visitor a boy sees from his window. *Sopa de frijoles/Bean Soup* (2009) and *Arroz con leche/Rice Pudding* (2010) show the joy derived from food that represents one's culture. *A Movie in My Pillow/Una película en mi almohada* (2001) explores painful experiences of immigration. In *Talking to Mother Earth/Hablando con Madre Tierra* (2008), a young child's awareness of the Earth allows him to find healing for the racism he has suffered.

This awareness of the Earth through the eyes of a child inspired Pat Mora's exquisite *The Desert Is My Mother/El desierto es mi madre* (1994) as well as *Listen to the Desert/Oye al desierto* (2001). Mora has also created *Confetti Poems for Children* (1996) edited *Love to Mamá: A Tribute to Mothers* (2004), and for the young adults written a book of poems of all sorts of manifestations of love: *Dizzy in Your Eyes. Love Poems* (2010). Gary Soto, one of the most prolific and recognized Latino authors, has cultivated all genres. He has written several books of poems for young readers: *A Fire in My Hands* (1990), *Neighborhood Odes* (1992), *Canto familiar* (1995), *Fearless Fernie* (2002), *Partly Cloudy. Poems of Love and Longing* (2002), and *Worlds Apart: Traveling with Fernie and Me.* (2005).

The book *Salta, Saltarín* includes poetry from both F. Isabel Campoy and Alma Flor Ada (2010). Besides writing poetry of their own, they have jointly edited a number of anthologies of poems by the best Spanish-speaking poets (*Gorrión, gorrión, El verde limón, La rama azul, Dulce es la sal, Nuevo día, Bosques de coral, Ríos de lava*). Four additional anthologies with parallel editions in English and Spanish also include Latino authors: *Pimpón* (2000) [in English *Dreaming Fish*], *Antón pirulero* (2000) [in English *Laughing Crocodiles*], *Mambrú* (2000) [in English *Singing Horse*], and *Chuchurumbé* (2000) [in English *Flying Dragon*].

Todo es canción (2010) is an extensive anthology of Alma Flor Ada's poetry mostly previously unpublished. She has also written other individual books: *Abecedario de los animales* (1990), *Coral y espuma: Abecedario del mar* (2003), and *Gathering the Sun: An Alphabet in Spanish and English* (1997). In 1991, Alma Flor Ada edited the anthology *Días y días de poesía* (1991), the most extensive anthology of poetry for children in Spanish, including that of Latino authors published in the United States at the time.

Reflection and Practice Related to Celebrating Latino Poetic Voices

- Open your class, daily or once a week, with the reading of a poem.
- Invite students to copy it to create their own personal anthology, and ask them to illustrate the poems either with illustrations of photographs.
- Weekly or monthly, invite them to write a poem of their own either modifying some words of one of the poems they have copied or writing one of their own.

Poetry Culminating Activities

- Have student share their anthologies, one on one, with students in another class.
- Have students create in groups, posters with an illustrated poem to place on the school walls.
- Have a school wide poetry celebration where students will recite poems they have memorized and/or ones they have written.

Writing for the Stage

The tradition of drama in Spanish is unsurpassed. Just as Cervantes contributed the genre of the modern novel to world literature, the dramas of the Spanish playwrights Lope de Vega, Calderón de la Barca, and Tirso de Molina created modern theatre when they broke away from the dichotomy of comedy versus tragedy to create plays in which the elements of comedy and tragedy coexist, as they do in real life.

Spanish drama, like the rest of the literature, has both a learned and a popular tradition. Unfortunately, plays are written to be performed, and contemporary public schools have failed for the most part to understand the enormous value of theatre in education. In most schools, performances are sporadic, and because they tend to be less in demand than other genres, it is hard to find publishers willing to publish dramas for children and youth.

Gary Soto has written several plays, among them *Novio Boy: A Play* (1997). *These Shoes of Mine* is included in the anthology *You're On! Seven Plays in English and Spanish*, (1999) edited by Lori Marie Carlson, which also contains plays by Elena Castedo, Oscar Hijuelos, and Denise Ruiz.

Alma Flor Ada and F. Isabel Campoy have published seven anthologies of plays in Spanish (*Primer acto, Risas y aplausos, Escenas y alegrías, Ensayo general, Actores y flores, Saludos al público, Acto final*) as well as four anthologies in Spanish and English separate editions *Teatro del gato garabato* (2000) [in English *Rat-A-Tat Cat*], *Teatrín de don Crispín* (2000) [in English *Roll-n-Role*], *Escenario de Polichinela* (2000) [in English *Top Hat*], and *Tablado de doña Rosita* (2000) [in English *Curtains Up!*]. These anthologies include both their original pieces and those of other writers.

Reflection and Practice Related to Writing for the Stage

- This section mentions a number of short plays that could serve as an introduction to theatre in the classroom. Whether it is done as Reader's Theatre or as a full theatrical experience, invite your students to select a play and present it to their class or the school.

Giving Free Rein to Fantasy

No author should feel compelled to write only within the parameters of one culture, field, or genre; all writers deserve the freedom to explore all fields and all topics, to navigate uncharted waters, and to contribute the products of their originality. No matter what genres or topics authors choose, their work will ultimately reveal their inner selves, their experiences, and their worldview. No matter how seemingly remote from the authors' historical background the topic may be, if the writing is of quality it must have been nourished by the author's own soul.

Because of the enormous need for more realistic fiction based on the authentic experiences of Latinos, it is hoped that more and more of these books will be produced. Yet it will be a symbol of coming of age when Latinos no longer feel compelled to remain within the boundaries of folklore and realistic narrative but feel the freedom to open the doors of the imagination and give vent to fantasy.

The books may have a more universal flavor, like some of the books of Pam Muñoz Ryan Carmen Agra Deedee, Marisa Montes, Alma Flor Ada. If they are fantasy books, they may sometimes have characters that very definitely carry some cultural weight. Consider, for example, the Chato books of Gary Soto (1995, 2000, 2005) depicting a low-riding cat, his picture book *The Cat's Meow* (1995) or the picture book *Martí and the Mango* (1993) in which Daniel Moretón playfully names his animal characters Martí and Gómez and models them after the great figures of Cuban Independence or René Colato Laínez, *The Tooth Fairy Meets el Ratoncito Pérez* (2010) in which the two characters responsible for bringing surprises to children in exchange for their fallen teeth get to meet each other, in a true bicultural experience. And Carmen Tafolla, *What Can You Do With a Rebozo/¿Qué puedes hacer con un rebozo?* (2008) and *What Can You Do With a Paleta/¿Qué puedes hacer con una paleta?* (2009). Whether the books incorporate direct references to the Latino culture or not, their underlying values or worldview would most likely reflect those of the authors.

Reflection and Practice Related to Giving Free Range to Fantasy

- Take the opportunity to ask students to reflect on the topics that are their favorites.
- Ask them to select one of their favorite books of the ones presented in this section and ask them to complete an answer sheet including:
  Title of the book
  Reason for choosing this book
  Topic
  Setting
  Period
  Main characters
  Principal events

LATINO ILLUSTRATORS AND AUTHOR ILLUSTRATORS

It is not surprising that a culture that has contributed some of the most important architects and plastic and visual artists of human history will also produce numerous outstanding illustrators of children's books. The limits of this chapter do not allow for a detailed presentation of their work; these remarks about some of the most recognized illustrators are an invitation to you to keep an eye out for their work and delight in their creativity.

Felipe Dávalos moved to the United States when he was already a world-renowned illustrator acknowledged by more than one generation of Mexican illustrators as their master. To his extensive academic preparation as an archaeologist, Dávalos adds his reflective experience as art director and book designer. Among the books he has recently illustrated is *The Lizard and the Sun* (1997), in which he depicts his archaeological knowledge of ancient Meso-American cultures. He served as art director for Alfaguara's *Puertas al Sol/Gateways to the Sun* and has contributed some of his own original art to this collection of books on Latino culture.

Dávalos is considered a *maestro*. He is one of exceptional Latin-American illustrators who see children's book illustration as an artistic expression for the transformation of Latin American and Latino children. That category also includes Antonio Martorell from Puerto Rico and Gian Calvi from Brasil; their profound expositions on this topic deserve publication and dissemination.

Lulú Delacre has illustrated her own compilations of oral folklore and has also illustrated books by other authors. Her illustrations for Lucía González's rendition of *The Bossy Gallito* (1994) use noteworthy combinations of animal characters in a realistic setting to capture the images and spirit of Miami's Little Havana. Lulú is also an author. Besides other titles previously mentioned she has created two charming frog characters, *Rafi and Rosi* (2004) inspired by the Puerto Rican coquí. *Rafi and Rosi Carnaval* (2006) shows some of the carnaval experiences. As in other books, Lulú utilizes the illustration's background to depict characteristic architecture, in this case, colonial Puerto Rican buildings.

Latinos feel enormous pride that the Latino illustrator David Díaz received the Caldecott Award for *Smoky Night* (1994). Díaz's work, which includes illustrations for *Roadrunner's Dance* (2000) by Rudolfo Anaya and for books about Frida Kahlo and César Chávez by Carmen Bernier-Grant, continues to receive the ample recognition it deserves.

Elizabeth Gómez a thoughtful researcher of art, finds in her art influences from the Mexican retablo to the Persian and Indian miniatures and Medieval illuminations. Of herself she says, "I strive for work that has the honesty and directedness of handmade craft."

Susan Guevara is best known for the striking characterization of Chato and his world in Gary Soto's *Chato's Kitchen* (1995), *Chato and the Party Animals* (2000), *Chato Goes Cruisin'* (2005). Yet her talent allows for many expressions of a wide range of always alluring styles.

Carmen Lomas Garza developed a naive style of art to depict in full detail the life of her childhood in Texas. Some of her paintings became the basis for two bilingual autobiographical books, *Family Pictures/Cuadros de familia* (1990) and *In my Family/En mi familia* (1996), in which the illustrations are accompanied by brief texts elaborating on the experience captured visually by the artist.

Rafael López divides his time between his native Mexico and San Diego, California. In 2010, he received the Pura Belpré Illustrator Award for his work in *Book Fiesta! Celebrate Children's Book Day* (2009) by Pat Mora. López's style fuses his skills as a muralist with strong graphic designs and the aesthetics of children's fantasy.

Antonio Martorell's woodcut illustrations for Isabel Freyre de Matos' *ABC de Puerto Rico* (1968) were a powerful statement of Puerto Rico's nationalist pride and a source, at the time of publication, of both controversy and an enormous following. Whereas Martorell's worldwide recognition as a painter and an author–illustrator of books for adults (*La piel de la memoria*, 1991) has left him with little time to illustrate many books for children, it is gratifying that he illustrated *Where the Flame Trees*

Bloom (1994) by Alma Flor Ada and *The Song of the Coqui and Other Tales of Puerto Rico* (1995) by Nicholasa Mohr.

An extraordinary presence among Latino illustrators is Yuyi Morales, who sometimes illustrates but also produces books as author–illustrator. In a very short time, Yuyi has developed a career as one of the best-known names in Latino children's literature through her illustrations for *Harvesting Hope: The Story of César Chávez* (2003) by Kathleen Krull and her own books *Little Night/Nochecita* (2007), *Just in Case: A Trickster Tale and Spanish Alphabet Book* (2008), and *Just a Minute: A Trickster's Tale and Counting Book* (2003).

Author-illustrator Daniel Moretón used the computer to create his bold and striking art for his original story *Martí and the Mango* (1993) and his new version of *La cucaracha Martina* (1997). The result, filled with extraordinary humor, is powerfully attractive.

The New-Mexican artist Amado Peña gathered some of his paintings in the book *Peña on Peña* (1995). Other paintings were collected in the book *Calor* (1995) by Juanita Alba.

In his prolific work, Enrique O. Sánchez has created a distinctive style with a palette that gives a Latino flavor to many books authored by Latinos (*Abuela's Weave*, 1993) and non-Latinos (*Saturday Market*, 1994; *Amelia's Road*, 1993). His illustrations are highly regarded for their tender renditions of children, the authenticity of the settings, and his playful use of coloring.

Simón Silva has inherited the boldness and strength of the Mexican muralists and particularly Diego Rivera's ability to present the people with tenderness, dignity, and respect. Drawing on his own experiences as the child of farm workers, Silva has rendered the colors and images of life in the fields in *Gathering the Sun* (1997), the first picture book he illustrated. In this ABC of farm-working life, his full-spread paintings create a powerful rendition of the experiences and feelings of migrant farm workers and their families.

Both author and illustrator, Leyla Torres has contributed to making everyday life in Latin America real to children in the United States. Her humanity, so transparent in her writing, is powerfully conveyed by her illustrations of people so realistically individualized that they become unforgettable characters the moment one opens her books. Some of her books are inspired by Colombia, her birthplace, like *The Kite Festival* (2004), others like *Subway Sparrow* (1993), by her New York experiences.

The masterful illustrations of Beatriz Vidal can be appreciated in her own book *Federico and the Magi's Gift* (2004) and in *A Gift of Gracias: The Legend of Altagracia* (2005) by Julia Álvarez.

Many other Latino illustrators of merit include Joe Cepeda, whose illustrations are light and playful. Raúl Colón, an extraordinary artist who, as is the case with many illustrators, has now begun to write his own books. Maya Christina González whose lively art, imbued with the colors and spirit of the barrio muralists, has complemented many titles from the Children's Book Press. Edel Rodríguez who besides illustrating with a very personal style also authors his own series of books for the initial readers about a young Argentina penguin named Sergio (2008, 2009) who manages to shine in the world of soccer scoring against the sea gulls.

Knowing the pain of Latinos as well as children of other multicultural groups who, while growing up could never find books that represented them, their families, and communities or showed them the richness of their heritage, it is fortunate that talented authors and illustrators are creating the books mentioned in this chapter and other chapters. It is fortunate that librarians, educators, and parents may learn from this book how to facilitate the magical encounter between children and books.

Latino and non-Latino youth alike deserve a literature that shares the rich Hispanic tradition of stories and folktales, nursery rhymes and songs, poetry, and plays. They should have access to a literature that celebrates the rich Hispanic heritage of art, music, celebrations, and creativity in all areas outside and inside the United States. They should have books that explore the complex reality of Latinos in the United States, portray the many unknown heroes of our communities, and reveal our varied manifestations of a zest for life, friendship, and solidarity; books in all genres and for all ages that recognize the diversity of our families, the strength of our creativity; and our ever-changing, always creative approach to life, its hardships and demands, its possibilities and hope.

REFERENCES

Ada, A. F. (Ed.). (1991). *Días y días de poesía*. Carmel, CA: Hampton-Brown.

Ada, A. F. (1991). *The gold coin*, illustrated by N. Waldman. New York, NY: Atheneum. [In Spanish (1991). *La moneda de oro*. Leon, Spain: Editorial Everest.]

Ada, A. F. (1993). *Dear Peter Rabbit*, illustrated by L. Tryon. New York, NY: Atheneum. [In Spanish: *Querido Pedrín*].

Ada, A. F. (1993). *My name is María Isabel*, illustrated by K. D. Thompson. New York, NY: Atheneum. [In Spanish: *Me llamo María Isabel*. New York, NY: Atheneum.]

Ada, A. F. (1993). *The rooster who went to his uncle's wedding*, illustrated by K. Kuchera. New York, NY: Putnam. [New edition: (2010). *The rooster who went to his uncle's wedding* illustrated by C. Legnazzi. Dallas, TX: Frog Street.]

Ada, A. F. (1994). *Where the flame trees bloom*, illustrated by A. Martorell. New York, NY: Atheneum. [In Spanish (2000). *Allá donde florecen los framboyanes*. Miami, FL: Alfaguara.]

Ada, A. F. (1995. *The lizard and the sun /La lagartija y el sol*, illustrated by F. Dávalos. New York, NY: Doubleday.

Ada, A. F. (1995). *Mediopollito/Half-Chicken*, translated by R. Zubizarreta, illustrated by K. Howard. New York, NY: Doubleday.

Ada, A. F. (1996). *Jordi's star,* illustrated by S. Gaber. New York, NY: Putnam.

Ada, A. F. (1997). *Gathering the sun: An alphabet in Spanish and English*, translated by R. Zubizarreta, illustrated by S. Silva. New York, NY: HarperCollins.

Ada, A. F. (1998). *Under the royal palms*. New York, NY: Atheneum. [In Spanish (2000). *Bajo las palmas reales*. Miami, FL: Alfaguara.]

Ada, A. F. (1999). *Three golden oranges*, illustrated by R. Cartwright. New York, NY: Atheneum.

Ada, A. F. (2000). *A magical encounter: The use of Latino literature in the classroom*. Boston, MA: Allyn & Bacon.

Ada, A. F. (2002). *I love Saturdays y domingos*, illustrated by E. Savadier. New York, NY: Atheneum. [In Spanish: *Me encantan los Saturdays y domingos*. Miami, FL: Alfaguara.]

Ada, A. F. (2003). *Coral y espuma. Abecedario del mar*, illustrated by V. Escrivá. Madrid, Spain: Espana.

Ada, A. F. (2007). *Extra! extra! fairy-tale news from hidden forest*, illustrated by L. Tryon. New York, NY: Atheneum. [In Spanish: *¡Extra! ¡extra! noticias del bosque escondido*. Miami, FL: Alfaguara].

Ada, A. F. (2010). *Todo es canción*, illustrated by M. J. Álvarez. Miami: Alfaguara.

Ada, A. F., & Zubizarreta, G. M. (2011). *Dancing home*. New York, NY: Atheneum. [In Spanish (2011). *Nacer bailando*. New York, NY: Atheneum.]

Alarcón, F. X. (1997). *Laughing tomatoes and other spring poems/Jitomates risueños y otros poemas de primavera*, illustrated by M. C. González. San Francisco, CA: Children's Book Press.

Alarcón, F. X. (1998). *From the bellybutton of the moon and other summer poems/Del ombligo de la luna y otros poemas de verano*, illustrated by M. C. González. San Francisco, CA: Children's Book Press.

Alarcón, F. X. (1999). *Angels ride bikes and other fall poems/Los ángeles andan en bicicleta y otros poemas de otoño*, illustrated by M. C. González. San Francisco, CA: Children's Book Press.

Alarcón, F. X. (2001). *Iguanas in the snow and other winter poems/Iguanas en la nieve y otros poemas de invierno*, illustrated by M. C. González. San Francisco Children's Book Press.

Alarcón, F. X. (2008). *Animal poems of the Iguazu/Animalario del Iguazú*, illustrated by M. C. González. San Francisco Children's Book Press.

Alba, J. (1995). *Calor*. Waco, TX: WRS.

Alire Sáenz, B. (1998). *A gift for papá Diego/Un regalo de papá Diego*. illustrated by Gerónimo García. El Paso, TX: Cinco Puntos Press.

Alire Sáenz, B. (2008). *He forgot to say goodbye*. New York, NY: Simon and Schuster.

Alire Sáenz, B. (2008). *A perfect season for dreaming / Un tiempo perfecto para soñar*, illustrated by Esaú Andrade Valencia. El Paso, TX: Cinco Puntos Press.

Álvarez, J. (2000). *The secret footprints*. New York, NY: Alfred A. Knopf.

Álvarez, J. (2001). *How Tía Lola came to [visit] stay*. New York, NY: Alfred A. Knopf.

Álvarez, J. (2002). *Before we were free*. New York, NY: Alfred A. Knopf.

Álvarez, J. (2004). *Finding miracles*. New York, NY: Alfred A. Knopf.

Álvarez, J. (2004). *Return to sender*. New York, NY: Alfred A. Knopf.

Álvarez, J. (2005). *A gift of gracias: The legend of Altagracia*, illustrated by B.Vidal. New York, NY: Alfred A. Knopf. [In Spanish: *Un regalo de gracias: La leyenda de la Altagracia*.]

Álvarez, J. (2008). *The best gift of all: The legend of la Vieja Belen/El major regalo del mundo: La historia de la Vieja Belén*. Miami, FL: Alfaguara.

Anaya, R. (1972). *Bless me, Ultima*. Berkeley, CA: Quinto Sol Publications.

Anaya, R. (1995). *The farolitos of Christmas*, illustrated by E. González. New York, NY: Hyperion.

Anaya, R. (1997). *Farolitos for Abuelo*, illustrated by E. González. New York, NY: Hyperion.

Anaya, R. (1997). *Maya's children: The story of La Llorona*. New York, NY: Hyperion.

Anaya, R. (1999). *My land sings: Stories from the Rio Grande*, illustrated by A. Córdova. New York, NY: Morow Junior Books.

Anaya, R. (2000). *Elegy on the death of César Chávez*, illustrated by G. Enríquez. El Paso, TX: Cinco Puntos Press.

Anaya, R. (2000). *Roadrunner's dance*, illustrated by D. Díaz. New York, NY: Hyperion.

Anaya, R. (2004). *The Santero's miracle: A bilingual story*, illustrated by A. Córdova. Albuquerque, NM: University of New Mexico Press.

Anaya, R. (2004). *Serafina's stories*. Albuquerque, NM: University of New Mexico Press.

Anaya, R. (2005). *The first tortilla*, illustrated by A. Córdova. Albuquerque, NM: University of New Mexico Press.

Anaya, R. (2009). *Juan and the Jackalope: A children's book in verse*. Albuquerque, NM: University of New Mexico Press.

Ancona, G. (1993). *Pablo remembers: The fiesta of the Day of the Dead*. New York, NY: Lothrop, Lee and Shepherd. [In Spanish: *Pablo recuerda la fiesta del Día de los Muertos*.]

Ancona, G. (1994). *The piñata maker*. New York, NY: Harcourt. [In Spanish: *El piñatero*.]

Ancona, G. (1995). *Fiesta USA*. New York, NY: Lodestar

Ancona, G. (1996). *In city gardens*. Celebrations. [In Spanish: *En los jardines de la ciudad*]

Ancona, G. (1997). *Mayeros: A Yucatan Maya family*. New York, NY: Lothrop, Lee and Shepherd.

Ancona, G. (1998). *Barrio: José's neighborhood*. New York, NY: Harcourt. [In Spanish: *El barrio de José*.]

Ancona, G. (1998). *Fiesta fireworks*. New York, NY: Lothrop, Lee and Shepherd.

Ancona, G. (1999). *Carnaval*. San Diego, CA: Harcourt.

Ancona, G. (1999). *Charro: The Mexican cowboy*. New York, NY: Harcourt.

Ancona, G. (2000). *Cuban kids*. New York, NY: Marshall Cavendish.

Ancona, G. (2001). *Harvest*. New York, NY: Marshall Cavendish.

Ancona, G. (2001). *Viva México: The fiestas*. New York, NY: Marshall Cavendish.

Ancona, G. (2001). *Viva México: The folkart*. New York, NY: Marshall Cavendish.

Ancona, G. (2001). *Viva México: The foods*. New York, NY: Marshall Cavendish.

Ancona, G. (2001). *Viva México: The past*. New York, NY: Marshall Cavendish.

Ancona, G. (2001). *Viva México! The people*. New York, NY: Marshall Cavendish.

Ancona, G. (2003). *Murals: Walls that sing*. New York, NY: Marshall Cavendish.

Ancona, G. (2004). *Somos Latinos/We are Latinos: Mis abuelos/My grandparents*. New York, NY: Chidren's Press. Scholastic.

Ancona, G. (2004). *Somos Latinos/We are Latinos: Mis amigos/My friends*. New York, NY: Chidren's Press. Scholastic.

Ancona, G. (2004). *Somos Latinos/We are Latinos: Mis bailes/My dances*. New York, NY: Chidren's Press. Scholastic.

Ancona, G. (2004). *Somos Latinos/We are Latinos: Mi barrio/My neighborhood*. New York, NY: Chidren's Press. Scholastic.

Ancona, G. (2004). *Somos Latinos/We are Latinos: Mi casa/My home*. New York, NY: Chidren's Press. Scholastic.

Ancona, G. (2004). *Somos Latinos/We are Latinos: Mis comidas/My foods*. New York, NY: Chidren's Press. Scholastic.

Ancona, G. (2007). *Capoeira: Dance. game, martial arts*. New York, NY: Lee and Low.

Anzaldúa, G. (1993). *Friends from the other side/Amigos del otro lado*, illustrated by M. C. González. San Francisco, CA: Children's Book Press.

Anzaldúa, G. (1995). *Prietita and the ghost woman/Prietita y la llorona*, illustrated by M. C. González. San Francisco, CA: Children's Book Press.

Argueta, J. (2001). *A movie in my pillow/Una película en mi almohada*, illustrated by E. Gómez. San Francisco, CA: Children's Book Press.

Argueta, J. (2003). *Xochitl and the flowers/Xochitl, la niña de las flores*, ilustrated by C. Angel. San Francisco, CA: Children's Book Press.

Argueta, J. (2005). *Money luna / Luna lunital lunera*, ilustrated by E. Gómez. San Francisco, CA: Children's Book Press.

Argueta, J. (2006). *La gallinita en la ciudad / The little hen in the city*. Miami, FL: Alfaguara.

Argueta, J. (2007). *Zipitio. El Zipitio*, illustrated by G. Calderon. Toronto, ON, Canada: Groundwood Books.

Argueta, J. (2008). *Talking to mother earth / Hablando con Madre Tierra*, illustrated by L. A. Pérez. Toronto, ON, Canada: Groundwood Books.

Argueta, J. (2009). *Sopa de frijoles/Bean soup. Un poema para cocinar/A cooking poem*, illustrated by R. Yockteng. Toronto, ON, Canada: Groundwood Books.

Argueta, J. (2010). *Arroz con leche/Rice pudding. Un poema para cocinar/A cooking poem*, illustrated by F. Vilela. Toronto, ON, Canada: Groundwood Books.

Argueta, J. (2010). *Alfredito flies home*. Illustrated by L. Garay. Toronto, ON, Canada: Groundwood Books.

Becerra de Jenkins, L. (1988). *The honorable prison*. New York, NY: Lodestar Books.

Becerra de Jenkins, L. (1996). *So loud a silence*. New York, NY: Lodestar Books.

Belpré, P. (1932). *Pérez and Martina*, illustrated by C. Sánchez. New York, NY: Frederick Warne.

Belpré, P. (1946). *The tiger and the rabbit and other tales*, illustrated by K. Petersen Parker. Boston, MA: Houghton Mifflin.

Belpré, P. (1961). *Santiago*, illustrated by S. Shimin. New York, NY: Warne Publishers.

Belpré, P. (1962). *Juan Bobo and the queen's necklace*, illustrated by C. Price. New York, NY: Warne Publishers.

Belpré, P. (1969). *Oté: A Puerto Rican folktale*, illustrated by P. Gardone. New York, NY: Pantheon.

Belpré, P. (1978). *The rainbow colored horse*, illustrated by A. Martorell. New York, NY: Warne Publishers.

Belpré, P. (1996). *Firefly summer*. Houston: Piñata Books.

Bernier-Grand, C. (1999). *In the shade of the níspero tree*. New York, NY: Orchard Books.

Bernier-Grand, C. (1994). *Juan Bobo: Four folktales from Puerto Rico*, illustrated by E.R. Nieves. New York, NY: HarperCollins.

Bernier-Grant, C. (2007). *Frida. ¡Viva la vida! Long live life!* Tarrytown, NY: Marshall Cavendish.

Brown, M. (2005). *My name is Celia/ Me llamo Celia*, illustrated by R. López. Lanham, MD: Luna Rising.

Brown, M. (2007). *My name is Gabito.· The life of Gabriel García Márquez/Me llamo Gabito. La vida de Gabriel García Márquez*, illustrated by R. Colón. Lanham, MD: Luna Rising.

Brown, M. (2010). *Side by side/Lado a lado*, illustrated by J. Cepeda. New York, NY: Rayo.

Brusca, M. C. (1991). *My mama's little ranch on the pampas*. New York, NY: Henry Holt.

Brusca, M. C. (1991). *On the pampas*. New York, NY: Henry Holt. [In Spanish: *En la pampa*. Buenos Aires, Argentina: Editorial Suramericana.]

Brusca, M. C. (1995). *When jaguars ate the moon and other stories about animals and plants of the Americas*. New York, NY: Henry Holt.

Bunting, E. (1994). *Smoky night*, illustrated by D. Díaz. San Diego: Harcourt.

Cabazos Peña, S. (Ed.). (1981). *Cuenta-ca-tún*. Houston: Arte Público Press.

Cabazos Peña, S. (Ed.). (1981). *Kikirikí*. Houston: Arte Público Press.

Campoy, F. I. (2002). *Rosa Raposa*, illustrated by J.Aruego and A. Dewey. New York, NY: Harcourt.

Campoy, F. I., & Ada, A. F. (2000). *Blue and green*. Miami, FL: Alfaguara. [In Spanish *Azul y verde*].

Campoy, F. I., & Ada, A. F. (Eds.). (2000). Gateways to the Sun/Puertas al Sol: Poetry/Poesía *Chuchurumbé*. [In English: *Flying dragon*]. *Mambrú*. [In English: *Singing horse*.]. *Pimpón*. [In English *Dreaming fish*] *Antón pirulero*. [In English *Laughing crocodiles*]. *Smiles*. [In Spanish *Sonrisas*]. Miami, FL: Alfaguara.

Campoy, F. I. & Ada, A. F. (Eds.). (2000). Gateways to the Sun/Puertas al Sol: Theatre/Teatro *Tablado de Doña Rosita*. [In English: *Curtains up!*].*Teatrín de don Crispín*. [In English *Roll-n-Role*.] *Teatro del Gato Garabato*. [In English: *Rat-A-Tat-Cat*]. *Escenario de Polichinela*. [In English: *Top hat*] Miami, FL: Alfaguara.

Campoy, F. I. & Ada, A. F. (2000). Gateways to the Sun/Puertas al Sol: Biographies/Biografías *Steps* (Rita Moreno, Fernando Botero, Evelyn Cisneros). [In Spanish *Pasos*] *Voices* (Luis Valdés, Judith Baca, Carlos J. Finlay). [In Spanish *Voces*]. *Smiles* (Pablo Picasso, Gabriela Mistral, Benito Juárez). [In Spanish *Sonrisas*], *Paths* (José Martí, Frida Kahlo, César Chávez), [In Spanish *Caminos*]. Miami, FL: Alfaguara.

Campoy, F. I., & Ada, A. F. (2003). *¡Pío Peep! Traditional Spanish nursery rhymes*, illustrated by V. Escrivá. New York, NY: HarperCollins.

Campoy, F. I., & Ada, A. F. (2004). *Mamá Goose: A Latino treasury. Un tesoro de rimas infantiles*, illustrated by M. Suárez. New York, NY: Hyperion Books for Children.

Campoy, F. I., & Ada, A. F. (2006). *Stories to celebrate/Cuentos para celebrar* [series of 12 bilingual titles]. Miami, FL: Alfaguara.

Campoy, F. I., & Ada, A. F. (2006). *Tales our abuelitas told*, illustrated by F.Dávalos, V. Escrivá, S. Guevara, L. Torres. [In Spanish: *Cuentos que contaban nuestras abuelas*] New York, NY: Atheneum.

Campoy, F. I., & Ada, A. F. (2007). *¡Merry Navidad!*, illustrated by V. Escrivá. New York, NY: HarperCollins.

Campoy, F. I., & Ada, A. F. (2010). *¡Muu, moo! Animal nursery rhymes*, illustrated by V. Escrivá. New York, NY: HarperCollins.

Campoy, F. I., & Ada, A. F. (2010). *Salta, saltarín*, illustrated by C. Legnazzi. Dallas, TX: Frog Street.

Campoy, F. I., & Ada, A. F. (2011). *Ten little puppies/Diez perritos*, illustrated by U. Wensell. New York, NY: HarperCollins.

Carling, A. L. (1998). *Mamá y papá have a store*. New York, NY: Dial Books. [In Spanish: (2003). *La tienda de mamá y papá*. Toronto, Canada: Groundwood Books.]

Carling, A. L. (2006). *Alfombras de aserrín/Sawdust carpets*. Toronto, Canada: Groundwood Books.]

Carlson, L. M. (Ed.). (1999). *You're on! Seven plays in English and Spanish*. New York, NY: Morrow Junior.

Castañeda, O. S. (1993). *Abuela's weave*, illustrated by E. O. Sánchez. New York, NY: Lee and Low. [In Spanish: *El tapiz de abuela*]

Castañeda, O. S. (1994). *Imagining Isabel*. New York, NY: Penguin.

Colato Laínez, R. (2004). *Waiting por papá / Esperando a papá*, illustrated by A. Accardo. Houston, TX: Arte Público Press.

Colato Laínez, R. (2005). *Play lotería/El juego de la lotería*, illustrated by J. Arena. Flagstaff, AZ: Luna Rising.

Colato Laínez, R. (2005). *I am René the boy/Yo soy René el niño*, illustrated by F. Graullera Ramírez. Houston: Arte Público Press.

Colato Laínez, R. (2010). *My shoes and I*, illustrated by F. Vanden Broeck. Honesdale, PA: Boyds Mill Press.

Colato Laínez, R. (2009). *René has two last names/René tiene dos apellidos*, illustrated by F. Graullera Ramírez. Houston, TX: Arte Público Press.

Colato Laínez, R. (2010). *From north to south*, illustrated by J. Cepeda. San Francisco, CA: Children's Book Press.

Colato Laínez, R. (2010). *The tooth fairy meets el Ratón Pérez*, illustrated by T. Lintern. Berkeley, CA: Tricycle Press.

Contreras, K. (2009). *Braids/Trencitas*. New York, NY: Lectorum.

Corpi, L. (1997). *Where fireflies dance /Allí donde bailan las luciérnagas*), illustrated by M. Reisberg. San Francisco, CA: Children's Book Press.

Crespo, G. (1995). *How Hwariwa the cayman learned to share: A Yanomami myth*. Boston, MA: Clarion Books.

Cumpiano, Ina. (2009). *Quinito neighborhood/ El barrio de Quinito*. San Francisco, CA: Children's Book Press.

Cumpiano, Ina. (2010). *Quinito day and night/ Quinito día y noche*. San Francisco, CA: Children's Book Press.

Day, F. A. (2003). *Latina and Latino voices in literature for children and teenagers*. Westport, CT: Greenwood Press.

Deedy, C. A. (2007). *Martina the beautiful cockroach*, illustrated by M. Austin. Atlanta, GA: Peachtree Publishers.

Delacre, L. (Ed.). (1989). *Arroz con leche: Popular songs and rhymes from Latin America*, selected and illustrated by L. Delacre. New York, NY: Scholastic.

Delacre, L. (Ed.). (1990). *Las Navidades: Popular Christmas songs from Latin America*, selected and illustrated by L. Delacre. New York, NY: Scholastic

Delacre, L. (1993). *Vejigante mascarader*. New York, NY: Scholastic Trade.

Delacre, L. (1996). *Golden tales: Myths, legends and folktales from Latin America*. New York, NY: Scholastic. [In Spanish *De oro y esmeraldas: Mitos, leyendas y cuentos populares de Latino América* Scholastic.]

Delacre, L. (2000). *Salsa stories*. New York, NY: Scholastic. [In Spanish: *Cuentos con sazón*]

Delacre, L. (2006). *Arrorró, mi niño: Latino lullabies*. New York, NY: Lee & Low Books.

Delacre, L. (2008). *Alicia afterimage*. New York, NY: Lee & Low.

Durango, J. (2008). *The walls of Cartagena*, illustrated by T. Pohrt. New York, NY: Simon and Schuster.

Engle, M. (2006). *The poet slave of Cuba: A biography of Juan Francisco Manzano*, illustrated by S. Qualls. New York, NY: Henry Holt.

Engle, M. (2008). *The surrender tree: Poems of Cuba's struggle for freedom*. New York, NY: Henry Holt.

Engle, M. (2009). *Tropical secrets: Holocaust refugees in Cuba*. New York, NY: Henry Holt.

Freire de Matos, I. (1968). *ABC de Puerto Rico*, illustrated by A. Martorell. Sharon, CN: Troutman Press.

Galarza, E. (1971). *Barrio boy: The story of a boy's acculturation*. Notre Dame, IN: University of Notre Dame Press.

Garay, L. (1997). *Pedrito's day*. New York, NY: Scholastic.

González, L. (1994). *The bossy gallito/El gallo de bodas. A traditional Cuban folktale*, llustrated by L. Delacre. New York, NY: Scholastic.

González, L. (1997). *Señor cat's romance and other stories from Latin America*, illustrated by L. Delacre. New York, NY: Scholastic.

González, L. (2008). *The storytelling candle*, illustrated by L. Delacre. San Francisco, CA: Children's Book Press.

Herrera, J. F. (1995). *Calling the doves/Canto de las palomas*. San Francisco, CA: Children's Book Press.

Herrera, J. F. (2002). *Grandma and me at the flea/ Los meros meros remateros*, illustrated by A. DeLucio-Brook. San Francisco, CA: Children's Book Press

Herrera, J. F. (2003). *Super cilantro girl/La superniña del cilantro*, illustrated by H. Robledo Tapia. San Francisco, CA: Children's Book Press

Herrera, J. F. (2004). *Desplumado/Featherless*, illustrated by E. Cuevas. San Francisco, CA: Children's Book Press

Hijuelos, O. (2008). *Dark dude*. New York, NY: Atheneum.

Igoa, C. (1995). *The inner world of the immigrant child*. New York, NY: St. Martin's Press.

Jiménez, F. (1997). *The circuit: Stories from the life of a migrant child*. Albuquerque: University of New Mexico Press.

Jiménez, F. (2000). *The Christmas gift /El regalo de Navidad*, illustrated by C. B. Coots. Boston, MA: Houghton Mifflin.

Jiménez, F. (2001). *La mariposa*, illustrated by S. Silva. Boston, MA: Houghton Mifflin.

Jiménez, F. (2002). *Breaking through*. Boston, MA: Houghton Mifflin.

Jiménez, F. (2009). *Reaching out*. Boston, MA: Houghton Mifflin.

Jiménez, J. R. (1914). *Platero y yo*, illustrated by F. Marco. Madrid: Ediciones de la lectura.

Krull. K. (2003). *Harvesting hope: The story of César Chávez*, illustrated by Y. Morales. New York, NY: Harcourt Publishers.

Lange, N. (1957). *Cuadernos de infancia*. Buenos Aires, Argentina: Editorial Losada.

Lázaro, G. (2006). *Julia*, illustrated by P. Marichal.Colección Cuando los grandes eran pequeños. New York, NY: Lectorum.

Lázaro, G. (2007). *José*, illustrated by M. Sánchez. Colección Cuando los grandes eran pequeños. New York, NY: Lectorum.

Lázaro, G. (2007). *Juana Inés*, illustrated by B. González Preza. Colección Cuando los grandes eran pequeños. New York, NY: Lectorum.

Lázaro, G. (2008). *Pablo*, illustrated by M. Donoso. Colección Cuando los grandes eran pequeños. New York, NY: Lectorum.

Lázaro, G. (2009). *Federico García Lorca*, illustrated by E. S. Moreiro. Colección Cuando los grandes eran pequeños. New York, NY: Lectorum.

Lázaro, G. (2009). *Jorge Luis Borges*, illustrated by G. Genovés. Colección Cuando los grandes eran pequeños. New York, NY: Lectorum.

Lomas Garza, C. (1990). *Family pictures/ Cuadros de familia*. San Francisco, CA: Children's Book Press.

Lomas Garza, C. (1996). *In my family/En mi familia*. San Francisco, CA: Children's Book Press.

Loya, O. (1997). *Momentos mágicos. Tales from Latin America*. Little Rock, AK: August House Publishers.

Martí, J. (1889/1979). *La Edad de Oro*. New York. Facsimile Edition. La Habana, Cuba. Centro de Estudios Martianos. Editorial Letras Cubanas.

Martí, J. (1982). *Cartas a María Mantilla*. Ciudad de La Habana, Cuba: Editorial Gente Nueva.

Martí, J. (1997). *Los zapaticos de rosa*, illustrated by L. Delacre. New York, NY: Lectorum.

Martí, J. (1998). "*Los zapaticos de rosa*." In A. F. Ada and F. I. Campoy (Eds.). *El son del sol*. Música amiga 10. Westlake, OH: Del Sol Books.

Martínez, C. G. (2008). *The smell of old lady perfume*. El Paso, TX: Cinco Puntos.

Martorell, A. (1991). *La piel de la memoria*. San Juan, Puerto Rico: Ediciones Envergadura.

Méndez Capote, R. (1964). *Memorias de una cubanita que nació con el siglo*. La Habana, Cuba: Bolsilibros Union.

Mohr, N. (1979). *Felita*. New York, NY: Bantam.

Mohr, N. (1986). *Going home*. New York, NY: Bantam.

Mohr, N. (1994). *In my own words: Growing up inside the sanctuary of my imagination*. New York, NY: Julian Messner/Simon & Schuster.

Mohr, N.(1995). *The song of the coqui and other tales of Puerto Rico/La canción del coquí*, illustrated by A. Martorell. New York, NY: Viking.

Mohr, N. (1996). *Old Letivia and the mountain of sorrows*, illustrated by R. Gutiérrez. New York, NY: Viking.

Montes, M. (2000). *Juan Bobo goes to work*, illustrated by J. Cepeda. New York, NY: Schwartz & Wode/Random

Montes, M. (2006). *A crazy mixed up Spanglish day*, illustrated by J. Cepeda. New York, NY: Scholastic.

Mora, P. (1994). *The desert is my mother/El desierto es mi madre*, illustrated by D. Lechón. Houston, TX: Piñata Books.

Mora, P. (1995). *The gift of the poinsettia: El regalo de la flor de Nochebuena*, illustrated by D. Lechón. Houston, TX: Piñata.

Mora, P. (1996). *Confetti poems for children*, illustrated by E. O. Sánchez. New York, NY: Lee & Low.

Mora, P. (1997). *A birthday basket for Tía*, illustrated by C. Long. New York, NY: Simon and Schuster.

Mora, P. (1998). *Delicious hullabaloo/Pachanga deliciosa*, illustrated by F. X. Mora, Houston, TX: Piñata.

Mora, P. (2001). *The bakery lady/La señora del panadero*, illustrated by P. Torrecilla. Houston, TX: Arte Público Press.

Mora, P. (2001). *Listen to the desert. Oye al desierto*, illustrated by F. X. Mora. New York, NY: Clarion.

Mora, P. (2002). *A library for Juana*, illustrated by B. Vidal. New York, NY: Knopf Books for Young Readers. [In Spanish: *Una biblioteca para Juana.*]

Mora, P. (Ed.). (2004). *Love to mamá: A tribute to mothers*, illustrated by P. S. Barragán. New York, NY: Lee & Low.

Mora, P. (2005). *Doña Flor. A tall tale about a giant woman with a great heart. Doña Flor un cuento de una mujer gigante con un gran corazón*, illustrated by R. Colón. New York, NY: Knopf Books for Young Readers.

Mora, P. (2008). *Abuelos*, illustrated by A. L. Carling. Toronto, Canada: Groundwood.

Mora, P. (2008). *Join hands! The ways we celebrate life*, illustrated by G. Ancona. Watertown, MA: Charlesbridge.

Mora, P. (2009). *Book fiesta! Celebrate children's book day*, illustrated by R. López. New York, NY: HarperCollins, Rayo.

Mora, P. (2009). *Gracias. Thanks*, illustrated by J. Parra. New York, NY: Lee & Low.

Mora, P. (2009). *A piñata in a pear tree: A Latino twelve days of Christmas*, illustrated by Y. Morales. New York, NY: Clarion.

Mora, P. (2010). *Dizzy in your eyes. Love poems*. New York, NY: Knopf.

Morales, Y. (2003). *Just a minute: A trickster's tale and counting book*. San Francisco, CA: Chronicle Books.

Morales, Y. (2007). *Little night/Nochecita*. New Milford, CT: Roaring Book Press.

Morales, Y. (2008). *Just in case: A trickster tale and Spanish alphabet book*. New Milford, CT: Roaring Book Press.

Moretón, D. (1993). *Martí and the mango*. New York, NY: Turtle Books.

Moretón, D. (1997). *La cucaracha Martina: A Caribbean folktale*. New York, NY: Turtle Books. [In Spanish: *La cucaracha Martina: Un cuento folklórico del Caribe.*]

Muñoz Ryan, P. (2000). *Esperanza rising*. New York, NY: Scholastic.

Muñoz Ryan, P. (2004). *Becoming Naomi León*. New York, NY: Scholastic.

Muñoz Ryan, P. (2010). *The dreamer*, illustrated by P. Sis. New York, NY: Scholastic.

Orozco, J. L. (Ed.). (1994). *De colores and other Latin American folk-songs for children*, illustrated by E. Kleven. New York, NY: Dutton.

Orozco, J. L. (Ed.). (1997). *Diez deditos: Ten little fingers and other play rhymes and action songs from Latin America*, illustrated by E. Kleven. New York, NY: Dutton.

Ortiz Cofer, J. (1990). *Silent dancing: A partial remembrance of a Puerto Rican childhood*. Houston, TX: Arte Público Press.

Osa, N. (2003). *Cuba 15*. New York, NY: Delacorte Press.

Paz, S. (1979). *From the sky of my childhood/Del cielo de mi niñez*. Smithsonian Folkways Record (audio cassette).

de la Parra, T. (1929). *Memorias de la Mamá Blanca*. Paris. Le Livre Libre. (1966). Buenos Aires, Argentina: EUDEBA.

Pellegrino, M. (2009). *Journey of dreams*. London: Frances Lincoln Publishers.

Peña, A. (1995). *Peña on Peña*. Waco, TX: WRS.

Peña. M. de la (2009). *We were here*. New York, NY: Delacorte.

Perera, H.(1998). *Cuentos de Apolo*. León, España: Ediciones Everest. [First published in 1947]

Perera, H. (2001). *Cuentos para chicos y grandes*, illustrated by R.Diego. New York, NY: Scholastic, Lectorum. [First Published in 1975]

Pérez, A. I. (2000). *My very own room/Mi propio cuartito*, illustrated by M. C.González. San Francisco, CA: Children's Book Press.

Pérez, A. I. (2002). *My diary from here to there/Mi diario de aquí hasta allá*, illustrated by M. C. González. San Francisco, CA: Children's Book Press.

Pico, F. (1997). *The red comb*, illustrated by M. A. Ordóñez. Caracas, Venezuela: EKARE.

Presilla, M. E. (1996). *Feliz Nochebuena, Feliz Navidad*, illustrated by I. E. Ferrer. New York, NY: Macmillan.

Presilla, M. E. (1996). *Mola: Cuna life stories and art*. New York, NY: Henry Holt.

Presilla, M. E., & Soto, G. (1996). *Life around the lake: Embroideries by the women of Lake Patzcuaro*. New York, NY: Henry Holt.

Soto, G. (1990). *A fire in my hands*: New York, NY: Harcourt.

Soto, G. (1990). *A summer life*. New York, NY: Bantam Doubleday.

Soto, G. (1990). *Baseball in April and other stories*. San Diego, CA: Harcourt Brace Jovanovich. In Spanish:*Béisbol en abril y otras historias*. México: Fondo de Cultura Económica.]

Soto, G. (1991). *Taking sides*. San Diego, CA: Harcourt Brace Jovanovich. [In Spanish: *Tomando partido*. México: Fondo de Cultura Económica.]

Soto, G. (1992). *Living up the street: Narrative recollections*. New York, NY: Dell.

Soto, G. (1992). *Neighborhood odes*, illustrated by D. Díaz. San Diego: Harcourt.

Soto, G. (1992). *Pacific crossing*. Needham MA: Silver Burdett Ginn.

Soto, G. (1993). *Local news*. New York, NY: Harcourt.

Soto, G. (1993). *The pool party*. New York, NY: Delacorte Press.

Soto, G. (1995). *Chato's kitchen*, illustrated by S. Guevara. New York, NY: Putnam. [In Spanish: *Chato y su cena*.]

Soto, G (1995). *Summer on wheels*. New York, NY: Scholastic.

Soto, G. (1995). *Canto familiar*. San Diego, CA: Harcourt.

Soto, G. (1995). *Crazy weekend*. New York, NY: Scholastic.

Soto, G. (1997). *Buried onions*. New York, NY: Harcourt.

Soto, G. (1997). *Novio boy: A play*. San Diego, CA: Harcourt.

Soto, G. (1997). *The skirt*, illustrated by Eric Velázquez. New York, NY: Bantam, Doubleday, Dell.

Soto, G. (1997). *The cat's meow*, illustrated by Joe Cepeda. New York, NY: Scholastic

Soto, G. (1998). *The bushy moustache*, illustrated by Joe Cepeda. New York, NY: Putnam.

Soto, G. (1998). *Petty crimes*. New York, NY: Harcourt.

Soto, G. (2000). *Chato and the party animals*, illustrated by S. Guevara. New York, NY: Putnam.

Soto, G. (2002). *Fearless Fernie*, illustrated by R. Dunnick. New York, NY: Putnam Juvenile.

Soto, G.(2002). *Partly cloudy. Poems of love and longing*. San Diego, CA: Harcourt.

Soto, G. (2002). *If the shoe fits*, illustrated by Terry Widener. New York, NY: Putnam.

Soto, G. (2005). *Chato goes cruisin'*, illustrated by S. Guevara. New York, NY: Putnam.

Soto, G. (2005). *Worlds apart: Traveling with Fernie and me*. New York, NY: Putnam.

Soto, G. (2006). *My little car*, illustrated by Pam Paparona. New York, NY: Putnam.

Soto, G. (2006). *Accidental love*. New York, NY: Harcourt.

Soto, G. (2006). *Taking sides*. Evanston, IL: Holt McDougal

Soto, G. (2007). *Help wanted*. New York, NY: Harcourt.

Soto, G. (2008). *Facts of life*. New York, NY: Harcourt.

Stork, F.X. (2009). *Marcelo in the real world*. New York, NY: Arthur Levine Books

Tafolla, C. (2008). *What can you do with a rebozo / ¿Qué puedes hacer con un rebozo?* Berkeley, CA: Tricycle Press.

Tafolla, C. (2009). *What can you do with a paleta ¿Qué puedes hacer con una paleta?* Berkeley, CA: Tricycle Press.

Thomas, P. (1967). *Down these mean streets*. New York, NY: Alfred A. Knopf.

Thomas, P. (1972). *Savior, savior, hold my hand*. New York, NY: Alfred A. Knopf.

Thomas, P. (1974). *Seven long times*. New York, NY: Praeger.

Thomas, P. (1978). *Stories from the barrio*. New York, NY: Alfred A. Knopf.

Torres, L. (1993). *Subway sparrow*. New York, NY: Farrar, Straus, Giraux. [In Spanish: *El gorrión del metro*.]

Torres, L. (1998). *Liliana's grandmothers*. New York, NY: Farrar, Straus, Giraux. [In Spanish: *Las abuelas de Liliana*.]

Torres, L. (2004). *The kite festivals*. New York, NY: Farrar, Straus, Giraux. [In Spanish: *El festival de las cometas*.]

Vega, D. (2009). *Grandmother, have the angels come?* illustrated by Erin Eitter Kono. New York, NY: Little Brown.

Vidal, B. (2004). *Federico and the Magi's gift: A Latin American Christmas story*. New York, NY: Random House Children's Books.

Villaseñor, V. (1994). *Walking stars. Stories of magic and power*. Houston, TX: Piñata Books.

Zamora Vicente, A. (1995). *Primeras hojas*. Madrid, España: Espasa-Calpe.

Zubizarreta, R. (1991). *The woman who outshone the sun/La mujer que brillaba más que el sol*, illustrated by F. Olivera. San Francisco, CA: Children's Book Press.

FURTHER READINGS

Ada, A. F. (1990). *Abecedario de los animales*, illustrated by V. Escrivá. Madrid: Espasa.

Ada, A. F. (1995). Colección cuentos con Alma: *Barquitos de papel, Barriletes, Días de circo, Pin pin sarabín. Pregones*, illustrated by P. Torrecilla. Beverly Hills, CA: Laredo Publishing.

Ada, A. F. (1998). *Yours truly, Goldilocks*, illustrated by L.Tryon. New York, NY: Atheneum. [In Spanish *Atentamente, Ricitos de Oro*. Miami, FL: Alfaguara].

Ada, A. F. (2001). *With love, little red hen*, iIllustrated by L. Tryon. New York, NY: Atheneum.

Álvarez, J. (2009). *Return to sender*. New York, NY: Alfred A. Knopf.

Ancona, G. (1981). *Dancing*. New York, NY: E. P. Dutton.

Ancona, G. (1995). *Ricardo's day*. New York, NY: Scholastic.

Argueta, J. (2007). *Trees are hanging from the sky*, illustrated by R. Yockteng. Toronto, ON, Canada: Groundwood Books.

Belpré, Pura. (1991). *Pérez and Martina*. New York, NY: Viking.

Bernier-Grand, C. (2004). *César ¡Sí se puede! Yes, We Can!*, illustrated by D. Díaz. Tarrytown, NY: Marshall Cavendish

Bernier-Grand, C. (2007). *Shake it, Morena and other folklore from Puerto Rico*, illustrated by L. Delacre. Minneapolis, MN: Lerner Publishing Group.

Bernier-Grand, C. (2009). *Diego:Bigger than life*, illustrated by D. Díaz. Tarrytown, NY: Marshall Cavendish.

Campoy, F. I. (2009). *My day from A to Z*, illustrated by S. Lavandeira. Miami, FL: Alfaguara [In Spanish: *Mi día de la A a la Z*].

Castillo, A. (2000). *My daughter, my son, the eagle, the dove: An Aztec chant*, illustrated by S. Guevara. New York, NY: E. P. Duttton.

Delacre, L. (2004). *Rafi and Roni*. New York, NY: Harper Collins.

Delacre, L. (2006). *Rafi and Roni Carnaval*. New York, NY: HarperCollins.

Galarza, E. (1971). *Aquí y allá en California*. San José, CA: Editorial Almadén.

Galarza, E. (1971). *Chogorróm*. San José, CA: Editorial Almadén.

Galarza, E. (1971). *Poemas Párvulos*. San José, CA: Editorial Almadén.

Galarza, E. (1971). *Zoo fun*. San José, CA: Editorial Almadén.

Galarza, E. (1971). *Zoo Risa*. San José, CA: Editorial Almadén.

Galarza, E.(1972). *Más poemas párvulos*. San José, CA: Editorial Almadén.

Galarza, E. (n/y). *Poemas pe-que pe-que pe-que-ñitos. Very Very Short Nature Poems*. San José, CA: Editorial Almadén.

Galarza, E. (n/y). *Rimas tontas*. San José, CA: Editorial Almadén.

Galarza, E. (n/y). *Todo mundo lee*. San José, CA: Editorial Almadén.

Lomas Garza, C. (1999). *Making magic windows/Ventanas mágicas*. San Francisco, CA: Children's Book Press.

Herrera, J. F. (2000). *The Upside Down Boy/El niño de cabeza*, illustrated by E. Gómez. San Francisco, CA: Children's Book Press

Martínez, V. (1996). *Parrot in the oven. Mi vida*. New York, NY: Harper Collins.

Mora, P. (1997). *Tomás and the library lady*, illustrated by R. Colon. New York, NY: Alfred A. Knopf. [In Spanish; *Tomás y la señora de la biblioteca*.]

Muñoz Ryan, P. (1998). *Riding freedom*, illustrated by B. Selznick. New York, NY: Scholastic.

Pérez, A. I. (2007). *Nana's big surprise/¡Nana, qué sorpresa!* San Francisco, CA: Children's Book Press.

Soto, G. (1993). *Too many tamales*, illustrated by E. Martínez. New York, NY: Putnam. [In Spanish: *¡Qué montón de tamales!]*

Soto, G. (1997). *Snapshots from the wedding*, illustrated by S. García. New York, NY: Putnam.

Torres, L. (1995). *Saturday sancocho*. New York, NY: Farrar, Straus, Giraux. [In Spanish: *El sancocho del sábado*.]

9

Stories from the Mountains: Appalachian Literature for Children and Adolescents

Carolyn S. Brodie

> When I was young in the mountains, I never wanted to go to the ocean, and I never wanted to go to the desert. I never wanted to go anywhere else in the world, for I was in the mountains. And that was always enough.
>
> —Rylant, 1982, unpaged

BRIEF OVERVIEW OF APPALACHIAN CULTURE

Appalachia the Place . . . the Culture . . . the People . . .

Appalachia is the name for a remarkably beautiful region of the United States with boundaries that are linked geographically to the eastern mountain regions of the country. Appalachian is the name for the people who call this region home and who are historically known to be determined, strong, filled with pride, integrity, and ingenuity. Generations of families who have lived in this region have handed down a culture and traditions centered on the arts and crafts, music, foods, spoken language, religious spirit, sense of beauty, independence, and love of place. The area was initially defined by the 1965 Appalachian Regional Development Act as a 182,000-square-mile region. Now defined by the Appalachian Regional Commission to include 200,000-square miles, it is home to 24.8 million people with a 42 percent rural population, versus a national rural population of 20 percent (Appalachian Regional Commission Web site). There are 420 counties in all or parts of 13 states that are included in this region of the United States including Alabama, Georgia, Kentucky, Maryland, Mississippi, New York, North Carolina, Ohio, Pennsylvania, South Carolina, Tennessee, Virginia, and all of West Virginia.

With the region's size, there is a great range of prosperity versus poverty; but over the last decades, there has been marked economic improvement in some areas of the region.

"In 1965, one in three Appalachians lived in poverty. In 2000, the region's poverty rate was 13.6 percent. The number of Appalachian counties considered economically distressed was 223 in 1965; in fiscal year 2010 that number is 82" (Appalachian Regional Commission Web site). The people of this region have in the past depended heavily on coal mining (or other mining), farming and forestry. In more recent years, industry and manufacturing have been important for the region's economic changes for the better. Some communities in the area have been more successful than others. With direct issues related to both a rural population and a historic link to poverty, there is no surprise that these factors have influenced the children's literature from and about the region.

In reference to the people of this region "the term *Appalachians*, usually refers to the ancestors of Scottish, Irish, English, Welsh, and German immigrants who settled in this region, isolated geographically, economically, and politically from the rest of the country and developed a unique culture" (Leeper, 2003, p. 34). "Like African Americans, Asian Americans, Latinos, and other racial and ethnic groups in the United States, modern Appalachians must define, or redefine, their culture in the wake of an ever growing homogenization of U.S. identity as well as stereotypes created and perpetuated by the media" (Leeper, 2003, p. 34).

The more common geographic interpretation and understanding of Appalachia is focused on the central and southern mountain ranges, including Alleghany of Virginia and West Virginia, Blue Ridge of the Carolinas and Great Smoky Mountains of Tennessee. The children's literature associated with Appalachia is primarily set in these three mountainous areas (Schmidt, 1992, p. 70). Schmidt's definition of the literature is similar to that used by the AppLit Web site at http://www.ferrum.edu/applit/about, accessed on October 03, 2010, which states, "in the interest of providing a point of reference, when AppLit pages use the term Appalachia, we are referring to the mountainous regions of Kentucky, Virginia, Tennessee, South Carolina, North Carolina, Georgia, and Alabama; all of the mountain state of West Virginia; and the hilly region of southern Ohio. Additionally, when we use the term Appalachian literature, we are referring to literature written about this particular region and its people."

Defining the exact area that constitutes Appalachian children's literature is sometimes difficult to pinpoint. There are differences in thought even among the scholars and other experts who study the region. So, for the purpose of this chapter, the definition will serve as a broader one, one that includes the mountain region literature as defined above. In reference to the important scholarship related to the area that began to arise in the 1960s and that has continued until the present, there have been a number of Appalachian studies, programs, and centers established in academic institutions within Appalachia that have various missions. Some of these include Loyal Jones Appalachian Center, Berea College, Berea, Kentucky; Appalachian Center, University of Kentucky, Lexington, Kentucky; Appalachian Center for Craft, Tennessee Tech University, Cookeville, Tennessee; Center for Appalachian Studies, East Tennessee University, Johnson City, Tennessee; and the Center for Appalachian Studies, Appalachian State University, Boone, North Carolina. Also an Appalachian Studies Association was created in 1977 to support those who are "writing, researching and teaching about Appalachia" (Appalachian Studies Association, http://www.appalachianstudies.org, accessed on October 03, 2010).

It was during the 1960s that B. Eliot Wiggington began to create a curriculum for his ninth grade students in Rabun County, Georgia, which resulted in the establishment of an educational and literary organization. The project connected the land, the culture, and the customs of the southern Appalachian region, which resulted in a student-produced magazine of their own inspiration. *The Foxfire Magazine* shared interviews and stories as told by the mountain people. The first *Foxfire* book was published in 1972 as an anthology of articles from the student magazine that presented the culture of the region. With the publication of this magazine and the subsequent series of books, there has been a greater understanding of the way of life of the people in this southern Appalachian mountain region. The series provides information about cooking, handcrafts, farming, toys and games, music, religious beliefs, and much more. *The Foxfire Museum & Heritage Center* is a learning and demonstration site in Rabun County, Georgia. It is also connected to the program's teacher training initiatives. You can visit the Foxfire Web site at http://www.foxfire.org/, accessed on October 03, 2010.

A BRIEF OVERVIEW OF APPALACHIAN CHILDREN'S LITERATURE

Available in a great variety of subjects, time frames, and age levels, Appalachian children's literature has, of course, the setting as integral to the story. The natural world is a focus of the literature from beauty of the region to the many ways that nature has affected the culture of the people through their family way of life, spiritual journey, work choice, and their creative expression through arts and music. Gary Schmidt said,

In a world of contrasts, of warm and green valleys and killing blizzards, of individuality and the importance of community, of bounty and poverty. And yet, in some measure it is those very contrasts which help to make the world of Appalachia as it is pictured in children's literature so appealing.

(Schmidt, 1992, p. 75)

Without a doubt, the most recent succinct overview of available Appalachian children's literature can be found in the preface (pp. 3–11) of Roberta Teague Herrin and Sheila Quinn Oliver's (2010) recently released *Appalachian Children's Literature: An Annotated Bibliography*. Though intended to be a discussion of how the book came to be published, the preface of this book also serves as an introduction to the available and important literature of the region. It also serves as a historical account of important authors and illustrators who contributed to the field. This important professional tool provides reviews for more than 2,000 titles and thus gives readers a timeline of Appalachian children's literature along with an annotated list of significant books through 2007. Herrin has researched the literature since the 1980s, and she is well aware of the difficulty in defining the region's literature. She includes literature from the 13 states as defined by the Appalachian Regional Commission, and makes note that selecting some books for the list was indeed difficult because using the ARC definition means that some counties in a state are included and some are not. This was particularly complicated when choosing which children's biographies to include. She describes the book as "by no means exhaustive; at best, it represents an exhaustive *attempt* to identify *most* of the significant Appalachian titles" (Herrin, 2010, p. 5). (Note: Though not exhaustive by Herrin's own definition, this resource is no doubt one of the most important reference tools ever produced about Appalachian children's literature, and this author was grateful that it was published in February 2010, just as this chapter was going to press).

Another significant overview of Appalachian children's literature is presented in Jennifer S. Smith's 2002 dissertation titled *Mining the Mountain of Appalachian Children's Literature: Defining a Multicultural Literature*. Smith's purpose for her descriptive study was "to develop a definition of Appalachian children's literature" (p. ii). For the purposes of her research, Smith states, "Appalachian children's literature is defined by setting and place and distinguished from other multicultural literature by the manner in which recurring traits manifest themselves across authors, genres, and decades" (p. ii). She goes on to say that "the definition formulated for this study is framed and informed by the history of published Appalachian children's literature with a Eurocentric perspective" (p. ii).

As for the writing of this chapter, the selection of Appalachian children's literature may differ somewhat from the other cultural or ethnic groups included in this professional book because in defining the literature, it is not only tied to the people of the region, but it is also tied very closely to the geographic landscape. The region and its people can be collectively studied via themes, values and characteristics that are reflected in the literature. They may also be studied through the selected national awards they have received such as Newbery and Caldecott. Another approach is to study Appalachian children's literature through information areas of geography and biography as well as through the genres of poetry and folklore.

HISTORICAL DEVELOPMENT

Herrin (2010) notes that the earliest known Appalachian literature published in the late 1700s was related to the land and its exploration. But it was not until the past century that there has been so much written about the region as well as written by authors from the region. Indeed, the region was not clearly defined until 1965 by the Appalachian Regional Commission.

In her dissertation, Jennifer S. Smith (2002) devotes an entire chapter to the history of Appalachian children's literature. The first part of the chapter provides a history of developments significant to the region and the culture of Appalachia. The majority of the chapter is an overview and historical timeline directly connected to Appalachian children's literature. This historical timeline is divided into a study by decades: prior to 1900; 1900–1919; 1920–1939; 1940–1969; 1970–1979; 1980–present (noting that the dissertation was published in 2002). Through this timeline, Smith notes the long standing importance of oral tradition in Appalachia, which has resulted in a wealth of folklore. Diversity within the region should also be noted. While European Americans are the focus for much of this regional literature, African Americans are also represented in the children's literature across the decades.

A few Appalachian children's publications were available prior to the 1920s. During the 1920s, children's literature in general was becoming more recognized and marketable, which was in part due to the significant changes in the publication industry and to technological advances. Children's literature was further legitimized in 1922 by the creation of the John Newbery Medal that is awarded by the American Library Association to the most distinguished contribution to American's children's literature in the preceding year. Following in 1938 was the creation of the Randolph Caldecott Medal that is awarded to the most distinguished American picture book for children published in the preceding year. It is important to note that over the decades a number of selections from Appalachian children's literature have been recognized in this prestigious national arena. For example, of Rebecca Caudill's numerous books for children, her Appalachian family novel titled *Tree of Freedom* (1949) was named a 1950 Newbery Honor. And, *A Pocketful of Cricket* (1964), a picture book written by Caudill and illustrated by Evaline Ness, was named a 1965 Caldecott Honor book.

It was not until the late 1930s and 1940s, that books were published and targeted toward a child audience (Asbury, 1995). At this time, regional writers who were from Appalachia were writing in varied genres and had begun to emerge and became more prevalent from 1940–1969. Their influence in the field became particularly notable. Smith notes the works of Rebecca Caudill, May Justus, William Steele, and Jesse Stuart as included during this period. These noted Appalachian authors were joined by James Still, Lillie Chapin, and Alexander Key from the 1970–1979 period (Smith, 2002, p. 55). Also, during the 1970s there were two important Newbery Medal books that were linked to Appalachia including Virginia Hamilton's *M. C. Higgins, the Great* (1974) and *Summer of the Swans* (1970) by Betsy Byars.

From 1980 to the present, Appalachian-centered literature became more widely available and recognized with new authors and illustrators entering the field. The 1980s were years of lasting contributions and tremendous artistic expression in Appalachian children's literature. Authors and illustrators who became nationally known for their contributions to Appalachaian children's literature during this time period include Cynthia Rylant, Gail E. Haley, George Ella Lyon, Ruth White, Gloria Houston, Jerrie Oughton, Paul Brett Johnson, Marc Harshman, Barry Moser, Phyllis Reynolds Naylor, and Anne Shelby.

WHY THIS LITERATURE IS IMPORTANT

Appalachian children's literature is important because the children and adults of the region need literature that validates, explains, and supports their way of life, culture, values, and their homeland. This regional literature signifies that there is importance and relevance to the experiences of the people who live there now and who have historically contributed to the region. Selections of this literature can help dispel stereotypes of the Appalachian people outside the region and provide a view of the positive and authentic cultural values and accurate details.

Perhaps Cynthia Rylant said it best about the importance of Appalachian children's literature. In her acceptance speech for the 1991 Boston Globe-Horn Book Award for nonfiction for *Appalachia: The Voices of Sleeping Birds* (1991), Rylant concluded her thank you remarks with the following:

I am most grateful, to my family and to the neighbors in Cool Ridge, West Virginia, who keep the book on their coffee tables and pick it up and read it again every few days and who always knew, deep down, that they were worth writing about.

(Rylant, 1992)

Rylant's use of descriptive language in this book provides the reader with a clear sense of the place of Appalachia with such passages as "in summer if you walk the roads you will smell honeysuckle and the odors of cows and that gritty aroma dirt roads in the mountains send up your nose. The dogs will have a different smell every day" (p. 19).

Appalachian scholar Bill Best (1995) makes a vital point about the importance of regional literature as children begin learning to read,

Reading and language arts should begin where the children are, in the most literal sense. It is not enough to have Dick and Jane passing through the mountains on their way to Florida from

New England. Early readers should contain stories about life as it is lived in the particular areas where children live.

(p. 661)

SELECTION CRITERIA

A chapter in a book such as this can only provide a selection of the rich and varied children's books that have been published about the Appalachian region and Appalachian people. *Appalachia Children's Literature* (Herrin & Oliver, 2010) included more than 2,000 titles connected to the region, so this chapter is selective in its approach.

Just as one would make selections for a school or public library, this researcher has followed the standard selection criteria for genres and types of literature. In addition, for the selection of multicultural literature, there are additional considerations.

The literature should provide:

- recognizable cultural identity,
- connection to a sense of place,
- cultural accuracy and authenticity in the writing,
- authentic visual details in the illustrations, and
- avoidance of stereotyping.

Stereotyping mentioned above is primarily connected to the earlier Appalachian children's literature that depicted the Appalachian people as hillbillies and backward people. Some of the descriptions serve to make the region and its people a distinctive culture. Some of the writings of May Hill Justus and William Steele in the 1950s and 1960s helped to establish the culture within children's literature. The hillbilly stereotype is seldom seen today. Cynthia Rylant (1991) says in *Appalachia: The Voices of Sleeping Birds*, "Those who don't live in Appalachia and don't understand it sometimes make the mistake of calling these people 'hillbillies.' It isn't a good word for them. They probably would prefer 'Appalachians.' Like anyone else, they're sensitive to words" (p. 7).

Many of the authors and illustrators of Appalachian children's literature are from the region, but many are not. Kurtz made the following comment about those who are not from a particular multicultural background,

In writing and illustrating another culture—as it is in writing within your own culture—the writer and illustrator should immerse themselves completely in the subject and know as much as possible before they start their work. There is too much stuff out there that is inaccurate, that insults those who know better.

(Kurtz, 1996, p. 41)

About Appalachian children's literature, Jo Ann Asbury (1995) stated,

Those from outside the region need to learn the diversity, characteristics, and values from different regions in order to prepare them for a multicultural world. They need to be able to recognize stereotypes for what they are and to accept differences in people

(p. 3)

PREVALENT THEMES

In a *Book Links* article, Susan Golden (1991) states about Appalachia that "some of the hallmarks of the culture are close-knit families, strong religious feelings, distinctive music, and crafts reflecting a keen awareness of nature. Individualism, interdependence, love of land, and pride in heritage are other continuing threads" (p. 14). These hallmarks found in Susan Golden's article are similar to the values that were defined by the noted Appalachian scholar, Loyal Jones, first in an essay that was published and reprinted many times over. Jones (1994) had written this piece on a value system to "counter persistent negative stereotypes about Appalachian people by listing and commenting on positive values or characteristics" (p. 7). An editor encouraged Jones to publish the essay in book form as a photographic essay and include photographs of Appalachian people. The book *Appalachian Values* (1994) was ultimately published in 1994 through The Jesse Stuart Foundation in Ashland, Kentucky.

Jones was the Director of the Appalachian Center at Berea College and an Appalachian studies educator and scholar who lived the mountain life, studied the surroundings, and knew the people. Speaking as an Appalachian, Jones (1994) notes in the first chapter of the book:

Life in the wilderness and the continuing relative isolation of Southern mountaineers made a strong imprint on us. The Appalachian value system that influences attitudes and behavior is different in some ways from that held by our modern countrymen, although it is similar to the value system of an earlier America

(p. 37)

This list of values includes religion, independence, self-reliance and pride, neighborliness, familism (strong family center), personalism (relate well to other people), humility and modesty, love of place, patriotism, sense of beauty, and sense of humor.

The Appalachian values described by Jones can be easily tied to the prevalent themes in Appalachian children's literature. In a doctoral dissertation, Valerie D. Valentine (2008) used Jones' work and content analysis to study "fifty-two children's realistic fiction picture books for evidence of authentic and accurate representation of Appalachian life and values" (p. 49).

The dissertation by Jennifer S. Smith (2002) titled *Mining the Mountain of Appalachian Children's Literature: Defining a Multicultural Literature* also provided insight into the research for this chapter. Within the construct of her work, Smith defines Appalachian literature and through her research with scholars in the field, she defines fifteen characteristics of Appalachian children's literature. Her research is more broadly defined than the study by Valentine (2008) because of the breadth of the genre studies and the input of the Appalachian scholars that she interviewed. One will note that her characteristics, again like that by Valentine, are also tied closely to the Appalachian values that were defined in 1994 by Loyal Jones.

Smith (2002) defines the fifteen characteristics of Appalachian children's literature that are listed below with her own statements of further explanation:

Education: very important to obtain
Family: includes intergenerational stories and very extended families

Independence: reluctant to depend on others for assistance; independent thinkers

Migration: stories of moving out of the mountains; also include stories of movement into as well as within

Modesty: simple living

Neighborliness: willing to share what they have with others

Patriotism: strong allegiance to home and country

Personalism: philosophy in which ultimate value lies in persons, either human or divine

Sense of beauty: includes music, art, handmade crafts, and nature

Sense of humor: apparent in jokes, yarns, tall tales, and other stories told

Setting: must include the mountains; more rural than urban; often depicts authors' homeplace

Socio-economic conditions: poor in material things, rich in relationships

Spirituality/Religion: not necessarily linked to a specific denomination; often linked to practice of folkways

Strong sense of place: includes emotional ties to the places and people that comprise home

Use of language: includes colloquialisms, regionalisms, metaphors, storytelling techniques, strong use of voice.

(p. 170)

Gary Schmidt, a professor at Calvin College in Michigan, spoke to the mythic dimension of Appalachia in a workshop presented at the 1992 Virginia Hamilton Conference. He stated,

Writers have used the myth of Appalachia to speak to the child audience of the beauty of the world and of its hardships, of the need for self-reliance and the need for community, of tenacity and sheer guts, and of wonder at the simplest moments of the child's life. (Schmidt, 1992, p. 70)

He defined four elements of the Appalachian myth as (1) physical splendor of the Appalachian natural world, though also filled with natural perils; (2) the Appalachian people living their lives closely tied to the natural world; (3) for either the good or the bad, lives are lived with a sense of community of family, neighbors, and small towns; and (4) there is "joy in the simple" (p. 74) experiences of daily lives such as a well-cooked meal, pride in a productive garden and sitting on a porch at the end of the day (Schmidt, 1992). These myths also further define the themes prevalent in Appalachian children's literature and are connected to Appalachian values by Jones and the dissertations by Valentine and Smith.

SELECTED APPALACHIAN CHILDREN'S LITERATURE AND SUGGESTED RESPONSES

The study of children's literature may be approached in several ways. This part of the chapter highlights selected literature and suggests responses to that literature. It is organized by sections that include selected themes, the Caldecott Award, the Newbery Award and selected genres. The first section looks at selected themes that were inspired by the work of Jones, Valentine, and Smith discussed previously. Numerous additional themes could be included here, but for the purposes of this chapter, five were selected: love of place; family, grandparent, and intergenerational; spirituality and religion; individualism, self-reliance, and pride; and neighborliness and hospitality. Table 9.1 lists these themes and the book titles included in these themes.

Table 9.1

Appalachian Children's Literature Themes

Themes	Book Titles
Love of Place	*Appalachia: The Voices of Sleeping Birds*
	Until the Cows Come Home
	My Great-Aunt Arizona
	Night in the Country
	This Year's Garden
	Halfway to the Sky
	The Final Tide
	Grandpa's Mountain
	When the Whippoorwill Calls
Family and Intergenerational Stories	*Basket*
	Hunting the White Cow
	Ragsale
	The Day the Picture Man Came
	Angel Coming
	Mountain Wedding
	You Hold Me and I'll Hold You
	Molasses Man
	The Ticky-Tacky Doll
	When Uncle Took the Fiddle
	My Mama Had a Dancing Heart
	In Coal Country
	My Mama is a Miner
	Cousins
	Chasing Redbird
Spirituality and Religion	*Missing May*
	A Fine White Dust
	When We Were Saints
	I Wonder as I Wander
Individualism, Self-reliance and Pride	*Vergie Goes to School With the Boys*
	Cecil's Story
	Miss Maggie
	The Rag Coat
	More Than Anything Else
Neighborliness and Hospitality	*Miss Maggie*
	Come a Tide
	Miss Ida's Porch

Appalachian children's literature is prevalent in every genre. For the purposes of this chapter, poetry, and folklore were selected for discussion. It should also be noted that Herrin (2010) includes an extensive number of biographies in the *Appalachian Children's Literature* reference tool. In addition, several Appalachian children's books from various genres have received recognition from the Newbery and Caldecott committees. It is interesting to study these books from different decades and to discuss how children could compare and contrast them in reference to the historical periods they depict.

THEMES

Love of Place

Cynthia Rylant's *Appalachia: The Voices of Sleeping Birds* (1991) provides a narrative description of the very essence of Appalachia that is illustrated by award-winning artist Barry Moser. This book is from the heart as both Rylant and Moser have deep roots in Appalachia and feel strongly about the region. The narrative is based on Rylant's experiences growing up in West Virginia and the illustrations are based on Moser's experiences growing up in Tennessee. As inspiration for his illustrations, Moser used family pictures and photographs taken in the region by Ben Shahn, Walker Evans, Marion Post Wolcott, and Dorothea Lange.

Response: To introduce a unit on Appalachia, Rylant's book is an excellent place to provide a foundation for the study of the region. In response to Rylant's use of multisensory experiences to depict the sights and feelings of Appalachia, students could make a chart of the five senses and talk about how this approach makes the place feel more realistic. A special book including hand-colored photographs is Patricia Mills' *Until the Cows Come Home* (1993), which shares spare text accompanied by photographs of a West Virginia farm, the land, and the people. Mills (flyleaf) wanted to capture "the simple pleasures and the great beauty of unspoiled rural life."

Response: Students can look through the photographs in the book and write a new story to accompany them, or they can use this book as a model and write a story that corresponds with photographs of their own region.

For an understanding of the sense of place, there are few children's informational books that provide an overview of the Appalachian region. *The Appalachians* (Maynard, 2004); *Appalachian Mountains* (Mader, 2004); and *Mist Over the Mountains* (Bial, 1997) provide brief introductions to the Appalachian region and its people.

Response: Read about the background and value of Appalachian culture in these books to better understand and appreciate the land and the people. Identify the region on a U.S. map and discuss the 13 states that make up Appalachia. Locate the mountain regions within the Appalachian region. Write a journal response about what the people in this broad geographic area have in common and share in small groups.

My Great-Aunt Arizona (1992) is a book that fits with many of the Appalachian values and characteristics. For this chapter, the author chose to place it with "love of place." This picture book is based on the true story of Gloria Houston's aunt who taught generations of school children in the Blue Ridge Mountains where she was born. Though Arizona never went to the places that she taught her students about during her 57 years of teaching, it is obvious through the text and the illustrations that Arizona indeed loved the place where she lived.

Response: Students can write about the places that they love most through poetry or prose or they could create a postcard from their special place and write to someone in their family.

Love of place stories can be about the small things in life. Two of Cynthia Rylant's books, *Night in the Country* (1986) and *This Year's Garden* (1984), share stories of simple pleasures in life. *Night in the Country* begins with, "There is no night so dark, so black as a night in the country" (unpaged) and then continues to explore the nighttime happenings such as swooping night owls, frogs singing at night, and an apple falling from the tree.

Response: Using *Night in the Country* as a model, students can write and illustrate a book titled *Day in the Country*. *This Year's Garden* follows a family as they attend to their garden during the winter for planning, the spring for planting, the summer for growing and eating the vegetables, and the winter for harvesting.

Response: Students can interview someone who loves gardening, write a report on their findings, and present the information to the class.

Written in journal format, Kimberly Brubaker Bradley's *Halfway to the Sky* (2002) follows 12-year-old Dani who begins to hike the Appalachian Trail after the death of her brother and the divorce of her parents. Dani's mother joins her on the Trail and they spend a two-month journey connecting with nature, learning more about each other, and becoming closer as mother and daughter.

Response: Students may identify the footpath of the 2,175 miles Appalachian Trail on the National Park Service's Web site at http://www.nps.gov/appa/index.htm, accessed on October 03, 2010. The Trail was completed in 1937 and runs through fourteen states from Maine's Mount Katahdin to Georgia's Springer Mountain. Using this book as a model, students could write journal entries during a field trip and then share their entries.

An interesting small collection of books is included in this theme of "love of place" and are also about "the loss of that place." These are stories about people who had strong connections with their land and found great difficulty in letting it go. Norma Cole's *The Final Tide* (1999) is set on the Cumberland River in 1948 and looks at the displacement of families at the time of the building of the Tennessee Valley Authority dams through the eyes of 14-year-old Geneva Haw. Carolyn Reeder's *Grandpa's Mountain* (1991) shares the story of 11-year-old Carrie and her grandparents' fight to keep their property in Virginia when the Shenandoah National Park is created. Another story of the creation of the Shenandoah National Park is Candice F. Ransom's *When the Whippoorwill Calls* (1995), which describes through words and pictures the story of Polly's family as they leave their Blue Ridge Mountain cabin when the land is sold to the federal government.

Response: Ransom's story connects with the theme of forced expulsion from home and could be used to prompt research and discussion of world refugees and why people must sometimes leave their homes.

Family and Intergenerational Stories

Family is always centrally important in Appalachian culture. As a result, there is a varied collection of Appalachian children's literature for both younger and older children with too many to include here, so this writer has selected a representative collection.

Basket (Lyon, 1990), a book that appeals to younger audiences, is about a basket that served many purposes for a grandmother and has been passed down from generation to generation.

Response: To respond to this story, children can make a basket from construction paper and put slips of paper in it with descriptions of favorite things they would keep in the basket. Or small, inexpensive baskets could be purchased so that each child has one to keep.

Tres Seymour's *Hunting the White Cow* (1993) shares the story of a family in search of their elusive white cow that has become legendary among the family, the neighbors, and the relatives. The reader has a sense that everyone is working together to get the cow back home from her wanderings, but at the same time, no one is super energetic about the task at hand.

Response: After reading this story, students can write a paragraph that outlines their solution for catching the cow and bringing her home.

The sense of family is strong in *Ragsale* (Bates, 1995). Jesann, her mom, sister Eunice, Mawmaw, Aunt Mary Jane, and Cousin Billie Jo all leave together for a much anticipated day of "ragsaling."

Response: In response to this book that details a wonderful family day in Jessann's family, students can draw a picture that captures one of their favorite family days and write a short story to accompany the picture. Another family story told from the point of view of a young girl is Faye Gibbons' *The Day the Picture Man Came* (2003) that shares the adventures that ensue when Cecil Bramlett, a traveling photographer, drives his wagon into the yard of the Howard family. There is a rambunctious outcome when the family's animals are included in the photograph.

Response: Children can draw their own family portrait in sepia tones as depicted in this picture book. Sometimes old sepia tone photographs can be found inexpensively in thrift shops. It would be interesting for students to be able to look at these old photographs and compare them to some taken on a digital camera of today. They could then write a description of the clothing and setting of the family portrait.

Throughout history, strong family bonds have been prevalent with families living close by or generations of families living together in the same house. Family get-togethers are important and sharing the stories from one generation to the next often play an important role in the family's cultural heritage. In addition to the stories shared from one generation to the next, families also share recipes, crafts, and traditions. Family celebrations such as a birth of a baby, a wedding, or a family reunion are all parts of this regional literature.

Henson's *Angel Coming* (2005) tells the story from the hills of Kentucky of an angel who comes to ride up the mountain on horseback to bring a baby in her saddlebag. An author's note plus three black and white photographs provide information about the women of the Frontier Nursing Services in Eastern Kentucky, which was established by the legendary Mary Breckinridge in 1925. Susan Gaber's illustrations portray the beauty of the mountainous regions and provide a careful, gentle look at this special family event of the birth of a baby.

Response: This picture book provides the answer for mountain children about where babies come from—they come with the angel in her saddleback and she delivers them after she has ridden up the mountain on horseback. While some educators may not wish to explore the issue of where babies come from with their classrooms, this picture book provides a unique answer to the question that originated with the mountain people.

Response: In response to this book, children can discuss the arrival of little brothers and sisters and how a new birth changed their home life such as requiring them to help take care of the new baby. In *Angel Coming*, the anticipation of the "big sister" (unpaged) and her excitement is a genuinely touching part of the story. Even though she wishes for a sister, she nevertheless finishes her story with a final thought: "Li'l brother is what I'll call him, not the sister I had wished for. . . . Can't help love him just the same" (Henson, 2005, unpaged).

In the springtime of the north Georgia Mountains, a *Mountain Wedding* (Gibbons, 1996) is planned for a widow, Mrs. Searcy, to marry another widower, Mr. Long. There is only one problem—the five Searcy children and the seven Long children do not want the wedding to happen until a chaotic event erupts at the ceremony, which results in the need for both families to work together and become one. As the scene is settled, the couple is finally joined in marriage with all members of both families joined together in a circle as the vows are repeated. Ted Rand's watercolor illustrations provide a realistic backdrop for the story that reminds one of a lovely spring day in the country. The endpages depict each family's children on opposing sides of the gutter with tongues stuck out and making faces at one another.

Response: Children may select the one passage from the book that is the focal point and discuss or write about how that scene changes the outcome of the story.

A family travels to Tennessee for Great-aunt Anne's funeral in Jo Carson's *You Hold Me and I'll Hold You* (1992). A little girl works through dealing with the death of her family member, how she should feel and react, and how she should seek comfort in a situation she doesn't clearly understand. Just at the moment during the funeral that she needs him most, her father reaches out to her while she is held safely in his arms and says, "you hold me and I'll hold you" (unpaged). Annie Cannon's soft watercolor paintings provide a realistic portrait of this intergenerational family story.

Response: Few books broach the subject of a child attending a funeral, and yet, this one shares this experience very gently and with love. This is a book that can be read by an adult to a child on the occasion of the loss of a loved one. It may be one that a counselor could use for grief counseling with children and their parents.

Kathy L. May's *Molasses Man* (2000) is set in late summer when it is just the right time to make molasses. Everyone helps Grandpa when the sorghum cane is ripe and ready to be cut in this intergenerational story. The book follows the process of how the molasses is made and of course, Grandpa makes the best molasses.

Response: Several books such as Ann Purmell's *Maple Syrup Season* (Holiday House, 2008); Jessie Haas' *Sugaring* (1996); and Marsha Wilson Chall's *Sugarbush Spring* (2000) describe the process of making maple syrup. Students can compare these titles with *Molasses Man* and discuss the process of how we obtain these substances as natural sweeteners and how they are used. It would also be interesting for children to taste molasses and to compare it with the taste of maple syrup. Students could then compare and contrast these sweeteners in a Venn diagram.

In Cynthia Rylant's *The Ticky-Tacky Doll* (2002), a little girl is forlorn and unhappy on her first day of school. Her Grandmama figures out that it is all because she had to leave her ticky-tacky homemade doll at home. To solve the problem, Grandmama sews her grandchild a little miniature of her special doll to fit in the corner of her book bag.

Response: Students can make handmade dolls using the reference book, *The Foxfire Book of Toys & Games*, which has an entire chapter devoted to handmade Appalachian dolls and playhouses (1993, pp. 85–122).

Two books by Libba Moore Gray, *When Uncle Took the Fiddle* (1999) and *My Mama Had a Dancing Heart* (1996) are also family-centered stories. *When Uncle Took the Fiddle* describes an early evening when all the family members are tired and then Uncle takes up the fiddle and the family comes to life and begins to play their own instruments. It is not long until the neighbors come to join in with the music playing and with the dancing.

Response: Students would certainly be entertained to listen to recordings of fiddle music from the Appalachian Mountains such as the Appalachian Fiddle Breakdown (Rural Rhythm, 2009) or have an invited fiddle player into the classroom.

My Mama Had a Dancing Heart (1996) tells the story of the closeness of a mother and daughter and shares the experiences of their dancing together barefoot in the spring rain, running together in the summer surf, kicking leaves in the autumn, and making snow angels in the winter.

Response: With the description of the seasons, this book could serve as a model for children to share their seasonal experiences with a parent or caregiver through poetry, writing, or painting a picture.

Coal mining is the focus for two family stories that also focus on parents. Judith Hendershot's *In Coal Country* (1987) is set in Neffs, Ohio, where a little girl tells the story of her family's life in the 1930s coal-mining town and the work of her father in the mines. The story takes place during the seasons of the year and provides a memorable look at family. The endpapers of the book look like coal dust has settled upon them. Another coalmining children's book is *Mama is a Miner* (1994) by George Ella Lyon. This picture book story is also told through the voice of a young girl, but the difference here is that the mother is the coal miner. Catalanotto's illustrations follow the mother as she makes the two-mile trip down into the earth to her job.

Response: Because these two stories are set in different time periods and one miner is a father and the other is a mother, these would be interesting books to compare similarities and differences by using a Venn diagram or a comparison chart. Students can learn about the history of coal mining by reading Susan Campbell Bartoletti's *Growing Up in Coal Country* (1996). Another response activity could be to study the historical and present day uses of coal and chart these uses.

An additional theme within the Appalachian family theme is stories of Christmas. Several noted titles include Rebecca Caudill's *A Certain Small Shepherd* (1965); Gloria Houston's *The Year of the Perfect Christmas Tree* (1988); Cynthia Rylant's *Silver Packages: An Appalachian Christmas Story* (1997); and Rylant's *Christmas in the Country* (2002). Christmas is also the theme for a collection of short stories by Cynthia Rylant titled *Children of Christmas: Stories for the Season* (1987). Appalachian children's novels that focus on Christmas include C. L. Davis' *The Christmas Barn* (2001) and Earl Hamner's *The Homecoming: A Novel about Spencer's Mountain* (1970).

Response: Students can locate a copy of *A Foxfire Christmas: Appalachian Memories and Traditions* (Wiggington, 1990) that focuses on "the food, the people, the decorations, and the customs" (flyleaf) of Appalachia. *A Foxfire Christmas* can be used to locate recipes such as gingerbread or molasses cookies, find instructions on rag dolls, or select stories to share from Christmas in the 1930s. Students might create Christmas decorations or bake cookies inspired by the examples in this book. Another suggestion is to read aloud selections from Cynthia Rylant's *Children of Christmas*. One of the stories from this collection, *Silver Packages*, was extracted and made into a stand-alone picture book. There is an extensive collection of activities connected to *Silver Packages* at http:// www.homeschoolshare.com/silver_packages.php, accessed on October 03, 2010.

For older students, Virginia Hamilton's *Cousins* (1990) follows the complicated relationship of two female cousins and their families. The families of the two girls are devastated when one of them accidentally drowns.

Response: Students can have a discussion about the book and talk about the advice that they would give to Cammie. They could write a diary entry based on what they think Cammie might write in her diary. Another title for an older audience is Sharon Creech's *Chasing Redbird* (1997), which tells the story of 13-year-old Zinny who discovers an overgrown trail behind her house that runs for 20 miles between Bybanks and Chocton. Zinny uses the summer to begin to clear the trail and along the way she discovers more about herself and her family.

Response: The Multnomah County Public Library's Talk it Up! page at http://www .multcolib.org/talk/guides.html, accessed on October 03, 2010 has a book discussion guide that includes ten discussion questions directly tied to *Chasing Redbird* and also suggests an activity and a snack of spaghetti and meatballs.

Other family-centered Appalachian children's novels include Bill and Vera Cleaver's *Where the Lilies Bloom* (1969); Katherine Paterson's *Come Sing, Jimmy Jo* (1985); Cynthia Rylant's *A Blue-Eyed Daisy* (1985); Lois Lowry's *Rabble Starkey* (1987); Sid Hite's *It's Nothing to a Mountain* (1994); and Barbara O'Connor's *Me and Rupert Goody* (1999).

Spirtuality and Religion

Religious themes and the search for faith have been prevalent themes in Appalachian children's literature. One book that features a quest to make a spiritual connection is Cynthia Rylant's 1993 Newbery Award book, *Missing May* that shares the story of 12-year-old Summer. This title is discussed below with the other Appalachian books that have received Newbery awards. Another Rylant title, *A Fine White Dust* (1986) is the story of 13-year-old Peter Cassidy who searches for truth and the meaning of faith. At this vulnerable time, Peter decides to follow an evangelist who has come to his small North Carolina town for a revival only to find that the Reverend James Carson was not as he appeared. *When We Were Saints* (2003) is a novel by Han Nolan that focuses on the story of 14-year-old Archie Caswell as he begins a spiritual quest after the death of his grandfather.

Response: These three books lend themselves to discussion. Teachers and librarians can connect to the Multnomah County Public Library's *Talk It Up!* book discussion page at http://www.multcolib.org/talk/start.html, accessed on October 03, 2010. The page includes suggestions on how to get started with a book club, a set of universal book discussion questions that could be used with the books mentioned previously, and a list of book discussion guidelines.

Gwenyth Swaim's picture book, *I Wonder as I Wander* (2003) is a fictionalized account of a young girl who wanders with her itinerant preacher father while he speaks God's message to anyone who will listen. The author notes that "I Wonder as I Wander" was written as a Christmas song and sung in 1933 by Annie Morgan in Murphy, North Carolina. The words were then captured by John Jacob Niles who collected Appalachian songs during the Depression. The song serves as a testament of Annie's religious questions.

Response: Children may be interested in researching the background of their own favorite Christmas song or any other song that they enjoy.

Individualism, Self-Reliance and Pride

Elizabeth Fitzgerald Howard's *Virgie Goes to School With the Boys* (2000) is a fine example of pride, self-reliance, and determination. Based on a family story, Howard depicts a fully realized Virgie who convinces her family that she can indeed walk the seven miles with her five brothers to attend the Quaker school each week for recently freed blacks in Jonesborough, Tennessee. Illustrations by E. B. Lewis perfectly capture both the rural landscape and the antics of a very determined Virgie.

Response: Since Virgie is away from her family all week, students could think about what Virgie might experience while she is away from home and in the school. Children can write a letter from Virgie back to her mother that describes the events that might have happened during a school week.

In *Cecil's Story* (1991) by George Ella Lyon, Cecil's father is away fighting in the Civil War, and then his mother must leave and go in search of her husband, leaving Cecil with neighbors. He shows self-reliance, bravery, and dependability while she is away. In this narrated third person text Cecil says "You'd know you could do it—chop wood, feed pigs and chickens" (1991, unpaged). He knows that he'd help take care of her when she comes back and even faces the fact that his father comes back with one arm missing.

Response: Children can write a story about what might happen next, after Cecil's father and mother have come home. They could also include a detailed description of how Cecil might help out on the family's farm.

Cynthia Rylant's *Miss Maggie* (1983) describes young Nat Crawford's observations of an older neighbor who lives in a "rotting log house on the edge of Crawford's pasture" (1983, unpaged). Miss Maggie lives independently, grows a few vegetables and supposedly has a snake in her house that Nat spends lots of time trying to see. During the winter, Miss Maggie's independence is threatened when she becomes ill, but Nat comes to her rescue.

Response: Students could discuss what it means to be independent and self-reliant.

The Rag Coat (1991) by Lauren Mills shares the story of a young girl named Minna who wants to go to school but cannot because she does not have a winter coat. The Quilting Mothers, a group of women who make quilts to sell, offer to make her a quilt from their various scraps of fabric that each tell a story. On the first day that Minna proudly wears her new coat to school, a little girl calls it a "pile of rags" until Minna begins to explain the stories behind each of the pieces of fabric.

Response: Using a simple outline of a coat pattern, students can create their own rag coat using scraps of paper that they color to match fabric patterns that are meaningful to them. Then they can write a story about of some of the paper scraps that make up their coat.

Marie Bradby's *More Than Anything Else* (1995) tells a fictionalized story of how young Booker T. Washington wanted to learn to read "more than anything else" (unpaged) and how he struggled to learn how to read until he was able to find a newspaper man to help him make sense of the letters on the page. It is a proud moment when Booker sees the letters that make up his own name written in the dirt.

Response: Children can share stories of how they learned to read and who helped them. They might also talk or write about the things in their lives they have wanted "more than anything else."

Neighborliness and Hospitality

Mentioned above in individualism, self-reliance and pride is Cynthia Rylant's *Miss Maggie* (1983) which relates how a young neighbor named Nat Crawford observes Miss Maggie from a distance as she goes about her life. The turning point in the story comes when Miss Maggie falls ill and needs Nat's help. Nat then begins to watch over Miss Maggie and the story indicates that from that point on "Nat saw a lot of Miss Maggie that winter, and for many winters after" (1983, unpaged).

Response: After reading *Miss Maggie*, students can create a character map of Nat Crawford using information from the book to support the characteristics they have chosen, such as kindness and neighborliness.

Come a Tide (Lyon, 1990) suddenly brings together neighbors after it has rained for four days, and the region is in for a mountain flood. "'It'll come a tide,' my grandma said" (unpaged) and then it does. So, the little girl and her family members leave their home when the warning whistle blows, but as they make their way to shelter, they check on neighbors along the way to make sure they know. Though some neighbors who have been through this drill before aren't in such a hurry, Mrs. Mac says, 'Joe won't go till he finds his teeth so I've put a pot of coffee on'" (unpaged).

Response: *Come a Tide* was featured by LeVar Burton in Reading Rainbow program 86. A teacher's guide to the book and to weather-related response ideas can be found at http://www.shopgpn.com/guides/rr/86.pdf, accessed on October 03, 2010.

In Sandra Belton's *From Miss Ida's Porch* (1993), neighbors gather on the front porch of a neighbor on Church Street in Beckley, West Virginia. Miss Ida's porch is "a telling place" (1993, p. 10) where both the young and old gather. On this night the neighbors all hear stories of Duke Ellington and Marian Anderson.

Response: Students can simulate a front porch and relate stories of some of their favorite figures from history or ask senior citizens from the community to share their own favorite stories on their imaginary front porch. They could use some of the storytelling techniques found in chapter 12 of this book.

CALDECOTT AND NEWBERY AWARDS

Appalachia and the Caldecott Award

"The Caldecott Medal was named in honor of nineteenth-century English illustrator Randolph Caldecott. It is awarded annually by the Association for Library Service to Children, a division of the American Library Association, to the artist of the most

Table 9.2

Appalachian Children's Literature Caldecott Medal Winners and Honor Books

Caldecott Award Year	Book Title
1954 Honor Book	*Journey Cake, Ho!*
1956 Medal Winner	*Frog Went A Courtin'*
1965 Honor Book	*A Pocket Full of Cricket*
1983 Honor Book	*When I was Young in the Mountains*
1986 Honor Book	*The Relatives Came*

distinguished American picture book for children" (http://www.ala.org/ala/mgrps/divs/alsc/awardsgrants/bookmedia/caldecottmedal/caldecottmedal.cfm, accessed on October 03, 2010.) Several books with an Appalachian setting or connection have been named as Caldecott Honor Books and one as a medal winner. It seems fitting that these Appalachian children's picture books have received this artistic distinction with the Appalachian people's sense of beauty and love of place. These books can each be studied on their own merit or they could be taken together as a unit and studied for themes, artistic merit, and cultural connections to Appalachia. Table 9.2 lists Appalachian children's literature Caldecott medal winners and Honor Books.

Ruth Sawyer's *Journey Cake, Ho!* (1953) illustrated by Robert McClosky describes the story of a boy named Johnny who leaves Tip Top Mountain. The older couple Johnny lives with send him on his way since all the farm animals have left and they can't support him. With a journey cake tucked inside his sack for nourishment, he sets off only to see his cake run away, but as he chases the cake, animals join the chase too until they all are back at the farm. Merry, the old woman captures up the journey cake, renames it Johnny Cake, and warms it on the griddle for Johnny's dinner. McClosky's two-toned blue, brown, and white illustrations are reflective of the 1950s picture books. *Journey Cake* takes place in a mountainous setting and though not attributed specifically to Appalachia, this book is listed on most Appalachian children's book lists and journey cake is a food related to the region.

Response: Students can compare *Journey Cake, Ho!* with other variants of stories about runaway foods. Particularly, they can study the art mediums and techniques used in book selections from the list below. Students may also find it interesting to graph the traditional events of the story and compare them. Events for a graph or chart might include

1. How does the story begin?
2. How does the runaway food get away?
3. Who are members of the chase?
4. How is the food recovered? And
5. How does the story end?

Other books that include a runaway food story include:

Aylesworth, J. (1998). *The Gingerbread Boy*. NY: Scholastic.
Brett, J. (1999). *The Gingerbread Baby*. NY: Putnam.

Brown, M. (1972). *The Bun: A Tale from Russia*. NY: Harcourt.

Eglielski, R. (1997). *The Gingerbread Boy*. NY: HarperCollins.

Galdone, P. (1979). *The Gingerbread Boy*. NY: Clarion.

Jacobs, J. (1986). Johnny cake. In T. dPaola, *Tomie dePaola's Favorite nursery tales* (pp. 11–15). NY: Putnam.

Kimmel, E. (2000). *The Runaway Tortilla*. Delray Beach, FL: Winslow Press.

Kimmelman, L. (2000). *The Runaway Latkes*, illustrated by P. Yalowitz. NY: Albert Whitman.

Lobel, A. (1978). *The Pancake*. NY: Morrow.

Rebecca Caudill's *A Pocketful of Cricket* (1964) illustrated by Evaline Ness, recounts the story of a six-year old boy named Jay who finds a number of interesting things for his pocket while he is driving the cows home at the end of the day. The most special thing he finds is Cricket who he takes home in his pocket and puts under the mesh of a tea strainer. Five days later, Jay begins first grade and decides to put Cricket in his pocket. When the teacher hears the "Chee! Chee!"(1964, unpaged) instead of making him put Cricket outside, the teacher turns this into a learning experience by having Jay share information as show and tell. The woodcuts, line drawings, and ink splatter illustrations by Evaline Ness are rendered in reds, blacks, and golds.

Response: Jay eats a snack of bread and butter as he sets out to the pasture to drive the cows home. Students can visit the Cornell University Cooperative Extension Web site for directions on how to make "glass jar butter" at http://senecacountycce.org/pdfs/p-c_headstart_butter.pdf, accessed on October 03, 2010.

Children may also be interested in seeing other picture books that are created from woodcuts. For a list of picture books featuring woodcuts connect to Nancy Keane's list at http://nancykeane.com/rl/152.htm, accessed on October 03, 2010. Children can create their own simulated woodblock print. The materials needed include a scratching utensil (example: blunt pencil, nail); Styrofoam tray bottom; printer's ink or paint; brayer; wooden dowel or wooden spoon; and paper. They can then follow these directions. Carefully using the pen-like object, create a drawing or design in the styrofoam tray, then cover it with ink or paint. Cover the impression with ink or paint. Place the paper on top. Rub the paper with a wooden dowel or the handle of wooden spoon to make sure ink is transferred evenly and firmly. Remove the paper and the result is your print that is a negative image of the design.

When I Was Young in the Mountains (1982) by Cynthia Rylant and illustrated by Diane Goode, was named a 1983 Caldecott Honor Book. The book opens with "When I was young in the mountains, Grandfather came home in the evening covered with the black dust of the coal mine. Only his lips were clean, and he used them to kiss the top of my head" (1982, unpaged). This eloquently written and beautifully told autobiographical account of Rylant growing up in the Appalachian Mountains is some of her finest writing. The smallest things are the important things such as Grandmother making corn bread, pinto beans, and fried okra for dinner; taking baths in the tin tubs filled with well water that were placed in front of the old black stove; going to the swimming hole; and relaxing on porch swings in the evening with the family. Goode's illustrations provide a nostalgic view of the time with soft pastel illustrations and a gentle look at what is important. Cynthia Rylant's *The Relatives Came* (1985) describes the joyous journey of a carload of family on their way to West Virginia to join their mountain family. After a number of hours of car time, their reunion is described, "Then it was hugging time. Talk about hugging! Those relatives just passed us all around their car, pulling us against their wrinkled Virginia clothes, crying sometimes. They hugged us for hours" (Rylant, 1985, unpaged). Gammell's color pencil illustrations that depict the family members splashed across the pages and all their happy activities together were the reason the book won a 1986 Caldecott Honor.

Response: After reading the story aloud, children can retell the story in their own words by answering the following questions: beginning, what happens first in the story?; middle, what happens in-between?; and end, what happens last in the story? Locate the "Retelling Rubric" at http://www.lessonplanspage.com/LARetellingThe RelativesCame13.htm, accessed on October 03, 2010.

A fun response activity to *The Relatives Came* is to share colored pencils with the class and allow children to create their own family members at a family reunion. Another family reunion title set in Appalachia is Faye Gibbons' *Emma Jo's Song* (2001), which describes the events of the big Puckett family reunion. Although not set in Appalachia, Tricia Tusa's *Family Reunion* (1996) is a fun, read-aloud about a family gathering like no other.

John Langstaff's *Frog Went A'Courtin'* (1955), illustrated by Feodor Rojankovsky, won the 1956 Caldecott Medal and is a picture book adaptation of a 400-year-old ballad "The Frog and the Mouse" from Scotland that has been both told and sung to children through the ages. A front piece note from the author titled "The Story of the Story" (unpaged) states that this version of the tune is sung by the children of the southern Appalachian Mountains. *Response*: The obvious response to *Frog Went A'Courtin* is to sing the song. The music is included on the last page of the book; a note on the flyleaf of the book states that this music is one of the earliest tunes associated with the ballad. Another response to this book is to employ creative dramatics and act out the story using character masks or paper bag puppets. Characters that would be needed include frog, horse, mouse, man rat, woman rat, white moth, big black bug, raccoon, snake, bumble bee, flea, gray goose, two ants, fly, chick, and tom cat. Although the lyrics listed on the page are different than what is provided by Langstaff, a recording of only the music can be found at the National Institute of Environmental Health http://kids.niehs.nih.gov/lyrics/ frog.htm, accessed on October 03, 2010 and children can sing along using the book. Another idea is to compare and contrast Langstaff's version with Gillian Tyler's *Froggy Went a-Courtin'* (2005).

Appalachia and the Newbery Award

"The Newbery Medal is awarded annually by the American Library Association for the most distinguished American children's book published the previous year" (http:// www.ala.org/ala/mgrps/divs/alsc/awardsgrants/bookmedia/newberymedal/aboutnewb-ery/aboutnewbery.cfm, accessed on October 03, 2010). Several Appalachian children's literature books have been awarded the Newbery Award and a few have been named as Honor Books. Table 9.3 lists the award-winning books discussed here. Cynthia Rylant's 1993 Newbery Award book, *Missing May*, is the heartfelt story of twelve-year-old May who has lived with and been loved by her aunt and uncle since she was just six years old. This family of three has made their home in a trailer in Deep Water, West Virginia. Now, May has passed away and Summer and her beloved, but grieving Uncle Ob must try to figure out how to get along without her there holding them together. Summer is

Table 9.3

Appalachian Children's Literature Newbery Award Winners and Honor Books

Newbery Award Year	Book Title
1950 Honor Book	*Tree of Freedom*
1970 Medal Winner	*Sounder*
1971 Medal Winner	*Summer of the Swans*
1975 Medal Winner	*M. C. Higgins the Great*
1992 Medal Winner	*Shiloh*
1993 Medal Winner	*Missing May*
1997 Honor Book	*Belle Prater's Boy*

now compelled to go on a journey with Uncle Ob and friend Cletus Underwood in search of the Reverend Miriam Young who is known to communicate with the dead. This is a story in which it is actually the journey that provides the answer.

Response: *Missing May* makes an excellent novel read aloud for a class. As the book is read aloud, make a list of words that students might not know and discuss their meanings. After each chapter is read aloud, students can write their thoughts and impressions in a literature response journal.

An Appalachian novel that children might be interested in reading after *Missing May*, is Ruth White's *Belle Prater's Boy* (1996), which was named a 1997 Newbery Honor book. Twelve-year-old Gypsy of Coal Station, Virginia wonders what has happened to her Aunt Belle since she disappeared early one October morning in 1953. After his mom has been missing, then Gypsy's cousin, Woodrow comes to live with their grandparents. Gypsy and Woodrow then become friends and come to understandings about themselves and their family. *The Search for Belle Prater* (White, 2005), a sequel to *Belle Prater's Boy*, follows Gypsy and Woodrow as they continue their search for Belle.

Response: The class can discuss the thematic connections of this story to friendship, family and relationships, and abandonment. *The Search for Belle Prater* and *Belle Prater's Boy* use Appalachian dialect. Children can identify these words in one or both of these books, make a list from the text, and discuss their meanings such as *figger* on p. 141. They could also discuss how the inclusion of Appalachian dialect provides a sense of place in these books.

Phyllis Reynolds Naylor's 1992 John Newbery Award book is titled *Shiloh* (1991), the first book in a trilogy that also includes *Shiloh Season* (1996) and *Saving Shiloh* (1997). *Shiloh* is set in Friendly, West Virginia. Eleven-year-old Marty Preston finds a beagle that has been mistreated and struggles with returning him to his owner. Ultimately, Marty decides he will do anything to save the dog he has named Shiloh.

Response: To respond after reading Shiloh, young people may choose sides for a discussion of what is right and wrong in relation to Marty's moral dilemma and what would be right by law. They can also use the discussion web strategy described and illustrated at http://www.educationworld.com/a_lesson/lesson/lesson032.shtml, accessed on October 03, 2010.

Virginia Hamilton was the first African American writer to win the Newbery Medal. The 1975 Newbery Medal was awarded to *M. C. Higgins the Great* (1974). The place for this story is Sarah's Mountain which is set in the strip-mining Appalachian hills of West Virginia and has been home to the Higgins family for three generations. Thirteen-year-old M.C. uses a 40-foot pole in the front yard of his home as an escape and a refuge to consider the problems in his life. This richly detailed story is also about M.C.'s quest to make his mother a country-western singing star when someone comes into the hills to record the ballads of the people. It is also about his relationship with Lurhetta Outlaw who helps him change his life.

Response: Students can imagine that they have a 40-foot pole in their yard that is a place of refuge for them to think about the problems in their life. They can discuss or write in response to questions such as why and how would such a place help them work out their own situation? What other places might they use as a place to think?

Other Appalachian children's novels that have won Newbery recognition include William H. Armstrong's *Sounder* (1969), which was awarded the 1970 Newbery Medal; Betsy Byars' *Summer of the Swans* (1970), which received the 1971 Newbery Medal, and Rebecca Caudill's *Tree of Freedom* (1949), which was named a 1950 Newbery Honor Book.

GENRES REPRESENTED IN APPALACHIAN CHILDREN'S BOOKS

Poetry

As Roberta Herrin notes in *Appalachian Children's Literature* (2010), poetry is perhaps the leanest of the regional literature genres, other than fantasy. However, there are some books of note. Three poems, spread across the pages of a 32-page picture book format, are featured in Nikki Giovanni's *Knoxville, Tennessee* (1994), which is a sunny tribute of a poem of almost 70 words that lend justice to summertime in a southern locale. Based on a family story and set in Tennessee, Jeff Daniel Marion's *Hello, Crow* (1992) relates the story in poetic form of a young boy who heard a crow call back to him and much later in his life as a grandfather he wonders if it really happened. A third title in this poetry format is George Ella Lyon's *Counting on the Woods* (1998) which is comprised of a poem that begins with "One path, a stick for a path. Two birds, day-break's words" (1998, unpaged). The poem is set with a lovely collection of captioned nature photos taken by Ann W. Olson in eastern Kentucky.

Known as a versatile writer in most literature genres, Cynthia Rylant has contributed two titles to the Appalachian poetry genre. *Waiting to Waltz: A Childhood* (1984) includes 30 free verse autobiographical poems of growing up in Beaver, West Virginia. *Soda Jerk* (1990) is a collection of narrative poems describing the events of life in a small Virginia town.

Response: Students could compare what they learn about Appalachian rural life in *When I Was Young in the Mountains* (Rylant, 1982) to what they learn about this way of life in these two books of poetry.

An authentic poetry collection of 49 poems written by Jo Carson is titled *Stories I Ain't Told Nobody Yet: Selections From the People Pieces* (1989). The collection is arranged in five categories: neighbors and kin, observations, relationships, work, and we say ourselves. Appropriate for grades seven and up, this collection of part poetry and part prose is suitable for dramatic readings and as a model for an oral history project.

Response: The most interesting response to poetry after reading poetry or hearing poetry read aloud is to write some of your own. Children can use Rylant's *Waiting to Waltz: A Childhood* (1984) as a model to write poetry of their own home town and experiences growing up.

Children are usually mesmerized when they hear their own recorded voices. They can also make their own recording of poetry read aloud from the selections listed above, or ask an older child to read *Hello, Crow* (Marion, 1992) *Knoxville, Tennessee* (Giovanni, 1994) aloud for recording and then share the recording along with a book with a younger child.

Response: Poetry sometimes evokes artistic response. Using *Knoxville, TN*, as a model, students can write and illustrate a class book with a collection of poems they have written about their home town. The book can then be placed in the classroom library or school library for others to enjoy. Using *Counting on the Woods* (1998) as a model, children can write a counting book comprised of a poem and photographs they have taken of nature in their part of the country.

Selections from Angela Johnson's *The Other Side: Shorter Poems* (Scholastic, 1998) can be read aloud for an upper elementary or middle school audience to enjoy.

Response: Students can respond to this poetry by creating their own scrapbook of photographs or illustrations, interspersed with poems they have written about their own hometown life as Angela Johnson did with these poems set in Shorter, Alabama.

Blue Bowl Down: *An Appalachian Rhyme* (Millen, 2004) shares a family's recipe and the process for making homemade bread. Beginning with "Lift the bowl to make our bread, down the blue bowl, little baby" (unpaged) and then getting the water and the flour. The important parts are to pat it down gently in the blue bowl, rest the dough, let it grow, sleep, and the next morning it is put in the oven. Of course, the eating part is fun, too. An author's note explains Millen's connection to the Appalachian highlands and her own family's tradition of making sourdough in the evening and then baking the bread the next morning.

Response: Of course, the response to this rhyme is to make sourdough bread possibly in a toaster oven to share with children and if that is not possible, then serve some that has been commercially prepared with jam and butter.

Granny Will Your Dog Bite and Other Mountain Rhymes (1999), collected by folk musician Gerald Milnes, is a collection of more than 40 mountain rhymes. The original release of this collection was accompanied by an audiocassette that may be still available in some libraries and collections.

Response: If the cassette is available, students will enjoy listening to Milnes perform the selections. Whether or not the cassette can be located, students will enjoy performing and recording selections from this book and listening to the efforts of their own work. A lesson plan for this book can be found at http://www.ferrum.edu/applit/Lessons/GrannyLP.htm, accessed on October 03, 2010.

"Appalachia: Music from Home" (Condon Music Group, 2009) is a collection of 20 tracks of contemporary mountain music by various artists. This collection was the background for the PBS Special titled "Appalachia: History of Mountains and People" and provides selections of old and new. Instruments included are banjos, fiddle, guitars, mandolins, and the upright bass.

Response: Students may enjoy listening to the music as background as they participate in writing projects or they may enjoy trying to play one of the instruments mentioned above or listening to someone invited to the class to demonstrate one of the instruments of traditional Appalachian music mentioned above.

Folklore: Traditional and Tall Tales

Before even opening the book, the reader can sense the power of Julius Lester's retelling of the tall tale, *John Henry* (1994). Jerry Pinkney's illustration on the book cover captures an African American man with strong, powerful arms and legs in a moment of rest, wearing a railroad cap, a bright red bandana, and carrying two pick-axes. Set in the Allegheny Mountains of West Virginia, Lester uses Summers County as the place to weave this legendary tale. The text is set against a selection of Jerry Pinkney's finest watercolors which depict the strong emotions of the story and celebrate the natural world. *John Henry* was also a 1995 Caldecott Honor book.

Response: Children can respond to the story by finding the geographic location of Summers County, West Virginia, on a U.S. map. They should be introduced to literary terms and then shown examples in *John Henry* (1994) that exemplify them, such as exaggeration, hyperbole, metaphor, and simile. After becoming familiar with these literary terms, they could look for examples in this book as well as in other tall tales. Another classic version of this tall tale was written and illustrated by Ezra Jack Keats (1965) and titled *John Henry: An American Legend*. Students could compare and contrast these two versions of the John Henry tall tale and then write their own version of the story.

While John Henry and Johnny Appleseed are traditional tales, *Swamp Angel* (1994) is an original tall tale written by Anne Issacs in response to the lack of tall tales featuring female characters. Issacs weaves the tale of Angelica Longrider, a Tennessee woodswoman, who was already two years old before she built her first log cabin. Her grandest feat is when she fights the huge bear named Thundering Tarnation all night long in her sleep. Lush, primitive oil paintings on boards of different woods provide the perfect period style of art for the story.

Another original tall tale is *Bewildered for Three Days: As to Why Daniel Boone Never Wore His Coonskin Cap* (Glass, 2000). Set in 1818, this adventurous story recounts how the young frontier folk hero, Daniel Boone, loses his coonskin cap to a bear one afternoon. The book contains a detailed author's note and a map of Cumberland Gap, Kentucky, and provides details about the life and times of Boone.

Response: All tall tales have certain elements in common. A key element is a main character who battles and overpowers an exaggerated force of nature much larger than a single person is normally able to overcome. Traditional tall tales were created in response to the hardships endured by the early American settlers who were faced with back-breaking work, such as digging up the earth and chopping down large trees.

Children can compare the forces of nature from one tall tale to another and discuss how tall tales could have brought some comfort and courage to early pioneers.

Two Appalachian Cinderella stories are *Ashpet: An Appalachian Tale* (Compton, 1994) and *Smoky Mountain Rose: An Appalachian Cinderella* (Schroeder, 1997). Ashpet, a servant girl, lives in a cabin by Eagle's Nest Mountain and works hard every day for Widow Hooper and her hard-to-please daughters. Because she is too busy, Ashpet is not allowed to attend the church picnic, but old Granny shows up just in time and with a special magic, Ashpet wins the heart of the doctor's son. The story of *Smoky Mountain Rose* is told in Appalachian dialect and set in Tarbelly Creek. Rose works hard on the farm for her step ma and two stepsisters. Then a "real rich feller by the name o' Seb" (unpaged) has a "fancy ol' party" so he can find a wife. In this Cinderella variant, the fairy godmother is a pig.

Response: Read aloud Paul Fleischman's *Glass Slipper, Gold Sandal: A World Wide Cinderella* (2007), which draws on Cinderella variants from around the world (including Appalachia) to create this new version of the story. Indeed, there are many Cinderella variants, a *Book Links* article that contains many of these classics can be found at http://www.ala.org/ala/aboutala/offices/publishing/booklinks/resources/multicultural.cfm, accessed on October 03, 2010. Students can compare and contrast the Appalachian versions of the Cinderella tale with each other and with other variants from other cultures. They can also look for examples in the two Appalachian versions of Appalachian culture such as dialect, mountainous setting, and homemade crafts.

One of the stories that can be found in Richard Chase's *Grandfather Tales* (1948) is "Sody Sallyratus." Joanne Compton's (1995) version of the story, *Sody Sallyratus*, opens when Ma runs out of sody sallyratus (baking soda). She sends her son, Tom, and then her son, Will, to the store, but when they don't come back, she goes herself. When no one comes back, son Jack waits and waits, but then decides to go himself to the store and finds out that a bear has been the problem. The next two versions are similar to each other. Teri Sloat's *Sody Sallyratus* (1997) follows family members as they each go to the store for the baking soda for biscuits, but each is eaten by a bear. The family's pet squirrel solves the problem. This version of the story includes information on baking soda and a biscuit recipe. Spelled slightly differently and told very differently is Aubrey Davis' *Sody Salleratus* (1996). The bear in this story eats the boy, girl, old man, and old woman who have each ventured to get the sody salleratus. Then the squirrel who lives with the family outsmarts the bear and he "busted wide open" (unpaged) and out steps the boy, girl, old man, and old woman.

Response: The perfect response to *Sody Sallyratus* is to make a batch of biscuits with baking soda and watch them rise. If a toaster oven is available, the students can watch them bake and then enjoy the product.

A collection of stories known as "Jack Tales" were collected by a folklorist and storyteller named Richard Chase. Published in 1943, *The Jack Tales* have been retold, shared, and published in various versions since then. They have the common element of a lead hero character named Jack who overcomes odds and outwits or tricks someone larger and more powerful, which is often a giant as in James Still's *Jack and the Wonder Beans* (1977) or Kenn and Joanne Compton's *Jack, The Giant Chaser* (1993) or Gail Haley's *Jack and the Bean Tree* (1986). Another version has Jack fending off the Fire Dragaman

in Gail Haley's *Jack and the Fire Dragon* (1988). Two other versions depict Jack as he encounters a variety of animals as he pursues his fortune including *Fearless Jack* (Johnson, 2001) and *Jack and the Animals: An Appalachian Folktale* (Davis, 1995). Ray Hicks shared three of these Appalachian stories in *The Jack Tales* (2000) including "Jack and the Northwest Wind," "Jack and the Bean Tree," and "Jack and the Robbers." This handsome, oversized book is accompanied by a compact disc with Hicks reading each of the tales in Appalachian dialect, accompanied by traditional music selections.
Response: Students can collect the Jack tales available in the school and public library and use a chart to compare the elements within each of these stories: Jack, the hero character; Jack's quest for his fortune; Jack's nemesis in each story; how Jack outwits or tricks the nemesis; and what is the outcome of the story. They can also listen to the Appalachian dialect of Ray Hicks as he reads selections from *The Jack Tales* (2000) and afterwards discuss how listening to Hicks' authentic pronunciation of the Appalachian dialect helps them get a sense of the cultural elements of the stories.

Two African American tales to share with young people are *Tailypo!* (1991) and *Little Eight John* (1992) told by Jan Wahl and illustrated by Wil Clay. *Tailypo!* tells the story of a man eating dinner in his cabin one night when a tail comes through the wall which he cuts off and eats up. Later, the Tailypo comes looking for his tail. In *Little Eight John* a young boy does mean things until trouble comes looking for him.
Response: Both of these stories lend themselves to creative dramatics. Teachers or teacher librarians can assign parts to different students and then have them dramatize the story. Students could also add props.

With the Cherokee connection to the Appalachian region, there are a number of folktales that could be included here. Joseph Bruchac is one of the most prolific Native American writers and storytellers today, and three of his stories were selected for this chapter. *The First Strawberries* (1993) tells the story of the creation of man and woman, which was blissful until they quarrel, and the woman leaves the man. In an effort to reunite them, the Sun creates raspberries, blueberries, blackberries, and finally, strawberries, which ultimately solves the problem.
Response: Serve fresh strawberries to students and talk about all the things made from them. Make a graph of the responses. Learn more about berries from Gail Gibbons' *The Berry Book* (2002). *How Chipmunk Got His Stripes* (2001) is a story told in the oral tradition that Bruchac had been told by his own father and that he has told to many audiences over the years. Bear and Brown Squirrel have a disagreement when Bear claims he can keep the sun from rising. The sun does indeed rise the next morning and when Brown Squirrel teases Bear unmercifully, he is scratched down the back and then becomes known as Chipmunk.
Response: This is a story that lends itself well to storytelling as evidenced by Bruchac's long history in telling the story. Students could incorporate some action into the story for a creative dramatics activity. Students may be interested in learning more about chipmunks who are the smallest members of the squirrel family. Locate Victoria Sherrow's *Chipmunks at Hollow Tree Lane* (1994). Learning the legend of how the Milky Way came to be is recounted in this version of a traditional Cherokee legend retold by Bruchac and Ross and titled *The Story of the Milky Way* (1995).
Response: This is another of Bruchac's tales that lends itself to storytelling and one that would be enhanced by glow-in-the-dark stars taped to the ceiling.

Other Cherokee legends to read and enjoy include Geri Keams' *Grandmother Spider Brings the Sun: A Cherokee Story* (1995); Gayle Ross' *How Rabbit Tricked Otter and Other Cherokee Trickster Stories* (1994); Jean Craighead George's *The Moon of the Bears* (1993); and Kay Thorpe Bannon's *Yonder Mountain: A Cherokee Legend* (2002). Students can learn more about the Cherokee in the informational book, *The Cherokees: A First Americas Book* (1996) by Virginia Driving Hawk Sneve, which includes a map of the North Carolina mountains and provides information about their history and their plight.

CONCLUSION

In this chapter, the author has strived to encourage teachers and librarians to learn more about the Appalachian region, its people, and its literature. The goal here is to present the positive images and values of Appalachian culture by focusing on books from Appalachian literary heritage about the people of this region who have pride in their land, their community, and their way of life.

Teaching children to understand and value people who are different from themselves helps build bridges across cultures and strengthens the possibility for peace in this world. Real-world experiences in many of these books about Appalachia help readers to gain insight and understanding into a people who have been misunderstood and sometimes mistreated by those outside this region. Sensitivity and understanding are a key part of multicultural education. It is hoped that through reading and discussing these wonderful children's books, readers will embrace Appalachia and its people and share their understanding and appreciation of this culture with others. In her acceptance speech for the 1991 Boston Globe-Horn Book Award for nonfiction for *Appalachia: The Voices of Sleeping Birds* (1991), Cynthia Rylant (1992) stated,

With each remembrance in the book, still I have left out a hundred others. And, my mother, my grandmother, and every one of my cousins—all could yet add thousands more. The best I can hope for is that you will have heard the place in my words.

This chapter represents only a selection of the rich literature that represents the Appalachian region and its people.

REFERENCES

Appalachia: Music from home. (2009). Nashville, TN: Condon Music Group.

Asbury, J. A. (1995, March 17). The changing image of Appalachian children's literature. In *Annual Appalachian Studies Conference*. Symposium conducted at Appalachian Studies Association, Morgantown, WV. Retrieved from ERIC database (ED385413).

Best, B. (1995). To see ourselves. In R. Hicks, A. Manning, & J. W. Miller (Eds.), *Appalachia inside out: Culture and custom* (p. 661). Knoxville, TN: University of Tennessee Press.

Gibbons, G. (2002). *The berry book*. New York, NY: Holiday House.

Herrin, R. T., & Oliver, S. Q. (2010). *Appalachian children's literature: An annotated bibliography*. Jefferson, NC: McFarland.

Jones, L. (1994). *Appalachian values*. Ashland, NC: The Jesse Stuart Foundation.

Kurtz, J. (1996). Multicultural children's books: The subtle tug-of-war. *School Library Journal*, *42*(2), 40–41.

Leeper, A. C. (2003). The "other America": Looking at Appalachian and Cajun/Creole resources. *Multicultural Review, 12*(1), 34–42.

Page, L. G. (1993). *The Foxfire book of toys & games*. Chapel Hill, NC: University of North Carolina Press.

Purmell, A. (2008). *Maple syrup season*, illustrated by J. Weber. Ashland, KY: Jesse Stuart Foundation.

Rylant, C. (1992). Appalachia: The voices of sleeping birds. *Horn Book Magazine, 68*(1), 131.

Tusa, T. (1996). *Family reunion*. New York, NY: Farrar Strauss Giroux.

Schmidt, G. (1992).The mythic dimensions of Appalachia. In A. L. Manna & C. S. Brodie (Eds.), *Many faces, many voices: Multicultural literary experiences for youth* (pp. 69–78). Ft Atkinson, WI: Highsmith Press.

Sherrow, V. (1994). *Chipmunk at hollow tree lane*. Norwalk, CT.

Smith, J. S. (2002). *Mining the mountain of Appalachian children's literature: Defining a multicultural literature* (Unpublished doctoral dissertation). The Ohio State University, Columbus, OH.

Valentine, V. (2008). Authenticity and accuracy in picture storybooks set in Appalachia. *Journal of Appalachian Studies, 14*(1), 49–61.

SELECTED APPALACHIAN CHILDREN'S LITERATURE

This selection of titles arranged by genre is not an exhaustive or comprehensive list. For a more comprehensive list, refer to *Appalachian Children's Literature* (Herrin, 2010).

Picture Books

Applet, K. (2003). *The best kind of gift.*, illustrated by P. Johnson. New York, NY: HarperCollins.

Bates, A. A. (1995). *Ragsale*, illustrated by J. Chapman-Crane. New York, NY: Houghton Mifflin.

Belton, S. (1993). *From Miss Ida's porch*, illustrated by F. Cooper. New York, NY: Four Winds.

Belton, S. (1994). *May'naise sandwiches & sunshine tea*, illustrated by G. Carter. New York, NY: Four Winds Press.

Birdseye, T. (1988). *Airmail to the moon*, illustrated by S. Gammel. New York, NY: Holiday House.

Birdseye, T. (1994). *A regular flood of mishap*, illustrated by M. Lloyd. New York, NY: Holiday House.

Bradby, M. (1995). *More than anything else*, illustrated by C. K. Soentpiet. New York, NY: Orchard.

Canyon, C. (2005). *John Denver's take me home, country roads*. Nevada City, CA: Dawn.

Carson, J. (1992). *You hold me and I'll hold you*, illustrated by A. Cannon. New York, NY: Orchard.

Caudill, R. (1964). *A pocketful of cricket*, illustrated by Evaline Ness. New York, NY: Holt, Rinehart & Winston.

Caudill, R. (1965). *A certain small shepherd*, illustrated by W. P. Du Bois. New York, NY: Holt, Rinehart and Winston.

Chall, M. W. (2000). *Sugarbush spring*, illustrated by J. Daly. New York, NY: HarperCollins.

Crum, S. (2004). *My mountain song*, illustrated by T. Rand. New York, NY: Clarion.

Davis, C. L. (2001). *The Christmas barn*. Middleton, WI: American Girl.

Gibbons, F. (1996). *Mountain wedding*, illustrated by T. Rand. New York, NY: Morrow.1.

Gibbons, F. (2001). *Emma Jo's song*, illustrated by S. Meidell. Honesdale, PA: Boyds Mills.

Gibbons, F. (2003). *The day the picture man came*, illustrated by S. Meidell. Honesdale, PA: Boyds Mills.

Gray, L. M. (1996). *My mama had a dancing heart*, illustrated by R. Colon. New York, NY: Orchard Books.

Gray, L. M. (1999). *When Uncle took the fiddle*, illustrated by L. Bloom. New York, NY: Orchard Books.

Hamner, E. (1970). *The homecoming: A novel about Spencer's Mountain*. New York, NY: Random House.

Harshman, M. (1989). *A little excitement*, illustrated by T. Rand. New York, NY: Cobblehill Books.

Harshman, M. (1990). *Snow company*, illustrated by L. W. Bowman. New York, NY: Dutton.

Harshman, M., & Ryan, C. (2001). *Red are the apples*, illustrated by W. Zahares. New York, NY: Harcourt.

Harshman, M., & Collins, B. (2002). *Rocks in my pockets*, illustrated by T. Goffe. New York, NY: Cobblehill.

Hendershot, J. (1987). *In coal country*, illustrated by T. B. Allen. New York, NY: Random House.

Hendershot, J. (1993). *Up the tracks to Grandma's*, illustrated by T. B. Allen. New York, NY: Random House.

Henson, H. (2005). *Angel coming*, illustrated by S. Gaber. New York, NY: Atheneum.

Henson, H. (2008). *That book woman*, illustrated by D. Small. New York, NY: Atheneum.

Houston, G. (1988). *The year of the perfect Christmas tree*, illustrated by B. Cooney. New York, NY: Dial.

Houston, G. (1992). *But no candy*, illustrated by L. Bloom. New York, NY: Philomel.

Houston, G. (1992). *My Great-Aunt Arizona*, illustrated by S. C. Lamb. New York, NY: Harper-Collins.

Howard, E. F. (2000). *Virgie goes to school with us boys*. New York, NY: Simon & Schuster.

Johnson, P. B. (1993). *The cow who wouldn't come down*. New York, NY: Orchard Books.

Johnson, P. B. (1999). *The pig who ran a red light*. New York, NY: Orchard Books.

Johnson, P. B. (2001). *The goose who went off in a huff*. New York, NY: Orchard Books.

Lambe, J. H. (2003). *Kudzu chaos*, illustrated by A. D. Lyne. Gretna, LA: Pelican Publishing.

Lyon, G. E. (1986). *A regular rolling Noah*, illustrated by S. Gammell. New York, NY: Macmillan.

Lyon, G. E. (1990). *Basket*, illustrated by M. Szilagyi. New York, NY: Orchard Books.

Lyon, G. E. (1990). *Come a tide*, illustrated by S. Gammell. New York, NY: Orchard Books.

Lyon, G. E. (1991). *Cecil's story*, illustrated by P. Catalanotto. New York, NY: Orchard Books.

Lyon, G. E. (1992). *Who came down that road?*, illustrated by P. Catalanotto. New York, NY: Orchard Books.

Lyon, G. E. (1994). *Mama is a miner*, illustrated by P. Catalanotto. New York, NY: Orchard Books.

Lyon, G. E. (1998). *A sign*, illustrated by C. K. Soentpiet. New York, NY: Orchard.

Lyon, G. E. (1998). *A traveling cat*, illustrated by P. B. Johnson. New York, NY: Orchard Books.

Lyon, G. E. (2004). *Weaving the rainbow*, illustrated by S. Anderson. New York, NY: Atheneum.

Marion, J. D. (1992). *Hello, crow*, illustrated by L. Bowman. New York, NY: Orchard Books.

May, K. (2000). *Molasses man*, illustrated by F. Marshall. New York, NY: Holiday House.

Mills, L. (1991). *The rag coat*. Boston, MA: Little, Brown.

Mills, P. (1993). *Until the cows come home*. New York, NY: North-South Books.

Purnell, A. (2002). *Apple cider-making days*. Minneapolis, MN: Millbrook Press.

Ranson, C. F. (1995). *When the whippoorwill calls*, illustrated by K. B. Root. New York, NY: Tambourine.

Ransom, C. F. (1999). *The promise quilt*, illustrated by E. Beier. New York, NY: Walker.

Ray, D. (1987). *My dog, Trip*. New York, NY: Holiday House.

Root, P. (2003). *The name quilt*, illustrated by M. Apple. New York, NY: Farrar, Straus Giroux.

Ryan, C. (1996). *Sally Arnold*, illustrated by B. Farnsworth. New York, NY: Dutton.

Rylant, C. (1982). *When I was young in the mountains*, illustrated by D. Goode. New York, NY: Dutton.

Rylant, C. (1983). *Miss Maggie*, illustrated by T. Di Grazia. New York, NY: Dutton.

Rylant, C. (1984). *This year's garden*, illustrated by M. Szilagyi. New York, NY: Bradbury.

Rylant, C. (1985). *The relatives came*, illustrated by S. Gammell. New York, NY: Bradbury Press.

Rylant, C. (1986). *Night in the country*, illustrated by M. Szilagyi. New York, NY: Bradbury Press.

Rylant, C. (1997). *Silver packages: An Appalachian Christmas story*, illustrated by C. Soentpiet. New York, NY: Orchard Books.

Rylant, C. (2002). *The ticky-tacky doll*, illustrated by H. Stevenson. San Diego, CA: Harcourt Brace.

Sawyer, R. (1953). *Journey cake, ho!*, illustrated by R. McClosky. New York, NY: Viking.

Schnur, S. (2000). *Spring thaw*, illustrated by S. Schuett. New York, NY: Viking.

Seymour, T. (1993). *Hunting the white cow*, illustrated by W. A. Halperin. New York, NY: Orchard.

Smucker, A. E. (1989). *No star nights*, illustrated by S. Johnson. New York, NY: Knopf.

Swain, G. (2003). *I wonder as I wander*, illustrated by R. Himler. Grand Rapids, MI: Eerdmans.

Vizuarraga, S. (2000). *Miss Opal's auction*, illustrated by M. Graham. New York, NY: Henry Holt.

Fiction

Armstrong, W. H. (1969). *Sounder*. New York, NY: Harper & Row.

Bradley, K. B. (2002). *Halfway to the sky*. New York, NY: Delacorte.

Bulla, C. R. (1966). *White bird*, illustrated by D. Cook. New York, NY: Random House.

Bulla, C. R. (1979). *Daniel's duck*, illustrated by J. Sandlin. New York, NY: Harper and Row.

Burch, R. (1980). *Ida early comes over the mountain*. New York, NY: Viking.

Byars, B. (1970). *Summer of the swans*. New York, NY: Viking.

Caudill, R. (1949). *Tree of freedom*, illustrated by D. B. Moore. New York, NY: Viking.

Caudill, R. (1962). *The best loved doll*. New York, NY: Henry Holt.

Caudill, R. (1965). *A certain small shepherd*, illustrated by W. P. Du Bois. New York, NY: Holt, Rinehart and Winston.

Caudill, R. (1966). *Did you carry the flag today, Charley?*, illustrated by N. Grossman. New York, NY: Holt, Rinehart & Winston.

Cleaver, V., & Cleaver, B. (1969). *Where the lilies bloom*, illustrated by J. Spanfeller. Philadelphia, PA: Lippincott.

Cole, N. (1999). *The final tide*. New York, NY: McElderry.

Creech, S. (1997). *Chasing redbird*. New York, NY: HarperCollins.

Fleishman, P. (1991). *The borning room*. New York, NY: HarperCollins.

Hamilton, V. (1974). *M. C. Higgins, the great*. New York, NY: Macmillan.

Hamilton, V. (1990). *Cousins*. New York, NY: Philomel.

Hesse, K. (1998). *Just juice*, illustrated by R. A. Parker. New York, NY: Scholastic.

Hite, S. (1994). *It's nothing to a mountain*. New York, NY: Henry Holt.

Houston, G. (1990). *Littlejim*, illustrated by T. B. Allen. New York, NY: Philomel.

Houston, G. (1994). *Littlejim's gift: An Appalachian Christmas story*, illustrated by T. B. Allen. New York, NY: Philomel.

Kassem, L. (1986). *Listen for Rachel*. New York, NY: Macmillan.

Lenski, L. (1946). *Blue Ridge Billy*. New York, NY: Dell.

Lenski, L. (1959). *Coal camp girl*. Philadelphia, PA: Lippincott.

Lowry, L. (1987). *Rabble Starkey*. New York, NY: Houghton Mifflin.

Lyon, G. E. (1998). *Borrowed children*. New York, NY: Orchard Books.

McDowell, M. T. (2009). *Carolina harmony*. New York, NY: Delacorte.

Naylor, P. R. (1991). *Shiloh*. New York, NY: Atheneum.

Naylor, P. R. (1996). *Shiloh season*. New York, NY: Atheneum.

Naylor, P. R. (1997). *Saving Shiloh*. New York, NY: Athenum.

Nolan, H. (2003). *When we were saints*. New York, NY: Harcourt.

O'Connor, B. (1999). *Me and Rupert Goody*. New York, NY: Farrar, Straus & Giroux.

Oughton, J. (1997). *Music from a place called Half-Moon*. New York, NY: Laurel Leaf.

Paterson, K. (1985). *Come sing, Jimmy Jo*. New York, NY: Dutton.

Reeder, C. (1991). *Grandpa's mountain*. New York, NY: Macmillan.

Rylant, C. (1985). *A blue-eyed daisy*. New York, NY: Bradbury Press.

Rylant, C. (1986). *A fine white dust*. New York, NY: Bradbury Press.

Rylant, C. (1992). *Missing May*. New York, NY: Orchard Books.

Rylant, C. (1987). *Children of Christmas: Stories for the season*. New York, NY: Orchard Books.

Smith, D. B. (1986). *Return to Bitter Creek*. New York, NY: Viking.

Tubb, K. O. (2008). *Autumn Winifred Oliver does things differently*. New York, NY: Delacorte.

Wells, R. (2000). *Mary on horseback: Three mountain stories*. New York, NY: Puffin Books.

White, R. (1996). *Bell Prater's boy*. New York, NY: Bantam Doubleday Dell.

White, R. (1998). *Sweet Creek Holler*. New York, NY: Farrar, Straus & Giroux.

White, R. (2004). *Buttermilk Hill*. New York, NY: Farrar, Straus and Giroux.

White, R. (2005). *The search for Belle Prater*. New York, NY: Farrar, Straus & Giroux.

Yep, L. (1991). *The star fisher*. New York, NY: Morrow.

Youmans, M. (2003). *The curse of the raven mocker*. New York, NY: Farrar, Straus & Giroux.

Nonfiction

Anderson, J. (1986). *Pioneer children of Appalachia*. New York, NY: Clarion.

Andryszewski, T. (1998). *Step by step along the Appalachian trail*. Brookfield, CT: Twenty-first Century.

Appelt, K. (2001). *Down Cut Shin Creek: The pack horse librarians of Kentucky*. New York, NY: Harper Collins.

Bartoletti, S. C. (1996). *Growing up in coal country*. Boston, MA: Houghton Mifflin.

Bauer, J. A. *Wildlife, wildflowers, and wild activities: Exploring southern Appalachia*, illustrated by J. Brown. Johnson City, TN: Overmountain.

Bial, R. (1997). *Mist over the mountains: Appalachia and its people*. Boston, MA: Houghton Mifflin.

Cheek, P. B. (1988). *An Appalachian scrapbook: An A-B-C of growing up in the mountains* (2nd ed.). Johnson City, TN: Overmountain Press.

Gravelle, K. (1997). *Growing up in a holler in the mountains*. New York, NY: Franklin Watts.

Hall, F. (1998). *Appalachian ABCs*. Johnson, TN: Overmountain Press.

Libal, J. (2005). *American regional cooking library: Culture, tradition, and history: Southern Appalachia*. Series Consultant: The Culinary Institute of America. Broomall, PA: Mason Crest.

Lyon, G. E. (1989). *A B Cedar: An alphabet of trees*, illustrated by T. Parker. New York, NY: Orchard.

Lyon, G. E. (1998). *Counting on the woods*, illustrated by A. Olson. New York, NY: DK Inc.

Mader, J. (2004). *Appalachian mountains*. New York, NY: Children's Press.

Maynard, C. W. (2004). *The Appalachians*. New York, NY: Rosen.

Pack, L. H. (2009). *A is for Appalachia!*, illustrated by P. Banks. Lexington, KY: University of Kentucky Press.

Rylant, C. (1989). *But I'll be back again*. New York, NY: Orchard Books.

Rylant, C. (1991). *Appalachia: The voices of sleeping birds*. San Diego, CA: Harcourt.

Rylant, C. (1992). *Best wishes*. Katonah, New York, NY: Richard C. Owen Publishers.

Sneve, V. D. H. (1996). *The Cherokees: A First Americans book*. New York, NY: Holiday House.

Poetry, Rhyme and Song

Aliki. (1974). *Go tell Aunt Rhody*. New York, NY: Macmillan.

Birdseye, T., & Birdseye, D. H. (1994). *She'll be comin' round the mountain*. New York, NY: Holiday House.

Carson, J. (1989). *Stories I ain't told nobody yet: Selections from the people pieces*. New York, NY: Orchard Books.

Frazee, M. (1999). *Hush, little baby*. San Diego, CA: Harcourt Brace.

Giovanni, N. (1994). *Knoxville, Tennessee*, illustrated by L. Johnson. New York, NY: Scholastic.

Johnson, A. (1998). *The other side. Shorter poems*. New York, NY: Scholastic.

Kidd, R. (1992). *On top of old Smoky: A collection of songs and stories from Appalachia*, illustrated by L. Anderson. Nashville, TN: Ideal Children's Books.

Lambert, P. L. (1995). *Evening: An Appalachian lullaby*. Boulder, CO: Roberts Rinehart.

Langstaff, J. M. (1955). *Frog went a-courtin'*, illustrated by F. Rojankovsky. New York, NY: Harcourt Brace.

Langstaff, J. M. (1957). *Over in the meadow*, illustrated by F. Rojankovsky. New York, NY: Harcourt Brace.

Langstaff, J. M. (1957). *The swapping boy*, illustrated by B. and J. Krush. New York, NY: Harcourt Brace.

Lyon, G. E. (1998). *Counting on the woods: A poem*, illustrated by A. W. Olson. New York, NY: DK Publishing.

Marion, J. D. (1992). *Hello, crow*, illustrated by L. Bowman. New York, NY: Orchard.

Millen, C. M. (2003). *Blue bowl down: An Appalachian rhyme*, illustrated by H. Meade. Boston, MA: Candlewick.

Milnes, G. (1999). *Granny will your dog bite and other mountain rhymes*, illustrated by K. B. Root. Little Rock, AR: August House.

Lyon, G. E. (2007). *Catalpa: Poems*. Nicholsville, KY: Wind Publications.

Quackenbush, R. (1973). *Go tell Aunt Rhody*. Philadelphia, PA: Lippincott.

Rylant. C. (1984). *Waiting to waltz: A childhood: Poems*, illustrated by S. Gammell. New York, NY: Bradbury.

Rylant, C. (1990). *Soda jerk*, illustrated by P. Catalanotto. New York, NY: Orchard.

Rylant, C. (1994). *Something permanent*, illustrated by W. Evans. New York, NY: Harcourt.

Still, J. (1977). *Jack and the wonder beans*, illustrated by M. Tomes. New York, NY: Putnam.

Still, J. (1998). *An Appalachian Mother Goose*, illustrated by P. B. Johnson. Lexington, KY: University Press of Kentucky.

Thornhill, J. (2004). *Over in the meadow*. Toronto, ON: Maple Tree Press.

Tyler, G. (2005). *Froggy went a-courtin'*. Cambridge: MA: Candlewick.

Traditional Literature

Anderson, H. C. (1990). *The tinderbox*, illustrated by B. Moser. Boston, MA: Little, Brown and Company.

Bannon, K. T. (2002). *Yonder mountain: A Cherokee legend*, illustrated by K. Rodanas. Tarrytown, NY: Marshall Cavendish.

Birdseye, T. (1993). *Soap! Soap! Don't forget the soap! An Appalachian folktale*, illustrated by A. Glass. New York, NY: Holiday House.

Bruchac, J. (1993). *The first strawberries: A Cherokee tale*. New York, NY: Dial.

Bruchac, J., & Dewey, A. (2001). *How chipmunk got his stripes: A tale of bragging and teasing*, illustrated by J. Aruego and A. Dewey. New York, NY: Dial.

Bruchac, J., & Ross, G. (1995). *The story of the Milky Way: A Cherokee tale*, illustrated by V. A. Stroud. New York, NY: Dial.

Chase, R. (1948). *Grandfather tales*. Boston, MA: Houghton Mifflin.

Chase, R. (1943). *The Jack tales: Folktales from southern Appalachians collected and retold*. Boston, MA: Houghton Mifflin.

Cohen, C. L. (1985). *Sally Ann Thunder Ann Whirlwind Crockett*, illustrated by A. Dewey. New York, NY: Greenwillow.

Compton, K., & Compton, J. (1993). *Jack, the giant chaser: An Appalachian tale*. New York, NY: Holiday House.

Compton, J. (1994). *Ashpet: An Appalachian tale*, illustrated by K. Compton. New York, NY: Holiday House.

Compton, J. (1995). *Sody Sallyratus*, illustrated by K. Compton. New York, NY: Holiday House.

Davis, A. (1996). *Sody Salleratus*, illustrated by A. & L. Daniel. Buffalo, NY: Kids Can Press.

Davis, D. (1992). *Jack always seeks his fortune*. Little Rock, AR: August House.

Davis, D. (1995). *Jack and the animals: An Appalachian folktale*, illustrated by K. Harvill. Little Rock, AR: August House.

Davis, D. (2004). *The pig who went home on Sunday: An Appalachian folktale*. Little Rock, AR: August House.

Fleischman, P. (2007). *Glass slipper, gold sandal: A worldwide Cinderella*. New York, NY: Henry Holt.

George, J. C. (1993). *The moon of the bears*, illustrated by R. Parker. New York, NY: Harper Collins.

Glass, A. (2000). *Bewildered for three days: As to why Daniel Boone never wore his coonskin cap*. New York, NY: Holiday House.

Haley, G. (1986). *Jack and the bean tree*. New York, NY: Crown.

Haley, G. (1988). *Jack and the fire dragon*. New York, NY: Crown.

Haley, G. (1992). *Mountain Jack tales*. New York, NY: Dutton.

Hicks, R., (2000). *The Jack tales*, illustrated by O. Smith. New York, NY: Callaway.

Hooks, W. H. (1989). *The three little pigs and the fox*, illustrated by S. D. Schindler. New York, NY: Macmillan.

Hunter, C. W. (1992). *The green gourd: A North Carolina folktale*, illustrated by T. Griego. New York, NY: Putnam.

Issacs, A. (1994). *Swamp Angel*, illustrated by P. O. Zelinsky. New York, NY: Dutton.

Johnson, P. B. (1999). *Old Dry Frye: A deliciously funny tall tale*. New York, NY: Scholastic.

Johnson, P. B. (2000). *Bearhide and crow*. New York, NY: Holiday House.

Johnson, P. B. (2001). *Fearless Jack*. New York, NY: Simon & Schuster.

Johnson, P. B. (2002). *Jack outwits the giants*. New York, NY: Simon & Schuster.

Keams, G. (1995). *Grandmother spider brings the sun*. Flagstaff, AZ: Northland Publishing.

Keats, E. J. (1965). *John Henry: An American legend*. New York, NY: Pantheon.

Lester, J. (1994). *John Henry*, illustrated by J. Pinkney. New York, NY: Dial.

MacDonald, M. R. (2007). *The old woman and her pig: An Appalachian folktale*, illustrated by J. Kanzler. New York, NY: HarperCollins.

Moser, B. (1994). *Tucker Pfeffercorn: An old story retold*. Boston, MA: Little, Brown.

Ross, G. (1995). *How turtle's back was cracked: A traditional Cherokee tale*, illustrated by M. Jacobs. New York, NY: Dial.

Ross, G. (1994). *How rabbit tricked otter and other Cherokee trickster stories*, illustrated by M. Jacobs. New York, NY: HarperCollins.

Schroeder. A. (1997). *Smoky Mountain Rose: An Appalachian Cinderella*, illustrated by B. Sneed. New York, NY: Dial.

Shelby, A. (2007). *The adventures of Molly Whuppie and other Appalachian folktales*. Chapel Hill, NC: University of North Carolina Press.

Shelby, A. (2009). *The man who lived in the hollow tree*, illustrated by C. Hazelaar. New York, NY: Atheneum.

Sloat, T. (1997). *Sody Sallyratus*. New York, NY: Dutton.

Small, T. (1994). *Legend of John Henry*. New York, NY: Delacorte.

Still, J. (1977). *Jack and the wonder beans*. New York, NY: Putnam.

Van Laan, N. (1998). *With a whoop and a holler*, illustrated by S. Cook. New York, NY: Atheneum.

Wahl, J. (1991). *Tailypo!*, illustrated by W. Clay. New York, NY: Henry Holt.

Wahl, J. (1992). *Little Eight John*. New York, NY: Lodestar.

Woolridge, C. N. (1995). *Wicked Jack*, illustrated by W.Hillenbrand. New York, NY: Holiday House.

SOURCES FOR THIS LITERATURE AND RELATED RESOURCES

Web Sites

Appalachian National Scenic Trail: Maine to Georgia (National Park Service) http://www.nps.gov/appa, accessed on October 03, 2010.

Appalachian Regional Commission http://www.arc.gov/, accessed on October 03, 2010.

Appalachian Studies Association http://www.appalachianstudies.org, accessed on October 03, 2010.

Appalachian Studies Association: Appalachian Studies: A resource directory for teaching Appalachian topics in elementary and secondary schools. http://www.appalachianstudies.org/resources/K12/, accessed on October 03, 2010.

AppLit: Resources for readers and teachers of Appalachian literature for children and young adults. http://www.ferrum.edu/applit/welcome.htm, accessed on October 03, 2010.

AppLit: Nature and the environment in Appalachian literature. http://www.ferrum.edu/applit/bibs/ecobib.htm, accessed on October 03, 2010.

AppLit. Appalachian Christmas books for children and young adults: http://www.ferrum.edu/AppLit/, accessed on October 03, 2010.

AppLit: "Miz Jackson was just talking outta her head, girl": A survey of realism in Appalachian picture books http://www.ferrum.edu/applit/articles/PicBkRealism.htm, accessed on October 03, 2010.

Digital Library of Appalachia http://www.aca-dla.org/, accessed on October 03, 2010.

Foxfire http://foxfire.org, accessed on October 03, 2010.

Resource Materials

Brodie, C. (1995). Appalachia. *School Library Media Activities Monthly, 12*(2), 45–47.

Burns, A. (1989). Mountain culture. In C. R. Wilson & W. Ferris (Eds.). *Encyclopedia of southern culture* (pp. 414–415). Chapel Hill, NC: The University of North Carolina Press.

Drake, R. B. (2001). *A history of Appalachia*. Lexington, KY: The University of Kentucky Press.

Edwards, G. T., Asbury, J. A., & Cox, R. L. (Eds.). (2006). *A handbook to Appalachia: An introduction to the region*. Knoxville, TN: University of Tennessee Press.

Evans, M. L., George-Warren, H., Santelli, R., & Robertson, T. (Eds.). (2004). *The Appalachians: America's first and last frontier*. New York, NY: Random House.

Garland, L. G., Smith, P., & Smith, H. (1993). *The Foxfire book of Appalachian toys & games*. Chapel Hill, NC: University of North Carolina Press.

Golden, S. (1996). Reading the Appalachia: An update. *Book Links, 5*(5), 34–40.

Goode, J. B. (1989). Appalachian literature. In C. R. Wilson & W. Ferris (Eds.). *Encyclopedia of Southern culture* (pp. 845–847). Chapel Hill, NC: The University of North Carolina Press.

Hanlon, T. L. (2005). Old and new stories from Appalachia. *The Five Owls, 17*(3), 59–60.

Hanlon, T. (2008). *Timeline of Appalachian folktales*. Retrieved from AppLit: http://www.ferrum.edu/applit/studyg/TimelineFolk.htm, accessed on October 03, 2010.

Harnish, M., & Oliver, S. Q. (1980). *Children's Appalachia: A study of themes and stereotypes in children's Appalachian literature*. Berea, KY: Berea College Appalachian Center.

Herrin, R. (1996). Gloria Houston and the burden of the "Old Culture" children's books. *Appalachian Journal, 24*(1), 30–42.

Herrin, R. (1991). Shall we teach 'em or learn 'em?: Attitudes toward language in Appalachian children's literature. *Journal of the Appalachian Studies Association, 3*, 192–198.

Hurst, C. O. (1994). Exploring Appalachia without a backpack. *Teaching Pre K-8, 24*(8).

Jones, L. (1975). Appalachian values. In R. J. Higgs & A. N. Manning (Eds.), *Voices from the Hills* (pp. 507–517). New York, NY: Frederick Ungar Publishing.

Lenski, L. (1972). *Journey into Childhood*. Philadelphia, PA: Lippincott.

Owens, W. T. (2001). An examination of picture books that teach children about Appalachia (Part 1). *Southern Social Studies Journal, 26*(2), 26–48.

Owens, W. T. (2001). An examination of picture story books that teach children about Appalachia (Part 2). *Southern Social Studies Journal, 27*(1), 3–19.

Owens, W. T. (2002). Picture story books that teach children about Appalachia: Problems, perplexities, and proposals (Part 3). *Southern Social Studies Journal, 28*(1), 3–21.

Roggenkamp, K. (2008) Seeing inside the mountains: Cynthia Rylant's Appalachian literature and the "Hillbilly" stereotype. *The Lion and the Unicorn, 32*(2), 192–215.

Sizemore, J. (2000). *Appalachian Literature, Appalachian Culture: Literature-Based, Cross-Curricular Activities for the Middle and high school Classrooms.* Prospect, KY: Harmony House Publishers.

Smith, J. (2007). The music of Appalachian children's literature. *Children and Libraries, 5*(2), 31–37.

Stafford, C. (1980). *Say that you love me: A teacher's guide to Appalachian awareness.* Cincinnati, OH: Cincinnati Association for the Education of Young Children.

Stokely, J. (1981). *An Appalachian studies teacher's manual.* Oak Ridge, TN: Children's Museum of Oak Ridge.

Troy, A. (1977). Appalachia in children's and adolescents' fiction. *Language Arts, 54*(1), 55–62.

Veltze, L. (Ed.). (1994). *Exploring the southeast states through literature.* Phoenix, AZ: Oryx Press.

Wiggington, E. (Ed.). (1990). *A Foxfire Christmas: Appalachian memories and traditions.* New York, NY: Doubleday.

Worthington, M. (2003). Reaching kids where they live: Appalachian artist and storyteller Paul Brett Johnson. *Now & Then, 20*(1), 31–34.

10

Representations not Representation: Exploring Middle East Children's Literature

Ruth McKoy Lowery

The twenty-first century has ushered in the continuation of various incidents of terrorism and wars around the globe. Many students growing up in the United States are inundated with the ongoing wars in Iraq and Afghanistan. Their familiarity is ascertained as many watch their parents, extended relatives, friends, and others go off on extended tours of active military duty in an effort to combat terror activities. Very often the images portrayed and displayed in public media presents a distorted view of people from Middle Eastern countries in general (Kayyali, 2006).

For many students the dramatic incidents of September 11, 2001; the apprehended shoe bomber; and most recently, the underwear bomber who attempted to blow up an airplane on Christmas Day 2009 generate images of fear as they hear references made to Muslims and Arabs, terminologies often used interchangeably but incorrectly (Al-Hazzá, 2006, p. 11). Still, for many children these images of fear, the uncertainty and instability of the ongoing wars, the lack of trust even of people they live among, learn, pray, and play with continues to deepen the divide and erode their understanding and tolerance of others around them (Henderson, 2008; Welch, 2006).

As many students become more aware of their peers of Middle Eastern origins, they may be unfamiliar with these peoples' history within the United States, the contributions they have made to the social and cultural milieu, and of the push and pull factors that draw these immigrant groups to this country (Banks, 2009; Kayyali, 2006; Lowery, 2000). Negative sentiments towards Arabs, Arab Americans, and Muslims have increased (Welch, 2006). Henderson (2008) proposed that the terrorist attacks of September 11, 2001 dramatically changed law enforcement in the United States but that the greatest impact of this change has been on Arab-American communities (p. ii). Many students are unaware that there are differentiations among the groups from the Middle Eastern countries and that like their own cultures and expressions of individuality, there is no one defining characteristic that can be used to identify all members of any particular group of people (Al-Hazzá & Bucher, 2008b, p. 211).

Al-Hazzá and Lucking (2007) determined that the incidents of terrorism and other forms of violence have resulted in a change in "politics, in social convention, in battle, and in the classroom" (p. 132). Al-Hazzá and Lucking further posited that these changes have resulted in dramatic shifts in the global perceptions of Arabs and Arab Americans (p. 132). Overwhelmingly, many of these views are negative. According to Banks (2009), this is "the best of times and the worst of times" for Arab Americans (p. 464). Banks delineated further that while many Arab Americans have prospered and are continuing to grow economically and educationally, anti-Arab sentiments are still deeply entrenched in "American popular culture and attitudes" (pp. 464–465).

School remains one of the most public environments in which diverse student populations come in contact with each other (Tanners, 1997). Particularly, it is the most accessible space that students will have contact with their Arab and Arab American peers. The stereotypical representations of these groups in public media, however, often affect how children acclimate to each other (Marston, 2004). Kirova and Emme (2006) established that peer relationships are important in students' overall adjustment to school (p. 152). Exposito and Favela (2003) also affirmed that the teacher is very important in helping immigrant children "feel at ease in their new surroundings" (p. 73). It is important then to provide a positive space for all students to feel welcome and confident that they belong.

Lowery (2000) proposed that "literature is one medium in which the world is presented to us" (p. 2). Literature then becomes an important conduit not only for learning about others but also about us (Bishop, 2000; Marston, 2004). Allowing children to see the experiences of diverse cultures, ethnicities, and more in stories can help them to become familiar with different customs, empathize with the traumatic experiences some of their immigrant peers have endured, and also allow them to aesthetically share some experiences they otherwise would not have had (Rosenblatt, 1994; Spiegel, 1998). Marston determined that good stories can appeal to students' emotions, offer characters they can identify, and can help them to form positive impressions that will positively impact them in the future (p. 647).

Books portraying experiences of Middle Eastern characters can illuminate for students that they share some of the same experiences as their peers. Al-Hazzá (2006) established that good "Arab literature portraying Arabs as individuals and realistically depicting their values, cultural heritage, and traditions" can help to eliminate negative perceptions by their American peers (p. 11). For many students who do not have physical contact with Arab Americans and Middle Eastern Americans in general, books can provide a vicarious experience as they explore the customs and experiences of these diverse groups of people.

In the remainder of this chapter the focus is on the representations of Arab Americans in children's literature but more broadly discuss the overall representations of Muslims in and around the Middle Eastern geographic region. The ongoing Allied military occupation of Iraq and Afghanistan has realized a significant increase in literature representing these groups. The stories in this discussion focus predominantly on books published within the last 10 years. The books have been espoused as quality literature to share the Muslim experience with young children and delineate stories of the vast experiences of different groups of people in recent years (Middle East Resources, 2000). Unfortunately, the number of contemporary realistic fiction stories readily available to young readers is still limited (Lems, 1999; Marston, 2004). A brief overview of Arab Americans and the larger Muslim communities is presented in an attempt to eradicate the misconceptions about Arabs, Muslims, and the Middle East in general (Al-Hazzá, 2006, Al-Hazzá & Bucher, 2008a; Hafiz, Hafiz, & Hafiz, 2009). Some of the push and pull factors that have brought Middle Eastern immigrants to the United States is briefly discussed. The books included in this chapter are representative of books available for the elementary through early adolescent audience (P–grade 6). A brief overview of the books is provided with suggestions for how teachers can integrate multicultural children's literature into their schools' curricula to help all students learn about the larger world outside their experiences, classrooms, homes, and communities.

MIDDLE EASTERN DEMOGRAPHY

Arabs comprise several different peoples who live in North Africa and western Asia, areas most commonly referred to as the Middle East, and they share a common culture (Naff, 1988, p. 13). The modern geographic regions of the Middle East "stretches from Egypt in the west, situated on the African continent, north to Turkey across to Iran then south to encompass the entire Arabian Peninsula with Yemen at its southernmost eastern edge" (Al-Hazzá & Bucher, 2008a, p. 7). The large geographic makeup of the Middle East ascertains that it is indeed difficult for everyone in the different countries to share the same cultural mores. Al-Hazzá and Bucher (2008a) noted further that Arabs are the largest ethnic group residing in 17 countries in the Middle East and number over 300 million (p. 12). Each country with Middle Eastern borders boasts its own traditions and values (p. 12). One major commonality among Arabs is the Arabic language, "a Semitic language that originated in the Arabian Peninsula" (Naff, 1988, p. 13).

According to Al-Hazzá and Bucher (2008a), the Arab countries "are held together by a cohesive bond" based on their common language, shared traditions such as their music, and their values (pp. 13–14). People of the Middle East are committed to the importance of tribal affiliations, generosity, and children (p. 12).

In recent years Americans have heard frequent and repetitive representations of countries in the Middle East. Representation is prevalent in mass media and many people pay particular attention depending on their involvement at different times and for different reasons. Many incorrectly assume that all countries in the geographic regions are related and all the inhabitants are the same. However, Al-Hazzá and Bucher (2008a) tell us that although the Turks, Afghans, Iranians, Armenians, and Pakistanis share the same geographic region, they are not Arabs (p. 14).

Al-Hazzá and Bucher (2008a) further argued that there are many more misconceptions particularly about Arab nations (p. 17). They pointed out that many Westerners incorrectly believe that the terms "Arab" and "Muslim" are the same, delineating further that while the Muslim population is the second largest religious population in the world, Arabs comprise only 20 percent of the group (p. 17). Although a majority of Arabs are indeed Muslims, the Arab world also includes large groups of "Christians, Jews, Maronites, Druze, Egyptian Copts, and Melokites" (p. 17). Of further note is the fact that the majority of the world's Muslim population does not live in the Middle East as is often assumed but rather in Indonesia (Al-Hazzá & Bucher, 2008a, p. 17; Naff, 1988). For this chapter, the broader Muslim group is included to share more of the literature that is being created for our elementary and young adolescent audiences.

People who adhere to the Islamic religion are called Muslims. Muslims believe that Muhammad was sent by Allah "to warn humanity of the consequences of its evil ways" (Naff, 1988, p. 20). The Quran or (Koran) consists of the teachings of Islam. Most Arabs are Muslims, but the majority of Muslims are not Arabs. According to Hafiz et al. (2009), Islam is the name that was "given to the message revealed by the Prophet Muhammad in AD 610 in Mecca" (p. 1). Hafiz et al. further proposed that Muslims can trace their ancestry back to Abraham. Contrary to popular belief by non-Muslim groups, Hafiz et al. explicated that Muslims do not worship Muhammad but rather see him as the "last chosen messenger" (p. 5).

Today, there are two predominant groups within the followers of Islam, the Shiite, and the Sunni. The Sunnis comprise 85 percent of the Muslim population, and a majority of Middle Easterners including the Arab Muslims identify with this group. The Shiites, however, are predominantly found in Iran and Iraq (Al-Hazzá & Bucher, 2008a, p. 10).

MIDDLE EAST IMMIGRANTS IN TWENTY-FIRST CENTURY AMERICA

Arab Americans have been a distinct part of the American fabric from the 1800s. Like other immigrant groups before them, most Arabs came motivated by the economic possibilities (Boosahda, 2003, p. 17). Kayyali (2006) delineated that the first immigrant wave occurred between 1880 and 1924. These immigrants came mostly from Lebanon and Syria. As immigration laws were tightened to keep out many hopefuls, fewer immigrants came during the second wave of 1925–1965. Most Arab Americans today are a part of the newest immigrants who have arrived since 1965 (p. 23). Most immigrants come in search of better living conditions and greater chances of upward mobility than in their home countries (Alfred, 2001/2002, p. 3).

While earlier Arab immigrants were Christians, today most are Muslims (Hoobler & Hoobler, 2003, p. 182). They come because they feel free to practice their religion in the United States. They add to the variety of American religions, and Islam is one of the fastest growing religions in the United States today. Hafiz, et al. (2009) posited that Islam is one of the most "misunderstood" religions (p. 103). In the last 10 years, however, Arab Americans have worked to heighten positive awareness in the United States, working hard "against ignorance, discrimination, and stereotyping" (Banks, 2009, p. 465). Alfred (2001/2002) determined that there are differences within geographic areas and even within each group or wave of immigrants, ranging from race, to class, to ethnicity, and to language.

The terrorist attacks of September 11, 2001, have made it harder for Arab nationals to immigrate to the United States. According to Kayyali (2006), after the attacks, United States security officials noted that the perpetrators were all male, Arab nationals who had entered the United States by land and air, many with visas in their real names (p. 24). As a direct result, immigration authorities have specifically targeted Arab and Muslim men (p. 24). Koppelman and Goodhart (2005) posited that negative sentiments toward Arabs, Muslims, and "Middle Eastern-looking" men have actually increased since the 1995 bombing of the federal building in Oklahoma City (p. 140). Al-Hazzá (2006) determined that "there is a great deal of misunderstanding and misinformation about Arabs," thus quality books portraying Arabs can help to alleviate these problems (p. 11).

REPRESENTATION IN MIDDLE EASTERN CULTURES IN CHILDREN'S LITERATURE

In this chapter, the experiences of Arabs and non-Arab Muslims who share the geographic regions of the Middle East are incorporated for two reasons. First, many of the children's books which have been published and are readily available in the United States, particularly in the last five years, heavily represent the experiences of children from Afghanistan and Iraq, the two countries that are currently occupied by the Allied forces. The new stories have predominantly representative themes encapsulating Muslim experiences. Second, teachers and school librarians who help incorporate children's stories in their curricula need to know the array of new titles.

This brief introduction to Middle Eastern/Middle Eastern American literature is not the only study to discovering the array of titles presented. Instead, it is intended to be an introduction to the rich and deep conversations that can be developed when readers are engaged in learning about others and in turn rotating the spotlight on themselves.

The list of books presented in this chapter consists of 24 titles: 6 novels and 18 picture books. They are representative of the culturally diverse groups from the Middle East (see Tables 10.1 and 10.2). The books feature stories that provide a window for the reader, illuminating diverse and varying experiences of young children. The books are divided into groups based on where the story happened. The main category is "Representations in Middle East Children's Literature." The book titles are subdivided into five categories, based on the theme they represented. The subcategories are

1. Immigrant experiences in the United States (five books),
2. American born experiences (six books),
3. Global experiences (one book),
4. Immigrant experiences outside the United States (two books), and
5. Middle Eastern native experiences (10 books).

The following key is used to classify each book discussed and to aid in easy recognition from the chart:

Represented Group (RG): AM=Arabs; M=Muslims, not Arab
Author: NW=Native Arab/Muslim Writers; NNW=Non-Native Arab/Muslim Writers
Genre: RF=Realistic Fiction; NF=Nonfiction; P=Picture Book; N=Novel

Represented groups is used to highlight if the book is about an Arab (AM) or Muslim (M). All the stories represent Muslim characters, but the M is used to code books that do not specifically feature Arab characters.

The Author key is used to highlight the cultural or ethnic affiliations of the author. NW represents Native Arab/Muslim authors and NNW represents non-native Arab/Muslim authors. Finally, Genre is used to highlight the broad story pattern and whether the book is a picture book or a novel.

Immigrant Experiences in the United States

As children immigrate to the United States and become part of school communities, literature describing their experiences can help them and other students they come in contact with (Isaacs, 2007). Immigrant literature helps readers to see life in the United

Table 10.1.
Representations in Middle East Children's Literature

Represented Group (RG): AM= Arabs; M= Muslims, not Arab

Author: NW= Native Arab/Muslim Writers; NNW=Non-Native Arab/Muslim Writers

Genre: RF=Realistic Fiction; NF=Nonfiction; P=Picture Book; N=Novel

Groups	Titles (P/N)	RG	Author	Genre
Immigrant Experiences in the United States	Budhos, M. (2006). *Ask Me No Questions* (N)	M	NNW	RF
	Bunting, E. (2006). *One Green Apple* (P)	AM	NNW	RF
	Howard, H. (2006). *Living as a Refugee in America: Mohammed's Story* (P)	M	NNW	NF
	Williams, K. L. & Mohammed, K. (2007). *Four Feet, Two Sandals* (P)	M	NW	RF
	Wolf, B. (2003). *Coming to America: A Muslim Family's Story* (P)	AM	NNW	NF
American Born Experiences	Clements, A. (2009). *Extra Credit* (N)	M	NNW	RF
	Hoyt-Goldsmith, D. (2002). *Celebrating Ramadan* (P)	AM	NNW	NF
	Mobin-Uddin, A. (2005). *My Name is Bilal* (P)	M	NW	RF
	Mobin-Uddin, A. (2007). *The Best Eid ever* (P)	M	NW	RF
	Mobin-Uddin, A. (2009). *A Party in Ramadan* (P)	M	NW	RF
Global Experiences	Nye, N. S. (1997). *Sitti's Secrets* (P)	AM	NW	RF
	Heiligman, D. (2006). *Celebrate Ramadan & Eid al-fitr* (P)	M	NNW	NF

States through the experiences of their immigrant peers. While images of immigrants to the United States are prominent across various media, for many children, their only real contact with immigrants may be through representations in children's literature. According to Bishop (2000), literature helps us to interpret and shape our experience, transcending time, place, and cultures (p. 73). It is important, then, that teachers engage children in critical and thoughtful reading of diverse literature (Harris, 1999).

In *Ask Me No Questions* (Budhos, 2006), an undocumented Bangladeshi Muslim family living in New York, works together to prevent being deported after the terrorist attacks of September 11, 2001. *One Green Apple* (Bunting, 2006) presents Farah, a young Muslim girl who has newly immigrated and started school in America. She wears a headdress and is concerned about making friends. She learns to adapt to her new life and warmly embraces the friendships extended by her classmates. *Coming to America: A Muslim Family's Story* (Wolf, 2003), is a photo essay of eight-year-old Rowan and her family's journey from Egypt to join their father in America. The family quickly adapts to life in America but also works very hard at preserving their Muslim culture.

Two stories in this subcategory relate the traumatic experiences of refugee children from Afghanistan. *Living as a Refugee in America: Mohammed's Story* (Howard, 2006) is a photo essay of Mohammed's family. After his father disappears, the family seeks refuge in Iran and Turkey. Soon they are granted asylum and now live in St. Louis. Mohammed helps his mother to care for his younger siblings, and the family works hard to adjust to life in America. In *Four Feet, Two Sandals* (Williams, 2007), Lina and Feroza become fast friends after each finds a sandal at the refugee camp where they live. Together they take turns wearing the sandals and sharing their dreams of a home and a new life. When Lina's family is selected to come to America, Feroza insists that they each keep a sandal to remember their friendship.

American Born Experiences

Many times students of a minority culture or ethnicity find it hard to adapt to their surroundings because of the labels others place on them. Sometimes these students have to remind their peers and others that they were born in the United States and are American citizens. Culturally responsive teachers and their teacher librarians are aware of the many little setbacks that may hinder their students' progress, and they work to find a comfortable middle ground where their students can grow. Ladson-Billings (1994) declared that teachers must demonstrate a connectedness with all students in their class (p. 55). She argued further that culturally relevant teachers use students' cultural experiences, teach them how to maintain their cultures, and help their students to transcend the negativity they face (p. 16).

In *Extra Credit* (Clements, 2009), Abby must complete an extra credit assignment to prevent flunking the sixth grade. She must find a pen pal in a foreign country. Soon she begins corresponding with a young boy, Sadeed, in Afghanistan. The two become fast friends sharing their experiences from both countries. However, the friendship is threatened as the adults on both continents determine that it is not safe for a young boy and girl to be corresponding. Three books in this subcategory were written by the same author. Asma Mobin-Uddin decided to write positive books about Muslim children because she felt there was not a good selection to choose from. In *My Name is Bilal* (Mobin-Uddin, 2005), Bilal is afraid to defend his sister, Ayesha, who is constantly teased for wearing her headscarf. As he struggles to embrace his Muslim faith, he also learns to defend his sister and stand up for himself.

The Best Eid Ever (Mobin-Uddin, 2007), celebrates the most special day on the Islamic calendar. However, Aneesa is sad because her parents have made the pilgrimage to Mecca in far away Saudi Arabia. Her grandmother tries to cheer her. Later, at the mosque, Aneesa meets two young girls, new refugees in the United States. Aneesa decides, with her grandmother's assistance, to help the girls; thus in helping, she has the best Eid celebration. *A Party in Ramadan* (Mobin-Uddin, 2009) portrays Leena, who wants to fast with her family for the Ramadan celebration. However, on the day the whole family will be together, Leena is also invited to her friend's birthday party. She decides to go to the party and still fast. Fighting the temptation to eat, she is able to celebrate her first day of fast with her family.

Celebrating Ramadan (Hoyt-Goldsmith, 2002) is a photo essay of how Ibraheem, a young Muslim living in New Jersey, and his family celebrate the month of Ramadan. Although Ibraheem is only in the fourth grade and does not have to fast, he is determined to be a part of the celebration with his family. With loving encouragement, Ibraheem fasts for the entire month with his parents. In *Sitti's Secrets* (Nye, 1997), Mona travels to Palestine to visit her grandmother. As she gets to know her grandmother, she learns her customs. She sees the uncertainty of life and wishes for change. Mona decides to write a letter to the President of the United States asking him to urge the leaders in the peace region to develop peaceful resolutions.

Global Experiences

Understanding, respecting and appreciating diversity can be approached from different angles. Most teachers and school media specialists will have to address this issue at some point in their careers. The frequency has increased as we see immigrants moving out of traditional familial areas and moving into school districts that were considered homogenous. When teachers and school media specialists are prepared to handle cultural diversity issues, they are more able to assist the students in adjusting to their classrooms (Johnson & Smith, 1993).

Celebrate Ramadan & Eid al-Fitr (Heiligman, 2006) is an informational book that delineates the celebration of Ramadan and the festival of Eid al-Fitr. Ramadan is the month of celebration, and Eid al-Fitr is a three-day festival celebration that is conducted at the end of Ramadan. People around the world are portrayed in different stages of their observance of this holy month.

Immigrant Experiences Outside the United States

Often, we think of immigrant experiences only if they occur only within our borders. However, as political unrest looms across the horizon, many individuals will seek refuge in various countries that will grant them asylum. The children affected by these crises will ultimately become students in the local schools. Gay (2000) admonished that teachers must be culturally responsive teachers who can teach their students how to appreciate and celebrate their own and others' cultural heritages. Gay further asserted that it takes just one individual to help children feel at ease in their new surroundings (p. 73). Teachers must be prepared to be global citizens. As such they develop tolerance and learn how to value every child in their classroom (Neuharth-Pritchett, Payne & Reiff, 2004).

Children of War: Voices of Iraqi Refugees (Ellis, 2009) is a candid portrayal of child refugees who had to flee Iraq with their families. Many are living in exile in Jordan, where they are not wanted, and a few have found asylum in Canada. Those in Jordan

Table 10.2.

Representations in Middle East Children's Literature

Represented Group (RG): AM= Arabs; M= Muslims, not Arab

Author: NW= Native Arab/Muslim Writers; NNW=Non-Native Arab/Muslim Writers

Genre: RF=Realistic Fiction; NF=Nonfiction; P=Picture Book; N=Novel

Groups	Titles (P/N)	RG	Author	Genre
Immigrant Experiences Outside the United States	Ellis, D. (2009). *Children of War: Voices of Iraqi Refugees* (N)	AM	NNW	NF
	Robinson, A. & Young, A.(2009). *Mohammed's Journey: A Refugee Diary* (P)	AM	NNW	NF
Middle Eastern Native Experiences	Addasi, M. (2008). *The White Nights of Ramadan* (P)	AM	NW	RF
	Heide, F. P. & Gilliland, J. H. (1992). *Sami and the Time of the Troubles* (P)	AM	NNW	RF
	Khan, R. (2009). *Wanting Mor* (N)	M	NW	RF
	Rumford, J. (2008). *Silent Music: A Story of Baghdad* (P)	AM	NNW	RF
	Stamaty, M. A. (2004). *Alia's Mission: Saving the Books of Iraq* (P)	AM	NNW	RF
	Whelan, G. (2009). *Waiting for the Owl's Call* (P)	M	NNW	RF
	Winter, J. (2005). *The Librarian of Basra: A True Story from Iraq* (P)	AM	NNW	NF
	Winter, J. (2009). *Nasreen's Secret School: A True Story from Afghanistan* (P)	M	NNW	NF
	Wrigley-Field, E. & Ross, J. (Eds.). (2009). *Iraqi Girl: Diary of a Teenage Girl in Iraq* (N)	AM	NW	NF
	Zenatti, V. (2008). *A Bottle in the Gaza Sea* (N)	AM	NW	RF

are waiting with their parents, hoping that other countries will offer them asylum. Many are angry at the United States because of the ongoing war. Their vivid recollections of their experiences are painfully haunting.

Mohammed's Journey: A Refugee Diary (Robinson & Young, 2009) is the story of a Kurdish family from northern Iraq, now living in England. When Mohammed's father is arrested, his mother escapes with him to protect them from further harm. The two suffer through traumatic circumstances but are finally able to start a new living in England where his mother has remarried, and Mohammed now has a little sister. His greatest wish is to see his father again, but he knows that will not happen.

Middle Eastern Native Experiences

Multicultural literature is a powerful medium that can help students to construct varying perspectives about their cultures and roles in society, as well as provide opportunities for understanding the cultural surroundings, insights, traditions and beliefs of others (Hefflin & Barksdale-Ladd, 2001; Yokota, 1993). Reading diverse literature cultivates an educated awareness to other cultural customs and values, promotes communication with people from other countries, and enhances experiences involving theirs and others' cultures. Through literature, readers vicariously explore lands and cultural mores that they would otherwise not experience. Children can develop empathy with characters whose life experiences are different from their own. Stories help to transmit values and perceptions of the world. Students then are exposed to diverse portrayals of family structures, gender roles, and different racial and cultural communities through literature (Johnson & Smith, 1993).

The stories in this subcategory, feature experiences of children in their homelands. For many immigrant children in American schools, these books can be beneficial in helping them to hold on to the memories of the homes and countries they had to leave behind. Native stories often portray ideas not widely available in mainstream media. Thus, these stories have the power to illuminate another view that many students and readers at large had not seen before. Books with ethnic themes can relate more personally to children who are of that particular racial or ethnic group depicted in a story. Often children in multiethnic classrooms do not want to discuss their cultural and religious differences for fear that the other students might tease them or misinterpret their traditions. Lindquist and Selwyn (2000) determined that teachers need to be sensitive to their students' needs (p. 84). Teachers need to build on students' experiences in order to better help them in the classroom (Sipe & Daley, 2005, p. 229). Before incorporating the various cultural novels into the curricula, teachers should seek to know more and understand the cultures, and how to handle students' fears.

In *The White Nights of Ramadan* (Addasi, 2008), Noor excitedly prepares for *Girgian*, a Muslim celebration observed in the Arabian Gulf states during the middle of the month of Ramadan when the moon is full. Noor helps to make candy to share with the neighbors and then helps her brothers to decorate their bags to receive candy when they go door-to-door. Anxiously awaiting the next day's busy activities, Noor is unable to go to sleep at night. In *Wanting Mor* (Khan, 2009), when Jameela's mother dies, she is left alone with her father who wants to move to the city, Kabul, immediately. Her father quickly remarries and just as quickly abandons Jameela. Born with a cleft lip and with no education, Jameela is lost without her mother. Her life changes for the better when she ends up at an orphanage, where she becomes one of the teachers.

Sami and the Time of the Troubles (Heide & Gilliland, 1992) is a tale of young Sami who lives in Beirut, Lebanon. Constant gunfire and bombing in the streets, prevents the family from enjoying a carefree life. Often, they have to hide in his uncle's basement. His mother is sad that things may never get better. She has already lost her husband to the war. When the fighting stops for a short time, the family heads for the beach, hoping for some semblance of the life they once knew. Sami is hopeful that life will get better. He refuses to believe that the war won't end soon. Similarly in *Silent Music: A Story of Baghdad* (Rumford, 2008), Ali lives in Baghdad. He loves playing soccer and listening to music but loves writing calligraphy most. As bombs and missiles fall over Bagdad, Ali finds solace practicing his calligraphy like the master calligrapher, Yakut, who lived in Baghdad in 1258.

Alia's Mission: Saving the Books of Iraq (Stamaty, 2004) and *The Librarian of Basra: A True Story from Iraq* (Winter, 2005) are two beautifully written books about Alia Muhammad Baker, the chief librarian of the Central Library in Basra, Iraq. When the Iraqi war seems imminent, Alia works tirelessly to preserve the library books and other government forms. As the government ignores her request to save the books, she turns to her neighbors for help. Together they smuggle over 30,000 books to safety. Nine days later, the library burns to the ground. *Waiting for the Owl's Call* (Whelan, 2009) is the tale of young Zulviya who weaves rugs alongside her grandmother, mother, and cousins. As she weaves, she dreams a pattern in her mind, complete with the vibrant colors of her homeland, Afghanistan. She hears a whisper about school and yearns to go there someday. Until then, she continues to dream in color.

Another story of the power of school and how it can impact young minds is the story of *Nasreen's Secret School: A True Story from Afghanistan* (Winter, 2009). Nasreen stops speaking after both her parents disappear. First her father is taken away, and then her mom goes looking for him but never returns. Her grandmother registers Nasreen in a secret school for girls in hopes that she will be happy around friends. Eventually, she opens up to making new friends.

Iraqi Girl: Diary of a Teenage Girl in Iraq (Wrigley-Field & Ross, 2009) is the story of Hadiya, a high school student in Mosul, who blogs about her experiences during the ongoing Iraqi war. She shares happy news about her family and her life but also presents the stark horrors that unceasingly threaten the family's very sense of survival. Hadiya cannot understand why others are fascinated with her blogs when they obviously lived in areas unaffected by the war she is experiencing. In *A Bottle in the Gaza Sea* (Zenatti, 2008), Tal, an Israeli teenager, longs to correspond with someone from the other side, Palestine. She writes a letter, places it in a bottle, and asks her brother, an Israeli soldier to throw the bottle into the Gaza Sea. A young Palestinian, with a sarcastic demeanor, gets the letter and begins corresponding with Tal via email. The rocky early correspondences soon become genuine conversations between friends, and Tal longs more than ever to be able to meet him soon.

RESPONSE ACTIVITIES FOR MIDDLE EASTERN CHILDREN'S LITERATURE

The books described in this chapter are a small, collective representation of the diverse themes found in children's literature written about the Middle East in the last two decades. These poignant stories have the power to pique students' interest, propelling them to delve into tales that can move them out of their familiar awareness into new understandings. Lehman (2007) positions that children's literature is important to integrate in schools' curricula. Lehman posited further that children need books in which they see reflections of themselves and their lived experiences (p. 65). They also need books that can open their imagination and experiences to others who are different from them so they can learn about these unfamiliar lives and settings (p. 65). Books portraying Middle Eastern children's experiences have the power to do just that in schools' curricula across the United States. Immigrant and Middle Eastern American students can read about their diverse cultures, mores, and practices represented in literature. Their peers can also learn about these diverse cultures, mores, and practices with which they would otherwise not be familiar. To further expose children to the diverse people of Middle Eastern heritage, there are many activities teachers can integrate across the curriculum. This section presents a sampling of the activities that can be implemented in language arts, reading, mathematics, science, social studies, and the arts.

Language Arts and Reading Activities

All the books cited in this chapter can be integrated in the literacy curriculum. Students can conduct literature circles, reading the books, and coming together in small groups to discuss their aesthetic and efferent readings of the books. For example, students could read and compare books about immigrant experiences in and out of the United States. *Living as a Refugee in America: Mohammed's Story* (Howard, 2006) could be compared with *Mohammed's Journey: A Refugee Diary* (Robinson & Young, 2009). One child has immigrated to the United States and the other to England. Students can discuss the reasons each family had to leave their homeland; what were their experiences traveling to the new country? How does each child adapt to life in his new country; how does each child reminisce about his homeland? Students can create a Venn diagram or comparison chart and list the information for each immigrant child's experiences.

Students can augment their writing classes by maintaining a response journal to record their thoughts and feelings about the books they read. They can note the countries of origin, the reason for moving to another country, how the families adapt to the new countries, and how things are different or the same in the new countries. The writing classes can also implement a creative element where students create a How to or an explorers list in which they offer suggestions for helping immigrant peers to adjust to life in the United States or another country. Letter writing as in *Extra Credit* (Clements, 2009), is another component that can be enhanced as students write letters welcoming immigrant children to their country, town, or classroom.

Children in the United States can quickly identify with visits to the library at their schools. *Alia's Mission: Saving the Books of Iraq* (Stamaty, 2004) and *The Librarian of Basra: A True Story from Iraq* (Winter, 2005) are two stories that can be used to solicit student responses. Students can create lists of their favorite books and generate detailed plans for how they would save the books in their school library or media center from an impending disaster. This can be augmented by having students conduct a book drive to collect books to donate to students in places that have experienced some form of disaster.

Mathematics Activities

Mathematics can easily be integrated into the curriculum as many of the stories highlight examples of measurement and distance. *Four Feet, Two Sandals* (Williams,

2007); *Children of War: Voices of Iraqi Refugees* (Ellis, 2009); and *Mohammed's Journey: A Refugee Diary* (Robinson & Young, 2009) are three stories that describe families who become refugees as they travel from their homelands to refugee camps in other regions or countries before being granted asylum by a host country like the United States or Canada. Students can track and add the distance these refugees traveled, often on foot and with very little possessions, to determine total mileage. Students can also research the contributions of Middle Easterners to the field of mathematics, especially in the development of algebra.

Science Activities

The people and regions of the Middle East are very diverse. Students can learn about the weather, plants, animals, and people in the different regions. In *Waiting for the Owl's Call* (Whelan, 2009), Zulviya weaves beautiful pictures in her mind about her loving surrounding. Students can learn about the animals that are native to the region. They can research the types of native plants and how they grow. In *Mohammed's Journey: A Refugee Diary* (Robinson & Young, 2009), Mohammed and his mother travel through dangerous conditions to get to safety. Students can research the climate of the different regions and how families traveling could be affected by the different weather conditions. Students can also research the contributions of Middle Easterners to the field of science, especially Ibn al-Haytham the noted Arab astronomer and mathematician.

Social Studies Activities

Topics normally covered in social studies can be easily integrated across various subject areas in studying the Middle East. Students can read about the region's various cultures, agriculture, architecture, and history. *Waiting for the Owl's Call* (Whelan, 2009) describes a family of weavers who create many of the rugs sold around the world. Students can learn about weaving, the materials used to create rugs, and how young children like themselves are being encouraged to go to school instead of sitting at a weaver's loom all day.

Students can learn about the different customs associated with different groups and regions of the Middle East. *The White Nights of Ramadan* (Addasi, 2008) describes the celebration of *Girgian*, and *Celebrate Ramadan & Eid al-Fitr* (Heiligman, 2006) describes the *Eid al-Fitr* holiday. Both are very important holidays Muslims celebrate during the month of Ramadan. Students can research the different customs and identify which holidays are celebrated by the different Muslim groups. They can compare and contrast the customs of different regions. The overall Social Studies curriculum can be augmented by learning about the specific regions in the Middle East where Arabs historically live and by incorporating a deeper focus on the different ethnicities and cultural mores of the region. Students can also research the contributions of Middle Eastern historians.

Art Activities

The arts normally represent a universal language which people around the world can understand. We are usually drawn to cultural expressions as we express our love of literature, song, and dance. Students can research the contributions of Middle Eastern cultures and incorporate some of these in their art and music curricula. In *Waiting for the Owl's Call* (Whelan, 2009), Zulviya describes the vivid colors of her homeland and weaves them into an imaginary pattern in her mind. Students can imitate the art of weaving in their art classes using various media like construction paper strips and colored yarn.

Ali, in *Silent Music: A Story of Baghdad* (Rumford, 2008), loves to practice calligraphy, the ancient art of drawing letters. Students can research the history of calligraphy and learn more about Yakut, the master calligrapher of Bagdad who lived in the thirteenth century. In *The White Nights of Ramadan* (Addasi, 2008), Noor helps her brothers to decorate their candy bags with bright paints and ribbons in anticipation of the Girgian celebration. Younger students often decorate paper bags in preparation for their class Halloween or holiday party. They can incorporate some of the art patterns they learn about in their research. Students can conduct extensive research about the art and artists of the Middle East.

CONCLUSION

Delving into the literature about Middle East cultures has piqued my interests as a teacher and emphasizes how much we need to learn about the greater world outside our immediate environment. The changing cultural composition of the United States also dictates that we should gain these insights. Castaneda (2004) presented that according to the 2000 U. S. census, the "racial, ethnic, and cultural composition" of the United States is dramatically changing to a multicultural society (p. 11). As teachers we have to facilitate our students' learning as we help them to understand the ways and mores of the cultures they explore (Louie, 2006). We have to provide authentic experiences for them and scaffold the learning to ensure optimal learning and engagement occurs. We must build on their experiences, knowledge, language, history, and culture in order to provide rich learning and engaged learning activities (Sipe & Daley, 2005, p. 238; Taylor, 2004, p. 43). White (2008) proposed that teachers need to imbed issues of social justice in their curriculum to effectively address the various social groups in their classrooms. This can be effectively done through the integration of children's literature.

Multicultural literature is not a panacea for cultural awareness, but its incorporation in schools' curricula is intended to expose students and their peers to the vast world outside their lived experiences. Schools are not equipped to cure all the ills of our global community; however, it is the space where children of various cultures will meet on a regular basis. Teachers must then be prepared to help students think in critical ways as they navigate their journey toward a discovery of learning. As we march on boldly into the twenty-first century, we are cognizant that the world we are experiencing today is not the world experienced by our fore parents and that it will be different for those who will follow in our footsteps. We must learn to understand others so that we will be better able to live peaceably together.

While many cultural groups are energized to see their cultures represented in children's literature, readers should be encouraged to engage in critical discussions and analyses of these representations. The literature can be explored from a critical sociological perspective (Lowery, 2000), enabling us to better understand ourselves and the greater world outside us. The changing demographics of the United States of America ascertain the need for us to learn about others. Positive representation of diverse groups in literature help to stifle continued negative stereotypes of others and like many of the characters discussed in this chapter, we can begin the road to healing.

Teachers can learn about appropriate books to use in their classrooms by developing a support network. These support groups could consist of other teachers who are already implementing multicultural children's literature in their classrooms, school media specialists, and local children's librarians who can be great sources of information. Support groups can help in the discussion of controversial issues, thus offering needed insights for these teachers. Members can share their experiences and offer viable ideas on how to approach particular topics.

REFERENCES

Al-Hazzá, T. C. (2006). Arab children's literature: An update. *Book Links, 15*(3), 11–12.

Al-Hazzá, T. C., & Bucher, K. T. (2008a). *Books about the Middle East: Selecting and using them with children and adolescents.* Columbus, OH: Linwood.

Al-Hazzá, T. C., & Bucher, K. T. (2008b). Building Arab Americans' cultural identity and acceptance with children's literature. *The Reading Teacher, 62,* 210–219.

Al-Hazzá, T. & Lucking, B. (2007). Celebrating diversity through explorations of Arab children's literature. *Childhood Education, 83,* 132–135.

Alfred, M. V. (2001/2002). Immigrants in America: Who are they, and why do they come? *Adult Learning, 4*(13), 1–5.

Banks, J. A. (2009). *Teaching strategies for ethnic studies* (8th ed.). Boston, MA: Pearson.

Bishop, R. S. (2000). Why literature? *The New Advocate, 13*(1), 73–76.

Boosahda, E. (2003). *Arab-American faces and voices: The origins of an immigrant community.* Austin, TX: University of Texas Press.

Castaneda, C. R. (2004). *Teaching and learning in diverse classrooms: Faculty reflections on their experiences and pedagogical practices of teaching diverse populations.* New York, NY: Routledge Falmer.

Exposito, S., & Favela, A. (2003). Reflective voices: Valuing immigrant students and teaching with ideological clarity. *The Urban Review, 35*(1), 73–91.

Gay, G. (2000). *Culturally responsive teaching: Theory, research and practice.* New York, NY: Teachers College Press.

Hafiz, D., Hafiz, Y., & Hafiz, I. (2009). *The American Muslim teenager's handbook.* New York, NY: Atheneum.

Harris, V. J. (1999). Applying critical theories to children's literature. *Theory into Practice, 38,* 147–154.

Hefflin, B.R. & Barksdale-Ladd, M.A. (2001). African American children's literature that helps students find themselves: Selection guidelines for grades k-3. *The Reading Teacher, 54,* 810–819.

Henderson, N. J. (2008). *Policing in Arab-American communities after September 11.* (Washington, DC): U.S. Dept. of Justice, Office of Justice Programs, National Institute of Justice. http://www.ncjrs.gov/pdffiles1/nij/221706.pdf.

Hoobler, D., & Hoobler, T. (2003). *We Are Americans: Voices of the immigrant experience.* New York, NY: Scholastic

Isaacs, K. T. (2007). New in America. *Book Links, 16*(3), 26–31.

Johnson, L., & Smith, S. (1993). *Dealing with diversity through multicultural fiction: Library to classroom partnership.* Chicago, IL: American Library Association.

Kayyali, R. A. (2006). *The Arab Americans*. Westport, CN: Greenwood Press.

Kirova, A., & Emme, M. (2006). Immigrant children's understandings of nonverbal peer interactions through the development of visual narratives. In L. D. Adams & A. Kirova (Eds.), *Global migration and education: Schools, children, and families* (pp. 151–168). Mahwah, NJ: Lawrence Erlbaum.

Koppelman, K. L., & Goodhart, R. L. (2005). *Understanding human differences: Multicultural education for a diverse America*. Boston, MA: Pearson.

Ladson-Billings, G. (1994). *The dreamkeepers: Successful teachers of African American children*. San Francisco, CA: Jossey-Bass.

Lehman, B. A. (2007). *Children's literature and learning: Literary study across the curriculum*. New York, NY: Teachers College Press.

Lems, K. (1999). The Arab world and Arab Americans. *Book Links*, 9(2), 31–39.

Lindquist, T., & Selwyn, D. (2000). *Social studies at the center: Integrating kids, content, and literacy*. Portsmouth, NH: Heinemann.

Louie, B.Y. (2006). Guiding principles for teaching multicultural literature. *The Reading Teacher*, 59, 438–448.

Lowery, R. M. (2000). *Immigrants in children's literature*. New York, NY: Peter Lang.

Marston, E. (2004). A window in the wall: Palestinians in children's literature. *The Horn Book Magazine*, 647–655.

Middle East Resources. (2000). Center for Middle Eastern Studies. Cambridge, MA: Harvard University.

Naff, A. (1988). *The Arab Americans*. New York, NY: Chelsea House.

Neuharth-Pritchett, S., Payne, B. D. & Reiff, J. C. (2004). *Perspectives on elementary education: A casebook for critically analyzing issues of diversity*. Boston, MA: Pearson.

Rosenblatt, L. M. (1994). *The reader, the text, the poem: The transactional theory of the literary work*. Carbondale, IL: Southern Illinois University Press.

Sipe, R. L. & Daley, P. A. (2005). Story-reading, story-making, story-telling: Urban African American kindergartners respond to culturally relevant picture books. In D. L. Henderson & J. P. May (Eds.), *Exploring culturally diverse literature for children and adolescents: Learning to listen in new ways* (pp. 229–242). Boston, MA: Pearson.

Spiegel, D. L. (1998). Reader response approaches and the growth of readers. *Language Arts*, 76, 41–48.

Tanners, L. (1997). Immigrant students in New York City schools. *Urban Education*, 32, 233–255.

Taylor, J. A. (2004). Teaching children who have immigrated: The new legislation, research and trends in immigration which affect teachers of diverse student populations. *Multicultural Education*, 11(3) 43–44.

Welch, M. (2006). *Scapegoats of September 11th: Hate crimes & state crimes in the war on terror*. New Brunswick, NJ: Rutgers University Press.

White, J. (2008). Teachers prepare to integrate social justice into the social studies curriculum. *The Social Studies*, 99, 83–84.

Yokota, J. (1993). Issues on selecting multicultural children's literature. *Language Arts*, 70, 156– 167.

MULTICULTURAL BOOKS

Addasi, M. (2008). *The white nights of Ramadan*, illustrated by N. Gannon. Honesdale, PA: Boyds Mills Press.

Budhos, M. (2006). *Ask me no questions*. New York, NY: Atheneum.

Bunting, E. (2006). *One green apple*, illustrated by T. Lewin. New York, NY: Clarion.

Clements, A. (2009). *Extra credit*, illustrated by M. Elliott. New York, NY: Atheneum.

Ellis, D. (2009). *Children of war: Voices of Iraqi refugees*. Toronto, ON: Groundwood.

Heide, F. P., & Gilliland, J. H. (1992). *Sami and the time of the troubles*, illustrated by T. Lewin. New York, NY: Clarion.

Heiligman, D. (2006). *Celebrate Ramadan & Eid Al-fitr*, consultant N. Yavari. Washington, DC: National Geographic.

Hoyt-Goldsmith, D. (2002). *Celebrating Ramadan*, photographs by L. Migdale. New York, NY: Holiday House.

Howard, H. (2006). *Living as a refugee in America: Mohammed's story*. Milwaukee, WI: World Almanac Library.

Khan, R. (2009). *Wanting mor*. Berkeley, CA: Groundwood.

Mobin-Uddin, A. (2005). *My name is Bilal*, illustrated by B. Kiwak. Honesdale, PA: Boyds Mills Press.

Mobin-Uddin, A. (2007). *The best Eid ever*, illustrated by L. Jacobsen. Honesdale, PA: Boyds Mills Press.

Mobin-Uddin, A. (2009). *A party in Ramadan*, illustrated by L. Jacobsen. Honesdale, PA: Boyds Mills Press.

Nye, N. S. (1997). *Sitti's secrets*, illustrated by N. Carpenter. New York, NY: Aladdin.

Robinson, A., & Young, A. (2009). *Mohammed's journey: A refugee diary*, illustrated by J.Allan. New York, NY: Frances Lincoln.

Rumford, J. (2008). *Silent music: A story of Baghdad*. New York, NY: Roaring Brook Press.

Stamaty, M. A. (2004). *Alia's mission: Saving the books of Iraq*. New York, NY: Alfred A. Knopf.

Whelan, G. (2009). *Waiting for the owl's call*, illustrated by P. Milelli. Chelsea, MI: Sleeping Bear Press.

Williams, K. L., & Mohammed, K. (2007). *Four feet, two sandals*, illustrated by D. Grand Rapids, MI: Eerdmans Books.

Winter, J. (2005). *The librarian of Basra: A true story from Iraq*. Orlando, FL: Harcourt

Winter, J. (2009). *Nasreen's secret school: A true story from Afghanistan*. New York, NY: Beach Lane.

Wolf, B. (2003). *Coming to America: A Muslim family's story*. New York, NY: Lee & Low.

Wrigley-Field, E., & Ross, J. (Eds.). (2009). *IraqiGirl: Diary of a teenage girl in Iraq*. Chicago, IL: Haymarket Books.

Zenatti, V. (2008). *A bottle in the Gaza Sea*, translated by A. Hunter. New York, NY: Bloomsbury.

11

Supporting English Language Learners' Literacy Development with Culturally Relevant Books

Nancy L. Hadaway and Terrell A. Young

In Chapter 1, Smolen and Oswald offer support for multicultural literature as a tool for educational reform and for creating equity and helping diverse groups achieve academically (Banks & Banks, 2001; Cai, 1998). Examining today's schools, one finds that English learners represent a particularly important diverse group as they are the fastest growing student population in the United States by a wide margin. From 1991 to 2002, the number of K–12 English learners increased 95 percent, while total enrollment increased only 12 percent (Padolsky, 2004). Current data from the National Center for Education Statistics (2008) reveal that 20 percent of school-age children speak a language other than English at home.

Yet, what underscores the importance of equity for this rapidly growing group of children in our schools is the persistent academic achievement gap when they are compared with their native English speaking peers. An analysis of data from 41 states reveals that only 18.7 percent of English learners met state norms for reading in English (Kindler, 2002). Further, language minority students have higher dropout rates, are more frequently placed in lower ability groups than their native English speaking peers, and are disproportionately clustered in segregated, high-poverty, and conflict-ridden schools (Orfield & Yun, 1999; Suarez-Orozco & Suarez-Orozco, 2001). While English learners come to school with positive social attitudes toward schooling, authority figures, and the future, they often face negative social mirroring that adversely affects their developing identities (Suarez-Orozco & Suarez-Orozco, 2001).

Central to addressing the needs of English learners is coherent, culturally sensitive curriculum and instruction. Research has identified several key factors that promote the academic success of English learners including:

- a positive school environment (Au, 2006; Battistich, Solomon, Watson, & Schaps, 1997; Berman, Minicucci, McLaughlin, Nelson, & Woodworth, 1995);

- meaningful and academically challenging curriculum (Berman et al., 1995; Doherty, Hilberg, Pinal, & Tharp, 2003);
- thematically integrated instruction (Freeman & Freeman, 2006);
- the use of research based best practices (Montecel & Cortéz, 2002);
- an enriched instructional model rather than a remedial one (Montecel & Cortez, 2002); and
- instruction based on theories of second language development (Au, 2006; Berman et al., 1995).

One example of research based instruction is the use of multicultural or culturally relevant literature. Teachers find that English learners' achievement is often greater when they are reading stories and books that are familiar or culturally relevant (Abu-Rabia, 1998; Goldenberg, Rueda, & August, 2008; Kenner, 2000). Indeed, "several studies converge in suggesting that language-minority students' reading comprehension performance improves when they read culturally familiar materials" (Hampton & Resnick, 2009, p. 13). Thus, the premise of this chapter is to encourage the use of culturally relevant children's literature as an integral part of instruction and curriculum with English learners.

LANGUAGE AS A FACTOR IN LITERATURE SELECTION CRITERIA

The multicultural nature of today's schools calls for literature that speaks to diverse cultures, and language is an integral part of any culture. In Chapter 1, Smolen and Oswald cite criteria for the selection of quality multicultural literature from Temple, Martinez, and Yokota (2006). These are excellent considerations, but additional concerns arise when choosing books for English learners. From refugees, immigrants, asylum seekers, and sojourners who move back and forth across borders to children who were born in the United States or who have lived here the majority of their lives, English learners are an incredibly diverse group. Other than the label, English learner, and the shared challenge of learning a new language, these students may have very little in common. They differ in the languages they speak and their cultural backgrounds, the socioeconomic status they hold, the level of fluency in their home language and English, their prior schooling and home literacy experiences, and their immigration or residency status.

The first step in creating a supportive learning environment is for teachers and teacher librarians to understand the individual. Positive learning environments acknowledge and affirm the learner's home language and culture, capitalize on the powerful social network of family and community, and help learners believe that there is a substantive payoff in working through the lengthy process of language acquisition from basic social communication through more developed academic language (Hadaway & Young, 2010). In such an atmosphere, learners can forge a new transcultural identity fusing the best of both worlds and avoiding the feeling that they must either abandon their language and culture (ethnic flight) or reject English and American culture (adversarial identity; Suarez-Orozco & Suarez-Orozco, 2001).

Clearly, in order to affirm the language and culture of English learners, we need bilingual and interlingual books and books that feature English learners and their backgrounds and concerns. As part of the literature selection process, the following factors should be considered.

- Does the text reflect the language, background, and experiences of recent immigrants or U.S. born English learners? Similarities and differences exist between these groups based on time in the United States and exposure to English and American culture.

- Is language used authentically? The use of other languages or dialects should show a respect for the cultural and linguistic background. Just as there is a cultural conglomerate notion (Yokota, 1993), there is a similar impression about language. We have the idea that there is one Spanish. Yet, there is language variation among different Spanish speakers (Spaniards, South Americans, Cubans/ Cuban Americans, Mexicans/ Mexican Americans, Puerto Ricans/ Puerto Rican Americans, etc.).
- In the case of interlingual or embedded language in a book, is the other language naturally integrated into the English text? Words and phrases from other languages should be used at meaningful junctures so that the text flows.
- When other languages are interspersed in English text, does the author provide a notation in the text or a glossary of terms? Defining terms in English helps all students, not just English learners or students who speak the language highlighted in the book, appreciate language diversity.
- In the case of bilingual or translated books, is the translation accurate and natural? Translations may be plagued by literal renditions that lack the flow of the native language as well as by incorrect lexical constructions, unclear phrases, awkward expressions and grammatical, spelling, and/or typographical errors (Schon, 2004).
- In the case of bilingual works, is one language given precedence over the other? For instance, the presentation on the page may give one language higher status through the order of appearance as well as differences in font size, boldness, or spacing between lines, difference in type quality between the scripts such as a non-Roman versus Roman alphabet, and differences in directionality, for example, English is read from left to right, Urdu is read from right to left (Multilingual Resources for Children Project, 1995; Walker, Edwards, & Blacksell, 1996).
- Is the selection of books for English learners balanced in terms of languages? Even though Spanish is the predominant language background of U.S. English learners, it is important to present children with books that feature many languages.

Again, the quality and accuracy of the literature and language use is a prime consideration, but when working with English learners, educators must also consider the different language proficiency levels of English learners. We want to choose familiar and culturally relevant books with rich cultural detail, but the literature selected must also be accessible to the English learner. Text selections that are beyond English learners' proficiency level will only frustrate them and negate the purpose of multicultural literature. In the tables in the chapter, we have coded the books according to two categories, proficiency level and grade level as indicated.

Proficiency level indicated by B, D, A, often more than one proficiency level is indicated.

- B = Beginning (Non-English-speaking to limited English)
- D = Developing (Basic English skills)
- A = Advanced (Developed English but some areas of difficulty continue)
- **Grade Level**
- P = Primary Grades K–2
- I = Intermediate Grades 3–5
- M = Middle Grades 6–8

We chose this system because grade level reading indications alone are not always helpful or accurate when working with English learners. Among English learners, we have beginning readers at every grade level. This coding scheme is merely an approximation depending on the objective of the lesson and the amount of support provided by educators.

While culturally explicit detail may be the ultimate goal for cultural relevance (Bishop, 1992), culturally specific books about unfamiliar cultures and topics may be difficult for English learners due to the vocabulary and background knowledge needed for comprehension. Books with specific cultural detail about religious and cultural celebrations (*Sawdust Carpets*, Carling, 2005; *The Best Eid Ever*, Mobin-Uddin, 2007); historical issues (Japanese internment camps in *A Place Where Sunflowers Grow*, Lee-Tai, 2006 and the bonfire signal system in *The Firekeeper's Son*, Park, 2004); and art forms (wood carving in *Julio's Magic*, Dorros, 2005; floor art in *Romina's Rangoli*, Iyengar, 2007; Japanese picture storytelling in *Kamishibai Man*, Say, 2005) may be challenging to English learners in the early stages of language acquisition, while books with universal themes and topics are more likely to provide a general cultural fit and be more accessible. For instance, themes of identity, family, acceptance, and cultural herit-age are familiar across cultures and may have a natural relevance for English learners. While specific elements of culture such as Korean mask dancing in *Behind the Mask* (Choi, 2006) and salsa music in Oye, *Celia!: A Song for Celia Cruz* (Sciurba, 2007) may be unfamiliar to some students, the overall themes of family life and pride in one's background and heritage are understandable. Simple concept books that explore the alphabet, counting, or colors such as *Just a Minute: A Trickster Tale and Counting Book* (Morales, 2003); *Ten Mice for Tet* (Shea & Weill, 2003); and *Spicy Hot Colors/Colores picantes* (Shahan, 2004) may be the most accessible for beginning English learners.

Bilingual Books and Language Themes

Language is a critical part of the identity of English learners. In the United States to-day, over 400 languages are spoken with Spanish the predominant language of 80 per-cent of English learners (Kindler, 2002). Among other English learners, 2 percent speak Vietnamese; 1.6 percent speak Hmong; 1 percent speak Cantonese; 1 percent speak Korean followed by Haitian Creole, Arabic, Russian, Tagalog, Navajo, Khmer, Mandarin, Portuguese, Urdu, Serbo-Croatian, Lao, and Japanese. Consequently, the task of creating a balanced literature collection for English learners is challenging.

The recent statistics do not tell the whole story, however. Language diversity has long been a part of life in America. However, the issue is more far-reaching than differ-ent languages alone. Related concerns include language learning and acquisition, language maintenance and language loss, language discrimination, bilingualism, and language adjustment. Early immigrants worked to maintain their home language and supported legislation mandating bilingual education in Swedish, Danish, Norwegian, Italian, Polish, Dutch, and Greek. After the swell of immigration from 1890–1920, restrictive national immigration quotas were enacted and many states passed laws for-bidding foreign languages in schools (Crawford, 1999). Students were often punished for using their home language as illustrated in the nonfiction picture book *Harvesting Hope: The Story of Cesar Chavez* (Krull, 2003).

During this same time, Native Americans were often encouraged or forced to send their children to government-run boarding schools, so they could "unlearn their Indian ways." At school, the children were forbidden to speak their native languages, situa-tions poignantly described in *Bright Path: Young Jim Thorpe* (Brown, 2006); *Home to Medicine Mountain* (Santiago, 1998); and *Shin-chi's Canoe* (Campbell, 2008).

After World War II, the launch of Sputnik brought a renewal of interest in foreign language instruction, and in 1965, the Bilingual Education Act was signed into law to assist growing numbers of non-English-speaking schoolchildren. These events spurred an increase in the number of bilingual books published for children. Currently, bilingual books are published in a variety of formats (Ernst-Slavit & Mulhern, 2003). Perhaps the format that is most commonly associated with bilingual books is the full text bilingual book with the complete text in two languages such as Carmen Lomas Garza's *In My Family/En mi familia* (1996) and Jorge Argueta's *Sopa de frijoles/Bean Soup* (2009). Table 11.1 is a compilation of some additional full text bilingual titles. While the majority of these examples are English/Spanish, many other languages are emerging in children's literature.

Table 11.1.
Full Text Bilingual Books

Book/Genre	Non-English Language	Proficiency Levels	Grades
Samira's Eid (Aktar, 2000), Fiction picture book	Arabic	D	P,I
The Swirling Hijaab (Robert, 2002), Fiction picture book	Arabic	B,D	P,I
Sequoyah: The Cherokee Man Who Gave His People Writing (Rumford, 2004), Nonfiction picture book	Cherokee	D,A	I,M
Mouse Match: A Chinese Folktale (Young, 1997)	Chinese	D,A	I,M
Niwechihaw, I Help (Nicholson, 2008), Fiction picture book	Cree	B	P,I
An Aboriginal Carol (Bouchard, 2008), Nonfiction picture song book	Inuktitut	D,A	I,M
Alego (Teevee, 2009), Fiction picture book	Inuktitut	B,D	P,I
A Place Where Sunflowers Grow (Lee-Tai, 2006), Fiction picture book	Japanese	D,A	I,M
The Magic Pocket: Selected Poems (Mado, 1998), Poetry	Japanese	B,D	P,I,M
The Tale of the Lucky Cat (Seki, 2007), Fiction picture folktale book	Japanese	B,D	P,I
Cooper's Lesson (Shin, 2004), Fiction picture book	Korean	D,A	P,I
A Gift for Abuelita: Celebrating the Day of the Dead/Un regalo para abuelita: En celebración del Día de los Muertos (Luenn, 1998), Fiction picture book	Spanish	D,A	I,M
A Movie in My Pillow/Una película en mi almohada (Argueta, 2001), Poetry	Spanish	B,D	P,I,M
Angels Ride Bikes and Other Fall Poems/Los ángeles andan en bicicleta: Y otros poemas de otoño (Alarcón, 1999), Poetry	Spanish	B,D	P,I,M

(*continued*)

Table 11.1. (continued)

Book/Genre	Non-English Language	Proficiency Levels	Grades
Animal Poems of the Iguazú/Animalario del Iguazú (Alarcón, 2008), Poetry	Spanish	D,A	I,M
Book Fiesta! Celebrate Children's Day/Book Day/ Celebremos El Día de los Niños/El Día de los Libros (Mora, 2009), Fiction picture book	Spanish	B,D	P,I
Calling the Doves/El canto de las palomas (Herrera, 2001), Nonfiction picture book memoir	Spanish	B,D	P,I
Colors! ¡Colores! (Lujan, 2008), Poetry	Spanish	B,D	P,I,M
Counting Ovejas (Weeks, 2006), Fiction picture (counting) book	Spanish	B	P
Family Pictures/Cuadros de familia (Garza, 2005), Nonfiction picture book	Spanish	B,D	P,I,M
Fiestas: A Year of Latin American Songs of Celebration (Orozco, 2002), Nonfiction song picture book	Spanish	B,D	P,I,M
From the Bellybutton of the Moon: And Other Summer Poems/Del ombligo de la luna: Y otros poemas de verano (Alarcón, 1998), Poetry	Spanish	B,D	P,I,M
Gracias/ Thanks (Mora, 2009), Fiction picture book	Spanish	B,D	P,I
Iguanas in the Snow: And Other Winter Poems/ Iguanas en la nieve: Y otros poemas de invierno (Alarcón, 2005), Poetry	Spanish	B,D	P,I,M
I Know the River Loves Me/Yo sé que el río me ama (Gonzalez, 2009), Fiction picture book	Spanish	B	P
In My Family/En mi familia (Garza, 1996), Nonfiction picture book	Spanish	B,D	P,I,M
Laughing Out Loud, I Fly: A carcajadas yo vuelo (Herrera, 1998), Poetry	Spanish	D,A	I,M
Laughing Tomatoes and Other Spring Poems/ Jitomates risueños: Y otros poemas de primavera (Alarcón, 1997), Poetry	Spanish	B,D	P,I,M
My Mexico/México mío (Johnston, 1996), Poetry	Spanish	B,D	P,I
Sopa de frijoles/Bean Soup (Argueta, 2009), Poetry	Spanish	B,D	P,I
Spicy Hot Colors/Colores picantes (Shahan, 2004), Nonfiction picture concept book	Spanish	B,D	P,I
The Tree Is Older Than You Are: A Bilingual Gathering of Poems & Stories from Mexico (Nye, 1995), Poetry	Spanish	D,A	I,M
Lakas and the Makibaka Hotel/ Si Lakas at Ang Makibaka Hotel (Robles, 2006), Fiction picture book	Tagalog	D,A	I,M

Table 11.2.

Bilingual Books—Different Language Versions

Book/Genre	Proficiency Level	Grade Level
Confetti: Poems for Children (Mora, 1998); *Confeti: Poemas para niños* [Spanish translation by Queta Fernandez & Pat Mora published in 2006], Poetry	B,I	P,I,M
Harvesting Hope: The Story of Cesar Chavez (Krull, 2003); *Cosechando esperanza: La historia de César Chávez* [Spanish translation by Alma Flor Ada & F. Isabel Campoy published in 2003], Nonfiction picture book biography	B,I	I
The Pot that Juan Built (Andrews-Goebel, 2002); *La vasija que Juan fabricó* [Spanish translation by Eunice Cortés published in 2004], Nonfiction picture book biography	I,A	I
Salsa Stories (Delacre, 2000); *Cuentos con sazón* [Spanish translation by Susana Pasternac published in 2001], Fiction short stories	I,A	M
Tomás and the Library Lady (Mora, 1997); *Tomás y la señora de la biblioteca* [Spanish translation by Pat Mora published in 1997], Fiction picture book	I,A	I,M

In addition to full text bilingual books, there are bilingual books published in different versions, one book for each language, for example, Pat Mora's *Tomás and the Library Lady* (1997) and *Tomás y la señora de la biblioteca*. The books in Table 11.2 were published first in the United States as interlingual bilingual books in English with embedded Spanish terms and phrases and then as complete Spanish version texts. Many popular books such as the Magic School Bus series and Clifford the Big Red Dog books have been translated into other languages. Finally, in addition to bilingual books published in the United States, many other books are first published outside the United States in another language and then brought to the United States in translated format. The annual Outstanding International Booklist, a project of the United States Board on Books for Young People, is an excellent resource for such works.

The most common type of bilingual book is the interlingual book with the majority of text in English and interspersed with words and phrases from another language. Just a few examples of recent interlingual children's books include the following. *I Am Latino: The Beauty in Me* (Pinkney & Pinkney, 2007) is a simple presentation of five senses, "listen/ to the melody of my language/ Buenos días (Good morning)." In *My Father's Shop* (Ichikawa, 2006), a noisy rooster follows a young boy into the marketplace in Morocco, and tourists from other countries begin to share how a rooster crows in their languages. Finally, In *What Should I Make?* (Nayar, 2009), readers learn about Indian flatbread as they are introduced to a few words in Hindi.

An analysis of the first ten years, 1996–2005, of the Notable Books for a Global Society, Pla K–12 Booklist reflects the growing number of bilingual books being published (Hadaway & Young, 2007) as there were six bilingual books with complete text in both English and Spanish, four bilingual books with separate versions in English and

Spanish, and 56 interlingual text books, for 25 percent of the total books selected over 10 years. The interlingual books reflected tremendous language diversity with 27 different languages; some books used more than one language other than English. Spanish was the most predominant language, but other languages included Amharic, Arabic, Chamoru, Chinese, Farsi/Dari, French, German, Hebrew, Hindi, Japanese, Korean, Maasia, Polish, Sanskit, Spanish, Swedish, Tamil, Vietnamese, Yiddish, and seven Native American languages, Abenaki, Ojibwa, Quiche, Athabascan, Lakota, Kwakwala, Iñupiaq. Table 11.3 provides a list of suggested interlingual books.

Certainly, bilingual books can be a reflection of the linguistic diversity of the classroom. All students need to see representations of themselves and their cultures in literature. "If children never see themselves in books, they receive the subtle message that they are not important enough to appear in books and that books are not for them" (Galda, Cullinan, & Sipe, 2010, p. 43). Moreover, bilingual books support children's English acquisition by connecting the new language to the more familiar home language. Children who are already literate in the first language don't need to learn to read in another language, but they need exposure to their new language in meaningful formats, ones that affirm their cultural background and encourage language maintenance not just a transition to English only.

"Conversely, if children see only themselves in the books they read, the message is that those who are different from them are not worthy of appearing in books" (Galda, Cullinan, & Sipe, 2010, p. 43). Bilingual books are not just for the culturally and linguistically diverse student. All children need opportunities to see the diversity of languages in the United States and how they differ from English. For example, readers learn several Japanese terms and some interesting characteristics of writing in Japanese in *Yoko Writes Her Name* (Wells, 2008).

Finally, it is important to acknowledge the many languages around the world that exist in spoken form only and the work of individuals who keep languages alive by creating a written form of the spoken words of a group. Crawford (1999) highlights the critical nature of language loss in Native American communities, noting "one-third of indigenous tongues have disappeared since the coming of Columbus" and cautioning that "virtually all Native American languages could be extinct within two or three generations" (not paginated). The publication of *Sequoyah* (Rumford, 2004) was especially timely then. Sequoyah was responsible for creating the Cherokee syllabary, thus, giving that language a written form. This bilingual biography in English/Cherokee tells the story of Sequoyah and how his work allowed the printing of materials in Cherokee, as a result, insuring the survival of that language. Over the last few years, it has been heartening to see several bilingual books in English and Native American languages including *Alego* (Teevee, 2009); *The Huron Carol* (Wallace, 2006); *The Delta Is My Home* (McLeod & Willett, 2008); and *We Feel Good out Here* (Andre & Willett, 2008).

ENGLISH LEARNERS IN LITERATURE

English learners need not only to see their language represented in books but also to glimpse individuals, similar to them, actively engaged in the midst of the language learning process. For English learners, there is much that is positive about seeing themselves reflected in stories in the classroom, but it is important to avoid books that may trivialize the transitions involved in learning a new language. Table 11.4 is a list of books that features English learners. A brief discussion of some common themes captured in these books follows.

Table 11.3.

Bilingual Books—Interlingual Text

Book/Genre	Non-English Language	Proficiency Levels	Grade Level
Faraway Home (Kurtz, 2000)	Amharic	B,D	P,I
The Storyteller's Beads (Kurtz, 1998)	Amharic	D,A	I,M
Celebrating Ramadan (Hoyt-Goldsmith, 2001)	Arabic	D,A	I,M
The Year of Miss Agnes (Hill, 2000)	Athabascan	D,A	I,M
Chu Ju's House (Whelan, 2004)	Chinese	A	M
Maples in the Mist: Poems for Children from the Tang Dynasty (Ho, 1996)	Chinese	D,A	I,M
Voices of the Heart (Young, 1997)	Chinese	D,A	I,M
Parvana's Journey (Ellis, 2002)	Farsi, Dari	A	M
Naming Maya (Krishnaswami, 2004)	Hindi	A	M
The Huron Carol (Wallace, 2006)	Huron, French	D,A	I,M
Whale Snow (Edwardson, 2003)	Iñupiaq	D,A	P,I
Grass Sandals: The Travels of Basho (Spivak, 1996)	Japanese	D,A	I,M
Tea with Milk (Say, 1999)	Japanese	D,A	P,I
The Trip Back Home (Wong, 2000)	Korean	B,D	P,I
Capoeira: Game! Dance! Martial Art! (Ancona, 2007)	Portuguese	D,A	I,M
Tree Girl (Mikaelsen, 2004)	Quiche, Spanish	A	M
El Barrio (Chocolate, 2009)	Spanish	B,D	P,I
Any Small Goodness: A Novel of the Barrio (Johnston, 2001)	Spanish	A	M
The Barking Mouse (Sacre, 2003)	Spanish	B,D	P,I
César: ¡Sí, se puede!/Yes, We Can! (Bernier-Grand, 2004)	Spanish	D,A	I,M
The Color of My Words (Joseph (2000)	Spanish	A	M
Esperanza Rising (Ryan, 2000)	Spanish	A	M
I Love Saturdays y domingos (Ada, 2002)	Spanish	B,D	P,I
Just a Minute: A Trickster Tale and Counting Book (Morales, 2003)	Spanish	B	P
Uncle Rain Cloud (Johnston, 2001)	Spanish	B,D	P,I
Cora Cooks Pancit (Lazo Gilmore, 2009)	Tagalog	B,D	P,I
Ten Mice for Tet (Shea & Weill, 2003)	Vietnamese	B,D	P,I

Individuals may feel mixed emotions about moving to a new country, going to a new school, and learning a new language. For instance, despite her parent's excitement, in *Good-Bye, 382 Shin Dang Dong* (Park & Park, 2002) Jangmi insists, "...I loved my home right here! I didn't want to go to America and make new friends" (n.p.).

Table 11.4.
Books about English Learners

Book/Genre	Themes	Cultural Background	Proficiency Levels	Grade Level
Good-bye, 382 Shin Dang Dong (Park & Park, 2002), Fiction	Immigration, adjustment to new country/language	Korean	B,D	P,I
Hannah Is My Name (Yang, 2004), Fiction	Residency status, adjustment to new country/language	Chinese	B,D	P,I
I Hate English (Levine, 1995), Fiction	Immigration, adjustment to new country/language	Chinese	B,D	P,I
I Love Saturdays y domingos (Ada, 2002), Fiction	Bicultural identity, language maintenance	Spanish	B,D	P,I
In English, Of Course (Nobisso, 2003), Fiction	Immigration, adjustment to new country/language	Italian	B,D	P,I
La mariposa (Jiménez, 1998), Fiction	Adjustment to new language in school	Spanish	B,D	P,I
Marianthe's Story/ Painted Words (Aliki, 1998), Fiction	Immigration, adjustment to new country/language	Unspecified	B,D	P,I
My Diary from Here to There (Pérez, 2002), Fiction	Immigration, adjustment to new country/language	Spanish	B,D	P,I
One Green Apple (Bunting, 2006), Fiction	Immigration, adjustment to new country/language	Arab	B,D	P,I
Papá and Me (Dorros, 2008), Fiction	Bicultural identity, language maintenance	Spanish	B,D	P,I
The Name Jar (Choi, 2001), Fiction	Americanization of names	Korean	B,D	P,I
The Upside Down Boy (Herrera, 2000), Nonfiction memoir	Adjustment to new language in school	Spanish	B,D	P,I
Tomás and the Library Lady (Mora, 1997), Fiction	Migrant life, bicultural identity, language maintenance	Spanish	B,D	P,I
Uncle Rain Cloud (Johnston, 2001), Fiction	Translating for adults, language maintenance	Spanish	B,D	P,I
My Name Is Sangoel (Williams & Mohammed, 2009), Fiction	Immigration, adjustment to new country/language, helps peers pronounce his name	Sudan	B,D	P,I
Home of the Brave (Applegate, 2007), Fiction	Immigration, adjustment to new country/language	Sudan	A	M
The Day of the Pelican (Paterson, 2009), Fiction	Refugees from Kosovo, adjustment to new country and language	Albanian	A	M

Meanwhile, in *My Diary From Here to There* (Pérez, 2002), Amada is anxious about her family's move from Mexico to Los Angeles, and she uses her diary to share her worries: "But what if we're not allowed to speak Spanish? What if I can't learn English?" (not paginated).

Language acquisition is a lengthy process and requires moving beyond basic social language toward the more specialized and academic language of school. Francisco in *La mariposa* (Jiménez, 1998) understands this challenge. He knows that caterpillars turn into butterflies, but how this happens is a mystery to him. Yet, Francisco recognizes that his school book holds the answer. "The words written underneath each picture in big black letters could tell him, he knew. So he tried to figure them out by looking at the pictures. But he still could not understand what they meant" (not paginated). This can be a confusing period as the learner sorts through a great deal of "noise" as described in *One Green Apple* (Bunting, 2006):

Our teacher gathers us around her. She talks to the class. Then she looks at me in a kind way. "One," she says. She touches an apple, then picks it. "One," she says again. I nod. I want to say, "I understand. It's not that I am stupid. It is just that I am lost in this new place." But I don't know how to tell her.

(p. 12)

Through books about language learning, English learners can see various strategies that others adopt such as a silent period just listening to the language as Mei Mei does in *I Hate English* (Levine, 1995). And, taking time to sort out and hear the sounds of a new language as shown in *Marianthe's Story/Painted Words/Spoken Memories* (Aliki, 1998, n.p.) "Every day Mari understood more and more. Misapeechi became Mr. Petrie. Waisha became Rachel, Kista became Kristin, Ahbe became Albert, and Patik became Patrick." Progress is slow but worthwhile as demonstrated in *The Day of the Pelican* (Paterson, 2009):

[Meli] didn't know for sure when the torrents of noise broke into sentences that actually made sense to her, but by her fourteenth birthday in June, English was no longer the headache-making racket it had been in September. Her ears had become accustomed to its strange sounds, and the new words began to feel far less clumsy in her mouth.

(pp. 114–115)

Along the way, English learners find creative means to communicate across language barriers. *Marianthe's Story: Painted Words/Spoken Memories* (Aliki, 1998) and *The Upside Down Boy* (Herrera, 2000), offer examples of communication through art. Though Mari is not able to speak English, she learns that art can transcend her language difficulties. As she explains to her mother, "I am drawing what I can't talk" (n.p.). Presenting a story through creative dramatics can also be an effective communication strategy as in *In English, Of Course* (Nobisso, 2003).

The adjustment process is filled with decisions for English learners, particularly those related to maintaining their heritage. Unhei (*The Name Jar*, Choi, 2001), for instance, initially considers adopting an Americanized name that would be easier for her peers at school to pronounce; while Na-Li (*Hannah Is My Name*, Yang, 2004) has already adopted a new name, Hannah. In *I Love Saturdays y domingos* (Ada, 2002), readers encounter a young girl who successfully navigates two language worlds, one with her paternal grandparents in English and the other with her maternal grandparents in Spanish. While in

Uncle Rain Cloud (Johnston, 2001), readers encounter a small glimpse of language maintenance as Uncle Tomás teaches nephew, Carlos, the stories of his ancestors, in the hopes of helping him hold onto his Spanish language heritage. Finally, in *My Diary From Here to There* (Pérez, 2002), Amada's grandmother tells her to "Keep your language and your culture alive in your diary and in your heart" (not paginated).

TEXT SETS FOR ENGLISH LEARNERS

Creating text sets is an excellent literacy support technique. Short and Harste with Burke (1996) describe text sets as collections of books that are conceptually related in some way such as a common theme or topic. The idea of text sets is most often used for students to read multiple texts to extend their understanding and to gain multiple perspectives (Lehman & Crook, 1998). With English learners, text sets may have books with different reading and content levels, which is ideal for the different language proficiencies of the students. Some English learners with more developed language proficiency may be able to read all the selections within a set, but others may only be able to access one book or a part of the set or may need support through paired reading or read aloud techniques. Such text collections are practical for the diverse conceptual and language backgrounds of English learners in a single classroom. This themed emphasis helps English learners encounter the same vocabulary and concepts multiple times. In the remainder of this section, we explore some possible themes for text sets targeted at English learners. Table 11.5 lists these themes with others and the associated books with notations as to the proficiency and grade level appropriateness.

Many English learners maintain close connections with family members in their country of origin or that of their parents, and several books depict visits with relatives and communicating across language barriers. In *Sitti's Secrets* (Nye, 1997), a young girl visits her grandmother, Sitti, in Palestine and in *The Trip Back Home* (Wong, 2000), a young girl goes with mother to visit family in Korea. In both of these books, the young girls speak only English, yet, they find ways to connect and communicate with their relatives. Visiting relatives in another country also means learning new customs as in *I Lost My Tooth in Africa* (Diakité, 2006). Amina visits her family in Mali, West Africa. While there, she loses her tooth and puts it under a gourd for the African tooth fairy who is supposed to exchange it for a chicken.

Cultural heritage is sometimes marked by special dress. *New Clothes for New Year's Day* (Bae, 2007) presents traditional Korean attire that a mother makes for her daughter, and end notes provide information about the custom of dressing up for the Lunar New Year. In *My Dadima Wears a Sari* (Sheth, 2007) a granddaughter wonders if her grandmother would ever want to wear something different besides the traditional sari. But, the grandmother shows her granddaughter all the positive things she can do in a sari, for instance, using it as a fan, collecting seashells, or using it as an umbrella. Food is also a cultural marker that varies tremendously across cultures. Instructions and recipes are included for Indian flatbread in *What Should I Make?* (Nayar, 2009) and for a popular Korean rice dish in *Bee-Bim Bop!* (Park, 2005). *Sopa de frijoles/Bean Soup* (Argueta, 2009) is a delightful recipe in poetic format that can reinforce the sequence of events in cooking. In *The Have a Good Day Café* (Park & Park, 2005), readers meet a Korean family that changes the strategy for their food cart business by selling Korean food items rather than typical American fare. A glossary of the food items is at the end of the book. *Hiromi's Hands* (Barasch, 2007) features a young Japanese American girl

Table 11.5.
Text Sets for English Learners

Theme	Text Set	Proficiency Levels	Grades
Artistic Endeavors	*To Be an Artist* (Ajmera & Ivanko, 2004)	B,D	P,I
	The Pot That Juan Built (Andrews-Goebel, 2002)	B,D	I,M
	A Song for Ba (Yee & Wang, 2004)	B,D	I
	José! Born to Dance (Reich, 2005)	B,D	I
	My Name Is Celia/Me llamo Celia (Brown, 2004)	B,D	I
	Kamishibai Man (Say, 2005)	D	I
	Julio's Magic (Dorros, 2005)	D	I
	Romina's Rangoli (Iyengar, 2007)	D	I,M
	Murals: Walls That Sing (Ancona, 2003)	D	I,M
	Frida: ¡Viva la vida!/Long Live Life! (Bernier-Grand, 2007)	D,A	I,M
Celebrations	*Up and Down the Andes: A Peruvian Festival Tale* (Krebs, 2008)	B,D	P,I
	N Is for Navidad (Elya & Banks, 2007)	B,D	P,I
	Yoon and the Christmas Mittens (Recorvits, 2002)	B,D	P,I
	Uncle Peter's Amazing Chinese Wedding (Look, 2006)	B,D	P,I
	This Next New Year (Wong, 2000)	B,D	P,I
	Celebrating Chinese New Year (Hoyt-Goldsmith, 1998)	D,A	I,M
	Celebrating Ramadan (Hoyt-Goldsmith, 2001)	D,A	I,M
	Cinco de Mayo: Celebrating the Traditions of Mexico (Hoyt Goldsmith, 2008)	D,A	I,M
	Celebrate Cinco de Mayo With Fiestas, Music and Dance (Otto, 2008)	D,A	I,M
	Fiesta Fireworks (Ancona, 1998)	D,A	I,M
	Days of the Dead (Lasky, 1994)	D,A	I,M
	Las Posadas: An Hispanic Christmas Celebration (Hoyt Goldsmith, 1999)	D,A	I,M
	Peiling and the Chicken-Fried Christmas (Chen, 2007)	A	M
Cultural Taste Sensations	*What Should I Make?* (Nayar, 2009)	B	P
	Bee-Bim Bop! (Park, 2005)	B	P
	Alego (Teevee, 2009)	B	P,I
	Sopa de frijoles/Bean Soup (Argueta, 2009)	B,D	P,I
	Yum! ¡Mm Mm! ¡Qué rico! America's Sproutings (Mora, 2007)	B,D	I,M

(*continued*)

Table 11.5. (continued)

Theme	Text Set	Proficiency Levels	Grades
	Hiromi's Hands (Barasch, 2007)	D	I,M
	The Have a Good Day Café (Park & Park, 2005)	D	I,M
	The Wakame Gatherers (Thompson, 2007)	D	I,M
Dressing the Part	*New Clothes for New Year's Day* (Bae, 2007)	B,D	P,I
	The Fiesta Dress: A Quinceañera Tale (McCormack, 2009)	B,D	P,I
	My Mother's Sari (Rao, 2007)	B,D	P,I
	What Can You Do With a Rebozo?/¿Qué puedes hacer con un rebozo? (Tafolla, 2009)	B,D	P,I
	The Swirling Hijaab (Robert, 2002)	B,D	P,I
	My Dadima Wears a Sari (Sheth, 2007)	D	I,M
Family Connections	*Sitti's Secrets* (Nye, 1997)	B,D	P,I
	The Trip Back Home (Wong, 2000)	B,D	P,I
	Kamal Goes to Trinidad (Frederick, 2008)	D	I
	I Lost My Tooth in Africa (Diakité, 2006)	B,D	P,I
	Shanghai Messenger (Cheng, 2005)	D,A	I,M
	Naming Maya (Krishnaswami, 2004)	A	M
Genre Study	Photo essays by Diane Hoyt-Goldsmith and George Ancona such as the examples listed below or others from the Children's Books Cited	D,A	I,M
	Celebrating Chinese New Year (Hoyt-Goldsmith, 1998)		
	Celebrating Ramadan (Hoyt-Goldsmith, 2001)		
	Murals: Walls That Sing (Ancona, 2003)		
	Capoeira: Game! Dance! Martial art! (Ancona, 2007)		
	Poetry collections such as those by Francisco Alarcón or Jorge Argueta, Pat Mora, Janet Wong and others listed in the Children's Books Cited	B,D,A	P,I,M
	Iguanas in the Snow: And Other Winter Poems/ Iguanas en la nieve y otros poemas de invierno (Alarcon, 2005)		
	Sopa de frijoles/Bean Soup (Argueta, 2009)		
	Yum!¡Mm Mm! ¡Qué rico! America's Sprouting (Mora, 2007)		
	Good Luck Gold (Wong, 2007)		
Immigration Journeys	*Ziba Came on a Boat* (Lofthouse, 2007)	B,D	P,I
	Gervelie's Journey: A Refugee Diary (Robinson & Young, 2008)	D,A	I,M
	La línea (Jaramillo, 2006)	A	M
	Crossing the Wire (Hobbs, 2006)	A	M

Table 11.5. (continued)

Theme	Text Set	Proficiency Levels	Grades
Language Discrimination	*Bright Path: Young Jim Thorpe* (Brown, 2006)	B,D	P,I
	Harvesting Hope: The Story of Cesar Chavez (Krull, 2003)	B,D	I
	Shin-chi's Canoe (Campbell, 2008)	D	I
	Home to Medicine Mountain (Santiago, 1998)	D	I
	Sweetgrass Basket (Carvell, 2005)	A	M
Migrant Life	*Tomás and the Library Lady* (Mora, 1997)	D	P,I
	César: Yes, We Can!/ César: ¡Sí, se puede! (2005)	D	I
	Papi's Gift (Stanton, 2007)	B,D	P,I
	Harvesting Hope: The Story of Cesar Chavez (Krull, 2003)	D	P,I
	Calling the Doves/El canto de las palomas (Herrera, 2001)	D	P,I
	Voices From the Field: Children of Migrant Farmworkers Tell Their Stories (Atkin, 2000)	D,A	I,M
	Harvest (Ancona, 2001)	D,A	I,M
	Breaking Through (Jiménez, 2001)	A	M
	Esperanza Rising (Muñoz Ryan, 2002)	A	M
School Days	*Running Shoes* (Lipp, 2007)	B,D	P,I
	Josias, Hold the Book (Elvgren, 2007)	B,D	P,I
	Armando and the Blue Tarp School (Fine, 2007)	D	I
	My Name Is Bilal (Mobin-Uddin, 2005)	D	I
	Going to School in India (Heydlauff, 2003)	D	I,M

who becomes a sushi chef in her family's New York restaurant. A two page spread on different sushi is included. Related to sushi, *The Wakame Gatherers* (Thompson, 2007) is the story of a bicultural girl, American and Japanese, who works with her grandmothers to gather Wakame, a type of seaweed.

Access to education and schooling in the United States differs from other settings. The difficulty of getting to school is presented in *Running Shoes* (Lipp, 2008) since school is eight kilometers from Sophy's small Cambodian village. Eventually, Sophy is given running shoes that enable her to run to school. Some schools are in very different settings as in *Armando and the Blue Tarp School* (Fine, 2007). The children in the *colonia* near the city dump in Tijuana, Mexico attend a summer school held outside on a blue tarp. *Going to School in India* (Heydlauff, 2003) offers a fascinating glimpse of India and the many places school is held. Finally, cultural differences can lead to difficulties at school. In *My Name Is Bilal* (Mobin-Uddin, 2005). Bilal and his sister, Ayesha, must adjust to a new school where they are the only Muslim students in attendance. Ayesha is teased by boys who grab her headscarf, but Bilal ignores this and later tells the class that his name is Bill, not Bilal, to avoid more teasing.

Holidays and family celebrations, even though they may be celebrated in very different ways, are universal. *This Next New Year* (Wong, 2000) highlights the lunar new year. Simple language and text explain many of the folk customs associated with this celebration. *Uncle Peter's Amazing Chinese Wedding* (Look, 2006) describes a traditional Chinese wedding amidst an amusing family story. *N is for Navidad* (Elya & Banks, 2007) is a rhyming alphabet book that targets the many sights, smells, and activities of a traditional Latino Christmas celebration.

A text set of books in the same genre might also be an excellent grouping. For instance, Diane Hoyt-Goldsmith (1998, 1999, 2001, 2002, 2008) and George Ancona (1998, 2001, 2003, & 2007) have numerous photo essays that spotlight features of Latino culture. There are also numerous bilingual and multicultural poetry collections including Francisco Alarcón's collections (1997, 1998, 1999, 2005, 2008) and Janet Wong's early work in *Good Luck Gold* (2007) or *Suitcase of Seaweed and Other Poems* (2008), which is clearly focused on her family roots and relationships as an American of both Chinese and Korean descent.

RESPONSE ACTIVITIES

Through literature, readers can gain an appreciation for language diversity and the issues surrounding language acquisition and language use. To draw readers further into the themes and topics highlighted in this literature, there are a variety of reader response activities.

Mapping Language Influence in Literature

A number of the books cited in this chapter introduce words from languages (other than English). Giorgis, Mathis, and Bedford (2007) suggest that students create a language chart listing the new words, English translations, language and country of origin, and the book in which they are found in the following manner.

This chart can be kept in the classroom and continually expanded as more books are read. See Figure 11.1.

Mapping Language Influence in U.S. Geography

In *Journey of English* (Brook, 1998, p. 43), readers discover the many words in English that have been borrowed from other languages—"camel from Hebrew, piano from Italian, zero from Arabic." Also, "over half of American states' names are from Native American languages. Alabama, Alaska, Connecticut, Idaho, Massachusetts,

Word	Meaning	Language	Country	Source
haraboji	Grandfather	Korean	Korea	*Trip Back Home*
halmoni	Grandmother	Korean	Korea	*Trip Back Home*

Figure 11.1.
Language Chart

Geographical name/term	Language of origin	Meaning
Sangre de Cristo Mountains	Spanish	literally the "blood of Christ" in reference to the red glow on the mountains from the setting sun
canyon	Spanish	deep gorge

Figure 11.2.
Geographic Chart

Oklahoma, and Tennessee are just a few of them" (p. 36). In *New York Is English, Chattanooga Is Creek* (2005), Chris Raschka reminds readers that "A thousand names, a hundred languages, a million, and a million, and a million people name one nation" (not paginated). To reinforce the influence that many languages have had on U.S. place names and geographic vocabulary, the class can research geographic names and terms that were borrowed from another language. A running list can also be kept on a class word wall (see Figure 11.2 which shows a possible format for a geographic chart) as students encounter new examples in different units of study.

Read Alouds and Read Alongs

Parents of English learners or other community members who are fluent in another language can be invited to read aloud to the class using a bilingual book with versions in two languages or with text in both languages. Or, as a class activity, the teacher can select bilingual or interlingual poetry, create a transparency of the poem, and lead the class in a read along. Different poetry performance or choral reading techniques can be used. For example, assigning words and phrases to students who speak that language and then, having them join in at the appropriate place in the read along.

CONCLUSION

Our most important goal should be to find the best books to share in classrooms and libraries that develop awareness and understanding of the diversity of languages used to communicate within the United States and outside our country as well and the role that language plays in self-identity and self-concept. For English learners, culture is a key criterion that must be considered when matching books to readers. Too often language minority students in the United States are pushed to learn English as quickly as possible to enable them to fully participate in school, work, and play. Yet, we also want children to read and listen to books that will help them maintain their linguistic heritage and promote bilingualism, biculturalism, and biliteracy (Au, 2006).

REFERENCES

Abu-Rabia, S. (1998). Attitudes and culture in second language learning among Israeli-Arab students learning Hebrew as a second language. *Curriculum and Teaching, 13* (1), 12–30.

Au, K. H. (2006). *Multicultural issues and literacy achievement*. Mahwah, NJ: Lawrence Erlbaum Associates.

Banks, J. A. & Banks, C. A. M. (Eds.). (2001). *Multicultural Education: Issues and Perspectives* (4th ed.). Boston, MA: Allyn & Bacon.

Battistich, V., Solomon, D., Watson, M., & Schaps, E. (1997). Caring school communities. *Educational Psychology, 32*, 137–151.

Berman, P., Minicucci, C., McLaughlin, B., Nelson, B., & Woodworth, K. (1995). *School reform and student diversity: Case studies of exemplary practices for LEP students*. Washington, DC: National Clearinghouse for English Language Acquisition.

Bishop, R. S. (1992). Multicultural literature for children: Making informed choices. In V. J. Harris (Ed.), *Teaching Multicultural Literature in Grades K–8* (pp. 37–53). Norwood, MA: Christopher-Gordon.

Cai, M. (1998). Multiple definitions of multicultural literature: Is the debate really just "ivory-tower" bickering? *The New Advocate, 11*(4), 311–324.

Crawford, J. (1999). Heritage languages in America: Tapping a "hidden" resource. Retrieved June 6, 2006 at http://www.languagepolicy.net/excerpts/heritage.html.

Doherty, R. W., Hilberg, R. S., Pinal, A., & Tharp, R. (2003, Winter). Five standards and student achievement. *NABE Journal of Research and Practice, 1*, 1–24.

Ernst-Slavit, G., & Mulhern, M. (2003, September/October). Bilingual books: Promoting literacy and biliteracy in the second-language and mainstream classroom. *Reading Online, 7*(2). Retrieved at http://www.readingonline.org/articles/art_index.asp?HREF=ernst-slavit/index.html.

Freeman, D. E., & Freeman, Y. S. (2006). Teaching language through content themes: Viewing our world as a global village. In T. A. Young & N.L. Hadaway (Eds.), *Supporting the literacy development of English learners: Increasing success in all classrooms* (pp. 61–78). Newark, DE: International Reading Association.

Galda, L., Cullinan, B. E., & Sipe, L. R. (2010). *Literature and the Child*. Belmont, CA: Wadsworth/Cengage.

Giorgis, C., Mathis, J., & Bedford, A. (2007). Finding our stories through her stories: Strong females in the global tapestry. In N. L. Hadaway & M. L. McKenna (Eds.), *Breaking boundaries with global literature: Celebrating diversity in K–12 classrooms* (pp. 55–72). Newark, DE: International Reading Association.

Goldenberg, C, Rueda, R. S., & August, D. (2008). Sociocultural contexts and literacy development. In D. August & T. Shanahan (Eds.), *Developing reading and writing in second-language learners: Lessons from the report of the National Literacy Panel on language-minority children and youth* (pp. 95–129). New York, NY: Routledge.

Hadaway, N. L., & Young, T. A. (2007). Language diversity in the United States and issues of linguistic identity in a global society. In N. L. Hadaway & M. L. McKenna (Eds.), *Breaking boundaries with global literature: Celebrating diversity in K–12 classrooms* (pp. 93–112). Newark, DE: International Reading Association.

Hadaway, N. L., & Young, T. A. (2010). *Matching books and readers: Helping English learners in grades K–6*. New York, NY: Guilford Press.

Hampton, S., & Resnick, L. B. (2009). *Reading and writing with understanding: Comprehension in fourth and fifth grades*. Newark, DE: International Reading Association.

Kenner, C. (2000). Biliteracy in a monolingual school system? English and Gujarati in south London. *Language and Education, 14* (1), 13–30.

Kindler, A. L. (2002). *Survey of the states' limited English proficient students and available educational programs and services: 2000–2001 summary report*. Washington, D.C.: National Clearinghouse for English Language Acquisition.

Lehman, B. A., & Crook, P. R. (1998). Doubletalk: A literary pairing of *The Giver* and *We Are All in the Dumps* with *Jack and Guy*. *Children's Literature in Education, 29*, 69–78.

Montecel, M. R., & Cortez, J. D. (2002). Successful bilingual education programs: Development and the dissemination of criteria to identify promising and exemplary practices in bilingual education at the national level. *Bilingual Research Journal, 26*, 122.

Multilingual Resources for Children Project. (1995). *Building bridges: Multilingual resources for children project*. Bristol, PA: Multilingual Matters.

Orfield, G., & Yun, J. T. (1999). *Resegregation in American schools*. Cambridge, MA: Civil Rights Project, Harvard University.

Padolsky, D. (2004). *How many school-aged English language learners (ELLs) are there in the U.S.? National Clearinghouse for English Language Acquisition*. Retrieved October 1 2010, from http://www.ncela.gwu.edu/faqs/

Schon, I. (2004). *Recommended books in Spanish for children and young adults, 2000–2004*. Lanham, MD: Scarecrow Press.

Short, K. G., & Harste, J. C. (with Burke, C.). (1996). *Creating classrooms for authors and inquirers* (2nd ed.). Portsmouth, NH: Heinemann.

Suárez-Orozco, C., & Suárez-Orozco, M. M. (2001). *Children of immigration*. Cambridge, MA: Harvard University Press.

Temple, C. A., Martinez, M. and Yokota, J. (2006). *Children's books in children's hands: An introduction to their literature*. Boston, MA: Allyn & Bacon.

Walker, S., Edwards, V., & Blacksell, R. (1996). Designing bilingual books for children. *Visible Language, 30*, 268–283.

Yokota, J. (1993). Issues in selecting multicultural children's literature. *Language Arts, 70*, 156–167.

CHILDREN'S BOOKS CITED

Ada, A. F. (2002). *I love Saturdays y domingos*, illustrated by E. Savadier. New York, NY: Atheneum.

Ajmera, M., & Ivanko, J. D. (2004). *To be an artist*. Watertown, MA: Charlesbridge.

Aktar, N. (2000). *Samira's Eid*, illustrated by E. Attard. London, UK: Mantra Lingua.

Alarcón, F. (1997). *Laughing tomatoes and other spring poems/Jitomates risueños y otros poemas de primavera*, illustrated by M. C. Gonzalez. San Francisco, CA: Children's Book Press.

Alarcón, F. (1998*). From the bellybutton of the moon: And other summer poems/Del ombligo de la luna y otros poemas de verano*, illustrated by M. C. Gonzalez. San Francisco, CA: Children's Book Press.

Alarcón, F. (1999). *Angels ride bikes: And other fall poems/Los ángeles andan en bicicleta y otros poemas de otoño*, illustrated by M. C. Gonzalez. San Francisco, CA: Children's Book Press.

Alarcón, F. (2005). *Iguanas in the snow: And other winter poems/Iguanas en la nieve y otros poemas d invierno*, illustrated by M. C. Gonzalez. San Francisco, CA: Children's Book Press.

Alarcón, F. (2008). *Animal poems of the Iguazú/Animalario del Iguazú*, illustrated by M. C. Gonzalez. San Francisco, CA: Children's Book Press.

Aliki. (1998). *Marianthe's story: Painted words/Spoken memories*. New York, NY: Greenwillow.

Ancona, G. (1998). *Fiesta fireworks*. New York, NY: Lothrop, Lee, & Shephard.

Ancona, G. (2001). *Harvest*. New York, NY: Marshall Cavendish.

Ancona, G. (2003). *Murals: Walls that sing*. New York, NY: Marshall Cavendish.

Ancona, G. (2007). *Capoeira: Game! Dance! Martial art!* New York, NY: Lee & Low.

André, J., & Willet, N. (2008). *We feel good out here*, photographs by T. MacIntosh. Markham, ON: Fifth House.

Andrews-Goebel, N. (2002). *The pot that Juan built*, illustrated by D. Diaz. New York, NY: Lee & Low.

Andrews-Goebel, N. (2004). *La vasija que Juan fabricó*, illustrated by D. Diaz, translated by E. Cortés. New York, NY: Lee & Low.

Applegate, N. (2007). *Home of the brave*. New York, NY: Feiwel & Friends.

Argueta, J. (2001). *A movie in my pillow/Una película en mi almohada*, illustrated by E. Gómez. San Francisco, CA: Children's Book Press.

Argueta, J. (2006). *Talking with Mother Earth/Hablando con Madre Tierra*, illustrated by L. A. Pérez. Toronto, CAN: Groundwood.

Argueta, J. (2009). *Sopa de frijoles/Bean soup*, illustrated by R. Yockteng. Toronto, CAN: Groundwood.

Atkin, S. B. (2000). *Voices from the field: Children of migrant farmworkers tell their stories*. Boston, MA: Little, Brown and Company.

Bae, H. (2007). *New clothes for New Year's Day*. La Jolla, CA: Kane/Miller.

Barasch, L. (2007). *Hiromi's hands*. New York, NY: Lee & Low.

Bernier-Grand, C. T. (2004). *César: ¡Sí, se puede!/Yes, we can!*, illustrated by D. Diaz. Tarrytown, NY: Marshall Cavendish.

Bernier-Grand, C. T. (2007). *Frida: ¡Viva la vida!/Long live life!* Tarrytown, NY: Marshall Cavendish.

Bouchard, D. (2008). *An Aboriginal carol*, illustrated by M. Beaver. Markham, ON: Red Deer Press.

Brook, D. (1998). *The journey of English*, illustrated by J. Zallinger. New York, NY: Clarion.

Brown, D. (2006). *Bright path: Young Jim Thorpe*. New Milford, CT: Roaring Brook Press.

Brown, M. (2004). *My name is Celia: The life of Celia Cruz/Me llamo Celia: La vida de Celia Cruz*. Flagstaff, AR: Rising Moon.

Bunting, E. (2006). *One green apple*, illustrated by T. Lewin. Boston. MA: Houghton Mifflin.

Campbell, N. (2008). *Shin-chi's canoe*, illustrated by K. LaFave. Toronto, CAN: Groundwood.

Carling, A. L. (2005). *Sawdust carpets*. Toronto, CAN: Groundwood.

Carvell, M. (2005). *Sweetgrass basket*. New York, NY: Dutton.

Chen, P. (2007). *Peiling and the chicken-fried Christmas*, New York, NY: Bloomsbury.

Cheng, A. (2005). *Shanghai messenger*, illustrated by E. Young. New York, NY: Lee & Low.

Chocolate, D. (2009). *El barrio*, illustrated by D. Diaz. New York, NY: Henry Holt.

Choi, Y. (2001). *The name jar*. New York, NY: Farrar, Straus, and Giroux.

Choi, Y. (2006). *Behind the mask*. New York, NY: Farrar, Straus, and Giroux.

Delacre, L. (2000). *Salsa stories*. New York, NY: Scholastic.

Delacre, L. (2000). *Cuentos con sazón*. New York, NY: Scholastic.

Diakité, P. (2006). *I lost my tooth in Africa*, illustrated by B. W. Diakité. New York, NY: Scholastic.

Dorros, A. (2005). *Julio's magic*, illustrated by A. Grifalconi. New York, NY: HarperCollins.

Dorros, A. (2008). *Papá and me*, illustrated by R. Gutierrez. New York, NY: HarperCollins.

Edwardson, D. D. (2003). *Whale snow*, illustrated by A. Patterson. Watertown, MA: Tradewinds.

Ellis, D. (2002). *Parvana's journey*. Toronto, CAN: Groundwood Books.

Elvegren, J. R. (2006). *Josias, hold the book*, illustrated by N. Tadgell. Honesdale, PA: Boyds Mills Press.

Elya, S. M. & Banks, M. (2007). *N is for Navidad*, illustrated by J. Cepeda. San Francisco, CA: Chronicle Books.

Fine, E. H. (2007). *Armando and the blue tarp school*, illustrated by J. P. Josephson. New York, NY: Lee & Low.

Fredrick, M. (2008). *Kamal goes to Trinidad*, photographs by P. Das. London, UK: Frances Lincoln.

Friedman, I. R. (1984). *How my parents learned to eat*, illustrated by A. Say. Boston, MA: Houghton Mifflin.

Garza, C. L. (2005). *Family pictures/Cuadros de familia*. San Francisco, CA: Children's Book Press.

Garza, C. L. (1996). *In my family/En mi familia*. San Francisco, CA: Children's Book Press.

Gonzalez, M. C. (2009). *I know the river loves me/Yo sé que el río me ama*. San Francisco, CA: Children's Book Press.

Herrera, J. F. (2001). *Calling the doves/El canto de las palomas*, illustrated by E. Simmons. San Francisco, CA: Children's Book Press.

Herrera, J. F. (1998). *Laughing out loud, I fly/ A carcajadas, yo vuelo*, illustrated by K. Barbour. New York, NY: HarperCollins.

Herrera, J. F. (2000). *The upside down boy/El niño de cabeza*, illustrated by E. Gómez. San Francisco, CA: Children's Book Press.

Heydlauff, L. (2003). *Going to school in India*. Watertown, MA: Charlesbridge.

Hill, K. (2000). *The year of Miss Agnes*. New York, NY: Simon & Schuster.

Ho, M. (1996). *Maples in the mist: Poems for children from the Tang Dynasty*. New York, NY: Lothrop, Lee and Shepard.

Hobbs, W. (2006). *Crossing the wire*. New York, NY: HarperCollins.

Hoyt-Goldsmith, D. (1998). *Celebrating Chinese New Year*, photographs by L. Migdale. New York, NY: Holiday House.

Hoyt-Goldsmith, D. (1999). *Las Posadas: An Hispanic Christmas celebration*, photographs by L. Migdale. New York, NY: Holiday House.

Hoyt-Goldsmith, D. (2001). *Celebrating Ramadan*, photographs by L. Migdale. New York, NY: Holiday House.

Hoyt-Goldsmith, D. (2002). *Celebrating a quinceañera: A Latina's 15th birthday celebration*, photographs by L. Migdale. New York, NY: Holiday House.

Hoyt-Goldsmith, D. (2008). *Cinco de Mayo: Celebrating the traditions of Mexico*, photographs by L. Migdale. New York, NY: Holiday House.

Ichikawa, S. (2006). *My father's shop*. La Jolla, CA: Kane/Miller.

Iyengar, M. M. (2007). *Romina's rangoli*, illustrated by J. Wanardi. Walnut Creek, CA: Shen's.

Jaramillo, A. (2006). *La línea*. New York, NY: Roaring Brook Press.

Jiménez, F. (1998). *La mariposa*, illustrated by S. Silva. Boston, MA: Houghton Mifflin.

Jiménez, F. (2001). *Breaking through*. Boston, MA: Houghton Mifflin.

Johnston, T. (1996). *My Mexico/México mío*. New York, NY: Putnam.

Johnston, T. (2001). *Any small goodness: A novel of the barrio*. New York, NY: Blue Sky.

Johnston, T. (2001). *Uncle Rain Cloud*, illustrated by F. Vanden Broeck. Watertown, MA: Charlesbridge.

Joseph, L. (2000). *The color of my words*. New York, NY: HarperCollins.

Krebs, L. (2008). *Up and down the Andes: A Peruvian festival tale*, illustrated by A. Fronty. Cambridge, MA: Barefoot Books.

Krishnaswami, U. (2004). *Naming Maya*. New York, NY: Farrar, Strauss and Giroux.

Krull, K. (2003). *Harvesting hope: The story of Cesar Chavez*, illustrated by Y. Morales. San Diego, CA: Harcourt.

Krull, K. (2003). *Cosechando esperanza: La historia de César Chávez*, translated by A. F. Ada & I. Campoy. San Diego, CA: Harcourt.

Kurtz, J. (1998). *The Storyteller's beads*. San Diego, CA: Gulliver.

Kurtz, J. (2000). *Faraway home*, illustrated by E.B. Lewis. San Diego, CA: Gulliver.

Lasky, K. (1994). *Days of the Dead*. New York, NY: Hyperion.

Lazo Gilmore, D. K. (2009). *Cora cooks pancit*, illustrated by K. Valiant. Walnut Creek, CA: Shen's.

Lee-Tai, A. (2006). *A place where sunflowers grow*, illustrated by F. Hoshino. San Francisco, CA: Children's Book Press.

Levine, E. (1995). *I hate English!* illustrated by S. Bjorkman. New York, NY: Scholastic.

Lipp, F. (2008). *Running shoes*, illustrated by J. Gaillard. Watertown, MA: Charlesbridge.

Lofthouse, L (2007). *Ziba came on a boat*, illustrated by R. Ingpen. La Jolla, CA: Kane/Miller.

Look, L. (2006). *Uncle Peter's amazing Chinese wedding*, illustrated by Y. Heo. New York, NY: Atheneum.

Luenn, N. (1998). *A gift for abuelita: Celebrating the Day of the Dead/Un regalo para abuelita: En celebración del Día de los Muertos*, illustrated by R. Chapman. Flagstaff, AZ: Rising Moon.

Luján, (2008). *Colors!¡Colores!* illustrated by P. Grobler. Toronto, CAN: Groundwood Press.

Mado, M. (1998). *The magic pocket: Selected poems*. New York, NY: Margaret K. McElderry.

Madrigal, A. H. (2000). *Blanca's feather/La pluma de Blanca*, illustrated by G. Suzán. Flagstaff, AZ: Rising Moon Press.

McLeod, T., & Willet, W. (2008). *The delta Is Our home*, photographs by T. MacIntosh. Markham, ON: Fifth House Books.

McCormack, C. M. (2009). *The fiesta dress: A quinceañera tale*, illustrated by M. Avilés. New York, NY: Marshall Cavendish.

Mikaelsen, B. (2004). *Tree girl*. New York, NY: Rayo/HarperCollins.

Mobin-Uddin, A. (2005). *My name is Bilal*, illustrated by B. Kiwak. Honesdale, PA: Boyds Mills Press.

Mobin-Uddin, A. (2007). *The best Eid ever*, illustrated by L. Jacobson. Honesdale, PA: Boyds Mills Press.

Mora, P. (1996). *Confetti: Poems for children*, illustrated by E. O. Sanchez. New York, NY: Lee & Low.

Mora, P. (1997). *Tomás and the library lady*, illustrated by R. Colón. New York, NY: Knopf.

Mora, P. (1997). *Tomás y la señora de la biblioteca*, illustrated by R. Colón. New York, NY: Knopf.

Mora, P. (2006). *Confeti: Poemas para niños*, illustrated by E. O. Sanchez. New York, NY: Lee & Low.

Mora, P. (2007). *Yum!¡Mm Mm! ¡Qué rico! America's sproutings*, illustrated by R. López. New York, NY: Lee & Low.

Mora, P. (2009). *Book fiesta! Celebrate Children's Day/Book Day/Celebremos el Día de los Niños/El Día de los Libros*, illustrated by R. López. New York, NY: Rayo/HarperCollins.

Mora, P. (2009). *Gracias/Thanks*, illustrated by J. Parra. New York, NY: Lee & Low.

Morales, Y. (2003). *Just a minute: A trickster tale and counting book*. San Francisco, CA: Chronicle.

Nayar, N. (2009). *What should I make?*, illustrated by P. Roy. Berkley, CA: Tricycle Press.

Nicholson, C. D. (2008). *Niwechihaw, I help*. Toronto, CAN: Groundwood Books.

Nobisso, J. (2003). *In English, of course*, illustrated by D. Ziborova. New York, NY: Gingerbread House.

Nye, N. S. (1995). *The tree is older than you are: A bilingual gathering of poems & stories from Mexico with paintings by Mexican artists*. New York, NY: Simon & Schuster.

Nye, N. S. (1997). *Sitti's secrets*, illustrated by N. Carpenter. New York, NY: Aladdin.

Orozco, J.-L. (2002). *Fiestas: A year of Latin American songs of celebration*, illustrated by E. Kleven. New York, NY: Dutton.

Otto, C. (2008). *Celebrate Cinco de Mayo with fiestas, music and dance*. Washington, DC: National Geographic.

Park, F., & Park, G. (2002). *Good-bye, 382 Shin Dang Dong*, illustrated by Y. Choi. Washington, DC: National Geographic.

Park, F., & Park, G. (2005). *The Have a Good Day Café*, illustrated by K. Potter. New York, NY: Lee & Low.

Park, L. S. (2004). *The firekeeper's son*, illustrated by J. Downing. New York, NY: Sandpiper.

Park, L. S. (2005). *Bee-bim bop!* illustrated by H. B. Lee. New York, NY: Clarion.

Paterson, K. (2009). *The day of the pelican*. New York, NY: Clarion.

Pérez, A. I. (2002). *My diary from here to there/Mi diario de aquí hasta allá*, illustrated by M.C. Gonzalez. San Francisco, CA: Children's Book Press.

Pinkney, M., & Pinkney, S. (2007). *I am Latino: The beauty in me*. New York, NY: Little, Brown and Company.

Rao, S. (2007). *My mother's sari*, illustrated by N. Sabnani. Chambersburg, PA: North-South Books.

Raschka, C. (2005). *New York is English, Chattanooga is Creek*. New York, NY: Atheneum.

Recorvits, H. (2006). *Yoon and the Christmas mittens*, illustrated by G. Swiatkowska. New York, NY: Farrar, Straus, and Giroux.

Reich, S. (2005). *José!: Born to dance:The story of José Limón*, illustrated by R. Colón. New York, NY: Simon & Schuster.

Robert, N. B. (2002). *The swirling hijaab*, illustrated by N. Mistry. London, UK: Mantra Lingua.

Robinson, A., & Young, A. (2008). *Gervelie's journey: A refugee diary*, illustrated by J. Allen. London, UK: Frances Lincoln.

Robles, A. D. (2006). *Lakas and the Makibaka Hotel/Si Lakas at Ang Makibaka Hotel*, illustrated by C. Angel. San Francisco, CA: Children's Book Press.

Rumford, J. (2004). *Sequoyah: The man who gave his people writing*. Boston, MA: Houghton Mifflin.

Ryan, P.M. (2002). *Esperanza rising*. New York, NY: Scholastic.

Sacre, A. (2003). *The barking mouse*, illustrated by A. Aquirre. Chicago, IL: Albert Whitman & Company.

Santiago, C. (1998). *Home to Medicine Mountain*, illustrated by J. Lowry. San Francisco, CA: Children's Book Press.

Say, A. (1999). *Tea with milk*. Boston, MA: Houghton Mifflin.

Say, A. (2005). *Kamishibai man*. Boston, MA: Houghton Mifflin.

Sciurba, K. (2007). *Oye, Celia! A song for Celia Cruz*, illustrated by E. Rodriguez. New York, NY: Henry Holt.

Seki, S. (2007). *The tale of the lucky cat*. Manhattan Beach, CA: East West Discovery Press.

Shahan, S. (2004). *Spicy hot colors/Colores picantes*. Little Rock, AR: August House.

Shea, P. D., & Weill, C. (2003). *Ten mice for Tet*, illustrated by T. N. Trang. San Francisco, CA: Chronicle Books.

Sheth, K. (2007). *My Dadima wears a sari*, illustrated by Y. Jaeggi. Atlanta, GA: Peachtree.

Shin, S. Y. (2004). *Cooper's lesson*, illustrated by K. Cogan. San Francisco, CA: Children's Book Press.

Spivak, D. (1997). *Grass sandals: The travels of Basho*, illustrated by Demi. New York, NY: Atheneum.

Stanton, K. (2007). *Papi's gift*, illustrated by R. K. Moreno. Honesdale, PA: Boyds Mills Press.

Tafolla, C. (2009). *What can you do with a rebozo?/¿Qué puedes hacer con un rebozo?* illustrated by A. Córdova. New York, NY: Random House.

Teevee, N. (2009). *Alego*. Toronto, CAN: Groundwood Books.

Thompson, H. (2007). *The Wakame gatherers*, illustrated by K. Wilds. Walnut Creek, CA: Shen's.

Wallace, I. (2006). *The Huron carol*. Toronto, CAN: Groundwood.

Weeks, S. (2006). *Counting ovejas*, illustrated by D. Diaz. New York, NY: Atheneum.

Wells, R. (2008). *Yoko writes her name*. New York, NY: Hyperion.

Whelan, G. (2004). *Chu Ju's house*. New York, NY: HarperCollins.

Williams, K. L., & Mohammad, K. (2009). *My name is Sangoel*, illustrated by C. Stock. Grand Rapids, MI: Eerdmans.

Wong, J. S. (2000). *This next New Year*, illustrated by Y. Choi. New York, NY: Frances Foster.

Wong, J. S. (2000). *The trip back home*, illustrated by B. Jia. San Diego, CA: Harcourt.

Wong, J. S. (2007). *Good luck gold*. Seattle, WA: BookSurge Publishing.

Wong, J. S. (2008). *A suitcase of seaweed and other poems*. Seattle, WA: BookSurge Publishing.

Yang, B. (2004). *Hannah is my name*. Cambridge, MA: Candlewick Press.

Yee, P., & Wang, J. P. (2004). *A song for Ba*. Toronto, CAN: Groundwood.

Young, E. (1997). *Mouse match: A Chinese folktale*. San Diego, CA: Harcourt.

Young, E. (1997). *Voices from the heart*. New York, NY: Scholastic.

12

Do Tell! Multicultural Folk Stories in the Classroom and Library

Jacqueline K. Peck

WHAT STORYTELLING IS . . . AND ISN'T

From cave paintings to the poems of bards and minstrels, from Brer Rabbit's tricks to the epic tales of Iranian *bakhshi*, from picture cards of the *kamishibai man* to the call and response of *griots* in Africa, storytelling is a universal human activity. Folk stories form a cultural record rooted in oral tradition. Because of these oral roots, folk stories changed as tellers traveled and incorporated the language and customs of ever new audiences (Garrity, 1999), often clouding their exact time and source of origin. These stories evolved until they were recorded in written form.

Yet in a subtler way, these folk stories continue to change when each teller gives them voice in her or his own way (Pellowski, 1990). Richard Chase (1943), renowned collector of the Appalachian Jack Tales told in North Carolina, describes the process this way: "No two individuals in Beech Mountain section ever tell the same story exactly alike; nor does the same man ever tell any one tale quite the same twice over . . . This is, of course, a part of the story-teller's art" (p. x). Further, the story is ultimately co-created by the listeners and teller in the moment of the telling. Doug Lipman (1999) describes a storytelling triangle within the context of the telling that is comprised of the teller, the audience, and the story. The teller has a connection to the story and the audience but exerts no control over the audience's connection to the story. The best a teller can do is to humbly nurture the listeners' cocreation of the story by observing their facial expressions and body language, and by maintaining eye contact throughout the telling. This cocreation renders storytelling more than mere acting or memorized recitation.

A story, after all, takes its final shape in the telling. When you tell a story . . . you are not giving a recitation or performing a dramatic monologue. You are sharing your own account of a series of interesting story events . . . A good story can be full of borrowings, spur-of-the-moment changes, interruptions, pauses, and exclamatory bursts. Ideally, a story will be somewhat loosely woven, with room for the listener to allow his or her imagination to roam freely—to fill in the gaps.

(Maguire, 1985, pp. 16–17)

THE THREE RS OF MULTICULTURAL STORYTELLING: RESEARCH, RESPECT, REFLECT

As the interviews with Doreen Rappaport and Joseph Bruchac (Chapter 1) clearly affirm, the first R of multicultural storytelling is research. Research the story you would like to tell, the culture of origin, its storytelling traditions, and what is known about the particular story's origin and variants. Lipman (2003) articulates the scope of this research process: ". . . before telling an Egyptian version of 'Rapunzel.' I referred to several books of Arab folktales, as well as articles about Egyptian society, and pictures representing goulas and djinns. I wanted to know more of what the tale would evoke in the mind of a member of Egyptian traditional culture" (What to Do with What You've Found section, paragraph 4).

Pellowski (1990) offers a powerful source for research into multicultural folk stories. Recognizing the difficulty in tracing origins of oral stories, Pellowski states that thorough descriptions of storytelling styles are only available for some traditions. Table 12.1 presents a sampling of such information that is easily accessed through the Internet and books. (Note: Because Europe is home to many discrete cultural traditions that have been cross-influenced by others, namely those summarized in the table, the diversity of European storytelling traditions is vast and therefore beyond the scope of this chapter. Additional resources are supplied at the chapter's end to facilitate research of these specific and diverse traditions.)

In addition, many collections of folk stories include statements about story origin. For example, following Bill Harley's adaptation of "The Freedom Bird" (Miller, 1988), the compiler and editor include these notes: "This story was brought back from Chang Mi, Thailand by David Holt, who heard it told in broken English by one of his guides, a 10 year old boy. David set it down on paper, worked with it and came up with this tale that Bill Harley recorded on his tape, *Monsters in the Bathroom*" (p. 22). [Listen to this story on the CD accompanying the book.]

Thorough research likely leads to development of the second R of multicultural storytelling: Respect. Respect the culture of origin, including the differences and similarities to one's own culture (Garrity, 1999). Learn the cultural storytelling style and employ it by using authentic characteristics culled from your research. Identify the culture of origin and known sources. Guard against telling stories from other cultural traditions with a Westernized style (Pellowski, 1990). Most importantly, respect the universality of human endeavor. Strive to be a storyteller who inherently communicates this respect through your eyes, your voice, and your gestures. Nurture a respect that grows from sincere research and learning of the culture, a respect that resides deep within. It is this respect that allows the story to unfold earnestly and engage the mutual respect of your listeners.

The third R follows from the first two. Grounded in research and filled with respect, reflect the universal themes with authenticity and integrity. Ask yourself if you can give an authentic telling. If not, introduce the story by saying, "Here's a story I like; the author set it in [country of origin] and imagined what it would be like if it happened there" (Pellowski, 1990, p. 228). Pellowski also suggests you tell your audience that even though you cannot tell the story as it was told in its original setting, you like it so much that you want to tell it in your own way. Consider showing authentic cultural

Table 12.1.

A Sampling of Cultural Storytelling Styles

Culture of Origin	Style Features	Suggested Resources
African	Call and Response: 'Koi!' 'Lya!'(Tanzania).	http://web.cocc.edu/cagatucci/ classes/hum211/afrstory.htm, accessed on September 28, 2010
	Griots are masters of storytelling whose training included spiritual and ethical dimensions.	
	Stories include frequent exchanges and interaction with the audience. Poetics and music are often included in the stories.	
	Storytellers mimic characters, often animals with human attributes, with use of voice, facial expression, and gesture.	
	Storytellers carry objects representing tales or riddles on a hat or net; audience chooses objects indicating which story they want the storyteller to tell.	
African American	Trickster tales (Brer Rabbit, Tortoise, Anansi the Spider brought from Africa to America by slaves) tell of physically weak characters who overcome their oppressors by using the power of their wit and wisdom.	Virginia Hamilton's *The People Could Fly* Julius Lester's *Tales of Brer Rabbit* and *More Tales of Brer Rabbit*
	Stories including riddles and devil tales also reflect African roots.	Badoe's *The Pot of Wisdom* http://www.blackstorytellers.com/, accessed on September 28, 2010 http://www.kotc.org/, accessed on September 28, 2010
Appalachian American	Traditionally, stories were shared during evening relaxation on the front porch, told during breaks from working tobacco or weeding turnips, and most interestingly, told as students helped with communal chores, such as preparing vegetables for canning. This practical use was termed, "keeping kids on the job" (Chase, 1943, p. viii).	Richard Chase's *Jack Tales*
Caribbean	Call and Response:	Diane Wolkstein's *The Magic Orange Tree*
	Teller asks audience if they want a story by saying, "Cric?" (creek); audience responds "Crac!" indicating they want a story (Haitian).	
	Ritual ending for humorous story:	
	"Billy ben	
	My story end" (Bahamas).	

(*continued*)

Table 12.1. (continued)

Culture of Origin	Style Features	Suggested Resources
Chinese	Stories are told in special recital halls where tea and snacks are served to the audience. Sometimes a bamboo clapper is used to start the story. This is similar to the *kamishibai* sounding of the *hyoshigi*. Storytellers use subtle voice changes to indicate characters. Hmong (Maio) tradition includes antiphonal singing by opposing teams, which each sing a section of the story and end with a question for the other team to answer. This continues until the story ends or one team cannot answer the question!	http://www.shuoshu.org/Chinese _Storytelling/History_and_milleu/The %20origins%20of%20professional% 20storytelling.shtml, accessed on September 28, 2010
Indian	*Par*, a special cloth that is handled by an assistant, portrays each scene as the story is told. This is similar to the Iranian *pardehdari* style. Singers and dancers may be included. The audience responds with "hum" or "mmm" to indicate their assent. *Puranas* are ancient stories of wisdom recorded in Sanskrit. Gypsies use a *burra* (a drum shaped like a human skull) to accompany their narration of folk stories.	http://www.carnatica.net/harikatha1 .htm, accessed on September 28, 2010
Iranian	*Pardehdari* storytelling is performed with the use of a cloth (similar to the *par* of India) portraying scenes of epics or religious stories. These stories are usually performed in the streets. Epics and mythical stories are also performed in coffee houses. *Bakhshi* are storytellers who narrate *dastan* (traditional Turkish epic) with self-accompaniment on the *dotar* (a two-stringed long-necked lute). Singing is traditionally done is three languages: Turkish, Persian, and Kurdish. They perform at village ceremonies, such as weddings, and also in coffeehouses. *Bakhshi* are also found in Central Asia.	www.tehrantimes.com/PDF/10652/ 10652-7.pdf, accessed on September 28, 2010 http://www.ancientsites.com/aw/Post/ 180638, accessed on September 28, 2010

Table 12.1. (continued)

Culture of Origin	Style Features	Suggested Resources
Japanese	*Kamishibai* storytelling uses large picture cards to illustrate the story. The *kamishibai* storyteller rides into a village on a bicycle, sets up the storytelling stage, sounds two wooden clappers called *hyoshigi* to call the children to buy candy and hear a story! Ritual ending: "Dondo harai" (With this, it's sold out).	Allen Say's *Kamishibai Man*
Jewish	*Klezmorim* are troubadours who play *klezmer* at joyful events. *Badkhn* (the master of ceremonies at weddings) creates rhymes and word plays about the wedding couple and tells stories at each stage of the event.	Howard Schwartz's *Elijah's Violin* Isaac Bashevis Singer's *Stories for Children* David Wisniewski's *Golem* http://www.jewishstorytelling.org/, accessed on September 28, 2010
Korean	*P'Ansori* are folk narratives sung with accompaniment on a *puk* (barrel drum). The audience holds primary importance in the storytelling and with the drummer, sends *ch'uimsae* (encouragement) to the teller at appropriate intervals in the story.	http://www.iias.nl/oideion/journal/issue03/um/index-a.html, accessed on September 28, 2010
American Indian	Emotions tend not to be conveyed through words but through gesture and voice. Audience responds with "ee-so" (ye-s indeed). Children are expected to listen attentively. American Indians do NOT tell stories during harvest season and neither should any tellers of Native American stories!	Joseph Bruchac (see Chapter 1) Gerald McDermott's *The Raven*
South American	Stories blend traditions of the indigenous Indian, African, and a bit of local Spanish culture.	http://www.unesco.org/courier/2001_05/uk/culture.htm, accessed on September 28, 2010
Southeast Asia	Bards play the chapay, a two-stringed lute, to alternate music and speech in folk and moral tales. (Cambodia—Kampuchea) Ethnic groups perform epic songs. (Viet Nam)	Thick Nhat Hanh's *The Dragon Prince: Stories and Legends from Vietnam*

Note: Information gathered and summarized from these sources: Chase, 1943; Lester, 1988; Lopez, 2001; Pellowski, 1990; Schwartz, 1983; Sheppard, 2004; Wolkstein, 1980.

artifacts, such as instruments or pieces of cloth from the county of origin, or embedding your telling with carefully chosen words in the original language of the story. These measures convey to your listeners the idea that "there's more to this story than what I'm telling" (Pellowski, 1990, p. 229). When I tell a Bantu story called "Uwungelema," I intentionally include several Bantu words ("uwungelema" and "uwelawela") and invite the audience to say them with me. In this way we all gain a sense of something more than what the story itself conveys.

Maintaining the integrity of a multicultural story is a more intuitive process. Ask yourself if your telling is able to uphold the integrity of the story and trust that it is all right to say "no" to telling a particular story. Not everyone can tell all stories. The most poignant example in my storytelling experience involved Virginia Hamilton's (1985) powerful story, "The People Could Fly." It was not possible for me to tell this story for several reasons; Primarily, slavery is not in my experience. It would be possible only to try to empathize with the enslaved condition, and it would be possible to select stories for telling that portray the inhumanity of this institution. However, it was not possible for me to maintain the integrity of "The People Could Fly" as it is told from the perspective of those enslaved. A second reason for choosing not to tell the story was because it includes slave dialect. It is my belief that this dialect's history of being mimicked and ridiculed by white people in many different contexts renders it disrespectful for a white storyteller to voice.

Adding to the debate on authenticity and integrity discussed in Chapter 1, Award-winning African American writer, Jacqueline Woodson (1998), offers these comments about people who would write about things outside their personal experience: "My hope is that those who write about the tears and the laughter and the language in my grandmother's house have first sat down at the table with us and dipped the bread of their own experiences into our stew" (p. 38). If fitting for writers, how much more it is required of storytellers.

THE VALUES OF TELLING MULTICULTURAL FOLK STORIES IN THE CLASSROOM AND LIBRARY

Multicultural folk stories hold widely documented values as the chapters in this book demonstrate. Through these stories we come to understand other cultures and our own from the inside out (Yolen, 1981). We can compare stories from different parts of the world and see similarities of character and situation that unite us (Maguire, 1985). We can trace the paths oral stories have traveled on slave routes, from conquerors to conquered peoples, and through courageous immigration to new places (Barton & Booth, 1990).

From a storytelling perspective, these multicultural folk stories hold additional values for both the teller and listeners. For tellers, it is possible to find just the right one to use for a specific audience or purpose, because these stories are available in many versions and variants (Livo & Reitz, 1987). Further, multicultural folk tales reside within the public domain making it possible to avoid sticky copyright issues.

For listeners, multicultural folk stories offer clear, uncomplicated patterns that support young students' development of story grammar; and the rich literary language of stories expands students' command of their own vocabulary (Livo & Reitz, 1987). The uncomplicated characters provide clear delineations of good and evil, just rewards, and earned consequences that support social-moral development. Indeed, through the ages multicultural folk stories have offered safe and fertile ground for students' emotional and psychological development (Blatt, 1993; Bettleheim, 1976). Listening to folk stories encourages the use of imagination and problem-solving strategies in a risk-free, supportive context. Further, the cultural information conveyed through these stories builds background knowledge that bolsters content area learning, particularly in the social studies.

The current commitment to robust multicultural understanding issues a call for greater use of this body of stories, for "[t]hese tales teach life lessons in a gentle way, expanding our view of humanity with their connections to the past and to other cultures. We often have a hard time cooperating on both personal and global levels . . ." (Kraus, 1998, p. vii). The daily news indicates this need for cooperation has never been greater. Exposure to a wide variety of cultural literature with its gentle teachings serves us and our students well.

THE PROCESS OF CLASSROOM AND LIBRARY STORYTELLING

Selecting just the right story to tell is the first consideration of the process. To find the just right story, read, read, read, and read more stories, and even read different versions of the same story. Listen to your own mind's voice as you read until you find the story that resonates with you. With practice, including some storytelling experiences that fall short of your expectations, you will more and more easily recognize the one story that fits your purpose, your audience, and your own telling style.

To select stories that are well suited for your intended audience, ask yourself if the audience will appreciate the characters' actions, understand the solution to the problem, and aesthetically and emotionally engage with the story. Also consider the curricular connections that the audience will be able to draw. Does the story touch relevant themes or times and places?

Preparation for a good telling requires repeated readings of the story. As you read, identify key words and phrases that evoke the culture. Research the key word pronunciations to accurately include this authentic language in your telling. As an aid to learning the story, you may find it helpful to map the story structure. Visualization of the setting and characters will also help you tap appropriate language as you describe these for your listeners. An important caveat: memorization impedes a good telling. It lessens your ability to *tell the story* by drawing your attention from the fluid cocreation of story with your audience to a static written form.

After you become comfortable with the story structure and message, you will want to practice techniques for effective telling. Experiment freely with gestures, voice, and facial expressions. Gestures can be used to indicate distance, size, and emotion. Try different voice volume, pitch, and speed. Another caveat exists: do not employ false voices, such as falsetto. These are difficult to maintain and can interfere with the flow of the telling. Use a mirror to evaluate various facial expressions.

When you are satisfied with some of the above techniques, practice, practice, practice! Tell your story to your pets and your plants. Become accustomed to hearing your voice. Practice with a trusted audience, such as your family and friends, to embed the use of eye contact in your telling and become comfortable with attending to the audience response.

Guiding students through the storytelling process is quite similar to your own process (Peck, 1989). Consider having the whole class work with only one story at first.

This enables your modeling of the process. Provide a variety of versions of the story. Guide your students' information gathering on the culture of the story using books or the Internet. Provide a story frame for mapping the structure and have the students work in small groups to complete maps of different versions of the story. Then guide the class to note similarities and differences and posit reasons for these (e.g., oral tradition, changes in locale). Give vocalization practice by having the students in unison repeat a repetitive phrase from the story in different voices (e.g., angry, timid). Give facial practice using a creative drama technique: students assume a self-space facing you and on cue, "show me a surprised face," produce that expression. Similarly, give gesture practice with in self-space taking your cues. Provide practice sessions of the whole storytelling in diads or triads with peers giving useful feedback on what worked well and what may need revision or more practice. As the students gain confidence in their storytelling abilities, provide a wide variety of multicultural stories that connect to curricular content and themes to encourage their continued work with the process.

EXTENSION ACTIVITIES

It is not difficult to locate resources for extending storytelling into the curriculum or into the community. Books previously cited in this chapter provide excellent starting points with activities linked to specific stories and story themes (Garrity, 1999; Livo & Reitz, 1987).

Much can be learned when students write about a story told to them. After telling "Stone Soup" (McGovern, 1968) to a class of seven-year olds, you can simply ask them to write in response to the story. You can talk about writing a character sketch or writing their version of the story as they remembered it. Some students may cast the old woman as a little old witch, complete with warts and crooked nose. Though these images are not included in the telling, it will be clear that these students cocreated this image as they listened to the story. Others may retell the story with the clear beginning, middle, and end, so characteristic of folk tales in their own words and voice. Another student may struggle to put words on the blank page and may ask if he/she could draw first. Encourage the student to do so. You may find the student drawing at the top of the page with a fully formed story following it.

Students might also write another version of the story, told in the voice of one of the characters. Indeed, a new genre of such folktales is available today, most notably the work of Jon Scieszka and Lane Smith (e.g., *The True Story of the Three Little Pigs*). Students might also write a sequel to the story in which another enemy is routed or challenge met.

Working beyond print to create visual representations in the style of *kamishibai* or *par* stories invites collaboration of art teachers and taps artistic talent that students may unknowingly hold. Students who excel at constructing in three dimensions may enjoy creating an electronic story complete with avatars and using virtual reality software. Others may enjoy a different technical process of building a diorama or model to portray story scenes.

Students may be inspired to tell their own personal stories. A good starting point is for them to tell the story of their name. This usually generates good conversation with parents about how they chose their name, who else in the family held the name, and perhaps the meaning of the name. As students gain understanding of multicultural stories and increase their own confidence in storytelling, encourage them to think about a personal story that relates to one of another culture and to prepare to tell it. This process will help the students realize the universality of the human condition, and ultimately provoke greater empathy for others.

Classes may engage the larger community by inviting families, civic groups, the school's business partners to a storytelling concert presented by the students. This will provide an expanded audience for the students' work, profoundly culminate the unit of study, and encourage wider appreciation for the students' work and your own.

CLOSING THOUGHTS

In the United States, storytelling enjoyed a robust renewal of interest during the 1980s. Festivals grew in number and attendance. Collections of stories gathered from the world, techniques on the process of storytelling, and classroom benefits and curricular connections (Peck, 1989) were all widely published during this time. Although activity and publication on storytelling appear to have waned, as long as people gather in community to remember their past, to bequeath their values to the young, to heal themselves, to laugh and to dream for what is yet to be, storytelling will thrive. And when we dip into the well of multicultural stories, we not only see the culture "from the inside out" (Yolen, 1981), we also see ourselves. May it be so for you and for all those whom you teach.

REFERENCES

Barton, B., & Booth, D. (1990). *Stories in the classroom: Storytelling, reading aloud and roleplaying with students*. Portsmouth, NH: Heinemann.

Bettleheim, B. (1976). *The uses of enchantment: The meaning and importance of fairy tales*. New York, NY: Knopf.

Blatt, G. (1993). *Once upon a folktale: Capturing the folklore process with students*. New York, NY: Teachers College.

Garrity, L. K. (1999). *The tale spinner: Folktales, themes and activities*. Golden, CO: Fulcrum Resources.

Lipman, D. (2003, November 28). *In search of the folktale*. Retrieved from http://storydynamics.com.

Lipman, D. (1999). *Improving your storytelling: Beyond the basics for all who tell stories in work or play*. Little Rock, AR: August House.

Livo, N. J., & Reitz, S. A. (1987). *Storytelling activities*. Littleton, CO: Libraries Unlimited.

Kraus, A. M. (1998). *Folktale themes and activities for students, Vol 1*.

Englewood, CO: Teacher Ideas. Lopez, A. (2001, May). Weaving magic with the spoken word. Retrieved from UNESCO: http://www.unesco.org/courier/2001_05/uk/culture.htm.

Maguire, J. (1985). *Creative storytelling: Choosing, inventing, and sharing tales for students*. New York, NY: McGraw-Hill.

Miller, T., Comp. with A. Pellowski, & Livo, N., Ed. (1988). *Joining in: An anthology of audience participation stories and how to tell them*. Cambridge, MA: Yellow Moon.

Peck, J. (1989). Using storytelling to promote language and literacy development. *The Reading Teacher*, 43(2), 138–141.

Pellowski, A. (1990). *The world of storytelling*. New York, NY: H. W. Wilson.

Sheppard, T. (2004, January 13). Traditional storytelling. http://www.timsheppard.co.uk/story/dir/traditions/.

Woodson, J. (1998, January/February). Who can tell my story? *The Horn Book Magazine*, 74, 34–38.

Yolen, J. (1981). *Touch magic: Fantasy, faerie and folklore in the literature of childhood.* New York, NY: Philomel.

CHILDREN AND YOUNG ADULT BOOKS

Badoe, A. (2001). *The pot of wisdom: Ananse stories*, illustrated by B. W. Diakite. Toronto, ONT: Groundwood Books/Douglas & McIntyre.

Chase, R. (1943). *The Jack tales: Folk tales from the southern Appalachians collected and retold by Richard Chas*, illustrated by B. Williams, Jr. Boston, MA: Houghton Mifflin.

Hamilton, V. (1985). *The people could fly: American Black folktales told by Virginia Hamilton*, illustrated by L. and D. Dillon. New York, NY: Knopf.

Lester, J. (1987). *Tales of Uncle Remus: The adventures of Brer Rabbit*, illustrated by J. Pinkney. New York, NY: Puffin.

Lester, J. (1988). *More tales of Uncle Remus: Further adventures of Brer Rabbit, his friends, enemies, and others*, illustrated by J. Pinkney. New York, NY: Dial.

McDermott, G (1993). *The raven: A trickster tale from the Pacific Northwest.* San Diego: Harcourt Brace Jovanovich.

McGovern, A. (1968). *Stone soup.* New York, NY: Scholastic.

Nhat Hanh, T. (2007). *Dragon prince: Stories and legends from Vietnam*, illustrated by N. Thi Hop, & N. Dong. Berkeley, CA: Parallax.

Say, A. (2005). *Kamishibai man.* New York, NY: Houghton Mifflin.

Schwartz, H. (1983). *Elijah's violin & other Jewish fairy tales*, illustrated by L. Heller. New York, NY: Harper Colophon.

Scieszka, J. (1996). *The true story of the three little pigs*, illustrated by L. Smith. New York, NY: Puffin.

Yolen, J. (1986). *Favorite folktales from around the world.* New York, NY: Pantheon.

Singer, I. B. (1984). *Stories for children.* New York, NY: Farrar Straus Giroux.

Wisniewski, D. (1996). *Golem.* New York, NY: Clarion.

Wolkstein, D. (1980). *The magic orange tree.* New York, NY: Schocken.

RESOURCES

American Library Association, www.ala.org, accessed on September 28, 2010.

Carrison, M. P., Kong, C. (1987). *Cambodian folk stories from the Gatiloke.* Singapore: Tuttle.

Cole, J. (1982). *Best-loved folk-tales of the world.* New York, NY: Anchor.

Cora Agatucci's African Storytelling, http://web.cocc.edu/cagatucci/classes/hum211/afrstory.htm, accessed on September 28, 2010.

Doug Lipman's In Search of the Folktale, http://storydynamics.com/Articles/Finding_and_Creating/types.html, accessed on September 28, 2010.

International Storytelling Center, www.storytellingfoundation.net/, accessed on September 28, 2010.

National Association for the Preservation and Perpetuation of Storytelling, www.storynet.org/, accessed on September 28, 2010.

13

Linking Audiovisuals with Multicultural Literature

Meghan Harper

Hannah enthusiastically greeted her fourth grade students as they streamed into the classroom. She hid a smile as she overheard them excitedly discussing their current multicultural literature unit exploring achievements of African Americans in the twentieth century. Hannah can hardly wait to share the success of this learning experience with her graduate school colleagues. This interdisciplinary unit enabled her to address multiple academic content standards while engaging ALL of the students' attention, a feat she endeavored to accomplish the entire school year. Hannah thought back to her first love, multicultural literature, and how this led to a wonderful learning experience for both her and the students. Hannah initially selected several of her favorite literature titles, *We Are the Ship* and *When Marian Sang* and then identified online audiovisual resources that would provide a context for the historical periods described in the books. The versatile format of the audiovisuals had enabled Hannah to enhance her whole group instruction as well as small group and individual work. The plethora of primary sources she found online directly connected with her literature titles and enabled her to address specific curricular concepts and skills. This cross-disciplinary unit addressed multiple content standards and skills and, most importantly, engaged the students' interest. Hannah was amazed at how this unit had stimulated many questions and opinions about individual rights. The students were already asking questions that tied in neatly with the next unit investigating the lives of Japanese Americans during World War II.

Audiovisual resources present unique opportunities for educators to enhance learning, stimulate dialogue and engage students in multisensory experiences with multicultural literature. Multisensory learning is defined as "learning that involves the processing of stimuli through two or more senses (e.g., through hearing as well as seeing)" ("Multisensory Learning," 2010, para. 1). Baines (2008) contends, "One of the greatest benefits of using multisensory stimuli is that they have the potential to involve students more fully in the learning experience" (p. 20). Multisensory experiences encourage associative learning and help readers make connections while reading. The versatility of audiovisual formats enables educators to integrate audiovisuals with multicultural literature across disciplines and age levels.

Technological innovations have greatly improved access to and availability of audiovisual resources so that educators can now easily locate, access, and use audiovisual resources and address academic content standards during instruction. Audiovisuals encourage children to actively participate in classroom discussions and activities. Baines (2008) suggests that, "At its core, multisensory learning is a way of teaching that requires students to activate their full faculties—seeing, hearing, smelling, tasting, moving, touching, thinking, intuiting, enjoying—in a variety of situations" (p. 21). The use of audiovisuals can help students to understand complex curricular concepts and extend their understanding of these concepts.

Support for the use of audio materials is cited in the document, *Recorded Books Work!*, "For students who are attempting to read informational text written at a level above their independent reading level, audiobook support has been shown to bridge the gap" (Recorded Books K–12, 2004). Audiovisual materials are flexible, making them useful resources for different learning styles and developmental levels. Additionally, audiovisuals use graphics and narration to describe and explain complex ideas, making academic content accessible to students who are not yet able to learn the content through reading. Through audiovisuals, learners can focus on meaning while reading rather than on decoding text. Audiovisuals provide opportunities for educators to enhance their instruction to appeal and appear more relevant to students with different learning styles. Baines (2008) points out,

Designing relevant and engaging interactions not only enhances student learning, it also affects students' long-term intellectual development. Using multisensory stimuli in instruction increases engagement, promotes deeper participation, and advances the prospect that learning can be fun.

(p. 23)

The fun factor of using audiovisuals and increasing student interest in learning cannot be underrated. Researchers, Pintrich and Schunk, (2002) claim, "The relationship between a positive attitude toward a subject and academic achievement in that subject is one of the strongest correlations in educational research." Furthermore, with audiovisuals, educators can use different formats to help students learn content in new ways.

Children's experiences with media today are vastly different from the experiences of their parents and teachers. Research suggests that before leaving college a student will spend over 10,000 hours playing video games, send and receive over 200,000 emails and text messages, spend 10,000 hours talking on cell phones, spend 20,000 hours watching television, and watch 500,000 commercials (Prensky, 2001a, p.1). Research findings indicate that children consistently and frequently have access to many forms of media and the number and variety of media they encounter on a daily basis is constant (American Institute for Research, 2004). The use of technology permeates most schools and impacts activities that children have access to on a daily basis. George Lucas reminds us that the "everyday experience" of young people is a media rich environment by stating:

Today we work with the written or spoken word as the primary form of communication. But we also need to understand the importance of graphics, music, and cinema, which are just as powerful and in some ways more deeply intertwined with young people's culture. We live and work in a visually sophisticated world, so we must be sophisticated in using all the forms of communication, not just the written word.

(Baines, 2008, p. 25)

Negative publicity about violence and excessive use of media such as television and the Internet is abundant. However, research on the benefits of developmentally appropriate uses of media is also prevalent. The fact is that children's exposure to and use of media makes a difference. Most children experience a variety of media formats for a large part of each day. In schools, audiovisual materials and multiple forms of media increase student access to the curriculum and increase their opportunities to engage in learning curricular concepts. In addition to facilitating a multisensory experience with curricular content, audiovisuals provide a bridge that enables many students to overcome difficulties with text-based activities. Audio materials motivate reluctant readers and decrease anxiety for struggling readers and English as a Second Language (ESL) students. The use of audiovisuals creates a dual experience when students see and hear a word at the same time; assisting them in decoding difficult words and deciphering unfamiliar concepts (Recorded Books, 2004). Ever-present audio materials enhance the learning experience. Furthermore, a multisensory approach stimulates and increases the development of associated memories and retention (Baines, 2008). Audiovisual materials foster cross-disciplinary investigation as students use different senses.Furthermore, they provide a rich context for learning about diverse cultures.

CURRENT TRENDS IN USING AUDIOVISUALS IN THE CLASSROOM

Today, a wealth of high quality audiovisual resources is available such as e-books, audio books, computer software, DVDs, and videos. The availability of free online resources that can be adapted for use with mobile technologies and easily accessed in the classroom has rapidly increased. Teachers only need to power up their classroom in order to take advantage of the variety of podcasts, video clips, and primary source materials that expand learning beyond the walls of the school. Audiovisual resources are flexible and present many educational opportunities for youth. Incorporating audiovisual resources in instruction helps to address differences in learning styles and helps to appeal to different interests. The use of audiovisuals in the classroom fosters "reading comprehension, fluency, language acquisition, vocabulary development and improved achievement" (Grover & Hannegan, 2008, p.17). As a result, students may experience more success in interpreting and understanding literature. The emphasis on nonfiction materials in academic testing and the increased availability of nonfiction-based audiovisual materials reflects educational standards at the state and national levels.

New audiovisual formats encourage children to be creators of information and ideas and not just consumers. Audiovisuals are becoming more accessible and available to educators due to the decreasing cost and the increasing ease of use. This is particularly the case for computer software. The emphasis on media literacies in academic content standards requires that students experience a variety of informational media. Audiovisuals also enable educators to efficiently make use of classroom instructional time. Students can use audiovisual materials independently and in small groups. Increased student interest and motivation in the subject area are added benefits for teachers who integrate audiovisuals in the classroom. Students are also highly motivated to use audiovisuals. As a result, educators can effectively make down time and wait time into quality instructional time. Students at all ability levels can benefit from the use of audiovisual materials to enhance their learning. Audiovisuals can be used to introduce complex topics, for remediation, practice, or to extend learning.

Research cited by Marc Prensky (2001a) from the field of neurobiology found that students' brains are physically different as a result of the exposure to large amounts of media. The new developments in brain research and published literature on how today's students learn have influenced the development of curricular and instructional materials that address students' learning preferences. *Brain based learning* is a term for instruction that is based on research from neuroscience that addresses how the brain learns. *Brain based education* takes into account how the brain learns naturally and is based on what we currently know about the actual structure and function of the human brain at varying developmental stages. Using the latest neural research, educational techniques are being developed that are brain friendly and provide a biologically driven framework for creating effective instruction and learning (Owens, 2007).

Marc Prensky (2001b) coined the term, *millennial learner*, and describes these students as having "Hypertext minds". The underlying rationale is that the "brain changes and organizes itself differently based on the inputs it receives" (p. 2). Students receive an amazing amount of information through digital mediums and process information differently than parents and teachers. Due to students' preference for receiving information quickly, Prensky (2001a) notes millennial learners seek choice and crave interactivity as well as expect instant gratification. Today's students are capable and actually prefer engaging in multitasking experiences. Thus, the use of audiovisuals is viewed favorably by these youth.

RATIONALE FOR USING AUDIOVISUAL MATERIALS WITH MULTICULTURAL LITERATURE

Using audiovisuals with multicultural literature assists students in relating to unfamiliar people and places in an authentic way. The use of audiovisuals with multicultural literature promotes awareness of cultures, illuminates shared commonalities, and celebrates differences. Indeed, audiovisuals affect individuals' multiple senses, and, thus, touch the heart and engage the soul. Students can witness first-hand the emotions of others' joy, pain, and sorrow. Depicting emotions visually and aurally facilitates understanding and empathy for others. In the article, "Music and Language Learning," Lake, (2002) asserts that optimum learning occurs in an environment of high stimulation and low anxiety. Lake, an ESL teacher, suggests teachers can create an optimal environment for learning through engaging students' minds, memories and senses.

In an audio book, a collection of music may accompany a narrated story. Such is the case with the audiobook title, *Ella Fitzgerald: The Tale of A Vocal Virtuosa*, which includes archival recordings of the singer. The value of pairing music with learning is discussed by Chris Brewer (2008) who provides a rationale for using music to enhance learning: it has a positive impact on the learning environment including students' concentration, attention, and memory. Indeed music is a valuable resource that can lead to a multisensory learning experience. In software products, features may include primary source materials such as music, interviews, speeches, photos, video clips, picture galleries or games. These unique features increase the opportunities that students have to make personal connections and identify with a culture intellectually and emotionally. For example, *When Marian Sang* by Pam Muñoz Ryan (2002) is a book about Marian Anderson, an African American opera singer in the early 1900s who led the way for other African Americans to break the color barrier. A CD accompanies the picture book with songs sung by Marian Anderson. By listening to the CD, the reader hears Marian Anderson's voice and, thereby, gains a deeper understanding of the story. Furthermore, an item's special features and versatile format ensure that students can use the item in varying ways independently or with a group. Authors Junko Yokota and Miriam Martinez (2007) suggest:

Multicultural audiobooks are particularly important in classrooms because teachers sometimes express a lack of confidence in reading these books aloud. They may feel uncomfortable reading unfamiliar words in a foreign language or hesitate to read aloud books in which the rhythm of the text feels unfamiliar when spoken.

(p. 1)

The availability and sheer volume of information available in a range of formats has greatly changed the attention and focus on media literacy education. According to the American Institute for Research (2004) media literacy is defined as the "ability to access, understand, analyze, evaluate and create messages in a wide range of media" (p. 11). Research suggests children's understanding and engagement with the world around them is better when media messages are moderated. Exposing children to a wide variety of formats and guiding them in the use and evaluation of media is crucial to their overall development of media literacy skills. The prolific use of mobile technologies and availability of audiovisual resources that students may access beyond the school day make it imperative that educators and parents make informed decisions about selection and use of media.

Gay & Hanley (1999) presented four concepts as support for multicultural education for middle school students:

1. the importance of civic participation, especially as it relates to democratic principles;
2. a sense of community membership that includes the contributions from many ethnic, racial, and gender groups;
3. the importance of cooperation and collaboration, where pooling efforts can contribute to the common good; and
4. the ability to solve problems, make decisions, using critical thinking skills. (as cited in Bishop, 2003, p. 35)

At all age levels, multicultural audiovisual materials connected with multicultural literature can be used to enable students to identify with their own backgrounds and experiences or expose students to new or unfamiliar life experiences of others.

Table 13.1 provides an example of the connections that can be made between multicultural literature and audiovisual materials, and how these materials correlate with academic content standards. Although the titles in this chart primarily reflect African American titles, many of the online sites listed in the table are useful across cultures.

Teachers can use Table 13.1 to assist them with designing instruction and incorporating audiovisual multicultural materials. Audiovisual materials provide excellent starting points to introduce students to a new topic or to generate discussion. For example, *Planting the Trees of Kenya: The Story of Wangari Maathai* by Claire A. Nivola (2008)

Table 13.1.
Multicultural Connections.

Theme	Books	Additional Materials	Academic Standards
Folktales	*Her Stories: African American Folktales, Fairy Tales, and True Tales* by Virginia Hamilton	Slavery and the Making of America Soundtrack (Music CD)	Social Studies • History • Grade 1 (B)
Slavery	*The People Could Fly* by Virginia Hamilton (audiobook)	Black Slavery Days (Music CD)	• Grade 2 (C–D) • Grade 3 (A) • People in Society
United States History	*Sojourner Truth: Preacher for Freedom and Equality* by Suzanne Slade	http://school.discoveryeducation.com/schooladventures/slavery/	• Grade 4 (A) • Skills and Methods • Grade 5 (A–B)
	An African American Alphabet: D is for Drinking Gourd by Nancy I. Sanders	http://www.pbs.org/wnet/slavery/	Science • Scientific Ways of Knowing
		http://www.negrospirituals.com/	
		http://www.loc.gov/rr/print/list/082_slave.html	• Kindergarten (B–C) • Grade 1 (B–C) • Grade 2 (B–C)
		http://www.nationalarchives.gov.uk/pathways/blackhistory/rights/abolition.htm	
Civil War	*The Civil War and Emancipation* by James A. Corrick	*Glory* (Movie)	• Grade 5 (A, C) Social Studies
Abolition	*Reconstruction* by Michael V. Uschan	*Voices of Black America: Historical Recordings of Speeches, Poetry, Humor & Drama* (Playaway)	• History • Grade 8 (G)
Reconstruction	*Ain't Nothing but a Man: My Quest to Find the Real John Henry* by Scott Reynolds Nelson with Marc Aronson	*Gone with the Wind* (Movie)	• Grade 7 (G) • People in Society • Grade 8 (B)

Table 13.1. (continued)

Theme	Books	Additional Materials	Academic Standards

Underground Railroad	*The Underground Railroad: An Interactive History Adventure* by Allison Lassieur
	
	Encyclopedia of the Underground Railroad by J. Blaine Hudson
		Race to Freedom: Story of the Underground Railroad (Movie)
		
		http://www.civil-war.com/
		
		http://www.civil-war.net/
		
		http://www.nationalgeographic.com/railroad/
		
		http://lcweb2.loc.gov/learn/start/keywords/undergrr.html
		
		http://www.ohiohistory.org/undergroundrr/#kids_and_teachers
			• Citizenship
			  • Grade 8 (B)
			• Skills and Methods
			  • Grade 8 (A–D)
			
			Science
			• Scientific Ways of Knowing
			  • Kindergarten (B–C)
			  • Grade 1 (B–C)
			  • Grade 2 (B–C)
			  • Grade 5 (A, C)

Music	*Duke Ellington: "I live with music"* by Carin T. Ford	*Inspiring figures: Jazz greats* (Playaway of books)
		Ella Fitzgerald: The Tale of a Vocal Virtuoso by Andrea Davis Pinkney
		Ellington was not a Street by Ntozake Shange
		Duke Ellington by Andrea Davis Pinkney
			Social Studies
			• History
			  • Grade 10 (F)
			• Citizenship
			  • Grade 10 (A)
			• Skills and Methods
			  • Grade 10 (A–B)

Jazz	*Louis Armstrong: "Jazz is played from the heart"* by Michael A. Schuman	*Masterpieces* by Ellington (Music CD)	Library • Media Literacy
Blues	*Jazz* by Walter Dean Myers (available with audio)	*The Definitive Collection* (Louis Armstrong) (Music CD)	• Grade 4 (A) • Grade 3 (A–B)

(continued)

Table 13.1. (continued)

Theme	Books	Additional Materials	Academic Standards
Art	Jazz ABZ by Wynton Marsalis	The Complete Ella Fitzgerald Songbooks (Music CD)	• Grade 7 (B) • Information Literacy
Famous People	Ella Fitzgerald: The Tale of a Vocal Virtuoso by Andrea Davis Pinkney	The Best of Art Tatum (Music CD)	• Grade 6 (A) Fine Arts
Segregation	Ellington was not a Street by Ntozake Shange	The Best of the Pablo Solo Masterpieces (Music CD)	• Dance, Music • Grade K–4 (A)
Civil Rights	Duke Ellington by Andrea Davis Pinkney	Martin Scorsese Presents: The Best of the Blues Soundtrack (Music CD)	• Music • Grade 5–12 (A)
	Piano Starts Here: The Young Art Tatum, by Robert Andrew Parker	Pure Blues (Music CD)	
	The Blues of Flats Brown by Walter Dean Myers (audiobook)	http://pbskids.org/jazz/	
	Getting to Know The World's Greatest Artists: Horace Pippin, by Mike Venezia	http://www.jazz.com/	
		www.jerryjazzmusician.com	
		www.redhotjazz.com	
		www.apassion4jazz.net	
		www.youtube.com: Search Art Tatum	
		http://afroamhistory.about.com/od/bluesmusic/a/bluesmusic.htm	
		http://www.scaruffi.com/history/blues.html	
Baseball	We Are the Ship: The Story of Negro League Baseball by Kadir Nelson	There was Always Sun Shining Someplace: Life in the Negro Baseball Leagues (PBS Documentary)	Science • Scientific Ways of Knowing

Table 13.1. (continued)

Theme	Books	Additional Materials	Academic Standards
Civil Rights	*Jackie Robinson Plays Ball* by Robyn O'Sullivan	http://www.coe.ksu.edu/nlbemuseum/resource/guide.html	• Kindergarten (B–C) • Grade 1 (B–C)
Segregation		www.baseballhalloffame.org	• Grade 2 (B–C)
Famous People		http://memory.loc.gov/ammem/collections/robinson	• Grade 5 (A, C)
		www.archives.gov/education/lessons/jackie-robinson	
		http://www.negroleaguebaseball.com/	
		http://www.blackbaseball.com/	
Civil Rights	*I Have a Dream An Illustrated Edition* by Dr. Martin Luther King, Jr.	*Martin's Big Words* by Doreen Rappaport (Video)	Social Studies • History • Grade 10 (F)
Segregation	*Freedom Walkers: The Story of the Montgomery Bus Boycott* by Russell Freedman	YouTube: Search "Rosa Parks"	Science • Scientific Ways of Knowing
Famous People	*Paul Robeson: "I Want to Make Freedom Ring"* by Carin T. Ford	YouTube: Search "I have a Dream"	• Kindergarten (B–C) • Grade 1 (B–C)
	The Civil Rights Movement: Marching in Birmingham by William J. Boerst	http://www.infoplease.com/spot/civilrightstimeline1.html	• Grade 2 (B–C) • Grade 5 (A, C)
	The Civil Rights Movement: Freedom Summer by David Aretha	http://lcweb2.loc.gov/ammem/aaohtml/exhibit/aopart9.html	
	The Civil Rights Movement: Striving for Justice by Tim McNeese	http://www.voicesofcivilrights.org/	

(continued)

Table 13.1. (continued)

Theme	Books	Additional Materials	Academic Standards
Civil Rights Segregation	*When Marian Sang* by Pam Munoz Ryan	Marian Anderson, Spirituals, (Music CD)	
	The Voice that Challenged a Nation: Marian Anderson and the Struggle for Equal Rights by Russell Freedman	*Marian Anderson: A Portrait in Music* (DVD)	
Famous People	*Getting to Know the World's Greatest Artists: Faith Ringgold* by Mike Venezia	*Faith Ringgold Paints Crown Heights* by Linda Freeman (Video)	
		http://www.mariananderson.org/home/index.html	
		http://www.pbs.org/newshour/bb/remember/1997/anderson_2-26a.html	
		http://www.afrovoices.com/anderson.html	
		http://www.learningtogive.org/lessons/unit292/lesson1.html	
Famous People	*Pele: Soccer Superstar* by Laurie Collier Hillstrom	*Soccer–"Pele": The Master & His Method* (DVD)	
	Muhammad Ali: American Champion Graphic Novel by Michael Burgan	*"Muhammad" Ali–The Whole Story* (DVD)	
		YouTube.com: search Pele	
		http://www.ifhof.com/hof/pele.asp	
		http://www.ali.com/	
		YouTube.com: search Muhammad	
Famous People	*I Dream a World: Portraits of Black Women Who Changed America* by Brian Lanker	*She's a Queen: A Collection of Hits* by Queen Latifah (Music CD)	
	Modern World Leaders: Thabo Mbeki by Dennis Abrams	*High School Phenoms* (DVD)	

Table 13.1. (continued)

Theme	Books	Additional Materials	Academic Standards
	People in the News: Queen Latifah by Judy Galens	http://www.mayaangelou.com/	
	People in the News: 50 Cent by Michael V. Uschan	http://www.anc.org.za/ancdocs/history/mbeki/	
		People in the News: LeBron James by Anne Wallace Sharp	
Famous People		Kenya: Afro-Cuban Jazz (Music CD)	Science
			• Science and Technology
			• Grade 1–2 (A)
Environment Protection	*Planting the Trees of Kenya: The Story of Wangari Maathai* by Claire A. Nivola	The Rough Guide of the Music of Kenya (Music CD)	
		http://www.greenbeltmovement.org/	
		http://nobelprize.org/nobel_prizes/peace/laureates/2004/maathai-bio.html	

can be used to initiate discussion about environmental issues as well as the impact of government and politics on environmental policies. This story is also a great testament to an individual's ability to make a difference in the world. To further enrich their experience, students can listen to several musical selections that depict the music of Kenya with these musical compilations, *Kenya: Afro-Cuban Jazz* (Music CD; Machito, 2000) and *The Rough Guide of the Music of Kenya (Music CD)* (Various Artists, 2004). In Nivola's book, the Green Belt Movement is introduced. Questions generated from reading the book can be categorized, and students can visit Web sites such as http://www .greenbeltmovement.org/, retrieved on October 2, 2010 to find out more information. While categorizing questions, teachers may want to brainstorm with students potential sources of information. This provides students with an excellent opportunity to hone their informational literacy skills. Students can identify what source of information is needed and where to search for the information. For example, if current information is needed, students may want to visit their school library's electronic periodical database. If country demographic facts or statistics are needed, an online or print almanac or government web site would be the best resource. Once students have found the needed information they may want to tap additional audiovisual resources, such as a video or audio recording, to share the information with their classmates.

CONNECTIONS TO ACADEMIC CONTENT

Audiovisuals can be connected to the different academic content areas in many ways. Below are some examples of audiovisual connections with English language arts, science, math and social studies.

English/Language Arts
- audio helps students with unfamiliar words and phrases,
- Audio helps improve phonological and decoding skills, and
- improves spelling.

Science
- explains concepts visually;
- shows interconnectedness of environment, politics, economic cause and effect; and
- application of scientific concepts and principles to real life.

Math
- assists with memory and imagination and
- sequencing of events and time.

Social Studies
- increases understanding of cultures,
- social issues,
- geography, and
- provides context to historical events.

SELECTION AND EVALUATION OF AUDIOVISUAL MATERIALS

Educators need to evaluate the content, value, cost, and use of the item when selecting or purchasing audiovisuals for use in instruction. The format of audiovisuals makes them inherently difficult to judge just by the cover. Audiovisuals often contain supplemental features that can increase the value and use potential. Thus, it is important to evaluate the item as a whole in addition to the separate components. Supplemental features include information in the form of video clips, graphics, interactive activities, additional programs, collections of art work images, or activities. To maximize use of audiovisual resources, educators should preview the resource itself as well as any available teacher guides and documentation. For many audiovisual resources, supplemental teacher guides or lesson plans are available online from the vendor or publisher Web site. All items must be reviewed for content accuracy and cultural sensitivity. Educators must consider that contemporary changes in knowledge and understanding of cultures may affect some presentations of topics. Van Orden and Bishop (2001) suggest that ethnic materials "contain authentic dialogue and depict realistic relationships" and "details in a story should help the reader gain a sense of the culture" (p. 213). One of the key considerations for evaluating multicultural audiovisual materials is the connection among all included information formats. For example, when evaluating a multicultural picture book, a teacher will have to evaluate how well the text and illustrations are connected in addition to the actual accuracy of cultural representation. Audiovisual formats are generally more complex; an audiobook will need to be evaluated in terms of quality of narration, accompanying music, text, and illustrations.

Evaluating materials for appropriateness and effectiveness for diverse audiences requires awareness and knowledge of common bias and inaccuracies with regard to cultural representations. Although each audiovisual format has specific considerations for use in the classroom, educators may use the following five savvy selection tips when evaluating materials for cultural sensitivity.

1. Authority
   Consider *who* has designed and created the item; consider the background, reputation, and credentials of the author, producer, publisher, sponsoring agent, or organization.
2. Accuracy and Currency
   Consider how the information compares with other instructional resources on the topic: the publication date; acknowledgment of opinions, biases, or limitations to the work; and contributions of specialists or experts in the field.
3. Appeal
   Consider criteria for the presentation of content such as organization, unity, scope, layout, and format. The content should be organized and arranged in a logical manner for ease of use and include organizational features such as indices, outlines, and content lists. Graphics and background music should be realistic, current, and avoid exoticism. For example, videos about other countries or cultures may include a visual of a landscape/place or background music that is unique or rare to the culture itself being studied, rather than reflect the mainstream experience of the culture (Waddell & Plummer, 1984, p. 95).
4. Appropriateness
   Consider the developmental, cognitive, and background knowledge of the intended audience. The content should be presented at a level that can be comprehended by the intended user. The length and medium should be suitable to the age and experience level of the intended audience.
5. Potential for Use
   Consider how the resource compares with other materials on the same subject and the connection to specific academic content standards and learning objectives. Educators must also

consider the flexibility and frequency of use within the classroom environment. In many classrooms, the availability of technology and power requirements dictates if the item can be used for multiple purposes.

Evaluating Audiovisuals

Each type of audiovisual format has its own strengths and considerations. Videos and DVDs content and quality are especially difficult to judge by a given title or packaging that has been primarily designed for marketing purposes. Educators should seek reviews or preview audiovisuals that incorporate both sound and music. Waddell and Plummer (1984) note that these types of media "make a deep and long-lasting impression . . . [can] form the basis of images and attitudes that will be extremely resistant to change or correction (p. 93). Reviewing videos and DVDs is an important prerequisite to selection and eventual purchase. In recent years, the review and preview of these materials has become significantly less time consuming and simplified. Many vendor Web sites include video clips on their Web sites with written reviews. These informational sources are adequate for selection purposes but should not be relied upon for a comprehensive understanding of the nature and presentation of the content. The availability of detailed reviews does not negate the need for previewing prior to use in the classroom, especially if the resources will be used for instruction or facilitating discussion. Video and DVD content descriptions can be misleading especially in regard to depth and breadth of topic coverage. Supplemental teaching guides and lesson resources may not be packaged with the item, thus, it behooves educators to allot time for previewing, planning, and in some instances, investigation in order to maximize the use of an item.

Sound recordings, audio books, and playaways are increasingly available on computer disks with accompanying quality print materials. When evaluating these types of audiovisuals, it is good to review the item's technical properties. The quality of narration, presence of clear instructions for use, and accuracy of content are very important. Quality of content is determined by the relevance of themes to children, presentation, and organization of the content. For example when evaluating a story audio book, it is important to first begin with high quality literature and then evaluate the presentation of the content. Narration should be aurally clear and expressive. Relevant themes should match the audience's age and interest level. Instructions should be clear and detailed enough so that use of the audiovisual is not based on intuitive skill or prior knowledge.

Playaways are prerecorded audio recordings that are in a small self-contained box. This small audio recording is usually circulated in public and school libraries with a lanyard and set of ear phones. Students can wear the playaway around their neck or the playaway can be used as a listening center with the addition of speakers plugged into the headphone jack.

Playaways require many of the same evaluative techniques as sound recordings. The narration and any background music should complement the text and add to an understanding of concepts. Playaways are versatile; they can be used with individual students, small groups or for class instruction. And they are highly mobile. Playaways based on nonfiction titles should be carefully previewed to ensure the audio format does not compromise the original content that exists in the corresponding print title. Print titles that have multiple sidebars, illustrations, or content that is primarily designed for a visual format are not necessarily the best titles to get on playaways. Some playaways contain more than one title and have supplementary materials that are wonderful educational resources. Thus, a table of contents or documentation that describes the playaway's contents should accompany the item.

Computer software should be evaluated based on content, use, and accompanying features. The Haugland/Shade Developmental Software Scale (Haugland & Gerzog, 1998) can be used as a guide for selecting quality software. The scale presents a checklist of features that include the presence of and attention to age appropriateness, child control, clear instructions, the fostering of independence, and technical features of the item. Age appropriateness is determined by the type of activities included in the software. The activities should be realistic and at varying levels of complexity to ensure children's independent use. Children should be able to control their progress and exploration of the software. The presence of written, picture, and oral instructions should facilitate students to use of the item. Clearly identified options for beginning or exiting the software should be visually apparent. Clear directions should also enable children to make choices and progress through activities. The item should offer creative opportunities for children to encourage independent use of the item and independent thinking about the content presented. Technical and printing capabilities should encourage use and not be prohibitive. Children should receive appropriate positive feedback as they engage in software activities or games. Compatibility with standard software and hardware is also essential for the continued and maximum use of the item. Educators can consult many of the wonderful online reviewing resources to make good purchasing decisions in addition to consulting their school library, public library, local bookstore, or online bookstores. Teachers and librarians should review each title in a series rather than rely on one item as a representative of the series. Often titles in series will be designed by multiple authors, thus quality from one item to the next can vary. The following checklists in Tables 13.2 and 13.3 can be used to evaluate audiovisual materials that contain audio features (playaways, audiobooks, CDs or cassettes, video) or interactive features (DVDs and CD Roms)

AWARDS FOR QUALITY CHILDREN'S AUDIOVISUALS

A good place to begin locating quality audiovisual materials is by surveying Notable Lists from the American Library Association, vendor Web sites, and professional organizations such as the National PTA. Educators and school librarians who have expertise in format and in content have compiled these lists. Professional journals published by many of these organizations include audiovisual reviews as a constant feature.

Selected Notable Lists

- American Library Association's (ALA's) Great Interactive Software for Children can be found at http://www.ala.org/ala/mgrps/divs/alsc/awardsgrants/notalists/gisk/index.cfm retrieved on October 2, 2010, and provides an annotated bibliography on the current year's ALA notable children's software with a link to past notable children's software dating back to 1996.
- Association for Library Service to Children (ALSC). (2010) ALSC's Notable Recordings According to the *School Library Journal*, 52(4), The Notable Children's videos, recordings, software, and subscription services lists are compiled annually by committees of the Association for Library Service to Children (ALSC). The items on these lists, intended for children 14 years of age and younger, were selected by three committees of librarians and educators

Table 13.2.

Resources with Audio Features (Audiobook, Podcasts, and Video)

Title:

Grade Levels:

Rate: E (excellent), G (good), F (fair), and P (poor)

Content	E	G	F	P	Technical	E	G	F	P
Age appropriateness					Controllable sound				
Freedom from bias/ prejudice					Professionally recorded				
Error-free information					Instructions for installation and operation				
Correct use of grammar, spelling, and sentence structure					Sound Quality				
Variety of activities, with options for increasing complexity					Performance Quality				
Potential of book to absorb students without text					Controllable Pace, including options for stop/pause/exit				
Relevance of themes					Speech is clear and distinct				
Quality and applicability of book					Appropriate narration speed				
Clear Instructions					Quality of narration (dialect, cadence accurate reflection of culture and connected to content of book				

from across the country on the basis of their originality, creativity, and suitability for young children (pp. 58–60).

- Parents Choice Awards http://www.parents-choice.org, retrieved on October 2, 2010. Established in 1978, Parents' Choice is the nation's oldest nonprofit guide to quality children's media and toys. This site is user-friendly. The advanced option enables searching by format, keyword search, award level, and cost as shown in Figure 13.1.

EXAMPLES OF AUDIOVISUAL FORMATS AND THEIR BENEFITS

The following are examples of audiovisual formats and their benefits:

Audio books

- foster reading comprehension, fluency, language acquisition, vocabulary development, and improved achievement;
- support children's focus on meaning and context rather than actual readings of the text; and
- assist with developing critical and active listening skills.

Table 13.3.

Resources with Interactive Features (DVD and CD Rom)

Title:

Grade Levels:

Rate: E (excellent), G (good), F (fair), and P (poor)

Content	E	G	F	P	Technical	E	G	F	P
Age appropriateness					Easy menus access				
Clear instructions					Simple and easy to use icons				
Fosters Independence					Ease of installation				
Realistic expectations					Printing ability				
Varying levels of complexity					Compatibility with computer hardware				
Child can control level of difficulty					Realistic models of objects and items				
Freedom to decide flow and direction of activities					Provides feedback				
Simple instructions					Child can control pace (stop/pause/exit)				
Uses spoken and picture instructions					Control of Sound				
Exiting navigation					Uncluttered screen displays				
Interactive					Legibility and appropriateness of text and print size				
Allows for exploration					Save features				
Offers opportunities for creative problem solving					Simple and precise directions				
Engages interest					Verbal instructions and help				

Books with CD
- provide access to primary source materials,
- enhance understanding of written text, and
- provide good models for reading aloud.

Computer software
- invites independent exploration and
- promotes understanding of how information is organized.

DVDs/Videos
- foster media literacies.

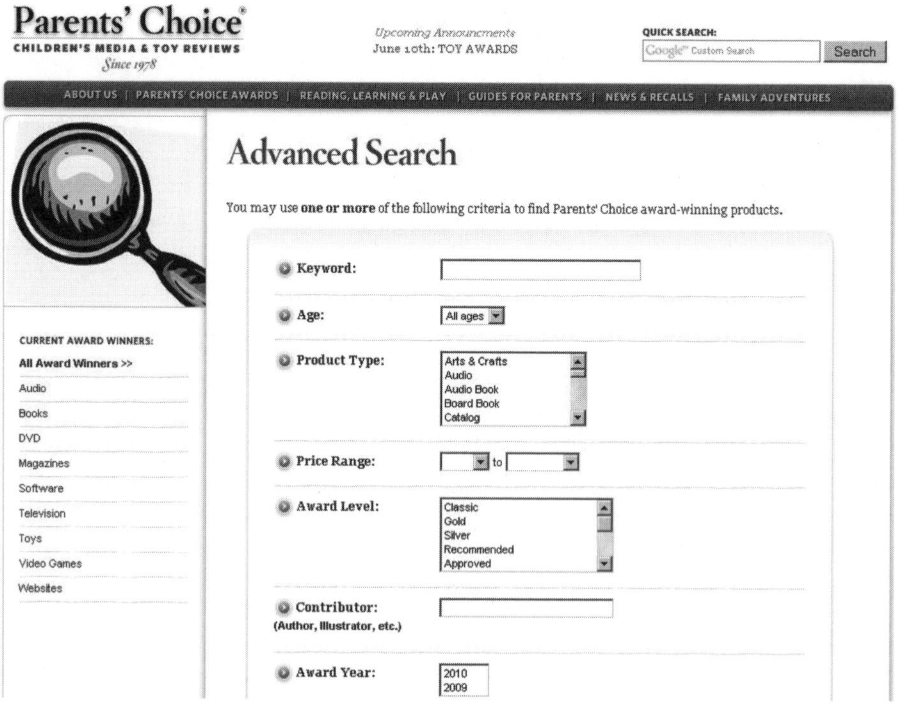

Figure 13.1.
Parents' Choice Advance Search.

Podcasts

- make children imagine the visuals and
- provide opportunities for children to create their own podcasts.

EXAMPLES OF MULTICULTURAL BOOKS CONNECTED TO AUDIOVISUALS

This section includes books and audiovisuals representing a variety of cultures (Native Americans, African Americans, Latinos, Asian Americans, Pacific Islanders, Appalachians, Jewish Americans, and Middle Eastern Americans). Teachers will find the following sites are excellent sources for multicultural audiovisual resources, many of which contain primary source materials and are excellent for enhancing instruction.

African American

Audiobooks/books with CD

A Thousand Never Evers by Shana Burg, Ages 9–12, Random House, 2008.
Through the tragedy of a missing brother, Addie Ann Pickett finds the voice to lead a civil rights march all her own, and maybe change the future for her people in 1963 Kuckachoo, Mississippi.

Blue's Journey by Walter Dean Myers Live Oak Media, 2008.
The evocative harmonica and guitar riffs bring to life Walter Dean Myer's original blues poetry.

Elijah of Buxton by Christopher Paul Curtis, Grades 5–8, Listening Library.
Elijah's life changes when he embarks on a dangerous journey to America and discovers the horrors of slavery (2009 Odyssey Honor Book).

Heroes of the Negro Leagues by Jack Morelli, Abrams Books, 2007.
The Negro leagues played a vital role in black history, with heroic athletes like Satchel Paige, Hank Aaron, and Jackie Robinson. This book is a great tribute and comes with the DVD *Only the Ball was White to* compliment and give more information about the Negro Leagues.

Jazz (sound recording) by Walter Dean Myers, Live Oak Media, 2007.
This is a collection of illustrated poems that celebrate the roots and various styles of jazz such as ragtime, bebop, and swing.

Jazz on a Saturday Night by Leo and Diane Dillon, Ages 5–10, Educational Record Center.
The bright colors and musical patterns make music skip off the page in this toe-tapping homage to many jazz greats (Coretta Scott King Honor Book).

March On! The Day My Brother Martin Changed The World by Dr. Christine King Farris, Grades 2–7, Scholastic, 2008.
Martin Luther King, Jr.'s sister remembers the day he gave his "I have a dream . . ." speech and of the man who inspired a nation.

Martin's Big Words by Doreen Rappaport, Grades PreK–7, Scholastic, 2002.
This title has selections from some of Martin Luther King, Jr.'s speeches and from freedom songs adds to the production as this biography and explores some of his most important beliefs and dreams.

The People Could Fly by Virginia Hamilton, Knopf Books for Young Readers, 2004.
This title is an American Black folktale about how the slaves could use magic words to help them fly away to freedom.

The Tales of Uncle Remus: The Adventures of Brer Rabbit by Julius Lester, Recorded Books.
Brer Rabbit's story is told, connecting it to African American roots.

When Marian Sang by Pam Muñoz Ryan, Grades K–4, Scholastic, 2007.
This title is an introduction to the life of one of our country's greatest singers that comes with a read-along CD. It also explores the affects of prejudice on the lives of African Americans in the early 1900's. It was awarded the ALA Notable Children's Recording for the use of original Anderson recordings.

Videos

Ella Fitzgerald: The Tale of a Vocal Virtuosa, Ages 6–12, Weston Woods Studios.
In celebration of the life of Ella Fitzgerald, this video tells of how she found her voice. It includes original recordings by Ella Fitzgerald.

Ellington Was Not a Street, Ages 5–12, Weston Woods Studios.
A young girl remembers famous African-American icons who visited her family home in Harlem, New York.

March On! The Day My Brother Martin Changed The World by Dr. Christine King Farris, Grades 2–7, Weston Woods Studios.
Martin Luther King, Jr.'s sister remembers the day he gave his "I have a dream ..." speech and of the man who inspired a nation. Combines the picture book's original artwork with vintage photos and enriched audio from the day of the speech.

Martin's Big Words, Grades PreK–7, Weston Woods Studios.
This video documentary of Doreen Rappaport's book explores some of Martin Luther King, Jr.'s most important beliefs and dreams.

Rosa, Ages 5–10, Weston Woods Studios.
The bravery of Rosa Parks is brought to life in this video version of Nikki Giovanni's picture book.

Playaways

Claudette Colvin—Twice Toward Justice by Phillip Hoose.
Phillip Hoose presents the first in-depth account of an important, yet largely unknown Civil Rights figure, skillfully weaving her dramatic story into the fabric of the historic Montgomery bus boycott and court case that would change the course of American history (2010 Newbery and Sibert Honor Book).

Inspiring Figures: Jazz Greats (sound recording) by Andrea Davis Pinkney, Findaway World, 2007.
Readings of *Ella Fitzgerald: The Tale of a Vocal Virtuoso* by Andrea Davis Pinkney; *Ellington Was Not a Street* by Ntozake Shange; and *Duke Ellington: The Piano Prince and His Orchestra* by Andrea Davis Pinkney. This also features an interview with author Andrea Davis Pinkney.

Voices of Black America: Historical Recordings of Poetry, Humor and Drama, Findaway World, 2007.
This features original recordings from 1908–1946 of Booker T. Washington's Atlanta Exposition Address, the poetry of Paul Laurence Dunbar and Langston Hughes, and the rarely heard humor of Charley Case and more.

We Are the Ship by Kadir Nelson.
This presents the history of Negro League baseball teams through colorful illustrations and descriptive text (2010 Odyssey Award Honor).

Hispanic

Audiobooks/books with CD

Celia Cruz: Queen of Salsa by Veronica Chambers, Grades K–5, Live Oak.
This charming read—along offers a glimpse into the life of Cuban-born salsa singer Celia Cruz.

Martina the Beautiful Cockroach: A Cuban Folktale by Carmen Agra Deedy, Grades K–5, Peachtree Publishers.
This retelling of the traditional Cuban tale of Martina's quest to find a husband includes a Spanish version and a storytelling performance (2009 Odyssey Honor Book).

The Pot That Juan Built by Nancy Andrews-Goebel, Grades 1–5, Scholastic, 2004.
Juan Quezada, one of Mexico's most famous potters, used his creative gifts to transform his impoverished village of laborers into a thriving artists' community.

Too Many Tamales by Gary Soto, Grades PreK–4, Scholastic, 2002.
While helping her mother prepare the *masa* to make tamales for Christmas dinner, Maria loses her mother's wedding ring and thinks it has been kneaded into the tamales.

The Skirt by Gary Soto, Grades 3 and up, Recorded Books.
Miata Ramirez is proud that she will be wearing her mother's old folklorico skirt while performing with her dance troupe, but what happens when she accidently leaves the precious skirt on the school bus?

The Surrender Tree by Margarita Engle, Random House.
In this history in verse, acclaimed poet Margarita Engle has created a lyrical, powerful portrait of Cuba in the midst of war and its struggle for freedom.

Under the Mango Tree: Stories from Spanish Speaking Countries by Elida Guardia Bonet, Grades 2 and up, Zarati Press.
Bonet's collection includes familiar folktales, such as "Juan Bob" and "La Cucharacha" from Spain and throughout Latin America.

Videos

A Box Full of Kittens, Ages 3–7, Nutmeg Media DVD.
This production of Sonia Manzano's book introduces Ruthie, a Puerto-Rican girl, who longs to do something heroic for her expectant aunt.

Playaways

Chato's Kitchen and Other Stories by Gary Soto and Nancy Andrews-Goebel, Grades PreK–5, Scholastic, 2009.
This Playaway compilation includes *Chato's Kitchen*, *Chato and the Party Animals*, and *The Pot That Juan Built*.

Native American

Audiobooks/books with CD

The Absolutely True Diary of a Part-Time Indian by Sherman Alexie, Ages 14 and up, Recorded Books, 2009.
Follow 14-year-old Arnold "Junior" Spirit through this earthy narration as he struggles to overcome physical, economic and social obstacles (2009 Odyssey Award Winner).

Good Thanks: A Native American Good Morning Message by Chief Jake Swamp, Grades PreK–4.
This book with CD is based on the belief that the natural world is a precious and rare gift, and it is narrated by Chief Jake Swamp in both English and in the Mohawk language.

Video

Chiefs, Ages 12–14, Active Parenting Publishers.
This documentary follows the Wyoming Indian High School basketball team through two seasons of adversity and perseverance (Best Documentary at 2002 Tribeca Film Festival).

Asian

Audiobooks/books with CD

Grandfather's Journey by Allen Say, Grades PreK–4, Scholastic, 2008.
Allen Say recounts his family's journey from Japan to America.

Lon Po Po by Ed Young, Grades PreK–5, Weston Woods.
With an elegant Chinese music accompaniment and powerful voices, this audio book brings Ed Young's Caldecott winning folktale to life.

Mao's Last Dancer: Young Reader's Edition by Li Conxin, Grades 7 and up, Bolinda Audio.
This autobiography details a boy's journey from a poverty-stricken Chinese village during the Cultural Revolution to ballet stardom in the West.

Videos

Grandfather's Journey, Ages 3–7, Weston Woods Studios.
  Allen Say recounts his family's journey from Japan to America.
Lon Po Po, Grades PreK–5, Weston Woods Studios.
Ed Young's Caldecott winning folktale is transformed into an animated video production.
Showa Shinzan, Ages 10–14, National Film Board of Canada.
A young Japanese girl experiences the tragedy of World War II and a volcanic eruption.

Playaways

All the Colors of the Earth by Sheila Hamanaka, Grades PreK–3.
This audiobook celebrates the diversity of children with multiethnic heritages.

Middle Eastern

Audiobooks

Blood Red Horse by K. M. Grant, Grades 5–9, Recorded Books, 2005.
This epic of the Crusades offers a historical perspective on modern conflicts in the Middle East.

Habibi by Naomi Shihab Nye (audio download), Audible.com, 2009.
When Liyana's American family moves to Jerusalem from St. Louis, 14-year-old Liyana confronts tensions between the Palestinians and the Jews.

Cybele's Secrest by Juliet Mallilier, Grades 8 and up, Listening Library, 2008.
Paula is required to travel with her father to Istanbul in order to assist him in procuring a mysterious religious artifact.

The Bronze Bow by Elizabeth George Speare, Grade 6 and up, Blackstone Audiobooks, 2001.
This story follows Daniel, a young outcast sworn to fight the Romans—who are occupying his Middle Eastern home—with the goal of throwing them out of the land altogether.

The Breadwinner by Deborah Ellis, Grades 4–6, Listening Library, 2002.
Set in the early years of the Taliban regime, Parvana is forced to disguise herself as a boy and become the "breadwinner" for her family after her father is hauled away.

Sami and the Time of the Troubles by Judith Heide Gilliland, Grades 1–3, Sandpiper, 2002.
Sami is a Lebanese boy whose everyday life is marred by gunfire and bombs. When things are good, Sami and his family can be outside, and he can play like other children, but during the bad times, they must hide in his uncle's basement.

Video

The Middle East, Grades 5–12, Schlessinger Media, 2001.
Since World War II, the United States has become increasingly drawn into the turbulence of the Middle East. In *The Middle East*, students will trace the rocky road toward peace in this part of the world.

What is Islam? Grades 5–12, Schlessinger Media, 2003.
In *What is Islam?* students take an in-depth look at the religion practiced by over one billion Muslims in countries worldwide. Students investigate the history of this religion by learning about Muhammad.

Muhammad: Legacy of a Prophet, Ages 14 and up, Unity Productions Foundation, 2002.
The film is interwoven with the story of Mohammad and the creation of Islam and stories of modern-day Muslims living in America post 9/11.

Playaway

Child of Dandelions by Shenaaz Nanji, Grades 7–12, Playaway, 2010.
Sabine is an Indian living in Uganda during the summer of 1972 when President Idi Amin issues his proclamation that all "foreign Indians" must leave the country within 90 days.

Three Cups of Tea by David Oliver Relin, Grades 3–6, Playaway, 2010.
This young reader's edition tells of how Mortenson, after being lost and ill in the mountains of Pakistan and cared for by the village of Korphe, repays their kindness by creating the Central Asia Institute and sending over 25,000 children to school.

Stories From Ancient Egypt I & II by David Angus, Playaway, 2007.
These are stories of struggle between good and evil, enacted by gods whom the Egyptians thought of as very like themselves.

ADDITIONAL AUDIOVISUAL RESOURCES

Audiobooks

Recorded Books has a Spanish imprint Audiolibros: http://www.recordedbooks.com/index.cfm?fuseaction=rb.show_imprint&show_by=imprint&imprint=audiolibros, retrieved on October 2, 2010.
Hawaiian Playground, All Ages/Musical Putumayo Kids.
Ukuleles, native Hawaiian language, and the sliding sounds of slack key guitars bring the Aloha state right into the room with this collection of fun songs (some in English, some in Hawaiian) by different performers.

Bud, Not Buddy by Christopher Paul Curtis, Grades 4–up, Listening Library.
In this Depression-era historical title, 10-year-old Bud lives in an orphanage, but is sure that if he could just find his long-lost father, he would have a home.

Locomotion by Jacqueline Woodson Grades 4–up, Recorded Books.
Lonnie Collins Motion, dubbed "Locomotion" by his mother, is orphaned after a tragic fire. To add to his sense of loss, he is sent to a foster home after a family decides to adopt his only sister but not him.

Interactive Computer Software

Arpilleras! The Colorful Appliqués of Peru, Grades 3–8.
Students can use this program to explore market scenes and landscapes of Peru, available at www.crizmac.com, retrieved on October 2, 2010.

Travel the World with Timmy!
This interactive program allows children to explore how people eat, dress, and live in other countries. Children will also hear and speak new languages.

Ebooks

Educational Resources www.edresources.com.
This Web site sells an eBook series called *Our Global Village*. The books explore the history, customs, lifestyles, games and more for different countries.

Video:

Family of the World DVD Series Master Communications, Inc., 2005, $29.95.
Titles include: *Families of Vietnam, Families of Australia, Families of Brazil, Families of Egypt*, and *Families of Sweden*.
Each video focuses on a different culture, their way of life, family attraction, communities, schools and homes of two families—from breakfast to bedtime.

Playaways

Almost Astronauts: 13 Women Who Dared to Dream by Tanya Lee Stone.
This chronicles the efforts of 13 women to gain admission into NASA's astronaut training program in the 1960s (2010 Sibert Medal).

Peace, Locomotion by Jacqueline Woodson.
In this chance to revisit Lonnie's world, the book is written as letters from Lonnie to his sister, Lili, who is in a different foster home; the story's backdrop is the unnamed war in which his foster brother, Jenkins, is fighting (2010 Odyssey Award Honor).

Library of Congress

One of the best sources for online collections of historical audiovisual resources is the Library of Congress, www.loc.gov, retrieved on October 2, 2010. This site is a virtual treasure of online collections in multiple formats. The *American Memory* collection is intended to serve as "a digital record of American history and creativity." The collection is comprised of historical resources such as original sound recordings, films, photos, prints, maps, and sheet music. Teachers may browse by topic or use the search box that enables all collections to be searched at once. A hyperlinked Teacher tab elicits ready-made classroom resources and suggestions for using the site (see Figure 13.2).

Many multicultural resources are available and have been designed for use by teachers. In the *American Library* collection, teachers will find an interface that has been designed for use by elementary children. *America's Story* (see Figure 13.3) contains age-appropriate audiovisual resources.

Biographies, games, and a digital collection of audio files are accessed under the heading See, Hear and Sing (see Figure 13.4), where children are encouraged to "Watch a movie, hear a song, and play a tune from America's past."

The collections at the Library of Congress are not limited to American history; educators and librarians have access to international and multicultural resources throughout the Library of Congress. The ability to search all collections from one search box makes this a time saver for teachers searching for audiovisual resources. A podcast collection with a series of podcasts is a constant feature on the site. Many of the topical categories relate to American history such as Slave Narratives; however, current topics and presentations by leading experts in various subject areas are included such as the Music and the Brain and the National Book Festival in the podcast series. From one site, teachers have access to a multitude of authentic, authoritative resources.

The History Channel

Teachers and librarians will find the range of video and audio clips on the History Channel Web site http://www.history.com, retrieved on October 2, 2010 very useful for linking with multicultural titles. The video and audio clips are short and concise and may be accompanied by either original photographs or videos that support the audio. The range of resources includes information on Native American code talkers, the life of Muhammad, Tuskegee Airmen, and an audio clip of Virginia Hamilton reading her book, *Zeely*.

Figure 13.2.
Teachers' Resources at www.loc.gov/teacher

Coretta Scott King Book Award Curricular Resources

This site http://www.teachingbooks.net, retrieved on October 2, 2010 has a user-friendly interface that quickly enables teachers to search for linked African American audio visual resources by title, age level, or award (See Figure 13.5). The Web site concisely describes the purpose of this site:

- hear directly from African American authors and illustrators as they talk about and read from their books;
- enjoy audio recordings, book readings, videos, and more; and
- teach the Coretta Scott King award-winning books with this free, online collection of primary source materials and lesson plans.

Asia Society

The Asia Society is an example of a professional organization that promotes cultural understanding. The Web site www.asiasociety.org, retrieved on October 2, 2010,

Figure 13.3.
America's Story from the Library of Congress

describes the purpose of this organization, "to strengthen relationships and promote understanding among the people, leaders, and institutions of the United States and Asia . . . to increase knowledge and enhance dialogue, encourage creative expression, and generate new ideas across the fields of arts and culture, policy and business, and education." This site has a page dedicated to educators and recommends high quality educational resources to use in the classroom. Many of these sites also include kid pages with suggested activities and audiovisual multicultural resources geared for children.

Special Collections on the Web

Teachers should be aware that there are many special collections of historical figures and events that are held by organizations and educational institutions. These collections are becoming increasingly available in digital formats with original documents, photos, interviews, and audio and video clips. The following figure (see Figure 13.6) is an example of the high-quality materials that can be located on the Web. This special collection of Marian Anderson contains original sound recordings of her singing at significant historical events in American history.

Figure 13.4.
See, Hear, and Sing

SOURCES OF AUDIOVISUAL MATERIALS FOR TEACHERS AND LIBRARIANS

Sources for locating audiovisual materials suitable for the classroom or student assignments have been compiled in the following section.

Annotated Bibliography of Resources

Boss, R. (2006). Software for Children. American Library Association. http://www.ala.org/ala/mgrps/divs/pla/plapublications/platechnotes/Educational_Software.pdf, retrieved on October 2, 2010.
This article discusses ways to select software for children and offers selection criteria used by ALSC to review media.

Coretta Scott King Book Award-winning Authors, Illustrators, & Books

- Hear directly from African American authors and illustrators as they talk about and read from their books.
- Enjoy audio recordings, book readings, videos, and more.
- Teach the Coretta Scott King Book Award-winning books with this free, online collection of primary source materials and lesson plans.

Search for Coretta Scott King Book Award curricular resources

...by name or book title

Enter author, illustrator, or title: [   ]   (See list of award recipients.)

...by grade level or curricular area

Select grade level or curricular area of interest:

☐ Pre-K to 2nd grade   ☐ Art
☐ 1st to 5th grade   ☐ Cultural Studies
☐ 4th to 8th grade   ☐ English Language Arts
☐ 7th to 12th grade   ☐ Health
                                      ☐ History
                                      ☐ Math
                                      ☐ Music
                                      ☐ Physical Education
                                      ☐ Science
                                      ☐ Social Studies
                                      ☐ Spanish

...by award type or year

Select further details:

[Select below   ▼]

...or see all

☐ All

[Go]   [Clear Form]

Figure 13.5.
Coretta Scott King Book Award

An Educator's Guide to Evaluating Claims about Educational Software. North Central Regional Educational Laboratory. http://www.ncrel.org/tech/claims/, retrieved on October 2, 2010.

The purpose of this site is to help individuals address whether software has been demonstrated to be effective with schools. This site will help teachers and librarians to use research to guide the progress of school level initiatives that use educational software to improve instruction.

Grover, S. & Hannegan, L. (May, 2005). Not just for listening: Integrating audio books into the curriculum. *Book Links*.

This article talks about the benefits of the audio books and a few evaluation tips. It also provides a bibliography of a few good audio book titles.

Hughes-Hassell, S. & Mancall, J.C. (2005). *Collection management for youth: Responding to the needs of learners*. Chicago, IL: American Library Association.

As education shifts to a learner-centered environment, collection development must address the dynamic interplay between all stakeholders in the school community. Drawing from the latest educational theory and research, the authors recommend a plan to operate school media centers in the midst of radical flux while meeting students' information needs in a holistic context.

Jabs, C. (2007) Raising a Computer-Smart Kit: Find out how home computers—used the right way—can speed up learning for your child. Reader's Digest. Retrieved from http://www.rd.com/content/raising-a-computer-smart-kid/ on October 2, 2010.

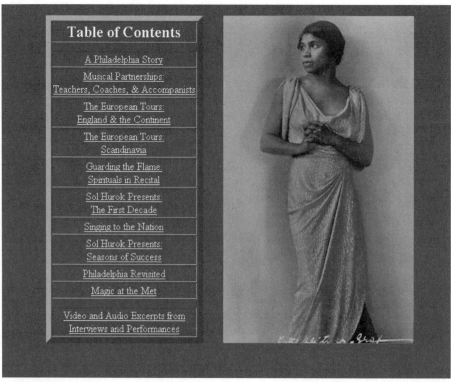

Figure 13.6.
Marian Anderson Special Collection

This article provides tips on how to introduce computers to children and how to choose the right software for your children.

Position Statement on Technology and Young Children: Ages 3 through 8. National Association for the Education of Young Children. http://www.naeyc.org/files/naeyc/file/positions/PSTECH98.PDF, retrieved on October 2, 2010.

NAEYC addresses, "several issues related to technology's use with young children: (1) the essential role of the teacher in evaluating appropriate uses of technology; (2) the potential benefits of appropriate use of technology in early childhood programs; (3) the integration of technology into the typical learning environment; (4) equitable access to technology, including children with special needs; (5) stereotyping and violence in software; (6) the role of teachers and parents as advocates; and (7) the implications of technology for professional development" (NAEYC).

Selecting Software for Young Children. Early Connections: Technology in Early Childhood Education. http://www.netc.org/earlyconnections/baschool/software.html, retrieved on October 2, 2010.

An article provided by Northwest Educational Technology Consortium (NETC) detailing ways in which technology can by used within an educational setting as well as ways in which to evaluate educational software.

Teacher's Store. (FEE BASED) Discovery Education: http://teacherstore.discovery
.com/stores/servlet/CategoryDisplay?storeId=10003&catalogId=10003&langId
=-1&categoryId=28833&parent_category_rn=28829&jzid=40602356-1-0.
The united streaming Internet-based video-on-demand service features 2,200 videos
and 22,000 video clips. Scientifically evaluated, correlated to national/state standards, and includes many teacher tools.

Yokota, J. & Martinez, M. Authentic Listening Experiences: Multicultural Audiobooks.
Book Links. http://www.ala.org/ala/aboutala/offices/publishing/booklinks/resources/
authenticlistening.cfm, retrieved on October 2, 2010. on
This article discuses the importance of multicultural literature. It provides a list of
audio books featuring African Americans, Asians, and Latinos.

An Annotated Bibliography Evaluation Tips

EvaluTech's Evaluation Review Criteria: http://www.evalutech.sreb.org/criteria/
index.asp, retrieved on October 2, 2010.
EvaluTech offers expanded access to resources that are aligned with the work of the
Educational Technology Cooperative. It is committed to providing high-quality
information to K-20 education agencies. Evalutech also provides criteria for selecting various audiovisual resources.

Kid's First. Coalition for Quality Children's Media. http://www.kidsfirst.org/kidsfirst/,
retrieved on October 2, 2010.
The Coalition for Quality Children's Media is a national; not-for-profit organization
founded whose mission is to teach children critical viewing skills and to increase the
visibility and availability of quality children's programs.

Haugland, S. W. (2005). Selecting or upgrading software and web sites in the
classroom. *Early Childhood Education Journal, 32(5).*
This article provides a discussion of considerations for selecting or updating software and/or web sites for children's use in classrooms or computer labs.

*How we Rate Interactive Media: About the Ratings and CTR's Software Evaluation
Instrument. http://www.childrenssoftware.com/rating.html, retrieved on October 2, 2010
This source provides six categories to evaluate quality children's software.

Queensland Government Library Services Evaluation Criteria: http://education.qld
.gov.au/information/service/libraries/resource/eval/evalc-criteria.html, retrieved on
October 2, 2010.
This Web site offers evaluation criteria to various materials, including audiovisual
items and software.

Review Corner: How we Rate Products (2007) www.reviewcorner.com/softwareevaluation
.html, retrieved on October 2, 2010.
This article explains how to select educational software programs.

A Teacher in the Living Room? Educational Media for Babies, Toddlers, and Preschoolers. The Henry J. Kaiser Family Foundation. http://www.kff.org/entmedia/
upload/7427.pdf, retrieved on October 2, 2010.
This 55-page report is based on an examination of DVDs, computer software, and
video games for which educational claims are made for children from infancy up to
age six. Researchers purchased and examined the products, measuring them against
the educational claims and the guidelines given to parents, and looked at the kind
of research behind the claims.

Reviewed Audiovisuals

Children's Technology Review: http://childrenstech.com/, retrieved on October 2, 2010.
> Available as a searchable database of over 7500 reviews dating back to 1985, and as a monthly PDF publication or in printed form, Children's Technology Review (CTR) is designed to help adults exploit the power of technology for children by providing accurate reviews of the latest products.

Learning Village: http://www.learningvillage.com/, retrieved on October 2, 2010.
> Learning Village reviews educational software and then recommends the best. Their software guide reviews some of the best learning software that educators have seen for either the home or classroom.

Super Kids: http://www.superkids.com/, retrieved on October 2, 2010.
> SuperKids provides several easy ways to find reviews related to children's software. Most readers choose to go first to the subject index where they can find the latest head-to-head product comparisons. Others look first at new reviews, or go to the title index to look up SuperKids' review of a specific title.

Queensland Government Library Resource Evaluation: http://education.qld.gov.au/ information/service/libraries/resource/eval/index.html, retrieved on October 2, 2010.
> This web site provides reviews and criteria for reviewing audiovisual resources. Ratings have been applied to reviewed work from "not recommended" to "highly recommended". The site also provides a searchable database of reviewed works within the Classroom Resource Review (CRR).

Free Audiovisual Resources

Federal Resources of Educational Excellence: http://www.free.ed.gov/, retrieved October 2, 2010
> This web site provides teaching and learning resources from federal agencies.

CONCLUSION

Multicultural literature supports both academic and individual student needs by celebrating the similarities and differences of diverse cultural backgrounds. Students have opportunities to see themselves in stories with universal themes on which they can reflect. Multicultural literature for many students becomes the bridge with which they can learn about other cultures, their contributions, and their influence on students' lives today.

Educators can tap into the wealth of easily accessible and versatile audiovisual formats that complement multicultural literature and enrich students' experiences with multicultural literature. Audio visuals enable educators to stimulate student interest by stimulating multiple senses. Instruction that is conducted in a sensory-rich environment heightens student engagement with the subject area and makes learning more relevant. Thus, students' overall participation in the learning process is intensified, positively influencing academic achievement.

Using audiovisuals to enrich and deepen students' experiences with multicultural literature enables educators and librarians to meet many students' individual and developmental learning needs. Creating multisensory experiences with multicultural literature helps teachers and librarians give life to the heart and soul of diverse cultures and communities and stimulate student understanding and appreciation of the student's own culture and the cultures of those who are different from them.

REFERENCES

American Institute for Research. (2004). *Navigating the children's media landscape: A parent and caregiver guide*. American Institutes for Research and released by Cable in the Classroom and National Parents and Teacher's Association. Retrieved from http://www.ciconline.org/parentsguide.

Baines, L. (2008) *A teacher's guide to multisensory learning: Improving literacy by engaging the senses*. Alexandria, VA. Association for Supervision and Curriculum Development.

Bishop, K. (2003). *Connecting libraries with classrooms: The curricular roles of the media specialist*. Worthington, OH. Linworth Publishing.

Brewer, C. (2008). *Music and learning: Integrating music in the classroom*. Retrieved from http://newhorizons.org/strategies/arts/brewer.

Cardillo, A., Coville, B., Ditlow, T., Myrick, E., & Lesesne T. (2007). Tuning in to audiobooks: Why should kids listen? *Children and Libraries: The Journal of the Association for Library Service to Children. 5(3), 42–46.*

Educational Resource Acquisition Consortium (ERAC) *A teacher view of video evaluations*. Retrieved from http://www.bcerac.ca/video/creatingEracsvideocatalogue.aspx

Gay, G., & Hanley, M. S. (1999). Multicultural empowerment in middle school social studies through drama pedagogy. *The Clearing House*, 72 (6), 364–370.

Grover, S. & Hannegan, L. (2008). Hear and now: Connecting outstanding audiobooks to library and classroom instruction. *Teacher Librarian* 35(3)17–21.

Harper, M. (2007). Awesome audiovisuals. *Congregational Libraries Today*, *11*, 1–5.

Haugland, S. and Gerzog, E. (1998) *Haugland Gerzog Developmental Scale*. Retrieved from http://ihashimi.aurasolution.com/hauglandgerzog_developmental_sc.htm.

Institute for Library and Information Literacy Education. *ILILE ODE Checklists*. Institute of Museum and Library Services and the U.S. Department of Education. Retrieved from http://www.ilile.org/instructionalRes/checklists/index.html.

Lake, B. (2002). Music and language learning. *Journal of the Imagination for Language Learning, 12.*

Machito. (2000). *Kenya: Afro-Cuban Jazz* [CD]. New York, NY: Blue Note Records.

Multisensory learning. *Education.com*. Retrieved from Glossary of Education: http://www.education.com/definition/multisensory-learning/.

Owens, L. (2007). An Overview of Brain Based Learning Retrieved from http://www.uwsp.edu/education/lwilson/brain/bboverview.htm.

Oxford University Press. (2006). First evidence that musical training affects brain development in young children. *Science Daily*. Retrieved from http://www.sciencedaily.com/releases/2006/09/060920093024.htm.

Palmer, H. (2006). The music, movement, and learning: A teacher view of video evaluations connection. *Young Children 82*(3).

Pintrich, P., & Schunk, D. (2002). *Motivation in education*. Upper Saddle River, NJ: Merrill.

Prensky, M. (2001a). Digital natives, digital immigrants. *On the Horizon*, 9(5).

Prensky, M. (2001b). Do they really think differently? *On the Horizon*, 9(6).

Ryan, P. M. (2002). *When Marian sang: The true recital of Marian Anderson*, illustrated by B. Selznick. New York, NY: Scholastic Press.

Reviewcorner.com. *How we rate products*. Retrieved from http://www.reviewcorner.com/
softwareevaluation.html.

Shamir, A. (2006). How to select CD-ROM storybooks for young children: The teacher's role.
The Reading Teacher, 59(6), 532–534. doi:10.1598/RT. 59.6.3

Van Orden, P., & Bishop, K. (2001). *The collection program in schools: Concepts, practices, and
information sources*. Englewood, CO: Libraries Unlimited.

Various Artists. (2004). *The rough guide to the music of Kenya* [CD]. London: World Music
Network.

Waddell, M., & Plummer, T. (1984). Assessing accuracy in materials on Asia. *School Library
Journal*, 31(2) 93–98.

Yokota, J., & Martinez, M. (2007). Authentic listening experiences: Multicultural audiobooks
Retrieved from http://www.ala.org/ala/aboutala/offices/publishing/booklinks/resources/
authenticlistening.cfm.

APPENDIX

Sources of Audiovisual Materials for Teachers

Arte Público Press
University of Houston
4800 Calhoun, 2-L
Houston, TX 77204-2090
(713) 743-2841
http://www.arte.uh.edu/

BBC Audiobooks America
http://www.bbcaudiobooksamerica.com/

The Bess Press
3565 Harding Ave.
Honolulu, HI 96816
(803) 734-7159
http://www.besspress.com/

Bilingual Press
Hispanic Research Center
Arizona State University
Box 872702
Tempe, AZ 85287-2702
(602) 965-3867
http://www.asu.edu/brp/

BookFLIX
http://teacher.scholastic.com/products/bookflixfreetrial/

Books on Tape, A Division of Random House, Inc.
School: http://school.booksontape.com/index3.cfm

CCV Software
http://www.ccvsoftware.com/

Childcraft Educators Corp
www.childcrafteducation.com

Children's Book Press
246 First St., Suite 101
San Francisco, CA 94105
(415) 995-2200
http://www.childrensbookpress.org/

Children's Poetry Archive
http://www.poetryarchive.org/childrensarchive/home.do

Crick Software
http://www.cricksoft.com/us/

Crimson Multimedia
www.crimsoninc.com

Crizmac
P.O. Box 65928
Tucson, AZ 85728
(800) 913-8555
http://www.crizmac.com/

Disney Educational Production
http://dep.disney.go.com/

Educational Activities
800-797-3223
www.edact.com

Educational Record Center
www.erckids.com

Educational Resources
http://www.edresources.com/
Follett Audiovisual Resources
http://www.flr.follett.com/intro/av.html

Interlink Publishing
46 Crosby St.
Northampton, MA 01060-1804
(413) 582-7054
http://www.interlinkbooks.com/

Kimbo Educational
www.kimboed.com

Knowledge Unlimited
P.O. Box 52
Madison, WI 53701-0052
(608) 836-6660/ (800) 356-2303
http://www.thekustore.com/

Library Video Company
http://www.libraryvideo.com

Lee and Low Books
95 Madison Avenue
New York, NY 10016
(212) 779-4400
http://www.leeandlow.com/

Listening Library
http://library.booksontape.com/s
_promo_pam_spencer.cfm

Live Oak Media
800-788-1121
www.liveoakmedia.com

Magic Maestro Music
http://www.magicmaestromusic.com

Melody House Music
800-234-9228
www.melodyhousemusic.com

Mitchell Lane Publishers
P.O. Box 200
Childs, MD 21916-0200
(410) 392-5036/ (800) 814-5484 (orders)
http://www.mitchelllane.com/

Multicultural Media
RR3, Box 6655
Granger Rd.
Barre, VT 05641
(802) 223-1294/
(800) 550-9675
http://www.multiculturalmedia.com/

New Press
450 W. 41st St.
New York, NY 10036
(212) 629-8802/ (800) 233-4830 (orders)
http://www.thenewpress.com/

Newsound Music
800-288-2007
www.newsoundmusic.com

Open Hand Publishing
P.O. Box 22048
Seattle, WA 98122
(206) 323-2187
http://www.openhand.com/index.php

Playaways
http://www.playawaydigital.com

Public Library
http://library.booksontape.com/index2.cfm

Reading Rainbow
http://www.shopgpn.com/Reading-Rainbow-Resources

Recorded Books, LLC
http://www.recordedbooks.com/

Shen's Books and Supplies
821 South First Ave.
Arcadia, CA 91006
(818) 445-6958/ (800)456-6660
http://www.shens.com/

Tilbury House
132 Water St.
Gardiner, ME 04345
(207) 582-1899/ (800) 582-1899
http://www.tilburyhouse.com/

Tundra Books
345 Victoria Ave., # 604 (Westmount)
P.O. Box 1030
Plattsburgh, NY 12901
(514) 932-5434
http://www.tundrabooks.com/

Vision Maker Video
P.O. Box 83111
Lincoln, NE 68501
(402) 472-3522/ (800) 835-7087
http://www.visionmaker.org/

Weston Woods
http://teacher.scholastic.com/products/westonwoods/

14

Using Multicultural Mentor Texts to Teach Writing

Barbara Moss and Christine Kane

Mentor, or touchstone texts, can be a powerful tool for teaching writing to children. Mentor texts refer to texts that are read and reread for a variety of purposes, and are studied and imitated in children's own writing (Dorfman & Cappelli, 2007). Most often, mentor texts are children's trade books, but a mentor text can also be a single sentence, a paragraph, a newspaper story, a magazine article, or any published piece written by a professional author.

Mentor texts capitalize on the reading-writing connection by engaging students in reading or listening to texts that can later become sources for language that they can use in their own written work. Mentors guide and teach younger or less experienced writers, teachers, or artists. Mentor texts guide or teach students by providing models or exemplars that can be imitated and adapted into children's own original work.

Jeff Anderson, author of *Mechanically Inclined* (2005) and *Everyday Editing* (2007), states that a mentor text is a well-written text, often written by a professional author, that can teach us something we need to know about writing. The wonderful thing about a well-crafted text is that we can learn endless things from gifted authors, from effectively using adjectives to creating a compelling plot.

Mentor texts can provide models of effective uses of sentence structure and punctuation, word choice, voice, dialogue, figurative language, and rhythm, rhyme, and repetition. In addition, they can help students see how authors craft their work at the macro level through particular text structures, both narrative and expository. By recognizing, understanding, and reflecting upon the ways authors create their works, children gain their own appreciation and understanding of what it means to be an author and develop increased recognition of the ways they, too, can craft stories and informational texts and assume their rightful roles as authors.

Mentor texts are also texts that teachers and students both love and know well. They are texts that are used over and over again and books that provide different insights each time they are read. They are texts that speak to the teacher and in turn to the students. According to Dorfman and Cappelli (2007) they "serve as snapshots into the future. They help students envision the kind of writer they can become; they help teachers move the whole writer, rather than each individual piece of writing, forward" (p. 3).

Through mentor texts, children learn to borrow from the texts they read and listen to. Through immersion in children's literature along with explicit writing instruction, children develop sensitivity to the language of books whether in terms of word choice, rhythm, onomatopoeia, or text structure. The next section will explore guidelines for teaching writing that apply to all students, but especially to English learners.

GUIDELINES FOR TEACHING WRITING TO ENGLISH LEARNERS

One of the greatest challenges in teaching today involves helping students develop their skills as writers. The findings of the *Report of the National Literacy Panel on Language-Minority Children and Youth* (August & Shanahan, 2006) analysis of research on English learners found that while students' word-level skills in literacy are often equal to that of their native speaking peers, text level skills such as comprehension and writing lag far behind those of native speakers. The report argues that developing oral English proficiency is associated with English reading comprehension and writing. They further note that writing proficiency in the first language is positively correlated to writing abilities in the second.

The National Council of Teachers of English offers the following guidelines for teaching writing to English learners (see Figure 14.1):

- Provide a positive writing environment.
- Use discussion-based collaborative writing activities.
- Promote peer interaction to support learning.
- Replace drills with time for writing practice.
- Provide frequent meaningful opportunities for students to generate their own texts.
- Design writing assignments for a variety of audiences, purposes, and genres.
- Provide model papers and point out specific aspects of the paper that demonstrate its quality.
- Provide positive feedback about areas where the student is meeting expectations.
- Provide explicit feedback (in written and in oral response). Begin with global comments (content and ideas, organization, thesis) then mechanical errors.
- Give multiple suggestions for change so that students maintain control of their writing.
- Talk explicitly about citation and plagiarism. Note that not all cultures ascribe to the same rules and guidelines. Provide students with strategies to avoid plagiarism.

Figure 14.1

Teaching Writing to English Learners (adapted from the NCTE Position Paper on the Role of English Teachers in Educating English Language Learners (ELLs), http://www.ncte.org/positions/statements/teacherseducatingell, accessed on August 10, 2010). *Source*: Copyright 2006 by National Council of Teachers of English.

These guidelines highlight the importance of providing a safe environment for students in which they feel that they can make mistakes and grow as writers. Students need time and multiple opportunities to practice their writing with teacher guidance. They also need explicit feedback that helps them target their areas of need. Teaching students to use and create rubrics for their writing can help to promote this type of feedback.

Improving English learners' writing abilities depends upon effective instruction for all students, but especially English learners. English learners and struggling native speakers of English need explicit modeling and writing instruction. Specific strategies in writing instruction that involve modeling, guided practice, and independent practice through mentor texts can support all students developmentally.

THE ROLE OF MENTOR TEXTS

An important goal of using mentor texts is for students to learn to read like writers; this means that students must develop the ability to notice how authors write, or how they practice their craft, and then see how this knowledge can impact their own writing. In this way children not only develop an ear for good writing, but also begin to see what good writing looks like in print, thereby developing the writer's eye (Ray & Cleaveland, 2004). As a part of this form of writing instruction, children begin by noticing how good writing sounds and ultimately progress to creating their own writing that reflects what they have learned.

MULTICULTURAL MENTOR TEXTS

Multicultural literature "refers to literature that focuses upon people of color— African, Asian, Hispanic, and Native Americans; religious minorities, such as the Amish or Jewish, regional cultures, for example Appalachian and Cajun; the disabled; and the aged" (Harris, 1993, p. 171). Such literature, regardless of genre, describes members of racial or ethnic minority groups, members of regional cultures, the disabled, the elderly, and other groups such as the homeless who might be considered outside the mainstream of American society. The best of these books reveal the experiences of members of parallel cultures with authenticity and accuracy.

Multicultural mentor texts differ from other forms of mentor texts in that they focus on multicultural characters, may be written by authors from parallel cultures, and address issues of particular interest to members of non-mainstream cultures. Multicultural mentor texts should, first and foremost, represent quality literature. They should be held to the same standards as other literature in terms of their quality and content.

The advantages of using multicultural mentor texts are many. Mentor texts that address multicultural themes allow students to interact with texts that portray people like themselves in circumstances that may be similar to their own. Books with multicultural themes let children see themselves at the same time they see children of other cultures; as Sims Bishop (1990) puts it, literature provides both a mirror and a window. High-quality multicultural books, like high-quality literature in general, provide students with powerful ideas about the ways in which literature connects with life.

Because multicultural mentor texts are often written by authors from parallel cultures, they not only provide students with models for their own writing, but they also help students see members of their own cultures as role models for writing, recognizing that authors come from a variety of cultures. In this way children can be empowered to see themselves as authors.

Multicultural mentor texts can contribute to children's growing understanding of particular discourse forms. Many English learners, for example, are familiar with the discourse forms of their native language, even though they may not be able to read or write their native language. For these children, reading books in their native languages can reinforce their understanding of these forms in the first language. They can then build on this understanding as they encounter such texts that are written in English. Such texts can provide rich models of the many discourse forms found in the English language that students may not encounter at home.

Through the exploration of fables, folklore, nonfiction, realistic fiction, biography, historical fiction and poetry from different cultures, children develop greater sensitivity to the structures and literary conventions which characterize each type of literature. As these understandings grow, so will reading comprehension. Exposure to these literary forms can provide children with models for developing their oral language and written discourse. By listening to and discussing multicultural literature, children enhance their own oral language and develop appreciation for the importance of the oral tradition within cultures.

SELECTING MULTICULTURAL MENTOR TEXTS

When selecting multicultural mentor texts, teachers should be sure to first evaluate the text as they would any other multicultural work. It goes without saying that these texts should be free of stereotyping and pejorative language, provide accurate depictions of life circumstances of members of parallel cultures, and visually depict members of a culture accurately.

As teachers identify potential multicultural mentor texts, they need to also consider their personal responses to the books. The best mentor texts are teacher favorites, books they return to again and again. In the same way, mentor texts must include titles that children feel connected to, titles that reflect their lives, their feelings, and their worlds. A further consideration of a mentor text is its connection to the curriculum. In this era of standards-based instruction, it is essential that such texts address an area of study that students will encounter during the school year. Many mentor texts can be used to not only teach writing, but also teach students about social studies and science. Finally, mentor texts should demonstrate aspects of literary craft that the teacher needs to share with students. They should be books that can be used again and again in the classroom because of the rich models they provide for writing.

Mem Fox's (1997) *Whoever You Are* is a book with rich possibilities for use as a multicultural mentor text. The book is one that children can readily connect with. They identify with the warm illustrations of children of different races from across the globe and the author's message that hearts are the same, joys are the same, smiles are the same and love is the same all over the world. The language of the text follows a rhythmic pattern and frequently repeated words which children can join in as they hear the book read aloud. This pattern is one that children can borrow from for their own writing. This book also has several text conventions that teachers can point out to children. For example, Fox consistently uses commas to denote pauses in the reading; children can not only see but hear the points at which the reading slows. The author even uses a colon (e.g., "But remember this:") to denote to the listener that something important is about to be said.

Another important consideration for multicultural mentor texts is the need to include a broad range of texts. Texts should be diverse in terms of representation of different cultures, in terms of genre represented, in terms of length and in terms of the variety of aspects of the writer's craft that they model. Mentor texts should be at students' independent reading levels.

WAYS TO LOOK AT MENTOR TEXTS

Katie Wood Ray & Lisa Cleaveland (2004) identify three different ways that teachers can direct students to look at mentor texts. The first way is simply to show students something specific from a book that illustrates a particular feature and help them think about how they can use it in their own writing. The teacher then asks students to locate examples of this feature in their own reading and try to use the feature in their writing. Using the earlier example, the teacher might read students the sentence from Mem Fox's (1997) *Whoever You Are* containing the colon and demonstrate how they might use this feature in their writing.

Ray also suggests using book walk throughs. This involves a more open-ended approach during which the teacher reads a book aloud and asks students what they notice about the way the book is written. It might also include more focused questions such as "What do you notice about the punctuation in this book?" Using the Mem Fox book described earlier, the teacher might ask, "What do you notice about the rhyme and repetition in this book?"

A third way to focus students on particular books is through small group inquiry. Using this approach, students work in pairs or small groups to analyze texts. Students can look at different texts but focus on looking for the same thing. For example, if students are focusing on poetry, they might consider question like "How does poetry look different from a story?" How do poets use words to create a poem?" Students can then record their responses on post it notes.

READING WRITING CONNECTIONS

Multicultural mentor texts also teach students about the conventions of the English language, which are important for students to understand when reading and writing. Titles like *Yo Yes* (Raschka, 1993), for example, illustrate the uses of punctuation marks, and the highly acclaimed *Martin's Big Words* (Rappaport, 2001) uses unique formats to help students recognize examples of Martin's exact words through the enlarged print that appears on each page. In this way younger students begin to recognize the role of direct quotations and the punctuation marks that signal these quotations. Through multiple experiences with such texts and effectively focused instruction, students learn to use quotation marks to demonstrate the use of quoted materials. Titles like *Amazing Grace* (Hoffman, 1991) provide more traditional examples of the use of quotation marks that denote the specific words of particular speakers.

USING MENTOR TEXTS IN THE CLASSROOM

This section of the chapter first outlines an instructional sequence that provides a framework for using multicultural mentor texts in the classroom. This sequence can be used, with modifications, for students of all ages. The second part of this section describes how three classroom teachers used this instructional sequence to teach various aspects of writing with their own students. The teachers in the section, Christine Kane, Linda Sennett, and Aja Booker are teachers at Nubia Leadership Academy, a predominantly African American elementary school in southeast San Diego, California.

An Instructional Sequence for Teaching with Multicultural Mentor Texts

After students have deconstructed a particular text for comprehension purposes, immersion in explicitly identifying elements of text structure for grammar or crafting purposes provides students with models of how these texts are constructed. A two-phase sequence, which employs the Gradual Release of Responsibility Model (Pearson & Gallagher, 1983), can facilitate student development using mentor texts. During phase 1, teachers use the mentor text exemplars to help students identify the model skill in the text and see it used by the teacher in a teacher-generated *model*. During phase 2, students need opportunities to *practice* the target skill, collaboratively as a whole class and independently.

Phase 1: Teacher Modeling of Exemplar Mentor Text

Students must engage with a familiar text multiple times for reading purposes before it becomes a mentor text used for writing purposes. During phase 1 teachers utilize a mentor text to provide explicit example of a target skill in writing instruction. Target skills are identified based on students' needs as identified by formal and informal writing assessments and grade level standards. During step 1 the teacher points out what the author does in the text to demonstrate a particular skill. During step 2 the teacher generates a model sentence illustrating the skill identified in the text.

Step 1: *Author Does*. The teacher presents a mentor text exemplar that highlights a target skill. The teacher presents the mentor text to the students and asks students, "What do you notice about this mentor text?" The teacher records the students' observations, adding academic language for identifying the target skill. Academic language is the language used in textbooks, in classrooms, and on tests that differs in structure and vocabulary from the everyday spoken English of social interactions. In the mentor text process teachers should explicitly name academic terms such as *adjective*, *simile*, and *interjection* as appropriate when highlighting text features in the mentor text exemplars. If students do not notice the target skill independently during this phase the teacher explicitly states the target skill and provides the formal academic term as well.

Step 2: *Teacher Does*. Using the target skill identified in the previous step, the teacher chooses a new topic and generates a new model sentence in front of students. The teacher then asks the students to evaluate the new model generated by the teacher for the target skill.

Phase 2: Students Practice of Exemplar Mentor Text

After students understand the concept of the target skill used in the exemplar mentor text, they need opportunities to practice. Involving students in large group or paired coconstruction of the target skill allows students to experience the process again with peer support. Once students are comfortable with the target skill, students can practice on their own independently.

Step 1: *Teacher and Student(s) Do*. The teacher and student(s) collaborate to write a new mentor text example on a topic of choice that includes the target skill. The teacher asks the student(s) to evaluate their new mentor text example for the target skill.

Step 2: *Student Does*. The teacher provides a set amount of time for students to choose a topic of their own and construct a mentor text example that includes the target skill. The teacher asks the student to evaluate their model for the target skill, provides feedback and evaluates the student's independent example.

Using Mentor Texts to Teach Grammar

After reading *When I Am Old With You* by Angela Johnson (1990) aloud to her first graders, teacher Christine Kane engaged her class in many discussions for comprehension purposes prior to using the text as a mentor text exemplar for teaching the target skill of adjectives. In this story, a small child imagines a future when he will be old with his grandaddy and will sit beside him in a rocking chair and talk about everything. They will go fishing, drink cool water from a jug, and play cards "till the lightning bugs shine in the trees." The African-American child and grandfather are distinct individuals, yet also universal figures, recognizable to anyone who has ever shared the bond of family love across generations.

The target skill for this lesson was derived from the teacher based upon informal student assessments in writing that showed a lack of descriptive language and addressed the requirement of state standards that students write compositions that describe and explain familiar objects, events, and experiences using sensory details.

The teacher selected this mentor text to help teach adjectives because it was a warm, family story to which her students could easily relate. Furthermore, the book was also included in the mandated literature curriculum that she was using for reading instruction, and each child had a copy of the entire story in their textbooks. After spending time deconstructing the text for comprehension purposes, Ms. Kane selected one
sentence from the text to use as an exemplar for the use of adjectives. She wrote this single sentence on a piece of chart paper for the whole class to observe.

Step 1: *Author Does*. The students were asked what they noticed about this sentence.

We'll go fishing too, Grandaddy, down by that old pond with the flat rocks all around.

The first graders correctly identified writing elements such as capital letter at the beginning of the sentence, capital letter for Grandaddy and a period used at the end of the sentence. Since they did not identify the target skill of adjectives, the teacher led them through a series of questions and explicitly stated the target skill:

Ms. Kane asked, "What do we know about the pond?"

Students responded that it was old. Ms. Kane used a green marker to draw a box around the word "old" and drew a line underneath the noun "pond."

She then asked, "What do we know about the kind of rocks that were at the old pond?"

Students responded that the rocks were flat. Ms. Kane used a green marker to draw a box around the word "flat" and drew a line underneath the noun "rocks." Ms. Kane then explicitly stated: Angela Johnson used "adjectives" to help her describe the pond and the rocks to help her readers draw a better picture in their minds about the setting for the story. Authors use adjectives as a way to describe another person or an object. Angela Johnson is going to be our writing mentor for learning about adjectives today.

Step 2: *Teacher Does*. The students observed Ms. Kane choose her own topic and constructed a sentence in front of the students and wrote it directly underneath the Angela Johnson's exemplar sentence on the chart. This provided students with two exemplar models of the correct way to use adjectives in a sentence before they were asked to practice the skill on their own. She said:

I know that Angela Johnson is a good writer who knows how to describe things so that readers can make a better picture in their minds about exactly how the pond looked when they went fishing. Angela Johnson's writing can help me learn how to add adjectives in my own writing too. If I wanted to write to someone who was not inside our classroom about the apple that is on my desk, I would want to make sure I described it clearly so that the reader could create a picture of it in their mind. I would want them to know that the apple was red and that my desk was shiny. I'm going to use Angela Johnson's writing as a mentor text to model how I will include adjectives in my own sentence.

Ms. Kane wrote the following sentence in front of her first grade students on the chart directly underneath the exemplar model from Angela Johnson:

> The red apple sat on the shiny desk in the classroom.

As she wrote the sentence, she made sure to make her thinking as a writer explicit for her students. She said:

I can see that when Angela Johnson wanted to describe the pond she put the word *old* in front of the word pond. She did the same thing when she wanted to describe the rocks. She added the word *flat* in front of the word rocks. When I want to describe my apple and my desk to my friend I will add the adjective *red* in front of apple and the adjective *shiny* in front of desk. Now my friend knows when they read my writing that the apple is red and my desk is shiny.

The first graders were then asked to evaluate if Ms. Kane had achieved the target skill for adjectives that author Angela Johnson had illustrated for them. As they correctly identified that the apple was described as red and that the desk was identified as shiny Ms. Kane drew a box around "red" and underlined the word apple with a green marker. She then repeated the same process for the adjective "shiny" and the noun "desk." She asked the students. "Did I use the target skill of adjectives in my own sentence the way I learned from my writing mentor Angela Johnson?"

The students responded in the affirmative. The teacher asked for volunteers to come up to the chart paper and prove that her model used adjectives appropriately. Two different students came up to the board to identify that Ms. Kane described the apple as red and the desk as shiny. Both students correctly used the academic term "adjective" in their reference to the describing words "red" and "shiny."

Step 3: *Teacher & Student(s) Do*. The students were asked to co-construct a sentence that included at least two adjectives using Angela Johnson's and Ms. Kane's exemplar sentences as mentor text. The following response from three student volunteers was transcribed on the chart underneath the exemplar sentences from Angela Johnson and Ms. Kane:

> The yellow pencils have small erasers in our black boxes.

The first graders were then asked to evaluate if they had achieved the target skill for adjectives that both Angela Johnson and Ms. Kane had illustrated for them. Student volunteers that did not assist in the creation of the collaboration sentence were asked to identify the adjectives in the sentence and the nouns that they described. Three separate student volunteers identified that the pencils were described as "yellow," their erasers were identified as "small" and they were located in black boxes. Ms. Kane drew a box around "yellow" and underlined the word pencils with a green marker. She then repeated the same process for drawing a box around the adjectives "small" and "black" and underlining their respective nouns "erasers" and "boxes." She asked the students:

"Did we use the target skill of adjectives in our sentence the way we learned from our mentor Angela Johnson?" The students again responded in the affirmative.

Step 4: *Student Does*. Each student independently wrote their own sentence without the assistance of the teacher and was specifically required to include at least one adjective in their sentence. Students were instructed to use the same evaluation format as they had seen modeled in Angela Johnson's, Ms. Kane's, and the class collaboration sentence. They identified their use of an adjective by putting a box around their adjective with a green crayon and underlining the noun that followed (see Figure 14.2 for an example). Ms. Kane walked around and took informal observation notes indicating which students were independently able to add at least one adjective into their own sentence and which students would require further reteaching of the target skill in future lesson plans.

As a follow up activity to the mentor text process, students were asked to reread the entire story, *When I Am Old With You*, with a partner and to generate a list of other adjectives that Angela Johnson had purposefully included as an author. Extension activities based upon this lesson continued throughout the remainder of the year as the teacher illustrated the target skill of adjective use in a wide variety of text by other authors. In this way, students were able to see how adjectives could be used in a variety of ways depending upon the author's purpose, rather than learning grammar rules through decontextualized worksheets.

Using Mentor Texts to Teach Similes

Third grade teacher, Linda Sennett, has found mentor texts to be extremely useful in helping her third graders become more accomplished authors. For this particular assignment, she used the picture book *The Talking Eggs* by Robert D. San Souci (1989), a folktale found in the mandated literature curriculum used at the school site. This adaptation of a Creole folktale highlights two sisters: Rose, who is spoiled and lazy but her mother's favorite, and sweet Blanche, who is forced to fetch and carry and do all the hard work for her mother and sister. Blanche's life is miserable until one day her kindness to an old witch-woman catapults her into a miraculous world where cows have two heads and bray like mules, and rabbits in fancy dress dance the Virginia reel. Strangest of all are the wondrous talking eggs, which dramatically prove that beauty may hide great ugliness while the plainest of objects may conceal treasure within.

Ms. Sennett has used this same text to highlight a variety of crafting purposes for third-grade students from similes to dialogue. This particular lesson highlighted the author's craft for inanimate objects talking and similes.

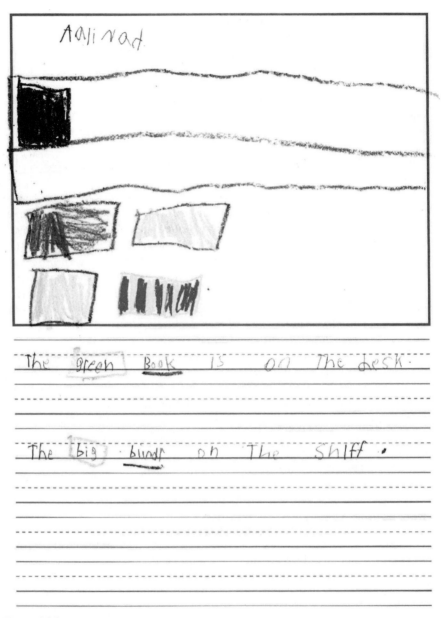

Figure 14.2
Aalinah's Sentences Containing Adjectives

After thoroughly discussing and evaluating the text for comprehension purposes, Ms. Sennett selected several sentences from the text to use as exemplars for writing similes. She wrote two examples on chart paper for the class to examine:

Step 1: *Author Does*. The students were asked to describe what they noticed about these sentences: "A cow with two heads, and horns like corkscrews, peered over the fence at Blanche and brayed like a mule" and "The old woman sat down near the fireplace and took off her head. She set it on her lap like a pumpkin." The third graders correctly identified capital letters at the beginning of each sentence and punctuation marks at each end. In order to introduce the idea of similes, the teacher brought their attention to the word "like" in both sentences by circling them with a blue marker:

Ms. Sennett stated, "I notice the author uses the word "like" in both of these sentences . . . I wonder why?" Students offered a variety of responses, including "The horns were twisty," "The cow didn't sound like a cow," and "He's saying her head is like a pumpkin."

Ms. Sennett had the students physically mimic the roundness of a pumpkin on their laps and asked the follow-up question, "Why do you think our mentor author chose to give this type of description?"

Students provided the following responses:

"Because you can really SEE what her head was like."
"And you can hear that the cow sounded like a donkey."

The teacher stated, "So her head is being COMPARED to a pumpkin? What else is being compared in these examples?" The students correctly identified that the horns were being compared to corkscrews (which Ms. Sennett helped clarify through an illustration), the cow's sound was being compared to the bray of a donkey, and the old woman's head was being compared to a pumpkin. Several other examples were analyzed in a similar fashion before proceeding to the next step, including the following excerpts from the text itself:

"Blanche was sweet and kind and as sharp as forty crickets."
"But their mother liked Rose the best, because they were as alike as two peas on a pod—bed-tempered, sharp-tongued, and always putting on airs."
"But out of the shells came clouds of whip snakes, toads, frogs, yellow jackets, and a big, old, gray wolf. These began to chase after her like a pig after a pumpkin."

Step 2: *Teacher Does*. The students observed Ms. Sennett construct several sentences containing similes in front of the class. These were written on chart paper underneath San Souci's examples. This allowed students to see yet another exemplar before creating similes with a partner and eventually independently. She explained the exemplar sentences in the following way:

I really like the way Robert San Souci used comparisons to help us visualize certain parts of the story, and we call these comparisons similes. His writing can help me learn how to include similes in my own writing too. For example, if I wanted someone to know what color our school uniforms are, I could say, 'Desiree's polo shirt is as blue as the evening sky.' Even though they may have never seen Desiree's shirt, they probably have seen the deep blue of the evening sky and would be able to get a clearer picture in their head. I could also say, 'Joshua's smile is as warm as a freshly baked muffin' to let my reader feel the same feeling of comfort and friendliness I get from his smile.

Ms. Sennett then asked, "Did I use similes in my own sentences like my mentor author Robert San Souci?" The students confirmed the correctness of her examples and volunteered the observations, "You compared her shirt to the night sky and his smile to muffins."

Step 3: *Teacher and Student(s) Do*. At this point the class was asked to co-create similes using Robert San Souci's and Ms. Sennett's examples as mentor text. The teacher provided students with the following sentence to prompt their responses: "It's pretty cold in here ... we could say it's as cold as ... " Students piped in "cold" words like an ice cube, ice cream, and winter. She then said: "I have a green sweater on today ... We could say it is green like what?" Students responded with "grass," "green beans," and "a frog." When the majority of students had a grasp on the idea of creating similes Ms. Sennett moved on to the next step.

Step 4: *Partners Do*. At this point, each student was assigned a partner and asked to brainstorm a list of similes. They then wrote their similes on index cards and returned to the rug to listen and evaluate each other's creations to see if they qualified as similes. The majority of students did quite well and volunteered examples like:

> "I am as tall as a tree."
> "Ms. Sennett is pretty like a flower."
> "My mom's hair is soft like a baby's skin."

Those pairs who experienced difficulty were aided by suggestions from their classmates, and they chose their favorite word from among those suggestions.

Step Five: *Student Does*. Once students were adept at creating similes with a partner, they were asked to write a fantasy about an inanimate object that could talk, and include at least one simile in their story (see Figure 14.3 for an example). Ms. Sennett emphasized the sections of the story where the eggs talked. Then she had her students brainstorm objects that they could make "talk."

The Talking Necklace

One day there was a boy named Max. Max was as short as a monkey. One morning Max found a necklace stand, they were all regular neckace except for one it was all the colors of the rainbow one was as bright as the sun. Everytime he would put the necklace on somebody's hand it would change colors. Red is for love, blue is for sadness, green is for happiness and black is for madness. When it was time to go to bed Max dreamed about doing everything with his necklace, skateboarding, swimming and running. The next day Max went to the park examining his necklace when he bumped into a line.

"I wonder what everyone is waiting for," Max wonders. Max saw a huge necklace store. He never saw a necklace store that big before! One houir later Max got in and checked out all the necklaces, one of them looked like his emotion necklace.

"There might be a million necklaces in here!" Max said. Once Max walked outside, a witch swooped in and took his necklace. The witch was mean so it didn't give back Max's necklace. So Max followed the witch, he wouldn't stop until he got his necklace back. But it was too late, the witch's broom was too fast, luckily when he stopped running he was by a cabin. Max sneaked inside and didn't see the witch anywere, so he searched for his missing necklace then saw the witch. Too bad for Max, because the witch saw him. The witch tried to smash the necklace, but Max got it back just in time! But once he got home, everyone in Proma City was sad.

"I know why everyone is sad. The necklace is on blue. I have to change it!" Max said. Max used his teeth, but that didn't work, so Max used all his strength to get to green, and it wored! Everybody is happy again! Then Max and Proma City lived happily ever after. Oh, and if your wrried about the witch, well Max took care of that.

"Um, could somebody untie me please?"

Figure 14.3

Kyevoni's Sample Story (Unedited Student Writing)

They came up with a variety of ideas such as a talking apple, pocket, table, and necklace. She then had each child choose a partner to help them develop their story by asking questions and giving feedback. Each student independently wrote their story without the teacher's assistance. Ms. Sennett then held individual conferences and made suggestions. Again, classmates who experienced difficulty were helped by peers who had a firmer grasp on the concept of writing similes. The most common error was thinking that just including the word "like" made a simile, for example, "I like to play football." As a follow up, students were asked to observe other author's use of similes, specifically in their independent reading. Many students have excitedly shared their findings with Ms. Sennett since the conclusion of this lesson.

TEACHING TEXT STRUCTURES

In addition to using multicultural mentor texts for teaching grammar and the author's craft, multicultural mentor texts can provide models for student writing in many other areas. Yet another area in which mentor texts can be useful is that of teaching text structure. By recognizing the structures authors use to frame their writing, students develop a wider repertoire of ideas for structuring their own writing.

As students work to create their own written work, they often struggle to identify a format that is appropriate to their topic. By using the instructional sequence described earlier, teachers can help students develop understanding of ways that their own written work can be structured. Sharing exemplary titles such as *Christmas in the Big House, Christmas in the Quarters* (McKissack & McKissack, 1999) with older students helps them to understand the potential range of structures possible for framing their writing. This book, for example, provides a rich example of structuring a text through a comparison contrast structure. In this excellent book the author juxtaposes the lives of slaves with that of slave owners during the Civil War. By reading the book aloud and sensitizing students to the many ways that the author signals the use of comparison/contrast through chapter titles, illustrations, signal words, and so on, teachers help students see how the author alternates chapters to compare and contrast the experiences of the two groups.

Other titles provide examples of other text structures. For example, titles like *Grandfather's Journey* by Allen Say (1993), details the plight of a man caught between his love of two different cultures, the American and Japanese, as he travels to Japan to assuage his sense of homesickness over living in the United States. The story follows a circular pattern in which the main character travels to Japan but misses the United States and returns to the United States only to miss Japan.

Alphabet books represent yet another interesting, yet familiar, way to structure a text. Tony Johnson's (1997) *Day of the Dead*, for example, provides information on the Day of the Dead holiday through entries for each letter of the alphabet. *Gathering the Sun* by Alma Flor Ada (1997) structures information in alphabetical order. By assigning students different letters of the alphabet, teachers can easily create a class alphabet book. Each student can be assigned a letter related to a particular topic under study. Each student can create and illustrate a page in a class book, and they review the information when all of the pages are complete.

Chronological order provides another structure for structuring a text. Biographies like *Harvesting Hope* (Krull, 2003) which details the life of César Chávez, are often arranged in time order. Children might enjoy creating their own life stories and arranging them in time order.

CONCLUSION

Multicultural mentor texts provide an incredibly rich resource for helping all students develop the skills necessarily to not only read like a writer, but master the many skills associated with writing. In an era dominated by accountability, multicultural mentor texts can sensitize students to the language of literature at the same time that they can teach students about the craft of writing. Literature itself, combined with excellent instruction, can empower students as both readers and writers and help them not only develop the literacy skills they need to succeed as readers and writers, but to develop the love of words and appreciation for literature that can serve them throughout their lifetimes.

REFERENCES

Anderson, J. (2007). *Everyday editing*. Portland, ME: Stenhouse.

Anderson, J. (2005). *Mechanically inclined: Building grammar, usage and style into writer's workshop*. Portland, ME: Stenhouse.

August, D., & Shanahan, T. (2006). *Developing literacy in second-language learners: Report of the National Literacy Panel on language-minority children and youth*. Mahweh, NJ: Lawrence Erlbaum Associates.

Bishop, R. S. (1990). Mirrors, windows, and sliding glass doors. *Perspectives: Choosing and using books for the classroom, 6*(3), ix–xi.

Dorfman, L. R., & Cappelli, R. (2007). *Mentor texts: Teaching writing through children's literature, k–6*. Portland, ME: Stenhouse.

Harris, V. J. (1993). *Teaching multicultural literature in grades k–8*. New York, NY: Christopher Gordon.

Pearson, P. D., & Gallagher, M. C. (1983). The instruction of reading comprehension. *Contemporary Educational Psychology, 8*(3), 317–344.

Ray, K. W., & Cleaveland, L. B. (2004). *About the authors: Writing workshop with our youngest writers*. Portsmouth, NH: Heinemann.

MULTICULTURAL LITERATURE

Flor Ada, A. (1997). *Gathering the sun: An alphabet in Spanish and English*. Illustrated by Simón Silva. New York, NY: Harper Collins Publishers.

Fox, M. (1997). *Whoever you are*. Illustrated by Leslie Staub. San Diego, CA: Harcourt Brace

Hoffman, M. (1991). *Amazing Grace*. Illustrated by Caroline Binch. New York, NY: Dial Books.

Johnson, A. (1990). *When I am old with you*. Illustrated by David Soman. New York, NY: Orchard Books.

Johnson, T. (1997). *Day of the Dead*. Illustrated by Jeanette Winter. Orlando, FL: Harcourt, Inc.

Krull, K. (2003). *Harvesting hope: The story of César Chávez*. Illustrated by Yuyi Morales. San Diego, CA: Harcourt.

McKissack, P. C. & McKissack, F. L. (1999). *Christmas in the big house, Christmas in the quarters*. Illustrated by John Thompson. New York, NY: Scholastic Inc.

Rappaport, D. (2001). *Martin's big words: The life of Dr. Martin Luther King, Jr.* Illustrated by Bryan Collier. New York, NY: Hyperion.

Raschka, C. (1993). *Yo yes*. New York, NY: Orchard Books.

San Souci, R. D. (1989). *The talking eggs*. Illustrated by Jerry Pinkney. New York, NY: Dial Books.

Say, A. (1993). *Grandfather's journey*. New York, NY: Houghton Mifflin Co.

15

Reading Fluency and Multicultural Literature

Belinda Zimmerman, Timothy Rasinski, and Tracy Foreman

The past two decades have seen remarkable advances in our understanding of how children learn to read and the most effective ways to teach reading. Knowledge of these advances was consolidated in the work of the National Reading Panel (2000). The Panel was mandated by the United States Congress to review the empirical research related to reading and reading instruction and identify those factors that were associated with success in learning to read based on research findings. In its report the panel identified five instructional factors associated with reading success: phonemic awareness, phonics or word decoding, reading fluency, vocabulary or knowledge of word meanings, and reading comprehension (National Reading Panel, 2000).

Of these five, reading fluency was the one that was least expected. For several previous decades reading fluency had been the neglected goal of the reading program (Allington, 1983). Indeed, in his review of the historical roots of reading fluency, Rasinski (2010) found that since the early part of the twentieth century, reading fluency had been ignored and in many cases discouraged as an area of instructional emphasis. Even as recently as the 1990s, a study of materials for elementary instruction in reading found very little mention of reading fluency as a goal or of instructional methods for teaching fluency. Although there are a number of reasons for the lack of interest in fluency, perhaps the greatest impediment to its inclusion in the reading curriculum was that it was associated with oral reading; and because oral reading was not thought to be an activity widely engaged in during adulthood, it was felt that there was little need to teach it or emphasize it in any focused way in the school reading curriculum.

More recent reviews of the research on fluency (e.g., Rasinski, Reutzel, Chard, Linan-Thompson, in press) have shown that fluency is a contributor to reading comprehension and achievement in reading, that there are identified methods for teaching fluency successfully, and that although fluency may be associated with oral reading, reading instruction aimed at improving fluency leads to improvements in silent reading as well. It is now recommended that fluency instruction be part of the daily reading curriculum.

Fluency has been identified as the link between phonics and word decoding and reading comprehension (Rasinski, 2003). Word recognition automaticity is one of two major components of fluency. It refers to the ability to read (decode) words not only accurately but also effortlessly or automatically. Automatic word decoding allows readers to be so effortless in their decoding that they can focus their attention on making meaning, the more important part of reading. Fluency also involves the ability to read orally in such a way that the reading sounds like real language. To read with appropriate prosody or expression means that a reader attends to the meaning and syntax of the passage. Reading with appropriate expression also allows for readers to elaborate on the meaning of the passage.

The most common form of assessment of reading fluency has been determining students' reading rate on grade and instructional level passages. It is suggested that as automaticity improves through guided oral assisted and repeated reading, automaticity improves. Automaticity is measured through reading rate or speed. Reading speed has been found to correlate substantially with measures of reading comprehension and overall reading proficiency (Rasinski, 2003).

This association of reading fluency with reading rate has led to the unintended consequence of improvements in reading fluency being associated with improvements in reading rate. What was a correlational relationship has come to be inferred as a causal relationship. As a result, over the past decade there has occurred a proliferation of instructional methods for improving reading fluency and overall reading proficiency by focusing primarily on increasing reading rate. Although, such programs and methods have been found to improve rate, there is little compelling evidence that such approaches improve the underlying competencies of fluency and comprehension.

A more authentic approach to teaching fluency comes when one considers the essence of fluency in oral language—the ability to make meaning through expressive reading at an appropriate rate that reflects the meaning of the passage. Materials that are meant to be performed orally for an audience and that manifest a strong voice are ideal for fluency. The voice embedded in the writing surfaces when one reads the text with appropriate prosody. Less proficient readers achieve appropriate levels of expression through assisted and repeated (rehearsed) readings of a passage.

Certain texts exist that lend themselves to oral interpretive reading and that contain a strong voice. Among these text types or genre are poetry, song lyrics, monologues (including letters, journals, and diaries) dialogues, and scripts. Such texts are meant to be rehearsed and performed with fluency. Moreover, when students rehearse such texts, fluency instruction becomes authentic, motivating, and effective. A growing body of research has demonstrated that when students engage in the rehearsal and performance of such materials, fluency and overall reading performance improves (Griffith & Rasinski, 2004; Martinez, Roser, & Strecker, 1999; Young & Rasinski, 2009). For example, Griffith and Rasinski describe a weekly instructional routine in which students practice poetry, scripts, monologues, and other material throughout the week and perform on Fridays. Over the course of employing such a routine, these researchers found that struggling readers make, on average, 2.9 years growth in overall reading achievement for one year of instruction.

While the materials used in the aforementioned studies tend to reflect mainstream American culture, it is not difficult to imagine poetry, song, and other such texts that reflect the diverse cultures represented in many classrooms in America today. Indeed, well chosen genre such as poetry, song lyrics, monologues, dialogues, and scripts have the potential for allowing students to examine, honor, and celebrate not only their own cultural backgrounds but also examine, honor, and celebrate the diverse cultural backgrounds of their classmates.

EFFECTIVE TEACHING OF FLUENCY FOR ENGLISH LANGUAGE LEARNERS

Earlier in their teaching careers, Tracy and Belinda had the opportunity to spend several exciting years team teaching a multicultural, multi-age, and inclusion classroom of students in grades one through three. One year, they were fortunate enough to have children from seven different countries in their classroom: United States, China, India, Korea, Israel, Poland, and Russia. In the university town where the school was located, it was not highly unusual to have one or two English Language Learners (ELLs) in the classroom since these students tended to be the children of new or visiting professors and of graduate students from many different parts of the world. However, during this particular year, having representation from seven different countries was considerable. The best way to instruct these children to become literate in the English language was often a topic of great discussion, as it most certainly is anywhere you have high or low populations of ELL students.

The school district provided some support by providing an English language tutor who worked with the children once a week for 30 minutes. The assistance was much needed and this capable tutor did her best to help the students to acquire English language literacy, especially considering her limited time and the fact that she was the sole English language tutor for all four elementary schools in the district. Understandably, the bulk of the children's learning was primarily the responsibility of Tracy and Belinda. The question became how to plan instruction that reaches each individual learner and promotes fluency in reading and writing in the English language.

Belinda and Tracy began to search for research-based strategies for answering this question. As part of their quest, they called upon their university colleague and the coauthor of this chapter, Dr. Timothy Rasinski. Much to their relief, he assured them that with adaptations, many of the methods they were currently using to promote fluency also applied to both first and second language learners (Padak & Rasinski, 2008). In the pages that follow, we highlight some of these successful strategies as well as some others we have learned since then. We also include in the Appendix some texts that classroom teachers, librarians, tutors, and, in some cases, parents may use to successfully implement the strategies, to enhance the fluency and reading progress of ELLs and to deepen all students' appreciation and acceptance of other cultures.

Pikulski & Chard (2005) specify nine steps that all fluency instructional programs should include. We endorse these as a checklist of characteristics to look for in selecting research-based fluency development strategies:

1. building the graphophonic foundations for fluency, including phonological awareness, letter familiarity, and phonics;
2. building and extending vocabulary and oral language skills;
3. providing expert instruction and practice in the recognition of high frequency vocabulary;
4. teaching common word parts and spelling patterns;

5. teaching, modeling, and providing practice in the application of a decoding strategy;
6. using appropriate texts to coach strategic behaviors and to build reading speed;
7. using repeated reading procedures as an intervention approach for struggling readers;
8. extending growing fluency through wide independent reading; and
9. monitoring fluency development though appropriate assessment procedures.

Similarly, Rasinski & Padak (2008) also emphasize that the following instructional practices are successful venues to fluency development:

1. the teacher or more expert reader models fluent reading;
2. repeated readings (individual or in partners);
3. supported reading (choral and echo);
4. paired reading (more fluent reader paired with less fluent reader; reading is done simultaneously).
5. shared reading (read to, read with, and listen to the child read);
6. tape recorded passages; and
7. careful text selection by the teacher (relatively easy, predictable, and patterned texts; predictable plots and characters; using poetry and song lyrics).

RESEARCH-BASED INSTRUCTIONAL ROUTINES FOR EFFECTIVE FLUENCY INSTRUCTION

An essential role of the teacher in planning fluency instruction for all learners, especially ELLs, is to develop and enact instructional routines in which reading fluency is the focus. An instructional routine is simply a set of strategic activities aimed at developing a particular skill in reading that is implemented on a regular schedule, usually on a daily or weekly basis and stems from targeting students' needs based on systematic observation and assessment. The routines provide varied, fun, and engaging ways to maximize time on task and to offer the ELLs greater depth and support in fluency instruction.

Fluency Development Lesson

The Fluency Development Lesson (FDL) is an instructional model that may be differentiated to meet the needs of all learners, yet it originated as a framework for fluency intervention. The FDL was developed by Rasinski, Padak, Linek, and Sturtevant (1994) as a supplement to the regular reading program to assist students experiencing difficulties in fluency and in learning to read. As it happens, this is often the case with ELLs, which makes the FDL an ideal support strategy for them. The goal is to provide instruction and practice in a focused routine that incorporates principles of effective fluency instruction and multiple opportunities to practice authentic reading (Padak & Rasinski, 2008).

The FDL model was designed for primary children, but has been found to work well with elementary and middle school students too. Depending on the age and the level of reading proficiency, the teacher selects and makes copies of brief passages such as poems, songs, speeches, readers theaters, or consecutive segments of a short story. It is suggested that teachers choose passages of 50–100 words. However, with emerging readers or those with extremely limited English language proficiency, it is very appropriate to choose texts with fewer words. See some example poems for these kinds of beginning readers at the end of the chapter. The routine requires that students and teachers work for 10 to 15 minutes each day with the carefully selected text in which the teacher models reading the text for the students and gradually hands over the responsibility for reading the text from himself/herself to the students. Oral support reading, word study, and at-home practice are also features of the intervention.

A day and time is reserved each week for the students to perform the text. In a year-long implementation of the FDL in urban, second-grade classrooms where students were generally struggling readers, students doing the FDL consistently and with fidelity made significant achievement in both reading fluency and overall reading progress when compared with their progress made during the prior year and when compared with students not engaged in the FDL (Rasinski, Padak, Linek, and Sturtevant, 1994). Perhaps the greatest evidence of the effectiveness of the FDL lies in its staying power. Rasinski (2010) reports that teachers in the study continued to practice it with their students well beyond the completion of the study. This is not surprising since we have used the FDL consistently in our university reading clinic with excellent results, regardless of the age of the students. A detailed outline of the FDL is presented in the following section.

Implementing the Fluency Development Lesson

Purpose

The FDL combines several aspects of effective fluency instruction in a way that maximizes students' reading in a relatively short period of time. The FDL is intended as a supplement to the regular reading curriculum. The lesson takes 10–15 minutes per day to complete.

Preparation

Teachers make copies of brief passages, usually poems of 50–150 words for each child. The teacher needs a copy of the passage to display on the SMART board, visual presenter (ELMO), or chart paper. This process is typically divided and spread out over the week, ensuring that the students are practicing the reading every day. Fridays are often designated as performance days.

ELLs

When working with ELLs on the FDL, the reading material may be provided in the child's native language and also in English. Some sample passages are provided at the end of the chapter. The repeated reading of the designated passage often results in increased comprehension as well as greater motivation, automaticity, reading rate, and proper phrasing and expression.

The Lesson

Monday

1. The teacher reads and rereads the text to the class, modeling his or her best fluent, phrased, and expressive reading. The job of the students is to relax and enjoy the teacher's lively and engaging performance.

2. The teacher discusses the meaning of the text with the class as well as the quality of his or her reading.
3. The teacher distributes copies of the text to each student.
4. The teacher reads the poem again aloud to the students. The students are directed to follow along silently with their own copies or with the copy that has been displayed. Again, the students are encouraged to relax and enjoy.
5. The entire class reads the text chorally several times. The teacher creates variety by having students read the passage or portions of it in groups. For example, the teacher might say, "All those whose favorite sport is football, please stand and read." or "All those with summer birthdays, please stand and read." The teacher may also ask the class to reread the poem in their deepest or highest voices; loud or soft voices; happy or sad voices. There are endless possibilities here.

Tuesday

6. The class reads and rereads the poem again chorally. Again, variations on choral reading may be requested by the teacher.
7. The class divides into pairs. Each pair finds a quiet spot, and one student practices reading the text to a partner three times. The partner's job is to follow along in the text, provide help when needed, and give positive feedback to the reader. After the first three readings, the roles are switched. If possible, one partner should be at least a slightly stronger English language speaker or reader. The partners should be taught to use positive feedback when they see improvement in the other's reading and/or effort.

Wednesday

8. The class reads and rereads the poem again chorally. Again, variations on choral reading may be requested by the teacher.
9. The teacher has children meet with partners again. The students find three–five words from the text that they find interesting, fun to say, or challenging. The teacher may select a couple of words for the students too. The students record each word on an index card. The growing collections of these cards may be stored in a baggy labeled with the child's name on it. Some teachers prefer to use inexpensive recipe card boxes purchased from the local dollar store since these stack easily for storage and tend to be a bit more durable.
10. The partners use the word cards for word sorts, building sentences, arranging the word cards in alphabetical order, and so forth. This helps the students to build word recognition, automaticity, and understanding. Also, this type of word study helps the students to understand how words work in the English language.

Thursday

11. The class reads and rereads the poem again chorally. Again, variations on choral reading may be requested by the teacher.
12. The teacher allows the children 5–10 minutes to prepare for poetry performances that will take place the following day. The children may present individually, in partners, or in small groups. The children enjoy having choice in how and with whom to present.

Friday

13. The teacher asks for volunteers to perform the text. Individuals, pairs, and groups of up to four perform the reading for the class. The teacher makes arrangements for students to perform the text for the school principal, secretary, other classes, etc. The performing students are lavished with praise and applause. Performance day is a real celebration of the students' developing fluency and facility with reading.

14. Students take a copy of the text home and read it to their parents/caregivers. Parents are asked to listen to their child read as many times as they would like and to praise their child's efforts.

Oral Recitation Lesson

The Oral Recitation Lesson (ORL) is a structured process involving modeling, guided and supported reading, repeated reading, and performance (Hoffman & Crone, 1985; Rasinski, 2003). This small group intervention requires several days to complete, takes about 30 minutes per session, and involves both direct and indirect instruction. The ORL was originally intended to be used with narrative text, but informational texts may be easily incorporated. In addition, the ORL works well with trade books, text books, or a basal reading series. This flexibility of materials is part of the appeal of the model.

Implementing the Oral Recitation Lesson

The ORL is designed for use in regular classroom settings with students struggling with reading. Because the process includes so many features of effective fluency instruction, it is especially useful when teaching ELLs.

Direct Instruction Phase (Small Groups)

(two–four days per story or passage; 30–45 minutes per day)

Part 1

1. The teacher reads the story aloud to the students in a very expressive and even dramatic way to model expression, intonation, stress, and phrasing patterns.
2. Following the read aloud, the teacher assists students in constructing a story map of the major elements in the passage such as setting, main characters, problem, and solution. To lend extra support to the ELLs, the teacher may serve as a scribe, recording the students' responses exactly as stated onto chart paper.
3. Next, the group works together with teacher guidance to construct a summary based on the completed story map.
4. The teachers and the students select a memorable portion of the selection that will be used in the next part of the direct instruction phase.

Part 2

5. The teacher provides a mini-lesson on the elements of effective oral presentation such as reading with appropriate expression, volume, pitch, phrasing and using the punctuation marks to capture the author's intended message. Then the teacher models a fluent oral reading of the memorable portion of the story selected in the previous step.
6. Now the students have the opportunity to practice reading the selected portion first chorally, then in pairs, and then individually when the students feel ready. The teacher coaches the students by offering feedback, support, and praise.

Part 3

7. Choice is honored as the students select their own portion of the text to perform and are supported in engaging in lots of practice. When students indicate that they are ready, they are invited to perform their text selection aloud to the class. Students should receive much positive feedback after each performance.

Indirect Phase

8. This part is done by the entire class. The teacher asks students to choose a story or a portion of a story that has been covered in the direct instruction phase.

9. Have students practice their selection by whisper reading, so that all students can practice without being interrupted or distracted by the other readers.

10. While students are practicing, the teacher checks in to see if students have achieved mastery in word recognition. Typically, this would mean about 98 percent for word recognition accuracy and 75 words per minute with good expression for fluency. However, with ELLs it may take them a bit more time to achieve these targets.

11. Assign the next story or passage to students who achieve mastery and repeat the process.

Book Bits

Book bits is a text introduction routine in which students engage in readings of short portions of texts (Johns & Berglund, 2006; Yopp & Yopp, 2001, 2003). For the ELL student, it involves repeated, choral, and paired reading plus a comprehension component in which the students are asked to predict the content of the selection based on their assigned short excerpt or book bit. They have the opportunity to reword, refine, change, and/or extend their predictions as the students hear the predictions of their classmates. Book bits is powerful because it encourages all students in the class to read while they make predictions, pose questions, and formulate purposes for reading (Yopp & Yopp, 2003). In addition, students are given the chance to engage in purposeful oral language conversations with their peers, which also promotes text understanding and English language learning.

Implementing Book Bits

1. The teacher selects a short text that the students will be reading. The text may be fiction or informational from such sources as a picture book, chapter book, poem, Reader's Theater, basal, or textbook.

2. The teacher writes short excerpts, or book bits, from the text on oversized post-its or sentence strips.

3. The students are placed into partners. Each set of partners receives one book bit.

4. The partners first do their best to read the excerpt silently. The teacher provides support to any student who appears to be struggling with the text.

5. The partners reread the text simultaneously using choral reading.

6. The partners now shift into paired reading in which they first read together and then read the passage to one another. Typically, the passages are read three times each.

7. They discuss their book bit and together they begin to make predictions as to what the text will be about.

8. Using words or pictures, the students come to consensus on the prediction and then one records the prediction on an oversized post-it note using words, pictures, or a combination of both.

   The partners find another pair of partners and read their passage and share their prediction and repeat this process with another pair of partners.

9. Then predictions are posted on the board for all to view.

10. The teacher gathers the students around the display of posted predictions. He or she invites several volunteers to share their predictions. Classmates may offer feedback on the prediction.

11. The teacher invites the partners to share whether or not they are keeping their prediction or changing it in some way. They need to provide reasons for any changes made.
12. The teacher assigns the reading of the text from which the book bits were extracted. Partners may find a spot in the room and read or take turns reading the whole text together.
13. After the reading, the teacher may engage the class in a whole group discussion of the whole text. Students will share questions or connections they made as a result of the reading. They will also want to share if their predictions were correct.

Audio-Assisted Reading

Some required reading material, especially nonfiction and informational texts, can be quite challenging for ELLs. Recorded texts are a manageable way to scaffold students in becoming more fluent readers. In fictional texts, the tapes help the students with fluency, word recognition, and comprehension. In nonfiction texts, tape recorded readings help the students build vocabulary and understand content.

A good way to test out the benefits of tape recorded reading is to apply this concept to the reading of fables. Fables are often short passages that are easy for teachers to record and for students to listen to multiple times. Fables enhance comprehension because they call for higher level thinking such as inferring, making connections, and evaluating the moral of the story for soundness and trustworthiness. Students in upper elementary, middle, and high school are ideal ages for teaching fables since those students are capable of grasping the higher order thinking needed to make sense of the moral or lesson which ends each fable. In addition, fables are well-suited to ELLs because they contain universal themes and messages. For example, consider the benefits of a fable a week using the following tale from Aesop:

SPANISH VERSION

El perro y su reflejo
Sucedió que un perro tenía un trozo de carne que llevaba a casa en su boca
para comerlo en paz. En su camino a casa tenía que atravesar un arroyo. Cuando
cruzaba, miró abajo y vió su sombra reflejada en
el agua. Pensando que era otro perro con otro trozo de carne, quiso
obtener ese también. Entonces hizo un gruñido a su reflejo en el agua, pero
cuando abrió su boca, el trozo de carne se cayó dentro del agua.

Moraleja: Los que son codiciosos siempre terminan sin nada.

ENGLISH VERSION

The Dog and His Shadow
A dog, bearing in his mouth a piece of meat that he had stolen, was crossing a river
on his way home when he saw his shadow reflected in the stream below. Thinking
that it was another dog with another piece of meat, he snapped at it greedily to get this
as well, but by opening his mouth merely dropped the piece that he had.

Moral: Those who are greedy often end up with nothing.

If possible, the teacher presents the ELL student with both a recorded and print version of the fable in the first language of the student and in English. Having the fable (text) in both languages is certainly not mandatory, but assists the student with comprehension. The recording of the poem needs to be phrased, expressive, and properly paced (not too fast; not too slow), because it serves as a model of fluent oral reading for the students. It is helpful for the teacher to be the one to record the piece in English to ensure that the pace is just right for the student(s). Often, commercially produced tapes are recorded much too quickly for the students to follow along. Podcasting is another alternative for teachers to create recorded texts. A podcast is simply a more technologically advanced form of audio recording. With podcasting, the recording is done on the computer and may be stored as an electronic file which can be accessed in the memory of the computer or on another electronic memory device such as an iPod device or MP3 player.

Another way to maximize the potential of recorded materials with ELLS is to allow students to take home the text and its corresponding recording for further practice and reinforcement. In the case of podcasts, the recording can be sent and distributed to students and families through e-mail. Researchers have found that incorporating this home-school component results in the increased reading achievement, motivation, and self confidence of the ELLs (Koskinen, Wilson, Gambrell, & Neuman, 1993; Rasinski & Padak, 2008).

To even further facilitate the reading progress of ELLs, the teacher may also want to incorporate a practice called tape, check, and chart into the tape assisted instructional routine. Here, after students have listened to and followed along with the recorded passage, students have an opportunity to record their own readings on audiotapes or to create a podcast of the written text (Johns & Berglund, 2006, pp.80–81).

In the case of our Aesop's fable, after the student listens to and follows along with the recorded passage, he or she would record themselves reading the fable aloud. Then the student would replay the tape and follow along with the text. When listening to his or her own recording, the student makes a mark above any miscues such as insertions, omissions, and/or mispronunciations. The student reads and records the fable again and repeats the marking of the miscues process. It is helpful for the student to mark the miscues with a different color each time. The process may be repeated several times. Each time the student tallies and charts the number of miscues. When the student indicates readiness, he or she offers an independent, performance reading to the teacher or to a partner. The student is praised for his improvement and progress.

Audio-assisted reading is certainly worth a look-see for teachers of ELLs. The evidence clearly shows that audio assisted reading results in dramatic payoffs in reading achievement for both struggling readers and ELLs, and these effects can be seen in anywhere from 8 to 27 weeks (Rasinski, 2010). In one example, Koskinen and colleagues (1993) had students listen to two recordings of the same story: one slower reading, and one more fluent rendering. Here, students had the opportunity to first focus on words and phrases and then to a more fluent model of the stories, which in turn facilitated the students' fluency. In another study, when 162 first grade ELL and non-ELL students read along with audio tape books both at school and at home, positive effects were reported in reading achievement, interest in reading, and self confidence (Koskinen, Blum, Bisson, Phillips, Creamer, & Baker, 2000; Koskinen et al., 1993). Further, a study of non-English speaking middle school students found that participating in tape assisted reading led to a 14 month increase in reading progress after just two months of participation in tape assisted reading (Langford, 2001). Similarly, in a study of 29 elementary and middle school students in which about half of the students were ELLs, the students participated in a tape assisted supplementary reading program for 4.5 months. Students were asked to conduct six–eight repeated readings of assigned passages while simultaneously listening to the audio taped recording. Once fluent reading of the assigned text was achieved, the students traded in that text for a more challenging text. The results revealed that the students increased their reading achievement by more than two years. In addition, spelling and oral language improved by 1 year and 1.5 years respectively. An important side effect was that students' attitudes toward reading as well as the teachers' ratings of students' classroom reading performance also yielded gains (Nalder & Elley, 2002). Given these positive results, audio assisted reading is indeed a worthwhile endeavor for teachers of both ELLs and those who find reading difficult.

Reader's Theater

Reader's theater is a type of performance reading where stories have been scripted like a play. Unlike traditional plays which require the memorization of lines and elaborate costumes, props, and scenery, reader's theater performers rely primarily on their voices to bring the story to life. In reader's theater, the students stand side-by-side or in a semicircle in front of an audience, often classmates, and read from scripts that they hold in their hands or place on music stands (Rasinski, 2010). Since the reader's theater process ends in a performance, the students must read and reread many times to prepare. This provides an authentic purpose for the students to engage in repeated reading and practice.

As we have established throughout the chapter, ELLs can greatly benefit from these repeated readings because this provides them with opportunities to further develop not only fluency, but also greater proficiency in word accuracy, word recognition, vocabulary, comprehension, and oral language skills. From the beginning of the reader's theater routine to the moment of performance, the students will read their scripts 15–20 times (Robertson, 2009; Rasinski, 2010). Given all of the reading and rereading necessary for students to deliver a quality presentation, it makes sense that classroom research is showing that reader's theater helps students, including ELLs, to make significant improvements in reading (Kozub, 2000; Martinez, Roser, & Strecker 1999).

Reader's theater is an enjoyable and captivating instructional procedure that may be used at any grade level to increase fluency and overall reading development. Rasinski recommends a five-day routine for successful classroom implementation. His guide to reader's theater follows (Rasinski, 2010, p. 109).

Implementing Reader's Theater (Adapted for ELL Students)

Before the week begins

1. Select or write a script to be performed. Make two copies for each member of the group. One for school practice and the other for home.

Sample text "Holding Up The Sky" is a traditional tale from China. Observe how the tale is transformed into a reader's theater script:

Holding Up the Sky (traditional tale from China)

One day an elephant saw a hummingbird
lying on its back with its tiny feet up in the air. "What
are you doing?" asked the elephant.

The hummingbird replied,
"I heard that the sky might fall today,
and so I am ready to help hold it up,
should it fall."

The elephant laughed cruelly.
"Do you really think," he said,
"that those tiny feet could help hold up the sky?"

The hummingbird kept its feet in the air,
intent on his purpose, as he replied,
"Not alone. But each must do what he can.
And this is what I can do."

Script Version for Reader's Theater

Narrator:	One day Big Elephant saw Little Hummingbird lying on his back with his tiny feet up in the air.
Elephant:	Oh my! What are you doing, Little Hummingbird? Why do you choose to lay like that? Are you feeling ill?
Narrator:	Little Hummingbird replied . . .
Little Hummingbird:	I am not ill. You see, I heard that the sky might fall today. So, I am ready to hold it up with my tiny feet should it fall.
Narrator:	Elephant laughed aloud in a mean and cruel way.
Elephant:	(laughing loudly) Do you really think that those tiny feet could actually help hold up the entire, enormous, sky? Puh-leeze!
Narrator:	Little Hummingbird kept his tiny feet up in the air. He was very sincere and determined as he replied:
Little Hummingbird:	Not alone. I may not be able to hold it all up on my own. But, Elephant, each of us must do whatever he can. And so this is what I can do.
Narrator:	Elephant suddenly stopped laughing. He had to think about that one!

Monday

2. Introduce or review the nature, purpose, and procedures for reader's theater with the class. Remind the students that they are working toward fluency (accuracy, rate, phrasing, and expression) and that they are to use voice and facial expressions to capture meaning.

3. Assign students to individual parts by having them volunteer or audition. When assigning parts, the teacher can match students' language proficiency and reading level with an appropriate part.

Tuesday—Thursday

4. Have students practice their parts on their own, in their group, under your guidance, and at home.

Friday

5. Invite students to perform their scripts for an audience. Suggested audiences include classmates, other classes, other grade levels, parents, the school secretary, and the principal. Try to make the performance a special event. Many teachers turn Friday afternoons into a classroom reader's theater festival and students who are ready get to perform their scripts.

Other Tips for Consideration When Working with ELLs

Nisbet and Tindall (2008) suggest the following tips to support the reader's theater experience for ELLs:

1. Teachers should write or select parts that are in keeping with the students' language and reading proficiency.
2. ELLs may be assigned to read parts with recurring content or lines that include choral reading of repeated text.
3. Culturally relevant literature should be used to assist children in making the connections needed to fully comprehend and enjoy the story.
4. When available, students should be encouraged to read the story in their native language before reading it in English.
5. The ELL should be paired with someone who is at least a slightly stronger reader for additional practice.
6. Teachers may find it beneficial to pre-teach important vocabulary and concepts from the story. This plants some of the language and critical ideas of the story in their heads prior to reading in order to set the ELL student up for success.
7. Story and character maps that have pictures to support the words will also help with language and story understanding. As students are preparing, the teacher acts as a coach for the upcoming performance. When offering constructive feedback, it is helpful to use the name of the character instead of the student's actual name. For example, "Remember, Big Elephant, try to make your laugh sound mean and cruel. Little Hummingbird, remember to sound very sincere even though Big Elephant is laughing at you."
8. It helps when students rehearse entrance and exits to the reader's theater stage. This reinforces the performance concept and gives students confidence because they know exactly how to begin and end.
9. A designated reader should announce the reader's theater by stepping forward and saying something like, "Welcome to our reader's theater performance. The title of our story is _____. The author of the story is _____." Then each reader steps forward and announces his or her name and the part being played. It also helps the audience if each character has a sign around his or her neck identifying the character being portrayed (Rasinski, 2010).
10. A signal should be established which indicates that the performance is beginning. One teacher we observed, glides her fingers over wind chimes to signal the start of the performance and another teacher has one of the performers gently ring a bell.
11. If possible, rehearse in front of an audience prior to the final performance. The audience may be the teacher or even a small group of students.
12. Teachers may want to videotape the rehearsal and the performance so specific feedback can be given and the students can assess the performance for themselves.
13. Readers should be coached to speak directly to the audience, rather than to the teacher or one another. Occasional eye contact should be encouraged and readers can be coached to focus their eyes slightly above the heads of the audience.

14. At the close of the performance, a student steps forward and announces, "This concludes our reader's theater. We hope you have enjoyed our performance."

CONCLUSION

There is little doubt that students learning English as a second language face a myriad of challenges as they make the transition from first language literacy learning to literacy development and acquisition in English. The ideas, strategies, and routines detailed throughout the chapter offer teachers highly effective, yet practical suggestions for assisting the ELL in successfully making this shift. While the topic of this chapter is to promote fluency development of ELLs using multicultural literature, we think that one of the best things educators can do to promote reading fluency is to help all of our students to fall in love with reading.

Teachers can do this by making books, stories, poems, songs come alive for students, surrounding students with print-rich environments that value diverse languages, and providing them with opportunities to experience wonderful stories. Furthermore, by acknowledging that all children bring to school rich linguistic abilities teachers can capitalize on the rich background experiences of ELLs to enhance everyone's learning. In classrooms where these opportunities are present teachers can create self-efficacious, motivated readers.

REFERENCES

Allington, R. L. (1983). Fluency: The neglected reading goal. *The Reading Teacher, 36*, 556–561.

Griffith, L. W., & Rasinski, T. V. (2004). A focus on fluency: How one teacher incorporated fluency with her reading curriculum. *The Reading Teacher, 58*(2), 126–137.

Hoffman, J. V., & Crone, S. (1985). The oral recitation lesson: A research-derived strategy for reading in basal texts. In J. A. Niles & R. V. Lalik (Eds.), *Issues in literacy: A research perspective, 34th Yearbook of the National Reading Conference* (pp. 76–83). Rockfort, NY: National Reading Conference.

Johns, J. L., & Berglund, R. L. (2006). *Fluency: Strategies and assessments* (3rd ed.). Newark, DE: International Reading Association.

Koskinen, P., Blum, I., Bisson, S., Phillips, S., Creamer, T., & Baker, T. (2000). Book access, shared reading, and author models: The effect of supporting the literacy learning of linguistically diverse students in school and at home. *Journal of Educational Psychology, 92*(1), 22–36.

Koskinen, P. S., Wilson, R. M, Gambrell, L. B., Neuman, S. B. (1993). Captioned video and vocabulary learning: An innovative practice in literacy instruction. *The Reading Teacher, 47*(1), 36–43.

Kozub, R. (2000). Reader's theater and its affect on oral language fluency. Retrieved from http://www.readingonline.org/editorail/august2000/rkrt.htm.

Langford, J. (2001). Tape-assisted reading for a group of low progress readers in a secondary school. *In Reading Today for Tomorrow*. Auckland Reading Association Newsletter, pp. 14–21.

Martinez, M., Roser, N., & Strecker, S. (1999). I never thought I could be a star: A reader's theater ticket to fluency. *The Reading Teacher, 52*, 326–334.

Nalder, S., & Elley, W. (2002). Rainbow Reading Research Report. Unpublished report.

National Reading Panel. (2000). *Report of the National Reading Panel: Teaching children to read. Report of the Subgroups*. Washington, DC: U.S. Department of Health and Human Services, National Institutes of Health.

Nisbet, D., & Tindall, E.R. (May, 2008). *Using reader's theater to promote literacy for English language learners*. Conference presentation at the International Reading Association Conference, Atlanta, GA.

Padak, N. D., & Rasinski, T. V. (2008). *Evidence-based instruction in reading: A professional development guide to fluency*. Boston, MA: Pearson.

Pikulski, J. J., & Chard, D. J. (2005). Fluency: Bridge between decoding and comprehension. *The Reading Teacher, 58,* 510–519.

Rasinski, T. V. (2003). *The fluent reader*. New York, NY: Scholastic.

Rasinski, T. V. (2010). *The fluent reader* (2nd ed.). New York, NY: Scholastic.

Rasinski, T. V., & Padak, N. D. (2008). *From phonics to fluency: Effective teaching of decoding and reading fluency in the elementary school*. Boston, MA: Pearson.

Rasinski, T. V., Padak, N., Linek, W., & Sturtevant, E. (1994). The effects of fluency development instruction on urban second grade readers. *Journal of Educational Research, 87,* 158–164.

Rasinski, T. V., Reutzel, C. R., Chard, D. & Linan-Thompson, S. (in press). Reading fluency. In M. L. Kamil, P. D. Pearson, P. Afflerbach, & E. B. Moje (Eds.), *Handbook of reading research, Volume IV*. New York, NY: Routledge.

Robertson, K. (2009). Reader's theater: Oral language enrichment and literacy development for ELLs. Retrieved from http://www.colorincolorado.org/article/30104?theme=print

Yopp, R. H., & Yopp, H. K. (2003). Time with text. *The Reading Teacher, 57*(3), 284–287.

Yopp, R. H., & Yopp, H. K. (2001). *Literature-based reading activities* (3rd ed.). Boston, MA: Allyn & Bacon.

Young, C., & Rasinski, T. (2009). Implementing readers theatre as an approach to classroom fluency instruction. *The Reading Teacher, 63*(1), 4–13.

RESOURCES

Bus Songs: Lyrics, videos and music for children's nursery rhymes and songs, http://www.bussongs.com *

Hebrew Songs, http://www.hebrewsongs.com

Images Australia, http://www.imagesaustralia.com

It's a Small World: International Nursery Rhymes, http://www.itsasmallworld.co.nz

KIDiddles: Children's Songs, Lullabies, Kid's Songs, Kid's Music, Songsheets, Music Sheets, http://www.kididdles.com/lyrics/world.html *

Mama Lisa's World: Children's Songs and Nursery Rhymes From Around the World, http://mamalisa.com

Motherland Nigeria: Kid Zone, http://www.motherlandnigeria.com/stories

Rasinski, T., & Griffith, L. (2005). *Texts for fluency practice: Grade 1*. Huntington Beach, CA: Shell Education Publishing.

Songs for Teaching, http://www.songsforteaching.com *

Texas State Library and Archives Commission: A Celebration of Childhood and Bilingual Literacy, http://www.tsl.state.tx.us/ld/projects/ninos/songsrhymes.html

*Note: Permission given by Web site to use for educational purposes

Note: To the best of our knowledge the materials in this chapter, unless otherwise noted, are in the public domain. Copyrighted materials found in the Web site noted previously grant permission for educational use. If any of the material is copyrighted, please contact chapter authors for corrections.

APPENDIX 15.1

Multicultural Texts for Practice and Performance

Multicultural Lullabies

Ballyeamon Cradle Song (Ireland)

Rest tired eyes a while
Sweet is thy baby's smile
Angels are guarding and they watch o'er thee

Sleep, sleep, *grah mo chree*
Here on your mama's knee
Angels are guarding
And they watch o'er thee

The birdies sing a fluting song
They sing to thee the whole day long
Wee fairies dance o'er hill and dale
For very love of thee

Dream, dream, *grah mo chree*
Here on your mama's knee
Angels are guarding and they watch over
And may they guard o'er thee

Twilight and shadows fall
Peace to His children all
Angels are guarding and they watch o'er thee
As you sleep
May angels watch over and
May they guard o'er thee

Note: grah mo chree means "sweetheart" in Gaelic.

Too-ra-loo-ra-loo-ra (Ireland)

Over in Killarney, many years ago
My mother sang this song to me
In tones so sweet and low
Just a simple little ditty
In her good old Irish way
And I'd give the world if she could sing
That song to me this day

Too-ra-loo-ra-loo-ra, Too-ra-loo-ra-li,
Too-ra-loo-ra-loo-ra, hush now don't you cry!
Too-ra-loo-ra-loo-ra, Too-ra-loo-ra-li,
Too-ra-loo-ra-loo-ra, that's an Irish lullaby!

Oft in dreams I wander
To that cot again
I fell her arms a-huggin' me

As when she held me then
And I hear her voice a-hummin'
To me as in the days of yore,
When she used to rock me fast asleep
Outside the cabin door

Too-ra-loo-ra-loo-ra, Too-ra-loo-ra-li,
Too-ra-loo-ra-loo-ra, hush now don't you cry!
Too-ra-loo-ra-loo-ra, Too-ra-loo-ra-li,
Too-ra-loo-ra-loo-ra, that's an Irish lullaby!

Ayo Nene Touti Senegal, Africa—(Wolof language)

Ayo nene, ayo nene, nene, touti
Baye Ma Lamine daara, bindal namai terre, terre
Yomboul Saloum
Saloumo narry negg-la nettelba di wan-wa
Wan-wa, wanou-bourla, bour-ba, bourrou Saloum
Baye Ma Lamine daara, bindal namai terre, terre
Yomboul Saloum

Saloumo narry negg-la nettelba di wan-wa
Wan-wa, wanou-bourla, bour-ba, bourrou Saloum

Kouiye aayeeeh khoobi mango do, thi mayeh Doome yow

Sweet Little Baby (English translation of Ayo Nene Touti)

Father Ma Lamine Daara wrote a blessing for me,
But it is not easy getting a blessing at Saloum
At Saloum there are only two rooms, the third one
Is in the kitchen,
A King's kitchen, it's the Ling of Saloum's (repeat)

If a person cannot give a mango leaf, will he give
a mango fruit?

Lullaby and Goodnight: Brahms Lullaby (Germany)

Lullaby and good night, with roses bedight With lilies o'er spread is baby's wee bed Lay thee down now and rest, may thy slumber be blessed Lay thee down now and rest, may thy slumber be blessed Lullaby and good night, thy mother's delight Bright angels beside my darling abide They will guard thee at rest, thou shalt wake on my breast They will guard thee at rest, thou shalt wake on my breast
(Brahms Lullaby in original German) Guten Abend, gute Nacht, Mit Rosen bedacht, Mit Naeglein besteckt, schlupf unter die Deck'Morgen frueh, wenn Gott will, wirst du wieder gewecktMorgen frueh, wenn Gott will, wirst du wieder geweckt
Guten Abend, gute Nacht, Von Englein bewacht
Die zeigen im Traum, dir Christkindleins Baum

Schlaf nun selig und suess, Schau im Traum's ParadiesSchlaf nun selig und suess,
Schau im Traum's Paradies

Frère Jacques (France)

Frère Jacques,
Frère Jacques,
Dormez vous?
Dormez vous?
Sonnez les matines,
Sonnez les matines,
Din, din, don!
Din, din, don!

Are You Sleeping? (English translation of Frère Jacques)

Are you sleeping,
Are you sleeping,
Brother John?
Brother John?
Morning bells are ringing,
Morning bells are ringing,
Ding, ding, dong,
Ding, ding, dong.

Nursery Rhymes, Chants, and Songs

Shiri Yakanaka (Zimbabwe)

Shiri yakanaka unoendepi?
Huya, huya huya titambe
Ndiri kuenda kumakore
Kuti ndifanane nemakore

Beautiful Bird (English translation of Shiri Yakanaka)

Beautiful bird where are you going? Come, come, come let's playI'm going to the
cloudsI want to be like the clouds

Tishe, Myshi, kot na Kryshe (Russia)

Tishe, myshi, kot na kryshe
On ne vidit i ne slyshit
Mysh, vedi sebia prilichno
Zanimaysia na otlichno!

Тише, мыши, кот на крыше,
Он не видит и не сИышит,
Мышь, веди себя приИично,
Занимайся на "отИично".

Hush You Mice (English translation of Tishe, Myshi, kot na Kryshe)

Hush you mice, a cat is near us,
He can see us, he can hear us
What if he is on a diet
Even then you should be quiet!

Kosi, Kosi, Lapki (Poland)

Kosi, kosi, lapki,
Pojedziem do babci
Babcia da nam mleczka,
A dziadzius pierniczka.

Clap Hands (English translation of Kosi, Kosi, Lapki)

Clap, clap, small hands!
We're going to see Grandma
Grandma will give us some milk
And Grandpa a gingerbread cookie.

Un gato (Spanish)

Había una vez un gato
con los pies de trapo
y los ojos al revés
¿Quieres que te lo cuente otra vez?

The Cat (English translation of Un gato)

Once upon a time there was a cat
Who had feet made of cloth
and the eyes are upside down
Should I tell it to you again?

This is a repeating rhyme. After saying the rhyme, the child answers "yes" or "no" and the rhyme is repeated until the child answers "no."

Ukuti (Kenya)

Ukuti, ukuti
Wa mnazi, Wa mnazi
Ukipata Upepo
Watete . . . Watete . . . Watete . . .

The Leaf (English translation of Ukuti)

The leaf, the leaf
Of the coconut tree, of the coconut tree
When the wind blows against it
It shakes . . . it shakes . . . it shakes . . .

Note: This is a circle rhyme. Children hold hands and skip around the circle. When they say "the wind blows," they skip faster. When "it shakes," they all fall down.

This song has the lyrics of the coastal community in Kenya known as the Mijikenda whose language borrows a lot from Kiswahili. It is a common children's song among the Mijikenda.

Mijikenda is the collective name referring to 10 tribes on the east coast of Africa who share a common dialect.

Cinco elefantitos (Mexico)

Cinco elefantitos, uno se cayó
Cuatro elefantitos, uno se perdió,
Tres elefantitos, uno se enfermó,
Dos elefantitos, uno se murió,
Ahora queda uno, uno se quedó,
Y este elefantito, ¡me lo llevo!, ¡me lo llevo yo!

Five Little Elephants (English translation of Cinco elefantitos)

Five little elephants, this one fell down
Four little elephants, this one lost its way
Three little elephants, this one fell sick
Two little elephants, this one passed away
Now there is one, one did stay
And this little elephant, I take it away! I take it away!

Note: This is a finger play.

Un elefante (Mexico)

Un elefante se balanceaba
Sobre la tela de una araña
Como veía que no se caía
Fue a llamar a otro elefante

Dos elefantes se balanceaban
Sobre la tela de una araña
Como veían que no se caían
Fueron a llamar otro elefante

Tres elefantes . . .
Cuatro elefantes . . .

One Elephant (English translation of Un elefante)

One elephant swung on a spider web
Seeing that the web would hold her
He went to get another elephant

Two little elephants swung on a spider web
Seeing that the web would hold them
They went to get another elephant

Three elephants . . .
Four elephants . . .

Note: This is a Spanish counting song.
(Spain)

Araña arañita

Araña, arañita sube la escalera
Araña, arañita súbela otra vez
¡Pum! ¡Se cayó! ¡Pum! Se cayó!
Vino un sapo gordo y se la comió.

Spider Spider (English translation of Araña arañita)

Itsy bitsy spider climbing up the stairs
Itsy bitsy spider climb up again
Crash! It fell down! Crash! It fell
Along came a toad and swallowed it down!

Kye Kye Kule (chay chay koo-lay) (West Africa)

Leader: Kye Kye Kule (chay chay koo-lay)
Chorus: Kye Kye Kule
Leader: Kye Kye Kofinsa (chay chay koh-feen-sah)
Chorus: Kye Kye Kofinsa
Leader: Kofisa Langa (koh-fee-sah lahn-gah)
Chorus: Kofisa Langa
Leader: Kaka Shilanga (kah kah shee lahn-gah)
Chorus: Kaka Shilanga
Leader: Kum Aden Nde (koom ah-dehn day)
Chorus: Kaka Shilanga
Leader: Kum Aden Nde (koom ah-dehn day)
Chorus: Kum Aden Nde
Leader: Kum Aden Nde (koom ah-dehn day)
Chorus: Kum Aden Nde-HEY!

Hands on Your Head (English translation of Kye Kye Kule)

Hands on your head
Hands on your shoulders
Hands on your waist
Hands on your knees
Hands on your ankles
Hands on your ankles
Hands on your ankles

This is a circle song. The leader is in the middle and chants the words. The children repeat the words and motions.

Note: This song is popular in West Africa and especially in the northern parts of Ghana. It could be from any of the following three tribes: Dugomba, Dagarti or Frara.

This is a fun activity that builds skills in leadership and in following directions. Children form a circle as the leader stands in the middle. The leader demonstrates a physical action, then the children in the circle repeat the leader's words and the movement. With each repetition of the song, the leader introduces a new action, each one moving closer and closer to the floor. After the last movement is performed on the floor, the leader jumps to his feet. The first child in the circle to get back up on his/her feet gets to be the next one to lead.

Multicultural Songs

De colores (Spain)

> De colores,
> De colores se visten los campos
> En la primavera
> De colores,
> De colores son los pajaritos
> Que vienen de afuera
> De colores,
> De colores es el arcoiris que
> Vemos lucir
>
> Coro:
> Y por eso los grandes amores
> De muchos colores me gustan a mí
> Y por eso los grandes amores
> De muchos colores me gustan a mí
>
> Canta el gallo, canta el gallo
> Con el kiri, kiri, kiri, kiri, kiri.
> La gallina, la gallina
> Con el kara, kara, kara, kara, kara.
> Los pollitos/polluelos, los pollitos/polluelos
> Con el pío, pío, pío, pío, pa.
> Coro . . .

Colors (English translation of De colores)

> Painted in colors,
> The fields are dressed in colors
> In the spring
> Painted in colors,
> Painted in colors are the little birds
> Who come from the outside
> Painted with colors
> Painted with the colors is the rainbow
> We see shining brightly above
>
> Chorus:
> And that is why I love
> So many colors

And that is why I love
So many colors

The rooster sings, the rooster sings
With a cock-a-doodle, cock-a-doodle-doo
The hen, the hen with a cluck, cluck, cluck, cluck, cluck
The chicks, the chicks
With a cheep, cheep, cheep, cheep, cheep

Chorus . . .

Zum Gali Gali (Israel)

Hechalutz lema'an avodah,
Avodah lema'an hechalutz

Zum gali gali gali
Zum gali gali
Zum gali gali gali
Zum gali gali

Hashalom lema'an ha'amin,
Ha'amin lema'an hashalom
Zum gali gali gali
Zum gali gali
Zum gali gali gali
Zum gali gali

Zum Gali Gali (no direct translation of this phrase)

Pioneers all work as one,
Work as one all pioneers

Zum gali gali gali
Zum gali gali
Zum gali gali gali
Zum gali gali

Peace shall be for the world,
All the world shall be for peace

Zum gali gali gali
Zum gali gali
Zum gali gali gali
Zum gali gali

Tremp' Ton Pain, Marie (France)

Tremp'ton pain,
dans la sauce
dans le vin
Nous irons dimanche
A la maison blanche

Toi en Nankin
Moi en bazin

Dip Your Bread, Marie (English translation of Tremp' Ton Pain, Marie)

Dip your bread
In the sauce
In the wine
We will go on Sunday
To the white house
You wearing yellow cotton cloth
Me wearing damask cloth

Waltzing Matilda (Australia)

Once a jolly swagman camped by a billabong
Under the shade of a coolibah tree,
And he sang as he watched and waited 'til his billy boiled
"You'll come a-Waltzing Matilda, with me"

Waltzing Matilda, Waltzing Matilda
"You'll come a-Waltzing Matilda, with me"
And he sang as he watched and waited 'til his billy boiled,
"You'll come a-Waltzing Matilda, with me".

Down came a jumbuck to drink at that billabong,
Up jumped the swagman and grabbed him with glee,
And he sang as he shoved that jumbuck in his tucker bag,
"You'll come a-Waltzing Matilda, with me".

Waltzing Matilda, Waltzing Matilda
"You'll come a-Waltzing Matilda, with me"
And he sang as he shoved that jumbuck in his tucker bag,
"You'll come a-Waltzing Matilda, with me".

Up rode the squatter, mounted on his thoroughbred
Down came the troopers, one, two, three,
"Where's that jolly jumbuck you've got in your tucker bag?"
"You'll come a-Waltzing Matilda, with me".

Waltzing Matilda, Waltzing Matilda
"You'll come a-Waltzing Matilda, with me"
"Where's that jolly jumbuck you've got in your tucker bag?",
"You'll come a-Waltzing Matilda, with me".

Up jumped the swagman and sprang into the billabong,
"You'll never take me alive", said he,
And his ghost may be heard as you pass by that billabong,
"You'll come a-Waltzing Matilda, with me".

Waltzing Matilda, Waltzing Matilda
"You'll come a-Waltzing Matilda, with me"

And his ghost may be heard as you pass by that billabong,
"You'll come a-Waltzing Matilda, with me."
"Oh, You'll come a-Waltzing Matilda, with me."

The Sailor Went to Sea (Australia)

The sailor went to sea, sea, sea
To see what he could see, see, see
But all that he could see, see, see
Was the bottom of the deep blue sea, sea, sea

The sailor went to chop, chop, chop
To see what he could chop, chop, chop
But all that he could chop, chop, chop
Was the bottom of the deep blue chop, chop, chop

The sailor went to knee, knee, knee
To see what he could knee, knee, knee
But all that he could knee, knee, knee
Was the bottom of the deep blue knee, knee, knee

The sailor went to toe, toe, toe
To see what he could toe, toe, toe
But all that he could toe, toe, toe
Was the bottom of the deep blue toe, toe, toe

The sailor went to Timbuktu,
To see what he could Timbuktu
But all that he could Timbuktu
Was the bottom of the deep blue Timbuktu

The sailor went to sea, chop, knee, toe, Timbuktu
To see what he could sea, chop, knee, toe, Timbuktu
That all that he could sea, chop, knee, toe, Timbuktu
Was the bottom of the deep blue sea, chop, knee, toe, Timbuktu

Las mañanitas (Mexico)

Estas son las mañanitas, que cantaba el Rey David,
Hoy por ser día de tu santo, te las cantamos a ti,
Despierta, mi bien, despierta, mira que ya amaneció,
Ya los pajarillos cantan, la luna ya se metió.
Qué linda está la mañana en que vengo a saludarte,
Venimos todos con gusto y placer a felicitarte,

Ya viene amaneciendo, ya la luz del día nos dio,
Levántate de mañana, mira que ya amaneció.

The Mexican Birthday Song (English translation of Las mañanitas)

This is the morning song that King David sang
Because today is your saint's day we're singing it for you

Wake up, my dear*, wake up, look it is already dawn
The birds are already singing and the moon has set
How lovely is the morning in which I come to greet you
We all came with joy and pleasure to congratulate you
The morning is coming now, the sun is giving us its light
Get up in the morning, look it is already dawn

*Note: *Often replaced with the name of the person who is being celebrated*

Little Snowman (Korea)

한겨울에 밀짚모자 꼬마 눈사람
눈썹이 우습구나 코도 삐뚤고
거울을 보여줄까 꼬마 눈사람

Little Snowman (English translation)

Little snowman wears a straw hat, in the winter time
His eyebrows look so funny, nose is pointy, too.
I'll show you in the mirror what you look like, little snowman friend.

Making a Circle Now (Korea)

둥글게 둥글게
둥글게 둥글게
빙글빙글 돌아가며
춤을춥시다
손뼉을 치면서
노래를 부르며
랄라 랄라 즐거웁게춤 추자
링가링가링가 링가링가링
링가링가링가링가링가링
손에손을 잡고 모두 다함께 즐거웁게 춤을
춥시다

Making a Circle Now (English translation of Korean song)

Making a circle now
Making a circle now
Turning turning in a circle
As we dance along
Lets clap our hands
Lets sing along

Lalalala have fun as we dance along
Lingalingalinga
Lingalingalinga
Hand in hand together, let's dance everybody now.

Poems for Emerging Readers

(Spanish)

Uno, dos, tres, cuatro, cinco

Uno, Dos, Tres, Cuatro, Cinco
Una vez pesqué a un pez vivo;
Seis, siete, ocho, nueve, diez,
Luego lo solté.
¿Por qué lo dejaste ir?
Porque me mordió un dedo.
¿Qué dedo te mordió?
Mi pequeño dedo meñique de la derecha.

One, Two, Three, Four, Five (English translation of Uno, dos, tres, cuatro, cinco)

One, two, three, four, five,
Once I caught a fish alive;
Six, seven, eight, nine, ten,
Then I let it go again.
Why did you let it go?
Because it bit my finger so.
Which finger did it bite?
This little finger on my right.

Dentro, fuera, al revés (Spanish)

By Timothy Rasinski

Dentro, fuera, al revés.
Tócate la nariz, luego date la vuelta.

Salta de alegría, luego toca el piso.
Dentro, fuera, al revés.

Dentro, fuera, al revés.
Sonríe, luego haz un gesto.

Anda al campo, anda a la ciudad.
Dentro, fuera, al revés.

Inside, Outside, Upside Down (English Version)

By Timothy Rasinski

Inside, outside, upside down.
Touch your nose, then turn around.

Jump for joy, then touch the ground.
Inside, outside, upside down.

Inside, outside, upside down.
Make a smile, then make a frown.
Go to the country, go to the town.
Inside, outside, upside, down.

Goma de mascar (Spanish version)

Goma de mascar, goma de mascar
mastica y sopla
Goma de mascar, goma de mascar
Rasca tu dedo del pie.
Goma de mascar, goma de mascar
sabes tan dulce.
¡Quítate esa goma de mascar
de tu pie!

Bubble Gum (English version of Goma de mascar)

Bubble gum, bubble gum,
chew and blow.
Bubble gum, bubble gum,
scrape your toe.
Bubble gum, bubble gum, tastes so sweet.
Get that bubble gum
off your feet!

La silla (Spanish version)

By Timothy Rasinski

Un insecto, un niño, y un oso
se sientan juntos en la
misma silla.

La silla era demasiado pequeña.
No cabían todos,
Ese insecto, ese niño, y ese oso.

The Chair (English version of La silla)

By Timothy Rasinski

A bug, a boy, and a bear
Sat themselves in the very
same chair.

The chair was too small.
It would not hold them all,
That bug, that boy, and that bear.

Estoy contento (Spanish version)

Estoy contento que el cielo este pintado de azul
Y la tierra esta pintada de verde
Con mucho aire fresco agradable
en la mitad.

I'm Glad (English version)

I'm glad the sky is painted blue
And the earth is painted green.
With such a lot of nice fresh air
All sandwiched in between.

Gatito (Spanish version)

By Timothy Rasinski

Pitty pat, pitty pat,
Aquí viene mi gatito,
Una bola de pelusa, regordete,
Lleno de alegría, mi gatito

Kitty Cat (English version)

By Timothy Rasinski

Pitty pat, pitty pat,
Here comes my kitty cat.
A ball of fur, plump and fat,
Full of fun, my kitty cat.

Multicultural Reader's Theatre Ideas

Holding up the Sky (traditional tale from China)

One day an elephant saw a hummingbird
Lying on its back with its tiny feet up in the air. "What
Are you doing?" asked the elephant.

The hummingbird replied,
"I heard that the sky might fall today,
And so I am ready to help hold it up,
Should it fall."

The elephant laughed cruelly.
"Do you really think," he said,
"that those tiny feet could help hold up the sky?"

The hummingbird kept its feet in the air,
Intent on his purpose, as he replied,
"Not alone. But each must do what he can.
And this is what I can do."

The Farmer and His Two Lazy Sons (Aesop's fable)

(two alternating voices with both voices reading the moral)

Once upon a time there lived a farmer who had two lazy sons. Every day the farmer got up early and worked very hard in the fields while his lazy sons just slept the day away in the fields.

One day the farmer became very sick and thought he might die soon, so he called his sons to his bedside and whispered weakly, "I do not have long to live, so I want to tell you about the treasure."

His sons leaned in closely at the sound of the word "treasure". They wanted to make sure they heard their father clearly. He told them, "It is a very large treasure and it is hidden in the vineyard."

The father died and the sons went to search for the treasure.

"We must dig in the dirt to find the treasure!" They did, but . . . No treasure!

"Then we must rake the soil to find the treasure!" They did, but . . .

No treasure!

"Then we must plow the soil to find the treasure!" They did, but . . .

No treasure!

"Where is the treasure? We have worked and worked but we haven't found anything!"

Meanwhile, all that digging, raking, and plowing had made the vines grow stronger and taller than ever before.

The grapes grew fatter and juicier than ever before. The brothers were very surprised and shared their grapes with friends and neighbors. Finally, they realized what their wise father was trying to teach them . . .

Moral: hard work will bring many rewards.

Anansi, Firefly and Tiger (traditional tale from Nigeria)

Narrator
Anansi
Firefly
Tiger

Narrator: One day Firefly went to Anansi the Spider's house and asked him if he would like to go egg hunting.

Firefly: If you would like to go with me, then come to my house later this evening.

Narrator: Anansi the Spider was very excited and of course, said

Anansi: Yes, I'll be there! See you later tonight!

Narrator: Anansi waited until it was getting dark and went to Firefly's house. They set off to find some eggs. Although it was dark now, Firefly helped them to find many eggs because he would open up his wings to light up the grass below where the eggs were illuminated in his light. Every time, however, that they found an egg, Anansi would grab it and yell:

Anansi: Mine! I saw it first!

Narrator: This continued through the night until Anansi's sack was so full of eggs he could hardly carry it. Firefly didn't get a single one.

Firefly: How rude! I didn't get a single egg! Good bye, Anansi. I'm going home.

Narrator: When Firefly left Anansi, he was left in the dark without knowing how to get home. He wandered through the dark until he bumped into an unknown house. Anansi, being the Trickster that he was, thought of a scheme. So he yelled

Anansi: Godfather! Godfather!

Tiger: Who is that outside my house?

Anasi: It is I, your godson, Anansi!

Narrator: Now, Tiger knew that he had no godsons and he also knew that Anansi had tricked him many times before. But Tiger was also clever.

Tiger: Come in, Godson, and we will boil those eggs and eat together.

Narrator: When they were ready, Tiger, his wife and all his children started to eat the eggs hungrily.

Tiger: Anansi, my Godson, would you like some eggs?

Anansi: No thank you, Godfather.

Tiger: Then at least you should sleep here and rest tonight.

Narrator: When everyone was getting ready to go to sleep, Tiger put a live lobster in the pot and added shells to make it look like there were still eggs inside. During the night, when everyone was asleep, Anansi crept over to the pot and reached inside the pot.

Anansi: OUCH! That hurt!

Tiger: Godson, are you OK?

Anansi: I was bitten by a dog flea. Please excuse me, Godfather.

Narrator: After a few minutes, he tried again.

Anansi: OUCH!

Tiger: Are you sure you're all right?

Anansi: Oh, Godfather, those dog fleas are eating me alive!

Tiger: What? Dog fleas? How dare you accuse us of having dog fleas in our house! We have even offered to feed you and give you a place to rest and in return you are ungrateful and rude. Get out of my house!

Narrator: Terrified, Anansi fled the house and never went back to Tiger's house again. And every time that he went to visit Firefly, Firefly's wife told Anansi that her husband was gone and to come back in a month. Anansi never did figure out where all the eggs were hidden and he had much time to think about his greediness.

16

Promoting Multicultural Literature and Literacy: Awards, Conferences, Library Initiatives, and Outreach Programs

Barbara A. Ward

Quality multicultural literature makes a difference in the lives of readers. It enriches the lives of all who encounter it, not just readers from the culture it happens to depict. Not only does multicultural literature expand our concepts about what it means to be an American, but it provides a way through which readers can explore sameness and differentness. It allows us to recognize ourselves as well as others with whom we may not be as familiar. Through the rich multicultural stories being published today, readers find ways to explore issues pertaining to belonging, family, self-identity, and cultural authenticity. By coming to understand the importance of cultural rituals, language, and family expectations, the unfamiliar world is drawn a little closer and becomes more familiar to readers. Multicultural literature does this exceptionally well.

However, unless someone introduces multicultural literature to young readers, using and celebrating this literature in some way, it is highly unlikely that children will find the books they need that mirror their own cultural experiences and books that provide a window into other worlds (Cullinan, 1989). Then, too, today's present attitude toward education means that teachers often find themselves preoccupied with various administrative tasks and a test-driven curriculum, leaving very little time for many of them to search out multicultural literature for themselves. This is often not the fault of the already overburdened teachers. Teachers may not have encountered culturally responsive pedagogy or received any training in meeting the needs of diverse learners during their preservice or graduate programs. They may have lacked the opportunities to learn about different ethnic groups in our society or be aware of the importance of multicultural literature for all students. They may not be aware of the high quality of this literature. Furthermore, it is often difficult to access multicultural literature. Regional libraries usually do not have a large collection of multicultural literature, and, typically, large chain bookstores do not feature this literature.

Bookstores promote what sells, and in the past multicultural literature has not been at the top of the bestselling lists. As small children's bookstores have given way to large chain stores, such as Borders and Barnes and Noble, customers often find sales clerks who know little or nothing about multicultural children's literature, or for that matter, children's literature.

Quality multicultural literature is often hidden on shelves in libraries and bookstores and is not brought to the attention of teachers, teacher librarians, and children. Librarians in regional libraries may be unfamiliar with the excellent children's literature that is now available on many diverse groups including African Americans, American Indians, Latinos, Asian Americans, Pacific Islanders, Arab Americans, Jewish Americans, Appalachians, and other groups. Therefore, we desperately need award lists, conferences, and Web sites that highlight and promote these wonderful books.

As our classrooms become increasingly culturally and linguistically diverse, it is more important than ever before that teachers teach in a culturally relevant manner (Ladson-Billings, 1995). One of the ways to do this is by using quality multicultural literature in the curriculum. In order to do this efficiently, teachers need to have tools and resources to help them identify and access quality multicultural literature. This chapter examines how multicultural literature is being promoted across the nation through ever-growing literature awards, conferences, library initiatives, and outreach programs that have multicultural literature as their main focus.

In this chapter, this author has compiled a list of the major awards for multicultural literature as well as conferences featuring multicultural literature as its main attraction. In addition, a list of useful Web sites that feature multicultural literature has been included. These resources are excellent starting places for teachers who want to begin to incorporate multicultural literature in their classrooms and librarians who want to include these books in their library programs. They also provide a quick way for teachers and librarians to stay informed about trends in the publishing of multicultural titles and to become familiar with the books cited for multicultural awards.

AWARDS FOR MULTICULTURAL LITERATURE

Paying attention to the traditional book awards lists from the American Library Association (ALA) helps teachers to become informed about quality literature, but for the most part, the books being recognized by organizations such as the ALA through the Caldecott and Newbery Medals tend to be books depicting the status quo and not the diverse world in which we live. There are several book awards that are given annually or biennially to outstanding multicultural books, and savvy teachers and librarians will be able to stay abreast on trends in the field of multicultural literature by perusing these lists and choosing some of the titles for their classrooms and libraries. Awards for excellence in children's literature have had a positive impact on the publication of quality multicultural literature. Many children's titles—especially multicultural books—rapidly go out of print while award-winning books tend to stay in print longer. These books are also more likely to be displayed prominently on shelves in the children's section of libraries. The following awards can serve as good resources for the selection of authentic and quality multicultural literature. Tables featuring major multicultural children's literature awards and award-winning books have been included throughout this chapter. Additionally, Appendix 16.1 lists

Table 16.1.

American Indian Youth Literature Award Winners

Year	Book
2010	*A Coyote Solstice Tale* by Thomas King, illustrated by Gary Clement
	Meet Christopher: An Osage Indian Boy from Oklahoma by Genevieve Simermeyer, photographs by Katherine Fogden
	Between the Deep Blue Sea and Me: A Novel by Lurline Wailana McGregor
2008	*Counting Coup: Becoming a Crow Chief on the Reservation and Beyond* by Joseph Medicine Crow & Herman Viola
	Crossing Bok Chitto by Tim Tingle, illustrated by Jeanne R. Bridges
	The Absolutely True Diary of a Part-Time Indian by Sherman Alexie, illustrated by Ellen Forney
2006	*Beaver Steals Fire: A Salish Coyote Story* by the Confederated Salish, illustrated by Kootenai Tribes
	The Birchbark House by Louise Erdrich
	Hidden Roots by Joseph Bruchac

the Carter G. Woodson Book Award winners and Appendix 16.2 lists the Notable Books for a Global Society books.

The American Indian Youth Literature Award

http://www.aila.library.sd.gov, accessed on September 25, 2010.

Newly created in 2008 by The AILA (American Indian Library Association, an affiliate of ALA), this new literary award identifies and honors the very best writing and illustrations by and about American Indians. Award-winning books depict Native Americans in the fullness of their humanity in present and past contexts. Table 16.1 lists the AILA award winners for 2006 through 2010.

The Américas Award

http://www.uwm.edu/Dept/CLACS/outreach/americas.html, accessed on September 24, 2010.

Given in recognition of U.S. works of fiction, poetry, folklore, or selected nonfiction (from picture books to works for young adults) published in the previous year in English or Spanish that authentically and engagingly portray Latin America, the Caribbean, or Latinos/as in the United States, the Américas Award is sponsored by the national Consortium of Latin American Studies Programs (CLASP) in the Center for Latin American and Caribbean Studies at the University of Wisconsin-Milwaukee.

By linking the American continent, the award reaches beyond geographic borders and multicultural-international boundaries, and honors books that focus on cultural heritages within the Western Hemisphere. Committee members look for titles that exemplify: (1) a distinctive literary quality; (2) cultural contextualization; (3) exceptional integration of text, illustration and design; and (4) potential for classroom use. Table 16.2 lists the winners of the Américas Award for books published between 2004 and 2008.

Table 16.2.

Américas Book Award Winners

Book	Author/Illustrator	Published
Just in Case: A Trickster Tale and Spanish Alphabet Book	Yuyi Morales	2008
The Surrender Tree: Poems of Cuba's Struggle for Freedom	Margarita Engle	2008
Red Glass	Lara Resau	2007
Yum! ¡Mm Mm! ¡Qué rico! America's Sproutings	Pat Mora, illustrated by Rafael López	2007
Josias, Hold the Book	Jennifer Elvgren, illustrated by Nicole Tadgell	2006
The Poet Slave of Cuba	Margarita Engle, illustrated by Sean Qualls	2006
Cinnamon Girl: Letters Found Inside a Cereal Box	Juan Felipe Herrera	2005
My Name is Celia/Me llamo Celia	Monica Brown, illustrated by Rafael López	2004
Sammy and Juliana in Hollywood	Benjamin Alire Sáenz	2004

The Arab American Book Award

http://www.arabamericanmuseum.org/bookaward, accessed on September 24, 2010.

Since 2007, the Arab American National Museum has selected titles to receive the Arab American Book Award. The award is given to encourage the publication of books that preserve and advance the understanding, knowledge, and resources of the Arab American community by celebrating the thoughts and lives of Arab Americans. The award is intended to inspire authors, educate readers, and foster a respect and understanding of the Arab American culture. Table 16.3 lists the winners of the Arab American Book Award for 2007 through 2009.

The Asian/Pacific American Award for Literature

http://www.apalaweb.org/awards/awards.htm, accessed on September 24, 2010.

The goal of the Asian Pacific American Librarians Association is to honor and recognize individual work about Asian/Pacific Americans and their heritage, based on

Table 16.3.

The Arab American Book Award Children's and Young Adult Literature Winners

Year	Book
2009	*Honeybee: Poems & Short Prose* by Naomi Shihab Nye
2008	*Tasting the Sky: A Palestinian Childhood* by Ibtisam Barakat
2007	*One Green Apple by Eve Bunting, illustrated* by Ted Lewin

Table 16.4.

Asian/Pacific American Award for Literature Winners

Year	Category	Book
2009	Picture Book	*Cora Cooks Pancit* by Dorina K. Lazo Gilmore, illustrated by Kristi Valiant
	Youth Literature	*Everything Asian* by Sung Woo
2008	Illustration in Children's Literature	*Surfer of the Century* by Ellie Crowe, illustrated by Richard Waldrep
	Young Adult Literature	*Hiroshima Dreams* by Kelly Easton
2004/2005	Illustration in Children's Literature	*The Firekeeper's Son* by Linda Sue Park, illustrated by Julie Downing
	Text in Children's and Young Adult Literature	*Kira Kira* by Cynthia Kadohata
2002/2003	Illustration in Children's Literature	*Apple Pie 4th of July* by Janet S. Wong, illustrated by Margaret Chodos-Irvine
	Text in Children's and Young Adult Literature	*A Step From Heaven* by An Na

literary and artistic merit. The Asian/Pacific American Award for Literature (APALA) is now given annually. Table 16.4 lists the winners of the APALA Award for 2002 through 2009.

The Batchelder Award

http://www.ala.org/ala/mgrps/divs/alsc/awardsgrants/bookmedia/batchelderaward/index.cfm, accessed on September 24, 2010.

The Batchelder Award is a citation awarded to an American publisher for a children's book considered to be the most outstanding of those books originally published in a language other than English in a country other than the United States and subsequently translated into English and published in the United States.

This award honors Mildred L. Batchelder, a former executive director of the Association for Library Service to Children. Convinced of the importance of good books for children in translation from all parts of the world, Batchelder began her career working at Omaha (Nebraska) Public Library, became a children's librarian at St. Cloud (Minnesota) State Teachers College, and she later served as librarian of Haven Elementary School in Evanston, Illinois. She joined the ranks of the American Library Association in 1936 where she spent 30 years with ALA, working as an ambassador to the world on behalf of children and books, encouraging and promoting the translation of the world's best children's literature. She wanted to eliminate barriers to understanding between people of different cultures, races, nations, and languages.

In 1979 and in subsequent years, the award has been given annually to a publisher for a book published in the preceding year. Before 1979, there was a lapse of two years between the original publication date and the award date. Two awards were announced in 1979: one for 1978 and one for 1979. Beginning in 1994, honor recipients were selected and announced as well. If the awards committee considers no book worthy of

Table 16.5.
Batchelder Award Winners

Year	Book	Author/ Translator
2010	*Faraway Island*	Annika Thor, translated by Linda Schenck
2009	*Moribito: Guardian of the Spirit*	Nahoko Uehashi, translated from the Japanese by Cathy Hirano
2008	*Brave Story*	Miyuki Miyabe, translated from the Japanese by Alexander O. Smith
2007	*The Pull of the Ocean*	Jean-Claude Mourlevat, translated from the French by Y. Maudet
2006	*An Innocent Soldier*	Josef Holub, translated from the German by Michael Hofmann
2005	*The Shadows of Ghadames*	Joëlle Stolz, translated from the French by Catherine Temerson
2004	*Run, Boy, Run*	Uri Orlev, translated from the Hebrew by Hillel Halkin
2003	*The Thief Lord*	Cornelia Funke, translated from the German by Oliver Latsch
2002	*How I Became an American*	Karin Gündisch, translated from the German by James Skofield
2001	*Samir and Yonatan*	Daniella Carmi, translated from the Hebrew by Yael Lotan
2000	*The Baboon King*	Anton Quintana, translated from the Dutch by John Nieuwenhuizen

the award for that year, none is given. The award is decided on and announced at the Midwinter Meeting of ALA, and the winning publisher receives a citation and commemorative plaque. Once announced on April 2, International Children's Book Day, the presentation is now given at the ALA Annual Conference held each summer. Table 16.5 lists the winners of the Batchelder Award for 2000 through 2010.

The Carter G. Woodson Book Award

http://www.socialstudies.org/awards/woodson/, accessed on September 24, 2010.

First presented in 1974, the Carter G. Woodson Book Award honors the most distinguished social science books appropriate for young readers that depict ethnicity in the United States. This award, sponsored by the National Council for the Social Studies, is intended to encourage the publishing of outstanding social studies books for young readers that treat topics related to ethnic minorities and race relations sensitively and accurately. Appendix 16.1 lists the book award and honor winners of the Carter G. Woodson Book Award for 2005 through 2010.

Children's Africana Book Awards

http://www.africaaccessreview.org/caba.cfm, accessed on September 24, 2010.

Established in 1989 to help schools, libraries, and parents improve book collections focusing on Africa, this organization has presented more than 40 awards to the best children's books about Africa since 1992 through the Outreach Council of the African Studies Association. They also maintain Africa Access Review, an online database containing over 1,000 annotations and reviews of children's books written by university professors, librarians, and teachers. Africa Access supports a book club that is African-oriented and provides useful reading and research activities.

The Coretta Scott King Award

http://www.ala.org/ala/mgrps/rts/emiert/cskbookawards/index.cfm, accessed on September 24, 2010.

Intended to commemorate the life and works of Dr. Martin Luther King, Jr. and to honor Coretta Scott King for her courage and determination to continue to work for peace, the Coretta Scott King Book Awards annually recognize outstanding books for young adults and children by African American authors and illustrators. The award encourages the artistic expression of the black experience via literature and the graphic arts in biographical, social, and historical treatments by African American authors and illustrators. Coretta Scott King Awards are given annually to an African-American author or illustrator whose work depicts or describes some aspect of the African American experience. Table 16.6 lists the winners of the Coretta Scott King

Table 16.6.
Coretta Scott King Book Awards—Author/Illustrator—2004–2010

Year	Category	Winner
2010	Author	*Bad News for Outlaws: The Remarkable Life of Bass Reeves, Deputy U.S. Marshal* by Vaunda Micheaux Nelson, illustrated by R. Gregory Christie
	Illustrator	*My People* by Langston Hughes, illustrated by Charles R. Smith Jr.
2009	Author	*We Are the Ship: The Story of Negro League Baseball* written & illustrated by Kadir Nelson
	Illustrator	*The Blacker the Berry* by Joyce Carol Thomas, illustrated by Floyd Cooper
2008	Author	*Elijah of Buxton* by Christopher Paul Curtis
	Illustrator	*Let it Shine* written and illustrated by Ashley Bryan
2007	Author	*Copper Sun* by Sharon Draper
	Illustrator	*Moses: When Harriet Tubman Led Her People to Freedom* by Carole Boston Weatherford, illustrated by Kadir Nelson
2006	Author	*Day of Tears: A Novel in Dialogue* by Julius Lester
	Illustrator	*Rosa* by Nikki Giovanni, illustrated by Bryan Collier
2005	Author	*Remember: The Journey to School Integration* by Toni Morrison
	Illustrator	*Ellington Was Not a Street* by Ntozake Shange, illustrated by Kadir A. Nelson
2004	Author	*The First Part Last* by Angela Johnson
	Illustrator	*Beautiful Blackbird* written & illustrated by Ashley Bryan

Award for authors and the Coretta Scott King Award for illustrators for the years 2004 through 2010.

The John Steptoe Award for New Talent

http://www.ala.org/ala/mgrps/rts/emiert/cskbookawards/johnsteptoe.cfm, accessed on September 24, 2010.

Established to acknowledge new talent and to offer visibility to excellence in writing and/or illustration which otherwise might be formally unacknowledged within a given year within the structure of the two awards given annually by the Coretta Scott King Task Force, the Steptoe Award spotlights the work of promising authors and/or illustrators.

The criteria for eligibility are the same as those for the writing and illustration awards, with the exception that the winner cannot have more than three publications. An author or illustrator who has already received or has just been selected to win one of the Coretta Scott King Awards in the current year is not eligible for the John Steptoe Award for New Talent. An author may receive this award one time.

One award is presented annually for text or illustrations. The Committee may choose to select one book for writing and a second book for illustration. The award might not be given if the committee so decides in a particular year.

Table 16.7 lists the award winners of the John Steptoe Award for New Talent for 2002 through 2010.

The Notable Books for a Global Society

http://mysite.verizon.net/vzeeioxu/index.html, accessed on September 24, 2010.

Every year since its establishment in 1995, this subcommittee of the International Reading Association's Children's Literature/Reading Special Interest Group has selected 25 titles that depict a wide range of diversity. Honored books enhance student

Table 16.7.
John Steptoe Award for New Talent

Year	Award Winner(s)
2010	Kekla Magoon for *The Rock and the River*
2009	Shadra Strickland for *Bird*
2008	Sundee T. Frazier for *Brendan Buckley's Universe and Everything in It*
2007	Traci L. Jones for *Standing Against the Wind*
2006	Jaime Adoff for *Jimi & Me*
2005	Author: Barbara Hathaway for *Missy Violet and Me* Illustrator: Frank Morrison for *Jazzy Miz Mozetta* by Brenda C. Roberts
2004	Author: Hope Anita Smith for *The Way a Door Closes, illustrated* by Shane W. Evans Illustrator: Elbrite Brown for *My Family Plays Music*
2003	Author: Janet McDonald for *Chill Wind* Illustrator: Randy DuBurke for *The Moon Ring*
2002	Jerome Lagarrigue for *Freedom Summer*

understanding of people and cultures throughout the world. Winning titles include fiction, nonfiction, and poetry written for students in grades K–12. Appendix 16.2 lists the books that have been chosen by the Notable Books for a Global Society for 2005 through 2010.

The Pura Belpré Award

http://www.ala.org/ala/mgrps/divs/alsc/awardsgrants/bookmedia/belpremedal/ index.cfm, accessed on September 24, 2010.

The Pura Belpré Award has been given to outstanding children's literature since 1996. Named in honor of Pura Belpré, the first Latina librarian at the New York Public Library, the award is presented annually to a Latino/Latina writer and illustrator whose work best portrays, affirms, and celebrates the Latino/a cultural experience in an outstanding work of literature for children and youth. It is co-sponsored by the Association for Library Service to Children (ALSC), a division of the American Library Association (ALA), and REFORMA, the National Association to Promote Library and Information Services to Latinos and the Spanish-Speaking, an ALA affiliate. Table 16.8

Table 16.8.
Pura Belpré—Narrative Awards

Year	Medal Winners	Honor Books
2010	*Return to Sender by* Julia Álvarez	*Diego: Bigger Than Life* by Carmen T. Bernier-Grand, illustrated by David Diaz
		Federico García Lorca by Georgina Lázaro, illustrated by Enrique S. Moreiro
2009	*The Surrender Tree: Poems of Cuba's Struggle for Freedom* by Margarita Engle	*Just in Case* by Yuyi Morales
		Reaching Out by Francisco Jiménez
		The Storyteller's Candle/La velita de los cuentos by Lucía González, illustrated by Lulu Delacre
2008	*The Poet Slave of Cuba: A Biography of Juan Francisco Manzano* by Margarita Engle	*Frida: ¡Viva la vida! Long Live Life!* by Carmen T. Bernier-Grand
		Martina the Beautiful Cockroach: A Cuban Folktale by Carmen Agra Deedy, illustrated by Michael Austin
		Los Gatos Black on Halloween by Marisa Montes, illustrated by Yuyi Morales
2006	*The Tequila Worm* by Viola Canales	*César: ¡Sí, se puede! Yes, We Can!* by Carmen T. Bernier-Grand, illustrated by David Diaz
		Doña Flor: A Tall Tale About a Giant Woman with a Great Big Heart by Pat Mora, illustrated by Raul Colón
		Becoming Naomi León by Pam Muñoz Ryan
2004	*Before We Were Free* by Julia Álvarez	*Cuba 15* by Nancy Osa
		My Diary From Here to There/Mi diario de aquí hasta allá by Amada Irma Pérez

Table 16.9.

Pura Belpré—Illustration Awards

Year	Medal Winners	Honor Books
2009	*Just in Case* by Yuyi Morales	*Papá and Me* by Arthur Dorros, illustrated by Rudy Gutierrez
		The Storyteller's Candle /La velita de los cuentos by Lucía Gonzalez, illustrated by Lulu Delacre
2008	*Los Gatos Black on Halloween*, illustrated by Yuyi Morales, written by Marisa Montes	*My Name Is Gabito: The Life of Gabriel García Márquez/Me llamo Gabito: la vida de Gabriel García Márquez* by Monica Brown, illustrated by Raúl Colón
		My Colors, My World/Mis colores, mi mundo by Maya Christina Gonzalez.
2006	*Doña Flor: A Tall Tale About a Giant Woman with a Great Big Heart*, by Raul Colón, written by Pat Mora	*Arrorró, mi niño: Latino Lullabies and Gentle Games*, selected and illustrated by Lulu Delacre
		César: ¡Sí, se puede! Yes, We Can! by Carmen T. Bernier-Grand, illustrated by David Diaz
		My Name Is Celia/ Me llamo Celia: The Life of Celia Cruz/ La vida de Celia Cruz by Monica Brown, illustrated by Rafael López
2004	*Just a Minute: A Trickster Tale and Counting Book* by Yuyi Morales	*First Day in Grapes* by L. King Pérez, illustrated by Robert Casilla, illustrated by L. King Pérez
		The Pot That Juan Built by Nancy Andrews-Goebel, illustrated by David Diaz
		Harvesting Hope: The Story of Cesar Chavez by Kathleen Krull, illustrated by Yuyi Morales

lists the narrative award winners and honor books for the Pura Belpré Award for 2004 through 2010. Table 16.9 lists the illustration award winners and honor books for the Pura Belpré Award for 2004 through 2010.

The Schneider Family Book Awards

http://www.duluth.lib.mn.us/YouthServices/Booklists/SchneiderFamily.html, accessed on September 24, 2010.

Presented by the American Library Association, the Schneider Family Book Award honors an author or illustrator for a book that embodies an artistic expression of the disability experience for child and adolescent audiences. The book must portray some aspect of living with a disability or that of a friend or family member, whether the disability is physical, mental or emotional.

The Annual Skipping Stones Honor Awards

http://www.skippingstones.org/, accessed on September 24, 2010.

The Skipping Stones Award encourages understanding of the world's diverse cultures, as well as nature and ecological richness. The books honored are those that promote cooperation, nonviolence, respect for differing viewpoints, and close relationships in human societies.

The Sydney Taylor Award

http://www.jewishlibraries.org/ajlweb/awards/st_books.htm, accessed on September 24, 2010.

Established in 1968, the Sydney Taylor Award is given to the book that best exemplifies the Jewish experience. The award is presented by The Association of Jewish Libraries.

Tomás Rivera Mexican American Children's Book Award

http://www.education.txstate.edu/departments/Tomas-Rivera-Book-Award-Project-Link/About.html, accessed on September 24, 2010.

Created by the College of Education of Texas State University in 1995, this award is given annually to authors and illustrators depicting the Mexican-American experience. The award seeks to increase awareness among librarians, teachers, parents and children so this literature will be used to educate, inspire, and entertain all children. The very first award went to Gary Soto and Susan Guevara.

As vital as book awards may be to draw attention to quality books, the importance of conferences and outreach programs whose primary focus is to promote excellent literature and/or literacy cannot be dismissed. Below this author has highlighted one well-established multicultural conference and two outreach programs that advance literacy for culturally diverse students.

CONFERENCES FOR MULTICULTURAL LITERATURE

The Virginia Hamilton Conference

http://dept.kent.edu/virginiahamiltonconf/, accessed on September 24, 2010.

Held each year at Kent State University in Kent, Ohio, the Virginia Hamilton Conference on Multicultural Literature for Youth, is the longest-running event in the United States to focus exclusively on multicultural literature for children and young adults. The conference, which is now in its twenty-sixth year, honors author Virginia Hamilton and seeks to reflect a commitment to promoting cultural awareness and to affirm cultural pride while addressing issues that surround the concept of culture. Virginia Hamilton was the recipient of nearly every major award and honor in her field. She was the first African American woman to win the coveted Newbery Award for *M. C. Higgins, the Great*. She also won many other prestigious literary awards.

OUTREACH PROGRAMS

A Cultural Exchange

http://www.aculturalexchange.org/, accessed on September 24, 2010.

In 1991, Deborah McHamm led a group of African-American women in establishing *A Cultural Exchange*, the largest literacy-based, nonprofit, multicultural arts organization for children in Northeast Ohio. The organization's innovative educational programs, events, and exhibits support her commitment to building a nation of readers who celebrate themselves and each other through reading. An example of this organization's innovative initiatives is the Busy Bookmobile, a colorful bus that is stocked with award-winning multicultural books and is available for bookings at schools, community events, churches, neighborhood organizations, libraries, and other places. Children can board the Busy Bookmobile and select their own books for less than a dollar.

El Día de los Niños

http://www.patmora.com/dia.htm, accessed on September 24, 2010.

Wishing to honor children while promoting childhood, author Pat Mora has spearheaded *El Día de los Niños/El Día de los Libros*/Day of the Child/Day of the Books since 1997 when the first festivity was celebrated. New Mexico's governor issued a proclamation and Santa Fe's mayor read her proclamation at Larragoite Elementary School at a reading by student writers in that first year. Events were also held in cities including Tucson, El Paso, and Austin. The celebration has grown each year to include cities and towns all across the United States and serves as an annual reminder of the joy of reading. From its inception, Mora envisioned this special day as one that would celebrate children and childhood, encourage literacy, emphasize the importance of linking all children to books, honor languages and cultures, respect home languages and cultures, and thus promote bilingual and multilingual literacy in the United States, which is a multicultural nation. She also viewed this day as one that would foster global understanding through reading, involve parents as valued members of the literacy team, and promote library collection development that reflects plurality.

USEFUL WEB SITES THAT PROMOTE MULTICULTURAL LITERATURE

The American Indians in Children's Literature Blog is available at http://americanindiansinchildrensliterature.blogspot.com/, accessed on September 24, 2010.

Nambe Pueblo Debbie Reese provides her critical thoughts on children's and young adult literature by and about American Indians through this blog, an outstanding resource for librarians, teachers, and others to expand their own critical thinking, analysis, and evaluation skills. Reese strives to read and review books depicting American Indians and often engages in lively dialogue with authors about cultural authenticity.

The Barahona Center for the Study of Books in Spanish for Children and Adolescents available at http://www2.csusm.edu/csb/english/, accessed on September 24, 2010, has recommended lists of books in Spanish as well as recommended lists of books in English about Latinos. This Web site was established by Isabel Schon whose research has centered on Latino/a literature. It provides a list of professional books and links to several useful Web sites. One link features Newbery titles that have been translated into Spanish.

Book Links Magazine is available at http://www.ala.org/ala/aboutala/offices/publishing/booklinks/index.cfm, accessed on September 24, 2010.

A quarterly supplement to *Booklist*, *Book Links* magazine is designed for teachers, youth librarians, school library media specialists, reading specialists, curriculum coordinators, and others interested in connecting children with high-quality literature-based resources. The magazine features interviews with authors and illustrators, ideas about using books in the classroom, and themed bibliographies, including one issue each year focusing on multicultural literature. Additionally, the Web site features a section titled "Web Connections," which provides teachers and librarians with Web site links to the books featured in each issue of *Book Links*.

The Cooperative Children's Book Center available at http://www.education .wisc.edu/ccbc/, accessed on September 24, 2010 is a treasure trove of book lists and resources for anyone wanting a crash course on multicultural literature. From this Web site, readers can follow links to the classic title *Multicultural Literature for Children and Young Adults Volume 2* by Kathleen T. Horning, Ginny Moore Kruse and Megan Schliesman which includes more than 350 children's books by and about people of color published in the United States between 1991 and 1996. An earlier volume is also available. A downloadable list of "50 Multicultural Books Every Child Should Know" and one of "30 Multicultural Books Every Teen Should Know" will surely provide useful titles for teachers and librarians. Additionally, the Web site offers links to bibliographies and teaching tips such as "10 Quick Ways to Analyze Children's Books for Racism and Sexism."

Coretta Scott King Book Awards Curriculum Resource Center is available at http://www.teachingbooks.net/crc.cgi?id=1, accessed on September 24, 2010.

This searchable database of Coretta Scott King award-winning books and honor books allows viewers to search by subject area and/or grade level and includes original interviews with the book creators about the books and links to additional resources about the books. Furthermore, there are audio taped responses from many of the Coretta Scott King winners.

Cynsations Cynthia Leitich Smith's Resource Pages is available at http:// www.cynthialeitichsmith.com/lit_resources/diversity/diversity.html, accessed on September 24, 2010.

There is a wealth of information about children's and young adult literature on author Cynthia Leitich Smith's site, including her commentary on multicultural literature and links to resources. She also features several author interviews.

Kay Vandergrift's Children's Literature Web site is available at http://comminfo .rutgers.edu/professional-development/childlit/ChildrenLit/, accessed on September 24, 2010, is filled with many wonderful resources, including up-to-date bibliographies of African-American, Asian-American, Hispanic American and Native American titles. She also has links to children's books on Islamic traditions and Muslim cultures and suggested titles and Web sites for exploring these traditions and cultures.

The National Center for Children's Illustrated Literature available at http://www .nccil.org/, accessed on September 24, 2010 highlights many multicultural illustrators. Thumbnail sketches and art samples from multicultural artists Ashley Bryan, Bryan Collier, Donald and Nina Crews, David Diaz, Leo and Diane Dillon, Brian Pinkney, Jerry Pinkney, and Ed Young. Not only can readers learn about the artists' creative processes, but they can also find additional information by following the links to the artists' Web sites.

Teaching Tolerance Web site is available at http://www.tolerance.org/, accessed on September 24, 2010.

A project of the Southern Poverty Law Center, *Teaching Tolerance* is a magazine and Web site that offers articles, lesson plans, bibliographies and other curriculum materials for teachers who want to teach their students about diversity. It also offers resources for parents, teens, and children. The site's search feature is helpful in locating specific types of materials according to subject and grade. Teaching Tolerance also sends to teachers, without charge, a selection of DVDs on tolerance.

The United States Board on Books for Young People is available at http://www .usbby.org/outstanding_international_books_list.htm, accessed on September 24, 2010.

This is an annual list of outstanding books originally published in countries other than the United States and published in the United States in the preceding year.

Colorín Colorado is available at http://www.colorincolorado.org/, accessed on September 24, 2010.

Colorín Colorado provides information, resources, reading strategies, activities and advice for teachers and Spanish-speaking families of English language learners. It includes lists of recommended quality books that reflect the language and cultural experiences of Spanish-speaking children in Pre-K through twelfth grade in the United States. The books are annotated and a suggested age level range and approximate reading level are given for each book. Featured are bilingual books as well as books in either English or Spanish. This Web site also includes a Meet the Authors section which offers videotaped interviews of outstanding multicultural authors who talk about their experiences and their writing. The following authors are featured in these interviews: Linda Sue Park, Pam Muñoz Ryan, Lulu Delacre, Alma Flor Ada, Francisco X. Alarcón, George Ancona, and Pat Mora.

REFERENCES

Cullinan, B. (1989). *Literature and the child.* New York, NY: Harcourt Brace Jovanovich.

Ladson-Billings, G. (1992). Culturally relevant teaching: The key to making multicultural education work. In C. A. Grant (Ed.), *Research and multicultural education* (pp. 106–121). London, UK: Falmer Press.

APPENDIX 16.1

List of Carter G. Woodson Book Award and Honor Winners— Elementary Grades

Shining Star: The Anna May Wong Story by Paula Yoo, illustrated by Lin Wang. (2010 Winner)

Bad News for Outlaws: The Remarkable Life of Bass Reeves, Deputy U.S. Marshal, by Vaunda Micheaux Nelson, illustrated by R. Gregory Christie. (2010 Honor)

Lincoln and Douglass: An American Friendship by Nikki Giovanni, illustrated by Bryan Collier. (2009 Winner)

A Boy Named Beckoning: The True Story of Dr. Carlos Montezuma, Native American Hero by Gina Capaldi. (2009 Honor)

Louis Sockalexis: Native American Baseball Pioneer by Bill Wise; illustrated by Bill Farnsworth. (2008 Winner)

Surfer of the Century by Ellie Crowe, illustrated by Richard Waldrep. (2008 Honor)

John Lewis in the Lead: A Story of the Civil Rights Movement by Jim Haskins & Kathleen Benson, illustrated by Benny Andrews. (2007 Winner)

Gordon Parks: No Excuses by Ann Parr, photographs by Gordon Parks. (2007 Honor)

Let Them Play by Margot Theis Raven, illustrated by Chris Ellison. (2006 Winner)

Roberto Clemente: Pride of the Pittsburgh Pirates by Jonah Winter, illustrated by Raúl Colón. (2006 Honor)

Jim Thorpe's Bright Path by Joseph Bruchac, illustrated by S. D. Nelson. (2005 Winner)
Alec's Primer by Mildred Pitts Walter, illustrated by Larry Johnson. (2005 Honor)

List of Carter G. Woodson Book Award and Honor Winners—Middle Grades

Claudette Colvin: Twice Toward Justice by Phillip Hoose. (2010 Winner)
With One Sky Above Us: The Story of Chief Joseph and the Nez Perce Indians by Nancy Plain. (2010 Honor)
Drama of African-American History: The Rise of Jim Crow by James Haskins & Kathleen Benson with Virginia Schomp. (2009 Winner)
Booker T. Washington and Education by John F. Wukovits. (2009 Honor)
Black and White Airmen: Their True History by John Fleischman. (2008 Winner)
Sophisticated Ladies: The Great Women of Jazz by Leslie Gourse, illustrated by Martin French. (2008 Honor)
Freedom Walkers: The Story of the Montgomery Bus Boycott by Russell Freedman. (2007 Winner)
Up Before Daybreak: Cotton and People in America by Deborah Hopkinson. (2007-Honor)
César Chávez: A Voice for Farmworkers by Bárbara Cruz. (2006 Winner)
Roberto Clemente: Baseball's Humanitarian Hero by Herón Márquez. (2006 Honor)
The Voice That Challenged a Nation: Marian Anderson and the Struggle for Equal Rights by Russell Freedman. (2005 Winner)
The Power of One: Daisy Bates and the Little Rock Nine by Judith Bloom Fradin & Dennis Brindell Fradin. (2005 Honor)

List of Carter G. Woodson Book Award and Honor Winners—Secondary Grades

Denied, Detained, Deported: Stories From the Dark Side of American Immigration by Ann Bausum. (2010 Winner)
Ang Lee by Clifford W. Mills. (2010 Honor)
Reaching Out by Francisco Jiménez. (2009 Winner)
When the Children Marched: The Birmingham Civil Rights Movement by Robert H. Mayer. (2009 Honor)
Don't Throw Away Your Stick Till You Cross the River: The Journey of an Ordinary Man by Vincent Collin Beach with Anni Beach. (2008 Winner)
United States v. Amistad: Slave Ship Mutiny by Susan Dudley Gold. (2008 Honor)
Dear Miss Breed: True Stories of the Japanese-American Incarceration During World War II and a Librarian Who Made a Difference by Joanne Oppenheim. (2007 Winner)
Growing Season: The Life of a Migrant Community by David Hassler, photographs by Gary Harwood. (2007 Honor)
No Easy Answers: Bayard Rustin and the Civil Rights Movement by Calvin Craig Miller. (2006 Winner)
Uh Huh! The Story of Ray Charles by John Duggleby. (2006 Honor)
The Civil Rights Act of 1964 by Robert H. Mayer. (2005 Winner)
Alvin Ailey: Celebrating African-American Culture in Dance by Barbara C. Cruz. (2005-Honor)

APPENDIX 16.2

List of Notable Books for a Global Society 2010

Ajmera, Maya, Magda Nakassis, & Cynthia Pon. *Faith.*

Baskin, Nora Raleigh. *Anything but Typical.*

Bausum, Ann. *Denied, Detained, Deported: Stories From the Dark Side of American Immigration.*

Bryan, Ashley. *Words to My Life's Song.*

Burg, Ann E. *All the Broken Pieces.*

Combres, Élisabeth. *Broken Memory: A Novel of Rwanda.*

Deedy, Carmen Agra. *14 Cows for America.*

Edwardson, Debby Dahl. *Blessing's Bead.*

National Geographic. *Every Human Has Rights: A Photographic Declaration for Kids.*

Griffin, Paul. *The Orange Houses.*

Hoose, Phillip. *Claudette Colvin: Twice Toward Freedom.*

Khan, Rukhsana. *Wanting Mor.*

Lin, Grace. *Where the Mountain Meets the Moon.*

Marshall, James Vance. *Stories From the Billabong.*

Murphy, Jim. *Truce: The Day the Soldiers Stopped Fighting.*

Naidoo, Beverley. *Burn My Heart.*

Napoli, Donna Jo. *Alligator Bayou.*

Nelson, Marilyn. *The Sweethearts of Rhythm: The Story of the Greatest All-Girl Swing Band in the World.*

Nelson, Vaunda Micheaux. *Bad News for Outlaws: The Remarkable Life of Bass Reeves, Deputy U. S. Marshal.*

O'Brien, Anne Sibley, & O'Brien, Perry Edmond. *After Gandhi: One Hundred Years of Nonviolent Resistance.*

Partridge, Elizabeth. *Marching for Freedom: Walk Together, Children, and Don't You Grow Weary.*

Perkins, Mitali. *Secret Keeper.*

Reynolds, Jan. *Cycle of Rice, Cycle of Life: A Story of Sustainable Farming.*

Russell, Ching Yeung. *Tofu Quilt.*

Stork, Francisco X. *Marcelo in the Real World.*

List of Notable Books for a Global Society 2009

Alarcón, Francisco X. *Animal Poems of the Iguazú/Animalario del Iguazú.*

Anderson, Laurie Halse. *Chains.*

Barker, M. P. *A Difficult Boy.*

Bartoletti, Susan Campbell. *The Boy Who Dared.*

Bellward, Stacy. *Ethiopian Voices: Tsion's Life.*

Bolden, Tonya. *George Washington Carver.*

Carter, Anne Laurel. *The Shepherd's Granddaughter.*

D'Aluisio, Faith. *What the World Eats.*

de la Peña, Matt. *Mexican Whiteboy.*

Erdrich, Louise. *The Porcupine Year.*

Fox, Mem. *Ten Little Fingers and Ten Little Toes.*

Gifaldi, David. *Listening for Crickets.*

Greenberg, Jan. *Side by Side: New Poems Inspired by Art From Around the World*.
Kuklin, Susan. *No Choirboy: Murder, Violence, and Teenagers on Death Row*.
LeZotte, Ann Clare. *T4*.
Milway, Katie Smith. *One Hen: How One Small Loan Made a Big Difference*.
Myers, Walter Dean. *Sunrise Over Fallujah*.
Nelson, Kadir. *We Are the Ship: The Story of Negro League Baseball*.
Nivola, Claire A. *Planting the Trees of Kenya: The Story of Wangari Maathai*.
Reibstein, Mark. *Wabi Sabi*.
Rumsford, James. *Silent Music*.
Schmidt, Gary. *Trouble*.
White, Ruth. *Little Audrey*.
Zenatti, Valerie. *A Bottle in the Gaza Sea*.

List of Notable Books for a Global Society 2008

Alexie, Sherman. *The Absolutely True Diary of a Part-Time Indian*.
Bae, Hyun-Joo. *New Clothes for New Year's Day*.
Barakat, Ibtisam. *Tasting the Sky*.
Beah, Ishmael. *A Long Way Gone: Memoirs of a Boy Soldier*.
Bryan, Ashley 2007. *Let It Shine*.
Compestine, Ying Chang. *Revolution is Not a Dinner Party*.
Curtis, Christopher Paul. *Elijah of Buxton*.
Fleischman, Paul. Glass Slipper, *Gold Sandal: A Worldwide Cinderella*.
Greenwood, Barbara. *Factory Girl*.
Judge, Lita. *One Thousand Tracings*.
Levine, Ellen. *Henry's Freedom Box*.
Marsden, Carolyn. *When Heaven Fell*.
Myers, Walter Dean. *Harlem Summer*.
O'Connor, Barbara. *How to Steal a Dog*.
Perkins, Mitali. *Rickshaw Girl*.
Sheth, Kashmira. *Keeping Corner*.
Sis, Peter. *The Wall: Growing Up Behind the Iron Curtain*.
Stanton, Karen. *Papi's Gift*.
Strauss, Rochelle. *One Well: The Story of Water on Earth*.
Tan, Shaun. *The Arrival*.
Thompson, Lauren. *Ballerina Dreams: A True Story*.
Toksvis, Sandi. *Hitler's Canary*.
Wells, Rosemary. *Red Moon at Sharpsburg*.
Williams, Karen Lynn & Mohammed, Khadra. *Four Feet, Two Sandals*.
Wise, Bill. *Louis Sockalexis: Native American Baseball Pioneer*.

List of Notable Books for a Global Society 2007

Boyne, John. *The Boy in the Striped Pajamas*.
Campoy, F. Isabel & Ada, Alma Flor. *Tales Our Abuelitas Told: A Hispanic Folktale Collection*.
Diakite, Penda. *I Lost My Tooth in Africa*.
Draper, Sharon. *Copper Sun*.

Freedman, Russell. *Freedom Walkers: The Story of the Montgomery Bus Boycott.*
Greenfield, Eloise. *When the Horses Ride By.*
Hobb, Will. *Crossing the Wire.*
Holm, Jennifer L. *Penny From Heaven.*
Hopkinson, Deborah. *Up Before Daybreak: Cotton and People in America.*
Kessler, Cristina. *Best Beekeeper of Lalibela: A Tale from Africa.*
Kroll, Virginia. *Selvakumar Knew Better.*
Lee-Tai, Amy. *A Place Where Sunflowers Grow.*
McCormick, Patricia. *Sold.*
McCutcheon, John. *Christmas in the Trenches.*
McKissack, Patricia. *Porch Lies: Tales of Slicksters, Tricksters, and Other Wily Characters.*
Myers, Walter Dean. *Jazz,* illustrated by Christopher Myers.
Raven, Margeret. T. *Night Boat to Freedom.*
Rubin, Susan Goldman with Ela Weissberger. *The Cat With the Yellow Star: Coming of Age in Terezin.*
Shoveller, Herb. *Ryan and Jimmy and the Well in Africa That Brought Them Together.*
Tingle, Tom. *Crossing Bok Chitto: A Choctaw Tale of Friendship and Freedom.*
Winthrop, Elizabeth. *Counting on Grace.*
Weatherford, Carol Boston. *Dear Mr. Rosenwald.*
Weatherford, Carol Boston. *Moses: When Harriet Tubman Led Her People to Freedom.*
Zalben, Jane B. *Paths to Peace.*
Zusak, Markus 2006. *The Book Thief.*

List of Notable Books for a Global Society 2006

Ahmadi, Farah. *The Story of My Life: An Afghan Girl on the Other Side of the Sky.*
Bartoletti, Susan Campbell. *Hitler Youth: Growing Up in Hitler's Shadow.*
Carling, Amelia Lau. *Sawdust Carpets.*
Carvell, Marlene. *Sweetgrass Basket.*
Chamberlin, Mary, & Chamberlin, Rich. *Mama Panya's Pancakes: A Village Tale From Kenya.*
Cheng, Andrea. *Shanghai Messenger.*
Giovanni, Nikki. *Rosa,* illustrated by Bryan Collier.
Hillman, Laura. *I Will Plant You a Lilac Tree: A Memoir of a Schindler's List Survivor.*
Johnson-Davis, *Denys. Goha the Wise Fool.*
Jurmain, Suzanne. *The Forbidden Schoolhouse: The True and Dramatic Story of Prudence Crandall and Her Students.*
Krinitz, Esther Nisenthal & Steinhardt, Bernice. *Memories of Survival.*
Lester, Julius. *The Old African.*
Millman, Isaac. *Hidden Child.*
Nelson, Marilyn. *A Wreath for Emmett Till.*
Park, Linda Sue. *Project Mulberry.*
Rappaport, Doreen. *The School is Not White! A True Story of the Civil Rights Movement.*
Reich, Susanna. *José!: Born to Dance: The Story of José Limón.*
Ruurs, Martriet. *My Librarian is a Camel: How Books are Brought to Children Around the World.*

Say, Allen. *Kamishibai Man*.

Staples, Suzanne Fisher. *Under the Persimmon Tree*.

Tal, Eve. *Double Crossing*.

Weatherford, Carole Boston. *A Negro League Scrapbook*.

Williams, Mary. Brothers in Hope: *The Story of the Lost Boys of Sudan*.

Woodson, Jacqueline. *Show Way*.

Yoo, Paula. *Sixteen Years in Sixteen Seconds*.

List of Notable Books for a Global Society 2005

Bernier-Grand, Carmen T. *César. ¡Sí, se puede!/Yes, We Can!*

Chotjewitz, David. *Daniel Half Human and the Good Nazi*.

Demi. *The Hungry Coat: A Tale From Turkey*.

Freedman, Russell. *The Voice That Challenged a Nation: Marian Anderson and the Struggle for Equal Rights*.

Hale, Marian. *The Truth About Sparrows*.

Hall, Bruce Edward. *Henry and the Kite Dragon*.

Hesse, Karen. *The Cats in Krasinski Square*.

Hill, Laban Carrick. *Harlem Stomp!: A Cultural History of the Harlem Renaissance*.

Kessler, Cristina. *Our Secret, Siri Aang*.

Krishnaswami, Uma. *Naming Maya*.

Kyuchukov, Hristo. *My Name Was Hussein*.

MacDonald, Margaret Read. *Three Minute Tales: Stories From Around the World to Tell or Read When Time Is Short*.

Mikaelsen, Ben. *Tree Girl*.

Myers, Walter Dean. *Here in Harlem: Poems in Many Voices*.

Oswald, Nancy. *Nothing Here but Stones*.

Raven, Margot Theis. *Circle Unbroken*.

Ryan, Pam Muñoz. *Becoming Naomi León*.

Singer, Marilyn (Ed.). *Face Relations: 11 Stories About Seeing Beyond Color*.

Stratton, Allan. *Chanda's Secrets*.

Turner, Pamela S. Hachiko: *The True Story of Loyal Dog*.

Warren, Andrea. *Escape From Saigon: How a Vietnam War Orphan Became an American Boy*.

Weber, Ednah New Rider. *Rattlesnake Mesa: Stories From a Native American Childhood*.

Whelan, Gloria. *Chu Ju's House*.

Woodson, Jacqueline. *Coming on Home Soon*.

Yee, Paul. *A Song for Ba*.

Appendix A

A Selected List of Multicultural Authors and Illustrators

AUTHORS AND ILLUSTRATORS OF AFRICAN AMERICAN LITERATURE

Arnold Adoff
Benny Andrews
Ysaye M. Barnwell
Sandra Belton
Tonya Bolden
Colin Bootman
Elbrite Brown
Ashley Bryan
R. Gregory Christie
Lesa Cline-Ransome
Bryan Collier
Floyd Cooper
Christopher Paul Curtis
Nancy Devard
Leo and Diane Dillon
Randy Duburke
Sharon M. Draper
Shane Evans
Tom Feelings
Peter M. Fiore
Jan Spivey Gilchrist
Nikki Giovanni
Libba Moore Gray
Eloise Greenfield

Nikki Grimes
Christy Hale
Virginia Hamilton
Cynthia Saint James
Leonard Jenkins
Angela Johnson
James Weldon Johnson
Jerome Lagarrigue
Julius Lester
Ellen Levine
E. B. Lewis
Cedric Lucas
Fredrick L. McKissack
Patricia C. McKissack
Frank Morrison
Toni Morrison
Shelia P. Moses
Christopher Myers
Walter Dean Myers
Kadir Nelson
Marilyn Nelson
Andrea Davis Pinkney
Brian Pinkney
Gloria Jean Pinkney

Jerry Pinkney
Sean Qualls
Doreen Rappaport
James Ransome
Margot Theis Raven
Faith Ringgold
Brian Selznick
Irene Smalls
Hope Anita Smith

Javaka Steptoe
John Steptoe
Stephanie Stuve-Bodeen
Natasha Anastasia Tarpley
Clifton L. Taulbert
Joyce Carol Thomas
Eric Velasquez
Carole Boston Weatherford
Jacqueline Woodson

AUTHORS AND ILLUSTRATORS OF ASIAN AND PACIFIC ISLANDER LITERATURE

Hyun-Joo Bae
Lynne Barasch
Rosemary Breckler
Da Chen
Andrea Cheng
George W. Chilcoat
Yangsook Choi
Helen Coutant
Linda Crew
Ellie Crowe
Demi
Stephanie Feeney
Jan Spivey Gilchrist
Justina Chen Headley
Sheila Hamanaka
John Hamamura
Naomi Hirahara
Yumi Heo
Minfong Ho
Felicia Hoshino
Cynthia Kadohata
Uma Krishnaswami
Amy Lee-Tai
Dom Lee
Huy Voun Lee
Milly Lee

Grace Lin
Lenore Look
Rafael López
Many Ly
Ken Mochizuki
An Na
Keiko Narahashi
Linda Sue Park
Ann Phong
Mark Reibstein
Allen Say
Kashmira Sheth
Roseanne Thong
Truong Tran
Michael O. Tunnell
Yoshiko Uchida
Vo-Dinh
Janet S. Wong
Joanna Yardley
Taro Yashima
Paul Yee
Laurence Yep
Yin
Paula Yoo
Ed Young
Ange Zhang

AUTHORS AND ILLUSTRATORS OF NATIVE AMERICAN LITERATURE

David Bouchard
Jeanne Rorex Bridges
Vee Browne

Joseph Bruchac
Shonto Begay
Nicola I. Campbell

Joseph Medicine Crow
Michael Dorris
Anthony Chee Emerson
Louise Erdrich
Paul Goble
Joy Harjo
Michael Lacapa
Charles Larry
George Littlechild

Jonathan London
Rafe Martin
Simon Ortiz
Jerrie Oughton
Gayle Ross
Cynthia Leitich Smith
Virginia Driving Hawk Sneve
Tim Tingle

AUTHORS AND ILLUSTRATORS OF LATINO/A LITERATURE

Francisco X. Alarcón
Alma Flor Ada
Julia Alvarez
Gloria Anzaldúa
Pura Belpré
Carmen T. Bernier-Grand
Isabel Campoy
Robert Casilla
Raúl Colón
Viola Canales
Becky Chavarría-Cháirez
Amy Córdova
Carmen Agra Deedy
Lulu Delacre
David Diaz
Arthur Dorros
Margarita Engle
Carmen Lomas Garza
Maya Christina Gonzalez
Susan Guevara
Rudy Gutierrez

Francisco Jiménez
Rafael López
Nicholasa Mohr
Marisa Montes
Pat Mora
Yuyi Morales
Nancy Osa
Argentina Palacios
Amada Irma Pérez
L. King Pérez
Tomás Rivera
Gina M. Rodríguez
Pam Muñoz Ryan
Linda Shute
Simón Silva
Gary Soto
Carmen Tafolla
K. Dyble Thompson
Pablo Torrecilla
Anne Vega
Beatriz Zapater

AUTHORS AND ILLUSTRATORS OF APPALACHIAN LITERATURE

Tom Birdseye
Clyde Robert Bulla
Jo Carson
Rebecca Caudill
Sharon Creech
Michelle Dionetti
Joanna Galdone
Marc Harshman
Judith Hendershot

Gloria Houston
Anne Isaacs
Tony Johnston
Lauren A. Mills
Phyllis Reynolds Naylor
Phyllis Root
Cynthia Rylant
Mary and William Steele
Nancy Van Laan

AUTHORS AND ILLUSTRATORS OF
ARAB AMERICAN LITERATURE

Maha Addasi

Ali Alalou

Elizabeth Alalou

Ashraf Abdel Azim

Kristen Balouch

Ehud Ben-Ezer

Kathleen Benson

Marina Budhos

Daniella Carmi

Cathryn Clinton

Deborah Durland DeSaix

Deborah Ellis

Aurélia Fronty

Suhaib Hamid Ghazi

Judith Heide Gilliland

Ramsay Harik

Florence Parry Heide

Deborah Heiligman

Kathy Henderson

Rebecca Hickox

Helen Howard

Diane Hoyt-Goldsmith

Laura Jacobsen

Denys Johnson-Davies

Rukhsana Khan

Eric A. Kimmel

Ted Lewin

Jonathon London

Elsa Marston

Claire Sidhom Matze

Asma Mobin-Uddin

Khadra Mohammed

Ann Morris

Suzan Nadimi

Mohammed Nazari

Naomi Shihab Nye

Jane Ray

Anthony Robinson

Karen Gray Ruelle

James Rumford

Rafik Schami

Jeffrey Schrier

Aaron Shepard

Chris Smith

Mark Alan Stamaty

Joelle Stolz

Gloria Whelan

Karen Lynn Williams

Jeanette Winter

Bernard Wolf

Annemarie Young

Ludmila Zeman

Valerie Zenatti

AUTHORS AND ILLUSTRATORS OF LITERATURE
ON MORE THAN ONE CULTURAL GROUP

Verna Aardema

Eve Bunting

Demi

Barry Moser

Patricia Polacco

Doreen Rappaport

Appendix B

Multicultural Book Awards

1. **Américas Children's and Young Adult Literature Award**
   This award, given annually, is in recognition of those who accurately portray Latin America, the Caribbean, or Latinos in the United States. The award is sponsored by the National Consortium of Latin American Studies Programs (CLASP).

2. **American Indian Youth Literature Award Winners**
   Created in 2006 by the American Indian Library Association, this award is given biannually to writers and illustrators who honor American Indian culture and humanity in past and present backgrounds.

3. **Arab American Book Award**
   This annual award began in 2006 and was established by the Arab American National Museum and faculty members of the University of Toledo. It is given to Arab American authors, editors, or illustrators who promote the understanding of the Arab American experience through their book. The three categories of awards include: adult fiction, adult non-fiction, and children's/young adult poetry.

4. **Asian Pacific American Award for Literature**
   This award, given by the Asian/Pacific American Librarians Association, is presented annually to writers who promote Asian/Pacific American culture and heritage, based on literary and artistic value. Among the four categories of awards, one is for picture book winner and one is for youth literature winner.

5. **Batchelder Award**
   The Batchelder Award is given to American publishers who print quality foreign language books translated into English in order to promote understanding and communication between all peoples of the world. This award is given in honor of Mildred L. Batchelder whose life work was to improve relationships between people of different cultures, races, nations, and languages.

6. **Carter G. Woodson Book Award**
   This award was created in 1974 by the National Council for the Social Studies (NCSS) to promote the publication of outstanding social science books that include sensitive and accurate portrayal of topics relating to ethnic minorities. The annual awards include an award

book and an honor book for three categories of readers: Elementary Level, Grades K–6; Middle Level, Grades 5–6; and Secondary Level, Grades 7–12.

7. **Children's Africana Book Awards**

   This annual award was established in 1991 by The Outreach Council of the African Studies Assocation (ASA). The purpose of the award is to honor outstanding authors and illustrators of children's books about Africa published in the United States and to promote the inclusion of these books in United States schools and libraries. Awards are granted in the following categories: Best Book for Young Children; Honor Books for Young Children; Best Book for Older Readers; and Honor Books for Older Readers.

8. **Coretta Scott King Book Award**

   This award is given annually to an African American writer and an African American illustrator for an outstandingly inspirational and educational contribution. It is given to writers and illustrators who promote the understanding of the realization of the American dream.

9. **Jane Addams Children's Book Award**

   This annual award was established in 1953 by the Women's International League for Peace and Freedom (WILPF) and the Jane Addams Peace Association. Awards are given in two categories: Books for Younger Children and Books for Older Children; honor books may be chosen in each category. In addition to the usual standards for excellence, the selection of these awards is limited to books that promote peace, social justice, world community, and equity of the sexes and all races.

10. **John Steptoe Award for New Talent**

    This award is presented annually to recognize new African-American talent and excellence in writing and/or illustration. The John Steptoe Award was established in 1994 by the Coretta Scott King Task Force.

11. **Notable Books for a Global Society**

    Each year, since 1996, the Notable Books for a Global Society (NBGS) Committee, part of the International Reading Association (IRA) Children's Literature and Reading Special Interest Group (CL/R SIG), selects a list of 25 outstanding trade books that promote student understanding of people and cultures throughout the world. Winning titles are chosen from fiction, nonfiction, and poetry for grades K–12. Winners are announced at the IRA annual convention, and each year the fall issue of *Dragon Lode*, published by CL/R SIG, includes the annual list of winners with annotations, teaching ideas, and related books for each of the 25 books.

12. **Pura Belpré Award**

    This award is given to a Latino/Latina writer or illustrator who best celebrates the Latino culture in children's and young adult literature. It is named for the first Latina librarian at the New York Public Library.

13. **Schneider Family Book Awards**

    These annual awards from the American Library Association recognize an author or illustrator for a book that includes an artistic interpretation of the disability experience for readers; the disability may be physical, mental or emotional. Three awards are granted in three age groups: birth through grade school (age 0–8); middle school (age 9–13); and teens (age 14–18). The Schneider Family Book Awards honor an author or illustrator for a book that embodies an artistic expression of the disability experience for child and adolescent audiences. Three annual awards, each consisting of $5000, and a framed plaque, are given annually in each of the following categories: birth through grade school (age 0–8), middle school (age 9–13) and teens (age 14–18).

14. **Skipping Stones Honor Awards**

    Skipping Stones is an award-winning multicultural magazine for today's youth. It is a global, non-profit publication that annually recognizes outstanding books and teaching resources to promote cooperation, awareness of diverse cultures, ecological sensitivity, and respect for differing points of view. Reviews of the winners are included in the summer issue of this magazine.

15. **Sydney Taylor Manuscript Award**

    This award was established by Sydney Taylor's husband in 1985 to encourage authors of Jewish children's books. Sydney Taylor began her writing career with one of her *All-of-a-Kind Family* stories. The Association of Jewish Libraries judges the Sydney Taylor Manuscript Competition. Submissions are limited to high quality manuscripts in the genre of Jewish children's fiction literature, written by unpublished authors.

16. **Tomás Rivera Mexican American Children's Book Award**

    This award is given to honor those who accurately portray the Mexican American experience in literature. It is named for Tomás Rivera who was a creative writer as well as an educator and a university administrator. His writings gave a voice to generations of migrant workers.

Appendix C

Publishers and Distributors of Multicultural Literature

Albert Whitman & Company: 250 South Northwest Highway, Suite 320 Park Ridge, Illinois; http://www.albertwhitman.com/
Albert Whitman & Company has been publishing children's books since 1919. They publish picture books, nonfiction books, and novels that speak to children of diverse backgrounds.

Arte Público: University of Houston, 452 Cullen Performance Hall, Houston, TX 77204-2004; http://www.latinoteca.com/arte-publico-press/
Arte Público is a major publisher of books by Hispanic authors that are contemporary and recovered works.

Piñata Books: http://www.latinoteca.com/app-home/
Piñata Books is Arte Público's imprint for children's books, strives to publish books that contain authentic and realistic portrayals of Hispanic people and their culture in the United States.

Bess Press: 3565 Harding Ave., Honolulu, HI 96816; http://www.besspress.com/
An independent publishing company, Bess Press publishes books for all ages about Hawaii as well as other groups from the Pacific region. Most of the authors live in Hawaii or the Pacific region.

Boyds Mills Press: 815 Church Street, Honesdale, Pennsylvania 18431; http://www.boydsmillspress.com/
This publisher has a long tradition of publishing books which enlighten and entertain. They are a trade division of Highlights for Children, Inc. Publishing under five

imprints, their books have won numerous awards and have been listed on several notable book lists.

Candlewick Press: 99 Dover Street, Somerville, MA 02144; http://www.candlewick .com/
Candlewick Press publishes books that include both quality writing and art. They are one of the largest independent publishing companies in the United States. Their books have won over 1500 honors and awards.

Children's Book Press: 965 Mission Street, Suite 425, San Francisco, CA 94103; http://www.childrensbookpress.org/
Founded in 1975, Children's Book Press is a non-profit, independent publisher that publishes books by and about people from the Latino, African American, Asian/Pacific Islander, and Native American cultures. Its goals are to help children build a sense of their history, culture, and importance, and to promote inter-cultural and cross-cultural awareness.

Chronicle Books: 680 Second Street, San Francisco, California 94107; http:// www.chroniclebooks.com/index/store,books/
Chronicle Books publish titles on a variety of cultures.

Cinco Puntos Press: 701 Texas, El Paso, Texas 79901; http://www.cincopuntos.com/ index.sstg
Cinco Puntos Press is an independent publishing company located in El Paso, Texas. Their books have won numerous awards. They particulary feature Chicano and Choctaw literature. They also offer Spanish/English bilingual books.

Del Sol Books 6574 Edmonton Avenue, San Diego, CA 92122; http://www .delsolbooks.com
This family-run business publishes books by Alma Flor Ada and F. Isabel Campoy. They also sell bilingual books and popular children's books translated into Spanish.

Harcourt Children's Books: 525 B Street, Suite 1900, San Diego, CA 92101; http://www .harcourtbooks.com/childrensbooks/
Harcourt Children's Books includes several imprints, including: Voyager Books, Green Light Readers, Magic Carpet Books, Gulliver Books, Silver Whistle, and Odyssey. Voyager Books publishes books by multicultural authors, including Alma Flor Ada, Eve Bunting, and Mem Fox.

HarperCollins: 10 East 53rd Street, New York, NY 10022. http://www.harpercollins childrens.com/?wt.mc_id=hchpkidscat
Harper Collins publishes numerous multicultural titles.
http://www.harpercollins.com/. This publishing company publishes multicultural books.

Amistad: http://www.harpercollins.com/imprints/index.aspx?imprintid=518006
Amistad publishes books by and about people of African ancestry and features a number of notable authors.

Houghton Mifflin Books for Children/Harcourt: 222 Berkeley Street, Boston, MA 02116-3764; http://www.houghtonmifflinbooks.com/hmcochild/
Houghton Mifflin publishes books by many notable multicultural authors, including: Allen Say, Toni Morrison, and Linda Sue Park.

Hyperion/Jump at the Sun: 114 Fifth Avenue, New York, NY 10011; http://www.hyperionbooksforchildren.com/jump/index.asp
Jump at the Sun publishes books that celebrate the African American experience. Hyperion was the first major publisher to create an imprint to publish African American children's books.

Interlink Publishing: 46 Crosby Street, Northampton, MA 01060-1804; http://www.interlinkbooks.com/
Interlink is an independent publishing company that specializes in publishing children's books from around the world in addition to world travel, world history, and world literature. They publish approximately 90 titles per year.

Just Us Books: 356 Glenwood Ave., East Orange, NJ 07017; http://aalbc.com/writers/justusbooks.htm
Just Us Books publishes books focusing on African American history, experiences, and culture and is now one of the leading publishers of African American literature for young people. It was originally founded in 1988 by Wade Hudson and Cheryl Willis Hudson.

Lee & Low Books: 95 Madison Avenue, Suite # 1205, New York, NY 10016; http://www.leeandlow.com/
This independent publishing company publishes books on a wide variety of different cultures. It was started by two Chinese Americans. Their books have won numerous awards.

Little Brown: 237 Park Avenue, New York NY 10017 http://www.hachettebookgroup.com/kids_index.aspx
Part of the Hachette Book Group, LB Books for Young Readers has published books by authors such as Jerry Pinkney and E.B. Lewis.

Macmillan Publishing: 175 Fifth Avenue, New York, NY 10010. This publishing company has a number of imprints that publish multicultural books.

• Farrar, Straus, & Giroux/Melanie Kroupa Books: http://us.macmillan.com/Content.aspx?publisher=fsgbyr&id=1393
  This imprint is known for its international list of fiction, non-fiction, and children's books.
• Henry Holt Books for Young Readers: http://us.macmillan.com/HoltYoungReaders.aspx
  An imprint of Macmillan, Henry Holt Books for Young Readers publishes quality literature to inspire preschoolers through young adults.
• Roaring Brook Press: http://us.macmillan.com/RoaringBrook.aspx
  This imprint of Macmillan aims to publish books that are entertaining and educating. They publish books for toddlers through young adults.
• Square Fish: http://us.macmillan.com/squarefish.aspx
  This imprint of Macmillan has published award winning books, including: *Francie* (Coretta Scott King Honor), *The Surrender Tree* (Pura Belpré Award), and *Rosa* (Caldecott Honor).

Oyate: 330 East Thomson Ave., Sonoma, CA 95476; http://www.oyate.org/index.php?
option=com_content&view=frontpage&Itemid=1
Oyate is a Native American organization which distributes books that accurately and
authentically portray Native Americans.

Pan Asian Publications: http://www.panap.com//aboutus.asp

Pan Asian Publications: This publishing company offers bilingual books featuring a
number of Asian languages such as Chinese, Hmong, Khmer, Korean, Tagalog, and
Thai.

Penguin: 375 Hudson Street, New York, NY 10014. This publishing company has a
number of imprints that publish multicultural books.

- Dial: http://us.penguingroup.com/static/pages/publishers/yr/dial.html
  Dial, an imprint of Penguin, publishes high quality books of literary merit and fine design.
  Their books focus on genuine and character-driven writing.
- Dutton: http://us.penguingroup.com/static/pages/publishers/adult/dutton.html
  Dutton is an imprint of Penguin publishing. They strive to publish high quality books that will
  transport readers. Philomel, an imprint of Penguin, publishes titles from all over the world and
  supports books with a social conscience.
- Putnam: http://us.penguingroup.com/static/pages/publishers/yr/putnam.html
  Putnam, an imprint of Penguin, recently published award-winning books by Jacqueline Wood-
  son and Nikki Grimes.

Random House: 1745 Broadway, 10th Floor, New York, NY 10019

- Delacorte, an imprint of Random House Books for Young Readers, aims to publish quality literature that nurtures the hearts and minds of children. http://www.jacketflap.com/pubdetail.asp
  ?pub=8150
- Knopf: http://knopf.knopfdoubleday.com/
  Knopf, an imprint of Random House, publishes distinguished fiction and nonfiction books to.

Scholastic, Inc./Blue Sky Press: 557 Broadway, New York, NY 10012; http://www
.scholastic.com/aboutscholastic/bookpublishing.htm
Scholastic is the largest publisher and distributor of children's literature.

Simon & Schuster: Children's Publishing Division, 1230 Avenue of the Americas,
New York, NY 10020; http://www.simonandschuster.biz/content/destination.cfm?
sid=33&pid=427745. Offers multicultural books.

Atheneum: http://www.simonandschuster.biz/content/destination.cfm?sid=33&pid=427747
Atheneum, an imprint of Simon & Schuster Books for Young Readers, focuses on quality fiction and picture books for preschool-young adults.

Tilbury House Publishers: 132 Water St., Gardiner, ME 04345; http://www.tilburyhouse
.com/home.html

Tilbury House strives to publish books with an emphasis on social justice, cultural diversity, and the environment. Their Web site offers resources for teachers to use with their books in the classroom.

Tortuga Press: P.O. Box 181, 2777 Yulupa Avenue, Santa Rosa, CA 95405; http:// www.tortugapress.com/tortwelcome.html
Tortuga Press publishes children's books in Spanish.

Zino Press: 2310 Darwin Road, Madison WI 53704: http://knowledgeunlimited.com/ coinfo.html
Zino Press is an independent publishing company that has been producing multicultural books and teacher resources for over 20 years. It is a division of Knowledge Unlimited. Its rhyming books promote phonemic awareness while at the same time providing important nonfiction multicultural subjects.

Index

About the Editors and Contributors

EDITORS

Lynn Atkinson Smolen, PhD, is Professor of Literacy Education and Teaching English as a Second Language and is the Director of the TESOL Program at The University of Akron. She has taught literacy courses and second language methods courses to preservice and inservice teachers for 30 years. Formerly, she was an elementary classroom teacher, a Title I reading teacher, and an ESL teacher in the Alachua County Public Schools, Florida. She earned her doctorate in curriculum and instruction with concentrations in bilingual education and reading at the University of Florida. As a strong advocate of multicultural literature, she has always included this literature in her teaching at all levels. Her scholarly interests are multicultural literature, reading in a second language, and diversity issues. She has presented at numerous international and national conferences and has published her research in international, national, and state journals.

Ruth A. Oswald, PhD, is Associate Professor of Literacy Education at The University of Akron with 25 years of teaching experience in elementary classrooms. She has always incorporated children's literature, including multicultural literature, into her teaching and currently instructs both undergraduate and graduate children's literature courses. She is a past president of The Ohio Council of The International Reading Association and is currently an active member of a consortium of higher education literacy leaders in Ohio to offer the Literacy Specialist program. She worked with a colleague to develop one of the online courses in this program: *Coaching in Diverse Classrooms*. Her areas of research focus on writing instruction, early literacy development, and multicultural literature.

CONTRIBUTORS

Francis S. Broadway, PhD, is Professor of Education at The University of Akron with 19 years as a middle and secondary science and mathematics teacher. As a science educator he contests and disrupts boundaries between disciplines and integrates children's literature into science instruction. He has immersed himself in children's literature, especially the narratives of illustrations, recognizing the beauty that exists in both art and science. He is mindful that there are many ways of knowing and each epistemology can learn from another.

Carolyn S. Brodie, PhD, has been Professor in the School of Library and Information Science at Kent State University (KSU) for more than 20 years, teaching youth and school librarianship courses. In 2005, she received KSU's Distinguished Teaching Award and in 2007 received the American Library Association's Scholastic Library Publishing Award. Her selection committee work has included the Association of Library Service Children's Notable Children's Books, the Newbery Award, and the Caldecott Award. She has worked with the Virginia Hamilton Conference on Multicultural Literature for Youth since 1989 and now serves as conference director.

F. Isabel Campoy is the award winning author of numerous children's books written in English and Spanish. She is a recognized speaker, researcher, and scholar devoted to the study of language acquisition and Latino children's literature. She obtained her degree in English Philology from Universidad Complutense in Madrid, Spain.

John A. Casper is pursuing an M.S. in Education with Licensure at The University of Akron, preparing to be a language arts teacher. He has served as a graduate assistant in the Department of Curricular and Instructional Studies and is currently teaching in France as an exchange teacher with The Franco-American Teachers-in-Training Institute..

Douglass Mark Conkle, BSED, is an early childhood literacy intervention specialist for the Akron Public Schools in Ohio and is currently working on completing his Master's degree at The University of Akron. He focuses on nurturing children to find their inner moral selves and on promoting caring communities. Besides children's picture books, teaching, and learning, Douglass also enjoys snowboarding and gardening.

Alma Flor Ada is the author of many multicultural books and is pleased that most of her books are published both in English and in Spanish. She grew up in Cuba and has compiled some of the stories of her childhood, as well as stories that she heard from her family as a child. Besides writing children's books, Alma Flor is a Professor at the University of San Francisco. She also works in schools with teachers, children, and parents. Alma Flor believes that knowing two languages has made the world richer for her and suggests that all children should be given the opportunity to learn more than one language when they are young because they can do so easily.

Michele M. Ebersole, PhD, is Associate Professor of Education at the University of Hawaii at Hilo. She has worked as an elementary classroom teacher and currently teaches literacy and children's literature courses to undergraduate and post-baccalaureate students.

Tracy Foreman, MEd, is a literacy specialist at Walls Elementary School in Kent, Ohio, where she has had many opportunities to celebrate diversity and multicultural learning. She is a Reading Recovery-trained Master Teacher with 19 years teaching experience in elementary classrooms. She is currently responsible for the Title I program at her school as well as for providing professional support to teachers.

Nancy L. Hadaway, PhD, is Professor of Literacy Studies at the University of Texas at Arlington with 35 years of experience in K–12 and university classrooms. She has been a member of several children's book award committees including the Orbis Pictus Committee, the Notable Books for a Global Society Committee, and the Outstanding International Book Committee and has coauthored or coedited several books about the use of children's literature with English learners.

Meghan Harper, PhD, is Assistant Professor at Kent State University in Kent, Ohio. She currently teaches youth and school librarianship courses in the School of Library and Information Science. Dr. Harper has been an administrator and a school librarian at levels K–12. In these positions, Dr. Harper collaborated with teachers to develop curricular units and incorporate the use of technology and media in the classroom. Dr. Harper is an advisory board member of the Virginia Hamilton Multicultural Literature Conference, the longest running national conference of its kind.

Darwin L. Henderson, EdD, is Associate Professor of Education at the University of Cincinnati where he teaches children's literature, multicultural literature, and emergent literacy. Darwin's committee service has included his leadership as chair of the Coretta Scott King Book Award and as a member of the Children's Notable Book Committee of the Association of Library Services to Children. His research interests lie in twentieth and twenty-first century African American writers and illustrators of literature for children and youth.

Sandra Jenkins, MA Ed, is an adjunct faculty member at The University of Akron where she teaches children's literature at the undergraduate level. She has 10 years of experience as a children's librarian. She currently teaches at a private early childhood center.

Christine Kane is a full-time, fourth-grade teacher, staff developer, and literacy coach for Nubia Leadership Academy, a charter school of San Diego Unified School District. She has 12 years of teaching experience in public schools. She is the codirector of the San Diego Area Writing Project, a local site of the National Writing Project at the University of California, San Diego (UCSD) and a part-time graduate literacy instructor for the University of San Diego (USD) and San Diego State University (SDSU). She is also completing a joint-doctoral program in Literacy from SDSU and USD.

Sarah King is a doctoral student at The University of Akron focusing on literacy for elementary students. Prior to beginning her doctoral work, she taught first grade for five years in a school that highlights religious and cultural diversity. In addition to her teaching duties, she organized Right to Read Week activities and a family literacy night. Sarah is passionate about children's literacy and is an avid children's book collector.

Avis M. Masuda, PhD, is Assistant Professor of Education at the University of Hawaii at Hilo with 20 years of teaching experience. She has worked with K–12 classroom teachers in the areas of literacy, assessment, and teacher learning communities. She currently teaches undergraduate and post-baccalaureate courses in literacy and secondary instructional methods.

Ruth McKoy Lowery, PhD, is Associate Professor in the College of Education at the University of Florida. She teaches courses in literature for children and adolescents. Her research incorporates students' responses to literature, multicultural literature in schools' curricula, immigrant populations, and teaching diverse student populations. She is the author of *Immigrants in Children's Literature* (2000), published by Peter Lang.

Claudette S. McLinn, EdD, is a District Field Librarian in Library Services at Los Angeles Unified School District in California with 34 years of experience as a teacher, librarian, and administrator in elementary and secondary education. She is also an Adjunct Professor at California State University, Long Beach, and currently teaches graduate courses in children's literature and young adult literature with a focus on multicultural literature. She has been active in the American Library Association, including serving on the Newbery, Coretta Scott King, and Pura Belpré Award Committees.

Barbara Moss, PhD, is Professor of Literacy Education at San Diego State University. She has been a classroom teacher, a reading supervisor, and a university professor during her educational career. She is the author of more than 100 articles and numerous books, including 35 *Strategies for Teaching Informational Text* from Guilford Press. She teaches classes at the credential, masters, and doctoral levels and presently works as a coach at an urban high school in San Diego, California.

Jacqueline K. Peck, PhD, is Visiting Associate Professor in the College of Education at The University of Akron in Ohio. She has published articles on storytelling, conducted workshops, and practiced the art for more than 20 years. She currently instructs both undergraduate and graduate literacy courses and regularly integrates storytelling into her teaching.

Timothy Rasinski, PhD, is Professor of Literacy Education at Kent State University. His scholarly interests include reading fluency and word study, reading in the elementary and middle grades, and readers who struggle. His research on reading has been cited by the National Reading Panel and has been published in journals such as *Reading Research Quarterly* and *The Reading Teacher*. He is coauthor of the Fluency Chapter for Volume IV of the *Handbook of Reading Research*. He has served as co-editor of *The Reading Teacher* and the *Journal of Literacy Research*. Rasinski is past-president of the College Reading Association and he has won the A. B. Herr and Laureate Awards from the College Reading Association for his scholarly contributions to literacy education. He is a member of the International Reading Hall of Fame. Prior to coming to Kent State, he taught for several years as an elementary and middle school classroom teacher.

Yolanda A. Reed has been a Lecturer in the Africana Studies Department at California State University Long Beach for over 15 years. Her teaching and research interests focus on ancient African civilizations, African American language, African and African American literature, Caribbean studies, and children's literature. She is an ardent bibliophile of African, Caribbean, and African American children's literature.

Donna Sabis-Burns, PhD, is an enrolled member of the Mohawk Band of Iroquois Six Nations and currently resides in the Washington, D.C. Metro area. She graduated from the University of Florida with her doctorate in Language and Literacy from the School of Teaching and Learning. Her research interests include social justice and Native American issues in children's literature. She is the Acting Assistant State Superintendent of Elementary and Secondary Education at the Office of the State Superintendent of Education in Washington, D.C. She is also a former first grade teacher and adjunct professor who taught courses in children's literature.. She is married with three children and ultimately hopes to contribute to the list of quality children's books on various social justice themes with her own publications.

Barbara A. Ward, PhD, is currently an eighth grade English/language arts teacher in Tallulah, Louisiana where multicultural literature is integral to her teaching practices. The immediate past chair of the Notable Books for a Global Society, she has taught literature courses for both the University of New Orleans and Washington State University and loves recommending global literature to others.

Teresa L. Young, EdD, is Assistant Professor in the Department of Childhood Education and Literacy at Xavier University in Cincinnati, Ohio. She has many years of experience working with preservice and graduate students in the areas of teacher preparation and early childhood education. She continues to focus her interest on literacy and early childhood education.

Terrell A. Young, EdD, is a Professor of Literacy Education at Washington State University where he teaches undergraduate and graduate courses in children's literature and literacy. He has had the honor of serving on several book award committees and served as president of both the IRA Children's Literature and Reading Special Interest Group and the NCTE Children's Literature Assembly. He currently serves on the Board of Directors of the International Reading Association. Young was the 2006 recipient of the IRA Outstanding Teacher Educator in Reading Award in 2006.

Belinda S. Zimmerman, PhD, is Assistant Professor of Literacy and Education at Kent State University in Ohio. In addition to many years of experience as a classroom teacher, she has also been a professional development consultant, literacy coach, and Reading Recovery teacher. Incorporating multicultural children's literature into her teaching with children, undergraduates, and graduate students has always been a passion and a priority.